African Americans in Congress:
A Documentary History

ERIC FREEDMAN
Michigan State University

STEPHEN A. JONES
Central Michigan University

CQ PRESS

A Division of Congressional Quarterly Inc.
Washington, D.C.

CQ Press
1255 22nd Street, NW, Suite 400
Washington, DC 20037

Phone: 202-729-1900; toll-free, 1-866-4CQ-PRESS (1-866-427-7737)

Web: www.cqpress.com

Cover design: Kimberly Glyder Design

Cover photos: *Top left,* Rep. Joseph H. Rainey (Library of Congress); *top center,* Rep. Barbara C. Jordan (AP Images); *top right,* Sen. Hiram R. Revels (Library of Congress); *middle,* Emancipation Proclamation (engraving by W. Roberts/Library of Congress); *bottom left,* Rep. Shirley A. Chisholm (Thomas J. O'Halloran/ Library of Congress); *bottom center,* Sen. Barack Obama (AP Images/Mannie Garcia); *bottom right,* Rep. Carol Moseley-Braun (Ron Sachs/CNP/Corbis).

Composition: MacPS

Text credits appear on pages 561–562, which are an extension of the copyright page.

∞ The paper used in this publication exceeds the requirements of the American National Standard for Information Sciences—Permanence of Paper for Printed Library Materials, ANSI Z39.48-1992.

Printed and bound in the United States of America

11   10   09   08   07   1   2   3   4   5

Library of Congress Cataloging-in-Publication Data

Freedman, Eric.
    African Americans in Congress : a documentary history / Eric Freedman, Stephen A. Jones.
        p. cm.
    Includes bibliographical references and index.
    ISBN 978-0-87289-385-6 (hardbound : alk. paper)   1. United States. Congress—History—Sources.   2. African American legislators—History—Sources.   3. Legislators—United States—History—Sources.   4. African Americans—Politics and government—Sources.   I. Jones, Stephen A. (Stephen Alan) II. Title.

JK1021.A47 2008
328.730089'96073—dc22

                                                          2007040318

For Ryan, Aedan, Evan, Drew and Kiersten,
in hopes that they will follow in
the steps of giants

For Alexander: May your passionate concern for what is true
and right never dim

Contents

3. RECONSTRUCTION: INCREASING RIGHTS AND POLITICAL EMPOWERMENT, 1868–1883   80

Documents

Preface

The history of African Americans in Congress is as long and complicated as the history of the United States. Sen. Hiram R. Revels, R-Miss., the first African American member of Congress, took his seat in 1870, but from the time of the Revolutionary War nearly 100 years before, Congress had been making decisions and enacting legislation determining the status of the nation's black population, free and slave. For just as long, African Americans had been struggling to influence Congress to guarantee their civil and political rights.

The United States' founding document, the Declaration of Independence, set the stage for this struggle. Its statement of principles makes the bold assertion that "all men are created equal" but remains silent on the issue of slavery. Ironically, one draft of the document had excoriated King George for foisting slavery—a "cruel war against human nature itself"—on his American colonies. Although the Declaration lacks a direct repudiation of slavery, its ringing claim of universal equality became a touchstone for African Americans. Frederick Douglass cited it in the 1850s as he prodded the nation to abolish slavery, and Martin Luther King Jr. referred to it as he stood on the steps of the Lincoln Memorial in 1963, a century after the Emancipation Proclamation, and called on the United States to live up to its professed ideals.

As the Continental Congress set about the task of winning the Revolutionary War, African Americans pressed states to grant them the political rights of citizenship. In 1780, as the war continued, John and Paul Cuffe and five other black men protested Massachusetts's refusal to allow them the vote, despite their paying taxes. At least as early as 1797, free blacks from the South were petitioning Congress for protection of their rights and their freedom.

Assembling the documents contained in *African Americans in Congress: A Documentary History* required us to approach the subject with a broad perspective. The collection begins in 1776, with the American Revolution, and ends in 2007, shortly after Democrats regained control of Congress and members of the Congressional Black Caucus assumed key leadership positions on high-profile House committees. We chose documents from periods when no African Americans served in Congress because at those times congressional actions—such as the Missouri Compromise and the Nineteenth Amendment to the Constitution—nonetheless affected the daily lives of blacks, including their civil and human rights, economic and educational opportunities, and access to political power. We also selected major Supreme Court decisions—such as *Dred Scott v. Sandford, Plessy v. Ferguson* and *Brown v. Board of Education*—which profoundly affected African Americans' lives. And to illuminate essential aspects of African Americans' struggle to win the free exercise of their rights, we included documents from African Americans who never served in Congress. Among these are the testimony of abolitionist Charles Remond to the Massachusetts legislature in 1842, a 1932 letter to President Herbert Hoover from NAACP official Walter White and the speech given by James W. Ford when he accepted the Communist Party's 1936 nomination for vice president.

The complex relationships between political, social and economic issues necessitated a twofold approach to organizing the documents selected. The first seven chapters are arranged chronologically to provide an overview of the development of African American participation in politics and in Congress. The remaining eight chapters are organized thematically to reflect the emergence over generations of issues concerning economic, political and social justice. These thematic chapters allow for attention to be paid to issues such as foreign affairs, war, peace and patriotism that might otherwise be overlooked and underappreciated in a strictly chronological presentation.

As of 2007, more than 120 African Americans—starting with Revels in 1870—had been elected to serve in the House of Representatives or the Senate. The 110th Congress, convened in January 2007, included forty-three African American members, the same record-setting number as had served in the 109th Congress. The African American men and women elected to Congress represent an extraordinary array of personal and political experiences. It is impossible to include a document representing each one, and yet some members have had such long or influential careers that their experiences are represented by multiple documents. The selections cover a range of historical events and political perspectives while also reflecting the voices and challenges—as well as the failings—of as many representatives and senators as possible.

Each document is a point of entry for exploring the broader issues at the heart of the political, social, economic, historic and cultural identity of the United States. Selecting them was sometimes difficult. Some documents—such as the U.S. Constitution, Reconstruction-era constitutional amendments, Rep. George H. White's 1901 valedictory speech and the Voting Rights Act of 1965—were obvious choices. In most cases, however, an array of options came into play for illuminating various issues and events, among them opposition to the wars in Vietnam and Iraq, segregation in the military, educational inequality and electoral campaigning. The documents comprise a range of original formats, including speeches, court decisions, debates, letters, press releases, memoirs, editorials, committee testimony, reports and legislation. The choice of documents, how to edit them and how to interpret them are ours; some scholars may disagree with some of the decisions we made.

Whenever possible, we relied on original sources, but the earlier research of documentary historians has enriched the writing of this first documentary history of African Americans in Congress. Although the selected bibliography, chapter notes, and source notes provide a complete list of such resources, we acknowledge those of particular importance written or edited by the following historians and commentators: Herbert A. Aptheker; Ira Berlin, Barbara J. Fields, Thavolia Glymph, Joseph P. Reidy and Leslie S. Rowland; Albert P. Blaustein and Robert L. Zangrando; Herb Boyd; Henry Steele Commager; Anthony J. Cooper; George Ducas and Charles Van Doren; Leslie H. Fishel Jr.

and Benjamin Quarles; Walter L. Fleming; Philip S. Foner; Thomas R. Frazier; Leon Friedman; Robert P. Green Jr.; Thomas C. Holt and Elsa Barkley Brown; Stephen Middleton; Gilbert Osofsky; and James P. Shenton. Documents' original spelling and punctuation, including errors, have been retained wherever possible. Brackets indicate additional information, such as first names and state and party affiliations, for clarity.

Acknowledgments

We are grateful to the many librarians who assisted us. At our institutions, they include Hui Hua Chua and Peter Berg at Michigan State University and David Shirley at Central Michigan University. We also appreciate the assistance of the professional staff who facilitated our work at the Gerald R. Ford Presidential Library in Ann Arbor, Michigan; the Herbert Hoover Presidential Library in West Branch, Iowa; the John F. Kennedy Presidential Library in Boston, Massachusetts; the Franklin D. Roosevelt Presidential Library in Hyde Park, New York; the Harlan Hatcher Graduate Library at the University of Michigan in Ann Arbor; the Center for American History at the University of Texas at Austin; and the Burton Historical Collection at the Detroit Public Library.

We received valuable suggestions from George A. Dalley, chief of staff to Rep. Charles B. Rangel of New York; former senator Carol Moseley-Braun of Illinois; Professor Emerita Roberta Sue Alexander of the University of Dayton; and Professor Reginald F. Hildebrand of the University of North Carolina at Chapel Hill. Also invaluable were recommendations from the four anonymous scholars and librarians who reviewed our proposal for CQ Press. At CQ Press, Mary Carpenter helped shape the initial structure of the project, and David Arthur, Jennifer Campi and Andrea Pedolsky guided us through the writing and editing processes.

We appreciate the support of Jane Briggs-Bunting, director of Michigan State University's School of Journalism; Charles T. Salmon, dean of MSU's College of Communication Arts and Sciences; and Timothy D. Hall, chair of the Department of History at Central Michigan University.

We express our deep gratitude to Professor David T. Bailey of the Department of History at Michigan State University for suggesting our collaboration on this volume and to undergraduate professorial assistant Tricia McCarthy for her research and proofreading contributions.

Eric Freedman
Stephen A. Jones

CHAPTER ONE

The Revolutionary War to *Dred Scott*
The Antecedents of Political Empowerment, 1776–1857

On Being Brought from Africa to America

'Twas mercy brought me from my *Pagan* land,
Taught my benighted soul to understand
That there's a God, that there's a *Saviour* too:
Once I redemption neither sought nor knew.
Some view our sable race with scornful eye,
"Their colour is a diabolic die."
Remember, *Christians, Negros,* black as *Cain,*
May be refin'd, and join th' angelic train.

—Phillis Wheatley, 1773[1]

Phillis Wheatley is pictured here in the frontispiece to the London edition of her 1773 book, the first book of poetry by an African American. The engraving of Wheatley was done by Scipio Moorhead, who was the slave of Rev. John Moorhead. Source: The Granger Collection, New York

Three years before the Declaration of Independence (**Document 1.1**) asserted the freedom of a new and sovereign nation on the North American continent, Phillis Wheatley's poetic reflection on her experience as an African in America illuminated the moral dilemma of American liberty. Brought to Boston as a slave at age seven, Wheatley was taught to read and write by her owners. Her 1773 book, entitled *Poems on Various Subjects, Religious and Moral,* was the first volume of poetry to be published by an African American. In that original piece of African American literature—with an understated dignity that would become a hallmark of black protest for the next two centuries—Wheatley attempted to pique the conscience of the nascent nation. If the United States were truly committed to the idea, expressed so eloquently three years later in the Declaration, that "all men are created equal" and therefore equally entitled to "life, liberty and the pursuit of happiness," and if its people were the Christians they professed to be, how could the country justify the continuation of human slavery, let alone the common discrimination against free black people? This question has haunted the nation for all of its existence.

America's founders clearly were aware of the contradiction. Slavery had already been debated for nearly a century when the Declaration was written. As early as 1688, a group of Mennonites from Germantown, Pennsylvania, wrote a protest against slavery:

> There is a saying, that we should do to all men like as we will be done ourselves; making no difference of what generation, descent, or colour they are. And those who steal or rob men, and

those who buy or purchase them, are they not all alike? Here is liberty of conscience, which is right and reasonable; here ought to be likewise liberty of the body.[2]

The signers of the Declaration debated the issue intensely as they prepared to assert their freedom from Britain. An early draft of the Declaration included slavery in the litany of evils for which King George III was to be held responsible. The founders removed the accusation regarding slavery from the final document, however, to avoid drawing attention to the fact that the colonists were demanding their own liberty while reserving the right to hold others in bondage. A little more than a decade later, the Constitution (**Document 1.4**) that enshrined the nation's political rights and structure in 1787 also avoided direct mention of slavery.

What emerged from these founding documents was a world of ambiguity and compromise over the presence of slavery in the South. Always divisive and a source of controversy and tension, slavery spread as the years passed and the nation grew. National growth was as central to the United States' first century as slavery. The two became inextricably intertwined as proslavery interests in the South and abolitionists in the North argued over the extension of slavery into the country's new territories and states. Moderates, meanwhile, struggled time and again to maintain a balance of political power that would keep the young nation from bursting apart at the seams.

For a while, compromise was a successful strategy; accommodations were made and a degree of political equilibrium was maintained in such documents as the Northwest Ordinance of 1787 (**Document 1.3**), the Constitution (1787), and the Missouri Compromise of 1820 (**Document 1.6**). The common ground of compromise, in general terms, involved limiting the northward extension of slaveholding territory as the country spread west, while admitting a mix of slave and free states to ensure even division of political power in the Senate, which would give the South the ability to block any federal attempts to abolish slavery. With each new compromise came a reassertion of the right of slave owners to reclaim runaway slaves, even if those runaways managed to escape to free territory in the North. But with each new conflict regarding slavery, the political balance became more fragile and difficult to sustain. Thomas Jefferson, who was responsible for the Declaration's language on liberty and equality, was so shaken by the controversy that led to the Missouri Compromise that he despaired for the nation's future. "This is a reprieve only, not a final sentence," he wrote in 1820 in one of the most prescient letters in American history. "But as it is, we have the wolf by the ears, and we can neither hold him, nor safely let him go. Justice is in one scale, and self-preservation in the other." [3]

Indeed, within thirty years compromise had begun to wear thin. The Compromise of 1850 (**Document 1.11**) and the Kansas-Nebraska Act of 1854 (**Document 1.13**) served to further polarize pro- and antislavery factions until violence erupted in "Bleeding Kansas." The Supreme Court's 1857 decision in *Dred Scott v. Sandford* (**Document 1.14**) was the last major action in a decades long legal and judicial fight that would erupt into war in 1861.

Throughout this period, African Americans found themselves in one of two circumstances: either they were held as slaves, entirely without rights; or they were considered "free" but struggled continually to be accorded and to retain the fundamental rights of citizens. Between the Revolution and the Civil War, the institution of slavery grew dramatically and became ever more entrenched. Although northern states generally, if gradually, abolished slavery, the number of slave states grew as the nation expanded westward. From 1775 to 1825, the number of slaves in the United States tripled, mainly due to reproduction, even though the federal government banned the import of slaves in 1808.

Although slavery was gradually outlawed in the northern states, the North was hardly a bastion of freedom for African Americans. The first eight decades of the nation's history saw a steady erosion of political and civil rights for free blacks throughout the nation. Political rights were universally diminished as new states were admitted to the Union with constitutions that forbade blacks from voting. Further, many states that had allowed free blacks to vote adopted statutes or new constitutions that withdrew that right. Either by law or by custom, segregation of the races on trains, on ships and in other public accommodations also became increasingly common.

The vast majority of African Americans during the revolutionary era were slaves, but there were free blacks residing in every state. As slavery spread, the presence of these free blacks became increasingly problematic. Southern states, resentful of northern abolitionists and fearful of violent slave uprisings, such as Nat Turner's rebellion in Virginia in 1831, placed more restrictions on free blacks and, in some cases, forbade individual whites from emancipating their slaves. Free blacks—particularly but not exclusively in the South—also were vulnerable to being taken captive, accused of being runaway slaves, and sold into slavery.

> # CAUTION!!
> ## COLORED PEOPLE
> ### OF BOSTON, ONE & ALL,
> You are hereby respectfully CAUTIONED and advised, to avoid conversing with the
> ## Watchmen and Police Officers of Boston,
> For since the recent ORDER OF THE MAYOR & ALDERMEN, they are empowered to act as
> # KIDNAPPERS
> AND
> ## Slave Catchers,
> And they have already been actually employed in KIDNAPPING, CATCHING, AND KEEPING SLAVES. Therefore, if you value your LIBERTY, and the *Welfare of the Fugitives* among you, *Shun* them in every possible manner, as so many *HOUNDS* on the track of the most unfortunate of your race.
> ## Keep a Sharp Look Out for KIDNAPPERS, and have TOP EYE open.
> *APRIL 24, 1851.*

An 1851 handbill from the abolitionist Boston Vigilance Committee warned the "Colored People of Boston" to avoid talking to watchmen and police officers as they were newly empowered by the Fugitive Slave Act to apprehend escaped slaves. Part of the Compromise of 1850, the act was conceived to appease southerners who opposed the entry of California into the Union as a free state. Source: The Granger Collection, New York

Slaves had no recourse from harsh or brutal treatment, and free blacks found their options for dealing with injustice extremely limited. Many states, even those that did not allow slavery, limited African Americans' access to the legal system, and many barred them from testifying in court. By the start of the Civil War in 1861, only a half dozen northern states still allowed blacks to vote. Even where they were allowed to vote, as in Pennsylvania before its 1838 constitutional revisions disenfranchised them, it was not uncommon for blacks to be discouraged from voting or to be turned away from the polls.

African Americans, therefore, had no effective avenue for political participation. As a result, black officeholders were nonexistent in the South and exceedingly rare in the North, although a few were elected or appointed to local positions. Examples include William A. Liedesdorff, a successful black merchant who was born in the West Indies, who was elected to the town council of San Francisco in 1847, three years before California was admitted to the Union; Macon B. Allen, who was appointed justice of the peace in 1848 in Middlesex County, Massachusetts; and John M. Langston, who was elected township clerk in 1855 in Brownhelm, Ohio, where abolitionist sentiment was strong.

Despite their limited opportunities for electoral participation, free African Americans were far from acquiescent. They regularly petitioned Congress and state legislatures to obtain or defend their rights. Related documents in this chapter include a petition to the state legislature of Massachusetts from a group of black men who objected to being taxed without being allowed to vote (**Document 1.2**) and a petition to Congress from several free black men who had been forced to flee North Carolina to avoid being sold back into slavery (**Document 1.5**). Such petitions were common, and sometimes—as in the Massachusetts case—they were successful.

African Americans also sought to organize themselves to generate political and social influence, and above all, they engaged passionately in the public debate over slavery, the rights of free blacks and even the rights of women. Frederick Douglass (**Document 1.12**) was the preeminent African American voice of the abolition movement, but he was hardly alone. Articulate and outspoken black activists such as Maria W. Stewart (**Document 1.7**), William Hamilton (**Document 1.8**) and Charles L. Remond (**Document 1.10**) made their marks, as did groups of concerned individuals. In 1838 a committee representing Pennsylvania's African American voters, who faced disenfranchisement, issued a detailed, passionate and carefully reasoned appeal, hoping to persuade the state's white voters that justice lay in protecting the rights of blacks (**Document 1.9**).

The period between the Revolution and the Civil War can be interpreted as a struggle to determine whether those five key words of the Declaration—"all men are created equal"—applied to blacks as well as whites. For African Americans and white abolitionists, the answer was a clear and resounding yes. But most southern whites, and even many white northerners who did not approve of slavery, dismissed the idea and rejected absolutely any notion of equality between blacks and whites. The latter position was in the ascendancy throughout the period. Segregation and disenfranchisement spread, even in the North, and with the *Dred Scott* decision, the nation's highest court asserted that blacks had no rights that whites were bound to respect. Taken as a whole, the documents in this chapter outline the arc of the African American struggle for freedom in the first eighty years of the Republic.

Document 1.1 in Context
"All Men Are Created Equal": Slavery Plagues a Fledgling Democracy

No document, not even the U.S. Constitution (**Document 1.4**), is more central to the struggle of African Americans for political and civil rights than the Declaration of Independence. The Constitution, of course, is of monumental importance because it defines the rights that are guaranteed to all citizens of the United States. The Declaration, however, established the very philosophical framework around which the Constitution was built. The Declaration is the nation's rationale for its very existence, its statement of principle, the promise by which the delivery of the Constitution is judged.

The Declaration identifies the rights to "Life, Liberty and the pursuit of Happiness" as so central to the human condition that they are "unalienable," incapable of being taken or even given away, and it asserts that the legitimacy of any government is dependent upon "the consent of the governed." But the language of the Declaration that has echoed most resoundingly across the years is the simple, five-word assertion that "all men are created equal."

That modest phrase has been the focal point of debate over the political and civil rights of African Americans for more than two centuries. Its presence in the Declaration underscored a fundamental dichotomy in American society. At the same time that the founders were declaring their absolute commitment to freedom and liberty, the colonies—particularly the southern ones—were relying increasingly on chattel slavery for economic prosperity.

The conflict was not lost on the Declaration's authors and signers, and it shaped the content of the final document. An early draft had included among the list of offenses ascribed to King George III a paragraph charging that the king was responsible for the existence of slavery in the colonies. Slavery, the paragraph stated, was a "cruel war against human nature itself," initiated and waged by "the Christian king of Great Britain." The passage was intended to underscore the hypocrisy of the king, but it was cut because it was undermined by the colonists' own continuing participation in the slave trade. Thus, all direct reference to slavery was removed from the Declaration, but the assertion that "all men are created equal" remained.

In 1854 Frederick Douglass threw the language of the Declaration back in the face of America, demanding to know how a nation that claimed to be committed to liberty and justice could countenance human slavery (**Document 1.12**). In November 1863, less than a decade later, when President Abraham Lincoln sought in the Gettysburg Address to persuade Americans that the Civil War was being fought—and *should* be fought—not merely to preserve the Union but also to preserve and advance the nation's commitment to freedom, he too recalled the words of the Declaration. A century later, in August 1963, Rev. Martin Luther King Jr. stood on the steps of the Lincoln Memorial in Washington, D.C., and once again called on America to fulfill its promise by recommitting itself to the words of the Declaration: "I have a dream that one day this nation will rise up and live out the true meaning of its creed: 'We hold these truths to be self-evident, that all men are created equal.' "

Document 1.1
Declaration of Independence, July 4, 1776

IN CONGRESS, July 4, 1776.

The unanimous Declaration of the thirteen united States of America,

When in the Course of human events, it becomes necessary for one people to dissolve the political bands which have connected them with another, and to assume among the powers of the earth, the separate and equal station to which the Laws of Nature and of Nature's God entitle them, a decent respect to the opinions of mankind requires that they should declare the causes which impel them to the separation.

We hold these truths to be self-evident, that all men are created equal, that they are endowed by their Creator with certain unalienable Rights, that among these are Life, Liberty and the pursuit of Happiness.—That to secure these rights, Governments are instituted among Men, deriving their just powers from the consent of the governed, —That whenever any Form of Government becomes destructive of these ends, it is the Right of the People to alter or to abolish it, and to institute new Government, laying its foundation on such principles and organizing its powers in such form, as to them shall seem most likely to effect their Safety and Happiness. Prudence, indeed, will dictate that Governments long established should not be changed for light and transient causes; and accordingly all experience hath shewn, that mankind are more disposed to suffer, while evils are sufferable, than to right themselves by abolishing the forms to which they are accustomed. But when a long train of abuses and usurpations, pursuing invariably the same Object evinces a design to reduce them under absolute Despotism, it is their right, it is their duty, to throw off such Government, and to provide new Guards for their future security.—Such has been the patient sufferance of these Colonies; and such is now the necessity which constrains them to alter their former Systems of Government. The history of the present King of Great Britain is a history of repeated injuries and usurpations, all having in direct object the establishment of an absolute Tyranny over these States. To prove this, let Facts be submitted to a candid world.

He has refused his Assent to Laws, the most wholesome and necessary for the public good.

He has forbidden his Governors to pass Laws of immediate and pressing importance, unless suspended in their operation till his Assent should be obtained; and when so suspended, he has utterly neglected to attend to them.

He has refused to pass other Laws for the accommodation of large districts of people, unless those people would relinquish the right of Representation in the Legislature, a right inestimable to them and formidable to tyrants only.

He has called together legislative bodies at places unusual, uncomfortable, and distant from the depository of their public Records, for the sole purpose of fatiguing them into compliance with his measures.

He has dissolved Representative Houses repeatedly, for opposing with manly firmness his invasions on the rights of the people.

He has refused for a long time, after such dissolutions, to cause others to be elected; whereby the Legislative powers, incapable of Annihilation, have returned to the People at large for their exercise; the State remaining in the mean time exposed to all the dangers of invasion from without, and convulsions within.

He has endeavoured to prevent the population of these States; for that purpose obstructing the Laws for Naturalization of Foreigners; refusing to pass others to encourage their migrations hither, and raising the conditions of new Appropriations of Lands.

He has obstructed the Administration of Justice, by refusing his Assent to Laws for establishing Judiciary powers.

He has made Judges dependent on his Will alone, for the tenure of their offices, and the amount and payment of their salaries.

He has erected a multitude of New Offices, and sent hither swarms of Officers to harrass our people, and eat out their substance.

He has kept among us, in times of peace, Standing Armies without the Consent of our legislatures.

He has affected to render the Military independent of and superior to the Civil power.

He has combined with others to subject us to a jurisdiction foreign to our constitution, and unacknowledged by our laws; giving his Assent to their Acts of pretended Legislation:

For Quartering large bodies of armed troops among us:

For protecting them, by a mock Trial, from punishment for any Murders which they should commit on the Inhabitants of these States:

For cutting off our Trade with all parts of the world:

For imposing Taxes on us without our Consent:

For depriving us in many cases, of the benefits of Trial by Jury:

For transporting us beyond Seas to be tried for pretended offences:

For abolishing the free System of English Laws in a neighbouring Province, establishing therein an Arbitrary government, and enlarging its Boundaries so as to render it at once an example and fit instrument for introducing the same absolute rule into these Colonies:

For taking away our Charters, abolishing our most valuable Laws, and altering fundamentally the Forms of our Governments:

For suspending our own Legislatures, and declaring themselves invested with power to legislate for us in all cases whatsoever.

He has abdicated Government here, by declaring us out of his Protection and waging War against us.

He has plundered our seas, ravaged our Coasts, burnt our towns, and destroyed the lives of our people.

He is at this time transporting large Armies of foreign Mercenaries to compleat the works of death, desolation and tyranny, already begun with circumstances of Cruelty & perfidy scarcely paralleled in the most barbarous ages, and totally unworthy the Head of a civilized nation.

He has constrained our fellow Citizens taken Captive on the high Seas to bear Arms against their Country, to become the executioners of their friends and Brethren, or to fall themselves by their Hands.

He has excited domestic insurrections amongst us, and has endeavoured to bring on the inhabitants of our frontiers, the merciless Indian Savages, whose known rule of warfare, is an undistinguished destruction of all ages, sexes and conditions.

In every stage of these Oppressions We have Petitioned for Redress in the most humble terms: Our repeated Petitions have been answered only by repeated injury. A Prince whose character is thus marked by every act which may define a Tyrant, is unfit to be the ruler of a free people.

Nor have We been wanting in attentions to our Brittish brethren. We have warned them from time to time of attempts by their legislature to extend an unwarrantable jurisdiction over us. We have reminded them of the circumstances of our emigration and settlement here. We have appealed to their native justice and magnanimity, and we have conjured them by the ties of our common kindred to disavow these usurpations, which, would inevitably interrupt our connections and correspondence. They too have been deaf to the voice of justice and of consanguinity. We must, therefore, acquiesce in the necessity, which denounces our Separation, and hold them, as we hold the rest of mankind, Enemies in War, in Peace Friends.

We, therefore, the Representatives of the united States of America, in General Congress, Assembled, appealing to the Supreme Judge of the world for the rectitude of our intentions, do, in the Name, and by Authority of the good People of these Colonies, solemnly publish and declare, That these United Colonies are, and of Right ought to be Free and Independent States; that they are Absolved from all Allegiance to the British Crown, and that all political connection between them and the State of Great Britain, is and ought to be totally dissolved; and that as Free and Independent States, they have full Power to levy War, conclude Peace, contract Alliances, establish Commerce, and to do all other Acts and Things which Independent States may of right do. And for the support of this Declaration, with a firm reliance on the protection of divine Providence, we mutually pledge to each other our Lives, our Fortunes and our sacred Honor.

Source: "Declaration of Independence," July 4, 1776, from the U.S. National Archives and Records Administration, www.ourdocuments.gov.

Document 1.2 in Context
"We Apprehend Ourselves to Be Aggrieved": African Americans Petition for the Right to Vote

The struggle of African Americans to obtain and exercise political rights dates to the earliest days of the Republic. At the time of the Revolution, the vast majority of African Americans were slaves and therefore had no political rights. But there were also free blacks in every state, and in some states, at some times, free blacks were allowed to vote.

Voting rights did not come easily to African Americans, however, and there was no guarantee that such rights would be sustained. In the period between the Revolution and the Civil War, blacks generally faced increasing exclusion and disenfranchisement as state after state adopted statutes—or was admitted to the Union with a state constitution—that barred them from voting. Some states, such as New York and Rhode Island, did not entirely disenfranchise African Americans but restricted their voting rights with property qualifications or poll taxes. Blacks had the greatest opportunity to vote in the New England states, but even there, obtaining the franchise took effort.

When they were denied their rights, African Americans regularly petitioned governmental bodies to seek redress. The petitioners in this 1780 Massachusetts case were already free; they were asking the state house of representatives to grant them the right to vote. Among the petitioners were Paul Cuffe, a successful shipowner who later was active in an effort to return African Americans to Africa, and his brother John. Both men had been jailed for refusing to pay their taxes to protest the fact that they were not allowed to vote. Their petition, written while the Revolutionary War was still being fought, is notable for the way in which it draws on the philosophy and slogans of the war to highlight the injustice and irony of their situation and to make the case for allowing blacks to vote. The Massachusetts petitioners emphasized the irony of their situation by noting in polite and understated tones the military service of "many of our color . . . against a similar exertion of power (in regard to taxation), too well known to need a recital in this place."

About five thousand African Americans had fought in the Continental army in support of American liberty. And yet, despite their sacrifice and service, black veterans found themselves still enslaved, or being taxed by the new state governments while being denied the right to vote for the representatives who assessed the taxes. In an unusual North Carolina case in 1784, a man named Ned Griffin petitioned the state's general assembly, asserting that he had served in the Continental army in the place of a white man named William Kitchen, who had promised Griffin his freedom in exchange for his military service. The assembly agreed that Griffin had fulfilled his part of the bargain and passed legislation granting him his freedom.

In the same year that the Massachusetts petition was written, the state adopted a constitution banning slavery. By 1783 the state allowed all free property-owning men to vote.

▬▬ Document 1.2 ▬▬
Petition for Voting Rights from Seven African American Men, Dartmouth, Massachusetts, March 1780

To the Honorable Council and House of Representatives, in General Court assembled, for the state of Massachusetts Bay, in New England:

The petition of several poor negroes and mulattoes, who are inhabitants of the town of Dartmouth, humbly showeth,—

That we being chiefly of the African extract, and by reason of long bondage and hard slavery, we have been deprived of enjoying the profits of our labor or the advantage of inheriting estates from our parents, as our neighbors the white people do, having some of us not long enjoyed our own freedom; yet of late, contrary to the invariable custom and practice of the country, we have been, and now are, taxed both in our polls and that small pittance of estate which, through much hard labor and industry, we have got together to sustain ourselves and families withall. We apprehend it, therefore, to be hard usage, and will doubtless (if continued) reduce to a state of beggary, whereby we shall become a burthen to others, if not timely prevented by the interposition of your justice and power.

Your petitioners further show, that we apprehend ourselves to be aggrieved, in that, while we are not allowed the privilege of freemen of the State, having no vote or influence in the election of those that tax us, yet many of our colour (as is well known) have cheerfully entered the field of battle in the defence of the common cause, and that (as we conceive) against a similar exertion of power (in regard to taxation), too well known to need a recital in this place . . .

. . . We most humbly request, therefore, that you would take our unhappy case into your serious consideration, and in your wisdom and power, grant us relief from taxation, while under our present depressed circumstances, and your poor petitioners, as in duty bound, shall ever pray, &c.

> (signed)
> John Cuffe
> Adventur Child
> Paul Cuffe
> Samuel X Gray
> Pero X Howland
> Pero X Russell
> Pero Goggeshall
> [X indicates the signer made his mark]

Source: "Petition For Voting Rights from Seven African American Men, Dartmouth, Massachusetts," 1780, SC1/series 45X, Massachusetts Archives Collection, vol. 186, 134–136.

Document 1.3 in Context
"Such Fugitive May Be Lawfully Reclaimed": Slavery and the Northwest Territory

In the summer of 1787, the newly independent United States of America was still operating under the Articles of Confederation. The Revolutionary War had ended barely five years earlier, and the Constitution had yet to be drafted and ratified. Already a great impetus was building for westward expansion. Now that the Americans were free of British rule, many were eager to assert and solidify the nation's claim to the vast territory north of the Ohio River and east of the Mississippi River.

In 1784 a congressional committee led by Thomas Jefferson had issued a report proposing guidelines for governing western territories and the process of admitting new states to the Union. However, the Northwest Territory (including the present-day states of Ohio, Michigan, Indiana, Illinois and Wisconsin) remained officially off-limits for development. That did not prevent increasing numbers of settlers from moving into the territory, and speculators, such as the Ohio Land Company, from pressing Congress to lift the restrictions.

The Northwest Ordinance that was adopted by Congress on July 13, 1787, essentially followed the proposals of Jefferson's committee. It contained three major provisions. First, it made clear that the Northwest Territory would eventually become part of the United States, and that the area would be divided into at least three but no more than five states.

Second, it established a three-phase process for admitting new states to the Union. In the first phase, a governor, secretary and three judges would be appointed by Congress to govern. When the population of a proposed state had grown to "five thousand free male inhabitants of full age," the second phase would begin. The territory would then establish an elected assembly and a nonvoting representative would be sent to Congress. In the third phase, once the territory's population had reached 60,000, the assembly would draft a state constitution and request admission to the Union.

Finally, the ordinance laid out a bill of rights to protect residents of the Northwest Territory. Religious freedom was guaranteed, as were the rights to habeas corpus and trial by jury. The ordinance also protected property rights, prohibited cruel and unusual punishments for crimes, and established a process for levying taxes.

The Northwest Ordinance accelerated the first great westward expansion of the United States. At the same time, it planted some of the seeds of a conflict that festered for nearly three-quarters of a century. In the final article of its last section, the ordinance proclaimed, "There shall be neither slavery nor involuntary servitude in the said territory." However, the article went on to guarantee the right of slave owners (though that indelicate term was not used) to reclaim runaway slaves who might escape into the free territory. It was a guarantee that was later written into the Constitution (**Document 1.4**) as well. In banning slavery in the Northwest but protecting the property rights of slave owners, the ordinance struck the awkward compromise by which the nation would live—and would be tormented—for the next seven decades.

Document 1.3
Northwest Ordinance, July 13, 1787

An Ordinance for the government of the Territory of the United States northwest of the River Ohio.

SECTION 1. Be it ordained by the United States in Congress assembled, That the said territory, for the purposes of temporary government, be one district, subject, however, to be divided into two districts, as future circumstances may, in the opinion of Congress, make it expedient . . .

SEC. 3. Be it ordained by the authority aforesaid, That there shall be appointed from time to time by Congress, a governor, whose commission shall continue in force for the term of three years, unless sooner revoked by Congress . . .

SEC. 4. There shall be appointed from time to time by Congress, a secretary, whose commission shall continue in force for four years unless sooner revoked . . . There shall also be appointed a court to consist of three judges, any two of whom to form a court, who shall have a common law jurisdiction, and reside in the district, and have each therein a freehold estate in 500 acres of land while in the exercise of their offices; and their commissions shall continue in force during good behavior.

SEC. 5. The governor and judges, or a majority of them, shall adopt and publish in the district such laws of the original States, criminal and civil, as may be necessary and best suited to the circumstances of the district, and report them to Congress from time to time: which laws shall be in force in the district until the organization of the General Assembly therein, unless disapproved of by Congress; but afterwards the Legislature shall have authority to alter them as they shall think fit.

SEC. 6. The governor, for the time being, shall be commander in chief of the militia, appoint and commission all officers in the same below the rank of general officers; all general officers shall be appointed and commissioned by Congress.

SEC. 7. Previous to the organization of the general assembly, the governor shall appoint such magistrates and other civil officers in each county or township, as he shall find necessary for the preservation of the peace and good order in the same: After the general assembly shall be organized, the powers and duties of the magistrates and other civil officers shall be regulated and defined by the said assembly; but all magistrates and other civil officers not herein otherwise directed, shall during the continuance of this temporary government, be appointed by the governor . . .

SEC. 9. So soon as there shall be five thousand free male inhabitants of full age in the district, upon giving proof thereof to the governor, they shall receive authority, with time and place, to elect a representative from their counties or townships to represent them in the general assembly: Provided, That, for every five hundred free male inhabitants, there shall be one representative, and so on progressively with the number of free male inhabitants shall the right of representation increase, until the number of representatives shall amount to twenty five; after which, the number and proportion of representatives shall be regulated by the legislature: Provided, That no person be eligible or qualified to act as a representative unless he shall have been a citizen of one of the United States three years, and be a resident in the district, or unless he shall have resided in the district three years; and, in either case, shall likewise hold in his own right, in fee simple, two hundred acres of land within the same; Provided, also, That a freehold in fifty acres of land in the district, having been a citizen of one of the states, and being resident in the district, or the like freehold and two years residence in the district, shall be necessary to qualify a man as an elector of a representative . . .

SEC. 13. And, for extending the fundamental principles of civil and religious liberty, which form the basis whereon these republics, their laws and constitutions are erected; to fix and establish those principles as the basis of all laws, constitutions, and governments, which forever hereafter shall be formed in the said territory: to provide also for the establishment of States, and permanent government therein, and for their admission to a share in the federal councils on an equal footing with the original States, at as early periods as may be consistent with the general interest:

SEC. 14. It is hereby ordained and declared by the authority aforesaid, That the following articles shall be considered as articles of compact between the original States and the people and States in the said territory and forever remain unalterable, unless by common consent, to wit:

Art. 1. No person, demeaning himself in a peaceable and orderly manner, shall ever be molested on account of his mode of worship or religious sentiments, in the said territory.

Art. 2. The inhabitants of the said territory shall always be entitled to the benefits of the writ of habeas corpus, and of the trial by jury; of a proportionate representation of the people in the legislature; and of judicial proceedings according to the course of the common law. All persons shall be bailable, unless for capital offenses, where the proof shall be evident or the presumption great. All fines shall be moderate; and no cruel or unusual punishments shall be inflicted. No man shall be deprived of his liberty or property, but by the judgment of his peers or the law of the land; and, should the public exigencies make it necessary, for the common preservation, to take any person's property, or to demand his particular services, full compensation shall be made for the same. And, in the just preservation of rights and property, it is understood and declared, that no law ought ever to be made, or have force in the said territory, that shall, in any manner whatever, interfere with or affect private contracts or engagements, bona fide, and without fraud, previously formed.

Art. 3. Religion, morality, and knowledge, being necessary to good government and the happiness of mankind, schools and the means of education shall forever be encouraged. The utmost good faith shall always be observed towards the Indians; their lands and property shall never be taken from them without their consent; and, in their property, rights, and liberty, they shall never be invaded or disturbed, unless in just and lawful wars authorized by Congress; but laws founded in justice and humanity, shall from time to time be made for preventing wrongs being done to them, and for preserving peace and friendship with them.

Art. 4. The said territory, and the States which may be formed therein, shall forever remain a part of this Confederacy of the United States of America, subject to the Articles of Confederation, and to such alterations therein as shall be constitutionally made; and to all the acts and ordinances of the United States in Congress assembled, conformable thereto . . .

Art. 5. There shall be formed in the said territory, not less than three nor more than five States; and the boundaries of the States, as soon as Virginia shall alter her act of cession, and consent to the same, shall become fixed and established . . . And, whenever any of the said States shall have sixty thousand free inhabitants therein, such State shall be admitted, by its delegates, into the Congress of the United States, on an equal footing with the original States in all respects whatever, and shall be at liberty to form a permanent constitution and State government: Provided, the constitution and government so to be formed, shall be republican, and in conformity to the principles contained in these articles; and, so far as it can be consistent with the general interest of the confederacy, such admission shall be allowed at an earlier period, and when there may be a less number of free inhabitants in the State than sixty thousand.

Art. 6. There shall be neither slavery nor involuntary servitude in the said territory, otherwise than in the punishment of crimes whereof the party shall have been duly convicted: Provided, always, That any person escaping into the same, from whom labor or service is lawfully claimed in any one of the original States, such fugitive may be lawfully reclaimed and conveyed to the person claiming his or her labor or service as aforesaid.

Be it ordained by the authority aforesaid, That the resolutions of the 23rd of April, 1784, relative to the subject of this ordinance, be, and the same are hereby repealed and declared null and void.

Done by the United States, in Congress assembled, the 13th day of July, in the year of our Lord 1787, and of their sovereignty and independence the twelfth.

Source: "Northwest Ordinance," July 13, 1787, from the U.S. National Archives and Records Administration, www.ourdocuments.gov.

Document 1.4 in Context
"Three Fifths of All Other Persons": The Constitution and the Three-Fifths Compromise

In some ways, the Constitution is a profoundly ambiguous document. That ambiguity has had enormous consequences for—and has raised difficult questions concerning—the political and civil rights of African Americans. The most fundamental issue is whether the Constitution included African Americans among "the people" who were to be considered citizens of the United States.

Remarkably, the Constitution never uses the word *slavery*. Everything that the Constitution has to say about slavery and the status of African Americans is said indirectly, by implication. The three clauses that most clearly carry those implications—Article 1, sections 2 and 9, and Article 4, section 2—had a profound impact on the status of blacks in the new nation and illustrate the complex balancing act the framers had to perform to win ratification of the document.

To win approval, the Constitution had to balance abolitionist sentiment against the economic interests of southern planters who had a huge financial investment in their slaves and a system of cash crop agriculture that required vast amounts of human labor. On one level, the Constitution deferred the issue, by putting off until 1808 any action on banning the foreign slave trade. It also protected slaveholders by requiring the return of fugitives who had escaped from service.

But the most delicate—and most significant—of the slavery-related provisions is contained in Article 1, section 3. Known as the Three-Fifths Compromise, the provision describes how state populations shall be counted for purposes of direct taxation and representation in Congress. In effect, while carefully avoiding use of the word, it states that three-fifths of slaves—

"all other Persons"—should be counted, which helped establish a balance of power in Congress that sustained the status quo on slavery.

Thus was the compromise cast, ensuring that slavery would continue for the time being. And because the Constitution appeared to condone slavery, it could be used to justify widely divergent views on the status of free blacks in American society. That ambiguity clearly worked to the disadvantage of African Americans, who for the next two centuries had to struggle to attain the rights that the document asserted were the birthright of all Americans.

▬ Document 1.4 ▬
Constitution of the United States, September 17, 1787

PREAMBLE
We the People of the United States, in Order to form a more perfect Union, establish Justice, insure domestic Tranquility, provide for the common defense, promote the general Welfare, and secure the Blessings of Liberty to ourselves and our Posterity, do ordain and establish this Constitution for the United States of America.

ARTICLE I
. . .

Section 2. Representatives and direct Taxes shall be apportioned among the several States which may be included within this Union, according to their respective Numbers, which shall be determined by adding to the whole Number of free Persons, including those bound to Service for a Term of Years, and excluding Indians not taxed, three fifths of all other Persons. The actual Enumeration shall be made within three Years after the first Meeting of the Congress of the United States, and within every subsequent Term of ten Years, in such Manner as they shall by Law direct. The Number of Representatives shall not exceed one for every thirty Thousand, but each State shall have at Least one Representative; and until such enumeration shall be made, the State of New Hampshire shall be entitled to chuse three, Massachusetts eight, Rhode-Island and Providence Plantations one, Connecticut five, New York six, New Jersey four, Pennsylvania eight, Delaware one, Maryland six, Virginia ten, North Carolina five, South Carolina five, and Georgia three . . .

Section 9. The Migration or Importation of such Persons as any of the States now existing shall think proper to admit, shall not be prohibited by the Congress prior to the Year one thousand eight hundred and eight, but a Tax or duty may be imposed on such Importation, not exceeding ten dollars for each Person . . .

ARTICLE IV
. . .

Section 2. No Person held to Service or Labour in one State, under the Laws thereof, escaping into another, shall, in Consequence of any Law or Regulation therein, be discharged from such Service or Labour, but shall be delivered up on Claim of the Party to whom such Service or Labour may be due . . .

Source: "Constitution of the United States," September 17, 1787, from the U.S. National Archives and Records Administration, www.ourdocuments.gov.

Document 1.5 in Context
"The Unconstitutional Bondage in Which Multitudes of Our Fellows in Complexion Are Held, Is to Us a Subject Sorrowfully Affecting": Free African Americans Petition Congress to Retain Their Freedom

Although the vast majority of African Americans were slaves when the American colonies won their independence from Britain, there were free black people living in every state of the new Union. Their freedom, however, was a tentative and fragile thing. Even legal manumission by a slave owner was no guarantee that the newly freed slave would remain free.

The following 1797 petition to Congress was submitted by Jacob Nicholson, Jupiter Nicholson, Job Albert and Thomas Pritchet, four free black men who had lived in North Carolina. All had been manumitted by their former masters but had been forced to flee North Carolina because of threats and attempts by whites to take them captive and sell them back into slavery.

All four had to leave members of their family behind, some of whom, despite being manumitted, were abducted and sold again into slavery. Nicholson explained in the petition: "I left behind me a father and mother, who were manumitted by Thomas Nicholson and Zachary Nickson; they have since been taken up, with a beloved brother, and sold into cruel bondage." Albert reported that the same thing happened to his mother and sister.

The petition sparked debate in the House of Representatives over how to respond. Rep. Thomas Blount, R.-N.C., said that the House should not even receive the petition because the petitioners were slaves under the law of North Carolina, where it was not legal for individuals to emancipate their slaves. But Rep. John Swanwick, R-Pa., who had presented the petition on January 30, said that all men had a right to petition Congress, although the House would have to decide whether to grant the relief they sought. Swanwick was particularly shocked by the petition's description of another former slave who had been manumitted in North Carolina only to be arrested later as a fugitive slave; an advertisement for his capture had offered a reward of ten dollars if he were captured alive, fifty dollars if he were found dead, a clear incitement to homicide. "Could gentlemen hear it and not shudder?" Swanwick asked the House.[4]

Although this is the first recorded petition to Congress by free blacks, it was followed by numerous others. In 1800, for example, a group of free blacks from Philadelphia submitted a petition asking Congress to end the African slave trade and to change laws requiring the return of fugitive slaves to their owners. Like the North Carolina petition, the Philadelphia petition set off heated debate in the House, especially over its suggestion that slavery violated the Constitution. Rep. John Rutledge Jr., Federalist-S.C., expressed irritation at the repeated presentation of petitions to Congress on the issue of slavery. He complained that "too much of this new-fangled French philosophy of liberty and equality" had found its way to the United States.[5]

In addition to detailing the struggles and suffering of the four North Carolina petitioners, the petition illuminates the vulnerability of all free black people in the United States at the time. Any free black person could find himself or herself suddenly accused of being a runaway slave and forced to justify his or her freedom. The disregard with which many whites and even state governments treated the rights of free African Americans before the Civil War would help give rise to an organized, and dedicated antislavery movement.

▬ Document 1.5 ▬
A Petition of Four Free Blacks to the United States House of Representatives, as Presented to Congress on January 30, 1797

To the President, Senate, and House of Representatives.

The Petition and Representation of the under-named Freemen, respectfully showeth:—

That, being of African descent, late inhabitants and natives of North Carolina, to you only, under God, can we apply with any hope of effect for redress of our grievances, having been compelled to leave the State wherein we had a right of residence, as freemen liberated under the hand and seal of humane and conscientious masters, the validity of which act of justice, in restoring us to our native right of freedom, was confirmed by judgment of the Superior Court of North Carolina, wherein it was brought to trial; yet, not long after this decision, a law of that State was enacted, under which men of cruel disposition, and void of just principle, received countenance and authority in violently seizing, imprisoning, and selling into slavery, such as had been so emancipated; whereby we were reduced to the necessity of separating from some of our nearest and most tender connexions, and of seeking refuge in such parts of the Union where more regard is paid to the public declaration in favor of liberty and the common right of man, several hundreds, under our circumstances, having in consequence of the said law, been hunted day and night, like beasts of the forest, by armed men with dogs and made a prey of as free and lawful plunder. Among others thus exposed, I, Jupiter Nicholson, of Perquimans county, North Carolina, after being set free by my master, Thomas Nicholson, and having been about two years employed as a seaman in the service of Zachary Nickson, on coming on shore, was pursued by men with dogs and arms; but was favored to escape by night to Virginia, with my wife, who was manumitted by Gabriel Cosand, where I resided about four years in the town of Portsmouth, chiefly employed in sawing boards and scantling; from thence I removed with my wife to Philadelphia, where I have been employed, at times, by water, working along shore, or sawing wood. I left behind me a father and mother, who were manumitted by Thomas Nicholson and Zachary Nickson; they have since been taken up, with a beloved brother, and sold into cruel bondage.

I, Jacob Nicholson, also of North Carolina, being set free by my master, Joseph Nicholson, but continuing to live with him till, being pursued night and day, I was obliged to leave my abode, sleep in the woods, and stacks in the fields, &c, to escape the hands of violent men who, induced by the profit afforded them by law, followed this course as a business; at length, by night, I made my escape, leaving a mother, one child, and two brothers, to see whom I dare not return.

I, Job Albert, manumitted by Benjamin Albertson, who was my careful guardian to protect me from being afterwards taken and sold, providing me with a house to accommodate me and my wife, who was liberated by William Robertson; but we were night and day hunted by men armed with guns, swords, and pistols, accompanied with mastiff dogs; from whose violence, being one night apprehensive of immediate danger, I left my dwelling, locked and barred, and fastened with a chain, being at some distance from it, while my wife was by my kind master locked up under his roof. I heard them break into my house, where, not finding their prey, they got but a small booty, a handkerchief of about a dollar value, and some provisions; but, not long after, I was discovered and seized by Alexander Stafford, William Stafford, and Thomas Creesy, who were armed with guns and clubs. After binding me with my hands behind me, and a rope around my arms and body, they took me about four miles to Hartford prison, where I lay four weeks, suffering much from want of provision; from thence, with the assistance of a fellow-prisoner, (a white man,) I made my escape and for three dollars was conveyed, with my wife, by a humane person, in a covered wagon by night, to Virginia, where, in the neighborhood of Portsmouth, I continued unmolested about four years, being chiefly engaged in sawing boards and plank. On being advised to move North-ward, I came with my wife to Philadelphia, where I have labored for a livelihood upwards of two years, in Summer mostly, along shore in vessels and stores, and sawing wood in the Winter. My mother was set free of Phineas Nickson, my sister by John Trueblood, and both taken up and sold into slavery, myself deprived of the consolation of seeing them, without being exposed to the like grievous oppression.

I, Thomas Pritchet, was set free by my master Thomas Pritchet, who furnished me with land to raise provisions for my use, where I built myself a house . . . This I was obliged to leave . . . being threatened by Holland Lockwood, who married my said master's widow, that if I would not come and serve him, he would apprehend me, and send me to the West Indies; Enoch Ralph also threatening to send me to jail, and sell me for the good of the country; being thus in jeopardy, I left my little farm, with my small stock and utensils, and my corn standing, and escaped by night into Virginia, where shipping myself to Boston, I was, through stress of weather landed in New York, where I served as a waiter for seventeen months; but my mind being distressed on account of the situation of my wife and children, I returned to Norfolk in Virginia, with a hope of at least seeing them, if I could not obtain their freedom; but finding I was advertised in the newspaper, twenty dollars the reward for apprehending me, my dangerous situation obliged me to leave Virginia, disappointed of seeing my wife and children, coming to Philadelphia, where I resided in the employment of a waiter upward of two years.

In addition to the hardship of our own case, as above set forth, we believe ourselves war-ranted, on the present occasion, in offering to your consideration the singular case of a fel-low-black now confined in the jail of this city under sanction of the act of General Government, called the Fugitive Law . . . This man, having been many years past manu-mitted by his master in North Carolina, was under the authority of the aforementioned law of that State, sold again into slavery, and, after serving his purchaser upwards of six years, made his escape to Philadelphia, where he has resided eleven years, having a wife and [f]our children; and, by an agent of the Carolina claimer, has been lately apprehended and com-mitted to prison, his said claimer, soon after the man's escaping from him, having advertised him, offering a reward of ten silver dollars to any person that would bring him back, or five times that sum to any person that would make due proof of his being killed, and no ques-tions asked by whom.

We beseech your impartial attention to our hard condition, not only with respect to our personal sufferings, as freemen, but as a class of that people who, distinguished by color, are therefore with a degrading partiality, considered by many, even of those in eminent stations, as unentitled to that public justice and protection which is the great object of Government . . .

If, notwithstanding all that has been publicly avowed as essential principles respecting the extent of human right to freedom; notwithstanding we have had that right restored to us, so far as was in the power of those by whom we were held as slaves, we cannot claim the privilege of representation in your councils, yet we trust we may address you as fellow-men, who, under God, the sovereign Ruler of the Universe, are intrusted with the distribution of justice, for the terror of evil-doers, the encouragement and protection of the innocent, not doubting that you are men of liberal minds, susceptible of benevolent feelings and clear conception of rectitude to a catholic extent, who can admit that black people (servile as their condition generally is throughout this Continent) have natural affections, social and domestic attachments and sensibilities; and that, therefore, we may hope for a share in your sympathetic attention while we represent that the unconstitutional bondage in which multitudes of our fellows in complexion are held, is to us a subject sorrowfully affecting . . . Is not some remedy for an evil of such magnitude highly worthy of the deep inquiry and unfeigned zeal of the supreme Legislative body of a free and enlightened people? . . .

> JACOB NICHOLSON,
> JUPITER NICHOLSON, his mark,
> JOB ALBERT, his mark
> THOMAS PRITCHET, his mark
> Philadelphia, January 23, 1797

Source: Annals of Congress, 4th Cong., 2d sess., January 30, 1797, 2015–2018, from the Library of Congress, http://memory.loc.gov/ammem/amlaw/lwac.html.

Document 1.6 in Context
"This Is a Reprieve Only, Not a Final Sentence": The Missouri Compromise

Throughout the first half of the nineteenth century, the westward expansion of the United States strained the delicate balance the founders had achieved on the issue of slavery to win ratification of the Constitution. Southerners feared the prohibition of slavery in new western states would give northern abolitionists the congressional majority they needed to outlaw slavery altogether, which would devastate the southern plantation economy. Northern opponents of slavery suspected that southern slave interests would not be satisfied until slavery was legal and acceptable throughout the nation.

Not surprisingly, tensions over slavery tended to peak during debates over the admission of new states to the Union. The first major challenge to the status quo came in 1818, when the Missouri Territory's population reached the level that qualified it to seek statehood. Missouri was the first area to seek statehood from the original Louisiana Territory, which had been purchased from France in 1803 by President Thomas Jefferson. Because most of its settlers had come from the South, many people assumed that Missouri would be admitted to the Union as a slaveholding state. But an intense national controversy was ignited when Rep. James Tallmadge Jr., a Democratic-Republican from New York, sought to amend the Missouri statehood bill to ban the importation of slaves into the state and require the eventual emancipation of all slaves born there. Although Tallmadge's amendment was passed by the House of Representatives, it was blocked by the Senate.

The bitter debate over Tallmadge's proposal illuminated the intensifying sectional differences over the slavery issue. In 1819 Alabama, a slave state, was admitted to the Union, which brought into balance the numbers of free and slave states and gave both sides equal representation in the Senate. When Maine sought admission in early 1820, an effort was made to admit both Maine, as a free state, and Missouri, as a slave state, with a single bill, thereby maintaining the deliberate balance. The House rejected the combined bill, but after intense negotiations, both states were admitted by separate bills. The key change was that Missouri was allowed to establish a state constitution that did not restrict slavery; the Missouri bill, however, established a westward line at 36°30' (the state's southern border) and declared that slavery would be forbidden in the remainder of the territory north of that line. South of that line, slavery would be allowed.

The Missouri Compromise eased the nation past the immediate political crisis and endured for more than three decades, until the Kansas-Nebraska Act of 1854 repealed the demarcation line (**Document 1.13**). But the compromise merely provided temporary relief from tensions that were steadily deepening. In an April 22, 1820, letter to Rep. John Holmes, a Massachusetts Democratic-Republican, Jefferson wrote that the Missouri controversy had, "like a firebell in the night, awakened and filled me with terror. I considered it at once as the knell of the Union. It is hushed, indeed, for the moment. But this is a reprieve only, not a final sentence." [6]

Document 1.6
Missouri Compromise, March 6, 1820

An Act to authorize the people of the Missouri territory to form a constitution and state government, and for the admission of such state into the Union on an equal footing with the original states, and to prohibit slavery in certain territories.

Be it enacted by the Senate and House of Representatives of the United States of America, in Congress assembled, That the inhabitants of that portion of the Missouri territory included within the boundaries herein after designated, be, and they are hereby, authorized to form for themselves a constitution and state government, and to assume such name as they shall deem proper; and the said state, when formed, shall be admitted into the Union, upon an equal footing with the original states, in all respects whatsoever . . .

SECTION 3. And be it further enacted, That all free white male citizens of the United States, who shall have arrived at the age of twenty-one years, and have resided in said territory: three months previous to the day of election, and all other persons qualified to vote for representatives to the general assembly of the said territory, shall be qualified to be elected and they are hereby qualified and authorized to vote, and choose representatives to form a convention, who shall be apportioned amongst the several counties . . .

And the election for the representatives aforesaid shall be holden on the first Monday, and two succeeding days of May next, throughout the several counties aforesaid in the said territory, and shall be, in every respect, held and conducted in the same manner, and under the same regulations as is prescribed by the laws of the said territory regulating elections therein for members of the general assembly . . .

SEC. 4. And be it further enacted, That the members of the convention thus duly elected, shall be, and they are hereby authorized to meet at the seat of government of said territory on the second Monday of the month of June next; and the said convention, when so assembled, shall have power and authority to adjourn to any other place in the said territory, which to them shall seem best for the convenient transaction of their business; and which convention, when so met, shall first determine by a majority of the whole number elected, whether it be, or be not, expedient at that time to form a constitution and state government for the people within the said territory, as included within the boundaries above designated; and if it be deemed expedient, the convention shall be, and hereby is, authorized to form a constitution and state government; or, if it be deemed more expedient, the said convention shall provide by ordinance for electing representatives to form a constitution or frame of government; which said representatives shall be chosen in such manner, and in such proportion as they shall designate; and shall meet at such time and place as shall be prescribed by the said ordinance; and shall then form for the people of said territory, within the boundaries aforesaid, a constitution and state government: Provided, That the same, whenever formed, shall be republican, and not repugnant to the constitution of the United States; and that the legislature of said state shall never interfere with the primary disposal of the soil by the United States, nor with any regulations Congress may find necessary for securing the title in such soil to the bona fide purchasers; and that no tax shall be imposed on lands the property of the United States; and in no case shall non-resident proprietors be taxed higher than residents.

SEC. 5. And be it further enacted, That until the next general census shall be taken, the said state shall be entitled to one representative in the House of Representatives of the United States . . .

SEC. 7. And be it further enacted, That in case a constitution and state government shall be formed for the people of the said territory of Missouri, the said convention or representatives, as soon thereafter as may be, shall cause a true and attested copy of such constitution or frame of state government, as shall be formed or provided, to be transmitted to Congress.

SEC. 8. And be it further enacted. That in all that territory ceded by France to the United States, under the name of Louisiana, which lies north of thirty-six degrees and thirty minutes north latitude, not included within the limits of the state, contemplated by this act, slavery and involuntary servitude, otherwise than in the punishment of crimes, whereof the parties shall have been duly convicted, shall be, and is hereby, forever prohibited: Provided always, That any person escaping into the same, from whom labour or service is lawfully claimed, in any state or territory of the United States, such fugitive may be lawfully reclaimed and conveyed to the person claiming his or her labour or service as aforesaid.

Source: "Conference Committee Report on the Missouri Compromise," March 1, 1820, from the U.S. National Archives and Records Administration, www.ourdocuments.gov.

Document 1.7 in Context
"Religion and the Pure Principles of Morality, the Sure Foundation on Which We Must Build": Maria W. Stewart's Philosophy of Black Autonomy and Self-Reliance

Although African Americans were excluded from political participation in most places and comprised only a tiny part of the body politic in others before the Civil War, many were eager and determined to have their voices heard on a variety of issues. Slavery and abolition were not the only subjects on which blacks held and expressed opinions.

One strong and distinctive voice was that of Maria W. Stewart, who was born Maria Miller in 1803 in Hartford, Connecticut, to free black parents. When she was orphaned at the age of five, she was sent to work for a white clergyman's family, with whom she stayed for the next ten years. In 1826 she married James W. Stewart, an outfitter of whaling and fishing ships in Boston; he died in 1829. The next year, following a religious conversion, Stewart began devoting her life to improving the circumstances of black Americans.

Stewart was the first American female political activist, speaking out in opposition to slavery as well as in support of full political and civil rights for African Americans and women. She became a friend and ally of the white abolitionist William Lloyd Garrison, who published her speeches in his antislavery journal, the *Liberator*. "Religion and the Pure Principles of Morality, the Sure Foundation on Which We Must Build," the essay from which the following excerpt is taken, was published in the *Liberator* and in pamphlet form in 1831.

In the essay, Stewart expressed a philosophy of black autonomy and self-reliance that put her among America's earliest black nationalists. She was adamant about the need for African Americans to establish their economic independence and to rely on their own judgment rather than that of whites. She also insisted that blacks must pursue education and uphold the highest moral standards.

But while she was philosophically a black nationalist, referring to whites as "the Americans" and to blacks as the "sons and daughters of Africa," Stewart was also a fervent opponent of the colonization movement that sought to emancipate blacks and then send them to Africa. She insisted that blacks should remain in the United States and demand their rights under the Constitution. Stewart said she would rather die than leave America and urged colonizers who were seriously interested in helping black people to use their money instead to create schools to educate those who had suffered the oppression of slavery.

Stewart's strong views and fearless expression of them offended many people, including some in Boston's black community. In 1833 she left Boston and gave up public speaking. She spent most of her remaining life, until her death in 1879, as a schoolteacher in New York, Baltimore and Washington, D.C. Her career as a public speaker was brief, but she was an important early voice, both in the struggle to abolish slavery and in the struggle to achieve equal rights for African Americans and for women.

▰▰▰ Document 1.7 ▰▰▰
Excerpt from Pamphlet by Maria W. Stewart, Published in Boston, October 1831

. . . I have been taking a survey of the American people in my own mind, and I see them thriving in arts, and sciences, and in polite literature. Their highest aim is to excel in political, moral and religious improvement. They early consecrate their children to God, and their youth indeed are blushing in artless innocence; they wipe the tears from the orphan's eyes, and they cause the widow's heart to sing for joy! and their poorest ones, [who] have the least wish to excel, they promote! And those that have but one talent, they encourage. But how very few are there among them that bestow one thought upon the benighted sons and daughters of Africa, who have enriched the soils of America with their tears and blood: few to promote their cause, none to encourage their talents. Under these circumstances, do not let our hearts be any longer discouraged; it is no use to murmur nor to repine; but let us promote ourselves and improve our own talents. And I am rejoiced to reflect that there are many able and talented ones among us, whose names might be recorded on the bright annals of fame. But, *"I can't,"* is a great barrier in the way. I hope it will soon be removed, and *"I will,"* resume its place . . .

How long shall the fair daughters of Africa be compelled to bury their minds and talents beneath a load of iron pots and kettles? Until union, knowledge and love begin to flow among us. How long shall a mean set of men flatter us with their smiles, and enrich themselves with our hard earnings; their wives' fingers sparkling with rings, and they themselves laughing at our folly? Until we begin to promote and patronize each other . . . Do you ask, what can we do? Unite and build a store of your own, if you cannot procure a license. Fill one side with dry goods, and the other with groceries. Do you ask, where is the money? We have spent more than enough for nonsense, to do what building we should want. We have never had an opportunity of displaying our talents; therefore the world thinks we know nothing. And we have been possessed of by far too mean and cowardly a disposition, though I highly disapprove of an insolent or impertinent one. Do you ask the disposition I would have you possess? Possess the spirit of independence. The Americans do, and why should not you? Possess the spirit of men, bold and enterprising, fearless and undaunted. Sue for your rights and privileges. Know the reason that you can attain them. Weary them with your importunities. You can but die, if you make the attempt; and we shall certainly die if you do not. The Americans have practised nothing but head-work these 200 years, and we have done their drudgery. And is it not high time for us to imitate their examples, and practise head-work too, and keep what we have got, and get what we can? We need never to think that any body is going to feel interested for us, if we do not feel interested for ourselves. That day we, as a people, harken unto the voice of the Lord our God, and walk in his ways and ordinances, and become distinguished for our ease, elegance and grace, combined with other virtues, that day the Lord will raise us up, and enough to aid and befriend us, and we shall begin to flourish.

Did every gentleman in America realize, as one, that they had got to become bondmen, and their wives, their sons, and their daughters, servants forever, to Great Britain, their very joints would become loosened, and tremblingly would smite one against another; their countenance would be filled with horror, every nerve and muscle would be forced into action, their souls would recoil at the very thought, their hearts would die within them, and death would be far more preferable. Then why have not Africa's sons a right to feel the same? Are not their wives, their sons, and their daughters, as dear to them as those of the white man's? Certainly, God has not deprived them of the divine influences of his Holy Spirit, which is the greatest of all blessings, if they ask him. Then why should man any longer deprive his fellow-man of equal rights and privileges? Oh, America, America, foul and indelible is thy stain! Dark and dismal is the cloud that hangs over thee, for thy cruel wrongs and injuries to the fallen sons of Africa. The blood of her murdered ones cries to heaven for vengeance against thee. Thou art almost become drunken with the blood of her slain; thou hast enriched thyself through her toils and labors; and now thou refuseth to make even a small return. And thou hast caused the daughters of Africa to commit whordoms and fornications; but upon thee be their curse.

O, ye great and mighty men of America, ye rich and powerful ones, many of you will call for the rocks and mountains to fall upon you, and to hide you from the wrath of the Lamb, and from him that sitteth upon the throne; whilst many of the sable-skinned Africans you now despise, will shine in the kingdom of heaven as the stars forever and ever. Charity begins at home, and those that provide not for their own, are worse than infidels. We know that you are raising contributions to aid the gallant Poles; we know that you have befriended Greece and Ireland; and you have rejoiced with France, for her heroic deeds of valor. You have acknowledged all the nations of the earth, except Hayti; and you may publish, as far as the East is from the West, that you have two millions of negroes, who aspire no higher than to bow at your feet, and to court your smiles. You may kill, tyrannize, and oppress as much as you choose, until our cry shall come up before the throne of God; for I am firmly persuaded, that he will not suffer you to quell the proud, fearless and undaunted spirits of the Africans forever; for in his own time, he is able to plead our cause against you, and to pour out upon you the ten plagues of Egypt. We will not come out against you with swords and staves, as against a thief; but we will tell you that our souls are fired with the same love of liberty and independence with which your souls are fired. We will tell you that too much of your blood flows in our veins, and too much of your color in our skins, for us not to possess your spirits. We will tell you, that it is our gold that clothes you in fine linen and purple, and causes you to fare sumptuously every day; and it is the blood of our fathers, and the tears of our brethren that have enriched your soils. AND WE CLAIM OUR RIGHTS . . .

Source: Maria W. Stewart, "Religion and the Pure Principles of Morality, the Sure Foundation on Which We Must Build," in *Productions of Mrs. Maria W. Stewart Presented to the First African Baptist Church & Society, of the City of Boston* (Boston: Friends of Freedom and Virtue, 1835); electronic transcript from New York Public Library, 1997, http://digilib.nypl.org/dynaweb/digs/wwm9722.

Document 1.8 in Context
"Why a Negro Convention Is Necessary": Opposition to African Colonization of Black Americans

In 1830 a group of African American leaders and political activists gathered in Philadelphia for what they called the National Negro Convention. The immediate purpose of the meeting was to discuss the question of whether blacks should be encouraged to migrate in large numbers to Canada to escape the oppression they faced in the United States. The first of the conventions brought together thirty-eight delegates from eight states under the leadership of the Rev. Richard Allen, senior bishop of the African Methodist Episcopal Church. Allen was elected president of the convention and of the organization it formed, the American Society of Free Persons of Color.

In his "Address to the Free People of Color of These United States," Allen laid out the convention's proposal for a settlement of African Americans in Canada, which was under British rule. He observed that in Canada blacks would not face the same discrimination, the language and climate were similar to those of the United States, and good farmland was available and relatively inexpensive. Allen and the convention attendees also called on African Americans to work energetically to improve their circumstances in the United States: "We cannot devise any plan more likely to accomplish this end, than by encouraging agriculture and mechanical arts: for by the first, we shall be enabled to act with a degree of independence, which as yet has fallen to the lot of but few among us; and the faithful pursuit of the latter, in connection with the sciences, which expand and ennoble the mind, will eventually give us the standing and condition we desire."[7] It was a philosophy adopted and made famous a half century later by Booker T. Washington.

From the beginning, the National Negro Convention was a strenuous opponent of the colonization movement to return blacks to Africa. Many African American leaders were skeptical of the movement's motives and were often contemptuous of the arguments put forward to support the idea. As Allen noted in his address, it was unjust for the United States to seek to repay its debt for exploiting Africa by placing the burden on American blacks—many of whose families had by that time lived in America for generations—who were being asked to uproot themselves and move across the ocean.

The National Negro Convention met annually for six years, then on a periodic basis into the mid-1860s. It spawned a number of other organizations and conventions that met at local, state and national levels as well. At those conventions, free blacks around the country demanded that slavery be abolished and that black people be granted the full and complete rights guaranteed to all U.S. citizens under the Constitution.

The following speech by William Hamilton—delivered as the keynote address "Why a Negro Convention Is Necessary" at the fourth National Negro Convention, held in New York City in June 1834—clearly illustrates the feelings many convention participants held toward the colonization movement.

Document 1.8
William Hamilton Addresses the Fourth Annual National Negro Convention, New York, June 1834

GENTLEMEN: It is with the most pleasing sensations and feelings of high gratification, that I, in behalf of my colored fellow citizens of New York, tender you of the delegation to this convention a hearty welcome to our city. And in behalf of the Conventional Board, I repeat the welcome. And, gentlemen, with regard to myself, my full heart vibrates the felicitation.

You have convened to take into consideration what may be the best means for the promotion of the best interest of the people of color of these United States, particularly of the free people thereof.

And that such convention is highly necessary, I think a few considerations will amply show.

First, the present form of society divides the interest of the community into several parts. Of these, there is that of the white man, that of the slave, and that of the free colored man. How lamentable, how very lamentable, it is that there should be, anywhere on earth, a community of castes, with separate interests! That society must be the most happy where the good of one is the common good of the whole. Civilization is not perfect, nor has reason full sway, until the community shall see that a wrong done to one is a wrong done to the whole; that the interest of one is or ought to be the common interest of the whole. Surely that must be a happy state of society where the sympathies of all are to all alike . . .

But alas for the people of color in this community! Their interest is not identified with that of other men. From them, white men stand aloof. For them the eye of pity hath scarcely a tear.

To them the hand of kindness is palsied, to them the dregs of mercy scarcely are given. To them the finger of scorn is pointed; contumely and reproach is continually theirs. They are a taunt, a hissing, and a by-word. They must cringe, and crouch, and crawl, and succumb to their peers. Long, long, long has the demon of prejudice and persecution beset their path. And must they make no effort to throw off the evils by which they are beset? Ought they not to meet to spread out their wrongs before one another? Ought they not to meet to consult on the best means of their relief? Ought they not to make one weak effort; nay, one strong, one mighty moral effort, to roll off the burden that crushes them?

Under present circumstances it is highly necessary the free people of color should combine and closely attend to their own particular interest. All kinds of jealousy should be swept away from among them and their whole eye fixed, intently fixed, on their own peculiar welfare. And can they do better than to meet thus, to take into consideration what are the best means to promote their elevation, and after having decided, to pursue those means with unabating zeal until their end is obtained?

Another reason why this convention is necessary, is, that there is formed a strong combination against the people of color, by some who are the master spirits of the day, by men whose influence is of the strongest character, to whom this nation bow in humble submission and submit to their superior judgment, who turn public sentiment whichever way they please.

You cannot but perceive that I allude to the Colonization Society. However pure the motives of some of the members of that society may be, yet the master spirits thereof are evilminded toward us. They have put on the garb of angels of light. Fold back their covering and you have in full array those of darkness.

I need not spread before you the proof of their evil purposes. Of that you have had a quantity sufficient; and were there no other good reason for this convention, the bare circumstance of the existence of such an institution would be a sufficient one. I do hope, confidently hope, that the time will arrive and is near at hand when we shall be in full possession of all the rights of men.

But as long at least as the Colonization Society exists, will a convention of colored people be highly necessary. This society is the great Dragon of the land, before whom the people bow and cry, Great Jehovah, and to whom they would sacrifice the free people of color. That society has spread itself over this whole land; it is artful, it suits itself to all places. It is one thing at the South, and another at the North; it blows hot and cold; it sends forth bitter and sweet; it sometimes represents us as the most corrupt, vicious and abandoned of any class of men in the community. Then again we are kind, meek and gentle. Here we are ignorant, idle, a nuisance and a drawback on the resources of the country. But as abandoned as we are, in Africa we shall civilize and Christianize all that heathen country.

And by thus preaching continually they have distilled into the minds of the community a desire to see us removed.

They have resorted to every artifice to effect their purposes.

By exciting in the minds of the white community the fears of insurrection and amalgamation;

By petitioning state legislatures to grant us no favors;

By petitioning Congress to aid in sending us away;

By using their influence to prevent the establishment of seminaries for our instruction in the higher branches of education.

And such are the men of that society that the community are blind to their absurdities; contradictions and paradoxes. They are well acquainted with the ground and the wiles by which to beguile the people.

It is therefore highly necessary we should meet, in order that we may confer on the best means to frustrate the purpose of so awful a foe.

I would beg leave to recommend an attentive consideration to this matter. Already you have done much toward the enervation of this giant: he begins to grow feeble; indeed he seems to be making his last struggle, if we may judge from his recent movements. Hang around him, assail him quickly. He is vulnerable. Well-pointed darts will fetch him down, and soon he breathes no more.

Cheer up my friends! Already has your protest against the Colonization Society shown the world that the people of color are not willing to be expatriated. Cheer up. Already a right feeling begins to prevail. The friends of justice, of humanity, and of the rights of man are drawing rapidly together and are forming a moral phalanx in your defense.

This hitherto strong-footed, but sore-eyed vixen, prejudice, is limping off, seeking the shade. The Anti-Slavery Society and the friends of immediate abolition are taking a noble, bold and manly stand in the cause of universal liberty. It is true they are assailed on every quarter, but the more they are assailed the faster they recruit. From present appearances the prospect is cheering, in a high degree. Anti-slavery societies are forming in every direction.

Next August proclaims the British dominions free from slaves.

These United States are her children, they will soon follow so good an example. Slavery, that Satanic monster, that beast whose mark has been so long stamped on the forehead of the nations, shall be chained and cast down into blackness and darkness forever.

Soon, my brethren, shall the judgment be set. Then shall rise in glory and triumph, reason, virtue, kindness and liberty, and take a high exalted stand among the sons of men. Then shall tyranny, cruelty, prejudice and slavery be cast down to the lowest depths of oblivion; yea, be banished from the presence of God and the glory of his power forever. Oh blessed consummation, and devoutly to be desired!

It is for you, my brethren, to help on in this work of moral improvement. Man is capable of high advances in his reasoning and moral faculties. Man is in the pursuit of happiness. And reason, or experience, which is the parent of reason, tells us that the highest state of morality is the highest state of happiness. Aside from a future day of judgment and retribution, there is always a day of retribution at hand. That society is most miserable that is most immoral—that most happy that is most virtuous. Let me therefore recommend earnestly that you press upon our people the necessity and advantage of a moral reformation. It may not produce an excess of riches, but it will produce a higher state of happiness and render our circumstances easier . . .

Source: William Hamilton, *Address to the Fourth Annual Convention of the Free People of Color of the United States,* New York, June 2, 1834 (New York: S. W. Benedict and Company Printers, 1834), from the Collection of Cornell University Library, Division of Rare and Manuscript Collections—Samuel J. May Anti-Slavery Collection.

Document 1.9 in Context
"Trusting in a God of Truth and Justice, We Lay Our Claim Before You": Pennsylvania African Americans Protest Their Disenfranchisement

Between the Revolution and the Civil War, free African Americans found their rights and freedoms constantly under attack in the North as well as the South. Increasingly, states restricted their voting rights and ability to testify in court. Their access to education became more limited, either by laws that barred them from public schools or by systems that segregated schools by race. It was common for blacks to be excluded from hotels and other public accommodations and to be segregated on public transportation.

Black voting rights, in particular, eroded in the first half of the nineteenth century. Until passage of the Fourteenth Amendment to the U.S. Constitution (**Document 3.2**) after the Civil War, voter qualifications were determined by individual states. Most of the states of the South barred even free blacks from voting, and most new western states adopted state constitutions that followed suit. The vote was more widely available to blacks in the North during this period (although that would change by the start of the Civil War). A half dozen states—Delaware, Kentucky, Maryland, Connecticut, New Jersey and Pennsylvania—had initially permitted free blacks to vote but, one by one, they rewrote their state constitutions to disenfranchise blacks.

By 1838 only Maine, Massachusetts, New Hampshire, Rhode Island, Vermont and New York still allowed free blacks to vote.

Even in those states, voting rights were not always equal or secure. New York, for example, passed a law in 1811 that regulated black suffrage by requiring black voters to provide proof they were free and to pay the costs the government incurred registering their eligibility to vote. That free blacks took the right to vote very seriously is demonstrated in a speech given by New Yorker Joseph Sidney in 1809, marking the first anniversary of the federal ban on the international slave trade. Sidney told his audience that it was the right and the duty of free blacks to vote, and he encouraged them to vote for Federalist candidates to help bring an end to slavery:

> All the democratic members of Congress, who have any considerable influence in directing the machine of government, belong to the South. And almost all of the free inhabitants of the southern section of the United States, are of the democratic party. And these are the very people who hold our African brethren in bondage. These people, therefore, are the *enemies* of our *rights*.[8]

In Pennsylvania, ambiguity regarding voting rights in the state's 1790 constitution lingered into the 1830s, when racial tensions in the state began to increase. During that decade, the state saw a significant increase in the number of antislavery organizations and became a focal point for the Underground Railroad, which helped runaway slaves escape to freedom in the North and Canada. Philadelphia also hosted the first of the National Negro Conventions in 1830. But when the slave uprising led by Nat Turner in Virginia stunned the nation in 1831, white state legislators in Pennsylvania began to propose ways to limit the migration of blacks to the state—and ways to increase restrictions on blacks already living there. Then, in August 1834, simmering economic and social resentments sparked three nights of racial rioting in Philadelphia; one black person was killed and dozens were injured. Another race riot shook the city a year later.

In that atmosphere of growing racial tension, the state called a convention in 1837 to write a new constitution. By January 1838 the convention had approved language that would allow only white men to vote in Pennsylvania. In the hope of persuading Pennsylvania voters not to approve the revised constitution, a group of free blacks in Philadelphia issued a written appeal, from which the following passages are excerpted. They argued, in very legalistic fashion, that blacks were entitled to the vote as taxpaying citizens and strenuously questioned what the black population had done to warrant disenfranchisement. The appeal, however, was unsuccessful; the state's voters ratified the new constitution in October 1838, albeit by a margin of just over 1,200 votes of the more than 226,000 cast.

<hr>

▬ Document 1.9 ▬
Appeal of Forty Thousand Citizens, Threatened with Disfranchisement, to the People of Pennsylvania, 1838

Appeal

Fellow Citizens:

We appeal to you from the decision of the "Reform Convention," which has stripped us of a right peaceably enjoyed during forty-seven years under the Constitution of this commonwealth. We honor Pennsylvania and her noble institutions too much to part with our birthright, as her free citizens, without a struggle. To all her citizens the right of suffrage is valuable in proportion as he is free; but surely there are none who can so ill afford to spare it as ourselves.

Was it the intention of the people of this commonwealth that the Convention to which the Constitution was committed for revision and amendment, should tear up and cast away its first principles? Was it made the business of the Convention to deny "that all men are born equally free," by making political rights depend upon the skin in which a man is born? or to divide what our fathers bled to unite, to wit, TAXATION and REPRESENTATION? We will not allow ourselves for one moment to suppose, that the majority of the people of Pennsylvania are not too respectful of the rights and too liberal towards the feelings of others, as well as too much enlightened to their own interests, to deprive of the right of suffrage a single individual who may safely be trusted with it. And we cannot believe that you have found among those who bear the burdens of taxation any who have proved, by their abuse of that right, that it is not safe in their hands. This is a question, fellow citizens, in which we plead *your* cause as well as our own. It is the safeguard of the strongest that he lives under a government which is obliged to respect the voice of the weakest. When you have taken from an individual his right to vote, you have made the government, in regard to him, a mere despotism; and you have taken a step towards, making it a despotism to all. — To your women and children, their inability to vote at the polls may be no evil, because they are united by consanguinity and affection with those who can do it. To foreigners and paupers the want of the right may be tolerable, because a little time or labor will make it theirs. They are candidates for the privilege, and hence substantially enjoy the benefits. But when a distinct class of the community, already sufficiently the objects of prejudice, are wholly, and for ever, disfranchised and excluded, to the remotest posterity, from the possibility of a voice in regard to the laws under which they are to live—it is the same thing as if their abode were transferred to the dominions of the Russian Autocrat, or of the Grand Turk. They have lost their check upon oppression, their wherewith to buy friends, their panoply of manhood; in short, they are thrown upon the mercy of a despotic majority. Like every other despot, this despot majority, will believe in the mildness of its own sway; but who will the more willingly submit to it for that?

To us our right under the Constitution has been the more precious, and our deprivation of it will be the more grievous, because our expatriation has come to be a darling project with many of our fellow citizens. Our abhorrence of a scheme which comes to us in the guise of Christian benevolence, and asks us to suffer ourselves to be transplanted to a distant and barbarous land, *because we are a "nuisance" in this,* is not more deep and thorough than it is reasonable. We love our native country, much as it has wronged us; and in the peaceable exercise of our inalienable rights, we will cling to it. The immortal Franklin, and his fellow laborers in the cause of humanity, have bound us to our homes here with chains of gratitude. We are PENNSYLVANIANS, and we hope to see the day when Pennsylvania will have reason to be proud of us, as we believe she has now none to be ashamed. Will you starve our patriotism? Will you cast our hearts out of the treasury of the commonwealth? Do you count our enmity better than our friendship? . . .

We were regarded as *citizens* by those who drew up the articles of confederation between the States, in 1778. The fourth of the said articles contains the following language: —"The free inhabitants of each of these States, paupers, vagabonds, and fugitives from justice excepted, shall be entitled to all privileges, and immunities of free *citizens* in the several

States." That we were not excluded under the phrase "paupers, vagabonds, and fugitives from justice," any more than our white countrymen, is plain from the debates that preceded the adoption of the article. For, on the 25th of June, 1778, "the delegates from South Carolina moved the following amendment *in behalf of their State*. In article fourth, between the words *free* inhabitants, insert *white*. Decided in the negative; ayes, two States; nays, eight States; one State divided." Such was the solemn decision of the revolutionary Congress, concurred in by the entire delegation from our own commonwealth. On the adoption of the present Constitution of the United States no change was made as to the rights of citizenship. This is explicitly proved by the Journal of Congress . . .

Be it remembered, fellow citizens, that it is only for the *"industrious, peaceable, and useful"* part of the colored people that we plead. We would have the right of suffrage only as the reward of industry and worth. We care not how high the qualification be placed. All we ask is, that no man shall be excluded on account of his *color*, that the same rule shall be applied to all.

Are we to be disfranchised, lest the purity of the white blood should be sullied by an intermixture with ours? It seems to us that our white brethren might well enough reserve their fear, till we seek such alliance with them. We ask no social favors. We would not willingly darken the doors of those to whom the complexion and features, which our Maker has given us, are disagreeable. The territories of the commonwealth are sufficiently ample to afford us a home without doing violence to the delicate nerves of our white brethren, for centuries to come. Besides, we are not intruders here, nor were our ancestors. Surely you ought to bear as unrepiningly the evil consequences of your fathers' guilt, as we those of our fathers' misfortune. Proscription and disfranchisement are the last things in the world to alleviate these evil consequences. Nothing, as shameful experience has already proved, can so powerfully promote the evil which you profess to deprecate, as the degradation of our race by the oppressive rule of yours. Give us that fair and honorable ground which self-respect requires to stand on, and the dreaded amalgamation, if it take place at all, shall be by your own fault, as indeed it always has been. We dare not give full vent to the indignation we feel on this point, but we will not attempt wholly to conceal it. We ask a voice in the disposition of those public resources which we ourselves have helped to earn; we claim a right to be heard, according to our numbers, in regard to all those great public measures which involve our lives and fortunes, as well as those of our fellow citizens . . .

We would not misrepresent the motives of the Convention, but we are constrained to believe that they have laid our rights a sacrifice on the altar of slavery. We do not believe our disfranchisement would have been proposed, but for the desire which is felt by political aspirants to gain the favor of the slaveholding States. This is not the first time that northern statesmen have "bowed the knee to the dark spirit of slavery," but it is the first time that they have bowed so low! Is Pennsylvania, which abolished slavery in 1780, and enfranchised her tax-paying colored citizens in 1790, now, in 1838, to get upon her knees and repent of her humanity, to gratify those who disgrace the very name of American Liberty, by holding our brethren as goods and chattels? . . . Firm upon our old Pennsylvania BILL OF RIGHTS, and trusting in a God of Truth and Justice, we lay our claim before you, with the warning that no amendments of the present Constitution can compensate for the loss of its foundation principle of equal rights, nor for the conversion into enemies of 40,000 friends.

Source: [Robert Purvis,] *Appeal of Forty Thousand Citizens, Threatened with Disfranchisement, to the People of Pennsylvania* (Philadelphia: Merrihew and Gunn, 1838).

Document 1.10 in Context
"It Is Justice I Stand Here to Claim": Opposing Public Discrimination and Segregation

Although slavery was the preeminent issue for African Americans in the decades before the Civil War, it was not their only concern. Nor was it the only question on which they sought to exercise political influence. Even in northern states that had abolished slavery, blacks found that neither the absence of slavery nor access to voting rights guaranteed truly equal rights. They faced all manner of race-based discrimination, regardless of their political status.

Massachusetts, for example, effectively outlawed slavery with its constitution of 1780, and by 1783 blacks could vote in the state. But African Americans in Massachusetts still faced discrimination and segregation on a daily basis, particularly in public transportation. In early 1842, as a committee of the Massachusetts House of Representatives met to examine the issue, Charles L. Remond gave testimony before the committee. Remond, a highly regarded orator who had been the first African American lecturing agent hired by the American Anti-Slavery Society in 1838, was the first black to speak directly to either house of the Massachusetts legislature.

The hearing and Remond's remarks were reported in the February 25, 1842, issue of the *Liberator,* abolitionist William Lloyd Garrison's antislavery journal. According to the article, the hearing was prompted by "various petitions" complaining that "respectable colored citizens, however well educated or estimable in their deportment, were not allowed the same measure of privilege as white citizens, but were obliged to take an unpleasant position in what is called the *Jim Crow Car.*" The *Liberator* identified Remond as one of three people, and the only person of color, to testify before the committee. "The speech of Remond, coming as it did from one of the proscribed race, and delivered in a manner at once graceful and pointed, seemed to produce much effect upon the assembly." [9]

In his testimony, Remond contrasted his experience on the Massachusetts railroads and steamships with his experience during a nineteen-month visit to England, Scotland and Ireland. In the British Isles, he told the committee, he was treated with dignity and respect, even when a clerical error resulted in his being booked in the same steamship stateroom as a white passenger. On another occasion, a British ship's officer spontaneously upgraded his accommodations to second-class when he discovered that Remond was the only passenger traveling in steerage.

By contrast, Remond testified, when he returned home to Massachusetts, he immediately found himself relegated to a segregated railway car on the ride from Boston to his family's home in Salem. A few days later, when two white friends attempted to sit with him in the segregated car during a business trip back into Boston, the train's conductor brusquely ordered them to leave. In addition to illustrating Remond's rhetorical skills, the testimony excerpted here helps illuminate the range of African American political activism in the antebellum period. It is also interesting to note in Remond's language a preemptive defense against "special pleading," the suggestion that he might be seeking special rights for African Americans rather than simply equal rights. Remond took pains to make it clear that he was seeking only justice.

▬ **Document 1.10** ▬
Charles L. Remond Decries Segregation before a Committee
of the Massachusetts House of Representatives, 1842

Mr. Chairman, and Gentlemen of the Committee:

In rising at this time, and on this occasion, being the first person of color who has ever addressed either of the bodies assembling in this building, I should, perhaps, in the first place, observe that, in consequence of the many misconstructions of the principles and measures of which I am the humble advocate, I may in like manner be subject to similar misconceptions from the moment I open my lips in behalf of the prayer of the petitioners for whom I appear, and therefore feel I have the right at least to ask, at the hands of this intelligent Committee, an impartial hearing . . . Complexion can in no sense be construed into a crime, much less be rightfully made the criterion of rights. Should the people of color, through a revolution of Providence, become a majority, to the last I would oppose it upon the same principle; for, in either case, it would be equally reprehensible and unjustifiable— alike to be condemned and repudiated. It is JUSTICE I stand here to claim, and not FAVOR for either complexion . . .

Our right to citizenship in this State has been acknowledged and secured by the allowance of the elective franchise and consequent taxation, and I know of no good reason, if admitted in this instance, why it should be denied in any other.

With reference to the wrongs inflicted and injuries received on rail-roads, by persons of color, I need not say they do not end with the termination of the route, but, in effect, tend to discourage, disparage and depress this class of citizens. All hope of reward for upright conduct is cut off. Vice in them becomes a virtue. No distinction is made by the community in which we live. The most vicious is treated as well as the most respectable, both in public and private.

But it is said we all look alike. If this is true, it is not true that we all behave alike. There is a marked difference; and we claim a recognition of this difference.

In the present state of things . . . color is made to obscure the brightest endowments, to degrade the fairest character, and to check the highest and most praiseworthy aspirations . . . And I submit, whether this unkind and unchristian policy is not well calculated to make every man disregardful of his conduct, and every woman unmindful of her reputation.

The grievances of which we complain, be assured, sir, are not imaginary, but real—not local, but universal—not occasional, but continual—every day matter of fact things—and have become, to the disgrace of our common country, [a] matter of history.

Mr. Chairman, the treatment to which colored Americans are exposed in their own country, finds a counterpart in no other; and I am free to declare, that, in the course of nineteen months' traveling in England, Ireland, and Scotland, I was received, treated and recognised, in public and private society, without any regard to my complexion. From the moment I left the American packet ship in Liverpool, up to the moment I came in contact with it again, I was never reminded of my complexion; and all that know anything of my usage in the American ship, will testify that it was unfit for a brute, and none but one could inflict it. But how unlike that afforded in the British steamer Columbia! Owing to my limited resources, I took a steerage passage. On the first day out, the second officer came to inquire after my health; and finding me the only passenger in that part of the ship, ordered the steward to give me berth in the second cabin; and from that hour until my stepping on shore at Boston, every politeness was shown me by the officers, and every kindness and attention by the stewards; and I feel under deep and lasting obligations to them, individually and collectively.

In no instance was I insulted or treated in any way distinct or dissimilar from other passengers or travelers, either in coaches, rail-roads, steampackets, or hotels; and if the feeling was entertained, in no case did I discover its existence.

I may with [propriety] here relate an accident, illustrative of the subject now under consideration. I took a passage ticket at the steam packet office in Glasgow, for Dublin; and on going into the cabin to retire, I found the berth I had engaged occupied by an Irish gentleman and merchant . . . On comparing tickets, we saw that the clerk had given two tickets of the same number; and it appeared I had received mine first. The gentleman at once offered to vacate the berth, against which I remonstrated, and took my berth in an opposite state room. Here, sir, we discover treatment just, impartial, reasonable; and we ask nothing beside.

. . . On my arrival home from England, I went to the rail way station, to go to Salem, being anxious to see my parents and sisters as soon as possible—asked for a ticket—paid 50 cents for it, and was pointed to the American designation car. Having previously received information of the regulations, I took my seat peaceably, believing it better to suffer wrong than do wrong . . . although I never, by any means, gave evidence that, by my submission, I intended to sanction usages which would derogate from uncivilized, much less long and loud professing and high pretending America.

Bear with me while I relate an additional occurrence. On the morning after my return home, I was obliged to go to Boston again, and on going to the Salem station I met two friends, who enquired if I had any objection to their taking seats with me. I answered, I should be most happy. They took their seats accordingly, and soon afterwards one of them remarked to me—"Charles, I don't know if they will allow us to ride with you." It was some time before I could understand what they meant, and; on doing so, I laughed—feeling it to be a climax to every absurdity I had heard attributed to Americans. To say nothing of the wrong done to those friends, and the insult and indignity offered me by the appearance of the conductor, who ordered the friends from the car in a somewhat harsh manner—they immediately left the carriage.

On returning to Salem some few evenings afterwards, Mr. Chase, the superintendent on this road, . . . enquired if I was not glad to get home after so long an absence in Europe. I told him I was glad to see my parents and family again, and this was the only object I could have, unless he thought I should be glad to take a hermit's life in the great pasture; inasmuch as I never felt to loathe my American name so much as since my arrival. He wished to know my reasons for the remark. I immediately gave them, and wished to know of him, if, in the event of his having a brother with red hair, he should find [himself separated] while travelling because of this difference, he should deem it just. He could make no reply . . .

Sir, it happens to be my lot to have a sister a few shades lighter than myself; and who knows, if this state of things is encouraged, whether I may not on some future occasion be mobbed in Washington-street, on the supposition of walking with a white young lady! . . .

Mr. Chairman, if colored people have abused any rights granted them, or failed to exhibit due appreciation of favors bestowed, or shrunk from dangers or responsibility, let it be made to appear . . . In view of these and many additional considerations, I unhesitatingly assert their claim on the naked principle of merit, to every advantage set forth in the Constitution of this Commonwealth.

Finally, Mr. Chairman, there is in this and other States a large and growing colored population, whose residence in your midst has not been from choice, (let this be understood and reflected upon,) but by the force of circumstances over which they never had control . . . If to ask at your hands redress for injuries, and protection in our rights and immunities, as citizens, is reasonable, and dictated alike by justice, humanity and religion, you will not reject, I trust, the prayer of your petitioners . . .

Source: Charles L. Remond, "Remarks of Charles Lenox Remond," *Liberator* 12, no. 8 (February 25, 1842): 30, from the University of Detroit Mercy Abolitionist Archive.

Document 1.11 in Context
"To Settle and Adjust Amicably All Existing Questions of Controversy . . . Arising Out of the Institution of Slavery": The Compromise of 1850

In 1850 a complicated mix of political and geographical issues posed the most serious challenge in a generation to the United States' seventy-five-year-old balancing act on the issue of slavery. The Mexican-American War of 1846–1848 had brought the United States huge new territories in the Southwest. California, swelling with Gold Rush settlement, had petitioned Congress for admission to the Union as a free state. Texas, which had joined the Union as a slave state five years earlier, was claiming territory as far west as Santa Fe in what is now New Mexico. Further, there was increasing debate over whether it was appropriate to continue to hold the biggest slave market in North America in the U.S. capital, Washington, D.C.

In an attempt to satisfy both slave- and free-state interests, a group in Congress led by Sen. Henry Clay, Whig-Ky., who had brokered the Missouri Compromise thirty years earlier (**Document 1.6**), and Sen. Stephen A. Douglas, D-Ill., devised a compromise they hoped would calm the debate. Clay introduced a resolution outlining a five-bill package of legislation to "settle and adjust amicably all existing questions of controversy . . . arising out of the institution of slavery upon a fair, equitable and just basis."

The legislation, known as the Compromise of 1850, set the western boundary of Texas and declared that the new southwestern territories would be organized without predetermining the issue of slavery; that decision would be left to each state's voters when they applied for statehood. Slavery would be permitted in Washington, D.C., although the slave trade would be banned within the capital. California, meanwhile, would be admitted to the Union as a free state.

The final bill in the package was designed to ease southern concerns that the admission of California would upset the slave- versus free-state balance of power in Congress. That bill, known as the Fugitive Slave Act, made it easier for slave owners to capture and reclaim runaway slaves. This addressed a longtime concern of southern states but enraged abolitionists in the North.

Under the act, law enforcement officials who failed to arrest an alleged runaway slave could be fined $1,000. A private citizen could also be fined $1,000 and jailed for six months simply for providing food or shelter to a runaway slave. Moreover, the standard of evidence was extremely low. A mere allegation that someone was an escaped slave was enough to require an arrest. Free blacks could be, and in some cases were, apprehended and shipped south as runaway slaves, with no way to defend themselves in the legal system.

The Compromise of 1850 did nothing to encourage a long-term settlement of the controversy over slavery; instead, it strengthened the resolve of northern abolitionists and, by leaving the status of slavery in new southwestern states up to voters, planted seeds of discord that would bear ugly fruit just four years later (see **Document 1.13**).

The Compromise of 1850 comprised six documents—Henry Clay's resolution and five statutes approved by Congress. Included here are Clay's resolution and the most controversial of the statutes, the Fugitive Slave Act.

▣ Document 1.11a ▣
Henry Clay's Resolution, January 29, 1850

It being desirable, for the peace, concord, and harmony of the Union of these States, to settle and adjust amicably all existing questions of controversy between them arising out of the institution of slavery upon a fair, equitable and just basis: therefore,

1. Resolved, That California, with suitable boundaries, ought, upon her application to be admitted as one of the States of this Union, without the imposition by Congress of any restriction in respect to the exclusion or introduction of slavery within those boundaries.
2. Resolved, That as slavery does not exist by law, and is not likely to be introduced into any of the territory acquired by the United States from the republic of Mexico, it is inexpedient for Congress to provide by law either for its introduction into, or exclusion from, any part of the said territory; and that appropriate territorial governments ought to be established by Congress in all of the said territory, not assigned as the boundaries of the proposed State of California, without the adoption of any restriction or condition on the subject of slavery.
3. Resolved, That the western boundary of the State of Texas ought to be fixed on the Rio del Norte . . .
4. Resolved, That it be proposed to the State of Texas, that the United States will provide for the payment of all that portion of the legitimate and bona fide public debt of that State contracted prior to its annexation to the United States . . . and upon the condition, also, that the said State of Texas shall . . . relinquish to the United States any claim which it has to any part of New Mexico.
5. Resolved, That it is inexpedient to abolish slavery in the District of Columbia whilst that institution continues to exist in the State of Maryland, without the consent of that State, without the consent of the people of the District, and without just compensation to the owners of slaves within the District.
6. But, resolved, That it is expedient to prohibit, within the District, the slave trade in slaves brought into it from States or places beyond the limits of the District, either to be sold therein as merchandise, or to be transported to other markets without the District of Columbia.
7. Resolved, That more effectual provision ought to be made by law, according to the requirement of the Constitution, for the restitution and delivery of persons bound to service or labor in any State, who may escape into any other State or Territory in the Union. And,

8. Resolved, That Congress has no power to promote or obstruct the trade in slaves between the slaveholding States; but that the admission or exclusion of slaves brought from one into another of them, depends exclusively upon their own particular laws.

Document 1.11b
Fugitive Slave Act, September 18, 1850

. . .

SECTION. 5. And be it further enacted, That it shall be the duty of all marshals and deputy marshals to obey and execute all warrants and precepts issued under the provisions of this act, when to them directed; and should any marshal or deputy marshal refuse to receive such warrant, or other process, when tendered, or to use all proper means diligently to execute the same, he shall, on conviction thereof, be fined in the sum of one thousand dollars, to the use of such claimant, on the motion of such claimant, by the Circuit or District Court for the district of such marshal; and after arrest of such fugitive, by such marshal or his deputy, or whilst at any time in his custody under the provisions of this act, should such fugitive escape, whether with or without the assent of such marshal or his deputy, such marshal shall be liable, on his official bond, to be prosecuted for the benefit of such claimant, for the full value of the service or labor of said fugitive in the State, Territory, or District whence he escaped . . . and all good citizens are hereby commanded to aid and assist in the prompt and efficient execution of this law, whenever their services may he required . . .

SEC. 6. And be it further enacted, That when a person held to service or labor in any State or Territory of the United States, has heretofore or shall hereafter escape into another State or Territory of the United States, the person or persons to whom such service or labor may be due, or his, her, or their agent or attorney . . . may pursue and reclaim such fugitive person, either by procuring a warrant from some one of the courts, judges, or commissioners aforesaid . . . or by seizing and arresting such fugitive, where the same can be done without process . . . In no trial or hearing under this act shall the testimony of such alleged fugitive be admitted in evidence; and the certificates in this and the first [fourth] section mentioned, shall be conclusive of the right of the person or persons in whose favor granted, to remove such fugitive to the State or Territory from which he escaped, and shall prevent all molestation of such person or persons by any process issued by any court judge, magistrate, or other person whomsoever.

SEC. 7. And be it further enacted, That any person who shall knowingly and willingly obstruct, hinder, or prevent such claimant, his agent or attorney, or any person or persons lawfully assisting him, her, or them, from arresting such a fugitive from service or labor, either with or without process as aforesaid, or shall rescue, or attempt to rescue such fugitive from service or labor, from the custody of such claimant . . . or shall aid, abet, or assist such person so owing service or labor as aforesaid, directly or indirectly, to escape from such claimant . . . or shall harbor or conceal such fugitive . . . shall, for either of said offences, be subject to a fine not exceeding one thousand dollars, and imprisonment not exceeding six months . . . and shall moreover forfeit and pay, by way of civil damages to the party injured by such illegal conduct, the sum of one thousand dollars, for each fugitive so lost as aforesaid, to be recovered by action of debt, in any of the District or Territorial Courts aforesaid, within whose jurisdiction the said offence may have been committed.

SEC. 8. And be it further enacted, That the marshals, their deputies, and the clerks of the said District and Territorial Courts, shall be paid, for their services, the like fees as may be allowed to them for similar services in other cases; . . . and in all cases where the proceedings are before a commissioner, he shall be entitled to a fee of ten dollars in full for his services in each case, upon the delivery of the said certificate to the claimant, his or her agent or attorney; or a fee of five dollars in cases where the proof shall not, in the opinion of such commissioner, warrant such certificate and delivery . . . The person or persons authorized to execute the process to be issued by such commissioners for the arrest and detention of fugitives from service or labor as aforesaid, shall also be entitled to a fee of five dollars each for each person he or they may arrest and take before any such commissioner . . .

Source: "Compromise of 1850," from the U.S. National Archives and Records Administration, www.ourdocuments.gov.

Document 1.12 in Context
"What to the American Slave Is Your Fourth of July?"
Frederick Douglass and the Abolitionist Fight

Frederick Douglass was the most famous and most influential African American prior to the Civil War, and only Booker T. Washington might claim comparable stature in the later decades of the nineteenth century. A powerful and gifted orator, Douglass transformed his own personal escape from slavery into a lifelong crusade to end slavery in America and to secure for blacks the rights guaranteed by the Constitution for all Americans.

Douglass was born in February 1818 in Talbot County, Maryland, the son of a field slave and a white man believed to be her master. He learned to read before he was a teenager and escaped to freedom when he was twenty. By 1839 he was married, living in New Bedford, Massachusetts, and speaking against slavery as a lay preacher. That year he met William Lloyd Garrison, the white antislavery activist and editor, whose journal, the *Liberator,* was one of the nation's foremost voices for abolition. Garrison was a key figure in launching Douglass's career as a public speaker.

In 1845 Douglass published a narrative of his life in which he told of his experiences as a slave and described his escape. The narrative added to his growing public reputation but also put him in danger of being captured as a runaway slave. For his own safety, Douglass left his wife and four children in Massachusetts and spent twenty-one months traveling and speaking against slavery to audiences in Britain. The tour gave him international stature, and British abolitionists formally purchased his freedom from his former master in late 1846.

As a legally free man, Douglass returned to the United States, where he continued speaking publicly and launched a small weekly newspaper, the *North Star,* to give voice to a black perspective in the national debates over slavery. He eventually split with Garrison, in part over his decision to produce his own newspaper but also on philosophical grounds. Garrison denounced the Constitution as irreparably flawed because he believed it endorsed slavery. Douglass, however, concluded that the Constitution and the Declaration of Independence actually opposed slavery and should be linchpins of the abolitionist argument (**Documents 1.1** and **1.4**).

On July 5, 1852, in Rochester, New York, Douglass outlined his philosophy in what may be his best and most famous speech. He began by praising the courage and honor of the nation's founders and their commitment to liberty. But he also took care to draw a sharp rhetorical distinction between himself, as a black man and a former slave, and his predominantly white audience.

In dramatic and impassioned language, Douglass contrasted the suffering of African Americans under the oppression of slavery with the promise of freedom and justice set out in the nation's founding documents. Douglass declared that both the Declaration and the Constitution were antislavery documents and urged his audience to embrace the commitment to freedom expressed in the Declaration. For the Fourth of July to have real meaning, he said, the United States must live up to its ideals and eliminate the abomination of slavery forever.

▬ Document 1.12 ▬
Frederick Douglass Outlines His Political Philosophy for the Rochester Ladies Anti-Slavery Society, Rochester, New York, July 5, 1852

Mr. President, Friends and Fellow Citizens: . . .

This, for the purpose of this celebration, is the 4th of July. It is the birthday of your National Independence, and of your political freedom. This, to you, is what the Passover was to the emancipated people of God . . . This celebration also marks the beginning of another year of your national life; and reminds you that the Republic of America is now 76 years old. I am glad, fellow-citizens, that your nation is so young . . . There is hope in the thought, and hope is much needed, under the dark clouds which lower above the horizon . . .

Citizens, your fathers . . . succeeded; and to-day you reap the fruits of their success. The freedom gained is yours; and you, therefore, may properly celebrate this anniversary. The 4th of July is the first great fact in your nation's history—the very ring-bolt in the chain of your yet undeveloped destiny.

Pride and patriotism, not less than gratitude, prompt you to celebrate and to hold it in perpetual remembrance. I have said that the Declaration of Independence is the ring-bolt to the chain of your nation's destiny; so, indeed, I regard it. The principles contained in that instrument are saving principles. Stand by those principles, be true to them on all occasions, in all places, against all foes, and at whatever cost . . .

Fellow-citizens, pardon me, allow me to ask, why am I called upon to speak here to-day? What have I, or those I represent, to do with your national independence? Are the great principles of political freedom and of natural justice, embodied in that Declaration of Independence, extended to us? and am I, therefore, called upon to bring our humble offering to the national altar, and to confess the benefits and express devout gratitude for the blessings resulting from your independence to us?

Would to God, both for your sakes and ours, that an affirmative answer could be truthfully returned to these questions! . . .

But, such is not the state of the case. I say it with a sad sense of the disparity between us. I am not included within the pale of this glorious anniversary! Your high independence only reveals the immeasurable distance between us. The blessings in which you, this day, rejoice, are not enjoyed in common. The rich inheritance of justice, liberty, prosperity and independence, bequeathed by your fathers, is shared by you, not by me. The sunlight that brought life and healing to you, has brought stripes and death to me. This Fourth [of] July is yours, not mine. You may rejoice, I must mourn . . .

Fellow-citizens; above your national, tumultuous joy, I hear the mournful wail of millions! whose chains, heavy and grievous yesterday, are, to-day, rendered more intolerable by the jubilee shouts that reach them . . . My subject, then fellow-citizens, is AMERICAN SLAVERY. I shall see, this day, and its popular characteristics, from the slave's point of view.

Standing, there, identified with the American bondman, making his wrongs mine, I do not hesitate to declare, with all my soul, that the character and conduct of this nation never looked blacker to me than on this 4th of July! . . .

What point in the anti-slavery creed would you have me argue? On what branch of the subject do the people of this country need light? Must I undertake to prove that the slave is a man? That point is conceded already. Nobody doubts it . . . It is admitted in the fact that Southern statute books are covered with enactments forbidding, under severe fines and penalties, the teaching of the slave to read or to write. When you can point to any such laws, in reference to the beasts of the field, then I may consent to argue the manhood of the slave. When the dogs in your streets, when the fowls of the air, when the cattle on your hills, when the fish of the sea, and the reptiles that crawl, shall be unable to distinguish the slave from a brute, there will I argue with you that the slave is a man! . . .

Would you have me argue that man is entitled to liberty? that he is the rightful owner of his own body? You have already declared it. Must I argue the wrongfulness of slavery? Is that a question for Republicans? . . .

What, am I to argue that it is wrong to make men brutes, to rob them of their liberty, to work them without wages, to keep them ignorant of their relations to their fellow men, to beat them with sticks, to flay their flesh with the lash, to load their limbs with irons, to hunt them with dogs, to sell them at auction, to sunder their families, to knock out their teeth, to burn their flesh, to starve them into obedience and submission to their masters? Must I argue that a system thus marked with blood, and stained with pollution, is wrong? No! I will not. I have better employments for my time and strength, than such arguments would imply . . .

At a time like this, scorching irony, not convincing argument, is needed . . . For it is not light that is needed, but fire; it is not the gentle shower, but thunder. We need the storm, the whirlwind, and the earthquake. The feeling of the nation must be quickened; the conscience of the nation must be roused; the propriety of the nation must be startled; the hypocrisy of the nation must be exposed; and its crimes against God and man must be proclaimed and denounced.

What, to the American slave, is your 4th of July? I answer: a day that reveals to him, more than all other days in the year, the gross injustice and cruelty to which he is the constant victim. To him, your celebration is a sham; your boasted liberty, an unholy license; your national greatness, swelling vanity; your sounds of rejoicing are empty and heartless; your denunciations of tyrants, brass fronted impudence; your shouts of liberty and equality, hollow mockery; your prayers and hymns, your sermons and thanksgivings, with all your religious parade, and solemnity, are, to him, mere bombast, fraud, deception, impiety, and hypocrisy—a thin veil to cover up crimes which would disgrace a nation of savages . . .

But a still more inhuman, disgraceful, and scandalous state of things remains to be presented.

By an act of the American Congress, not yet two years old, slavery has been nationalized in its most horrible and revolting form . . .

In glaring violation of justice, in shameless disregard of the forms of administering law, in cunning arrangement to entrap the defenceless, and in diabolical intent, this Fugitive Slave Law stands alone in the annals of tyrannical legislation . . .

But it is answered in reply to all this, that precisely what I have now denounced is, in fact, guaranteed and sanctioned by the Constitution of the United States; that the right to hold and to hunt slaves is a part of that Constitution framed by the illustrious Fathers of this Republic . . .

Fellow-citizens! there is no matter in respect to which, the people of the North have allowed themselves to be so ruinously imposed upon, as that of the pro-slavery character of the Constitution. In that instrument I hold there is neither warrant, license, nor sanction of the hateful thing; but, interpreted as it ought to be interpreted, the Constitution is a GLORIOUS LIBERTY DOCUMENT. Read its preamble, consider its purposes. Is slavery among them? Is it at the gateway? or is it in the temple? It is neither. While I do not intend to argue this question on the present occasion, let me ask, if it be not somewhat singular that, if the Constitution were intended to be, by its framers and adopters, a slave-holding instrument, why neither slavery, slaveholding, nor slave can anywhere be found in it . . .

Now, take the constitution according to its plain reading, and I defy the presentation of a single pro-slavery clause in it. On the other hand it will be found to contain principles and purposes, entirely hostile to the existence of slavery . . .

Allow me to say, in conclusion, notwithstanding the dark picture I have this day presented of the state of the nation, I do not despair of this country. There are forces in operation, which must inevitably work the downfall of slavery. "The arm of the Lord is not shortened," and the doom of slavery is certain. I, therefore, leave off where I began, with hope . . .

Source: Frederick Douglass, *Oration, Delivered in Corinthian Hall, Rochester* (Rochester, N.Y.: Lee, Mann and Company, 1852), from the Department of Rare Books and Special Collections, University of Rochester Libraries, www.library.rochester.edu.

Document 1.13 in Context
"Received into the Union with or without Slavery, as Their Constitution May Prescribe": Westward Expansion and Slavery Collide in "Bleeding Kansas"

In 1854 the pressure for westward expansion and the simmering conflict over slavery came crashing together once again in the halls of Congress. The need for territorial organization in the lands immediately west of Missouri had been apparent—and growing—for some time. Demand for the millions of acres of rich farmland in the region was driving increasing settlement, and railroad developers were eager to expand into the area. In the face of southern opposition, Congress had already tried and failed four times to pass legislation that would organize the land that is now Kansas and Nebraska as a single territory.

Southern proslavery lawmakers had long been unhappy about the restriction against slavery in the territories north of the 36°30' line established by the Missouri Compromise (**Document 1.6**). That restriction meant that the entire area immediately west of Missouri should be organized as free territory. Proslavery interests considered it an obstruction to the westward extension of slavery and worried that it would eventually shift the nation's balance of political power in favor of abolition. Antislavery forces, meanwhile, were adamant that the restriction should be retained.

In January 1854 Sen. Stephen A. Douglas, D-Ill., proposed a solution. Under Douglas's bill, the land west of Missouri would be organized into two territories instead of one: the Kansas Territory south of the 40th parallel, and the Nebraska Territory north of that line. Moreover,

Douglas's bill called for residents of the two territories to vote to determine the status of slavery. It was the same approach that had been applied to the new southwestern territories in the Compromise of 1850 (**Document 1.11**). The implication was that Kansas would probably approve slavery while Nebraska would probably reject it.

The change, however, meant repeal of the Missouri Compromise, a repeal that was specifically written into the final version of the Kansas-Nebraska Act. That outraged opponents of slavery, and the intense and often bitter debate over the bill went on for months. In the end, Douglas managed to push the bill through Congress in late May 1854 with support from southern lawmakers and President Franklin Pierce, a Democrat from New Hampshire.

Fallout from passage of the act was rapid, chaotic and violent. For four years, conflict raged as supporters and opponents of slavery rushed to Kansas in an attempt to sway the decision on slavery by becoming territorial voters. Bloody violence killed dozens, elections were held and challenged, fraud was alleged, opposing legislatures were formed and federal troops were sent in to restore order. It was not until 1861, on the eve of the Civil War, that Kansas was finally admitted to the Union as a free state.

The chaos of "bleeding Kansas" intensified the hostility between North and South and made reconciliation or further compromise on the issue of slavery virtually impossible. The turmoil in Kansas also launched the violent career of John Brown, whose attempt to spark a slave rebellion at Harpers Ferry, Virginia, five years later would add yet another provocation to the litany of resentments and recriminations. And it also helped inspire organization of the Republican Party, which was able in just six years to elect its candidate, Abraham Lincoln, as president of the United States.

▬▬ Document 1.13 ▬▬
An Act to Organize the Territories of Nebraska and Kansas, May 30, 1854

Be it enacted by the Senate and House of Representatives of the United States of America in Congress assembled, That all that part of the territory of the United States included within the following limits . . . is hereby, created into a temporary government by the name of the Territory Nebraska; and when admitted as a State or States, the said Territory or any portion of the same, shall be received into the Union with or without slavery, as their constitution may prescribe at the time of the admission . . .

SECTION 5. *And be it further enacted,* That every free white male inhabitant above the age of twenty-one years who shall be an actual resident of said Territory, and shall possess the qualifications hereinafter prescribed, shall be entitled to vote at the first election, and shall be eligible to any office within the said Territory . . .

SEC. 9. *And be it further enacted,* That the judicial power of said Territory shall be vested in a Supreme Court, District Courts, Probate Courts, and in Justices of the Peace . . . Writs of error, and appeals from the final decisions of said Supreme Court, shall be allowed, and may be taken to the Supreme Court of the United States, in the same manner and under the same regulations as from the circuit courts of the United States . . . except only that in all cases involving title to slaves, the said writs of error, or appeals shall be allowed and decided by the said Supreme Court, without regard to the value of the matter, property, or title in controversy; and except also that a writ of error or appeal shall also be allowed to the Supreme Court of the United States, from the decision of the said Supreme Court created by this act, or of any judge thereof, or of the district courts created by this act, or of any judge thereof, upon any writ of habeas corpus, involving the question of personal freedom: *Provided,* that nothing herein contained shall be construed to apply to or affect the provisions to the "act respecting fugitives from justice, and persons escaping from the service of their masters," approved February twelfth, seventeen hundred and ninety-three, and the "act to amend and supplementary to the aforesaid act," approved September eighteen, eighteen hundred and fifty . . .

SEC. 10. *And Be it further enacted,* That the provisions of an act entitled "An act respecting fugitives from justice, and persons escaping from the service of their masters," approved February twelve, seventeen hundred and ninety-three, and the provisions of the act entitled "An act to amend, and supplementary to, the aforesaid act," approved September eighteen, eighteen hundred and fifty, be, and the same are hereby, declared to extend to and be in full force within the limits of said Territory of Nebraska . . .

SEC. 14. *And be it further enacted,* . . . That the Constitution, and all Laws of the United States which are not locally inapplicable, shall have the same force and effect within the said Territory of Nebraska as elsewhere within the United States, except the eighth section of the act preparatory to the admission of Missouri into the Union approved March sixth, eighteen hundred and twenty, which, being inconsistent with the principle of non-intervention by Congress with slaves in the States and Territories, as recognized by the legislation of eighteen hundred and fifty, commonly called the Compromise Measures, is hereby declared inoperative and void; it being the true intent and meaning of this act not to legislate slavery into any Territory or State, nor to exclude it therefrom, but to leave the people thereof perfectly free to form [and] regulate their domestic institutions in their own way, subject only to the Constitution of the United States: *Provided,* That nothing herein contained shall be construed to revive or put in force any law or regulation which may have existed prior to the act of sixth March, eighteen hundred and twenty, either protecting, establishing, prohibiting, or abolishing slavery . . .

SEC. 19. *And be it further enacted,* That all that part of the Territory of the United States included within the following limits, . . . is hereby, created into a temporary government by the name of the Territory of Kansas; and when admitted as a State or States, the said Territory, or any portion of the same, shall be received into the Union with or without slavery, as their Constitution may prescribe at the time of their admission . . .

SEC. 23. *And be it further enacted,* That every free white male inhabitant above the age of twenty-one years, who shall be an actual resident of said Territory, and shall possess the qualifications hereinafter prescribed, shall be entitled to vote at the first election, and shall be eligible to any office within the said Territory . . .

SEC. 27. *And be it further enacted,* That the judicial power of said Territory shall be vested in a supreme court, district courts, probate courts, and in justices of the peace . . . Writs of error, and appeals from the final decisions of said supreme court, shall be allowed, and may be taken to the Supreme Court of the United States, in the same manner and under the same regulations as from the Circuit Courts of the United States . . . except only that in all cases involving title to slaves, the said writ of error or appeals shall be allowed and decided by said supreme court, without regard to the value of the matter, property, or title in controversy; and except also that a writ of error or appeal shall also be allowed to the Supreme Court of the United States, from the decision of the said supreme court created by this act, or of any judge thereof, or of the district courts created by this act, or of any judge thereof, upon any writ of habeas corpus, involving the question of personal freedom . . .

SEC. 28. *And be it further enacted,* That the provisions of the act entitled "An act respecting fugitives from justice, and persons escaping from, the service of their masters," approved February twelfth, seventeen hundred and ninety-three, and the provisions of the act entitled "An act to amend, and supplementary to, the aforesaid act," approved September eighteenth, eighteen hundred and fifty, be, and the same are hereby, declared to extend to and be in full force within the limits of the said Territory of Kansas . . .

SEC. 31. *And be it further enacted,* That the seat of government of said Territory is hereby located temporarily at Fort Leavenworth; and that such portions of the public buildings as may not be actually used and needed for military purposes, may be occupied and used, under the direction of the Governor and Legislative Assembly, for such public purposes as may be required under the provisions of this act.

SEC. 32. *And be it further enacted,* . . . That the Constitution, and all laws of the United States which are not locally inapplicable, shall have the same force and effect within the said Territory of Kansas as elsewhere within the United States, except the eighth section of the act preparatory to the admission of Missouri into the Union, approved March sixth, eighteen hundred and twenty, which, being inconsistent with the principle of non-intervention by Congress with slavery in the States and Territories, as recognized by the legislation of eighteen hundred and fifty, commonly called the Compromise Measures, is hereby declared inoperative and void; it being the true intent and meaning of this act not to legislate slavery into any Territory or State, nor to exclude it therefrom, but to leave the people thereof perfectly free to form and regulate their domestic institutions in their own way, subject only to the Constitution of the United States: *Provided,* That nothing herein contained shall be construed to revive or put in force any law or regulation which may have existed prior to the act of sixth of March, eighteen hundred and twenty, either protecting, establishing, prohibiting, or abolishing slavery . . .

Source: "An Act to Organize the Territories of Nebraska and Kansas," 1854, from the U.S. National Archives and Records Administration, www.ourdocuments.gov.

Document 1.14 in Context
"No Rights Which the White Man Was Bound to Respect": The *Dred Scott* Decision and the Path toward War

On March 6, 1857, the United States Supreme Court issued a landmark ruling that not only concluded one black man's eleven-year court battle to win his freedom, but also underscored the irreconcilable differences that had evolved over the role of slavery in America. In a long and sweeping opinion, Chief Justice Roger B. Taney declared that the plaintiffs, Dred Scott and his wife, Harriet Robinson Scott, were not free and that they did not even have the right to sue to seek their freedom. As if that were not bad enough, the decision, which many modern legal scholars consider the worst ever issued by the Court, went even further. Taney asserted that black people had "no rights which the white man was bound to respect." The chief justice also demolished the foundation on which decades of delicate political compromise over slavery had been built by declaring that Congress did not have the authority to forbid slavery in any of the federal territories. It was a dramatic reversal of a public policy that had been established in the Northwest Ordinance of 1787 (**Document 1.3**).

The saga of Dred Scott began in 1834 when Dr. John Emerson, an army surgeon, moved with his slave from their home in Missouri to residences first in the state of Illinois and then in the Wisconsin Territory, both of which were areas where slavery was outlawed. Emerson and Scott lived on free soil for seven years before returning to Missouri. Emerson died not long after their return to Missouri, and in 1846 Scott sued for his freedom. Scott's suit argued that living for seven years in free territory had established his freedom.

The Supreme Court in 1857 was not a friendly venue for the appeal of a slave. Seven of the court's nine justices had been appointed by presidents who supported slavery; five, including Taney, owned or had owned slaves or belonged to families that owned slaves. At least one had fathered a child by a slave woman. Moreover, the case was argued in an atmosphere of growing national tension over slavery. The Kansas-Nebraska Act (**Document 1.13**) had repealed the Missouri Compromise (**Document 1.6**), and violence was erupting in Kansas between slavery supporters and foes.

In the Court's opinion, Taney took direct aim at the philosophical dilemma with which the nation had been wrestling since 1776: how could a nation that professed to believe "that all men are created equal" permit slavery to continue? He sought to resolve the issue by slicing through the Gordian knot of the Declaration (**Document 1.1**). The Declaration's pivotal phrase, Taney determined, simply did not mean what it appeared to mean. "[I]t is too clear for dispute," he wrote, "that the enslaved African race were not intended to be included, and formed no part of the people who framed and adopted this declaration." Taney declared that African Americans were property, not people—as the Declaration and Constitution used the term—and though they might be manumitted, they could never be considered citizens. Therefore they had no rights.

Far from settling the issue of slavery—either legally or politically—the *Dred Scott* decision added fuel to the angry and contentious public debate. It inflamed abolitionist passions, which in turn intensified southern fears and contributed to the election of Abraham Lincoln, ultimately accelerating the nation's rush toward civil war.

▭ Document 1.14 ▭
Judgment in the U.S. Supreme Court Case
Dred Scott v. Sandford, March 6, 1857

. . . The question is simply this: Can a negro whose ancestors were imported into this country, and sold as slaves, become a member of the political community formed and brought into existence by the Constitution of the United States, and as such become entitled to all the rights and privileges and immunities guaranteed to the citizen? One of which rights is the privilege of suing in a court of the United States in the cases specified in the Constitution . . .

The words "people of the United States" and "citizens" are synonymous terms, and mean the same thing. They both describe the political body who, according to our republican institutions, form the sovereignty, and who hold the power and conduct the Government through their representatives. They are what we familiarly call the "sovereign people," and every citizen is one of this people and a constituent member of this sovereignty. The question before us is, whether the class of persons described in the plea in abatement compose a portion of this people, and are constituent members of this sovereignty? We think they are not, and that they are not included, and were not intended to be included, under the word "citizens" in the Constitution, and can therefore claim none of the rights and privileges which that instrument provides for and secures to citizens of the United States . . .

The question then arises, whether the provisions of the Constitution, in relation to the personal rights and privileges to which the citizen of a State should be entitled, embraced the negro African race, at that time in this country, or who might afterwards be imported, who had then or should afterwards be made free in any State; and to put it in the power of a single State to make him a citizen of the United States, and endue him with the tall rights of citizenship in every other State without their consent? Does the Constitution of the United States act upon him whenever he shall be made free under the laws of a State, and raised there to the rank of a citizen, and immediately clothe him with all the privileges of a citizen in every other State, and in its own courts?

The court think the affirmative of these propositions cannot be maintained. And if it cannot, the plaintiff in error could not be a citizen of the State of Missouri, within the meaning of the Constitution of the United States, and, consequently, was not entitled to sue in its courts . . .

In the opinion of the court, the legislation and histories of the times, and the language used in the Declaration of Independence, show, that neither the class of persons who had been imported as slaves, nor their descendants, whether they had become free or not, were then acknowledged as a part of the people, nor intended to be included in the general words used in that memorable instrument . . .

They had for more than a century before been regarded as beings of an inferior order, and altogether unfit to associate with the white race, either in social or political relations; and so far inferior, that they had no rights which the white man was bound to respect; and that the negro might justly and lawfully be reduced to slavery for his benefit. He was bought and sold, and treated as an ordinary article of merchandise and traffic, whenever a profit could be made by it. This opinion was at that time fixed and universal in the civilized portion of the white race . . .

The language of the Declaration of Independence is equally conclusive: . . .

It then proceeds to say: "We hold these truths to be self-evident: that all men are created equal; that they are endowed by their Creator with certain unalienable rights; that among them is life, liberty, and the pursuit of happiness; that to secure these rights, Governments are instituted, deriving their just powers from the consent of the governed."

The general words above quoted would seem to embrace the whole human family, and if they were used in a similar instrument at this day would be so understood. But it is too clear for dispute, that the enslaved African race were not intended to be included, and formed no part of the people who framed and adopted this declaration; for if the language, as understood in that day, would embrace them, the conduct of the distinguished men who framed the Declaration of Independence would have been utterly and flagrantly inconsistent with the principles they asserted; and instead of the sympathy of mankind, to which they so confidently appealed, they would have deserved and received universal rebuke and reprobation.

Yet the men who framed this declaration were great men—high in literary acquirements—high in their sense of honor, and incapable of asserting principles inconsistent with those on which they were acting. They perfectly understood the meaning of the language they used, and how it would be understood by others; and they knew that it would not in any part of the civilized world be supposed to embrace the negro race, which by common consent, had been excluded from civilized Governments and the family of nations, and doomed to slavery . . .

This state of public opinion had undergone no change when the Constitution was adopted, as is equally evident from its provisions and language . . .

But there are two clauses in the Constitution which point directly and specifically to the negro race as a separate class of persons, and show clearly that they were not regarded as a portion of the people or citizens of the Government then formed.

One of these clauses reserves to each of the thirteen States the right to import slaves until the year 1808, if it thinks proper. And the importation which it thus sanctions was unquestionably of persons of the race of which we are speaking, as the traffic in slaves in the United States had always been confined to them. And by the other provision the States pledge themselves to each other to maintain the right of property of the master, by delivering up to him any slave who may have escaped from his service, and be found within their respective territories. By the first above-mentioned clause, therefore, the right to purchase and hold this property is directly sanctioned and authorized for twenty years by the people who framed the Constitution. And by the second, they pledge themselves to maintain and uphold the right of the master in the manner specified, as long as the Government they then formed should endure. And these two provisions show, conclusively, that neither the description of persons therein referred to, nor their descendants, were embraced in any of the other provisions of the Constitution; for certainly these two clauses were not intended to confer on them or their posterity the blessings of liberty, or any of the personal rights so carefully provided for the citizen . . .

It is very true, that in that portion of the Union where the labor of the negro race was found to be unsuited to the climate and unprofitable to the master, but few slaves were held at the time of the Declaration of Independence; and when the Constitution was adopted, it had entirely worn out in one of them, and measures had been taken for its gradual abolition in several others. But . . . some of the States, where it had ceased or nearly ceased to exist, were actively engaged in the slave trade . . . And it can hardly be supposed that, in the States where it was then countenanced in its worst form—that is, in the seizure and transportation—the people could have regarded those who were emancipated as entitled to equal rights with themselves . . .

And upon a full and careful consideration of the subject, the court is of opinion, that, upon the facts stated in the plea in abatement, Dred Scott was not a citizen of Missouri within the meaning of the Constitution of the United States, and not entitled as such to sue in its courts; and, consequently, that the Circuit Court had no jurisdiction of the case, and that the judgment on the plea in abatement is erroneous . . .

Upon these considerations, it is the opinion of the court that the act of Congress which prohibited a citizen from holding and owning property of this kind in the territory of the United States north of the line therein mentioned, is not warranted by the Constitution, and is therefore void; and that neither Dred Scott himself, nor any of his family, were made free by being carried into this territory; even if they had been carried there by the owner, with the intention of becoming a permanent resident . . .

Source: Dred Scott v. Sandford, 60 U.S. 393 (1857), from the U.S. National Archives and Records Administration, www.ourdocuments.gov.

NOTES

1 Phillis Wheatley, Poems on Various Subjects, Religious and Moral (London: A. Bell, 1773), from the New York Public Library, Digital Schomburg Collection, http://digital.nypl.org=writers_aa19/.

2 "The Earliest Protest against Slavery," in *Documents of American History*, ed. Henry Steele Commager (Englewood Cliffs, N.J.: Prentice-Hall, 1973), 37–38.

3 Thomas Jefferson to Rep. John Holmes, letter, April 22, 1820 in *The Life and Selected Writings of Thomas Jefferson*, ed. Adrienne Koch and William Peden (New York: Random House, 1972), 698.

4 Rep. John Swanwick of Pennsylvania, speaking on January 23, 1797, *Annals of Congress*, 4th Cong., 2nd sess., 2019.

5 Rep. John Rutledge Jr. of South Carolina, speaking on January 2, 1800, *Annals of Congress*, 6th Cong., 1st sess., 230.

6 Thomas Jefferson to Rep. John Holmes, letter, April 22, 1820, in Koch and Peden, *The Life and Selected Writings of Thomas Jefferson*, 698.

7 Richard Allen, "Address to the Free People of Colour of these United States," in *Minutes of the Proceedings of the National Negro Conventions, 1830–1864*, ed. Howard Holman Bell, 1913 (New York: Amo Press, 1969), from Public Broadcasting Service, *Africans in America*, www.pbs.org/wgbh/aia/part3/3h512t.html.

8 Joseph Sidney, "African American Political Oration, 1809," in *Jim Crow New York: A Documentary History of Race and Citizenship, 1777–1877*, ed. David N. Gellman and David Quigley (New York: New York University Press, 2003), 61.

9 "Equal Rights of All Citizens in the Cars," *Liberator* 12, no. 8 (February 25, 1842): 32.

CHAPTER TWO

The Civil War

The Slavery Debate Erupts, 1860–1865

braham Lincoln's plurality victory in the three-way contest of the 1860 presidential election made him the nation's first Republican president. Simultaneously, his win guaranteed that the proslavery Southern states would carry out their threat to secede from the Union (**Document 2.1**), set up their own national government (**Document 2.2**) and thus ignite a civil war. About a month after Lincoln took office, war erupted on April 12, 1861, when Confederate artillery fired at Fort Sumter in the harbor off Charleston, South Carolina—the opening shot in what would become the transformational conflict in U.S. history.

At the start of the war, Lincoln made it clear that saving the Union was his primary goal. Since his inauguration on March 4, 1861, a fundamental question had confronted Lincoln and the Northern states: How would the Confederacy be defeated and the United States preserved?

The answer to this question was rooted largely in the North's transportation, manufacturing, population and financial advantages over the South, giving it a military edge in a

In May 1862 Robert Smalls, then a slave, took over the Confederate ship Planter *and delivered it to Union forces, with whom he served for the rest of the Civil War. After the war, Smalls served in the South Carolina legislature before being elected to the U.S. House of Representatives.*
Source: Library of Congress

four-year war of attrition. A Northern naval blockade of Southern ports significantly impaired the Confederacy's ability to import essential arms and supplies from Europe, and Southern efforts to enlist Britain and France as allies failed. Richmond, Virginia, the Confederate capital, was close to Washington, D.C., and thus within easy striking distance of Federal forces. As a matter of strategy, Confederate efforts to relieve the overburdened Virginia countryside, by invading the North in such battles as Antietam in Maryland and Gettysburg in Pennsylvania, cost the South large numbers of irreplaceable troops. As the war dragged on, Confederate troop desertions mounted amid deteriorating living conditions both in the army and on the home front and in the face of the growing likelihood of defeat.

Assuming that the Confederacy would be defeated and the Union restored, Lincoln faced the question of what would happen to the former slaves on whose labor rested much of the Southern economy. Finding answers proved complex. Lincoln wrestled with the scope of a declaration of emancipation, including whether to extend its geographic reach to cover the slaveholding border states that had not seceded. Leading up to the Emancipation Proclamation he ultimately signed (**Document 2.3**), Lincoln remained ambivalent, as evidenced by his reaction to General Order Number 11, issued on May 9, 1862, by Gen. David Hunter:

> The three States of Georgia, Florida and South Carolina, comprising the military department of the south, having deliberately declared themselves no longer under the protection of the United States of America, and having taken up arms against the said United States, it becomes a military necessity to declare them under martial law. This was accordingly done on the 25th day of April, 1862. Slavery and martial law in a free country are altogether incompatible; the persons in these three States—Georgia, Florida, and South Carolina—heretofore held as slaves, are therefore declared forever free.[1]

Lincoln worried about the political effects of this order on the border states and quickly overruled Hunter. But whether or not it fit Lincoln's original plan, the Union army's expanding occupation of Southern territory brought to millions of slaves emancipation, although sometimes accompanied by dislocation, poverty and illiteracy. Similarly, Lincoln would wrestle with proposals to encourage or require black emigration from the United States (**Document 2.5**), a constitutional ban on slavery that would culminate in the Thirteenth Amendment (**Document 2.8**) and the public services the federal government should provide to support former slaves in the subsequently defeated South (**Document 2.10**).

More subtle but also of critical importance were the military and political contributions that former slaves and free-born African Americans could make as supporters of the Union and the Republican Party. Many, including fugitive slaves or "contrabands," sought the chance to serve in the armed forces. In an October 1861 letter to Secretary of War Simon Cameron, a black physician from Michigan offered to recruit 5,000–10,000 "free men," preferably for sharpshooting assignments: "We are all anxious to fight for the maintenance of the Union and the preservation of the principles promulgated by President Lincoln and we are sure of success if allowed an opportunity." [2] In his newspaper *Douglass' Monthly,* abolitionist Frederick Douglass editorialized, "Men of Color, to Arms!"[3] Lincoln and his commanders debated the role African Americans could play in the Union army and navy, eventually recognizing that they would be important assets in providing essential manpower for the war effort (**Document 2.7**). Although they frequently were relegated to menial and support assignments, some blacks saw combat. After a two-hour battle in which a Confederate force was defeated, Union Gen. James Blunt wrote of the First Kansas Colored Infantry: "I never saw such fighting as was done by the Negro regiment . . . The question that negroes will fight is settled; besides they make better soldiers in every respect than any troops I have ever had under my command." [4]

In the South, although Confederate generals were desperate for troops, the use of black soldiers was a much more divisive issue—the *Charleston Mercury* labeled it "insane, demoralizing, destructive, hopeless" [5]—and it was not until the end of the war that the Confederate Congress reluctantly authorized the enlistment of blacks (**Document 2.9**). The Confederacy surrendered, however, before the new policy could be actively implemented. Overall, approximately 3 million troops fought and about 620,000 died on both sides, among them about 37,000 black Union soldiers and officers.

The Civil War provided opportunities for the men who would become the first African Americans in Congress during and immediately after Reconstruction. Some of those opportunities were military in nature. In an article about the death of former representative Robert B. Elliott, R-S.C., in 1892, the *African Methodist Episcopal Church Review* observed:

> The first shot that was fired upon Fort Sumter opened the pathway to many a notable event in the history of this country, to the development of great soldiers and great statesmen, whose lives otherwise might have been as "flowers born to blush unseen"; but the most unexpected of events was the black legislator in the State and Nation . . . From the battle-field to the halls of legislation was but a natural step.[6]

Elliott, the piece continued, joined the Union navy, "and when the war was over he went from the cannon's mouth to the halls of legislation." [7]

Legislation passed in July 1862 permitted escaped slaves, or "contrabands," and free blacks to serve in the Union forces as laborers or to enlist in military service "if competent." Most African Americans were used as laborers, but several black military units distinguished themselves in combat. Here, two contrabands sit outside a tent in General George G. Meade's camp in Culpeper, Virginia, in late 1863.
Source: Library of Congress

Other future black lawmakers made military contributions as well. Former slave Robert Smalls, R-S.C., emerged as a naval hero (**Document 2.4**). Bricklayer Charles E. Nash, R-La., rose from private to sergeant major in the Union army. John M. Langston, R-Va., recruited black troops for regiments. And future senator Hiram R. Revels, R-Miss., both recruited African American troops and served as the chaplain for a black regiment. Yet others made more modest contributions to the war effort. As a recently freed slave, future representative John R. Lynch, R-Miss., was paid a meager $2 for six weeks' work as a cook for an Illinois regiment. He later wrote, "Of this I did not complain and found no fault, because I felt that I had rendered some service to a few of those who had contributed something to the salvation of the Union and the abolition of slavery." [8] He later worked as a cook for another army unit and as a pantryman aboard a government transport.

For some future members, the outcome of the war opened financial and political doors. For example, Blanche K. Bruce, who was born a slave in Virginia, moved to Mississippi after the war, where he became a planter, a local official and later a U.S. senator. Similarly, James E. O'Hara, who was born free in New York City, moved to North Carolina, where he won state legislative office and went on to the U.S. House of Representatives.

The coming of war did not, however, herald the end of discrimination. During the war, blacks in the North faced their own challenges, such as lack of political power, violence and pervasive, everyday racism. In December 1862 two brothers in Hartford, Connecticut, petitioned Congress about the taxation of their tailoring business without representation, protesting that by the Constitution of Connecticut because of our Negro blood, and for no other reason, we are deprived on the right of Suffrage and of the privilege of taking any part whatever in matters of Government, both State and National . . . [and] we are required to pay from our little business about one hundred dollars per month for the support of a Government we have no voice in administering.[9]

In July 1863 New York City erupted into violence as white citizens and immigrants protested Lincoln's call for the conscription of 300,000 more soldiers and vented their anger about the competition free blacks posed for jobs (**Document 2.6**). African Americans were beaten and lynched, and a black church and orphanage were burned to the ground. The violence was quelled only after Lincoln ordered Northern troops fresh from combat at Gettysburg into the city as peacekeepers.

Even when antiblack sentiments were not expressed violently, they created a hostile environment. Black residents of Philadelphia complained in 1864 that they suffered "very serious inconveniences and hardships daily, by being excluded from riding in the City Passenger Cars," or streetcars.[10]

In the 1864 presidential election, Democrat George McClellan, a former commander of the Union army whom Lincoln had twice relieved of command, challenged the president as an antiwar candidate who was committed to negotiating with the Confederacy to end the war. Lincoln won reelection easily.

On April 9, 1865, Confederate Gen. Robert E. Lee surrendered the Army of Northern Virginia to Union Lt. Gen. Ulysses S. Grant at Appomattox Court House, Virginia. Although other forces had yet to surrender, the war was effectively over. Less than a week later, on April 14, Southern sympathizer John Wilkes Booth fatally shot Lincoln, who died the next day. The succession of Vice President Andrew Johnson, a Democrat, to office and his deep political and policy disagreements with a Republican Congress over postwar policies for the South would set the stage for the election of the first black members of the House and Senate.

Document 2.1 in Context
"The Union Heretofore Existing between This State and the Other States of North America, Is Dissolved": South Carolina Secedes from the Union

Abraham Lincoln's victory in the November 1860 presidential election over Democrats Stephen A. Douglas and John C. Breckinridge triggered the long-anticipated secession of eleven Southern states, with South Carolina taking the lead. In fact, South Carolina had set the stage in 1852, when it held a convention to complain about federal "encroachment" on states' rights and to reserve the option of withdrawing from the Union. Its formal declaration of secession, adopted on December 24, 1860, couched itself in the mantle of the American Revolution—the authority of the people to abolish a "destructive" government and the purported sovereignty of individual states. However, without mentioning race, the declaration went on to make clear that preservation of slavery as an institution that treated slaves as property was a paramount motivation. It both attacked the antislavery movement and criticized Lincoln as a man "whose opinions and purposes are hostile to slavery." [11] The Alabama legislature, anticipating the "contingency" of a Republican presidential victory, took preparatory steps as well; its resolution of February 24, 1860, lashed out at "anti-slavery agitation" in the "non-slaveholding States of this Union" and scheduled a secession convention to be held after the presidential election.[12]

For all its harsh language, the South Carolina declaration was tame compared with Mississippi's secession declaration of January 9, 1861. That document focused on slavery from its second paragraph on and was permeated with explicit racism, such as the statement that slave labor "supplies the product which constitutes by far the largest and most important portions of commerce of the earth. These products are peculiar to the climate verging on the tropical regions, and by an imperious law of nature, none but the black race can bear exposure to the tropical sun." Even more important as a predictor of the South's future hostility to black political empowerment was the statement that those opposed to slavery advocate "negro equality, socially and politically." [13] The Texas secession declaration of February 2, 1861, also emphasized both slavery and race, and noted that the state had been accepted into the United States "holding, maintaining and protecting the institution known as negro slavery— the servitude of the African to the white race." In addition, it attacked abolitionists who demanded "the recognition of political equality between the white and negro races." [14] And in its defense of the right of slavery, Georgia's declaration of January 29, 1861, asserted that when the U.S. Constitution was drafted, "the subordination of the African race was fully conceded by all." [15]

▬ Document 2.1 ▬
Declaration of the Immediate Causes Which Induce and Justify the Secession of South Carolina from the Federal Union, Adopted December 24, 1860

The people of the State of South Carolina, in Convention assembled, on the 26th day of April, A.D., 1852, declared that the frequent violations of the Constitution of the United States, by the Federal Government, and its encroachments upon the reserved rights of the States, fully justified this State in then withdrawing from the Federal Union; but in deference to the opinions and wishes of the other slaveholding States, she forbore at that time to exercise this right. Since that time, these encroachments have continued to increase, and further forbearance ceases to be a virtue.

And now the State of South Carolina having resumed her separate and equal place among nations deems it due to herself, to the remaining United States of America, and to the nations of the world, that she should declare the immediate causes which have led to this act.

In the year 1765, that portion of the British Empire embracing Great Britain, undertook to make laws for the government of that portion composed of the thirteen American Colonies. A struggle for the right of self-government ensued, which resulted, on the 4th of July, 1776, in a Declaration, by the Colonies, "that they are, and of right ought to be, FREE AND INDEPENDENT STATES; and that, as free and independent States, they have full power to levy war, conclude peace, contract alliances, establish commerce, and to do all other acts and things which independent States may of right do" . . .

In pursuance of this Declaration of Independence, each of the thirteen States proceeded to exercise its separate sovereignty; adopted for itself a Constitution, and appointed officers for the administration of government in all its departments—Legislative, Executive and Judicial. For purposes of defense, they united their arms and their counsels; and, in 1778, they entered into a League known as the Articles of Confederation, whereby they agreed to entrust the administration of their external relations to a common agent, known as the Congress of the United States, expressly declaring, in the first Article "that each State retains its sovereignty, freedom and independence, and every power, jurisdiction and right which is not, by this Confederation, expressly delegated to the United States in Congress assembled" . . .

Thus were established the two great principles asserted by the Colonies, namely: the right of a State to govern itself; and the right of a people to abolish a Government when it becomes destructive of the ends for which it was instituted. And concurrent with the establishment of these principles, was the fact, that each Colony became and was recognized by the mother Country a FREE, SOVEREIGN AND INDEPENDENT STATE.

In 1787, Deputies were appointed by the States to revise the Articles of Confederation, and on 17th September, 1787, these Deputies recommended for the adoption of the States, the Articles of Union, known as the Constitution of the United States . . .

By this Constitution, certain duties were imposed upon the several States, and the exercise of certain of their powers was restrained, which necessarily implied their continued existence as sovereign States. But to remove all doubt, an amendment was added, which declared that the powers not delegated to the United States by the Constitution, nor prohibited by it to the States, are reserved to the States, respectively, or to the people . . .

Thus was established, by compact between the States, a Government with definite objects and powers, limited to the express words of the grant. This limitation left the whole remaining mass of power subject to the clause reserving it to the States or to the people, and rendered unnecessary any specification of reserved rights . . .

We maintain that in every compact between two or more parties, the obligation is mutual; that the failure of one of the contracting parties to perform a material part of the agreement, entirely releases the obligation of the other; and that where no arbiter is provided, each party is remitted to his own judgment to determine the fact of failure, with all its consequences.

In the present case, that fact is established with certainty. We assert that fourteen of the States have deliberately refused, for years past, to fulfill their constitutional obligations, and we refer to their own Statutes for the proof.

The Constitution of the United States, in its fourth Article, provides as follows: "No person held to service or labor in one State, under the laws thereof, escaping into another, shall, in consequence of any law or regulation therein, be discharged from such service or labor, but shall be delivered up, on claim of the party to whom such service or labor may be due" . . .

The same article of the Constitution stipulates also for rendition by the several States of fugitives from justice from the other States.

The General Government, as the common agent, passed laws to carry into effect these stipulations of the States. For many years these laws were executed. But an increasing hostility on the part of the non-slaveholding States to the institution of slavery, has led to a disregard of their obligations, and the laws of the General Government have ceased to effect the objects of the Constitution. The States of Maine, New Hampshire, Vermont, Massachusetts, Connecticut, Rhode Island, New York, Pennsylvania, Illinois, Indiana, Michigan, Wisconsin and Iowa, have enacted laws which either nullify the Acts of Congress or render useless any attempt to execute them. In many of these States the fugitive is discharged from service or labor claimed, and in none of them has the State Government complied with the stipulation made in the Constitution . . . Thus the constituted compact has been deliberately broken and disregarded by the non-slaveholding States, and the consequence follows that South Carolina is released from her obligation . . .

The right of property in slaves was recognized by giving to free persons distinct political rights, by giving them the right to represent, and burthening them with direct taxes for three-fifths of their slaves; by authorizing the importation of slaves for twenty years; and by stipulating for the rendition of fugitives from labor.

We affirm that these ends for which this Government was instituted have been defeated, and the Government itself has been made destructive of them by the action of the non-slave-holding States. Those States have assumed the right of deciding upon the propriety of our domestic institutions; and have denied the rights of property established in fifteen of the States and recognized by the Constitution; they have denounced as sinful the institution of slavery; they have permitted open establishment among them of societies, whose avowed object is to disturb the peace and to eloign the property of the citizens of other States. They have encouraged and assisted thousands of our slaves to leave their homes; and those who remain, have been incited by emissaries, books and pictures to servile insurrection.

For twenty-five years this agitation has been steadily increasing, until it has now secured to its aid the power of the common Government. Observing the *forms* of the Constitution, a sectional party has found within that Article establishing the Executive Department, the means of subverting the Constitution itself. A geographical line has been drawn across the Union, and all the States north of that line have united in the election of a man to the high office of President of the United States, whose opinions and purposes are hostile to slavery. He is to be entrusted with the administration of the common Government, because he has declared that that "Government cannot endure permanently half slave, half free," and that the public mind must rest in the belief that slavery is in the course of ultimate extinction . . .

On the 4th day of March next, this party will take possession of the Government. It has announced that the South shall be excluded from the common territory, that the judicial tribunals shall be made sectional, and that a war must be waged against slavery until it shall cease throughout the United States.

The guaranties of the Constitution will then no longer exist; the equal rights of the States will be lost. The slaveholding States will no longer have the power of self-government, or self-protection, and the Federal Government will have become their enemy . . .

We, therefore, the People of South Carolina, by our delegates in Convention assembled, appealing to the Supreme Judge of the world for the rectitude of our intentions, have solemnly declared that the Union heretofore existing between this State and the other States of North America, is dissolved, and that the State of South Carolina has resumed her position among the nations of the world, as a separate and independent State; with full power to levy war, conclude peace, contract alliances, establish commerce, and to do all other acts and things which independent States may of right do.

Source: "Declaration of the Immediate Causes which Induce and Justify the Secession of South Carolina from the Federal Union," December 24, 1860, from the Avalon Project at Yale Law School, www.yale.edu/lawweb/avalon/csa/scarsec.htm.

Document 2.2 in Context
"No . . . Law Denying or Impairing the Right of Property in Negro Slaves Shall Be Passed": Slavery and the Confederate Constitution

The permanent Constitution of the Confederate States of America was adopted March 11, 1861, in Montgomery, Alabama, to replace a provisional one signed February 8, 1861. It bore close resemblance to the U.S. Constitution (**Document 1.4**), outlining a strong, three-branch federal government with a president as the head of the executive branch, a bicameral congress with a popularly elected house of representatives and a senate elected by state legislatures, and a judiciary with a supreme court at the top. The powers allocated to each branch were also similar. (The Confederate Congress, however, never enacted legislation to create that supreme court, a failure that reflected "an arguably exaggerated concern for states' rights." [16]) In addition, the individual rights guaranteed in the Confederate Constitution were virtually identical in wording to the first eight amendments in the Bill of Rights, including freedoms of speech, press and assembly, the right to a jury trial, and a prohibition against cruel and unusual punishments.

Such similarities are not surprising, given that almost two dozen of the signers had served in the U.S. Congress, including former Speaker of the House Howell Cobb, D-Ga., who was president of the provisional Confederate Congress. All had lived under the United States' federal system of government, and those who had held federal office before the war had taken an oath to support the U.S. Constitution. In his first inaugural address, Confederate president and former U.S. senator Jefferson Davis said, "We have changed the constituent parts but not the system of our government. The constitution formed by our fathers is that of these Confederate States, in their exposition of it; and, in the judicial construction it has received, we have a light that reveals its true meaning." [17] In other words, Davis was saying that the Confederate Constitution was a return to the founders' original intent.

Even when it came to slavery, there were key similarities: neither constitution outlawed slavery, and both counted a slave as two-thirds of a person in apportioning congressional districts. Article I, section 9, of the Confederate Constitution prohibited "the importation of negroes of the African race" from foreign countries, partly out of concern that European nations would refuse to recognize the new government. Although the U.S. Constitution had not banned slavery outright, it had allowed the importation of slaves only until 1808, forty-three years earlier. The Confederate Constitution, however, cemented the legality of slavery as a cornerstone of the South's government. For example, Article I, section 9, also empowered Congress to ban the introduction of slaves from states that did not secede; the same section prohibited laws that would deny or impair the status of slaves as property. Article IV, section 2, guaranteed citizens the right to travel in any state of the Confederacy with their slaves, and its fugitive slave provision required citizens to turn in any escaped slave. Further, Article IV, section 3, required Congress to recognize and protect slavery as a legal institution in any state or territory wanting to join the Confederacy in the future. Yet at the same time, no provision explicitly denied free blacks political rights, including the right to vote.

▬▬ Document 2.2 ▬▬
Permanent Constitution of the Confederate States of America, March 11, 1861

We, the people of the Confederate States, each State acting in its sovereign and independent character, in order to form a permanent federal government, establish justice, insure domestic tranquillity, and secure the blessings of liberty to ourselves and our posterity—invoking the favor and guidance of Almighty God—do ordain and establish this Constitution for the Confederate States of America.

ARTICLE I

Section 1

All legislative powers herein delegated shall be vested in a Congress of the Confederate States, which shall consist of a Senate and House of Representatives.

Section 2

1. The House of Representatives shall be composed of members chosen every second year by the people of the several States; and the electors in each State shall be citizens of the Confederate States, and have the qualifications requisite for electors of the most numerous branch of the State Legislature; but no person of foreign birth, not a citizen of the Confederate States, shall be allowed to vote for any officer, civil or political, State or Federal . . .
3. Representatives and direct taxes shall be apportioned among the several States, which may be included within this Confederacy, according to their respective numbers, which shall be determined by adding to the whole number of free persons, including those bound to service for a term of years, and excluding Indians not taxed, three-fifths of all slaves. The actual enumeration shall be made within three years after the first meeting of the Congress of the Confederate States, and within every subsequent term of ten years, in such manner as they shall by law direct . . .

Section 3

1. The Senate of the Confederate States shall be composed of two Senators from each State, chosen for six years by the Legislature thereof, at the regular session next immediately preceding the commencement of the term of service; and each Senator shall have one vote . . .

Section 8

The Congress shall have power –

. . .

11. To declare war, grant letters of marque and reprisal, and make rules concerning captures on land and water: . . .
13. To provide and maintain a navy:
14. To make rules for the government and regulation of the land and naval forces:

15. To provide for calling forth the militia to execute the laws of the Confederate States, suppress insurrections, and repel invasions:

16. To provide for organizing, arming, and disciplining the militia, and for governing such part of them as may be employed in the service of the Confederate States; reserving to the States, respectively, the appointment of the officers, and the authority of training the militia according to the discipline prescribed by Congress: . . .

Section 9

1. The importation of negroes of the African race from any foreign country other than the slaveholding States or Territories of the United States of America, is hereby forbidden; and Congress is required to pass such laws as shall effectually prevent the same.

2. Congress shall also have power to prohibit the introduction of slaves from any State not a member of, or Territory not belonging to, this Confederacy.

3. The privilege of the writ of habeas corpus shall not be suspended, unless when in cases of rebellion or invasion the public safety may require it.

4. No bill of attainder, ex post facto law, or law denying or impairing the right of property in negro slaves shall be passed . . .

12. Congress shall make no law respecting an establishment of religion, or prohibiting the free exercise thereof; or abridging the freedom of speech, or of the press; or the right of the people peaceably to assemble and petition the Government for a redress of grievances.

13. A well-regulated militia being necessary to the security of a free State, the right of the people to keep and bear arms shall not be infringed . . .

ARTICLE II

Section 1

1. The executive power shall be vested in a President of the Confederate States of America. He and the Vice President shall hold their offices for the term of six years; but the President shall not be reeligible . . .

7. No person except a natural-born citizen of the Confederate States, or a citizen thereof at the time of the adoption of this Constitution, or a citizen thereof born in the United States prior to the 20th of December, 1860, shall be eligible to the office of President; neither shall any person be eligible to that office who shall not have attained the age of thirty-five years, and been fourteen years a resident within the limits of the Confederate States, as they may exist at the time of his election . . .

Section 2

1. The President shall be Commander-in-Chief of the Army and Navy of the Confederate States, and of the militia of the several States, when called into the actual service of the Confederate States; he may require the opinion, in writing, of the principal officer in each of the Executive Departments, upon any subject relating to the duties of their respective offices; and he shall have power to grant reprieves and pardons for offenses against the Confederate States, except in cases of impeachment . . .

ARTICLE III

Section 1

1. The judicial power of the Confederate States shall be vested in one Supreme Court, and in such inferior courts as the Congress may, from time to time, ordain and establish. The judges, both of the Supreme and inferior courts, shall hold their offices during good behavior, and shall, at stated times, receive for their services a compensation which shall not be diminished during their continuance in office . . .

ARTICLE IV

. . .

Section 2

1. The citizens of each State shall be entitled to all the privileges and immunities of citizens in the several States; and shall have the right of transit and sojourn in any State of this Confederacy, with their slaves and other property; and the right of property in said slaves shall not be thereby impaired.
2. A person charged in any State with treason, felony, or other crime against the laws of such State, who shall flee from justice, and be found in another State, shall, on demand of the executive authority of the State from which he fled, be delivered up, to be removed to the State having jurisdiction of the crime.
3. No slave or other person held to service or labor in any State or Territory of the Confederate States, under the laws thereof, escaping or lawfully carried into another, shall, in consequence of any law or regulation therein, be discharged from such service or labor; but shall be delivered up on claim of the party to whom such slave belongs; or to whom such service or labor may be due.

Section 3

1. Other States may be admitted into this Confederacy by a vote of two-thirds of the whole House of Representatives and two-thirds of the Senate, the Senate voting by States; but no new State shall be formed or erected within the jurisdiction of any other State, nor any State be formed by the junction of two or more States, or parts of States, without the consent of the Legislatures of the States concerned, as well as of the Congress.
2. A person charged in any State with treason, felony, or other crime against the laws of such State, who shall flee from justice, and be found in another State, shall, on demand of the executive authority of the State from which he fled, be delivered up, to be removed to the State having jurisdiction of the crime.
3. The Confederate States may acquire new territory; and Congress shall have power to legislate and provide governments for the inhabitants of all territory belonging to the Confederate States, lying without the limits of the several States; and may permit them, at such times, and in such manner as it may by law provide, to form States to be admitted into the Confederacy. In all such territory the institution of negro slavery, as it now exists in the Confederate States, shall be recognized and protected by Congress and by the Territorial government; and the inhabitants of the several Confederate States and Territories shall have the right to take to such Territory any slaves lawfully held by them in any of the States or Territories of the Confederate States . . .

ARTICLE VI

. . .

3. This Constitution, and the laws of the Confederate States made in pursuance thereof, and all treaties made, or which shall be made, under the authority of the Confederate States, shall be the supreme law of the land; and the judges in every State shall be bound thereby, anything in the constitution or laws of any State to the contrary notwithstanding . . .

Source: "Constitution of the Confederate States of America," March 11, 1861, from the Hargrett Rare Book and Manuscript Library, University of Georgia Libraries, www.libs.uga.edu/hargrett/selections/confed/trans.html.

Document 2.3 in Context
"I Never, in My Life, Felt More Certain That I Was Doing Right": Lincoln Signs the Emancipation Proclamation

On April 16, 1862, Abraham Lincoln signed legislation ending slavery in the District of Columbia, responding to political pressure to stop what abolitionists labeled "the national shame" of slavery in the capital. Then, on September 22, 1862, five days after Federal troops ended a string of military setbacks by repulsing a Confederate invasion of the North at the Battle of Antietam in Maryland, the president took political advantage of the good news and presented the Preliminary Emancipation Proclamation. This signaled his intention to declare free all slaves in those states still in rebellion on January 1, 1863.

When the official proclamation was released on January 1, 1863, it reflected the mix of pragmatic political and military considerations—such as the continuation of slavery in several states that had not seceded—and of moral considerations of ideology and humanitarianism that had characterized earlier congressional proposals advocated by Republicans. Significant additions and subtractions from the preliminary version were evident. Perhaps most importantly, Lincoln added a provision allowing blacks to enlist in the Union army and navy. By the end of the war, close to 200,000, both those born free and former slaves, had served as soldiers and sailors. The final version also omitted two of Lincoln's preliminary and most controversial policy provisions, one to compensate loyalist slave owners for the loss of their slaves and the other to "colonize persons of African descent, with their consent, upon this continent, or elsewhere."

As he prepared to sign the proclamation on New Year's Day 1863, the president said, "I never, in my life, felt more certain that I was doing right than I do in signing this paper." [18] The proclamation was the subject of joyful sermons in black churches, but abolitionist Frederick Douglass acknowledged its limitations when he described it as "the first step on the part of the nation in its departure from the thralldom of the ages." [19] It triggered celebrations among abolitionists and blacks in the war-weary North, and further anti-Lincoln vitriol among many whites in the South.

Despite its symbolic value, the proclamation actually freed no slaves because it applied only to areas in rebellion and not under Union control—places where the federal government could not enforce it. That meant, for example, that slavery could continue in border states such as Maryland that had not seceded and in Union-occupied territory in the South, such as New Orleans. Slavery would not be formally abolished until the Thirteenth Amendment (**Document 2.8**) was ratified in December 1865.

Even in the North, the Emancipation Proclamation was not uniformly welcomed. On January 7, 1863, the Democratic-controlled Illinois legislature adopted a resolution characterizing Lincoln's proclamation as:

> unwarrantable in military as in civil law; a gigantic usurpation, at once converting the war, professedly commenced by the administration for the vindication of the authority of the constitution, into the crusade for the sudden, unconditional and violent liberation of 3,000,000 negro slaves; a result which would not only be a total subversion of the Federal Union but a revolution in the social organization of the Southern States, the immediate and remote, the present and far-reaching consequences of which to both races cannot be contemplated without the most dismal foreboding of horror and dismay.[20]

Nonetheless, with the stroke of his pen Lincoln had transformed the Northern war effort from a fight solely to preserve the Union into a fight also to end slavery. The complexion of the war had changed forever.

Document 2.3a
Preliminary Emancipation Proclamation, September 22, 1862

By the President of the United States of America.
A Proclamation.

I, Abraham Lincoln, President of the United States of America, and Commander-in-Chief of the Army and Navy thereof, do hereby proclaim and declare that hereafter, as heretofore, the war will be prosecuted for the object of practically restoring the constitutional relation between the United States . . .

That it is my purpose, upon the next meeting of Congress to again recommend the adoption of a practical measure tendering pecuniary aid to the free acceptance or rejection of all slave States, so called, the people whereof may not then be in rebellion against the United States and which States may then have voluntarily adopted, or thereafter may voluntarily adopt, immediate or gradual abolishment of slavery within their respective limits; and that the effort to colonize persons of African descent, with their consent, upon this continent, or elsewhere, with the previously obtained consent of the Governments existing there, will be continued.

That on the first day of January in the year of our Lord, one thousand eight hundred and sixty-three, all persons held as slaves within any State, or designated part of a State, the people whereof shall then be in rebellion against the United States shall be then, thenceforward, and forever free . . .

That the executive will, on the first day of January aforesaid, by proclamation, designate the States, and part of States, if any, in which the people thereof respectively, shall then be in rebellion against the United States . . .

That attention is hereby called to an Act of Congress entitled "An Act to make an additional Article of War" approved March 13, 1862, and which act is in the words and figure following:

"Be it enacted by the Senate and House of Representatives of the United States of America in Congress assembled, That hereafter the following shall be promulgated as an additional article of war for the government of the army of the United States, and shall be obeyed and observed as such:

"Article-All officers or persons in the military or naval service of the United States are prohibited from employing any of the forces under their respective commands for the purpose of returning fugitives from service or labor, who may have escaped from any persons to whom such service or labor is claimed to be due, and any officer who shall be found guilty by a court martial of violating this article shall be dismissed from the service" . . .

Also to the ninth and tenth sections of an act entitled "An Act to suppress Insurrection, to punish Treason and Rebellion, to seize and confiscate property of rebels, and for other purposes," approved July 17, 1862, and which sections are in the words and figures following:

"SEC.9. And be it further enacted, That all slaves of persons who shall hereafter be engaged in rebellion against the government of the United States, or who shall in any way give aid or comfort thereto, escaping from such persons and taking refuge within the lines of the army; and all slaves captured from such persons or deserted by them and coming under the control of the government of the United States; and all slaves of such persons found on (or) being within any place occupied by rebel forces and afterwards occupied by the forces of the United States, shall be deemed captives of war, and shall be forever free of their servitude and not again held as slaves.

"SEC.10. And be it further enacted, That no slave escaping into any State, Territory, or the District of Columbia, from any other State, shall be delivered up, or in any way impeded or hindered of his liberty, except for crime, or some offence against the laws, unless the person claiming said fugitive shall first make oath that the person to whom the labor or service of such fugitive is alleged to be due is his lawful owner, and has not borne arms against the United States in the present rebellion, nor in any way given aid and comfort thereto; and no person engaged in the military or naval service of the United States shall, under any pretence whatever, assume to decide on the validity of the claim of any person to the service or labor of any other person, or surrender up any such person to the claimant, on pain of being dismissed from the service."

And I do hereby enjoin upon and order all persons engaged in the military and naval service of the United States to observe, obey, and enforce, within their respective spheres of service, the act, and sections above recited.

And the executive will in due time recommend that all citizens of the United States who shall have remained loyal thereto throughout the rebellion, shall (upon the restoration of the constitutional relation between the United States, and their respective States, and people, if that relation shall have been suspended or disturbed) be compensated for all losses by acts of the United States, including the loss of slaves . . .

Source: Abraham Lincoln, "Preliminary Emancipation Proclamation," September 22, 1862, from the U.S. National Archives and Records Administration, www.archives.gov/exhibits/american_ originals_ iv/sections/preliminary_emancipation_proclamation.html.

▬▬ Document 2.3b ▬▬
Emancipation Proclamation, January 1, 1863

By the President of the United States of America:
A Proclamation.

Whereas, on the twenty-second day of September, in the year of our Lord one thousand eight hundred and sixty-two, a proclamation was issued by the President of the United States, containing, among other things, the following, to wit:

"That on the first day of January, in the year of our Lord one thousand eight hundred and sixty-three, all persons held as slaves within any State or designated part of a State, the people whereof shall then be in rebellion against the United States, shall be then, thenceforward, and forever free; and the Executive Government of the United States, including the military and naval authority thereof, will recognize and maintain the freedom of such persons, and will do no act or acts to repress such persons, or any of them, in any efforts they may make for their actual freedom.

"That the Executive will, on the first day of January aforesaid, by proclamation, designate the States and parts of States, if any, in which the people thereof, respectively, shall then be in rebellion against the United States; and the fact that any State, or the people thereof, shall on that day be, in good faith, represented in the Congress of the United States by members chosen thereto at elections wherein a majority of the qualified voters of such State shall have participated, shall, in the absence of strong countervailing testimony, be deemed conclusive evidence that such State, and the people thereof, are not then in rebellion against the United States."

Now, therefore I, Abraham Lincoln, President of the United States, by virtue of the power in me vested as Commander-in-Chief, of the Army and Navy of the United States in time of actual armed rebellion against the authority and government of the United States, and as a fit and necessary war measure for suppressing said rebellion, do, on this first day of January, in the year of our Lord one thousand eight hundred and sixty-three, and in accordance with my purpose so to do publicly proclaimed for the full period of one hundred days, from the day first above mentioned, order and designate as the States and parts of States wherein the people thereof respectively, are this day in rebellion against the United States, the following, to wit:

Arkansas, Texas, Louisiana, (except the Parishes of St. Bernard, Plaquemines, Jefferson, St. John, St. Charles, St. James Ascension, Assumption, Terrebonne, Lafourche, St. Mary, St. Martin, and Orleans, including the City of New Orleans) Mississippi, Alabama, Florida, Georgia, South Carolina, North Carolina, and Virginia, (except the forty-eight counties designated as West Virginia, and also the counties of Berkley, Accomac, Northampton, Elizabeth City, York, Princess Ann, and Norfolk, including the cities of Norfolk and Portsmouth[)], and which excepted parts, are for the present, left precisely as if this proclamation were not issued.

And by virtue of the power, and for the purpose aforesaid, I do order and declare that all persons held as slaves within said designated States, and parts of States, are, and henceforward shall be free; and that the Executive government of the United States, including the military and naval authorities thereof, will recognize and maintain the freedom of said persons.

And I hereby enjoin upon the people so declared to be free to abstain from all violence, unless in necessary self-defence; and I recommend to them that, in all cases when allowed, they labor faithfully for reasonable wages.

And I further declare and make known, that such persons of suitable condition, will be received into the armed service of the United States to garrison forts, positions, stations, and other places, and to man vessels of all sorts in said service.

And upon this act, sincerely believed to be an act of justice, warranted by the Constitution, upon military necessity, I invoke the considerate judgment of mankind, and the gracious favor of Almighty God . . .

Source: Abraham Lincoln, "Emancipation Proclamation," January 1, 1863, from the U.S. National Archives and Records Administration, www.ourdocuments.gov.

Document 2.4 in Context
"A Degree of Courage, Well Directed by Intelligence and Patriotism": Robert Smalls, War Hero and Member of Congress

It was not unusual for the Confederacy to impress free blacks into military service, usually to perform menial work. After the Emancipation Proclamation (**Document 2.3**), it was common for former slaves to enlist in the Union military. It was unusual, however, for a former slave to serve on both sides— fighting involuntarily for the South and then voluntarily for the North. The story of Robert Smalls, who was born into slavery in South Carolina, is such a tale, one that is extraordinary not merely because of his bravery and adventures but because he later served in the U.S. House of Representatives.

Some details of the story vary: Smalls was either impressed into the Confederate navy, as most historical accounts state, or was hired as a civilian sailor, as the Robert Smalls Foundation maintains.[21] In May 1862, while serving as a wheelman who piloted the Confederate steam transport boat *Planter,* Smalls led the takeover of the ship, with its "valuable cargo of guns and ammunition," and ensured its safe navigation into Union custody under the cover of darkness.[22] A January 12, 1898, House Committee on War Claims report detailed the incident, Smalls's continuing service and his promotion to captain in the Union navy. (The foundation indicates that he was always paid as a civilian.) The committee supported a bill to belatedly compensate Smalls for the actual value of the *Planter* and its cargo. In doing so, the committee adopted the findings of an earlier House inquiry that had concluded that Smalls had demonstrated "a degree of courage, well directed by intelligence and patriotism, of which the nation may well be proud, but which for twenty years has been wholly unrecognized by it." [23] Congress never awarded him that compensation.

Smalls was among almost 18,000 black sailors who, unlike their army counterparts, served in a largely racially integrated environment. The Union navy had never prohibited blacks; many had served in the Continental and state navies during the Revolution and, later, in the War of 1812. In the 1840s, however, the navy had capped the proportion of blacks allowed in the service at 5 percent. During the Civil War, Union navy recruitment guidelines channeled black enlistees into laborer positions such as stewards and cooks. During the war, African Americans accounted for approximately 20 percent of the navy's enlisted personnel, a majority of them fugitive slaves known as "contrabands." Many other enlistees had been born free in coastal states along the Atlantic and had maritime backgrounds. One reason the navy welcomed large numbers of black sailors was that the army, with its enlistment bonus, was more attractive than the navy to whites. But despite overall integration of black and white enlistees, former slaves often found themselves treated as inferior to, and paid less than, other sailors, regardless of color, and subjected to segregation aboard some vessels.

After the war, Smalls jumped into Republican politics and was elected to the South Carolina legislature before first winning his House seat in 1874. His tenure was interrupted when a white supremacist Democrat claimed victory in the 1880 election, but Smalls successfully contested the election and regained his seat. In Congress, he spoke articulately and passionately about black voting rights, segregation and civil rights.

Here are letters from DuPont to Navy Secretary Gideon Welles in 1862, Cdr. E. G. Parrott to Adm. Samuel F. DuPont in 1862, and from Gen. Alex J. Perry to Smalls in 1883. These official letters detail Smalls's exploits and verify that the North's highest ranking naval official was aware of his accomplishments on behalf of the Union.

▬▬ Document 2.4 ▬▬
Correspondence about the Union Naval Service of Robert Smalls, May 1862 and January 1883

Adm. Samuel F. DuPont to Navy Secretary Gideon Welles

Flagship Wabash,
Port Royal Harbor, S.C., May 14, 1862.

Sir: I inclose a copy of a report from Commander E. G. Parrott, brought here last night by the late rebel steam tug Planter, in charge of an officer and crew from the engineer department at Charleston, under Brigadier-General Ripley, whose barge, short time since, was brought out to the blockading fleet by several contrabands.

The bringing out of this steamer, under all the circumstances, would have done credit to anyone. At 4 o'clock in the morning in the absence of the captain, who was on shore, she left her wharf close to the Government office and headquarters, with Palmetto and Confederate flags flying passed the successive forts, saluting as usual by blowing her steam whistle. After getting beyond the range of the last gun she quickly hauled down the rebel flags and hoisted a white one.

The Onward was the inside ship of the blockading fleet in the channel, and was preparing to fire when her commander made out the white flag. The armament of the steamer is a 32-pounder, or pivot, and a fine 24-pounder howitzer. She has, besides, on her deck four other guns, one 7-inch rifled, which were to have been taken the morning of the escape to the new fort on the middle ground. One of the four belonged to Fort Sumter, and had been struck in the rebel attack on the fort on the muzzle. Robert, the intelligent slave and pilot of the boat, who performed this bold feat so skillfully, informed me of this fact, presuming it would be a matter of interest to us to have possession of this gun. This man, Robert Smalls, is superior to any who have come to our lines, intelligent as many of them have been. His information has been most interesting and portions of the utmost importance.

The steamer is quite an acquisition to the squadron by her good machinery and very light draft. The officer in charge brought her through St. Helena Sound and by the inland passage down Beaufort River, arriving here at 10 o'clock last night.

On board the steamer when she left Charleston were 8 men, 5 women, and 3 children.

I shall continue to employ Robert as a pilot on board the Planter for the inland waters, with which he appears to be very familiar. I do not know whether, in the views of the government, the vessel will be considered a prize; but, if so, I respectfully submit to the Department the claims of this man Robert and his associates.

Very respectfully, your obedient servant,

S. F. DU PONT,

Flag Officer, Commanding, etc.

Cdr. E. G. Parrott to Adm. Samuel F. DuPont

United States Steamship Augusta,
Off Charleston, May 13, 1862.

Sir: I have the honor to inform you that the rebel armed steamer Planter was brought out to us this morning from Charleston by eight contrabands, and delivered up to the squadron. Five colored women and three children are also on board. She carried one 32-pounder and one 24-pounder howitzer, and has also on board four large guns, which she was engaged in transporting.

I send her to Port Royal at once, in order to take advantage of the present good weather. I send Charleston papers of the 12th, and the very intelligent contraband who was in charge will give you the information he has brought off.

I have the honor to request that you will send back, as soon as convenient, the officer and crew sent on board.

I am, respectfully, etc., your obedient servant,

E. G. PARROTT,

Gen. Alex J. Perry to Rep. Robert Smalls

War Dept., Quartermaster-General's Office,
Washington, D.C., January 3, 1883.

Sir: Your communication of the 26th, ultimo, in relation to your services on the steamer Planter during the rebellion, and requesting copies of any letters from General Gillmore and other officers on the subject, has been received.

The records of this office show that the name of Robert Smalls is reported by Lieut. Col. J. J. Elwell, Hilton Head, S.C., as a pilot, at $50 per month, from March 1, 1863, to September 30, 1863; and from October 1, 1863, to November 20, 1863, at $75 per month.

He was then transferred to Capt. J. L. Kelly, assistant quartermaster, November 20, 1863, by whom he was reported as pilot from November 21 to November 30, 1863. He is reported by that officer in same capacity from December 1, 1863, until February 29, 1864, at $150 per month.

The name of Robert Smalls is then reported by Captain Kelly as captain of the steamer Planter, at $150 per month, from March 1, 1864, until May 15, 1864, when transferred to the quartermaster in Philadelphia.

He is reported by Caps. C. D. Schmidt, G. R. Orme, W. W. Van Ness, and John R. Jennings, assistant quartermasters, at Philadelphia, as captain of the Planter, at $150 per month from June 20, 1864, to December 16, 1864, when transferred to Capt. J. L. Kelly, assistant quartermaster, Hilton Head, S.C., by whom he is reported to January 31, 1865.

From February 1, 1865, he is reported as a "contractor," victualing and manning the steamer Planter.

I respectfully inclose herewith a copy of a letter, dated September 10, 1862, from Capt. J. J. Ellwell, chief quartermaster, Department of the South, in relation to the capture of the steamer Planter, which is the only one found on file in this office on the subject.

Very respectfully, your obedient servant,

ALEX. J. PERRY,

Deputy Quartermaster General, U. S. A.,

Acting Quartermaster-General.

Source: House Committee on War Claims, *Report to Accompany H.R. 1333,* 55th Cong., 2d sess., January 12, 1898.

Document 2.5 in Context
"The Policy of the President toward the Colored People of This Country Is . . . Mistaken:" African Americans Oppose Colonization Proposals

Abraham Lincoln—along with some other Republican officials—endorsed schemes to promote voluntary black colonization outside the United States—in Africa, the Caribbean or South America—which had been called for by earlier leaders such as Thomas Jefferson and Henry Clay. The April 1862 statute that emancipated slaves in the District of Columbia included $100,000 for the purpose of encouraging colonization, with $100 to be paid to each voluntary emigrant. The same law authorized $300 in compensation to slaveholders in the capital for each of their slaves who was freed. Lincoln defended the concept at a meeting with African Americans in August 1862, not long before drafting the Emancipation Proclamation, which originally included a colonization provision (**Document 2.3a**).

Such proposals resonated poorly among African Americans, however. For example, a group in Philadelphia praised Lincoln for his "generous efforts in our behalf" but appealed to him on political, humane, patriotic and financial grounds to stop pushing for emigration:

> If statistics prove anything, then we constitute, including our property qualifications, almost the entire wealth of the Cotton States, and make up a large proportion of that of the others. Many of us, in Pennsylvania, have our own houses and other property, amounting, in the aggregate, to millions of dollars. Shall we sacrifice this, leave our homes, forsake our birth-place, and flee to a strange land, to appease the anger and prejudice of the traitors now in arms against the Government? Will the country be benefited by sending us out of it, and inviting strangers to fill our places? Will they make better citizens, prove as loyal, love the country better, and be as obedient to its laws as we have been? [24]

Despite such arguments, Lincoln reiterated his support for colonization in his December 1, 1862, annual report to Congress, and the matter was discussed in Congress and by his cabinet.

As one alternative, a large group of African Americans meeting in Newtown, New York, in September 1862 suggested instead that the president promote black colonization of the rebellious states. The sentence in the following document about a "different race of people" refers to a comment Lincoln had made.

As late as April 1865, as the Civil War ended, Lincoln was still considering colonization:

> I can hardly believe that the South and North can live in peace unless we get rid of the Negroes. Certainly they cannot, if we don't get rid of the Negroes whom we have armed and disciplined and who have fought with us, to the amount, I believe, of some 150,000 men. I believe that it would be better to export them all to some fertile country with a good climate, which they could have to themselves.[25]

▬ Document 2.5 ▬
Petition of the Colored Citizens of Queens County, New York, September 1862

. . . We the colored citizens of Queens County, N.Y., having met in mass meeting, according to public notice, to consider the speech of Abraham Lincoln, President of the United States, addressed to a committee of Free Colored Men, called at his request at the White House in Washington, on Thursday, August 14, 1862, and to express our views and opinions of the same; and whereas, the President desires to know in particular our views on the subject of being colonized in Central America or some other foreign country, we will take the present opportunity to express our opinions most respectfully and freely, since as loyal Union colored Americans and Christians, we feel bound to do so.

First. We rejoice that we are colored Americans, but deny that we are a "different race of people," as God has made of one blood all nations that dwell on the face of the earth, and has hence no respect of men in regard to color, neither ought men to have respect to color, as they have not made themselves or their color.

Second. The President calls our attention particularly to this question—"Why should we leave this country?" This, he says, is perhaps the first question for proper consideration. We will answer this question by showing why we should remain in it. This is our country by birth, consequently we are acclimated, and in other respects better adapted to it, than any other country. This is our native country; we have as strong attachment naturally to our native hills, valleys, plains, luxuriant forests, flowing streams, mighty rivers, and lofty mountains, as any other people. Nor can we fail to feel a strong attachment to the whites with whom our blood has been commingling from the earliest days of this country. Neither can we forget and disown our white kindred. This is the country of our choice, being our fathers' country.

Third. Again, we are interested in its welfare above every other country; we love this land, and have contributed our share to its prosperity and wealth. This we have done by cutting down forests, subduing the soil, cultivating fields, constructing roads, digging canals . . .

Fourth. Again, we believe, too, we have the right to have applied to ourselves those rights named in the Declaration of Independence . . . While bleeding and struggling for her life against slaveholding traitors, and at this very time, when our country is struggling for life, and one million freemen are believed to be scarcely sufficient to meet the foe, we are called upon by the President of the United States to leave this land . . . But at this crisis, we feel disposed to refuse the offers of the President since the call of our suffering country is too loud and imperative to be unheeded . . .

. . . Our answer is this: There is no country like our own. Why not declare slavery abolished, and favor our peaceful colonization in the rebel States, or some portion of them? . . . We would cheerfully return there, and give our most willing aid to deliver our loyal colored brethren and other Unionists from the tyranny of rebels to our Government . . .

In conclusion, we would say that, in our belief, the speech of the President has only served the cause of our enemies, who wish to insult and mob us, as we have, since its publication, been repeatedly insulted, and told that we must leave the country. Hence we conclude that the policy of the President toward the colored people of this country *is a mistaken policy.*

Source: "Reply to the President, by the Colored People of Newton, L.I.," *Liberator* 32, no. 37 (September 12, 1862): 248.

Document 2.6 in Context
"The Diabolical Outrages of the Mob Last Night":
The New York City Draft Riots

The political atmosphere in New York City in July 1863 was divisive; the city had elected Democratic leaders, but there were Republicans in the White House and in control of Congress. The federal government's new draft lottery, through which citizens were randomly selected for mandatory service in the Union military, only exacerbated existing social and political tensions, as did the policy that enabled men of means to pay $300 for a waiver exempting them from military service if they were selected in the draft.

Five days and nights of rioting broke out on July 13, 1863, two days after New York City's first draft lottery. Disquiet over the draft served as the catalyst, but these riots were years in the making. Although they erupted six and one-half months after the Emancipation Proclamation (**Document 2.3b**) and four and one-half months after passage of the Conscription Act, they were rooted in long-running racial, economic and political conflicts. Police were assaulted, property was burned and telegraph lines were cut. African Americans were attacked and murdered in the streets; casualty estimates diverge widely, with some estimates putting the toll above 1,000, mostly blacks.

Many of the rioters were white longshoremen opposed to the hiring of blacks to work on the docks. Indeed, the city's Democratic politicians and Democratic newspapers had consistently stoked the fears of working men, warning that emancipated slaves coming North would displace white workers, especially unskilled Irish and German immigrants. The *New York Herald* had insisted during the 1860 campaign season, "Hundreds of thousands will emigrate to their friends—the republicans—North, and be placed by them side by side in competition with white men. Are you ready to divide your patrimony with the negro?" [26] In reality, far more former slaves, or "contrabands," had emigrated to such midwestern states as Illinois, Ohio and Indiana than to New York in 1862–1863.

During the Civil War, there were smaller draft riots in Boston, Massachusetts, Newark, New Jersey, and Troy, New York. But even without opposition to the draft as a motivator, violence against African Americans erupted elsewhere in the North as white workers—afraid of labor competition—demonstrated their hostility. In July 1862 the *Cincinnati Enquirer* reported on an influx of low-wage black laborers from the South to Pennsylvania and asked, "How do our white laborers relish the prospect that the emancipation of the blacks spreads before them?" [27] A few days later, Irish workers assaulted African Americans in Cincinnati and torched their homes. In August 1862 white employees at a tobacco factory in Brooklyn, New York, attacked their black coworkers, and antiblack riots occurred in Buffalo.

This white eyewitness's account of the draft riots provides a vivid look at the violence, racism, antigovernment sentiments and destruction that swept New York City. Such antiblack violence showed that despite laws banning slavery in the North, racist attitudes among whites and societal upheaval concerning roles for newly freed slaves remained widespread.

══ Document 2.6 ══
Letters about the New York City Draft Riots from Eyewitness Edward Markoe Wright to His Mother, July 1863

New York July 14/63

My dear mother

Fearing that you may be frightened by learning of the diabolical outrages of the mob last night, I write a few lines to say that I am safe & sound, and, although I will be obliged to go out to Felsenhof this afternoon, I hope to see you tomorrow . . .

As I was an eyewitness to many of the fearful scenes of yesterday I will endeavor to give you an account of my adventures from the middle of the day. All day the lower portion of the city resembled a holiday—so few people were to be seen about the streets compared to the usual crowds—and about two o'clock a crowd of men passed the square in front of our office chasing a negro. They had assaulted one at the foot of Wall Street, nearly killing him, and an old gentleman that attempted to help the negro was also set upon and badly beaten & left for dead on the dock. The negro that was being chased & passed our office was overtaken by the crowd, which really only consisted of about a dozen men & boys—at Broad Street and there killed—being badly cut up by the heavy hooks that carmen use. This crowd could easily have been dispersed by a half dozen resolute policemen—but they were all afraid to move—and the only one in sight as the crowd passed walked off very deliberately in another direction . . .

. . . Crowds of men assembled in 3rd Avenue, filling up the streets for blocks—and afterwards a small force of soldiers—of the invalid corps—was ordered to the scene of the disturbance, about fifty all together. These soldiers—being resisted by the mob fired upon them—but very foolishly fired over their heads—and, before a second volley could be fired—there was not a gun left in the hands of a single soldier—being completely disarmed by the people. The mob then made a descent upon Allerton's Bulls Head Hotel and after seizing upon all the brandy, whiskey & cigars they could find—set fire to the building & burnt it to the ground . . . The next place attacked was the armory on 21st St. & 2nd Avenue where government stores were kept. The mob demanded that the establishment should be closed but those from the inside replied by firing upon the people—which so incensed them that they forced entrance into the building by breaking down the doors with heavy beams and setting fire to the building by throwing camphene upon the floors and setting it on fire . . .

Returning to the house for my tea, we started out again at eight o'clock. It seemed as if the whole city was on fire—the sky in every direction was lurid with the light from the burning houses—the deep tones of the fire bells & the distant shouting of the people. Attracted by the light we made our way out Sixth Avenue to 40th St.—then across to Fifth Avenue—to where we heard the shouting of the mob—and to my horror & surprise discovered that the diabolical fiends had set the colored orphan asylum on fire. There was the building flaming in every part—every room appearing to have separate flame of its own—and the fire rising above the roof against the dark sky. In front [of] the court yard men & boys hurrying to & fro with bundles, bushes or anything they could lay hands upon . . . We took refuge on the steps of a large house and the mob surged past—and reaching the end of the block surged back again. The number of people composing the mob was very small—and many of them quite young—shouting Jeff Davis—No draft—Horace Greeley to be hung—but we were obliged to remain quiet until many minutes had elapsed before we thought it advisable to venture to go home . . . Yet no one dared to lift a hand. It would have been perfect madness to have attempted to reply—for there were no policemen to be seen . . .

. . . In Grand St. during the evening they killed another Negro—and one of the clerks on his way home saw the mob chasing them in every direction. This morning I passed Carmine St. where they hung a Negro—just in front of a churchyard—and under this tree they afterwards kindled a bonfire burning the body above—and when I saw the place today the body had been taken down but the ground was blackened in every direction by the fire . . .

New York July 15/63

Dear Mother

While the scenes that are passing remain vividly impressed on my mind I hasten to send you an account of yesterday & today.

Up to the present time the riot has continued—but it would seem now to have abated in violence. Yesterday after I wrote to you the mob continued to attack negro boarding houses—against which there seems to be the utmost animosity—and enrolling offices in different parts of the city . . .

All railroad communication on the New Haven, Harlem & Hudson River RRs with the neighboring towns is entirely cut off—the rioters having taken up the tracks in a number of places to keep the military from arriving, which had been sent for . . .

. . . As I afterwards learned, the rioters in the course of the evening sacked two large clothing stores of Brooks Bros.—completely robbing & taking away the entire stock jewelry stores, boot stores & numbers of private houses & negro boarding houses were sacked & plundered & many of them set on fire. The mob now seemed perfectly wild with their success & wandered through the streets in different directions committing violence of every kind & destroying thousands of dollars worth of property. They have had several collisions with the soldiery—who have fired upon them & numbers have been killed . . . More fires have commenced in other parts of the city and last night the alarms were more frequent than the day before . . .

Source: Ann Wright Brown, ed., *July 1863 Draft Riots,* 2002, www.bklyn-genealogy-info.com/Military/1863.DraftLetters.html.

Document 2.7 in Context
"All Persons of Color . . . Mustered into the Military Service of the United States Shall Receive the Same . . . as Other Soldiers": Black Soldiers Seek Equal Treatment

Former slaves and blacks born free were permitted to serve in the Union army after Congress in July 1862 authorized the president to accept them to build entrenchments, perform camp service and other labor, or undertake naval or military service if they were competent.

Later enlistment-related legislation faced vocal criticism, however. In a February 1863 debate on a bill "to raise additional soldiers for the service of the Government," for example, Rep. William Allen, D-Ohio, said, "When this bill becomes a law, as I presume it will, it will complete a system heretofore inaugurated, the effect of which will be to seal the perpetual separation of the States of this Union." Allen predicted that black troops would never be assigned to combat, because the Republican Party would "not be likely to place the negro in any such perilous position." [28]

Many African Americans were eager to fight. In a speech at Avery College, a black institution in Pennsylvania, Francis Williams urged the faculty and his fellow students to do their duty and "show their courage." [29] African Americans' zeal to take part in the fight was reflected in a variety of ways, including music. The cover for the sheet music of an 1864 song, "How Do You Like It, Jefferson D?" shows the devil holding Confederate president Jefferson Davis by the pants over a fire while a black Union soldier, armed with a rifle, looks on and thumbs his nose.

Many white officers were reluctant to command African Americans. In March 1863 Maj. Gen. Henry Halleck wrote to Maj. Gen. Ulysses S. Grant about the government's commitment to use black troops, especially "as a military force for the defence of forts, depots, etc. . . . . If they can be used to hold points on the Mississippi during the sickly season, it will afford much relief to our armies." [30] Some black units, such as the Fifty-fourth Infantry, the Massachusetts regiment memorialized in the 1989 film *Glory,* played crucial battlefield roles, but black soldiers more often confronted segregation, abusive white officers and menial assignments.

The mere presence of African American soldiers in battle riled the Confederate enemy, and captured black troops were often dealt with even more harshly than white prisoners of war. The killing of numerous, ostensibly already surrendered, African American Union soldiers at the April 1864 Battle of Fort Pillow in Tennessee was one of the most notorious examples.

African Americans suffered significant, disproportionately high casualties. One army figure for "U.S. Colored Troops" calculated that 324 of 7,122 black officers and 36,523 of 178,975 black enlisted men died during the war, most from disease rather than wounds. Mortality among blacks was about one in five—more than one-third higher than among white troops even though blacks could not enlist until eighteen months into the war.[31]

In January 1864 a black sergeant was court martialed and executed for mutiny because he protested discriminatory pay. But needing more manpower as the war grinded onward, Congress passed an army appropriations bill in June 1864 with stipulations that whites and "persons of color" in the military be paid the same bounty, or enlistment bonus, and receive the same pay, uniform, weapons and rations.[32] Sections of the bill, excerpted here, also authorized retroactive equalization of pay, clothing and bounties—dating back to their enlistment date—for African Americans who had been free as of April 19, 1861.

Despite pay equity, segregation in the army would continue even after the war. In an April 1878 speech an African American senator, Blanche K. Bruce, R-Miss., backed a bill that would have abolished all-black units, saying, "The day is not far distant when all men, without regard to complexion or previous condition, will be received into the Army as they are to-day admitted into the Navy." [33]

▬ Document 2.7 ▬
Army Appropriations Bill Mandating Equal Treatment of African American Soldiers in the Union Army, June 15, 1864

An Act making Appropriations for the Support of the Army for the Year ending the thirtieth June, eighteen hundred and sixty-five, and for other Purposes. . . .

SECTION 2. *And be it further enacted,* That all persons of color who have been or may be mustered into the military service of the United States shall receive the same uniform, clothing, arms, equipments, camp equipage, rations, medical and hospital attendance, pay and emoluments, other than bounty, as other soldiers of the regular or volunteer forces of the United States of like arm of the service, from and after the first day of January, eighteen hundred and sixty-four; and that every person of color who shall hereafter be mustered into the service shall receive such sums in bounty as the President shall order in the different states and parts of the United States, not exceeding one hundred dollars.

SEC. 3. *And be it further enacted,* That all persons enlisted and mustered into service as volunteers under the call, dated October seventeen, eighteen hundred and sixty-three, for three hundred thousand volunteers, who were at the time of enlistment actually enrolled and subject to draft in the state in which they volunteered, shall receive from the United States the same amount of bounty without regard to color.

SEC. 4. *And be it further enacted,* That all persons of color who were free on the nineteenth day of April, eighteen hundred and sixty-one, and who have been enlisted and mustered into the military service of the United States, shall, from the time of their enlistment, be entitled to receive the pay, bounty, and clothing allowed to such persons by the laws existing at the time of their enlistment. And the Attorney-General of the United States is hereby authorized to determine any question of law arising under this provision. And if the Attorney-General aforesaid shall determine that any of such enlisted persons are entitled to receive any pay, bounty, or clothing, in addition to what they have already received, the Secretary of War shall make all necessary regulations to enable the pay department to make payment in accordance with such determination.

SEC. 5. *And be it further enacted,* That all enlistments hereafter made in the regular army of the United States, during the continuance of the present rebellion, may be for the term of three years.

Source: Statutes at Large of the United States of America 13 (1866): 126–130, from the Library of Congress, http://memory.loc.gov/ammem/amlaw/lwsllink.html.

Document 2.8 in Context
"Neither Slavery nor Involuntary Servitude . . . Shall Exist within the United States": The Thirteenth Amendment Abolishes Slavery

Historians generally categorize the Thirteenth Amendment as the first of the three Reconstruction amendments because it was finally ratified and took effect after the South surrendered. An alternative way to regard it, however, is as a crucial bridge or transition between the Civil War and the Reconstruction era.

The concept of a constitutional ban on slavery predated the war, but support for the resolution in Congress was far from universal, with much of the criticism focusing on how such an amendment would expand national power. After winning approval in the House and Senate, Congress proposed the amendment to the states on January 31, 1865, months before the war ended. The Illinois legislature moved quickly, ratifying it on February 1, with Rhode Island, Michigan, Maryland, New York, Pennsylvania and West Virginia acting within the following two days.

After the South surrendered, the ratification debate in the legislatures of former Confederate states was sometimes heated. An account of the Alabama constitutional convention, during which the state prepared for readmission to the Union, described one delegate as arguing that Congress had no right to seize property—slaves—without compensation and accusing the federal government of relying on bayonets rather than the voluntary decision of state residents. Secretary of State William H. Seward declared the amendment ratified by the required number of states on December 18, 1865, after Georgia on December 6 became the twenty-seventh to approve it.

The Thirteenth Amendment represented a constitutionally binding commitment to carry out the principles of the 1863 Emancipation Proclamation (**Document 2.3**), and it went further than Abraham Lincoln had been able to go. Its short but sweeping language covered the entire United States, including its territories, and it gave Congress direct authority to legislatively enforce the prohibition against slavery. It also laid a foundation for a key amendment to the 1865 Freedman's Bureau Act and the 1866 Civil Rights Act, both of which would be enacted over vetoes by President Andrew Johnson.

While abolishing slavery, however, the Thirteenth Amendment did not establish a constitutional guarantee of individual rights and equal protection of the laws; these would have to await the Fourteenth Amendment (**Document 3.2**). Nor did the Thirteenth Amendment eliminate proslavery advocacy among the die-hards: David Quinn, a Chicago lawyer, even submitted a "petition and memorial" in June 1866—six months after ratification—asking Congress to reinstate "Negro slavery" on the grounds of white superiority.[34]

▬ Document 2.8 ▬
Thirteenth Amendment, Passed by Congress January 31, 1865, Ratified December 6, 1865

SECTION 1. Neither slavery nor involuntary servitude, except as a punishment for crime whereof the party shall have been duly convicted, shall exist within the United States, or any place subject to their jurisdiction.

SEC. 2. Congress shall have power to enforce this article by appropriate legislation.

Source: "Thirteenth Amendment to the U.S. Constitution: Abolition of Slavery," 1865, from the U.S. National Archives and Records Administration, www.ourdocuments.gov.

Document 2.9 in Context
"To Ask for and Accept . . . the Services of Such Number of Able-Bodied Negro Men": The Confederacy Authorizes Enlisting Black Soldiers

African Americans, both free-born and former slaves, made up a considerable proportion of the Union army and navy. Few blacks voluntarily served the Confederacy, although some were coerced into providing manual labor for the South, such as future member of Congress Joseph H. Rainey, R-S.C., who was forced to work on the fortification at Fort Sumter, South Carolina. The Confederates were wary of using black troops; one widespread fear was that armed blacks would lead a slave insurrection, and some critics argued that enlisting slaves would demoralize the South. Only when they faced virtually inevitable defeat did the Confederate Congress finally authorize the enlistment of slaves.

The idea of recruiting blacks had been raised earlier—and swiftly shot down—when doing so could have helped solve the Confederacy's increasingly dire manpower needs. In January 1864 Maj. Gen. Patrick Cleburne made such a proposal to the other generals of the Army of Tennessee. He cited "the exigency in which our country is now placed," including an enemy that "menacingly confronts us at every point with superior forces" and the potential "loss of all we now hold most sacred—slaves and all other personal property, lands, homesteads, liberty, justice, safety, pride, manhood." He recommended that

> We immediately commence training a large reserve of the most courageous of our slaves; and further that we guarantee, within a reasonable time, freedom to every slave in the South who shall remain true to the Confederacy in this war. As between the loss of independence and the loss of slavery, we assume that every patriot will freely give up the latter—give up the negro slave rather than be a slave himself.[35]

But Cleburne's fellow generals refused to forward the proposal to the War Department in Richmond.

In January 1865 the Confederate House of Representatives began closed-door discussions of the issue. The Virginia legislature endorsed such a move, as did Gen. Robert E. Lee. Finally, the Confederacy passed a law on March 13, 1965, allowing enlistment of slaves, but only with their own consent and that of their owners. Interestingly, it also required that they receive the same pay, food and clothing as their free white counterparts but did not mandate that black volunteers be emancipated after completing their military service.

To implement the new law, on March 23 the Confederate army's adjutant and inspector general, Gen. Samuel Cooper, announced a system for "the collection, enrollment and disposition" of the black recruits in each state, including their placement in squads and companies. It provided, for example, that "enlistment of colored persons . . . will be made upon printed forms, to be furnished for the purpose, similar to those established for the regular service." The superintendent in each state was directed to submit monthly reports with "the names of all the slaves recruited, with their age, description and the names of their masters." As for treatment of black recruits, the regulations ordered officers to provide "provident, considerate and humane attention to whatever concerns the health, comfort, instruction and discipline of those troops, and to the uniform observance of kindness, forbearance and indulgence to their treatment of them, and especially that they will protect them from injustice and oppression." [36]

The legislation came far too late to matter. Within weeks, on April 9, Lee surrendered to Union Gen. Ulysses S. Grant at Appomattox Court House, Virginia, marking the beginning of the end of the Confederacy.

<hr>

▦ Document 2.9 ▦
Confederate Authorization to Enlist Slaves, as Promulgated by the Confederate Adjutant and Inspector General's Office, March 23, 1865

ADJ. AND INSP. GENERAL'S OFFICE,
Richmond, Va., March 23, 1865.

GENERAL ORDERS NO. 14
I. The following act of Congress and regulations are published for the information and direction of all concerned:

AN ACT to increase the military force of the Confederate States.

The Congress of the Confederate States of America do enact, That, in order to provide additional forces to repel invasion, maintain the rightful possession of the Confederate States, secure their independence, and preserve their institutions, the President be, and he is hereby, authorized to ask for and accept from the owners of slaves, the services of such number of able-bodied negro men as he may deem expedient, for and during the war, to perform military service in whatever capacity he may direct.

SEC 2. That the General-in-Chief be authorized to organize the said slaves into companies, battalions, regiments, and brigades, under such rules and regulations as the Secretary of War may prescribe, and to be commanded by such officers as the President may appoint.

SEC 3. That while employed in the service the said troops shall receive the same rations, clothing, and compensation as are allowed to other troops in the same branch of the service.

SEC 4. That if, under the previous sections of this act, the President shall not be able to raise a sufficient number of troops to prosecute the war successfully and maintain the sovereignty of the States and the independence of the Confederate States, then he is hereby authorized to call on each State, whenever he thinks it expedient, for her quota of 300,000 troops, in addition to those subject to military service under existing laws, or so many thereof as the President may deem necessary to be raised from such classes of the population, irrespective of color, in each State, as the proper authorities thereof may determine: *Provided,* That not more than twenty-five per cent of the male slaves between the ages of eighteen and forty-five, in any State, shall be called for under the provisions of this act.

SEC 5. That nothing in this act shall be construed to authorize a change in the relation which the said slaves shall bear toward their owners, except by consent of the owners and of the States in which they may reside, and in pursuance of the laws thereof.

Approved March 13, 1865.

Source: U.S. War Department, *The War of the Rebellion: A Compendium of the Official Records of the Union and Confederate Armies* (Washington, D.C.: U.S. Government Printing Office, 1880–1901), ser. 4., vol. 3, 1161–1162, from the Freedmen and Southern Society Project, University of Maryland, College Park, www.history.umd.edu/Freedmen/csenlist.htm.

Document 2.10 in Context
"A Bridge from Slavery to Freedom": Congress Establishes the Freedmen's Bureau

Following two years of debate and about a month before the war ended, Congress established a relief agency for "refugees, freedmen and abandoned lands" [37] within the War Department. The agency, known as the Freedmen's Bureau, was created with a one-year lifespan. The March 1865 statute set out its organizational structure and empowered the secretary of war to provide clothing, fuel, temporary shelter and provisions to an estimated 4 million former slaves. Radical Republican proponents described it as a "bridge from slavery to freedom," [38] intending that freedom to be both economic and political. The act's most controversial provision allowed former slaves to receive up to forty acres each of "land within the insurrectionary states as shall have been abandoned" [39] or which the Union had seized, with low rent and the right to eventually buy it.

President Andrew Johnson appointed Maj. Gen. Oliver O. Howard as the bureau's commissioner general. Initially the bureau did well financially, but when Johnson later returned confiscated and abandoned lands to their prewar owners, the bureau lost most of its revenue from rents and property sales. The president's February 1866 veto of a two-year extension of the bureau helped set the stage for his impeachment (see **Document 3.1**). He characterized the bureau as an "immense patronage," a "permanent branch of the public administration," corrupt and too costly in light of "the condition of our fiscal affairs." [40] *Harper's Weekly* commented disapprovingly, "The national disgrace of an abandonment of the freedmen in their present condition to those who lately held them as slaves would be overwhelming." [41]

Congress, which had passed the extension almost unanimously, overrode the president's veto. The bureau continued to function until it was formally dissolved in June 1872, but its principal operating period concluded in December 1868.

Although hampered by inadequate funding, white apathy, administrative weaknesses and political opposition, the bureau helped African Americans negotiate labor contracts, fed and clothed them, provided information to reunite families split by slavery and war, offered advice on legal problems and land purchases, and in some cases engaged in social innovations. For example, it set up four self-sustaining "home colonies," or agricultural collectives, in Louisiana to provide a livelihood, protection, education and training. It also extended its operations beyond the former Confederacy into Washington, D.C., dealing with public housing and sanitation for thousands of former slaves and relocating unemployed workers to the North.

At the same time, corruption, incompetence and graft undermined the bureau's mission. Illiterate former slaves were exploited, supplies were stolen, bribes were paid to dishonest agents and black veterans were cheated of their bounties and back pay. In early 1866 Emily Howland, a white Quaker educator monitoring the bureau's work, received a letter from a Virginia volunteer, who wrote, "I think General Howard wants to do right by all, but he has not the right ones under him. They do not all work for the people; some of them are for their own pockets only." [42]

Some critics considered the bureau to be a mad experiment, but despite its limitations and constraints it helped resettle more than 30,000 people, set up about 50 hospitals and established more than 4,300 schools, including Howard, Hampton, Fisk and Clark Atlanta universities—some of which produced future black lawmakers.

▬ Document 2.10 ▬
Freedmen's Bureau Act, March 3, 1865

An Act to establish a Bureau for the Relief of Freedmen and Refugees.

Be it enacted by the Senate and House of Representatives of the United States of America in Congress assembled, That there is hereby established in the War Department, to continue during the present war of rebellion, and for one year thereafter, a bureau of refugees, freedmen, and abandoned lands, to which shall be committed, as hereinafter provided, the supervision and management of all abandoned lands, and the control of all bureau subjects relating to refugees and freedmen from rebel states, or from any district of country within the territory embraced in the operations, of the army, under such rules and regulations as may be prescribed by the head of the bureau and approved by the President. The said bureau shall be under the management and control of a commissioner to be appointed by the President, by and with the advice and consent of the Senate, whose compensation shall be three thousand dollars per annum, and such number of clerks as may be assigned to him by the Secretary of War, not exceeding one chief clerk, two of the fourth class, two of the third class, and five of the first class. And the commissioner and all persons appointed under this act, shall, before entering upon their duties, take the oath of office prescribed in an act entitled "An act to prescribe an oath of office, and for other purposes," approved July second, eighteen hundred and sixty-two, and the commissioner and the chief clerk shall, before entering upon their duties, give bonds to the treasurer of the United States, the former in the sum of fifty thousand dollars, and the latter in the sum of ten thousand dollars, conditioned for the faithful discharge of their duties respectively, with securities to be approved as sufficient by the Attorney-General, which bonds shall be filed in the office of the first comptroller of the treasury, to be by him put in suit for the benefit of any injured party upon any breach of the conditions thereof.

SEC. 2. *And be it further enacted,* That the Secretary of War may direct such issues of provisions, clothing, and fuel, as he may deem needful for the immediate and temporary shelter and supply of destitute and suffering refugees and freedmen and their wives and children, under such rules and regulations as he may direct.

SEC. 3. *And be it further enacted,* That the President may, by and with the advice and consent of the Senate, appoint an assistant commissioner for each of the states declared to be in insurrection, not exceeding ten in number, who shall, under the direction of the commissioner, aid in the execution of the provisions of this act . . . Each of said commissioners shall receive an annual salary of two thousand five hundred dollars in full compensation for all his services. And any military officer may be detailed and assigned to duty under this act without increase of pay or allowances. The commissioner shall, before the commencement of each regular session of congress, make full report of his proceedings with exhibits of the state of his accounts to the President, who shall communicate the same to congress, and shall also make special reports whenever required to do so by the President or either house of congress; and the assistant commissioners shall make quarterly reports of their proceedings to the commissioner, and also such other special reports as from time to time may be required.

SEC. 4. *And be it further enacted,* That the commissioner, under the direction of the President, shall have authority to set apart, for the use of loyal refugees and freedmen, such tracts of land within the insurrectionary states as shall have been abandoned, or to which the United States shall have acquired title by confiscation or sale, or otherwise, and to every male citizen, whether refugee or freedman, as aforesaid, there shall be assigned not more than forty acres of such land, and the person to whom it was so assigned shall be protected in the use and enjoyment of the land for the term of three years at an annual rent not exceeding six per centum upon the value of such land, as it was appraised by the state authorities in the year eighteen hundred and sixty, for the purpose of taxation, and in case no such appraisal can be found, then the rental shall be based upon the estimated value of the land in said year, to be ascertained in such manner as the commissioner may by regulation prescribe. At the end of said term, or at any time during said term, the occupants of any parcels so assigned may purchase the land and receive such title thereto as the United States can convey, upon paying therefor the value of the land, as ascertained and fixed for the purpose of determining the annual rent aforesaid . . .

Source: Statutes at Large of the United States of America 13 (1866): 507–509, from the Library of Congress, http://memory.loc.gov/ammem/amlaw/lwsllink.html.

NOTES

1 David Hunter, General Orders No. 11, May 9, 1862, from Freedmen and Southern Society Project, University of Maryland, /www.history.umd.edu/Freedmen/hunter.htm#HUNTER.

2 G. P. Miller to Simon Cameron, Letter, October 30, 1861, in *A Documentary History of the Negro People in the United States,* ed. Herbert Aptheker (New York: Citadel Press, 1969), 460.

3 Frederick Douglass, "Men of Color, to Arms!" in *Life and Times of Frederick Douglass,* from Library of Congress, http://memory.loc.gov.

4 National Park Service, Civil War Soldiers and Sailors System, "History of African Americans in the Civil War," www.itd.nps.gov/cwss/history/aa_history.htm.

5 "Men Run Mad," *Charleston Mercury,* January 26, 1865, in *African American History in the Press, 1851–1899: From the Coming of the Civil War to the Rise of Jim Crow as Reported and Illustrated in Selected Newspapers of the Time,* ed. Schneider Collection, vol. 1, *1851–1869* (Detroit: Gale, 1996), 366.

6 Theophilus J Minton, "Robert Brown Elliott," *African Methodist Episcopal Church Review 8,* no. 4 (April 1892): 363.

7 Ibid.

8 John Roy Lynch, *Reminiscences of an Active Life: The Autobiography of John Roy Lunch,* ed. John Hope Franklin (Chicago: University of Chicago Press, 1970), 36.

9 T. P. Saunders and P. H. B. Saunders, "Petition to Congress," December 17, 1862, in Aptheker, *A Documentary History,* 500.

10 William Still, Isaiah C. Wears, S. M. Smith, and I. C. Gibbs, "Letter to the Board of Managers of the Various Passenger Cars," *The Liberator,* December 23, 1864, in Aptheker, *A Documentary History,* 502.

11 "Declaration of the Immediate Causes which Induce and Justify the Secession of South Carolina from the Federal Union," December 24, 1860, from the Avalon Project at Yale Law School, www.yale.edu/lawweb/avalon/csa/scarsec.htm.

12 "An Ordinance to Dissolve the Union between the State of Alabama and the Other States United Under the Compact Styled 'The Constitution of the United States of America,' January 11, 1861, from the Civil War Home Page, www.civil-war.net/pages/ordinances_secession.asp.

13 "A Declaration of the Immediate Causes which Induce and Justify the Secession of the State of Mississippi from the Federal Union," January 9, 1861, from the Avalon Project at Yale Law School, www.yale.edu/lawweb/avalon/csa/missec.htm.

14 "A Declaration of the Causes which Impel the State of Texas to Secede from the Federal Union," February 2, 1861, from the Avalon Project at Yale Law School, www.yale.edu/lawweb/avalon/csa/texsec.htm.

15 "A Declaration of the Causes which Impel the State of Georgia to Secede from the Federal Union," January 29, 1861, from the Avalon Project at Yale Law School, www.yale.edu/lawweb/avalon/csa/geosec.htm

16 David P. Currie, "Through the Looking Glass: The Confederate Constitution in Congress," *Virginia Law Review* 90, no. 5 (September 2004): 1267.

17 Jefferson Davis, "Inaugural Address of the President of the Provisional Government," February 18, 1861, from the Avalon Project at Yale Law School, www.yale.edu/lawweb/avalon/csa/csainau.htm.

18 Quoted in John Hope Franklin, "The Emancipation Proclamation: An Act of Justice," *Prologue* 25, no. 2: 1993.

19 Frederick Douglass, *Life and Times of Frederick Douglass, Written by Himself* (New York: Pathway Press, 1941), 359.

20 "Resolutions of the Illinois State Legislature," *Illinois State Register,* January 7, 1864, in *Documents of American History,* 9th ed., ed. Henry Steele Commager (Englewood Cliffs, N.J.: Prentice-Hall, 1973), 422.

21 Kitt Alexander, e-mail message to Eric Freedman, April 24, 2007.

22 House Committee on War Claims, *Report to Accompany H.R. 1333,* 55th Cong., 2d sess., January 12, 1898, 53.

23 Ibid., 52.

24 "An Appeal from the Colored Men of Philadelphia to the President of the United States," 1862, in Aptheker, *A Documentary History,* 474.

25 Quoted in Charles H. Wesley, "Lincoln's Plan for Colonizing the Emancipated Negroes," *Journal of Negro History* 4 (January 1919): 20.

26 *New York Herald,* November 15, 1860, quoted in Albon P. Man Jr., "Labor Competition and the New York Draft Riots of 1863," *Journal of Negro History* 36, no. 4 (October 1951): 378–379.

27 *Cincinnati Enquirer,* July 15, 1862, quoted in William H. Lofton, "Northern Labor and the Negro during the Civil War," *Journal of Negro History* 34, no. 3 (July 1949): 259.

28 *Congressional Globe,* 37th Cong., 3d sess., Appendix, 83–86, February 2, 1863, from Library of Congress, http://memory.loc.gov/ammem/amlaw/lwcg.html.

29 Francis Williams, "Duty of Colored Men in the Present National Crisis," *Christian Recorder,* April 23, 1864, in *The Voice of Black America: Major Speeches by Negroes in the United States, 1797–1971,* ed. Philip S. Foner (New York: Simon & Schuster, 1972), 282.

30 Henry Halleck to Ulysses S. Grant, Letter, March 31, 1863, quoted in Herbert Aptheker, "Negro Casualties in the Civil War," *Journal of Negro History* 32, no. 1 (January 1947): 21.

31 Aptheker, "Negro Casualties in the Civil War," 12.

32 *Statutes at Large of the United States of America* 13 (1866): 129.

33 Blanche K. Bruce, "Enlistment of Colored Soldiers," April 10, 1878, quoted in *Black Congressmen during Reconstruction: A Documentary Sourcebook,* ed. Stephen Middleton (Westport, Conn.: Praeger, 2002), 23.

34 David Quinn, "Petition and Memorial of David Quinn, Asking for the Re-establishment of Negro Slavery in the United States," Chicago, June 13, 1866, from Library of Congress, African American Pamphlet Collection, http://memory.loc.gov.

35 Patrick Cleburne to Commanding General, the Corps, Division, Brigade, and Regimental Commanders of the Army of Tennessee, January 2, 1864, in *Confederate Correspondence, Orders, and Returns Relating to Operations in Southwestern Virginia, Kentucky, Tennessee, Mississippi, Alabama, West Florida, and Northern Georgia,* no. 24, O.R. Series 1, volume L.11/2 [S#110]. First Sentence quoted in Thomas Robson Hay, "The South and the Arming of the Slaves," *Mississippi Valley Historical Review* 6, no. 1 (June 1919): 43. Second sentence quoted in Don H. Doyle, "Review of *A Shattered Nation: The Rise and Fall of the Confederacy, 1861–1868,* by Anne Sarah Rubin," *Southern Cultures* 12, no. 1 (Spring 2006): 112.

36 S. Cooper, General Orders No. 14, March 23, 1865, available at the Freedmen and Southern Society Project, University of Maryland, www.history.umd.edu/Freedmen/csenlist.htm.

37 *Statutes at Large of the United States of America* 13 (1866): 507.

38 Charles Sumner, "Bridge from Slavery to Freedom," in *Congressional Globe,* 38th Cong., 1st sess., June 13, 1864. Speech available in pamphlet form from the Ohio Historical Society, http://dbs.ohiohistory.org/africanam/page.cfm?ID=811.

39 *Statutes at Large of the United States of America* 13 (1866): 508.

40 Andrew Johnson, "Veto Message" to the Senate, February 19, 1866, in *A Compilation of the Messages and Papers of the Presidents,* ed. James D. Richardson, vol. 6, pt. 2, *Andrew Johnson* (Project Gutenberg, 2004), www.gutenberg.org/files/12755/12755-8.txt

41 "The Freedmen's Bureau," *Harper's Weekly,* March 10, 1866, 146, in Schneider Collection, *African American History in the Press,* vol. 1, 432.

42 Mrs. Harvey Bailey to Emily Howland, letter, February 6, 1866, original in Cornell University Library, Division of Rare and Manuscript Collections.

Reconstruction

Increasing Rights and Political Empowerment, 1868–1883

Even before the last Confederate soldiers had surrendered, politicians in Washington were clashing over their drastically divergent visions of how the rebellious states should be reintegrated into the Union. They were sharply divided on the roles and rights that should be granted to freed slaves and to white southerners who had been loyal to the Confederacy. Presidents Abraham Lincoln and Andrew Johnson—who took office after Lincoln was assassinated—favored a softer, more liberal and more rapid reintegration of the South into the national political fabric than did the Radical Republicans. The nearly immediate resurgence of formerly Confederate white Democrats into public offices across the South and the racist legislation those states adopted, known as "black codes," widened that philosophical gap and led to confrontations between Democrat Johnson and the Radical Republicans, which culminated in the president's impeachment in 1868.

Reconstruction was a complex era in U.S. history. It occasioned epic power struggles as the residents, both white and black, of a region devastated by war struggled to reconstitute their governments, economies and

"Time Works Wonders." This 1870 cartoon from Harper's Weekly *comments on the irony of Hiram R. Revels representing Mississippi from the U.S. Senate seat once filled by Jefferson Davis, who resigned to serve as president of the Confederacy. The original caption quoted Shakespeare's* Othello: Davis, depicted here as the villain Iago, thinks that Revels has "leap'd into my seat: the thought wherof doth like a poisonous mineral gnaw my inwards."
Source: Library of Congress

cultures. It was an era that witnessed the first great empowerment of African Americans, along with actual and alleged political corruption, economic struggle and overt race-related violence. But it also was an era that should not be cast in stereotypes of black versus white, Democrats versus Republicans, North versus South or even good versus evil. Tragically harsh economic conditions existed for both blacks and whites, particularly the poor, in the South after the war. Reconstruction's direct and indirect effects were not limited to the South, however, and the era must be examined in the context of such national trends and events as economic downturns, the 1867 crop failure, Western migration, political corruption, the spread of free public education, the restructuring of state governments and the reinterpretation of the role of the federal government.

Reconstruction in the Radical Republican model started in 1867 and led to African Americans winning high political offices. One made it all the way to the governor's office: Pinckney B. S. Pinchback of Louisiana became the state's governor for a month, after moving up from the lieutenant governorship to fill a vacancy. He then made unsuccessful bids for U.S. House and Senate seats (**Document 3.8**). Others had more success in their bids.

This 1872 group portrait by Currier & Ives *depicts the first African American legislators, who served in the Forty-first and Forty-second Congresses. From left to right, they are Sen. Hiram R. Revels, R-Miss.; Rep. Benjamin S. Turner, R-Ala.; Rep. Robert C. De Large, R-S.C.; Rep. Josiah T. Walls, R-Fla.; Rep. Jefferson F. Long, R-Ga.; Rep. Joseph H. Rainey, R-S.C. and Rep. Robert B. Elliott, R-S.C.* Source: The Granger Collection, New York

For the first time in U.S. history, starting with Rep. Joseph H. Rainey of South Carolina, who took office in 1870, and ending with Rep. George H. White of North Carolina, who left office in 1901, twenty black men—all southern Republicans—served in the House and two in the Senate during Reconstruction and its aftermath. They came from states and districts with a high proportion of African American citizens, which gave them an advantage at a time when many white supporters of the former Confederacy were unable to vote. For example, Mississippi, Alabama, Florida, Louisiana and South Carolina had majority-black populations, and all but two African American representatives of the period came from majority-black congressional districts; African Americans accounted for more than 40 percent of the residents of the two other districts.

Black politicians arrived in Washington with an array of backgrounds. Some had been born slaves, others free. Some had college educations and professional careers such as the ministry and law, while others were largely self-educated and practiced such occupations as tailor and shipping clerk. Several had seen military service for the Union or the Confederacy—or in the case of Rep. Robert Smalls of South Carolina, for both (**Document 2.4**). Most had held local or state political office, had taken part in state Reconstruction conventions, had filled Republican Party posts or had engaged in a combination of such activities before going to Washington.

Their principal legislative activities—as reflected in bills and petitions they sponsored and speeches they gave—fell into two broad categories: those relating to civil rights (**Document 3.9**), discrimination and racism (**Document 3.6**), education (**Document 3.5**) and the economic interests of former slaves (**Document 3.11**), and those relating to local interests of their own districts. As the documents in this chapter illustrate, some Reconstruction-era black politicians participated passionately in debates over legislation addressing issues such as enforcement of the Fourteenth Amendment (**Document 3.2**), lynching, amnesty for former Confederates (**Document 3.7**) and voting rights (**Document 3.3**). But like many of their white colleagues, they also devoted considerable attention to bills to help their districts with public works projects, what today are characterized as "pork barrel" projects or "earmarks"—such as an orphanage in Charleston, South Carolina, navigation improvements on the Mississippi River, a survey of Louisiana's Bayou Courtableau and construction of a public building in Selma, Alabama. They also worked to resolve individual constituents' pension disputes and other personal problems. They were involved in other issues of the day, including tariffs, shipping, the cotton tax, celebration of the centennial of independence, the Cuban revolution, congressional salaries and the rights of Native Americans. Most of their proposals, however, died in committee or, if they survived committee, on the floor, even though the Republicans held the majority in the Senate when the first two black senators served and they controlled the House until 1875 and again in 1881–1883.

Neither collectively nor individually did they wield significant influence or power. To begin with, there were never enough black members at any one time to constitute an effective voting block in the House, thus contributing to their marginalization; at the peak, there were seven. Further, they did not always vote the same way in roll calls, and although they were more racially liberal than their white Republican colleagues, they sometimes split even on race-related legislation such as amnesty for former Confederates. John A. Hyman of North Carolina and Jeremiah Haralson of Alabama never even delivered a speech on the House floor.

Another major factor in their lack of clout was the brevity of their tenures. No African American lawmaker served long enough to accumulate meaningful seniority, although South Carolina's Rainey—who earned the symbolic achievement of becoming the first black member of the House— presided over the House during a floor debate about an Indian appropriations bill in 1874. Some members who served multiple terms had gaps in their service when they lost or did not run in intervening elections, including Smalls and Richard H. Cain of South Carolina. Others served only partial terms of a year or less; party leaders in their states nominated them to fill vacancies as a way to woo black voters, while choosing to run white candidates for the subsequent full term. For example in Georgia, Rep. Jefferson F. Long was elected in December 1870 to fill the last few months of a term, took the oath of office on January 16, 1871, and sat only until the session ended that March 3. The *Atlanta Constitution* reported that Long arrived at his seat before each day's session began, sat quietly and rarely left the floor; "he wrote no letters, franked no documents." [1] In elections, some black members faced other black candidates, as in 1876 when Alabama Republicans dumped incumbent Jeremiah Haralson and instead nominated former representative James T. Rapier; Haralson ran anyway as an independent, and a white Democrat won the seat in the three-way contest.

Some representatives spent more time seeking the office than holding it. James E. O'Hara of North Carolina unsuccessfully sought the Republican nomination in 1874, withdrew from the 1876 race, lost a three-way election in 1878 that was marked by fraud in the vote count that gave the seat to a Democrat, and decided not to compete in 1880 while fighting a malfeasance indictment. He won the 1882 and 1884 elections but lost in 1886. Election challenges were also a limiting factor on longevity and influence; significant portions of a two-year term could be eaten up before the House accepted election results, as Hyman and John M. Langston of Virginia learned.

Certainly other factors constrained black members' accomplishments as well, among them the shift of control in the House to the Democrats in 1875 (**Document 3.10**). Not only did the change in leadership preclude race-related legislation from coming to the floor but it also made it unlikely that any Republican-backed legislation would pass, whether the sponsors were black or white. In addition, African Americans encountered a hostile work environment created by racist attitudes among their white colleagues in both parties, executive branch officials and bureaucrats; paternalistic attitudes among their white Republican colleagues; and partisanship, as Democrats sought to regain control of Congress as well as the governments of the southern states that had sent blacks to Washington, D.C.

From the beginning, African American lawmakers recognized that high public office was no shield against racism, on or off Capitol Hill. Racism was a major motivation in Democratic opposition to swearing in Hiram R. Revels as the first black senator, for example (**Document 3.4**). Even after he was seated, Revels rode in the segregated section of Mississippi River steamboats when traveling between Washington and Mississippi. The master of one steamer testified that Revels "informed me that the separate cabin was the only way to give satisfaction to the white and colored race." [2] In 1874 Mississippian Blanche K. Bruce was elected to be the second black senator—and the last until Edward W. Brooke III, R-Mass., in 1966. When Bruce arrived in the chamber in March 1875, his fellow Mississippi senator, white Democrat James L. Alcorn, declined the customary honor of escorting him down the aisle to be sworn in. Alcorn "was buried behind a newspaper," Bruce later recalled.[3] Republican Roscoe Conkling of New York escorted him instead. Membership in Congress certainly was no insurance against racism beyond Washington. In 1882, for instance, the *Christian Recorder*, published by the Philadelphia-based African Methodist Episcopal Church in the United States, described an incident involving Rep. Smalls, who was a Civil War naval hero: "How hard prejudice dies, even in the North, may readily be seen in the refusal of the proprietor of the Revere House, Boston, to entertain Captain Robert Smalls." [4]

Many Reconstruction-era African American members remained politically active in state government or party politics after they finished their terms in Washington. For example, Smalls became a port collector in South Carolina, Haralson was appointed a customs agent in Baltimore and Bruce worked in the Treasury Department.

Dramatic changes in the national political scene had significant implications for black political power. The 1876 presidential election was scarred by racial violence in parts of the South. Republican Rutherford B. Hayes lost the popular vote to Democrat Samuel J. Tilden, but Tilden failed to secure an electoral college majority. This led to a congressional compromise creating an electoral commission that gave Hayes the White House. At odds with his party, Hayes backed home rule for the southern states and contended that Reconstruction had ended with ratification of the Fifteenth Amendment in 1870 (**Document 3.3**). Many African Americans distrusted Hayes and viewed his policy as placating former rebels at the expense of civil and political rights for blacks.

By 1877 Democrats governed all states in the former Confederacy and many blacks continued to lose faith in the Republican Party. In 1882 blacks in Rhode Island adopted a resolution stating that "the Republican party of our State has failed to properly recognize the worthiness and faithful devotion of its colored adherents; . . . it continues to do so in the face of earnest but respectful remonstrances." [5]

Three and one-half decades later, former representative John R. Lynch, R-Miss., who had served in the House during the Hayes-Tilden battle, looked back at Reconstruction and its aftermath. He wrote:

> While it is true that Hayes . . . was finally declared elected according to the forms of law, yet the terms and conditions upon which he was allowed to be peaceably inaugurated were such as to complete the extinction and annihilation of the Republican party at the South. The price that the Hayes managers stipulated to pay,—and did pay,—for the peaceful inauguration of Hayes was that the South was to be turned over to the Democrats and that the administration was not to enforce the Constitution and the laws of the land in that section against the expressed will of the Democrats thereof. In other words, so far as the South was concerned, the Constitution was not to follow the flag.[6]

For most practical purposes, the year 1877 marked the end of Reconstruction when Hayes ordered the withdrawal of Federal occupation troops from the Southern states. The result was a devastating neutralization of the political power and participation of blacks across the South. The number of blacks elected to Congress began to shrink. As for Lynch, his own concerns about the South proved true: he would be the last African American representing Mississippi in Congress until 1987.

The documents in this chapter begin with Johnson's articles of impeachment in 1868 (**Document 3.1**) and end with the 1883 U.S. Supreme Court decision striking down most guarantees of the 1875 Civil Rights Act (**Document 3.12**). Together, they illustrate the rise and rapid fall of black political power, both in the postwar South and in the national political arena, as racial bias and electoral expediency dashed hopes and expectations for equal rights.

Document 3.1 in Context
"Unmindful of the High Duties of His Office": Congress Impeaches President Andrew Johnson

Elected to the U.S. Senate from Tennessee in 1857, Democrat Andrew Johnson remained staunchly pro-Union, characterized secession as "treason"[7] and was the sole senator from the South not to leave Congress when the Civil War erupted in 1861. In 1862 he became military governor of the Union-occupied sections of his home state, and in 1864 he was elected vice president on the Republican ticket, replacing incumbent Hannibal Hamlin, whose views on rehabilitating the South were viewed by Abraham Lincoln as too harsh. Lincoln also hoped that in the upcoming election Johnson would help him attract the support of Democrats in the North and voters in southern "border states," like Maryland and Kentucky, that had refused to join the Confederacy.

When Johnson assumed the presidency after Lincoln was assassinated in April 1865, he began a rocky relationship with the Republican majority in Congress, particularly the Radical Republicans. Johnson pursued Lincoln's more conciliatory approach to Reconstruction and the restoration of civil government to the southern states, resisting congressional demands for a strong federal role in Reconstruction. He opposed the Fourteenth Amendment (**Document 3.2**) and its guaranty of equal protection, vetoed some early civil rights and Reconstruction bills, ignored a law requiring appointees to federal civil and military jobs to swear that they had not assisted the rebellion, and generally used his executive authority to thwart

Congress. By pardoning numerous former Confederate military and political figures and ordering their confiscated land returned, he precluded the Freedmen's Bureau from renting land to former slaves at low cost (see **Document 2.10**). Under these lenient federal policies, state legislatures across the South soon enacted discriminatory "black codes," disenfranchised black voters and allowed high-level former Confederates to resume political office.

In the 1866 election, the Radical Republicans gained decisive control over Congress and on March 2, 1867, passed the First Reconstruction Act over Johnson's veto. It established martial law in the South pending the states' adoption of constitutions that assured equal political and legal rights to their citizens and granted universal suffrage to blacks. Johnson became the first president to face impeachment after he fired Secretary of War Edwin M. Stanton, a Lincoln appointee and ally of the Radicals, in a test of the constitutionality of the Tenure of Office Act of 1867 that Congress had also passed over his veto.

The House of Representatives passed an eleven-article resolution of impeachment on February 24, 1868, charging that Johnson had unlawfully removed Stanton from office, had violated the Command of the Army Act and—in a reflection of bitterness over what was perceived as the president trampling on Congress's reputation as well as its constitutional authority—had defamed Congress through "intemperate, inflammatory, and scandalous harangues." [8] Like other news outlets, African American publications covered the three-month Senate trial closely; for example, weekly reports appeared in the Philadelphia-based *Christian Recorder,* which took an anti-Johnson stance and at one point described a pro-Johnson speech as "adroit and indeed almost wonderful as a piece of fine spun sophistry." [9]

Johnson was acquitted on May 26, 1868, when the final vote fell one short of the two-thirds majority needed to convict. After the trial, some representatives proposed alternative grounds for impeachment, citing corrupt abuse of the patronage system, usurpation of congressional authority, subornation of perjury and the pardons granted for political purposes to 193 Union army deserters. Those allegations went nowhere.

After Johnson's acquittal, the Radical Republicans continued to push for the federal government to guarantee political and civil rights to African Americans. Their success led Congress to demand that the states of the former Confederacy formally adopt the Fifteenth Amendment (**Document 3.3**), giving African Americans the right to vote, as a condition to readmission to the Union. Ratification of the amendment occurred early in the administration of President Ulysses S. Grant.

In a 2006 survey, presidential scholars ranked Johnson's Reconstruction policies among the top ten presidential mistakes in U.S. history.[10] Had the president's approach to Reconstruction prevailed, it is likely that few—if any—African Americans would have been elected to Congress during the Reconstruction era.

▬▬ Document 3.1 ▬▬
Articles of Impeachment of President Andrew Johnson, Presented to the Senate by Rep. John A. Bingham, R-Ohio, March 4, 1868

Articles exhibited to the House of Representatives of the United States, in the name of themselves and all the people of the United States, against Andrew Johnson, President of the United States, in maintenance and support of their impeachment against him for high crimes and misdemeanors.

ARTICLE I.

That said Andrew Johnson, President of the United States, on the 21st day of February, in the year of our Lord 1868, at Washington, in the District of Columbia, unmindful of the high duties of his office, of his oath of office, and of the requirement of the Constitution that he should take care that the laws be faithfully executed, did unlawfully and in violation of the Constitution and laws of the United States issue and order in writing for the removal of Edwin M. Stanton from the office of Secretary for the Department of War, said Edwin M. Stanton having been theretofore duly appointed and commissioned, by and with the advice and consent of the Senate of the United States, as such Secretary, and said Andrew Johnson, President of the United States, on the 12th day of August, in the year of our Lord 1867, and during the recess of said Senate, having been suspended by his order Edwin M. Stanton from said office, and within twenty days after the first day of the next meeting of said Senate, that is to say, on the 12th day of December, in the year last aforesaid, having reported to said Senate such suspension, with the evidence and reasons for his action in the case and the name of the person designated to perform the duties of such office temporarily until the next meeting of the Senate, and said Senate, thereafterward, on the 13th day of January, in the year of our Lord 1868, having duly considered the evidence and reasons reported by said Andrew Johnson for said suspension, and having refused to concur in said suspension, whereby and by force of the provisions of an act entitled "An act regulating the tenure of certain civil offices," passed March 2, 1867, said Edwin M. Stanton did forthwith resume the functions of his office, whereof the said Andrew Johnson had then and there due notice, and said Edwin M. Stanton, by reason of the premises, on said 21st day of February, being lawfully entitled to hold said office of Secretary for the Department of War, which said order for the removal of said Edwin M. Stanton is, in substance, as follows, that is to say:

EXECUTIVE MANSION,
WASHINGTON, D.C., *February 21, 1868*

SIR: By virtue of the power and authority vested in me as President by the Constitution and laws of the United States you are hereby removed from office as Secretary for the Department of War, and your functions as such will terminate upon receipt of this communication.

You will transfer to Brevet Major General Lorenzo Thomas, Adjutant General of the Army, who has this day been authorized and empowered to act as Secretary of War *ad interim,* all records, books, papers, and other public property now in your custody and charge.

Respectfully yours, ANDREW JOHNSON.
Hon. EDWIN M. STANTON, *Washington D.C.*

Which order was unlawfully issued with intent then and there to violate the act entitled "An act regulating the tenure of certain civil offices," passed March 2, 1867; and, with the further intent contrary to the provisions of said act, in violation thereof, and contrary to the provisions of the Constitution of the United States, and without the advice and consent of the Senate of the United States, the said Senate then and there being in session, to remove said Edwin M. Stanton from the office of Secretary for the Department of War, the said Edwin M. Stanton being then and there Secretary of War, and being then and there in the due and lawful execution of the duties of said office, whereby said Andrew Johnson,

President of the United States, did then and there commit, and was guilty of a high misdemeanor in office . . .

ARTICLE X.

That said Andrew Johnson, President of the United States, unmindful of the high duties of his office and the dignity and proprieties thereof, and of the harmony and courtesies which ought to exist and be maintained between the executive and legislative branches of the Government of the United States, designing and intending to set aside the rightful authorities and powers of Congress, did attempt to bring into disgrace, ridicule, hatred, contempt and reproach the Congress of the United States and the several branches thereof, to impair and destroy the regard and respect of all the good people of the United States for the Congress and legislative power thereof, (which all officers of the Government ought inviolably to preserve and maintain,) and to excite the odium and resentment of all the good people of the United States against Congress and the laws by it duly and constitutionally enacted; and in pursuance of his said design and intent, openly and publicly and before divers assemblages of the citizens of the United States, convened in divers parts thereof to meet and receive said Andrew Johnson as the Chief Magistrate of the United States, did, on the 18th day of August, in the year of our Lord 1866, and on divers other days and times, as well before as afterward, make and deliver with a loud voice certain intemperate, inflammatory, and scandalous harangues, and did therein utter loud threats and bitter menaces as well against Congress as the laws of the United States duly enacted thereby, amid the cries, jeers, and laughter of the multitudes then assembled and within hearing, which are set forth in the several specifications hereinafter written, in substance and effect, that is to say: . . .

Specification Second.—In this, that at Cleveland, in the State of Ohio, heretofore, to wit, on the 3d day of September, in the year of our Lord 1866, before a public assemblage of citizens and others, said Andrew Johnson, President of the United States, speaking of and concerning the Congress of the United States did, in a loud voice, declare in substance and effect among other things, that is to say:

"I will tell you what I did do. I called upon your Congress that is trying to break up the government."

. . .

"In conclusion, beside that, Congress had taken much pains to poison their constituents against him. But what had Congress done? Have they done anything to restore the union of these States? No; on the contrary, they had done everything to prevent it: and because he stood now where he did when the rebellion commenced, he had been denounced as a traitor. Who had run greater risks or made greater sacrifices than himself? But Congress, factious and domineering, had undertaken to poison the minds of the American people."

Specification Third.—In this, that at St. Louis, in the State of Missouri, heretofore, to wit, on the 8th day of September, in the year of our Lord 1866, before a public assemblage of citizens and others, said Andrew Johnson, President of the United States, speaking of and concerning the Congress of the United States, did, in a loud voice, declare in substance and effect, among other things, that is to say: . . .

"Well, let me say to you, if you will stand by me in this action; if you will stand by me in trying to give the people a fair chance, soldiers and citizens, to participate in these offices, God being willing, I will kick them out. I will kick them out just as fast as I can" . . .

Which said utterances, declarations, threats, and harangues, highly censurable in any, are peculiarly indecent and unbecoming in the Chief Magistrate of the United States, by means whereof said Andrew Johnson has brought the high office of the President of the United States into contempt, ridicule, and disgrace, to the great scandal of all good citizens, whereby said Andrew Johnson, President of the United States, did commit, and was then and there guilty, of a high misdemeanor in office . . .

ARTICLE XI.

. . . And the House of Representatives, by protestation, saving to themselves the liberty of exhibiting at any time hereafter any further articles or other accusation or impeachment against the said Andrew Johnson, President of the United States, and also of replying to his answers which he shall make unto the articles herein preferred against him, and of offering proof to the same and every part thereof, and to all and every other article, accusation, or impeachment which shall be exhibited by them, as the case shall require, do demand that the said Andrew Johnson may be put to answer the high crimes and misdemeanors in office herein charged against him, and that such proceedings, examinations, trials, and judgments may be thereupon had and given as may be agreeable to law and justice.

Source: Congressional Globe, 40th Cong., 2d sess., March 4, 1868, 1647–1649, from the Library of Congress, http://memory.loc.gov/ammem/amlaw/lwcg.html.

Document 3.2 in Context
"An Effort to Force Negro Suffrage upon the States": The Fourteenth Amendment Confronts the "Black Codes"

Congress proposed the Fourteenth Amendment on June 13, 1866, after extensive debate. It took effect following South Carolina's ratification on July 9, 1868, in the face of considerable dispute. In December 1866, for example, the Arkansas legislature rejected the amendment as "an effort to force negro suffrage upon the states"; it did, however, approve the amendment in April 1868.

The Fourteenth Amendment guaranteed equal protection of the law, citizenship to all people born or naturalized in the United States and voting rights for men at least twenty-one years of age. It also denied federal posts to some Civil War rebels, addressed congressional apportionment and federal debts, and prohibited governmental compensation to slave owners for the "loss or emancipation" of their slaves, something President Abraham Lincoln had once considered offering to slave owners in loyal states.

Before the Civil War, abolitionists laid the groundwork for the amendment's citizenship and equal protection provisions, but the need for a constitutional standard of national citizenship became apparent following the 1857 decision in *Dred Scott v. Sanford* (**Document 1.14**). In that case, the Supreme Court ruled that blacks could not become U.S. citizens, even if they had been born free in the United States.

After the Civil War ended, strong opposition remained to black citizenship and equal protection in both the South and the North. For example, a plank in the 1865 Louisiana Democratic Party platform stated:

Resolved, That we hold this to be a Government of white people, made and to be perpetuated for the exclusive benefit of the white race; and . . . people of African descent cannot be considered as citizens of the United States, and that there can, in no event, nor under any circumstances, be any equality between the white and other races.[11]

Responding to discrimination in the North, the 1867 Illinois State Convention of Colored Men adopted a resolution protesting that "the constitutional disability under which colored men labor in this State calls loudly for redress; it insults our manhood, and disgraces the name of our great State." [12]

Much of the impetus for action in Congress was a political reaction to "black codes" enacted in southern states immediately after the war, including statutes that restored a virtual slave–master relationship in employment arrangements. These included a South Carolina statute passed in December 1865 that stated, "All persons of color who make contracts for service or labor, shall be known as servants, and those with whom they contract shall be known as masters," and provided that such contracts could be approved only with a white witness.[13] These repressive measures extended beyond employment; a Mississippi law, for example, made it a crime for a "freedman, free negro or mulatto" to carry a firearm without a license.[14]

Although the Fourteenth Amendment promised rights, it proved insufficient to ensure those rights. Congress soon found that it had to rely on the authority of section 5 to enact enforcement-related legislation.

▬ Document 3.2 ▬
Fourteenth Amendment to the U.S. Constitution, Proposed to the States by Congress June 16, 1866, Ratified July 9, 1868

SECTION 1. All persons born or naturalized in the United States, and subject to the jurisdiction thereof, are citizens of the United States and of the state wherein they reside. No state shall make or enforce any law which shall abridge the privileges or immunities of citizens of the United States; nor shall any state deprive any person of life, liberty, or property, without due process of law; nor deny to any person within its jurisdiction the equal protection of the laws.

SEC. 2. Representatives shall be apportioned among the several states according to their respective numbers, counting the whole number of persons in each state, excluding Indians not taxed. But when the right to vote at any election for the choice of electors for President and Vice President of the United States, Representatives in Congress, the executive and judicial officers of a state, or the members of the legislature thereof, is denied to any of the male inhabitants of such state, being twenty-one years of age, and citizens of the United States, or in any way abridged, except for participation in rebellion, or other crime, the basis of representation therein shall be reduced in the proportion which the number of such male citizens shall bear to the whole number of male citizens twenty-one years of age in such state.

SEC. 3. No person shall be a Senator or Representative in Congress, or elector of President and Vice President, or hold any office, civil or military, under the United States, or under any state, who, having previously taken an oath, as a member of Congress, or as an officer of the United States, or as a member of any state legislature, or as an executive or judicial officer of any state, to support the Constitution of the United States, shall have engaged in insurrection or rebellion against the same, or given aid or comfort to the enemies thereof. But Congress may by a vote of two-thirds of each House, remove such disability.

SEC. 4. The validity of the public debt of the United States, authorized by law, including debts incurred for payment of pensions and bounties for services in suppressing insurrection or rebellion, shall not be questioned. But neither the United States nor any state shall assume or pay any debt or obligation incurred in aid of insurrection or rebellion against the United States, or any claim for the loss or emancipation of any slave; but all such debts, obligations and claims shall be held illegal and void.

SEC. 5. The Congress shall have power to enforce, by appropriate legislation, the provisions of this article.

Source: "Fourteenth Amendment to the U.S. Constitution: Civil Rights," 1868, from the U.S. National Archives and Records Administration, www.ourdocuments.gov.

Document 3.3 in Context
"Including the Negro in the Body Politic": Guaranteeing Equal Voting Rights Nationwide

Black suffrage was a divisive issue. After legislation was introduced to enfranchise black men in the nation's capital, it took Congress about two years to pass it, and even then "An Act to Regulate the Elective Franchise in the District of Columbia," which granted voting rights "without any distinction on account of color or race," did not take effect until the House and Senate overrode President Andrew Johnson's veto in January 1867.[15]

Although the Fifteenth Amendment guaranteeing voting rights nationally was proposed by Congress in February 1869 and ratified in February 1870, its origins were older. For example, soon after the Civil War ended in 1865, Sen. Carl Schurz, R-Mo., reported to Johnson:

> As the most difficult of the pending questions are intimately connected with the status of the negro in southern society, it is obvious that a correct solution can be more easily obtained if he has a voice in the matter. In the right to vote we would find the best permanent protection against oppressive class-legislation, as well as against individual persecution.[16]

Early versions of the amendment were introduced in 1867, the year that abolitionist and editor Frederick Douglass appealed to Congress for "impartial suffrage, and for including the negro in the body politic." He argued that the "work before Congress" was "to save the people of the South from themselves and the nation from detriment on their account." [17]

Ratification moved quickly, and black members of several southern legislatures helped secure their states' approval of the amendment. During the ratification process, the *Christian Recorder*, the Philadelphia-based newspaper of the African Methodist Episcopal Church, called the amendment "this Constitutional leveler—not leveler, but uplifter," but also cautiously tempered its optimism: "Were not the most certain (apparently) of human events liable to failure we might commence our hallelujah over the passage of the 15th amendment."[18] Once the amendment was approved, there was widespread celebration; in Monticello, Arkansas, "the streets were so thronged that they were almost impassable." [19] On the other hand, critics contended that Republican supporters of the amendment were motivated as much, if not more, by politics—their desire to win black votes throughout the country—as by a philosophical commitment to equal rights.

Popular history stresses the impact of the Fifteenth Amendment on the South, but until the amendment took effect, the only place in the country where black suffrage was mandatory was in the South, under the First Reconstruction Act—also passed over Johnson's veto, in March 1867. Meanwhile, the majority of the other states denied voting rights to African Americans. In February 1866, for example, the Pennsylvania State Equal Rights League petitioned Congress, writing:

> Prior to the year 1838 we voted without any distinctive qualification, and went side by side to the polls with our white fellow citizens to deposit the ballot—that palladium of American Citizenship . . . We have been disenfranchised twenty-eight years, and suffered all the insults and outrage consequent upon it—which legitimately flow from an act disenfranchising us, and determining our rights by the texture of our hair, and our citizenship by the color of our skin.[20]

It was the two-sentence Fifteenth Amendment, not the Civil War itself, that enfranchised African Americans. By guaranteeing equal voting rights nationwide, the amendment provided a fundamental and essential step toward political participation for African Americans and made it possible for blacks to win congressional seats.

▰▰▰ Document 3.3 ▰▰▰
Fifteenth Amendment to the Constitution, Passed by Congress February 26, 1869, Ratified February 3, 1870

SECTION 1. The right of citizens of the United States to vote shall not be denied or abridged by the United States or by any state on account of race, color, or previous condition of servitude.

SEC. 2. The Congress shall have power to enforce this article by appropriate legislation.

Source: "Fifteenth Amendment to the U.S. Constitution: Voting Rights," 1870, from the U.S. National Archives and Records Administration, www.ourdocuments.gov.

Document 3.4 in Context
"Never Before in the History of This Government Has a Colored Man Been Elected to Senate of the United States": Hiram R. Revels Becomes the First Black Senator

Sen. Hiram R. Revels's tenure in Washington, D.C., lasted little more than a year. Although no major legislation carries his name, his election as the first African American senator tested the fabric of Reconstruction values and the willingness of at least part of the nation to abide by the results of the Civil War as they pertained to political rights. Born free in North Carolina, Revels was ordained an African Methodist Episcopal minister before the war. Once war erupted, he recruited black soldiers in Maryland for the Union army and served as chaplain of a black regiment stationed in Mississippi, where he settled and won a state senate seat after the war in 1869. The Republican-controlled state legislature elected him to the U.S. Senate—ironically to fill the seat vacated by Confederate president Jefferson Davis—but Revels's arrival on Capitol Hill in February 1870, when Mississippi was readmitted to the Union, triggered three days of searing debate over whether to seat him.

On the surface, Democratic opposition was couched largely in constitutional terms. If, as the Supreme Court's notorious 1857 *Dred Scott* decision held (**Document 1.14**)—a ruling that was not technically overturned until the Fourteenth Amendment took effect in 1868 (**Document 3.2**)—then blacks could not be U.S. citizens. Therefore, the Democrats argued that Revels did not meet the constitutional requirement that members of Congress be "nine years a citizen" before being sworn in. Their argument was legally irrelevant since he had never been a slave and had voted in Ohio. Senate Democrats also accused their Republican colleagues of partisanship, a motivation that was true on both sides. But as the excerpts from the debate over seating Senator-elect Revels illustrate, racism was the implicit, and occasionally explicit, basis for the strident opposition.

The press followed the controversy closely. A few days before the debate, the pro-Republican *Harper's Weekly* described Revels as "thoroughly respected by his own people, and by whites" and commented that "it is no less striking and significant that the papers which always toadied the great slave-drivers in Congress gibe and sneer at the new Senator, not because of any want of capacity, any fault of character, or any defect of manner, but solely because of color." [21] After Revels was sworn in and had delivered his maiden speech, the pro-Democratic *New York World* sneered, "To-day's session of the Senate was signalized by the first speech ever delivered by the lineal descendant of an orang-outang in Congress," and described him sitting at his desk "tranquilly pawing his lower visage and beard with hands resembling claws, and eying the assemblage aloft with a greasy and complacent smile." [22]

After his brief Senate term, Revels returned to Mississippi, where he later became president of Alcorn Agricultural College. His political conservatism became even more evident in a partisan controversy over the fraud-riddled 1875 election in which Democrats regained control of the Mississippi government (**Document 3.10**). Revels testified before a U.S. Senate investigative committee that he knew of no voting irregularities in his part of the state.

Document 3.4
Senate Debate on the Seating of Hiram R. Revels of Mississippi, February 23–25, 1870

Mr. [Henry] WILSON [R-Mass.]: I present the credentials of Hon. H. R. Revels, Senator-elect from Mississippi, and I ask that they be read, and that he be sworn in.

The VICE PRESIDENT [Schuyler Colfax, R-Ind.]: The credentials will be read, after which, if there be no objection, the Senator-elect will present himself to take the oath of office; but if there be objection the question will be submitted to the Senate . . .

Mr. [Willard] SAULSBURY [Sr.] [D-Del.]: I object to the reception of the paper on the ground that it is not such a certificate of election as is required by law, being a paper signed by a military officer who styles himself "provisional governor" . . .

Mr. [George F.] EDMUNDS [R-Vt.]: I ask the Senator whether with him and his friends who are making this opposition there is anything behind this mere technical objection; whether there is not objection to the reception of the Senator? . . .

Mr. [Garrett] DAVIS [D-Ky.]: Mr. President, this is certainly a morbid state of affairs. Never before in the history of this Government has a colored man been elected to Senate of the United States. To-day for the first time one presents himself and asks admission to a seat in it. How does he get here? Did he come here by the free voices, by the sponta-neous choice of the free people of Mississippi? No, sir; no. The sword of a military dic-tator has opened the way for his easy march to the Senate of the United States, and but for that sword and that dictator he never would have been presented here for a seat in this body . . .

The black race. I do not know why the law of the universe permitted that race to be brought here; and, above all, I do not know why the Yankees were made their instruments in bring them here, unless it was to curse and to create another devil for the white man! . . .

Mr. [James] NYE [R-Nev.]: I repudiate the idea that we shall refer this question to the Com-mittee on the Judiciary to determine whether a man who comes here commissioned from a great State shall be excluded because of his color! . . .

Sir, it seems to me that this is the crowning glory of a long series of measures. It seems to me this is the day long looked for, when we put into practical effect the theory that has existed as old as man. We say that men are brothers; whatever their color, all as sub-ject to the same law, and all are eligible to fill any place within the gift of the people . . .

Mr. DAVIS: To the honorable Senator who has just taken his seat I have a word to say. He has twitted me with my prejudice against color. Well, now, Mr. President, I would put it to the Senate's candor, if I were disposed to do so, but I am not, whether if he knew that every enfranchised negro would vote against him and his party he would be so anxious in his support of their rights as he is, I will not ask him to answer such a question; but in rela-tion to my prejudice, I will say that the honorable Senator and every Radical Senator in this body is as much prejudiced against that color as I am, if I have any prejudice at all. Now, I have not seen that the honorable Senator has ever waited upon some colored Dinah to a ball. I have not seen that he has ever extended any of his gallantries to them. I have not known a solitary Senator who is so clamorous in favor of the rights of the negro and the equality of the races, that he has made sedulous court to any one fair black swan, and offered to take her singing to the altar of Hymen. [Laughter.] . . .

Mr. [Simon] CAMERON [R-Pa.]: I remember very well, Mr. President, that just before the southern Senators left this Chamber, in 1861, I had a conversation with Mr. Jefferson Davis, in which he complained that the people of the North had interfered with the rights of the South, especially in taking from them their slaves. I remember that I said to him, "You of Mississippi have no right to complain; I do not think a single slaveholder in the whole State of Mississippi ever lost a slave in the way you speak of; you are too remote from the border to be interfered with in that way." The conversation continued some time. I said to him, "Sir, let me tell you that if you recede from here, the moment a gun has been fired against the flag of this country slavery ceases; and the logical conclusion after that will be that the slave will be recognized as a citizen; and he will come into the Halls of Congress; and I believe, in the justice of God, that a negro some day will come and occupy your seat." [Laughter.] I am glad to believe to-day that what I thought then might hap-pen in the future has come to pass . . .

Mr. WILSON: Mr. President, neither the Senate nor the country will be surprised that nearly three days have been spent in the consideration of the simple question of administering the oath to the Senator-elect from Mississippi. Senators upon the other side of the Cham-ber have avowed their opposition to the administration of that oath. The country will note it; the eight hundred thousand colored voters of the country will remember it; history will record it. We have heard much of dying in the last ditch. Here is that last ditch. This is the last battle. These lamentations, these wailings we now hear are the notes of the dying swan . . .

Now, sir, I am glad this Senator is here from the State of Mississippi; that he comes here as the representative of the black race . . . Their eyes are fixed upon him. They will remember these three days of debate. They will understand its significance, and so will their tried and trusted friends . . . When he takes his seat with us will be closed this great struggle of forty years. He will be an illustration of the power of the Constitution and the laws . . . By this act Mississippi, which nine years ago withdrew her delegation from Congress, raised the flag of revolt against the country, and undertook to establish a government founded on the crushed, palpitating, bruised hearts of a race in chains, will be represented in the Senate of the redeemed Republic by one in whose veins courses the blood of the African race.

Mr. [Eugene] CASSERLY [D-Calif.]: Mr. President, we have to thank the Senator from Massachusetts who last spoke [Mr. Wilson] for his remarks. Bitter, vituperative, taunting as they were toward those of us on this side of the Chamber who have exercised our right here of differing from him, we should be grateful to him for the frankness with which he spoke. He appeals to the eight hundred thousand black voters of the country to take note of what he says has occurred here during the past three days. He appeals to them for their votes and for their support for his own party, and against the Democratic party, which he seeks to hold responsible for the debate of those three days . . .

Mr. [Charles] SUMNER [R-Mass.]: For a long time it has been clear that colored persons must be Senators, and I have often so declared. This was only according to the irresistible logic of the situation, to say nothing of inherent right . . .

The vote on this question will be an historic event, marking the triumph of a great cause. From this time there can be no backward step. After prolonged and hard-fought battle, beginning with the Republic, convulsing Congress, and breaking out in blood, the primal truths declared by our fathers are practically recognized. All men are created equal, says the great Declaration, and now a great act attests this verity. To-day we make the Declaration a reality. For a long time a word only, it now becomes a deed. The Declaration was only half established by Independence. The greater duty remained behind. In assuring the Equal Rights of all we complete this work . . .

Mr. WILSON: In presenting the credentials of Mr. Revels I ask that they be read, and that the oaths of office be administered to him. I now make the motion that the oaths of office be administered to him . . .

The question being taken by yeas and nays resulted—yeas 48, nays 8.

The VICE PRESIDENT: The Senator-elect will present himself at the chair of the Vice President to take the oaths of office.

Mr. REVELS was escorted to the desk by Mr. WILSON, and the oaths prescribed by law having been administered to him, Mr. REVELS took his seat in the Senate.

Source: Congressional Globe, 41st Cong., 2d sess., February 23–25, 1870, 1503–1505, 1509–1510, 1514, 1544, 1561–1562, from the Library of Congress, http://memory.loc.gov/ammem/amlaw/lwcg.html.

Document 3.5 in Context
"A Bill Abolishing the Separate Colored Schools": The Failed Effort to Desegregate Public Schools in Washington, D.C.

A national ban on racial segregation in public schools was a goal of some Radical Republicans. Efforts to achieve that policy encountered significant social and political criticism, including arguments that public education properly fell in the bailiwick of state and local governments, not the federal government. While advocates of a ban succeeded in requiring the new constitutions of states readmitted to the Union, such as Mississippi, Virginia, Texas, South Carolina and Louisiana, to prohibit school segregation—at least on paper—they failed to win inclusion of such a provision in the Second Reconstruction Act of 1867, an 1870 bill to provide federal aid to the states to support public schools, the Amnesty Act of 1872, the Civil Rights Act of 1875 or in other Reconstruction-era legislation.

In 1871 advocates sought to use a proposed reform of the Washington, D.C., education system as a vehicle to mandate what were commonly called "mixed schools" in the nation's capital. At the time, the city had separate systems for black and white children, and both the House and Senate debated bills that contained desegregation provisions. The proposed Senate language read, "And no distinction on account of race, color, or previous condition of servitude shall be made in providing the means of education, or in the mode of education or treatment of pupils in such schools." The debate concerned whether to remove that provision. One Senate opponent of integration, Allen G. Thurman, D-Ohio, argued:

> Now it is proposed that we shall go one step further and say not only that Government shall exercise the power of taxing all men for the support of the common schools, disregarding all political opinions of the parents and the children, and disregarding all religious creeds too, but that it shall also disregard the marked differences that the Almighty himself has stamped upon the people. Sir, what is this but despotism? [23]

Sen. Hiram R. Revels, R-Miss., the only black senator (**Document 3.4**) and a member of both the Education and Labor Committee and District of Columbia Committee, was among those favoring the politically doomed provision. He took the floor immediately after Sen. Thomas W. Tipton, R-Neb., had advocated a separate-but-equal approach to public education. In his speech, Revels discussed the integrated schools he had visited in the North and placed school segregation into a broader social context.

Congress's failure to mandate integrated schools in the District of Columbia foreshadowed the U.S. Supreme Court's 1896 "separate-but-equal" decision in *Plessy v. Ferguson* (**Document 4.5**) and the contentious decades-long national battle to outlaw school segregation that would culminate in 1954 with *Brown v. Board of Education* in 1954 (**Document 5.9**).

<hr>

▬ Document 3.5 ▬
Sen. Hiram R. Revels, R-Miss., Speaks in Support of School Desegregation in Washington, D.C., February 8, 1871

Mr. REVELS: Mr. President, I rise to express a few thoughts on this subject. It is not often that I ask the attention of the Senate on any subject, but this is one on which I feel it to be my duty to make a few brief remarks.

In regard to the wishes of the colored people of this city I will simply say that the trustees of colored schools and some of the most intelligent colored men of this place have said to me that they would have before asked for a bill abolishing the separate colored schools and putting all children on an equality in the common schools if they had thought they could obtain it. They feared they could not; and this is the only reason why they did not ask for it before.

I find that the prejudice in this country to color is very great, and I sometimes fear that it is on the increase. For example, let me remark that it matters not how colored people behave themselves, how well they deport themselves, how intelligent they may be, how refined they may be—for there are some colored persons who are persons of refinement; this must be admitted—the prejudice against them is equally as great as it is against the most low and degraded colored man you can find in the streets of this city or in any other place.

This, Mr. President, I do seriously regret. And is this prejudice right? Have the colored people done anything to justify the prejudice against them that does exist in the hearts of so many white persons, and generally of one great political party in this country? Have they done anything to justify it? No, sir. Can any reason be given why this prejudice should be fostered in so many hearts against them, simply because they are not white? I make these remarks in all kindness, and from no bitterness of feeling at all . . .

Mr. President, let me here remark that if this amendment is rejected, so that the schools will be left open for all children to be entered into them irrespective of race, color, or previous condition, I do not believe the colored people will act imprudently. I know that in one or two of the late insurrectionary States the Legislatures passed laws establishing mixed schools, and the colored people did not hurriedly shove their children into those schools; they were very slow about it. In some localities where there was but little prejudice or opposition to it they entered them immediately; in others they did not do so. I do not believe that it is in the colored people to act rashly and unwisely in a matter of this kind.

But, sir, let me say that it is the wish of the colored people of this District, and of the colored people over this land, that this Congress shall not do anything which will increase that prejudice which is now fearfully great against them. If this amendment be adopted you will encourage that prejudice; and, perhaps, after the encouragement thus given, the next step may be to ask Congress to prevent them from riding in the street cars, or something like that. I repeat, let no encouragement be given to a prejudice against those who have done nothing to justify it, who are poor and perfectly innocent, as innocent as infants. Let nothing be done to encourage that prejudice. I say the adoption of this amendment will do so.

Mr. President, I desire to say here that the white race has no better friend than I. The southern people know this. It is known over the length and breadth of this land. I am true to my own race. I wish to see all done that can be done for their encouragement, to assist them in acquiring property, in becoming intelligent, enlightened, useful, valuable citizens. I wish to see this much done for them, and I believe God makes it the duty of this nation to do this much for them; but, at the same time, I would not have anything done which would harm the white race . . .

Let me ask, will establishing such schools as I am now advocating in this District harm our white friends? Let us consider this question for a few minutes. By some it is contended that if we establish mixed schools here a great insult will be given to the white citizens, and that the white schools will be seriously damaged. All that I ask those who assume this position to do is to go with me to Massachusetts, to go with me to some other New England States where they have mixed schools, and there they will find schools in as prosperous and flourishing a condition as any to be found in any part of the world. They will find such schools there; and they will find between the white and colored citizens friendship, peace, and harmony.

When I was on a lecturing tour in the State of Ohio, I went to a town, the name of which I forget. The question whether it would be proper or not to establish mixed schools had been raised there. One of the leading gentlemen connected with the schools in that town came to see me and conversed with me on the subject. He asked me, "Have you been to New England, where they mixed schools?" I replied, "I have, sir." "Well," said he, "please tell me this: does not social equality result from mixed schools?" "No, sir; very far from it," I responded. "Why;" said he, "how can it be otherwise?" I replied, "I will tell you how it can be otherwise, and how it is otherwise. Go to the schools and you see there white children and colored children seated side by side, studying their lessons, standing side by side, and reciting their lessons, and perhaps, in walking to school, they may walk along together; but that is the last of it. The white children go to their homes; the colored children go to theirs; and on the Lord's day you will see those colored children in colored churches, and the white children in white churches; and if an entertainment is given by a white family, you will see the white children there, and the colored children at entertainments given by persons of their own color." I aver, sir, that mixed schools are very far from bringing about social equality . . .

In the next place, I desire to say that school boards, and school trustees, and railroad companies, and steamboat companies are to blame for the prejudice that exists against the colored race, or to their disadvantage in those respects. Go to the depot here, now, and what will you see? A well-dressed colored lady, with her little children by her side, whom she has brought up intelligently and with refinement, as much so as white children, comes to the cars; and where is she shown to? Into the smoking car where men are cursing, swearing, spitting on the floor; where she is miserable, and where her little children have to listen to language not fitting for children who are brought up as she has endeavored to bring them up, to listen to.

Now, sir let me ask, why is this? Is it because the white passengers in a decent, respectable car are unwilling for her to be seated there? No, sir; not as a general thing. It is a rule that the company has established, that she shall not go there.

Let me give you a proof of this. Some years ago I was in the State of Kansas and wanted to go on a train of cars that ran from the town where I was to St. Louis, and this rule prevailed there, that colored people should go into the smoking car. I had my wife and children with me, and was trying to bring up my children properly, and I did not wish to take them into the smoking car. So I went to see the superintendent who lived in that town, and I addressed him thus: "Sir, I propose to start for St. Louis to-morrow on your road, and wish to take my family along; and I do not desire to go into the smoking car. It is all that I can do to stand it myself; and I do not wish my wife and children to be there and listen to such language as is uttered there by men talking, smoking, spitting, and rendering the car very foul; and I want to ask you now if I cannot obtain permission to take my family into a first-class car, as I have a first-class ticket?" Said he: "Sir, you can do so; I will see the conductor and instruct him to admit you." And he did admit me, and not a white passenger objected to it, not a white passenger gave any evidence of being displeased because I and my family were there . . .

Source: Congressional Globe, 41st Cong., 3d sess., February 8, 1871, 1059–1060, from the Library of Congress, http://memory.loc.gov/ammem/amlaw/lwcg.html.

Document 3.6 in Context
"Would to God, Sir, That the Fair Fame of the State of My Birth . . . Had Not Been Marred by the Wicked Deeds of These Outlaws": The Ku Klux Klan Act of 1871

In 1871 Congress passed the sixth of a series of post–Civil War civil rights laws, the Ku Klux Klan Act, which was intended to enforce Fourteenth Amendment guarantees of equal protection. The measure came amid lawless intimidation of African Americans in the South by the Ku Klux Klan, the Knights of the White Camellia and other secret supremacist groups. The Klan's 1868 statement of principles professed to "recognize . . . the supremacy of the Constitution [and] the Constitutional Laws thereof"; labeled the organization "an institution of Chivalry, Humanity, Mercy, and Patriotism"; and asked prospective members, "Are you opposed to negro equality, both social and political?" [24] Klan victims testified before a joint congressional committee in 1871 about terrorist incidents. For instance, Harriet Hernandes of South Carolina described for the committee how armed men had come to her house and whipped her and her fifteen-year-old daughter. The attack was retaliation because her husband had voted for Radical Republicans, who supported protecting the rights of African Americans.

The statute made it a "high crime," carrying potential prison terms and fines, for terrorist conspiracies to seek to overthrow the government, impede public officials, intimidate witnesses and jurors, threaten voters or obstruct justice. One provision referred explicitly to violators who "go in disguise upon the public highway or upon the premises of another for the purpose, directly or indirectly, of depriving any person or any class of persons of the equal protection of the laws." The act also empowered the president to use military force or "other means, as he may deem necessary for the suppression of such insurrection, domestic violence, or combinations." [25]

During the House debate, Rep. Joseph H. Rainey, an African American Republican from South Carolina, told his colleagues how, six years after the Civil War ended, "we can yet see the traces of the disastrous strife and the remains of disease in the body-politic of the South. In proof of this witness the frequent outrages perpetrated upon our loyal men. The prevailing spirit of the southerner is either to rule or to ruin." [26] On the other side, Rep. Abraham E. Garrett, a white Democrat from Tennessee, took the floor to denounce the proposal, both for bestowing "extraordinary powers" on the president and for further victimizing the South, which had already endured "the carpet-bagger and scalawag" and "military despots." [27] As the bill awaited final congressional action, the Charleston (S.C.) Daily Courier described the measure as "hostile legislation" and "one of false pretenses. It is a blow at free institutions, under carefully covered and deceiving words." [28]

In his floor speech in support of the legislation, Rep. Robert C. De Large, R-S.C., said both major parties shared some responsibility for conditions in the South but lambasted the Democrats for encouraging armed secret organizations and lawlessness.

Document 3.6
Rep. Robert C. De Large, R-S.C., Supports the Ku Klux Klan Act, April 6, 1871

The House having under consideration the bill (H.R. No. 320) to enforce the provisions of the fourteenth amendment to the Constitution of the United States, and for other purposes—

Mr. DE LARGE: Mr. Speaker, I had supposed that in the consideration of this matter of legislation for the South party lines would not have been so distinctly drawn, but that we would have at least first endeavored to ascertain whether or not there was any necessity for the legislation, and then decide what kind of legislation would be best. I say I did not expect that party lines would be drawn so distinctly while considering a matter of such grave import.

I believe that if there was a single gentleman upon the floor of this House who, before the commencement of this debate, doubted that lawlessness, confusion, and anarchy existed in some portions of the South, he is at least cured of that doubt by this time. Gentlemen upon both sides of the House have in their speeches acknowledged, and, by the evidence produced, proven to my satisfaction, and, I believe, to the satisfaction of a majority of the members of this House, that such a state of affairs does exist in some portions of the southern States.

I am free to say that none can bring the charge to my door of ever having acted in a manner that would be termed illiberal. I am also free to say that I, like other gentlemen upon the floor of this House, have the honor of representing a district in which no case of outlawry has ever occurred. Since the time of reconstruction no outrage has been committed in my district; and I say frankly to you to-day that until within the last few months no one upon the face of God's earth could have convinced me that any secret organization existed in my state for the purpose of committing murder, arson, or other outrages upon the lives, liberty, and property of the people; and, sir, I sincerely deplore and lament the abundance of that evidence which so plainly proves the existence of such an organization to-day. Would to God, sir, that the fair fame of the State of my birth, and which I have the honor in part to represent, had not been marred by the wicked deeds of these outlaws, who shrink from no cruelty, who spare no sex nor station to carry out their devilish purposes.

But, sir, I cannot shut my eyes to facts; I cannot refuse to yield my faith to tales of horror so fully proven; and I am thoroughly convinced that it is necessary to do something to cure these awful wrongs. I am free to admit that neither the Republicans of my State nor the Democrats of that State can shake their garments and say that they have had no hand in bringing about this condition of affairs. Both parties are responsible for it. As a member of the Republican party I may state, while demanding legislation on behalf of all the citizens there, that both parties to a considerable extent are responsible for this condition of things. Sir, it is necessary that we should legislate upon this subject. The Governor of my State has called upon the Executive of this country for assistance and protection. He has stated distinctly in that call that he is unable to preserve the public peace in some districts of that State. That is something which we must all admit. That is not denied by the Democrats of South Carolina. Some of them doubtless rejoice in this, because they can throw the blame, as they think, upon the administration of the State, which is in the hands of their political foes. It is not now the question, what is the cause which has brought about this condition of affairs? It is useless, except for the purpose of gaining partisan credit or fixing partisan odium, now to charge the blame here or there. But, sir, the naked facts stare us in the face, that this condition of affairs does exist, and that it is necessary for the strong arm of the law to inter-pose and protect the people in their lives, liberty, and property . . .

Mr. Speaker, when the Governor of my State the other day called in council the leading men of that State, to consider the condition of affairs there and to advise what measure would be best for the protection of the people, whom did he call together? The major por-tion of the men whom he convened were men resting under political disabilities imposed by the fourteenth amendment. In good faith I ask gentlemen on this side of the House, and gentlemen on the other side, whether it is reasonable to expect that these men should be interested, in any shape or form, in using their influence and best endeavors for the preser-vation of the public peace, when they have nothing to look for politically in the future? You say they should have the moral and material interest of their State at heart, though even always to be denied a participation in its honors. You may insist that the true patriot seeks no personal ends in the acts of patriotism. All this is true; but, Mr. Speaker, men are but men everywhere, and you ought not to expect of those whom you daily call by opprobrious epi-thets, whom you daily remind of their political sins, whom you persistently exclude from places of the smallest trust in the Government you have created, to be very earnest to coop-erate with you in the work of establishing and fortifying governments set up in hostility to the whole tone of their prejudices, their convictions, and their sympathies. What ought to be is one thing, what in the weakness and fallibility of human nature will be is quite another thing. The statesman regards the actual and acts upon it; the desirable, the possible, and even the probable furnishes but poor basis for political action.

If I had time I would enumerate some of the causes which have brought about the exist-ing state of affairs. I am not here to apologize for murderers; I am not here to defend any one who has committed any act of impropriety or wrong. But, sir, it is a fact, I do not give it as any or even the slightest excuse for the Democrats of my State, who, by their influence secretly or by joining in armed organization, have brought about this condition of affairs—it is a fact, unfortunately for us, that our party had done some things which give color to the charge that it is responsible to some degree for the evils which afflict us.

When I heard the gentleman from New York [Mr. Samuel COX, D] on Tuesday last hurl his shafts against the members of my race, charging that through their ignorance they had brought about these excesses, I thought he should have remembered that for the ignorance of that portion of the people he and his party associates are responsible, not those people themselves. While there may have been extravagance and corruption resulting from the plac-ing of improper men in official positions—and this is part of the cause of the existing state of things—these evils have been brought about by men identified with the race to which the gentleman from New York belongs, and not by our race.

Many men like himself, in order to get a better position in society or officially, came down among us, and, not knowing them, we placed them in position. If we, through ignorance, have placed them in position, have placed them in power, and they have deceived us, it is no fault of ours . . .

Source: Congressional Globe, 42d Cong., 1st sess., April 6, 1871, Appendix, 230–231, from the Library of Congress, http://memory.loc.gov/ammem/amlaw/lwcg.html.

Document 3.7 in Context
"I Must Here and Now Enter My Solemn Protest against Any Such Proposition": Opposition to Political Amnesty for Former Confederates

Amnesty for former Confederate civil and military officers was a contentious issue after the end of the Civil War. Under the lenient policies advocated by Presidents Abraham Lincoln and Andrew Johnson, white southerners who had backed secession quickly regained power, enacting "black codes." These regressive state laws abridged the political and property rights of the recently freed slaves under the guise of regulating such areas as employment, parenthood, marriage, entrepreneurship and vagrancy. The Fourteenth Amendment (**Document 3.2**), adopted in 1868, barred from federal and state civil and military offices anyone "who, having previously taken an oath, as a member of Congress, or as an officer of the United States, or as a member of any state legislature, or as an executive or judicial officer of any state, to support the Constitution of the United States," had nonetheless "engaged in insurrection or rebellion against the same, or given aid or comfort to the enemies thereof." The amendment also empowered Congress to "remove such disability" by a two-thirds vote.

The debate over whether to allow those men to again hold public office stretched on, and African American members of Congress were divided on the issue. Some, such as Sen. Hiram R. Revels, R-Miss., favored restoration of full political rights to those who took an oath of loyalty to the United States, as Revels explained in a May 17, 1870, speech:

> If you can find one man in the South who gives evidence that he is a loyal man, and gives that evidence in the fact that he has ceased to denounce the laws of Congress as unconstitutional, has ceased to oppose them and respects them and favors the carrying of them out, I am in favor of removing his disabilities; and if you can find one hundred men that the same is true of I am in favor of removing their disabilities.[29]

Taking the opposite position, Rep. Jefferson F. Long, R-Ga., argued against amnesty on February 1, 1871, suggesting that some white southerners were feigning loyalty as a means to regain power. Further, he said, "We propose to remove political disabilities from the very men who were the leaders of the Ku Klux Klan and have committed midnight outrages" in his state.[30] Rep. Robert B. Elliott, R-S.C., also made an impassioned speech against amnesty, which is excerpted here. Elliott appealed to sentiment against the Klan, called for justice for white and black southerners who had remained loyal to the Union and reminded his colleagues of the political self-interest of Republicans who hoped to retain control of the House in the 1872 election.

On May 22, 1872, after years of debate, Congress passed the General Amnesty Act by the necessary two-thirds margin. It provided

> that all political disabilities imposed by the third section of the fourteenth article of amendments of the Constitution of the United States are hereby removed from all persons whomsoever, except Senators and Representatives of the Thirty-Sixth and Thirty-Seventh Congresses, officers in the judicial, military, and naval service of the United States, heads of Departments, and foreign ministers of the United States.[31]

Thus the only southerners still blocked from holding state or federal offices were the approximately 500 former military officers, ambassadors, and members of Congress, the judiciary and the president's cabinet who had violated their oath to uphold the U.S. Constitution by switching their allegiance to the Confederacy.

<hr>

Document 3.7
Rep. Robert B. Elliott, R-S.C., Opposes Legislation Offering Amnesty to Former Confederates, March 14, 1871

Mr. ELLIOTT: Mr. Speaker, the House now has under consideration a bill of vast importance to the people of the section that I have the honor in part to represent. It is a proposition to remove the political disabilities of persons lately engaged in rebellion against the sovereignty of the Government of the United States. I believe, sir, that I have been noted in the State from which I come as one entertaining liberal views upon this very question; but, sir, at a time like this, when I turn my eyes to the South and see the loyal men of that section of the country suffering at the hands of the very men whom it is proposed to-day by this Forty-Second Congress of the United States to relieve of their political disabilities, I must here and now enter my solemn protest against any such proposition.

Sir, it is nothing but an attempt to pay a premium for disloyalty and treason at the expense of loyalty. I am not surprised that the gentleman from Kentucky [James BECK, D-Ky.] should introduce such a proposition here. It was due to the class of men that it is proposed to relieve that such a proposition should come from the gentleman from Kentucky and gentlemen upon that side of the House. I can appreciate the feeling of sympathy that the gentleman from Kentucky entertains for these men in the South who are to-day prohibited from holding Federal offices. They are his allies. They are his compatriots. They are to-day disfranchised simply because they rushed madly into rebellion against this, the best Government that exists under heaven, at their own distance, with the advice, and with the consent of such gentlemen as the gentleman from Kentucky. But when I hear gentlemen like the gentleman from Illinois, [Mr. John F. FARNSWORTH, R-Ill.] who spoke upon this question on Friday last, advance views and opinions such as that gentleman then advanced I must be allowed to express my surprise, ay, sir, my regret, that at this time such words should fall from the lips of a man whom I have been taught long to regard as one of those who are unflinching in their devotion to the cause of liberty and the preservation and maintenance of this great Government.

The gentleman from Illinois [Mr. FARNSWORTH] took occasion, in his argument on Friday last, to compare the condition of the man who is to-day disfranchised and the man who is allowed to hold office in the South. He drew a parallel between the disfranchised old man and his servant, or slave, who to-day holds office or may do so. He tells you that you should take into consideration the condition of this poor old man who, because he simply happened to join the rebellion after having taken an oath to support the Constitution of the Government of the United States, is prohibited from holding office, while his slave is allowed to hold office under the State and the United States governments. Ay, sir, the reason of this difference between the political status of the two is simply this: that while this old man, with whom the gentleman from Illinois sympathizes in his heart, was rebellious against the Government which had fostered and sustained and protected him, his slave was loyal to that Government, loyal to its Army, and loved its flag, which the man who had been reared under it, who had been fostered and protected by it, had learned only to despise. The difference is this; that while that "poor old man," of whom the gentleman speaks so sympathizingly, would only curse the Government, would only ill-treat and murder its loyal adherents, the slave was the friend of that Government, and the protector and defender of those who were endeavoring to uphold it.

In discussing this question, and as a reason why this bill should pass, the gentleman from Illinois [Mr. FARNSWORTH] stated that the removal of disabilities would do good, and that to maintain those disabilities could effect no good purpose. Sir, I say that this removal would be injurious, not only to the loyal men of the South, but to the Government itself. To relieve those men of their disabilities at this time would be regarded by the loyal men of the South as an evidence of the weakness of this great Government, and of an intention on the part of this Congress to foster the men who to-day are outraging the good and loyal people of the South. It would be further taken as evidence of the fact that this Congress desires to hand over the loyal men of the South to the tender mercies of the rebels who to-day are murdering and scourging the loyal men of the southern States.

The gentleman from Illinois, in his argument, was pleased to ask this question, which he proposed to answer himself: are these men who are disfranchised and prohibited from holding offices the men who commit the murders and outrages of which complaint is made? And his answer to that question was that they are not. But permit me to say to that gentleman that those men are responsible for every murder, responsible for every species of outrage that is committed in the South. They are men who, by their evil example, by their denunciations of Congress, by their abuse of the President of the United States, and of all connected with this Government, have encouraged, aided, and abetted the men who commit these deeds. They contribute to this state of things by their social influence, by their money and the money sent from the northern States—money furnished by Tammany Hall for the purpose of keeping up these outrages in order to insure a Democratic triumph in the South in 1872.

And I am here to-day to tell you, in the name of the loyal men of the South, that it is the fact that money is sent to the South by the Democratic party of the North to aid these men in keeping up this state of lawlessness for the purpose of overawing the loyal people there and preventing them from expressing their preferences at the ballot-box; that the number of arms shipped to the southern States, and which are brought there upon every New York steamer that arrives, is an evidence of the fact that these men who have the means, who have the influence, are responsible for these outrages, and not the poor, miserable tools who are their instruments in carrying them out.

I ask this House, I ask gentlemen on this side especially, whether they are willing to join hands with those who propose to-day to relieve these men of their disabilities? Are they willing to tell the loyal men of the South, whose only offense is that they have been true to the Government, that they have sustained Congress in its just and lawful acts, that they have maintained the authority of Congress; are gentlemen willing to tell these loyal men that Congress is not disposed to protect them, but, on the contrary, is willing at their expense to pay a premium for disloyalty?

Sir, I speak not to-day in behalf of the colored loyalists of the South alone. I wish it to be distinctly understood that I represent here a constituency composed of men whose complexions are like those of gentlemen around me as well as men whose complexions are similar to my own. I represent a constituency as loyal as the constituency of any other gentleman upon this floor. Those men appeal to you to-day to do justice to them. They ask you to protect them by legislation, instead of placing them under the heel of those men who have ruled in the South with an iron hand since the reconstruction acts were passed. Sir, I come here backed up by a majority as large probably as that of any gentleman on this floor; I come here representing a Republican district; but unless this Congress will aid those loyal men of the South, unless, instead of passing propositions of this kind, it will turn its attention, and that speedily, to the protection of property and life in the South, the Republican party in this House cannot expect the support of those whom I represent.

Source: Congressional Globe, 42d Cong., 1st sess., March 14, 1871, 102–103, from the Library of Congress, http://memory.loc.gov/ammem/amlaw/lwcg.html.

Document 3.8 in Context
"I Demand Simple Justice": P. B. S. Pinchback Argues for a Seat in Congress

Pinckney B. S. Pinchback, who was the Mississippi-born son of a freed slave and served as acting governor of Louisiana briefly in late 1872 and early 1873, holds a unique position in U.S. history: He attempted to simultaneously claim seats in both the House, based on the popular vote in the 1872 election, and in the Senate, based on an 1872 vote of the Louisiana legislature. In both instances, he argued that his official certificates of election gave him a *prima facie,* or "on its face," right to serve unless a later inquiry proved his election invalid. That was the traditional practice at the time, and a privilege often granted to white candidates in contested elections. However, Pinchback's efforts fell short for a combination of reasons tied to Louisiana's bitterly divisive Republican politics, racism, partisanship in Congress, a double standard and a feud with his former ally, ex-Louisiana governor Henry C. Warmoth.

Warmoth was impeached in 1872, primarily because Republican state legislators were outraged by his support for Democratic candidates in that year's election and for his opposition to the reelection of President Ulysses S. Grant, a Republican. At the time, Pinchback was lieutenant governor—a post he had assumed as state senate president when the incumbent died in office—and he stepped into the governor's office. He served only thirty-five days before William P. Kellogg, who was elected in a contentious and bitter contest, resigned his U.S. Senate seat and was sworn in as the new governor.

There was apparently an understanding that as a reward for supporting Kellogg's gubernatorial ambitions, Pinchback would be nominated for a House seat and, if Kellogg's legislative slate were elected, Pinchback would get Kellogg's vacant Senate seat. At the time, senators were elected by state legislatures. Following the November 1872 elections, Pinchback claimed that he had won the popular vote for the House seat, and Kellogg's legislative allies claimed victory as well.

The rival Republican faction did not agree, and two competing state legislatures met, each claiming to be the legitimate winner of the election. The one allied with Kellogg elected Pinchback to the Senate seat. Pinchback arrived under challenge in Washington, D.C., at the start of the term in March 1873; the Senate, however, refused to seat him and took until 1876 to formally reject his claim by a 32–29 vote. The Senate did award him $16,666, the amount he would have received for salary and mileage during the contested period. By the time the Senate voted on his claim, Democrats controlled the Louisiana legislature, which elected a Democrat to fill the balance of the term.

The dispute over Pinchback's election to the House, although shorter in duration, provided high drama and insights into political thought of the times, more so than the House's refusal in 1869 to seat African American claimant J. Willis Menard, also a Louisiana Republican (see **Document 8.1**). The 1872 election for an at-large House seat pitted Republican nominee Pinchback against George A. Sheridan, a Massachusetts-born former brigadier general of the militia on Warmoth's staff and a nominal Republican, who ran on a fusion ticket that united some Democrats with anti-Grant, anti-Kellogg Republicans. Most districts submitted two sets of returns, one favoring Sheridan and the other Pinchback. The House Committee on Elections was not persuaded that either Pinchback or Sheridan had established a right to the seat, and both contestants pled their case on the floor on June 8, 1874.

Pinchback spoke following a race-laden speech by Rep. Lucius Q. C. Lamar, D-Miss., who not only sided with Sheridan but also justified the southern states' decision to secede and attacked Reconstruction. Pinchback's arguments to be seated included the vote totals, electoral fraud, his longtime Republican credentials, hypocrisy among House members, the ascendancy of the Democratic Party and the legitimacy of Louisiana's government under Kellogg. He also noted that two northern-born white candidates, elected at the same time in Louisiana under questioned circumstances, had been seated based on the *prima facie* validity of their election certificates. Sheridan, for his part, argued fraud, the illegitimacy of the Kellogg government and the dysfunctionality of the Republican Party, while attacking Pinchback. Ultimately, the House sided with Sheridan, who won only a Pyrrhic victory because he was not sworn in until March 3, 1875, the last day of the two-year term.

▬ Document 3.8 ▬
P. B. S. Pinchback Argues for a Seat in Congress, June 8, 1874

Mr. PINCHBACK, (contestant.): Mr. Speaker, I appear under great disadvantage, from the fact that I have not had an opportunity of acquiring that knowledge which would enable me to indulge in such high flights of oratory as the distinguished gentleman who preceded me. The remarks of the gentleman from Mississippi [Mr. Lucius Q. C. LAMAR] were expressed with a beauty and a power such as I have scarcely ever heard before; but his argument I came near saying was full of sophistry. I will not, however, be so harsh as that; but it was the more calculated to deceive, because it seemed to come from a spirit of conviction and of honesty. Sir, there is no argument so fraught with evil, so fraught with the power of deception, as that which seems to emanate from an honest purpose and an honest conviction . . .

Mr. Sheridan comes before this House without any claim whatever. He has not even a *prima facie* case. He has no authority before this House, on the admission of the committee itself, to show that he is entitled to a seat, except so far as the report of the minority goes. And why? Why, sir, the only authority that he has brought here, in the language and by the admissions of the committee, is a certificate—from whom? From ex-Governor H. C. Warmoth, which certificate was made, it appears, on the 4th day of December, when the report of the committee abundantly shows that no promulgation of the vote for Congressmen at large of the State had been made until the 11th day of December—seven days thereafter . . .

Sir, I demand simple justice. I am not here as a beggar. I do not care so far as I am personally concerned whether you give me my seat or not. I will go back to my people and come here again; but I tell you to preserve your own consistency. Do not make fish of me while you have made flesh of everybody else . . .

But, Mr. Speaker, I have a clear and unimpeached party record. From the first day when you clothed me with the right to vote to the present, I have voted at every election the straight republican ticket. And what is more than that, I have done that in Louisiana which few men have done in any portion of this country . . .

I repeat, I am not arraigning the committee, because it has done just the thing I desired. I want a full investigation. But I do hope that no republican will for any reason allow himself to be prejudiced against admitting my claim at least on the *prima facie* case. I say that to do so is unmanly and unjust, not only to me as an individual but to the State of Louisiana. It is unjust to Louisiana, because as long as these contests are kept up both here and in the Senate I am made the instrument by which the sovereign State of Louisiana is deprived at this crisis of her life of two votes in the national Congress . . .

One other very important point was made by the gentleman from Mississippi. He stated that no party can sustain the iniquity, the rascality, the corruption, and the fraud of the southern governments. Now, have the members of this Congress, have the people of this country, ever stopped to consider what was after all the true cause of all the evils that are now the subject of complaint in the South. I know not what is true of the other Southern States, but I can state here, without fear of contradiction, that in the State of Louisiana the responsibility is largely upon the democracy. I can show here by irrefutable facts that in the first election held under the reconstruction acts the democracy of Louisiana . . . treated the reconstruction acts as a nullity, and in many portions of the State instigated and thrust forward the most ignorant colored men that could be found for election to the constitutional convention, with the view of making that convention a farce; and in order to make success certain they put no competing candidates in the field. Of course these men were elected, held seats in the convention, in which they voted with their friends. The constitution was framed, submitted to the people, and ratified. The illiterate men returned home successful statesmen, and from that day to this nearly every man in Louisiana has found himself every inch a statesman, and from this policy has arisen in a great degree the ignorance that has found its way into the public offices of our State.

But that is not the worst of it. In many instances this policy has been resorted to by white republicans when they have found a colored man with intelligence, cultivation, and sagacity, that they disliked and desired to destroy. The colored people have begun to understand this trick and to appreciate intelligence among their class, and to realize that they are held responsible for bad governments in the South; and I say if you will let them alone and only treat them with fair play, encourage them when they make an effort to do what is right, they will work out their own salvation. When they understand that all bad laws, all peculations, iniquities, frauds, and corruption which are charged upon these governments will at last be laid upon their shoulders and they will be held responsible for the same, in my judgment they will be swift to move in the right direction to rectify any wrongs which may exist by the selection of honest, intelligent, and competent men to administer the affairs of the Government . . .

Gentlemen on the other side have told us that the white people of the South accept the situation. I thought they had, at least I began to think they had, just before the last general election. It was believed at that time that I was inclined to favor the liberal republican movement in Louisiana. These gentlemen then began to find out that I was not so bad as they had been in the habit of charging. They had prior to this alleged that I was a fire-brand, that I was corrupt, and that I was everything that was bad; just as they say about republicans generally. But when they thought that I was inclined to democracy through the liberal republican party, and would accept a place on their ticket, the fusion convention of Louisiana tendered to me the unanimous nomination for Congress from the State at large on their ticket, the very place which was afterward given to General Sheridan. When they found that they could not get me, because I would not accept the position, not many days elapsed after this failure to compromise before they were restored to their former opinion . . .

. . . For notwithstanding I am a republican, working hard and earnestly always in the interests of the republican party, certain men in Louisiana who claim to be republicans have insidiously labored to destroy my power and influence in my State. I have been stabbed in the house of my friends. For two long years these men published a paper professedly republican, whose columns daily teemed with the vilest and bitterest denunciations of my character, only equaled, as I once told President Grant, by the New York Sun in its attacks upon him. The baneful influence of these assaults has overshadowed me in my contest in the Senate, and hangs like an ominous cloud over this body, and may prevent my obtaining a recognition *prima facie* to a seat upon the floor of this House . . .

But I shall hold those false friends responsible at home. I have skirmished heretofore; I shall fight hereafter. I do not believe you gentlemen will be biased by these reports, so far as your action upon this case is concerned, but they may affect your opinion of me as an individual, and I humbly beg your pardon if I have trespassed upon your time in introducing this personal feature. But when you consider the attitude I have been in for two years nearly—that I have been held up before the American people in a manner that two of your ablest and best men could not stand, still I live. I will be pardoned I suppose for having made these personal references, for you know it is a trying ordeal for any man to pass when he is held up for two years before the American press, especially if he is an aspirant for office, and as in my case claiming a seat in the Senate of the United States. You may be sure if he ever committed an indiscretion of any kind in all his life they will be certain to find it out and hurl it at him greatly magnified . . .

Source: Congressional Record, 43d Cong., 1st sess., June 8, 1874, Appendix, 431–434.

Document 3.9 in Context
"Has the Federal Government the Constitutional Right to Enforce by Suitable and Appropriate Legislation the Guarantees Herein Referred To?" The Civil Rights Act of 1875

The Civil Rights Act of 1875 was the last in a series of seven post-war statutes intended to guarantee equal rights. The first had been enacted in 1866 over President Andrew Johnson's veto. The 1875 statute—an act to protect all citizens, which in the context of political rights of the day meant male citizens, in their civil and legal rights—contained a broad reassertion of equal rights under the law, regardless of color, race, religion, political persuasion or place of birth. It included specific guarantees of equal rights to public accommodations and facilities, as well as the right to serve on juries, and it authorized criminal sanctions for violations. There was extensive debate over the bill. It became law more than a year after Rep. Robert B. Elliott, R-S.C., made one of the most ardent and articulate arguments for its passage. His

House speech delved into constitutional law, U.S. history, the racist motivations of some opponents of the bill and lingering intransigent attitudes toward equal rights. He especially criticized white Democratic representatives Alexander H. Stephens of Georgia, the former vice
president of the Confederacy, and James B. Beck of Kentucky, for their racially charged
remarks.

Elliott was not the only black lawmaker to take the floor to confront blatantly racist remarks
by white colleagues. For example, during one debate, Rep. Richard H. Cain, R-S.C., blasted
a white North Carolina Democrat who had called whites "the superior race" and labeled
blacks "barbarians" who should go to the West Indies or Africa.[32] One of the sharpest
moments in the debates came when Rep. John T. Harris, a white Democrat from Virginia, said
the bill

> seeks to enforce by law a doctrine which is not accepted by the minds nor received
> in the hearts of the people of the United States—that the negro in all things is the
> equal of the white man. And I say there is not one gentleman upon this floor who
> can honestly say he really believes that the colored man is created his equal.[33]

Rep. Alonzo J. Ransier, R-S.C., retorted, "I can," leading Harris to lash back, "Of course you
can; but I am speaking to the white men of the House." [34]

Rep. John R. Lynch, R-Miss., a former slave and Civil War veteran, was visible and vocal
on civil rights issues during his three terms in Washington. He had served as speaker of the
state house of representatives before coming to Congress, and his own campaign experiences
were marred by racism and fraud (**Document 8.2**). In February 1875 he took to the House
floor in defense of what would prove to be the last major civil rights legislation to pass Congress until 1957.

▭▭▭ Document 3.9 ▭▭▭
Rep. John R. Lynch, R-Miss., Speaks in Support of the Proposed
Civil Rights Bill, February 3, 1875

Mr. LYNCH: Mr. Speaker, I was not particularly anxious to take part in this debate, and
would not have done so but for the fact that this bill has created a great deal of discussion
both in and outside of the halls of Congress. In order to answer successfully the arguments
that have been made against the bill, I deem it necessary, if my time will allow me to do so,
to discuss the question from three stand-points—legal, social, and political . . .

CONSTITUTIONALITY OF THE BILL
It is a fact well known by those who are at all familiar with the history of our Government
that the great question of State rights—absolute State sovereignty as understood by the Cal-
houn school of politicians—has been a continuous source of political agitation for a great
many years. In fact, for a number of years anterior to the rebellion this was the chief topic
of political discussion. It continued to agitate the public mind from year to year and from
time to time until the question was finally settled upon the field of battle. The war, however,
did not result in the recognition of what may be called a centralized government, nor did it
result in the destruction of the independent functions of the several States, except in certain particulars. But it did result in the recognition, and I hope the acceptance, of what may
be called a medium between these two extremes; and this medium position or liberal policy

has been incorporated in the Federal Constitution through the recent amendments to that instrument . . .

. . . What are those particulars wherein the fourteenth amendment confers upon the Federal Government additional powers which it did not have before? The right to prevent distinctions and discriminations between the citizens of the United States and of the several States whenever such distinctions and discriminations are made on account of race, color, or previous condition of servitude; and that distinctions and discriminations made upon any other ground than these are not prohibited by the fourteenth amendment . . .

But there are some democrats, and if I am not mistaken the gentleman from Georgia [Mr. Alexander H. STEPHENS] is one among the number, who are willing to admit that the recent amendments to the Constitution guarantee to the colored citizens all of the rights, privileges, and immunities that are enjoyed by white citizens. But they say that it is the province of the several States, and not that of the Federal Government, to enforce these constitutional guarantees. This is the most important point in the whole argument. Upon its decision this bill must stand or fall . . . The question that now presents itself is, has the Federal Government the constitutional right to enforce by suitable and appropriate legislation the guarantees herein referred to?

. . . The constitutional right of Congress to pass this bill is fully conceded by the Supreme Court . . .

. . . Any State can, without violating the fourteenth or fifteenth amendments and the provisions of this bill, prohibit any one from voting, holding office, or serving on juries in their respective States, who cannot read and write, or who does not own a certain amount of property, or who shall not have resided in the State for a certain number of months, days, or years. The only thing these amendments prevents them from doing in this respect is making the color of a person or the race with which any person may be identified a ground of disqualification from the enjoyment of any of these privileges . . .

CIVIL RIGHTS AND SOCIAL EQUALITY

. . . That the passage of this bill can in any manner affect the social status of any one seems to me to be absurd and ridiculous. I have never believed for a moment that social equality could be brought about even between persons of the same race. I have always believed that social distinctions existed among white people the same as among colored people. But those who contend that the passage of this bill will have a tendency to bring about social equality between the races virtually and substantially admit that there are no social distinctions among white people whatever, but that all white persons, regardless of their moral character, are the social equals of each other; for if by conferring upon colored people the same rights and privileges that are now exercised and enjoyed by whites indiscriminately will result in bringing about social equality between the races, then the same process of reasoning must necessarily bring us to the conclusion that there are no social distinctions among whites, because all white persons, regardless of their social standing, are permitted to enjoy these rights . . . I cannot believe that gentlemen on the other side of the House mean what they say when they admit as they do, that the immoral, the ignorant, and the degraded of their own race are the social equals of themselves and their families. If they do, then I can only assure them that they do not put as high an estimate upon their own social standing as respectable and intelligent colored people place upon theirs; for there are hundreds and thousands of white people of both sexes whom I know to be the social inferiors of respectable and intelligent colored people. I can then assure that portion of my democratic friends on the other side of the House whom I regard as my social inferiors that if at any time I should meet any one of you at a hotel and occupy a seat at the same table with you, or the same seat in a car with you, do not think that I have thereby accepted you as my social equal . . .

No, Mr. Speaker, it is not social rights that we desire. We have enough of that already. What we ask is protection in the enjoyment of *public* rights. Rights which are or should be accorded to every citizen alike. Under our present system of race distinction a white woman of a questionable social standing, yes, I may say, of an admitted immoral character, can go to any public place or upon any public conveyance and be the recipient of the same treatment, the same courtesy, and the same respect that is usually accorded to the most refined and virtuous; but let an intelligent, modest, refined colored lady present herself and ask that the same privileges be accorded to her that have just been accorded to her social inferior of the white race, and in nine cases out of ten, except in certain portions of the country, she will not only be refused, but insulted for making the request . . .

CIVIL RIGHTS FROM A POLITICAL STAND-POINT

I now come to the most important part of my subject—civil rights from a political standpoint. In discussing this branch or the subject, I do not deem it necessary to make any appeal to the republican members whatever in behalf of this bill. It is presumed, and correctly, too, I hope, that every republican member of the House will vote for this bill. The country expects it, the colored people ask it, the republican party promised it, and justice demands it . . .

But is has been suggested that it is not necessary for me to make an appeal to the democratic, conservative, or liberal republican members in behalf of this measure; that they will go against it to a man. This may be true, but I prefer to judge them by their acts. I will not condemn them in advance. But I desire to call the attention of the democratic members of the House to one or two things in connection with the history of their organization. Your party went before the country in [the elections of] 1872 with a pledge that it would protect the colored people in all of their rights and privileges under the Constitution, and to convince them of your sincerity you nominated as your standard-bearer [Horace Greeley] one who had proved himself to be their life-long friend and advocate. But the colored people did not believe that you were sincere, and consequently did not trust you. As the promise was made unconditionally, however, their refusal to trust you does not relieve you from the performance of the promise. Think for a moment what the effect of your votes upon this bill will be. If you vote in favor of this measure, which will be nothing more than redeeming the promises made by you in 1872, it will convince the colored people that they were mistaken when they supposed that you made the promise for no other purpose than to deceive them. But if you should vote against this bill, which I am afraid you intend to do, you will thereby convince them that they were not mistaken when they supposed that you made the promise for no other purpose than to deceive them . . .

Source: Congressional Record, 43d Cong., 2d sess., February 3, 1875, 943–947.

Document 3.10 in Context
"Force, Fraud, and Intimidation Were Used Generally and Successfully": Investigating the 1875 Mississippi Elections

Angered by the results of the 1875 election that restored Democrats to power in Mississippi—and that foreshadowed the resurgence of Democratic political power across the South—the Republican-controlled U.S. Senate voted primarily along party lines to investigate allegations of fraud, as well as charges of violence against and intimidation of black voters in that state. The authorizing resolution by Sen. Oliver H. P. T.Morton, R-Ind., cited "the late alleged killing of people and outrages committed near the Mississippi and Louisiana line, and at or near Bayou Tunica, and on Red River." [35] The inquiry took place in uncertain political times: a year earlier, Democrats had recaptured the House, and Senate Republicans worried about losing the upcoming 1876 presidential election.

In calling for the inquiry, African American senator Blanche K. Bruce, R-Miss., said the conduct of the election had "affected not merely the fortunes of partisans—as the same were necessarily involved in the defeat or success of the respective parties to the contest—but put in question and jeopardy the sacred rights of the citizens." [36] Not incidentally, the election created Democratic dominance of the state legislature, destroying Bruce's own prospects for a second Senate term during an era when state legislatures rather than voters elected U.S. senators. Rep. John R. Lynch was the only incumbent Republican member of the House to win reelection from Mississippi in 1875.

A special Senate committee of three Republicans and two Democrats held hearings in Washington, D.C., and Mississippi; 162 witnesses testified, most of them Republicans or African Americans. Among them was former senator Hiram R. Revels, R-Miss. (**Document 3.4**), whom the Senate report described as "colored" and who testified that he was "satisfied that the canvass was characterized by order and quiet" in his county.[37] His testimony supported the Democrats' claim that the election had been fairly and properly conducted.

Not surprisingly, the rival sides reached sharply different conclusions. The Republican majority concluded that the evidence "will fully support the allegation that force, fraud, and intimidation were used generally and successfully in the political canvass of 1875," and that the election results put political control into the hands of those whose "common purpose is to deprive the negroes of the free exercise of the right of suffrage." Their report recommended new laws to protect the rights of citizens and to deny congressional representation to "states in anarchy, or wherein the affairs are controlled by bodies of armed men," but Congress took no such steps.[38] On the other side, the minority report labeled the investigation as an "inquisition" and accused Republicans of relying on unverified hearsay, opinion and "wild rumor," commenting that "the great bulk of the testimony which has been taken is such as would not be received in any court of justice in this country to convict the meanest culprit of the pettiest offense." [39]

Document 3.10
Mississippi in 1875, Report of the Senate Select Committee to Inquire into the Mississippi Election of 1875, August 7, 1876

. . . The testimony will fully support the allegation that force, fraud, and intimidation were used generally and successfully in the political canvass of 1875.

But before proceeding to a detailed statement of the facts and conclusions sustained and warranted by the proof, the committee think it proper to refer to the suggestions and excuses offered in justification of the outrages committed.

It has been alleged that [Republican] Governor [Adelbert] Ames was an unfit person to hold the office to which he was elected in the year 1873; but, on the contrary, the committee find from the evidence, as well as from general report in Mississippi, that Governor Ames was not only not amenable to any just charge affecting his personal integrity, his character as a public officer, or his ability for the duties of chief magistrate of that State, but that his fitness in all these particulars was sustained by the testimony of those who were not in accord with him politically . . .

The evidence submitted tends strongly to show, what cannot be denied, that there were many persons in office in the State of Mississippi, especially in elective offices, in the several counties, who were either incapable or dishonest; and there were a few of the same character connected with the State government. The conduct of these persons, however, was not approved by the governor nor by the masses of the republican party.

Complaints and charges against a class of persons called "carpet-baggers" are frequent in the depositions of witnesses opposed to the republican party in the State. It is to be admitted that a small number of the immigrants from other States misused the confidence of the black people, secured office, and betrayed the trusts confided to them. But the number of such persons, compared to the whole number of immigrants, was very small; and it is but just to say that the great majority are intelligent, upright, and brave men from the North who are entirely incorruptible, and who, in peril of their lives, are now struggling against serious odds to maintain their political opinions and to secure a just administration of the Government . . .

It is to be observed, also, that previous to the war taxes were not levied for the support of schools in Mississippi; indeed, there was no system of public instruction; and that since the war school-houses have been erected in all parts of the State for the education of the children of both races, and large sums of money have been expended annually for the maintenance of schools, including schools for training teachers . . .

It is also alleged in justification of the acts of intimidation, and of the crimes committed during the canvass and at the election, that Governor Ames had organized, or attempted to organize, a force, termed the negro militia . . .

Some of the officers selected by him were native-born white citizens who had served in the late war on the side of the confederates, and he solicited and accepted recruits from the white as well as from the black population . . .

This effort on the part of the governor, it is now claimed, was the occasion seized by the democrats for organizing and arming themselves, ostensibly to resist the black militia; but, in fact, . . . it became the means by which the colored inhabitants and the white republicans of the State were overawed, intimidated, and deprived of their rights as citizens . . .

These organizations were the instruments also by which numerous murders were committed upon persons who were then active, or who had been active, in the republican party . . .

The outrages perpetrated by the white people in the canvass and on the day of election find no justification whatever in the acts or the policy of Governor Ames concerning the State militia.

The effort on his part to organize the militia for the preservation of the public peace seems to the committee to have been not only lawful but proper, and the course of the democrats in organizing and arming themselves to resist the governor in his efforts to preserve the public peace was unlawful . . .

Nor do these outrages find any excuse in the statement made repeatedly by witnesses, that the negroes were organizing or threatened or contemplated organizing themselves into military bands for the destruction of the white race. The evidence shows conclusively that there were not only no such organizations, but that the negroes were not armed generally; that those who had arms were furnished with inferior and second-hand weapons, and that their leaders, both religious and political, had discountenanced a resort to force. Many rumors were current among the whites that the negroes were arming and massing in large bodies, but in all cases these rumors had no basis . . .

On the other hand, it is to be said, speaking generally, that a controlling part, and, as we think, a majority, of the white democratic voters of the State were engaged in a systematic effort to carry the election, and this with a purpose to resort to all means within their power, including on the part of some of them the murder of prominent persons in the republican party, both black and white . . .

(1.) The committee find that the young men of the State, especially those who reached manhood during the war, or who have arrived at that condition since the war, constitute the nucleus and the main force of the dangerous element . . .

(2.) There was a general disposition on the part of white employers to compel the laborers to vote the democratic ticket . . .

(3.) Democratic clubs were organized in all parts of the State, and the able-bodied members were also organized generally into military companies and furnished with the best arms that could be procured in the country. The fact of their existence was no secret, although persons not in sympathy with the movement were excluded from membership . . .

(8.) The committee find that in several of the counties the republican leaders were so overawed and intimidated, both white and black, that they were compelled to withdraw from the canvass those who had been nominated, and to substitute others who were named by the democratic leaders, and that finally they were compelled to vote for the ticket so nominated, under threats that their lives would be taken if they did not do it . . .

(9.) The committee find that the candidates, in some instances, were compelled, by persecution or through fear of bodily harm, to withdraw their names from the ticket and even to unite themselves ostensibly with the democratic party . . .

(12.) The committee find in several cases, where intimidation and force did not result in securing a democratic victory, that fraud was resorted to in conducting the election and in counting the votes . . .

(13.) The evidence shows that the civil authorities have been unable to prevent the outrages set forth in this report, or to punish the offenders . . .

(17.) The evidence shows, further, that the State of Mississippi is at present under the control of political organizations composed largely of armed men whose common purpose is to deprive the negroes of the free exercise of the right of suffrage and to establish and maintain the supremacy of the white-line democracy, in violation alike of the constitution of their own State and of the Constitution of the United States.

The events which the committee were called to investigate by the order of the Senate constitute one of the darkest chapters in American history . . .

Mississippi, with its fertile soil, immense natural resources, and favorable commercial position, is in fact more completely excluded from the influence of the civilization and capital of the more wealthy and advanced States of the Union than are the distant coasts of China and Japan . . .

. . . The nation cannot witness with indifference the dominion of lawlessness and anarchy in a State, with their incident evils and a knowledge of the inevitable consequences. It owes a duty to the citizens of the United States residing in Mississippi, and this duty it must perform. It has guaranteed to the State of Mississippi a republican form of government, and this guarantee must be made good.

The measures necessary and possible in an exigency are three:

1. Laws may be passed by Congress for the protection of the rights of citizens in the respective States.

2. States in anarchy, or wherein the affairs are controlled by bodies of armed men, should be denied representation in Congress.

3. The constitutional guarantee of a republican form of government to every State will require the United States, if these disorders increase or even continue, and all milder measures shall prove ineffectual, to remand the State to a territorial condition, and through a system of public education and kindred means of improvement change the ideas of the inhabitants and reconstruct the government upon a republican basis . . .

Source: Senate Select Committee to Inquire into the Mississippi Election of 1875, *Mississippi in 1875,* 44th Cong., 1st sess., 1876, S. Rep. 527, IX–X, XII–XV, XXVII–XXIX, from the University of Michigan Digital Library Production Service, http://quod.lib.umich.edu/m/moagrp/.

Document 3.11 in Context
"They Have Placed Responsibility for All Questionable Acts upon Their Dead Associates": The Failure of the Freedman's Savings and Trust Company

Created in March 1865 of altruistic—even paternalistic—intentions to assist and encourage thrift and savings among freed slaves, black military veterans and their descendants, the Freedman's Savings and Trust Company started strong but eventually disintegrated into fiscal ruin. At its height, the congressionally chartered bank expanded to thirty-three branches, including one in Washington, D.C., and its 72,000 patrons put an aggregate of $57 million into savings during its ten years of active operation. The bank's failure in 1874 came at a devastating cost to its depositors.

A yearlong Senate select committee investigation chaired by Sen. Blanche K. Bruce, R-Miss., identified a variety of causes leading to the bank's collapse, including Congress's initial failure to legislate criminal sanctions for breach of trust by bank officers and trustees engaged in financial improprieties such as self-dealing and conflicts of interest, disregard for depositors' well-being, financial recklessness, disregard for legal and regulatory mandates, unauthorized and uncollateralized loans, fraud, mismanagement and lack of oversight. The report named wrongdoers and chastised other governmental units for failing to prosecute criminal misconduct. In doing so, it provided a nineteenth-century model for future congressional panels to follow in subsequent investigations of war profiteering, organized crime, high-level corruption and voting rights abuses.

In 1874 Congress passed remedial legislation to reorganize bank operations at the urging of Frederick Douglass, who was serving as the bank's president by then. However, even the congressional attempt to wind up the bank's affairs under new management proved excessively costly, as the committee noted in the report that Bruce presented to the Senate in April 1880. The committee estimated the damage to depositors to that point at $1.5 million; by the time the bank closed in 1884, the losses were calculated at almost $3 million across about 61,000 depositors, most of them black. The next year, Congress empowered the Comptroller of the Currency to take over the bank, marshal any assets, collect whatever loans were still collectible and wrap up the liquidation.

After Bruce left the Senate at the end of his term in 1881, proposals to reimburse the depositors—including legislation by Rep. John R. Lynch, R-Miss.—and lobbying by a series of Comptrollers of the Currency failed. As an 1886 article in the *Cleveland* (Ohio) *Gazette,* an African American weekly newspaper, noted, "Congress couldn't see it and the bill is still due with large prospects of remaining in that condition unless some of the leeches who helped to extract the life blood from the *deceased* make up a purse between them for that amount." [40] Futile compensation proposals continued until 1920, forty years after the Bruce committee report.

Bruce's investigation marked the first time an African American member of Congress chaired a committee. As of mid-2007, this has not been repeated in the Senate.

▬▬ Document 3.11 ▬▬
Senate Select Committee Report on Freedman's Savings and Trust Company, April 2, 1880

Mr. [Blanche K.] BRUCE, from the Select Committee on the Freedman's Savings and Trust Company, submitted the following REPORT: . . .

Resolved, That the Select Committee on the Freedman's Savings and Trust Company, appointed by resolution of the Senate of April 7, 1879, is authorized and directed to investigate the affairs of said savings and trust company and its several branches, to ascertain and report to the Senate all matters relating to the management of the same and the cause or causes of failure, with such other facts relating thereto as may be important to a full understanding of the management and present condition of the institution, and to a more economical administration and speedy adjustment of its affairs . . .

Your committee, under the authorization and direction of the preceding resolution, have considered carefully the affairs and managements of the Freedman's Savings and Trust Company, and respectfully report the results of their investigation, together with the testimony and other evidence upon which their conclusions are based.

The resolution directing this investigation proposed an inquiry into the affairs of this institution for the purpose of ascertaining the causes of its failure under the management provided in the original charter, and, also, to ascertain the condition of the institution as administered by the commissioners appointed under the act of 1874, with the view to reduce the present cost of management, and the speedy and final adjustment of the affairs of the bank . . .

Pending the continuance of the civil war, and soon after the colored race became a considerable element in the military forces of the United States, the safe-keeping of the pay and bounty moneys of this class became a matter of great importance to them and their families, and to meet this exigency, military savings banks were created at Norfolk, Va., and Beaufort, S. C., centers at that time of colored troops. At the close of the war the emancipation of this race increased the necessity of some financial agency to meet their economic and commercial wants, and in response to this demand, taking suggestions and counsel of the expedients that military experience had suggested for the benefit of this people, the National Congress incorporated, March 1865, the Freedman's Savings and Trust Company.

As its name imports, the institution was designed to perform for a particular class of our people the simple but important functions of a savings bank; its declared purpose being "to receive on deposit such sums of money as may from time to time be offered therefor, by or on behalf of persons heretofore held in slavery in the United States or their descendants, and investing the same in the stocks, bonds, treasury notes, or other securities of the United States" . . .

Until 1868 the spirit and letter of the charter seemed to have been recognized very faithfully by the trustees and officers who administered the affairs of the company, and until the beginning of 1870 there do not appear to have been in the administration any serious and practical departures from the kindly and judicious programme indicated in the act creating the institution.

In May, 1870, an amendment to the charter was secured, which embodied a radical and what subsequent events proved to be a dangerous and hurtful change in the character of securities in which the trustees were empowered to invest the deposits of the institution . . .

If the trustees who conducted this bank had been men of great discretion, great integrity, and entire devotion to the purpose of the enterprise under their control, there is no reason why either loss to the depositors should have followed or disaster to the institution should have come. Even the crisis of 1873 could not have affected this institution if it had been honestly and intelligently conducted as originally projected. We are to look, therefore, for the causes of failure to other than the absence of these protective clauses to the charter.

The trustees, after 1870, evidently either misapprehended the declared purposes of the charter relative to the character of the available fund, or else they intentionally perverted and violated the charter requirements . . .

Section 15 of the charter contemplates and provides that the president, vice-president, and subordinate agents of the company "shall give security for their fidelity and good conduct while in office." It does not appear from the testimony that a bond was generally exacted, or that when given it was adequate . . . It is a tax on our credulity to expect us to believe that sane and honest men could so trifle with a serious trust and so recklessly administer the funds of others.

Section 12 declares that "no president, vice-president, trustee, or servant of the corporation shall, directly or indirectly, borrow the funds of the corporation or its deposits, or in any manner use the same or any part thereof, except to pay necessary expenses."

There are instances in which this provision has been disregarded directly; repeated instances in which members of a stock company, while holding office in the Freedman's Bank, would negotiate loans for the companies to which they belonged from said bank . . .

In maintenance of the conclusions that we have reached in this connection, and as illustrative of the questionable management of the bank, we call attention in some detail to several out of many of the transactions to which we have referred . . .

The men who appear to have been most prominent in the questionable transaction that we have detailed, and in others, were . . . all members of the board of trustees, and a majority of them at one time or another members of some one of the administrative committees of the bank; and Messrs. Eaton and Stickney, the actuaries of the bank, who, under its loose administration and despite the charter, seemed to have exercised as much power in the management of the institution as the trustees themselves.

Mr. Alvord, the president from 1868 to 1873; Mr. Eaton, the actuary until 1872, and Mr. Huntington, a member of the finance committee, are now dead, and the parties sharing their responsibility, so far as they have come before your committee to be questioned on their official acts, have pleaded forgetfulness or ignorance of the violated law, or good intentions and philanthropic motives, and, all other excuses failing, they have placed responsibility for all questionable acts upon their dead associates . . .

J. C. KENNEDY LOAN.

A loan was made to J. C. Kennedy, March 27, 1872, for $12,000, on $20,000 second-mortgage bonds of the Seneca Sandstone Company. This loan was made just after the questionable transactions between the bank, the Seneca Stone Company, and Kilbourn and Evans, and made on the same kind of worthless security. This loan has never been paid, and the question of settlement is now pending in the courts on suit brought by the commissioners. The probabilities are that this amount will be lost to the bank.

EVAN LYONS LOAN.

The loan of $34,000 to Evan Lyons, made on the 23d of July, 1872, has caused a loss of $25,000 to the bank. The collateral given consisted of 60 acres of land, known as the Lyons mill seat, in Washington County. Lyons made four applications for loans of smaller amounts, offering in each case the same collateral. Upon presentation of the application to the finance committee it was repeatedly rejected, and on the 8th of May, 1872, it was rejected absolutely. Yet on the 23d of the July following the same finance committee approved this loan to him for $34,000 . . .

R. I. FLEMING LOANS.

The loans made to R. I. Fleming aggregated about $224,000. A balance is still due from Fleming of $35,026.98. The securities taken for the loans made to Fleming were often insufficient, consisting mainly of approved bills against the District of Columbia, Young Men's Christian Association stock, and collaterals of that character, and in some cases no security was taken. Fleming is now bankrupt, and there is very little prospect of the Freedman's Savings and Trust Company ever realizing anything on his indebtedness. The estimated loss on the Fleming loans will aggregate $32,000 . . .

Source: Senate Select Committee on the Freedman's Savings and Trust Company, *Report to Accompany Bills S. 711 and S. 1581,* 46th Cong., 2d sess., 1880, S. Rep. 440, I–VI, VII–IX.

Document 3.12 in Context
"The Colored People of the United States Feel To-day as if They Had Been Baptized in Ice Water": The Supreme Court's Civil Rights Decision of 1883

Just as the 1875 Civil Rights Act (**Document 3.9**) marked the end of congressional activism on civil rights for nearly ninety years, the 1883 U.S. Supreme Court decision invalidating most of that statute signaled a decades-long judicial hostility to using federal legislation as a vehicle to ensure equal protection under the law. The question of the statute's constitutionality came to the Court through a combination of cases from the North and South: four involved criminal prosecutions for discrimination against black patrons in theaters in California and New York and in hotel accommodations in Missouri and Kansas, while the fifth was a Tennessee civil suit alleging that a railroad illegally refused to allow an African American woman to ride in the ladies' car.

In its decision, the Court struck down all the act's provisions providing federal protection for race-neutral access to public accommodations and facilities; it let stand only the prohibition against race-based discrimination in jury service. Writing for the eight-member majority, Justice Joseph P. Bradley said Congress lacked constitutional authority to enact the invalidated provisions, which fell within the regulatory powers of the states. The Court held that the Thirteenth Amendment (**Document 2.8**) applies only to "slavery and involuntary servitude" and concluded that a private individual's or company's refusal to provide equal accommodations in inns, public transportation and places of public amusement does not impose any badge of slavery or involuntary servitude. The Court further held that the Fourteenth Amendment (**Document 3.2**) was not intended to protect individual rights against individual violations, only to nullify any state laws or actions that impaired citizens' rights and privileges. The sole dissenter, Justice John M. Harlan, found the statute constitutionally sound.

In an October 20, 1883, *New York Globe* editorial, black journalist and civil rights advocate T. Thomas Fortune wrote:

> The colored people of the United States feel to-day as if they had been baptized in ice water . . . Public meetings are being projected far and wide to give expression to the common feeling of disappointment apprehension for the future . . . The Supreme Court now declares that we have no civil rights—declares that railroad corporations are free to force us into smoking cars or cattle cars; that hotel keepers are free to make us walk the streets at night; that theatre managers can refuse us admittance to their exhibitions for the amusement of the public—it has reaffirmed the infamous decision of the infamous Chief Justice [Roger B.] Taney [in the *Dred Scott* case; see Document 1.14] that "a black man has no rights that a white man is bound to respect." [41]

Document 3.12
U.S. Supreme Court Decision in the *Civil Rights Cases*, October 15, 1883

"THE CIVIL RIGHTS CASES"
UNITED STATES v. STANLEY
UNITED STATES v. RYAN
UNITED STATES v. NICHOLS
UNITED STATES v. SINGLETON
ROBINSON and wife v. MEMPHIS & CHARLESTON R. CO.

BRADLEY, J.

These cases are all founded on the first and second sections of the act of congress known as the "Civil Rights Act," passed March 1, 1875, entitled "An act to protect all citizens in their civil and legal rights." Two of the cases, those against Stanley and Nichols, are indictments for denying to persons of color the accommodations and privileges of an inn or hotel; two of them, those against Ryan and Singleton, are . . . for denying to individuals the privileges and accommodations of a theater, the information against Ryan being for refusing a colored person a seat in the dress circle of Maguire's theater in San Francisco; and the indictment against Singleton being for denying to another person, whose color is not stated, the full enjoyment of the accommodations of the theater known as the Grand Opera House in New York . . . The case of Robinson and wife against the Memphis & Charleston Railroad Company was . . . to recover the penalty of $500 given by the second section of the act; and the gravamen was the refusal by the conductor of the railroad company to allow the wife to ride in the ladies' car, for the reason, as stated in one of the counts, that she was a person of African descent . . .

Has congress constitutional power to make such a law? . . . The power is sought, first, in the fourteenth amendment, and the views and arguments of distinguished senators, advanced while the law was under consideration, claiming authority to pass it by virtue of that amendment, are the principal arguments adduced in favor of the power . . .

The first section of the fourteenth amendment,—which is the one relied on,—after declaring who shall be citizens of the United States, and of the several states, is prohibitory in its character, and prohibitory upon the states . . . It is state action of a particular character that is prohibited. Individual invasion of individual rights is not the subject-matter of the amendment. It has a deeper and broader scope. It nullifies and makes void all state legislation, and state action of every kind, which impairs the privileges and immunities of citizens of the United States, or which injures them in life, liberty, or property without due process of law, or which denies to any of them the equal protection of the laws . . .

. . . The last section of the amendment invests congress with power to enforce it by appropriate legislation. To enforce what? To enforce the prohibition. To adopt appropriate legislation for correcting the effects of such prohibited state law and state acts, and thus to render them effectually null, void, and innocuous . . . It does not invest congress with power to legislate upon subjects which are within the domain of state legislation; but to provide modes of relief against state legislation, or state action, of the kind referred to . . .

If this legislation is appropriate for enforcing the prohibitions of the amendment, it is difficult to see where it is to stop. Why may not congress, with equal show of authority, enact a code of laws for the enforcement and vindication of all rights of life, liberty, and property? If it is supposable that the states may deprive persons of life, liberty, and property without due process of law, (and the amendment itself does suppose this,) why should not congress proceed at once to prescribe due process of law for the protection of every one of these fundamental rights, in every possible case, as well as to prescribe equal privileges in inns, public conveyances, and theaters . . .

In this connection it is proper to state that civil rights, such as are guaranteed by the constitution against state aggression, cannot be impaired by the wrongful acts of individuals, unsupported by state authority in the shape of laws, customs, or judicial or executive proceedings . . . An individual cannot deprive a man of his right to vote, to hold property, to buy and to sell, to sue in the courts, or to be a witness or a juror; he may, by force or fraud, interfere with the enjoyment of the right in a particular case; he may commit an assault against the person, or commit murder, or use ruffian violence at the polls, or slander the good name of a fellow-citizen; but unless protected in these wrongful acts by some shield of state law or state authority, he cannot destroy or injure the right; he will only render himself amenable to satisfaction or punishment; and amenable therefor to the laws of the state where the wrongful acts are committed . . .

. . . The law in question, without any reference to adverse state legislation on the subject, declares that all persons shall be entitled to equal accommodation and privileges of inns, public conveyances, and places of public amusement, and imposes a penalty upon any individual who shall deny to any citizen such equal accommodations and privileges. This is not corrective legislation; it is primary and direct; it takes immediate and absolute possession of the subject of the right of admission to inns, public conveyances, and places of amusement . . .

This amendment, as well as the fourteenth, is undoubtedly self-executing without any ancillary legislation, so far as its terms are applicable to any existing state of circumstances. By its own unaided force and effect it abolished slavery, and established universal freedom . . .

When a man has emerged from slavery, and by the aid of beneficent legislation has shaken off the inseparable concomitants of that state, there must be some stage in the progress of his elevation when he takes the rank of a mere citizen, and ceases to be the special favorite of the laws, and when his rights as a citizen, or a man, are to be protected in the ordinary modes by which other men's rights are protected. There were thousands of free colored people in this country before the abolition of slavery, enjoying all the essential rights of life, liberty, and property the same as white citizens; yet no one, at that time, thought that it was any invasion of their personal status as freemen because they were not admitted to all the privileges enjoyed by white citizens, or because they were subjected to discriminations in the enjoyment of accommodations in inns, public conveyances, and places of amusement. Mere discriminations on account of race or color were not regarded as badges of slavery . . .

HARLAN, J., dissenting.

The opinion in these cases proceeds, as it seems to me, upon grounds entirely too narrow and artificial. The substance and spirit of the recent amendments of the constitution have been sacrificed by a subtle and ingenious verbal criticism . . . Constitutional provisions, adopted in the interest of liberty, and for the purpose of securing, through national legislation, if need be, rights inhering in a state of freedom, and belonging to American citizenship, have been so construed as to defeat the ends the people desired to accomplish, which they attempted to accomplish, and which they supposed they had accomplished by changes in their fundamental law . . .

The thirteenth amendment, my brethren concede, did something more than to prohibit slavery as an institution, resting upon distinctions of race, and upheld by positive law. They admit that it established and decreed universal civil freedom throughout the United States. But did the freedom thus established involve nothing more than exemption from actual slavery? Was nothing more intended than to forbid one man from owning another as property? Was it the purpose of the nation simply to destroy the institution, and then remit the race, theretofore held in bondage, to the several states for such protection, in their civil rights, necessarily growing out of freedom, as those states, in their discretion, choose to provide? . . .

Congress has not, in these matters, entered the domain of state control and supervision. It does not assume to prescribe the general conditions and limitations under which inns, public conveyances, and places of public amusement shall be conducted or managed . . .

My brethren say that when a man has emerged from slavery, and by the aid of beneficent legislation has shaken off the inseparable concomitants of that state, there must be some stage in the progress of his elevation when he takes the rank of a mere citizen, and ceases to be the special favorite of the laws, and when his rights as a citizen, or a man, are to be protected in the ordinary modes by which other men's rights are protected. It is, I submit, scarcely just to say that the colored race has been the special favorite of the laws. What the nation, through congress, has sought to accomplish in reference to that race is, what had already been done in every state in the Union for the white race, to secure and protect rights belonging to them as freemen and citizens; nothing more. The one underlying purpose of congressional legislation has been to enable the black race to take the rank of mere citizens . . .

Source: Civil Rights Cases, 109 U.S. 3 (1883), from FindLaw, http://laws.findlaw.com/us/109/3.html.

NOTES

1 John M. Matthews, "Jefferson Franklin Long: The Public Career of Georgia's First Black Congressman," *Phylon* 42, no. 2 (June 1981): 148.

2 *Decuir v. Benson,* 27 La. Ann. 1 (1875).

3 Samuel Shapiro, "A Black Senator from Mississippi: Blanche K. Bruce (1841–1898)," *Review of Politics* 44, no. 1 (January 1982): 89.

4 *Christian Recorder,* June 1, 1882.

5 "Rhode Island Negroes on Republican Party, 1882," in *A Documentary History of the Negro People in the United States,* ed. Herbert Aptheker (New York: Citadel Press, 1969), 685.

6 John R. Lynch, *The Facts of Reconstruction* (New York: Arno Press and New York Times, 1968), 157–158.

7 Andrew Johnson, speech in Nashville, Tennessee, June 9, 1864, in *Documentary History of Reconstruction: Political, Military, Social, Religious, Educational and Industrial, 1865 to 1906,* ed. Walter L. Fleming, vol. 1 (New York: McGraw-Hill, 1966), 116.

8 *Congressional Globe,* 40th Cong., 2d sess., March 4, 1868, 1648.

9 "Affairs at the Capital," *Christian Recorder* (Philadelphia, Pa.), April 18, 1868.

10 McConnell Center, University of Louisville, "Results of Presidential Mistakes Survey," February 2006, http://louisville.edu/mcconnellcenter/news/presidentialmoments/results.html.

11 "Louisiana Democratic Platform," October 2, 1865, *Annual Cyclopedia,* 1865, 512, in Fleming, *Documentary History of Reconstruction,* vol. 1, 229.

12 "Proceedings of the Illinois State Convention of Colored Men, Assembled at Galesburg," in Aptheker, *A Documentary History,* 615.

13 *Statutes at Large of South Carolina,* December 21, 1865, vol. 13, 269, in Fleming, *Documentary History of Reconstruction,* vol. 1, 268.

14 *Laws of Mississippi,* November 29, 1865, 165, in Fleming, *Documentary History of Reconstruction,* vol. 1, 289.

15 *An Act to Regulate the Elective Franchise in the District of Columbia,* 39th Cong., 2d sess., *Statutes at Large of the United States of America* 14 (1868): 375, from the Library of Congress, http://memory.loc.gov/ammem/amlaw/lwsllink.html.

16   Carl Schurz to President Andrew Johnson, Letter, December 18, 1865, in *Report on the Condition of the South*, Senate Ex. Doc. no. 2, December 19, 1865, from Project Gutenberg, ftp://ibiblio.org/pub/docs/books/gutenberg/etext05/cnsth10.txt.

17   Frederick Douglass, "Appeal to Congress for Impartial Suffrage," January 1867, from the University of Oklahoma College of Law, www.law.ou.edu/ushistory/suff.shtml.

18   "The Fifteenth Amendment," *Christian Recorder*, July 3, 1869.

19   "Celebration of the Fifteenth Amendment, Big Day at Monticello, Ark.," *Christian Recorder*, April 25, 1889.

20   William Nesbit, Joseph C. Bustill, and William D. Forten, on Behalf of the Pennsylvania State Equal Rights League, *To the Honorable the Senate and House of Representatives of the United States, in Congress Assembled . . .*, February 20, 1866, 2, from the Library of Congress, http://memory.loc.gov/ammem/aapchtml/aapchome.html.

21   "Hon. H. R. Revels" and "Senator Revels," *Harper's Weekly*, February 19, 1870, in *African American History in the Press, 1851–1899: From the Coming of the Civil War to the Rise of Jim Crow as Reported and Illustrated in Selected Newspapers of the Time*, ed. Schneider Collection vol. 2, *1870–1899* (Detroit: Gale, 1996), 624.

22   "From Washington," *New York World*, February 24, 1870, in Schneider Collection, *African American History in the Press*, vol. 2, 628.

23   *Congressional Globe*, 41st Cong., 3d sess., February 8, 1871, 1057.

24   "The Ku Klux Klan," in *Documents of American History*, 9th ed., ed. Henry Steele Commager (Englewood, N.J.: Prentice-Hall, 1973), 499–500.

25   *Statutes at Large of the United States*, 42d Cong., 1st sess., April 20, 1871, 13–15.

26   Joseph H. Rainey, "Enforcement of the Fourteenth Amendment," in *Black Congressmen during Reconstruction: A Documentary Sourcebook*, ed. Stephen Middleton (Westport, Conn.: Praeger, 2002), 293.

27   *Congressional Globe*, 42d Cong., 1st sess., April 5, 1871, Appendix, 203.

28   "American Liberty and the So-Called Ku-Klux Bill," *Charleston Daily Courier*, April 8, 1871, in Schneider Collection, *African American History in the Press* vol. 2, 652–653.

29   "The Amnesty Bill," excerpts from remarks by Hiram R. Revels, May 17, 1870, in Middleton, *Black Congressmen during Reconstruction*, 327–328.

30   "The Amnesty Bill," excerpts from remarks by Jefferson F. Long, February 1, 1871, in Middleton, *Black Congressmen during Reconstruction*, 143.

31   *An Act to Remove Political Disabilities Imposed by the Fourteenth Article of the Amendments of the Constitution of the United States*, Statutes at Large of the United States of America, 42d Cong., 2d sess., May 22, 1872, 142.

32   "Civil Rights," excerpts from remarks by Richard H. Cain, in Middleton, *Black Congressmen During Reconstruction*, 50, 52.

33   *Congressional Record*, 43d Cong., 1st sess., January 5, 1874, 376.

34   Ibid.

35   *Congressional Record*, 44th Cong., 1st sess., May 19, 1876, 20. The Senate adopted the resolution appointing the committee on March 31, 1876. It is reprinted on page III of the report.

36   "Election in Mississippi," excerpt from the speech of Sen. Blanche K. Bruce, March 31, 1876, in Middleton, *Black Congressmen during Reconstruction*, 6.

37   Senate Select Committee to Inquire into the Mississippi Election of 1875, *Mississippi in 1875*, 44th Cong., 1st sess., August 7, 1876, S. Rep. 527, 1015–1016.

38   Ibid., IX, XXVIII, XXIX.

39   Ibid., XXXVI.

40   J. E. Bruce, "Freedman's Bank: Present Condition of Its Affairs," *Cleveland* (Ohio) *Gazette*, July 24, 1886.

41   T. Thomas Fortune, "The Civil Rights Decision," *New York Globe*, October 20, 1883, in *The Black American: A Brief Documentary History*, ed. Leslie H. Fishel Jr. and Benjamin Quarles (New York: William Morrow, 1970), 315.

CHAPTER FOUR

After Reconstruction

Political Disenfranchisement and Banishment, 1880–1904

With the collapse of congressional Reconstruction, African Americans in the South continued to find themselves living in subservient and second-class political, economic, social and educational conditions. While they had become free people with ostensibly guaranteed constitutional rights, they faced a resurgent white political establishment that sought to exclude them from the body politic.

The disenfranchisement of black voters took many forms, some of them formal, such as poll taxes, literacy tests and property ownership requirements. Other means of denying African Americans the vote relied on intimidation, chicanery and violence. Former member of Congress Robert Smalls detailed the extralegal practices used by the Democrats in the late 1880s in his own state of South Carolina, where black Republican voters outnumbered white Democrats: so-called rifle clubs terrorized the state, ballot boxes were stuffed and ballots were stolen and destroyed; election officials chose not to open the polls in many Republican precincts; and officials deliberately failed to sign the returns of some precincts that did open. Smalls wrote:

An 1878 handbill issued by Benjamin "Pap" Singleton in Nashville, Tennessee, urging blacks to move west. Singleton testified in 1880 before a Senate committee about the mass migration, saying "we are going to leave the South. We are going to leave it if there ain't an alteration and signs of change."
Source: The Granger Collection, New York

> Having perfect immunity from punishment, the encouragement, if not the active participation of the State government, and the protection of the courts of the State, the rifle clubs committed their outrages without restraint, and the election officers their frauds without even the thin veneer of attempted concealment. Elections since then have been carried by perjury and fraud.[1]

Gerrymandering was another effective tool of disenfranchisement. In South Carolina, for example, Democrats redrew congressional districts so that six districts had white majorities and only one bizarrely shaped district had a black majority. Even then, a white candidate quickly captured the seat representing the black-majority district.

Across the South, the white establishment in the state legislatures wielded the tools of legal disenfranchisement, amending constitutions and passing discriminatory statutes (**Document 4.7**). At the same time, there was a violent white supremacist movement developing, in which the visible roles were played mainly by poor whites. Members of one organization, the Red Shirts, did not hide their identities under hoods and robes as did members of the Ku Klux Klan. Instead, they paraded, raided, rallied, brandished weapons and attacked blacks openly, wearing "the red-shirt badge of Southern manhood." [2]

In 1896 North Carolina Populists and Republicans, including most black voters, allied themselves to oust the Democrats and elect a Republican governor on a fusion, or multiparty, ticket. Shortly before the state's 1898 election, the governor issued a proclamation "commanding all ill-disposed persons, whether of this or that political party, or of no political party, to immediately desist from all unlawful practices and all turbulent conduct." [3] The Red Shirts—bolstered by a recent appearance by Sen. Benjamin R. "Pitchfork Ben" Tillman, a racist South Carolina Democrat who spoke at political rallies in North Carolina shortly before the election—refused to comply. They intimidated black voters with shotguns and Winchester rifles, and Democrats won the election. Their tactics of intimidation continued beyond the 1898 election. Two years later, the *Cleveland Gazette*, an African American newspaper published in Ohio, reported:

> The North Carolina white man who had the temerity, last week, to express himself as being opposed to the amendment disenfranchising the Afro-Americans of that state, was severely thrashed, if not beaten to death by "red shirts," who are democrats largely, with a sprinkling of republicans, who wish to eliminate the Negro from North Carolina politics. And yet we boast of the freeness of this country, especially when it comes to the matter of speech.[4]

Not surprisingly, many blacks opted to leave the South and sought economic and political opportunities elsewhere (**Document 4.1**). In 1892 the Associated Press quoted a "well-known real estate dealer in Chattanooga," Tennessee, describing the economic reasons why so many black residents of his city had left for Colorado and Kansas. The shutdown of local businesses and manufacturers threw "hundreds, I may almost say, thousands of men out of employment, the majority of them being negroes. The result has been that these poor fellows have not been able to pay their rents, and scarcely to find food for their families." [5]

Others left because they distrusted their state and local governments, which had failed or chosen not to protect them. The 1879 Louisiana Negro Convention heard that the principal cause for the exodus from that state

> lies in the absence of a republican form of government to the people of Louisiana. Crime and lawlessness existing to an extent that laughs at all restraint and the misgovernment naturally induced from a State administration, itself the product of violence, have created an absorbing and constantly increasing distrust and alarm among our people throughout the State.[6]

Nine years later, that distrust of government remained in Louisiana, where an 1888 mass meeting of African Americans asserted

> that a reign of terror exists in many parts of the state; that the laws are suspended and the officers of the government, from the governor down, afford no protection to the lives and property of the people against armed bodies of whites, who shed innocent blood and commit deeds of savagery unsurpassed in the dark ages of mankind.[7]

Antiblack activity by government was by no means limited to the state and local levels. The 1880s and 1890s were marked by ongoing measures in Washington, D.C., to undo

Reconstruction, including the repeal of laws intended to protect voting rights and the failure to pass new civil rights legislation. For example, a May 1880 rider to the Army Appropriation Act prohibited federal troops from enforcing political rights in the South. It barred the use of any funds "for the subsistence, equipment, transportation, or compensation of any portion of the Army of the United States to be

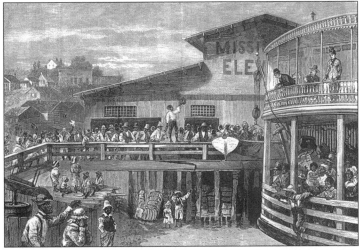

This American wood engraving from 1879 depicts the wharf at Vicksburg, Mississippi, from which many black migrants departed following the end of Reconstruction. They headed for points north and west, including Kansas.
Source: The Granger Collection, New York

used as a police force to keep the peace at the polls at any election held within any State," unless requested by the governor or legislature.[8] In 1890 Congress failed to pass a broad civil rights measure (**Document 4.4**). And in 1894 Congress repealed the statute allowing federal supervision of state elections.

The third branch of government, the Supreme Court, hammered more nails into the coffin of civil rights. Despite its unanimous 1884 decision to uphold the convictions of Klan members for intimidating black voters (*Ex parte Yarbrough*, **Document 4.2**), the Court in 1896 turned its back on African American rights in the pro-segregation, "separate but equal" ruling of *Plessy v. Ferguson* (**Document 4.5**).

Meanwhile, the dwindling number of black representatives continued to face major obstacles such as election fraud, at home, and in Washington, where their voices were usually ignored, especially when the Republican Party was in the minority. Even so, they continued to push ultimately doomed legislation on civil rights—including the first bill to make lynching a federal capital crime (**Document 4.9**)—and economic issues—as illustrated by the maiden speech of Rep. George W. Murray, R-S.C., backing the Populist position favoring free silver, and a speech by Rep. James E. O'Hara, R-N.C., opposing legislation to protect the dairy industry against competition from margarine manufacturers (**Document 4.3**).

Thus by the dawn of the twentieth century, black political power at the national, state and local levels was minimal. As a result, some activists chose to create their own independent organizations outside the structure of the two major political parties, which were uninterested in or hostile toward protecting the rights of black Americans, or to establish their own parties (**Document 4.12**). In New York, for example, the Afro-American League and the more militant Afro-American Council emerged, yet both lacked the clout to influence white leaders and were more like debating societies than political forces. Those who wanted to remain within the party structures were relegated to separate affiliated organizations, such as the United Colored Democracy formed by the Tammany Democratic machine that governed New York City.

The major parties made overtures to those black voters who still had the right to vote (**Document 4.6**) but paid little attention to their concerns. Republicans continued to rely rhetorically—if not through their deeds—on the Lincoln legacy to woo black voters (**Document 4.11**), while some components of the Democratic Party made no effort to hide their racist appeal (**Document 4.8**). In 1889 one of the most outspoken white supremacists in Congress, Sen. John T. Morgan, D-Ala., acknowledged in his magazine article "Shall Negro Majorities Rule?" that nearly 40 percent of the population in thirteen states was black, and that blacks outnumbered whites in three states. However, he said:

> The laws that give the ballot to one-fifth of the Negro race appeal to the race prejudice which incites them to persistent effort to accomplish the impossible result of race equality . . . We have not accomplished any good to either race by conferring upon 1,500,000 Negroes the privilege of voting.[9]

Albion W. Tourgée, a black lawyer who later represented Homer Plessy in *Plessy v. Ferguson*, responded in "Shall White Minorities Rule?" He wrote:

> Even if the claim of inherent superiority of the white race be admitted, it does not follow that it constitutes a sufficient ground for disenfranchisement of the inferior race . . . There cannot be any security for our institutions or any guarantee of our domestic peace, so long as the question of depriving a majority of the qualified electors of any State of the rights which they are solemnly guaranteed by law through any unlawful means is coolly discussed as a living issue in the great organs through which popular thought finds expression.[10]

Overall, the post-Reconstruction period would be what Rep. William L. Clay, D-Mo., later described as the "barren years" of "taxation without representation" for African Americans.[11] In a literal sense that was true. When Rep. George H. White, R-N.C., left Congress in 1901 (**Document 4.10**), there would be no black lawmaker on Capitol Hill for twenty-seven years.

Document 4.1 in Context
"We Are Going to Leave It If There Ain't an Alteration and Signs of Change": African Americans Begin to Depart the South

With the failure of congressional Reconstruction, black southerners experienced deteriorating economic, social and political conditions, as well as violence and intimidation. The final withdrawal of Federal occupation troops from the South in 1877 left African Americans even more exposed. Many blacks soon seized on the promise of migration out of the South as a means of improvement. It was not the type of foreign colonization Abraham Lincoln had advocated (**Document 2.5**), but it would have profound implications for black political power in and out of the South. Many of those who migrated within the United States were entrepreneurial, educated and able to afford the costs of the move and the expense of buying land or starting a business in their new locations—in other words, the type of people who might have wielded political and economic influence in their southern communities under different circumstances.

Migration also took hold among the less affluent. *Harper's Weekly* reported that in parts of Louisiana and Mississippi emigration by plantation laborers "became a stampede" in the spring of 1879, and that colonization organizations "are now universal throughout the

Southern States." As for the economic impact of the movement, the magazine continued: "How serious a matter this is, appears from a few figures. The value of the combined cotton, sugar, and rice crops for the year 1878 was $256,000,000, made almost entirely by negro labor. Whatever seriously affects such production touches the interests of the whole country." [12]

The wisdom of the exodus divided African Americans. Frederick Douglass, the former abolitionist and newspaper editor and future U.S. minister to Haiti, criticized the migration west, saying it "leaves the whole question of equal rights on the soil of the South open, and still to be settled." [13] But "with the downfall of Reconstruction," Howard University Law School Dean Richard T. Greener, who was the first black graduate of Harvard University, advocated emigration. He argued that blacks would benefit by leaving an environment where "no jury will convict for political offenses committed against" them, where "the exclusive devotion of the Negro to the culture of cotton and rice is demoralizing" and where those who remain in the South may raise their wages and the demand for their labor. As for the future of black political power, Greener acknowledged: "I assume that the predominance of the Negro in politics in the South is gone for a generation at least. The South will not have it and the North has exhibited no very marked disposition to enforce it." But he looked to the future: "Let it come when the children of the present black colonists go back to the mother land"—referring to the South—"improved in all that makes good citizens by a sojourn in the West." [14]

The large number of emigrants was viewed with such concern that the U.S. Senate appointed a select committee to investigate what it called the "Negro Exodus from the Southern States." The committee heard from hundreds of witnesses, black and white, including Benjamin "Pap" Singleton—described by the committee as "colored" and nicknamed "the Moses of the Colored Exodus"—who testified about his efforts to recruit thousands of African Americans to move to two colonies he had established in Kansas. His activities, he told the committee in response to questioning by Sen. William Windom, R-Minn., were motivated by the economic plight of blacks across the South.

▬ Document 4.1 ▬
Benjamin Singleton Testifies before the Senate Select Committee to Investigate the Causes of the Removal of the Negroes from the Southern States to the Northern States, April 17, 1880

BENJAMIN SINGLETON (colored) sworn and examined.
By Mr. [William] WINDOM [R-Minn.]:

Question: Where were you born, Mr. Singleton?
Answer: I was born in the State of Tennessee, sir.
Q.: Where do you now live?
A.: In Kansas.
Q.: What part of Kansas?
A.: I have a colony sixty miles from Topeka, sir . . .
Q.: What is your colony called?
A.: Singleton colony is the name of it, sir.
Q.: How long has it been since you have formed that colony?
A.: I have two colonies in Kansas—one in Cherokee County, and one in Lyon, Morris County.

Q.: When did you commence the formation of that colony—the first one?

A.: It was in 1875, perhaps.

Q.: That is, you first began this colonizing business in 1875?

A.: No; when I first commenced working at this it was in 1869.

Q.: You commenced your colony, then, in 1869?

A.: No, I commenced getting the emigration up in 1875; I think it was in 1875 . . .

Q.: When did you change your home from Tennessee to Kansas?

A.: I have been going there for the last six or seven years, sir.

Q.: Going between Tennessee and Kansas, at different times?

A.: Yes, sir; several times.

Q.: Well, tell us about it?

A.: I have been fetching out people; I believe I fetched out 7,432 people.

Q.: You have brought out 7,432 people from the South to Kansas?

A.: Yes, sir; brought and sent.

Q.: That is, they came out to Kansas under your influence?

A.: Yes, sir; I was the cause of it . . .

Q.: How did you happen to send them out?

A.: The first cause, do you mean, of them going?

Q.: Yes; What was the cause of your going out, and in the first place how did you happen to go there, or to send these people there?

A.: Well, my people, for the want of land—we needed land for our children—and their disadvantages—that caused my heart to grieve and sorrow; pity for my race, sir, that was coming down, instead of going up—that caused me to go to work for them. I sent out there perhaps in '66—perhaps so; or in '65, any way—my memory don't recollect which; and they brought back tolerable favorable reports; then I jacked up three or four hundred, and went into Southern Kansas, and found it was a good country, and I thought Southern Kansas was congenial to our nature, sir; and I formed a colony there, and bought about a thousand acres of ground—the colony did—my people.

Q.: And they went upon it and settled there?

A.: Yes, sir; they went and settled there.

Q.: Were they men with some means or without means?

A.: I never carried none there without means.

Q.: They had some means to start with?

A.: Yes; I prohibited my people leaving their country and going there without they had money—some money to start with and go on with a while . . .

Q.: Have they any property now?

A.: Yes; I have carried some people in there that when they got there they didn't have fifty cents left, and now they have got in my colony—Singleton colony—a house, nice cabins, their milch cows, and pigs, and sheep, perhaps a span of horses, and trees before their yards, and some three or four or ten acres broken up, and all of them has got little houses that I carried there. They didn't go under no relief assistance; they went on their own resources; and when they went in there first the country was not overrun with them; you see they could get good wages; the country was not overstocked with people; they went to work, and I never helped them as soon as I put them on the land.

Q.: Well, they have been coming continually, and adding from time to time to your colony these few years past, have they?

A.: Yes, sir; I have spent, perhaps, nearly six hundred dollars flooding the country with circulars . . .

Q.: Did you do that at the instance of Governor [John P.] St. John and others in Kansas?

A.: O, no, sir; no white men. This was gotten up by colored men in purity and confidence; not a political negro was in it; they would want to pilfer and rob at the cents before they got the dollars. O, no, it was the muscle of the arm, the men that worked that we wanted.

Q.: Well, tell us all about it.

A.: These men would tell all their grievances to me in Tennessee—the sorrows of their heart. You know I was an undertaker there in Nashville, and worked in the shop. Well, actually, I would have to go and bury their fathers and mothers. You see we have the same heart and feelings as any other race and nation. (The land is free, and it is nobody's business, if there is land enough, where the people go. I put that in my people's heads.) Well, that man would die, and I would bury him; and the next morning maybe a woman would go to that man (meaning the landlord), and she would have six or seven children, and he would say to her, "Well, your husband owed me before he died" and they would say that to every last one of them, "You owe me." Suppose he would? Then he would say, "You must go to some other place; I cannot take care of you." Now, you see, that is something I would take notice of. That woman had to go out, and these little children was left running through the streets, and the next place you would find them in a disorderly house, and their children in the State's prison.

Well, now, sir, you will find that I have a charter here. You will find that I called on the white people in Tennessee about that time. I called conventions about it, and they sat with me in my conventions, and "Old man," they said, "you are right." The white people said, "You are right; take your people away." And let me tell you, it was the white people—the ex-governor of the State, felt like I did. And they said to me, "You have tooken a great deal on to yourself, but if these negroes, instead of deceiving one another and running for office, would take the same idea that you have in your head, you will be a people."

I then went out to Kansas, and advised them all to go to Kansas; and, sir they are going to leave the Southern country. The Southern country is out of joint. The blood of a white man runs through my veins. That is congenial, you know, to my nature. that is my choice. Right emphatically, I tell you today, I woke up the millions right through me! The great God of glory has worked in me. I have had open air interviews with the living spirit of God for my people; and we are going to leave the South. We are going to leave it if there ain't an alteration and signs of change. I am going to advise the people who left that country (Kansas) to go back.

Q.: What do you mean by a change?

A.: Well, I am not going to stand bulldozing and half pay and all those things. Gentlemen, allow me to tell you the truth; it seems to me that they have picked out the negroes from the Southern country to come here and testify who are in good circumstances and own their homes and not the poor ones who don't study their own interests. Let them go and pick up the men that has to walk when they goes, and not those who have money.

There is good white men in the Southern country, but it ain't the minority (majority); they can't do nothing; the bulldozers has got possession of the country, and they have got to go in there and stop them; if they don't the last colored man will leave them. I see colored men testifying to a positive lie, for they told me out there all their interests were in Louisiana and Mississippi. Said I, "You are right to protect you own country," and they would tell me, "I am obliged to do what I am doing." Of course I have done the same, but I am clear footed . . .

Q.: And you attribute this movement to the information you gave in your circulars?

A.: Yes, sir; I am the whole cause of the Kansas immigration!

Q.: You take all that responsibility on yourself?

A.: I do, and I can prove it; and I think I have done a good deal of good, and I feel relieved!

Q.: You are proud of your work?

A.: Yes, sir; I am! (Uttered emphatically.) . . .

Source: Senate Select Committee to Investigate the Causes of the Removal of the Negroes from the Southern States to the Northern States, "Testimony of Benjamin Singleton," April 17, 1880, in the Committee report, 379–382, from the Schomburg Center for Research in Black Culture, New York Public Library, http://www.inmotionaame.org/home.cfm.

Document 4.2 in Context
"The Temptations to Control These Elections by Violence and by Corruption Is a Constant Source of Danger": The Supreme Court Upholds Enforcement of Voter Protection Laws

To gain and maintain Democratic control of federal and state political offices across the South, white supremacists engaged in violence and intimidation of black voters, in violation of federal voter protection laws. Armed and sometimes disguised groups disrupted Republican political rallies that attracted African Americans and threatened and assaulted not only men who voted for—or were expected to vote for—Republican candidates, but their family members as well.

In an exception to the usual impunity with which such intimidation operated, a federal grand jury in Georgia indicted white Ku Klux Klan members on charges of conspiring in July 1883 to prevent black voters from participating in a congressional election. Specifically, they were charged with a conspiracy to "injure, oppress, threaten and intimidate" their victims, "on account of [their] race, color, and previous condition of servitude, in the full exercise and enjoyment of the right and privilege of suffrage in the election of a lawfully qualified person as a member of the congress of the United States of America." They also were accused of "unlawfully, willingly, and feloniously" disguising themselves "with the intent to prevent and hinder" their victims' "free exercise and enjoyment of [their] right to vote" for a federal office.[15]

The defendants were convicted and sentenced to two years in prison under a statute that provided for fines of $500–$5,000 and imprisonment "with or without hard labor" of six months to six years."[16] They sought from the U.S. Supreme Court a writ of habeas corpus to compel their release, challenging the constitutionality of the statute and arguing that only the states had the authority to regulate elections, even those for congressional office.

In a landmark opinion written by Justice Samuel F. Miller, the Supreme Court in 1884 unanimously upheld the statute as a valid exercise of congressional power to enforce the Fifteenth

Amendment and thus safeguard the integrity of the federal election process. More broadly, the decision also reinforced the authority of the national government to enact criminal laws "necessary and proper" to protect federal property and federal rights beyond voting. Yet it would prove an elusive victory, as the federal government had already abandoned efforts to protect voting rights and had legislatively barred the use of Army troops to safeguard voting rights in the South. Further, southern states systematically amended their constitutions, enacted statutes that restricted political rights, gerrymandered congressional and legislative districts, tolerated massive fraud at the polls and pursued policies and practices of disenfranchisement (**Documents 4.3** and **4.6**).

▬ **Document 4.2** ▬
The Ku-Klux Cases, Ex parte Yarbrough, March 3, 1884

This case originates in this court by an application for a writ of *habeas corpus* on the part of Jasper Yarbrough and seven other persons, who allege that they are confined by the jailer of Fulton county in the custody of the United States marshal for the Northern district of Georgia, and that the trial, conviction, and sentence . . . under which they are held, were illegal, null, and void . . .

This . . . leaves for consideration the more important question . . . whether the law of congress, as found in the Revised Statutes of the United States, under which the prisoners are held, is warranted by the constitution, or, being without such warrant, is null and void . . .

"Sec. 5508. If two or more persons conspire to injure, oppress, threaten, or intimidate any citizen in the free exercise or enjoyment of any right or privilege secured to him by the constitution or laws of the United States, or because of his having so exercised the same, or if two or more persons go in disguise on the highway, or on the premises of another, with intent to prevent or hinder his free exercise or enjoyment of any right or privilege so secured, they shall be fined . . . and imprisoned . . . and shall, moreover, be thereafter ineligible to any office or place of honor, profit, or trust created by the constitution or laws of the United States."

"Sec. 5520. If two or more persons in any state or territory conspire to prevent, by force, intimidation, or threat, any citizen who is lawfully entitled to vote from giving his support or advocacy, in a legal manner, towards or in favor of the election of any lawfully qualified person as an elector for president or vice-president, or as a member of the congress of the United States, or to injure any citizen in person or property on account of such support or advocacy, each of such persons shall be punished by a fine . . . or by imprisonment . . . or by both such fine and imprisonment . . ."

. . . That a government whose essential character is republican, whose executive head and legislative body are both elective, whose numerous and powerful branch of the legislature is elected by the people directly, has no power by appropriate laws to secure this election from the influence of violence, of corruption, and of fraud, is a proposition so startling as to arrest attention and demand the gravest consideration. If this government is anything more than a mere aggregation of delegated agents of other states and governments, each of which is superior to the general government, it must have the power to protect the elections on which its existence depends, from violence and corruption. If it has not this power, it is left helpless before the two great natural and historical enemies of all republics, open violence and insidious corruption . . .

We know of no express authority to pass laws to punish theft or burglary of the treasury of the United States. Is there therefore no power in congress to protect the treasury by punishing such theft and burglary? Are the mails of the United States, and the money carried in them, to be left at the mercy of robbers and of thieves who may handle the mail, because the constitution contains no express words of power in congress to enact laws for the punishment of those offenses? The principle, if sound, would abolish the entire criminal jurisdiction of the courts of the United States, and the laws which confer that jurisdiction . . .

So, also, has the congress been slow to exercise the powers expressly conferred upon it in relation to elections by the fourth section of the first article of the constitution. This section declares that 'the times, places, and manner of holding elections for senators and representatives shall be prescribed in each state by the legislature thereof; but the congress may at any time make or alter such regulations, except as to the place of choosing senators.' It was not until 1842 that congress took any action under the power here conferred, when, conceiving that the system of electing all the members of the house of representatives from a state by general ticket, as it was called,— that is, every elector voting for as many names as the state was entitled to representatives in that house,— worked injustice to other states which did not adopt that system, and gave an undue preponderance of power to the political party which had a majority of votes in the state, however small, enacted that each member should be elected by a separate district, composed of contiguous territory . . .

. . . Will it be denied that it is in the power of that body to provide laws for the proper conduct of those elections? To provide, if necessary, the officers who shall conduct them and make return of the result? And especially to provide, in an election held under its own authority, for security of life and limb to the voter while in the exercise of this function? Can it be doubted that congress can, by law, protect the act of voting, the place where it is done, and the man who votes from personal violence or intimidation, and the election itself from corruption or fraud? . . .

This proposition answers, also, another objection to the constitutionality of the laws under consideration, namely, that the right to vote for a member of congress is not dependent upon the constitution or laws of the United States, but is governed by the law of each state respectively. If this were conceded, the importance to the general government of having the actual election—the voting for those members—free from force and fraud is not diminished by the circumstance that the qualification of the voter is determined by the law of the state where he votes . . . But it is not correct to say that the right to vote for a member of congress does not depend on the constitution of the United States. The office, if it be properly called an office, is created by that constitution, and by that alone. It also declares how it shall be filled, namely, by election . . . The fifteenth amendment of the constitution, by its limitation on the power of the states in the exercise of their right to prescribe the qualifications of voters in their own elections, and by its limitation of the power of the United States over that subject, clearly shows that the right of suffrage was considered to be of supreme importance to the national government, and was not intended to be left within the exclusive control of the states . . .

While it is quite true . . . that this article gives no affirmative right to the colored man to vote, and is designed primarily to prevent discrimination against him whenever the right to vote may be granted to others it is easy to see that under some circumstances it may operate as the immediate source of a right to vote . . . In such cases this fifteenth article of amendment does, *proprio vigore*, substantially confer on the negro the right to vote, and congress has the power to protect and enforce that right . . .

. . . This new constitutional right was mainly designed for citizens of African descent. The principle, however, that the protection of the exercise of this right is within the power of congress, is as necessary to the right of other citizens to vote as to the colored citizen, and to the right to vote in general as to the right to be protected against discrimination . . .

It is as essential to the successful working of this government that the great organisms of its executive and legislative branches should be the free choice of the people, as that the original form of it should be so . . . In a republican government, like ours, where political power is reposed in representatives of the entire body of the people, chosen at short intervals by popular elections, the temptations to control these elections by violence and by corruption is a constant source of danger. Such has been the history of all republics, and, though ours has been comparatively free from both these evils in the past, no lover of his country can shut his eyes to the fear of future danger from both sources. If the recurrence of such acts as these prisoners stand convicted of are too common in one quarter of the country, and give omen of danger from lawless violence, the free use of money in elections, arising from the vast growth of recent wealth in other quarters, presents equal cause for anxiety. If the government of the United States has within its constitutional domain no authority to provide against these evils,—if the very sources of power may be poisoned by corruption or controlled by violence and outrage, without legal restraint,—then, indeed, is the country in danger, and its best powers, its highest purposes, the hopes which it inspires, and the love which enshrines it, are at the mercy of the combinations of those who respect no right but brute force on the one hand, and unprincipled corruptionists on the other . . .

Source: Ex parte Yarbrough, 110 U.S. 651 (1884), from FindLaw, http://laws.findlaw.com/us/110/651.html.

Document 4.3 in Context
"Let Not This Engine of Favoritism and Injustice Mar the Pages of Our Statutes": Rep. James E. O'Hara, R-N.C., Speaks on Food Safety Legislation

Like many other African American lawmakers, New York–born James E. O'Hara began his political career after the Civil War as a Republican Party activist in the South. He won a House seat representing North Carolina in 1882 after two failed bids. During his first term, he was the only black member of the House of Representatives.

Soon after being sworn in, O'Hara proposed a constitutional amendment on civil rights. Like his black colleagues of the Reconstruction and post-Reconstruction eras, he focused many of his speeches and legislative initiatives on civil rights issues such as lynching, segregated railroad travel, discriminatory pricing at restaurants and compensation to depositors of the failed Freedman's Savings and Trust Company (**Document 3.11**). He also proposed—unsuccessfully—equalizing pay for male and female teachers in Washington, D.C.

O'Hara and his black colleagues also took part in debates on more pedestrian issues, including an 1886 bill intended to protect butter—and thus the dairy industry—against margarine by taxing the latter at 2 cents per pound and charging annual license fees to the product's manufacturers, wholesalers and retailers. At the time, margarine frequently was sold fraudulently as butter, at half the price. Some proponents of the measure argued that margarine was a threat to public health, some claimed that advertising and selling the product as butter would be deceptive, and others admitted their intent was to restrict competition. Critics called the measure "protection run mad." [17]

In his speech opposing the legislation, O'Hara took issue with supporters' assertions that the measure would protect poor people, and he sharply criticized it as a partisan-inspired device to create government jobs for Democratic loyalists and build the federal bureaucracy. He also argued that any regulation should be left to the states; in fact, twenty states already regulated margarine packaging and licensing, while seven others banned its sale. (In the following excerpt, his comment about "an army of Jean Valjeans" is a reference to the relentless French police detective in Victor Hugo's *Les Miserables*.)

When the bill became law in 1886, margarine became the first domestic food subjected to federal regulation.

Later the same year, O'Hara lost a three-way contest for election to a third term. Although his district was predominantly black, most black voters in North Carolina had effectively been disenfranchised by then.

▓▓▓▓ Document 4.3 ▓▓▓▓
Rep. James E. O'Hara, R-N.C., Speaks against a Bill to Regulate the Oleomargarine Industry, June 2, 1886

. . . No member of this House will go further than I am ready to go to protect the people from the adulteration of food. But this bill, as I understand it, proposes not to prevent the adulteration of food as such. On the contrary, under the guise of protecting the poor man from oleomargarine and spurious butter, it seeks to destroy one industry of the country for the purpose of building up another. More than that, it proposes to create a number of new offices and to revivify and set in motion all the odious features of the internal-revenue system. The fourteenth section of this bill, which I propose to strike out, does not only create additional officers at large salaries, but it gives to the Commissioner of Internal Revenue the power, whenever in his judgment the necessity of the service may require it, to add to this already large army of officers other officers . . .

. . . If places are needed for party favorites, let gentlemen say so. Let the country so understand it . . . Let us make it clear and sure there should be no attempt here to throttle any interest or to strangle any industry of the country. I am no advocate of oleomargarine; but it is said that this bill is made in the interest of the poor man, and I ask, where are the petitions of poor men crying out against this abuse?

. . . The poor man is not here clamoring for this proposed legislation, but it is the rich dairymen of the country who by this bill are saying you should have only what we desire to give you at whatever price we may demand, whether it be butter made from pure milk of fancy and well-kept cows, or from milk of diseased and swill-fed cows as they do from oleomargarine or any of the other manufactures mentioned in the bill.

The crowning piece of infamy of the bill, however, is found in the nineteenth section. This section proposes to give a premium to every spy and informer in the land who shall become a self-appointed guardian of this law; it offers a reward, holds out an inducement, to the lazy and worthless to spy upon his neighbor's action, that he may satisfy his avarice and cupidity by securing one-half of the penalty imposed by the bill. It has a tendency to create an army of Jean Valjeans to follow with sleuthhound tenacity every imaginable violator of this law . . .

I have heard the cry of the Democratic party for the past ten years: "Reduction of taxes!" "Relief of the masses from an army of officeholders!" "Help from the merciless, red-legged grasshoppers and 'golden-winged butterflies,' " as the revenue officers were once called in my State. But, I suppose all this has changed, and the cry of war taxes has changed to the cry of protection to the people from the spurious and death-dealing food, and the slogan of reform. The revenue officer, the spy, the accuser of his neighbors, the United States prosecuting attorney are no longer tyrants but guardian angels to the health and liberty of the poor man.

The hard-wrung taxes to keep up and feed this vast additional army of cormorants becomes a free-will offering of spices and ointment of sweet-smelling savor. I do not believe that the people of my State or of any State in this Union are in favor of this bill; it savors of class legislation, of favoritism to one industry and oppression of another; it is not protection—it is destruction; and as such it must work to the detriment of the poorer classes. I will willingly go as far as any gentleman upon this floor to protect the people from adulterated food, and I say here and now that whenever the Committee on Agriculture, or any committee of this House, shall bring in a bill to remedy that evil, placing its enforcement with the ordinary courts of the country, without the creation of additional officers and spies and informers, separate and apart from the Internal Revenue Bureau, I am ready to give it my hearty approval.

As between natural butter and the manufactured article I am decidedly in favor of natural butter, and am of the opinion that if the dairymen of the country need protection they ought to have it; but I would ask the friends of the bill, a large number of whom are in favor of State rights, are not the respective State Legislatures competent to deal with this question? Has an effort been made by the dairymen of any particular State or number of States to secure protection against this so-called false representation of butte and refusal by the Legislature? . . .

That a single industry shall be crushed out, or that a rival industry, both to the manner born, shall be protected, or that political favorites, henchmen, and bosses shall have places? . . . By all means protect the poor from adulterated and deleterious food, but in the name of common fairness let us do it in one general bill. Enact a law that will make no invidious distinction, but one that will bear alike upon all, that will be wise and beneficial, but let not this engine of favoritism and injustice mar the pages of our statutes . . .

Source: Congressional Record, 49th Cong., 1st sess., June 2, 1886, 5163–5164.

Document 4.4 in Context
"It Will Be a Sad Day for This Republic When the People Can Be No Longer Trusted with the Ballot Box": The Federal Elections Bill of 1890

The Republican Party's 1892 platform proclaimed:

> The free and honest popular ballot, the just and equal representation of all the people, as well as their just and equal protection under the laws, are the foundation of our Republican institutions, and the party will never relax its efforts until the integrity of the ballot and the purity of elections shall be fully guaranteed and protected in every State.[18]

Unfortunately, such rhetoric, even from the party of Lincoln, was largely empty, coming as it did on the heels of the Republicans' failure to pass legislation guaranteeing at least some of the voting rights that African Americans had lost when U.S. troops withdrew from the South, ending Reconstruction and permitting states to systematically disenfranchise blacks (**Document 4.7**).

The Federal Elections Bill of 1890 was intended to build on the Fifteenth Amendment (**Document 3.3**) and the post–Civil War Enforcement Acts; it was to apply across the nation, not only in the South. Although its provisions were limited to House elections—state and local elections were deemed beyond the pale of federal authority, and until 1913 senators were chosen by state legislatures rather than at the polls (**Document 5.1**)—the measure could have been a powerful tool against intimidation and corruption. Major provisions included empowering federal courts to appoint bipartisan election supervisors upon the petition of at least 100 voters in a congressional district. Although the bill did not authorize a role for federal marshals or troops, opponents attacked it as the "Force Bill" that would destroy states' rights, even though 1871 statutes had authorized federal supervision of congressional elections in northern cities.

By the same token, the bill's Republican champions, led by Rep. Henry Cabot Lodge and Sen. George F. Hoar of Massachusetts, were not motivated solely by a belief in equal rights. Between 1875 and 1891, Republicans had controlled both Congress and the presidency for only four years, 1881–1883 and 1889–1891. Their difficulties had two main sources: a loss of support from African American and small-farmer voters in the South, and the large number of undecided voters in several midwestern and eastern states.

The Republican-controlled House narrowly passed the Federal Elections Bill by a 155–149 vote in July 1890, but Senate Republicans decided to delay consideration until after the November elections. When the Senate returned for its post-election lame duck session, however, the Republican leadership deemed two other issues more pressing—tariffs and free coinage of silver—and gave the elections bill lackluster support. Some Republicans feared that it would impair the flow of northern capital being invested in the South. Furthermore, Democrats filibustered.

While the measure languished in the Senate, Rep. John M. Langston, an African American Republican from Virginia, took to the House floor on January 16, 1891, to characterize the Senate's focus on currency as a betrayal of blacks: "Why, the feeling in the country seems to be to-day that silver is the thing; and a man said to me the other day, when the [elections] bill had been laid aside for the time being, 'Ah, Sir, your cause has been sold for thirty pieces of silver.' " Interrupted by frequent applause from fellow Republicans, Langston criticized Democrats, recalled the bravery of black soldiers during the Civil War and evoked constitutional guarantees of political rights. He proclaimed, "Fair elections! Sir, it will be a sad day for this Republic when the people can be no longer trusted with the ballot box." [19]

During the House debate on the bill, excerpted here, supporters and critics of the legislation raised arguments that would arise repeatedly in congressional debates in the twentieth century, including states' rights, disguised and undisguised racism, political equality and partisanship. The Senate never voted on the bill; thus died the last major congressional legislation for black voting rights until the civil rights movement of the 1960s.

▬ **Document 4.4** ▬
Excerpts from House Debate on the Federal Elections Bill, July 1890

Mr. [William S.] HOLMAN [D-Ind.]: The pending bill . . . proposes an absolute and complete change in our system of government. For over a hundred years our government has been administered on the theory that the people themselves were the only safe depository of political power, that the people themselves in their townships, villages, towns, counties, parishes, and States should control all public affairs which could, under our system of government, be brought within their reach. Hence, for more than a hundred years all elections, local and Federal, have been under the control of the people of each community, exercising their authority under the laws of their respective States . . .

This bill bristles with extraordinary and arbitrary provisions . . .

Mr. [Abner] TAYLOR [R-Ill.]: Mr. Speaker, a person listening to the debate on this question for a number of days past would have gone away from the House with the idea that this measure was local, was being passed simply for one portion of these United States . . .

I say we do "need something" in Chicago. There has never been an election held in Chicago within my recollection when there has not been illegal voting and cheating at the polls. After nearly every election we have to arrest, try, and convict some persons for violating the elective franchise . . . Ninety-nine times out of a hundred it is a Democrat that is sent to the penitentiary . . .

Mr. [William J.] STONE [D-Mo.]: . . . Sir, we hear much talk of treason and traitors in these latter days. It is not an unusual thing to hear Representatives on this floor denounced as traitors for their participation in the great civil war thirty years ago. But I affirm it is as much a crime under the Constitution and against the Constitution to assault the authority and the sovereignty of the State as it is to assault the authority and sovereignty of the nation. The men who, thirty years ago, upon the battle-fields yonder across the broad Potomac, with rifles in their hands and flashing swords, sought to destroy the autonomy of the nation were no more guilty of high treason than are the men who assemble here under the marble arches and swelling Dome of the Capitol and conspire to destroy the autonomy of the States. [Applause on the Democratic side.] . . .

Mr. [William C.] BRECKINRIDGE [D-Ky.]: . . . I am not now speaking as a Democrat denouncing this bill as a weapon forged by Republican committees and brought out of a Republican caucus into a Republican House by orders which that caucus dare not disobey, but I am speaking as an American citizen looking to the future. The present operation of the law in the pending election will be, or it is supposed that it will be, for the benefit of the Republican Party. But in a broad sense of the word, parties are not permanent. I have lived to see the Whig, the Knownothing, and other parties go to pieces. I expect to see the Republican party pass into history . . .

It is a step in the wrong direction. It is not only unwise in that it turns over the elections to a single machine dominated by the will of the party in power, but it is iniquitous in that it directs that party to go into any community and by the bribery of office and the pay attached to those offices use "the lewd fellows of the baser sort" who exist in every community, to corrupt the elections of the people and really take from them the right of choosing their Representatives . . .

Mr. [Asher G.] CARUTH [D-Ky.]: . . . Could partisan ingenuity devise a more wicked, diabolical plot against the liberty of the citizen? . . .

. . . It is to be paid by the honest tax-payers of this country out of their scant earnings, and will be a tax of from five to ten millions of dollars. What is the excuse for this? We know that if the Republican party thought it could maintain its supremacy without it, it would not be urging with all its power the passage of this bill . . .

It refers to the census for an argument and tells us how many negroes fail to vote at each election. It claims that if these votes were polled they would all be cast for the Republican ticket. Does the Republican party own the negro vote? By what right or authority do they claim it? Because Lincoln signed the emancipation proclamation and Grant forced Lee's surrender at Appomattox? . . .

President [Benjamin] Harrison holds office by virtue of the colored vote . . . The reading negro knows this . . .

Mr. [Jonathan P.] DOLLIVER [R-Iowa]: . . . A republic with an outcast industrial population rapidly increasing in number can spend its time to better advantage than by debating old questions about State rights and negro supremacy . . .

I support his bill because in some small degree it offers to the industrious millions of the South the prospect of citizenship under national protection . . . I want to see the Republican party stand faithful to the obligation laid upon it by the providence of God in the emancipation of an unfortunate race—united as one man to defend the sanctity of American citizenship. [Loud applause on the Republican side.] . . .

Mr. [Henry L.] MOREY [R-Ohio]: . . . Why this cry of pain from the South?

Why this sudden fear of a war of races? Has any white voter in the South been deprived of his vote by the colored men? Certainly not. Why should the white men of the South constantly decry against a war of races? Has the white man of the South suffered in any such conflict? Is it not always the colored man who gets hurt? . . .

No man on that side, no Northern Democratic Representative, in all this discussion, has dared to speak of any political right of the colored men that white men are bound to respect . . .

Mr. [Charles E.] HOOKER [D-Miss.]: . . . Why, therefore, are you attempting to make this change in the Constitution and in the laws of elections? Because you hear the rumblings of the coming storm which will overtake you on the ides of November, when you will be called to account by the people for this effort to usurp the power of the States and centralize it in the Federal Government of the United States, and thus by a bold and defiant step perpetuate the power and permanency of the Republican party in this House . . .

Mr. [Alfred A.] TAYLOR [R-Tenn.]: . . . Do gentlemen on the other side tell us that this will cost money—millions of money—and that therefore it must not come to pass?

I say, in the name of liberty and of law, perish money, perish property, perish life itself! Save the sanctity of the ballot-box! Survive the Government of the people! Preserve the unity and sovereignty of the American Republic! [Prolonged applause on the Republican side.] . . .

Mr. [William] McKINLEY [R-Ohio]: . . . This bill may not be, in all of its provisions, what I would like to have, but it is a bill looking to an honest representation on the floor of the American House of Representatives and to honest voting and the fair counting of votes in every part and section of the American Republic. [Applause on the Republican side.]

That is all of the bill, and no honest man can object to it and no lover of fair play can afford to oppose it.

Ah, but they say this measure is harsh. This measure will rest heavily upon only districts and upon States which violate the laws and the Constitution of our common country. Let every citizen of this Republic vote and then see to it that his vote is counted as it is cast and returned as counted, and you never need invoke any of the provisions of the bill or subject yourselves to what you term its harsh provisions. [Applause on the Republican side.] . . .

Source: Congressional Record, 51st Cong., 1st sess., July 1–2, 1890, 6844-6846, 6848, 6853, 6860, 6861–6862, 6897, 6927, 6929, 6933.

Document 4.5 in Context
"The Judgment This Day Rendered Will, in Time, Prove to Be Quite as Pernicious as the Decision Made by This Tribunal in the *Dred Scott* Case": The Supreme Court Rules on *Plessy v. Ferguson*

By 1896 the Supreme Court that had in 1884 upheld a voting rights statute in *Ex parte Yarbrough* (**Document 4.2**) was no more. Instead of equal rights, "separate but equal" became the law of the land with the Court's *Plessy v. Ferguson* decision. The ruling's adverse implications would reverberate through Jim Crow laws and other discriminatory measures and would blight America until it was reversed in *Brown v. Board of Education* in 1954 (**Document 5.9**).

Plessy v. Ferguson centered on Homer Adolph Plessy, an African American man who violated an 1890 Louisiana law mandating "equal but separate accommodations for the white and colored races" by refusing to use a segregated car on an East Louisiana Railroad Company train. Under the law, railroad companies could provide separate passenger coaches or divide a single coach "by a partition so as to secure separate accommodations." Passengers convicted of violations faced a $25 fine or twenty days in jail; railroad officers, directors and employees could also face prosecution for failing to enforce the law. Plessy sued to block enforcement of the law on the grounds that it conflicted with the Thirteenth and Fourteenth Amendments (**Documents 2.8** and **3.2**).

Plessy's brief argued, in part, that the law was not only unconstitutional but also impractical:

> A man may be white and his wife colored, a wife may be white and her children colored. Has the State the right to compel the husband to ride in one car and his wife in another? Or to assign the mother to one car and the children to another? . . .
> In all parts of the country, race-intermixture has proceeded to such an extent that there are great numbers of citizens in whom the preponderance of the blood of one race or another, is impossible of ascertainment, except by careful scrutiny of the pedigree. . . But even if it were possible to determine preponderance of blood and so determine racial character in certain cases, what should be said of those cases in which the race admixture is equal. Are they white or colored?[20]

In a 7–1 decision (one justice did not participate), the majority ruled on May 18, 1896, that states could determine their own criteria for enforcing race-based segregation and other abridgements of civil rights. For example, an 1877 Alabama criminal law mandated a prison term of two to seven years for "any white person and any negro, or the descendant of any negro, to the third generation inclusive" who "intermarry or live in adultery or fornication with each other." [21]

Dividing the population into two categories created an irony that the lone dissenter, Justice John Marshall Harlan, a Democrat, touched on in his minority opinion where he referred to the status of Chinese:

> There is a race so different from our own that we do not permit those belonging to it to become citizens of the United States . . . But by the statute in question, a Chinaman can ride in the same passenger coach with white citizens of the United States, while citizens of the black race in Louisiana, many of whom, perhaps, risked their lives for the preservation of the Union . . . are yet declared to be criminals, liable to imprisonment, if they ride in a public coach occupied by citizens of the white race.[22]

The decision provoked outrage at a Colored National League meeting in Boston, where one speaker said, "I want to call your attention to the fact that five of the nine judges are republicans, the other four are democrats, and all profess to be Christians." [23]

▬ Document 4.5 ▬
U.S. Supreme Court Decision in *Plessy v. Ferguson*, May 18, 1896

MR. JUSTICE [Henry B.] BROWN . . . delivered the opinion of the court.

This case turns upon the constitutionality of an act of the General Assembly of the State of Louisiana, passed in 1890, providing for separate railway carriages for the white and colored races . . .

The information filed in the criminal District Court charged in substance that Plessy, being a passenger between two stations within the State of Louisiana, was assigned by officers of the company to the coach used for the race to which he belonged, but he insisted upon going into a coach used by the race to which he did not belong . . .

The petition for the writ of prohibition averred that petitioner was seven eighths Caucasian and one eighth African blood; that the mixture of colored blood was not discernible in him, and that he was entitled to every right, privilege and immunity secured to citizens of the United States of the white race; and that, upon such theory, he took possession of a vacant seat in a coach where passengers of the white race were accommodated, and was ordered by the conductor to vacate said coach and take a seat in another assigned to persons of the colored race, and having refused to comply with such demand he was forcibly ejected with the aid of a police officer, and imprisoned in the parish jail to answer a charge of having violated the above act.

The constitutionality of this act is attacked upon the ground that it conflicts both with the Thirteenth Amendment of the Constitution, abolishing slavery, and the Fourteenth Amendment, which prohibits certain restrictive legislation on the part of the States.

1. That it does not conflict with the Thirteenth Amendment, which abolished slavery and involuntary servitude, except as a punishment for crime, is too clear for argument. Slavery implies involuntary servitude—a state of bondage; the ownership of mankind as a chattel, or at least the control of the labor and services of one man for the benefit of another, and the absence of a legal right to the disposal of his own person, property and services . . .

A statute which implies merely a legal distinction between the white and colored races—a distinction which is founded in the color of the two races, and which must always exist so long as white men are distinguished from the other race by color—has no tendency to destroy the legal equality of the two races, or reestablish a state of involuntary servitude . . .

2. By the Fourteenth Amendment, all persons born or naturalized in the United States, and subject to the jurisdiction thereof, are made citizens of the United States and of the State wherein they reside; and the States are forbidden from making or enforcing any law which shall abridge the privileges or immunities of citizens of the United States, or shall deprive any person of life, liberty or property without due process of law, or deny to any person within their jurisdiction the equal protection of the laws . . .

The object of the amendment was undoubtedly to enforce the absolute equality of the two races before the law, but in the nature of things it could not have been intended to abolish distinctions based upon color, or to enforce social, as distinguished from political equality, or a commingling of the two races upon terms unsatisfactory to either. Laws permitting, and even requiring, their separation in places where they are liable to be brought into contact do not necessarily imply the inferiority of either race to the other . . .

. . . It is also suggested by the learned counsel for the plaintiff in error that the same argument that will justify the state legislature in requiring railways to provide separate accommodations for the two races will also authorize them to require separate cars to be provided for people whose hair is of a certain color, or who are aliens, or who belong to certain nationalities, or to enact laws requiring colored people to walk upon one side of the street, and white people upon the other, or requiring white men's houses to be painted white, and colored men's black, or their vehicles or business signs to be of different colors, upon the theory that one side of the street is as good as the other, or that a house or vehicle of one color is as good as one of another color. The reply to all this is that every exercise of the police power must be reasonable, and extend only to such laws as are enacted in good faith for the promotion for the public good, and not for the annoyance or oppression of a particular class . . .

We consider the underlying fallacy of the plaintiff's argument to consist in the assumption that the enforced separation of the two races stamps the colored race with a badge of inferiority. If this be so, it is not by reason of anything found in the act, but solely because the colored race chooses to put that construction upon it. The argument necessarily assumes that if, as has been more than once the case, and is not unlikely to be so again, the colored race should become the dominant power in the state legislature, and should enact a law in precisely similar terms, it would thereby relegate the white race to an inferior position. We imagine that the white race, at least, would not acquiesce in this assumption. The argument also assumes that social prejudices may be overcome by legislation, and that equal rights cannot be secured to the negro except by an enforced commingling of the two races. We cannot accept this proposition. If the two races are to meet upon terms of social equality, it must be the result of natural affinities, a mutual appreciation of each other's merits and a voluntary consent of individuals . . . Legislation is powerless to eradicate racial instincts or to abolish distinctions based upon physical differences, and the attempt to do so can only result in accentuating the difficulties of the present situation. If the civil and political rights of both races be equal one cannot be inferior to the other civilly or politically. If one race be inferior to the other socially, the Constitution of the United States cannot put them upon the same plane . . .

MR. JUSTICE [John Marshall] HARLAN dissenting.

. . . Every one knows that the statute in question had its origin in the purpose, not so much to exclude white persons from railroad cars occupied by blacks, as to exclude colored people from coaches occupied by or assigned to white persons. Railroad corporations of Louisiana did not make discrimination among whites in the matter of accommodation for travellers. The thing to accomplish was, under the guise of giving equal accommodation for whites and blacks, to compel the latter to keep to themselves while travelling in railroad passenger coaches. No one would be so wanting in candor as to assert the contrary . . .

If a State can prescribe, as a rule of civil conduct, that whites and blacks shall not travel as passengers in the same railroad coach, why may it not so regulate the use of the streets of its cities and towns as to compel white citizens to keep on one side of a street and black citizens to keep on the other? . . . And why may it not also prohibit the commingling of the two races in the galleries of legislative halls or in public assemblages convened for the considerations of the political questions of the day? . . .

The white race deems itself to be the dominant race in this country. And so it is, in prestige, in achievements, in education, in wealth and in power. So, I doubt not, it will continue to be for all time, if it remains true to its great heritage and holds fast to the principles of constitutional liberty. But in view of the Constitution, in the eye of the law, there is in this country no superior, dominant, ruling class of citizens . . . Our Constitution is color-blind, and neither knows nor tolerates classes among citizens . . .

In my opinion, the judgment this day rendered will, in time, prove to be quite as pernicious as the decision made by this tribunal in the Dred Scott case . . . Sixty millions of whites are in no danger from the presence here of eight millions of blacks. The destinies of the two races, in this country, are indissolubly linked together, and the interests of both require that the common government of all shall not permit the seeds of race hate to be planted under the sanction of law. What can more certainly arouse race hate, what more certainly create and perpetuate a feeling of distrust between these races, than state enactments, which, in fact, proceed on the ground that colored citizens are so inferior and degraded that they cannot be allowed to sit in public coaches occupied by white citizens? . . .

The thin disguise of "equal" accommodations for passengers in railroad coaches will not mislead any one, nor atone for the wrong this day done . . .

Source: Plessy v. Ferguson, 163 U.S. 537 (1896), from FindLaw, http://laws.findlaw.com/us/163/537.html.

Document 4.6 in Context
"Let the Mercenary Mud Slingers Do Their Worst": The *Afro-American Sentinel* on William Jennings Bryan

In 1888 a former slave and teacher from North Carolina named Henry P. Cheatham won a House seat as a Republican, making him the sole African American newly elected to, and only the third serving in, Congress that year. A white Nebraska Democrat named William Jennings Bryan joined Cheatham in the House in 1891. Bryan backed a Cheatham-sponsored bill to provide support for public schools, but the measure ultimately failed out of a widespread belief that education was a state rather than a federal obligation. Cheatham's position on other legislative issues also mirrored aspects of the populism that Bryan would later symbolize. For example, Cheatham sponsored a bill to compensate defrauded depositors of the Freedman's Savings and Trust Company (**Document 3.11**), opposed legislation that would allow small farmers in the South to use hog fat and cottonseed oil to make synthetic lard, and advocated the regulation of trusts.

In 1896, with President Grover Cleveland leaving office, Democrats tried to retain the White House by nominating Bryan, who also had Populist and Silver Republican party nominations. By then, millions of African Americans had been disenfranchised, especially in the South, and those black voters who remained registered tended to vote Republican.

During the campaign, the *Afro-American Sentinel* newspaper in Omaha, Nebraska, recalled Bryan's support for Cheatham's education bill to remind its black readers that Bryan, although a Democrat, favored civil rights and opposed lynching. The following editorial endorsement, which might be attributed to his favorite-son status as a Nebraskan, referred to Bryan's nickname, "Boy Orator of the Platte"—a reference to his comparative youth, his speaking skills and a river in Nebraska.

Bryan's own views on race were contradictory. On one hand, he espoused popular rule and democratic values, including equal constitutional rights; on the other, he reflected contemporary pro-segregation opinions. For example, he criticized President Theodore Roosevelt's White House dinner invitation to Booker T. Washington and defended white political supremacy in the South.

Bryan did not secure significant support from African Americans. Even if he had, it was a time of escalating disenfranchisement and the black vote would not have been enough to win the election. Republican William McKinley defeated Bryan in 1896 and again in 1900. William H. Taft's victory in 1908 ended Bryan's third and final White House bid; Bryan later became President Woodrow Wilson's secretary of state.

Cheatham, like his former congressional colleague, went on to encounter multiple political defeats. He lost his 1892 bid for a third term in the House, done in by redistricting, election fraud and the candidacy of a Populist who split the non-Democratic votes. He lost another three-way contest in 1894, and the House rejected his challenge to the results, finding insufficient evidence to support his claim that the election was unfair. And in 1896, his brother-in-law George H. White (**Document 4.9**) edged him out for a Republican congressional nomination.

▬ Document 4.6 ▬
Afro-American Sentinel Editorial on William Jennings Bryan and His Support of Rep. Henry P. Cheatham, R-N.C., August 29, 1896

Some New York Negro, heretofore unheard of, whose leading trait is brass and whose principal lack is brains, has lately written a communication to Mr. Bryan asking him (1) whether he thinks Negroes in the South should have the same rights as whites? (2) whether he condemns lynching in the South? And (3) whether he thinks "the separate car outrage as practiced in Louisiana is just?" The fool concludes his communication with what he doubtless intended as a terrifying remark: "Ten million of colored people will be interested in your reply . . ."

What fact is there in the life of Wm. J. Bryan, whether inquiry be directed to his public or private career, that would justify the slightest suspicion that he would be in the least degree inclined to condone the outrages and injustices under which the colored people of the South—aye, and of some part of the North, including New York—suffer?

During Mr. Bryan's first term in Congress, some five or six years ago, the Hon. H. P. Cheatham, an Afro-American Congressman from North Carolina, introduced a certain measure in the House designed particularly to promote the interest of the colored people of the South. Although a large part—we think a majority—of the Republican members of that House opposed, and eventually defeated Mr. Cheatham's measure, the nobleman, Wm. J. Bryan, with that generosity of heart and earnest eloquence that are his brightest and most conspicuous characteristics, did his best from first to last for its success. The editor of this paper had the good fortune of getting possession of Mr. Cheatham's letter to Mr. Bryan acknowledging the latter's splendid and disinterested services in behalf of this race at that time. As our readers doubtless remember, we printed Mr. Cheatham's letter through several editions of this paper during the memorable campaign which ended in Mr. Bryan's second election to Congress from a district which was believed and conceded to be hopelessly Republican.

Let the mercenary mud slingers do their worst in their attempts to bedaub the character of the "boy orator from the Platte." The buzzards, whether blacks or whites, will find no carrion here upon which to feast their foul appetites.

Source: "A Pro-Bryan Editorial" from the *Afro American Sentinel,* August 29, 1896, in *A Documentary History of the Negro People in the United States,* ed. Herbert Aptheker (New York: Citadel Press, 1969), 818–819.

Document 4.7 in Context
"A View to the Elimination of Every Negro Voter": Constitutional Disenfranchisement in Louisiana

The amendments to Louisiana's constitution enacted in 1898 to disenfranchise African American voters were representative of developments across the post-Reconstruction South. To maintain their political influence and to prevent state retrenchment of civil and economic rights, southern reformers and Populists tried but failed to unite African Americans and poor whites against the growing power of the conservative, mostly wealthy, Democrats who dominated political offices. But the issue of race still trumped appeals to class commonality. Indeed, many Democratic politicians sought to assure poor whites that they had more in common with wealthier whites than with poor blacks.

The results were evident in the imposition of literacy tests, property ownership requirements and poll taxes as prerequisites to vote in many southern states. For example, the Louisiana constitution of 1898 required male citizens aged twenty-one or older to read and write in English or their "mother tongue." Those who could not pass the literacy test could still vote if they owned property worth at least $300 and paid taxes on it, but few blacks held land worth that much.

The concept of a poll tax dated to colonial days when it was used to help finance public schools. The rationale was that people who owned no property—and thus paid no property taxes—should be required to pay some tax to support government services. But by the late nineteenth century, southern states were beginning to find the imposition of such a tax as a prerequisite for voting useful in dissuading poor blacks from casting ballots.

A so-called grandfather clause inserted among the amendments provided an alternative qualification that served almost exclusively as a loophole allowing poor, illiterate whites to vote: if a potential voter, his father or his grandfather had been eligible to vote in any state before January 1, 1867, he was constitutionally exempted from Louisiana's literacy and property requirements. Very few African Americans had been eligible to vote in 1866 because most were former slaves, making the grandfather clause intrinsically racially biased.

States adopted other legal measures to restrain black suffrage, including residency requirements, proof-of-age requirements, disenfranchisement for certain criminal convictions and the absence of procedures to appeal an election registrar's arbitrary decisions. The racial motivations behind these laws were sometimes blatant. Virginia, for example, exempted descendants of Confederate veterans from its voter qualification requirements. Carter Glass, a future white Democratic senator from Virginia, acknowledged the motives behind efforts to disenfranchise blacks during his state's 1901 constitutional convention:

> By fraud, no; by discrimination yes. But it will be discrimination within the letter of the law . . . Why, that is precisely [what] we proposed; that, exactly, is what this convention was elected for—to discriminate to the very extremity of permissible action under the limitation of the Federal Constitution, with a view to the elimination of every Negro voter who can be gotten rid of, legally, without materially impairing the numerical strength of the white electorate.[24]

The president of the 1898 Louisiana constitutional convention, Ernest B. Kruttschnitt, was also blunt, admitting the convention had been called "to eliminate from the electorate the mass of corrupt and illiterate voters who have during the last quarter of a century degraded our politics." He claimed that the "solution of the question of the purification of the electorate" was entrusted to the Democratic party.[25]

The impact of the poll tax and other disenfranchisement tools would be dramatic and long lasting. In 1867 there were 82,907 black voters on the Louisiana rolls. By January 1898—a month before the state's constitutional convention—that number had dropped to 12,902. After Louisiana enacted the amendments, the ranks of black voters decreased rapidly. By 1940, only 897 blacks were registered in the state. The situation was similar across the South. In the seven southern states that still had a poll tax in 1940, an average of only 3 percent of the population voted, contrasted with an average of 25 percent participation in states without such a tax.

The Twenty-fourth Amendment, ratified in 1964, abolished the poll tax for all federal elections.

▬▬ Document 4.7 ▬▬
Amended Constitution of Louisiana, 1898

. . .

ARTICLE 197

Every male citizen of this State and of the United States, native born or naturalized, not less than twenty-one years of age, and possessing the following qualifications, shall be an elector, and shall be entitled to vote at any election in the State by the people, except as may be herein otherwise provided . . .

SECTION 3. He shall be able to read and write, and shall demonstrate his ability to do so when he applies for registration, by making, under oath administered by the registration officer or his deputy, written application therefore, in the English language, or his mother tongue, which application shall contain the essential facts necessary to show that he is entitled to register and vote, and shall be entirely written, dated and signed by him, in the presence of the registration officer or his deputy, without assistance or suggestion from any person or any memorandum whatever, except the form of application hereinafter set forth; provided, however, that if the applicant be unable to write his application in the English language, he shall have the right, if he so demands, to write the same in his mother tongue from the dictation of an interpreter; and if the applicant is unable to write his application by reason of physical disability, the same shall be written at his dictation by the registration officer or his deputy, upon his oath of such disability . . .

SEC. 4. If he be not able to read and write, as provided by Section three of this article, then he shall be entitled to register and vote if he shall, at the time he offers to register, be the bona fide owner of property assessed to him in this State at a valuation of not less than three hundred dollars on the assessment roll of the current year in which he offers to register, or on the roll of the preceding year, if the roll of the current year shall not then have been completed and filed, and on which, if such property be personal only, all taxes due shall have been paid. The applicant for registration under this section shall make oath before the registration office or his deputy, that he is a citizen of the United States and of this State, over the age of twenty-one years; that he possesses the qualifications prescribed in section one of this article, and that he is the owner of property assessed in this State to him at a valuation of not less than three hundred dollars, and if such property be personal only, that all taxes due thereon have been paid.

SEC. 5. No male person who was on January 1st, 1867, or at any date prior thereto, entitled to vote under the Constitution or statutes of any State of the United States, wherein he then resided, and no son or grandson of any such person not less than twenty-one years of age at the date of the adoption of this Constitution, and no male person of foreign birth, who was naturalized prior to the first day of January, 1898[,] shall be denied the right to register and vote in this State by reason of his failure to possess the educational or property qualifications prescribed by this Constitution; provided, he shall have resided in this State for five years next preceding the date at which he shall apply for registration, and shall have registered in accordance with the terms of this article prior to September 1, 1898, and no person shall be entitled to register under this section after said date.

ARTICLE 198

No person less than sixty years of age shall be permitted to vote at any election in the State who shall not, in addition to the qualifications above prescribed, have paid on or before the 31st day of December, of each year, for the two years preceding the year in which he offers to vote, a poll tax of one dollar per annum, to be used exclusively in aid of the public schools of the parish in which such tax shall have been collected; which tax is hereby imposed on every male resident of this State between the age of twenty-one and sixty years. Poll taxes shall be a lien only upon assessed property, and no process shall issue to enforce the collection of the same except against assessed property . . .

ARTICLE 200

No person shall vote at any primary election or in any convention or other political assembly held for the purpose of nominating any candidate for public office, unless he is at the time a registered voter. And in all political conventions in this State the apportionment of representation shall be on the basis of population . . .

Source: "State Constitution of Louisiana, 1898, Suffrage and Elections," from Yale University, Gilder Lehrman Center for the Study of Slavery, Resistance, and Abolition, www.yale.edu/glc/archive/1154.htm.

Document 4.8 in Context
"North Carolina . . . Is the Only State in the Union Where Negro Domination Is Possible": *The Democratic Hand Book* of 1898

By 1898 North Carolina was the only state with an African American representative serving in Congress: Republican George H. White, who was running for reelection. But race was a divisive issue in North Carolina politics at the end of the nineteenth century, as was clearly set out in a publication of the state's Democratic Executive Committee. The rationale for the *Democratic Hand Book,* released before the 1898 elections, was given in a short, seemingly benign introduction by party leaders: "The condition of public affairs that confronts us calls for the most strenuous efforts on the part of all patriotic North Carolinians to restore good government to our beloved State." [26] For 199 pages, however, the handbook lambasted "the negro and his white ally" for lawlessness, fraud, favoritism, incompetence, high taxes and extravagant governmental spending.[27] It also criticized Populists who had allied themselves with Republicans in the state's Fusion movement, an anti-Democratic coalition that allocated political offices among candidates of each party to form unified election slates.

The handbook waved a red flag in front of white voters, warning of the possibility of black rule, which could lead to blacks migrating into the state:

> It is a well-known fact that South Carolina and other Southern States, in defense of good government in those States, have made negro rule in those States impossible. In the States to the north of us it cannot be, for the negro is too few in number. It may now be stated as a fact that North Carolina, under Republican rule, is the only State in the Union where negro domination is possible. Who can say, if Republican rule is to go on in this State, that we are not to have an influx of negroes from other States, drawn here by that condition, and that communities that are now exempt from the dangers of negro rule may not soon be subjected to it? [28]

It also quoted an eight-year-old letter in which the state's sitting Republican governor, Daniel Russell, wrote that "the negroes of the South are largely savages." The Democrats commented:

> We do not agree with Mr. Russell when he calls these people savages. They are not savages. They are civilized beings, made so in the providence of God by being brought into contact with the Anglo-Saxon race . . . But we do agree with Mr. Russell when he says they are unfit to govern. The difference between him and us is that he says they are unfit to govern but he puts them at it, while we say they are unfit for it and we do not put them at it.[29]

While the handbook did not explicitly advocate violent suppression of black political and civil rights, its release coincided with, and in effect condoned, such violence in North Carolina. The 1898 campaign was marked by the threatening presence of armed Red Shirts at pro-Democratic events and parades, some attended by Sen. Benjamin R. "Pitchfork Ben" Tillman, D-S.C., the nation's best-known white supremacist. Shortly before the election, Governor Russell issued a proclamation

> commanding all ill-disposed persons, whether of this or that political party, or of no political party, to immediately desist from all unlawful practices and all turbulent conduct . . . And I do further command and enjoin it upon all good and law abiding citizens not to allow themselves to become excited by any appeals that may be made to their passions and prejudices by the representatives of any political party whatsoever.[30]

The Red Shirts ignored the proclamation. Intimidated Republicans and Populists of both races stayed away from the polls, and Democrats won most offices; George White, however, managed to hold his House seat. Two years later, Ohio's African American *Cleveland Gazette* reported that Red Shirts fatally beat a white North Carolina man "who had the temerity . . . to express himself as being opposed to the amendment disfranchising the Afro-Americans of that state." [31]

▬ Document 4.8 ▬
The Democratic Hand Book, 1898, North Carolina

. . . In our State the men who have been chosen by the Democratic people as their leaders, or as their candidates, or who may hereafter be chosen, are so chosen because they are in touch with the people and are steadfast believers in the principles of Democracy as taught by Jefferson and promulgated by [William Jennings] Bryan . . .

Republican Rule in North Carolina.

On the first day of July, 1868, the Republican Party took complete control of North Carolina. It had the Executive, Legislative and Judicial Departments of the Government, and nearly all the counties and towns were likewise under its control. No party ever had a better opportunity to serve a people and win their gratitude, but no party ever treated a people worse. It found a people poor and struggling amid the ruins of a desolating war. They needed good laws, the party gave them bad. They needed peace and rest, the party gave them violence and disorder. They needed low taxes, the party made them high . . . They needed encouragement, the party gave them the bitter dregs of disappointment. They needed protection, the party gave them a reign of lawlessness. They needed economy, the party gave them reckless extravagance. They needed honesty in government, the party gave them an era of corruption. They needed patriots for legislators, the party gave them knaves . . . The Legislature became a stench in the nostrils of decent men. Gloom settled over the State and the people, sore and oppressed, turned to the Democratic Party for deliverance. . .

Democratic Rule in North Carolina.

The election in 1870 for members of the General Assembly was hotly contested by the Republican and Democratic parties. The Republican Party made a supreme effort to retain control of the law-making branch of the government. The Democrats made the fight against the Republicans, then as now, on their bad, extravagant, disgraceful record, and they carried both houses by large majorities. It is true there was no Populist Party then to help the Republicans. Many men who are now acting with the Populist Party were then found in the Democratic ranks manfully struggling to rescue the State from the Republican Party. As the campaign progresses in this second great battle for the rescue of the law-making branch of the government and these men learn more of the evils of Republican rule, it is hoped they will again be found doing battle for Good Government and White Supremacy.

So, in 1870, the Democratic Party obtained control of the legislative branch of the government and held it continuously till 1894—a period of twenty-four years . . .

When this party came into power in the Legislature it proceeded to repeal bad laws and to enact in their stead good ones; to reduce taxes and expenditures; to economize in every possible way; to restore law and order; to provide for better schools, and to do all things within the power of the legislative branch of the government for the protection and betterment of the people . . .

The Common Schools.

. . . The Democratic Party believes in education . . .

Appreciating the importance of having trained teachers for the common schools, the Democratic Party established normal schools at various points in the State for the training of these teachers. It began, as we now remember, with the Normal School at the University for the white teachers, and the State Normal School at Fayetteville for the colored teachers. These were followed by others at different points in the State for each race . . .

The Democratic Party in its last Convention has declared that, if returned to power, it will by appropriate legislation make it impossible for a negro to be put upon a white school committee. Now let it be well understood that the party does not mean to take any back steps in the cause of education; but it does propose to obey the spirit as well as the letter of the Constitution. When the people ratified that instrument, in 1876, they decreed that the white and colored schools should forever be kept separate, and that is just what the Democratic Party proposes to do . . . It will give to each race, and to the schools of each race all that properly belongs to them, without any unjust discrimination, but it will put white men in charge of white schools and colored men in charge of colored schools . . .

Democratic Administration in County, City and Town.

. . . When the Democratic Party came into power it found that in many of the counties and towns of the East heavy taxes had been levied and collected, and the money had been stolen or squandered. The Republican Party then, as now, was weighed down by the negro, and to appease him, counties and towns, then as now, were turned over to him to pillage and plunder . . . Negro magistrates and negro officials then, as now, went through the farce of administering the law . . .

The Democratic Party addressed itself to the work of bringing order out of chaos in those communities. Ignorant, vicious, worthless officials were replaced by competent white men; the levying and collecting of the taxes were closely scrutinized; rigid economy was practiced; honesty prevailed in every department; expenses were decreased, and all laws were faithfully and impartially administered . . . Under Democratic rule these same counties and towns were under the control of honest, capable white men . . . The blacks, as well as the whites, were vastly better off . . .

The Republican Party has the negro on its hands, and it has to pay some respect to his wishes. The negro makes up about four-fifths of the Republican Party in this State, and he must be consulted and appeased. A party thus constituted cannot give good government to the people. To hold the negro solid the party must give him the local offices in the counties and towns where he is numerous. If the party gives him these local offices, then bad government must follow . . .

The Composition of the Republican Party.

. . . Go to a Republican convention in the counties where a majority of the Republicans are black, and you will see the worst element of the white Republicans mixing with the blacks and controlling these conventions. The more decent white Republicans hold themselves aloof and look on with disgust. The men who can best control and manipulate the negroes are most in evidence at these conventions, while the better class of Republicans are conspicuous by their absence. One of the results of this condition of things is that it often happens that bad or incompetent white men are chosen by the negroes to fill the local offices in county and town . . .

The Democratic Party and the Negro.

. . . It is likewise equally manifest that it is a matter of public interest to inquire into the attitude of the Democratic Party towards the negro. Is it one of hostility, or one of genuine interest in his real welfare? . . .

No well-informed, truthful man, black or white, can deny that the negro owes about all he has, in the way of public school facilities, to the Democratic Party; and no one knows better than the negro himself to whom and to what class of people he goes for help in his church work and in his various enterprises for the intellectual and moral elevation of his race . . . Under the benign rule of the Democratic Party during the long period it held unbroken power in North Carolina, the negro race enjoyed peace and quiet, and had the full protection of the laws, and the conditions were such that the negro made rapid improvement and realized to the utmost the blessings of good government. But there is one thing the Democratic Party never has done and never will do—and that is to set the negro up . . .

To Rule Over White Men.

It is no fault of the negro that he is here, and he is not to be punished for being here; but this is a white man's country and white men must control and govern it. They must govern it not only because they are white men, but because they can do it better than the negro. The negro has, whenever tried, demonstrated his unfitness and inability to rule. It is better for the negro, as well as for the white man, that the white man should make and administer the laws. It is a mercy to the negro himself to save him from his own ruin. It has been in the past, and is to-day, the special mission of the Democratic Party to rescue the white people of the east from the curse of negro domination . . .

Difference of Republican and Democratic Treatment of the Negro.

The Republican party uses the negro for all he is worth for election purposes, and in pursuance of this general purpose it sets him up to rule over white men. The fact that he is unfit for the position to which he aspires makes no difference. He must have enough of the local pie to appease his hunger, or else those who manipulate his vote may have trouble . . .

Source: State Democratic Executive Committee of North Carolina, *The Democratic Hand Book, 1898* (Raleigh, N.C.: Edwards and Broughton, 1898), from the University Library, University of North Carolina at Chapel Hill, http://docsouth.unc.edu/nc/dem1898/menu.html.

Document 4.9 in Context
"The Citizens Took into Their Own Hands the Law": Failed Efforts to Enact Federal Anti-Lynching Legislation

In the aftermath of Reconstruction, violent acts motivated by discrimination against African Americans escalated as far as murders committed by vigilante lynch mobs. In 1900 the only black member of Congress, Rep. George H. White, R-N.C., introduced a bill to make lynching a federal crime, but it went nowhere, despite widespread evidence of lynchings and similar lawlessness, and despite at least token presidential attention. In a February 1890 speech, White claimed that 166 people had been lynched in the United States, 155 of them in the South, between January 1, 1898, and April 25, 1889, alone; 145 were black and 10 white.

As early as 1892, the lynching issue was put before Congress by Sen. William A. Peffer, a white Populist from Kansas, who read on the Senate floor a petition in the form of a resolution "adopted by the colored people of Riley," a city in his state. He told his colleagues, "Many poor people, particularly colored people, are being hounded and hunted up when merely suspected of a crime, and hanged or shot to death," and he urged Congress to "take prompt action." [32] The brief petition said of Kansas:

> That we deplore the failure of the General Government to adequately protect our race in the enjoyment of the rights guaranteed to it in the Constitution. In that mob or lynch law has been permitted to take the place of the regular orderly procedure of the established tribunals of justice, so that trials by jury for members of our race accused or even suspected of crime [have] practically ceased in many parts of our country.[33]

Peffer's petition died in the Senate Judiciary Committee.

In his December 1891 State of the Union address, President Benjamin Harrison had characterized the lynching of "eleven men of Italian nativity by a mob of citizens" in New Orleans "a most deplorable and discreditable incident" but did not mention violence against blacks.[34] In December 1892, however, he condemned the lynching of African Americans:

> The frequent lynching of colored people accused of crime is without the excuse, which has sometimes been urged by mobs for a failure to pursue the appointed methods for the punishment of crime, that the accused have an undue influence over courts and juries. Such acts are a reproach to the community where they occur, and so far as they can be made the subject of Federal jurisdiction the strongest repressive legislation is demanded.[35]

The 1896 GOP platform took a stand against the violence and drew no distinction between foreign and American victims: "We proclaim our unqualified condemnation of the uncivilized and barbarous practices well known as lynching and killing of human beings, suspected or charged with crime, without process of law." [36] The plight of victimized noncitizens, however, took precedence in a Washington concerned about treaty obligations. President William McKinley's December 1899 State of the Union Address mentioned five more Italian victims in Louisiana, but was silent on the fate of black victims.

Dozens of anti-lynching proposals failed in the decades after White's bill, whether they focused on the rights of aliens or those of U.S. citizens, black or white. Any bills that managed to emerge from committee and win approval in one chamber of Congress, inevitably died in the other chamber. Frustrated by the lack of progress, the NAACP in 1916 launched a national campaign against lynching, including investigations of incidents and protests to state officials.

The Democratic party platform consistently failed to address the issue in any capacity, although President Woodrow Wilson, the titular head of the national party, condemned lynching in 1918. Southern Democrats, however, challenged any potential federal legislation as an unconstitutional intrusion into state authority to punish criminal activity.

The following accounts from the African American and mainstream press give a sense of the lawlessness from the early 1890s through the early years of the 1900s. They include an account of lynchings in Georgia by African American journalist Ida B. Wells, who spent much of her career engaged in a crusade against lynching, and a letter to a newspaper by Booker T. Washington.

<hr>

▬▬ Document 4.9 ▬▬
Newspaper Accounts Chronicling Lynching and Vigilantism, 1891–1904

From the New York Times, *March 27, 1891:*

Middlesborough, Ky., March 26—A terrible tragedy took place this morning at Cumberland Gap, Tenn., a few miles from here, in which A. J. Burke, the telegraph operator at that place was shot and instantly killed by Thomas Hunter, a negro. Reports are conflicting as to what caused Hunter to commit the deed, but from what can be learned it seems that Burke and Hunter fell out over some trifling matter in a saloon . . .

The murderer then fled, but was captured here this morning, and on the way back to the Gap the officers were met by sixty armed men, who took Hunter from them and hanged him. His body was then riddled with bullets.

From the New York Times, *December 12, 1892:*

Wheeling, West Va., Dec. 11—Police Officer James Dillon was killed and Constable Burton mortally wounded near Bluefield yesterday by a colored man named Cornelius Coffee. Coffee made his escape and boarded a Chesapeake and Ohio train, but was arrested in Pocahontas, Va., and held until the arrival of Detective Eugene Robinson . . . who brought the prisoner over the line into West Virginia. At Keystone, a little hamlet a few miles from the State line, a band of men stopped the train, entered the car, quietly relieved Robinson of his prisoner, and proceeded to the nearest tree, where Coffee was strung up and his body riddled with bullets.

From the **New York Times,** *February 2, 1893:*

Paris, Texas, Feb. 1—Henry Smith, the negro assailant of four-year-old Myrtle Vance, has expiated, in part, his crime by death at the stake . . .

When the news came last night that he had been captured, that he had been identified . . . the city was joyful over the apprehension of the brute.

Hundreds of people poured into the city from the adjoining country, and the word passed from lip to lip that the punishment should fit the crime, and that death by fire was the penalty that Smith should pay for the most atrocious murder and outrage in Texas history . . .

Officers saw the futility of checking the passions of the mob, so the law was laid aside, and the citizens took into their own hands the law and burned the prisoner at the stake . . .

Here Smith was placed upon a scaffold six feet square and ten feet high, securely bound, within the view of all beholders.

Here the victim was tortured for fifty minutes by red-hot irons being thrust against his quivering body. Commencing at the foot, the brands were placed him inch by inch until they were thrust against the face.

Then, being apparently dead, kerosene was poured upon him, cottonseed hulls placed beneath him, and he was set on fire. Curiosity seekers have carried away already all that was left after the memorable event, even to pieces of charcoal . . .

From the **Cleveland Gazette,** *July 17, 1897:*

Birmingham, Ala.—Four men (white) of Blossburg, a mining camp 15 miles west, are in jail here, charged with lynching Jim Thomas, the Afro-American who said he knew who crawled into Mrs. James Brown's room at Blossburg and attempted an assault, but who never gave the name. Afro-Americans at Blossburg became indignant over the lynching and began arming themselves. Sheriff O'Brien, learning of shipments of rifles and ammunition from the city to Blossburg, telegraphed the governor of the state for authority to stop the shipments. Of course authority was given but the sheriff missed the lot. The men were arrested on warrants sworn out by Afro-Americans, and for fear of a conflict, had a preliminary trial in Birmingham on Thursday . . .

From the **Atlanta Constitution,** *June 18, 1898:*

Shreveport, La., June 3—A thousand people gathered at Doyline, which is situated on the Vicksburg, Shreveport and Pacific railroad, about eighteen miles from here, to witness the burning at stake of William Street, a negro who attempted the ruin and murder of Mrs. Parish . . .

The people erected a post beside the railroad track near the town, quietly laid the lightwood and kindling, saturated with coal oil, preparatory to chaining Street to the post. Street was a gingerbread colored man of about twenty-eight years. He confessed the crime to a colored minister, but said a negro minister named John Rhodes was implicated.

When going to the stake he looked frightened and refused to have anything to say . . . The flames were started at 1 o'clock.

It was a sickening sight which lasted ten minutes, when Street was a charred mess.

From Ida B. Wells-Barnett, Lynch Law in Georgia, *June 20, 1899:*

During six weeks of the months of March and April just past, twelve colored men were lynched in Georgia, the reign of outlawry culminating in the torture and hanging of the colored preacher, Elijah Strickland, and the burning alive of Samuel Wilkes, alias Hose, Sunday, April 23, 1899.

The real purpose of these savage demonstrations is to teach the Negro that in the South he has no rights that the law will enforce. Samuel Hose was burned to teach the Negroes that no matter what a white man does to them, they must not resist. Hose, a servant, had killed Cranford, his employer. An example must be made. Ordinary punishment was deemed inadequate. This Negro must be burned alive . . . The daily press offered reward for the capture of Hose and then openly incited the people to burn him as soon as caught. The mob carried out the plan in every savage detail.

Of the twelve men lynched during that reign of unspeakable barbarism, only one was charged with an assault upon a woman. Yet Southern apologists justify their savagery on the ground that Negroes are lynched only because of their crimes against women.

From the Cleveland Gazette, *January 5, 1901:*

Indianapolis, Ind.—On the night of September 14, 1897, a mob broke into Ripley county jail at Versailles and brutally beat and afterward hanged five of the prisoners, among them being William H. Jenkins. His widow went to Illinois and there took out letters of administration and afterward brought suit in the Federal court here against Sheriff Bushing for failure to protect her husband from the mob, and against 70 citizens of the county, charging each with complicity in her husband's murder. To-day the suits were all compromised and withdrawn, the defendants paying Mrs. Jenkins $5,000.

From Booker T. Washington's Letter in the Birmingham Age-Herald, *February 29, 1904:*

Within the last fortnight three members of my race have been burned at the stake; of these one was a woman, Not one of the three was charged with any crime even remotely connected with the abuse of a white woman . . . All of these burnings took place in broad daylight and two of them occurred on Sunday afternoon in sight of a Christian church . . .

If the law is disregarded when a Negro is concerned, it will soon be disregarded when a white man is concerned . . .

Worst of all these outrages take place in communities where there are Christian churches; in the midst of people who have their Sunday schools, their Christian Endeavor Societies and Young Men's Christian Associations, where collections are taken up for sending missionaries to Africa and China and the rest of the so-called heathen world . . .

Sources, in order of first appearance: Schneider Collection, ed., *African American History in the Press, 1851–1899: From the Coming of the Civil War to the Rise of Jim Crow as Reported and Illustrated in Selected Newspapers of the Time* (Detroit: Gale, 1996), vol. 2: *New York Times,* March 27, 1891, reprinted as "A Negro Murderer Lynched," 1173; *New York Times,* December 12, 1892, reprinted as "Taken from a Detective and Lynched," 1186; *New York Times,* February 2, 1893, reprinted as "Another Negro Burned," 1190–1192; *Atlanta Constitution,* June 18, 1898, reprinted as "Negro Outlaw Is Burned at Stake," 1250. *Cleveland Gazette,* from the Ohio Historical Society: "Arrested for a Lynching," July 17, 1897, http://dbs.ohiohistory.org/africanam/det.cfm?ID=18755; "A $5,000 Lynching," January 5, 1901, http://dbs.ohiohistory.org/africanam/det.cfm?ID=19439. Ida B.

Wells-Barnett, *Lynch Law in Georgia* (Chicago: Chicago Colored Citizens, June 20, 1899). Booker T. Washington, "A Protest against the Burning and Lynching of Negroes," *Birmingham Age Herald,* February 29, 1904, from Library of Congress, http://memory.loc.gov/ammem/aap/ aaphome.html.

Document 4.10 in Context
"Defense of the Negro Race—Charges Answered": Rep. George H. White's Valedictory Speech

When Rep. George H. White, R-N.C., the last former slave to serve in Congress, delivered his final House floor speech on January 29, 1901, he was nearing the end of his second term. He had spent the prior four years as the lone African American in Congress, and he would be the last to serve until Republican Oscar S. De Priest of Illinois was elected in 1928. With Democrats in firm control of North Carolina politics, White had chosen not to seek reelection in November 1900. Most southern states already had largely disenfranchised African American voters (**Document 4.6**), and White's departure in March 1901 would end a quarter century of continuous black representation of North Carolina's Second District.

Measured by legislative accomplishments, White's tenure at the Capitol had been unproductive. His landmark bill (**Document 4.9**) to make lynching a capital crime akin to treason died in committee; as he put it, "I took occasion to address myself in detail to this particular measure, but with all my efforts the bill still sweetly sleeps in the room of the committee to which it was referred." [37] Nor did his colleagues act on his proposals to compensate the cheated depositors of the Freedman's Savings and Trust Company (**Document 3.11**), former representative Robert Smalls, R-S.C. (**Document 2.4**), and would-be Republican representative and senator P. B. S. Pinchback of Louisiana (**Document 3.8**).

The vehicle for White's final speech was a debate over agricultural appropriations, a topic he addressed briefly before launching into a defense of black Americans and a critique of several of his white colleagues by name—Reps. William W. Kitchin, D-N.C., Oscar W. Underwood, D-Ala., and Peter J. Otey, R-Va. His candid remarks were greeted with what the *Congressional Record* described as "loud applause" and, not surprisingly, attracted widespread attention in the black press. In its account, the *African Methodist Episcopal Church Review* noted the death of the first African American senator, Republican Hiram R. Revels of Mississippi, two weeks before the speech and editorialized:

> Mr. White gave his congressional death a dramatic tinge in a speech that was in his manliest vein, but whose chief worth, in our opinion, lies in his prophecy that the Negro will return to these halls again. No thoughtful Negro doubts this. The Negro has never doubted his destiny and his capability . . . He saw the disenfranchisement long ago that has come but to-day when the North should forget its humanitarianism in its commercialism. [38]

After his term ended, White opted not to return to politically hostile North Carolina. Instead, he practiced law until 1905 in Washington, then moved to Philadelphia, where he engaged in business, invested in real estate and founded the city's first black-owned bank.

▬▬ Document 4.10 ▬▬
Rep. George H. White, R-N.C., Delivers His Valedictory Speech on the Floor of the House of Representatives, January 29, 1901

. . . In the consideration of the bill now under debate the Committee on Agriculture has had a wide and very varied experience . . .

But, Mr. Chairman, there are others on this committee and in this House who are far better prepared to enlighten the world with their eloquence as to what the agriculturists of this country need than your humble servant . . . I shall consume the remainder of my time in reverting to measures and facts that have in them more weighty interests to me and mine than that of agriculture—matters of life and existence.

I want to enter a plea for the colored man, the colored woman, the colored boy, and the colored girl of this country. I would not thus digress from the question at issue and detain the House in a discussion of the interests of this particular people at this time but for the constant and the persistent efforts of certain gentlemen upon this floor to mold and rivet public sentiment against us as a people and to lose no opportunity to hold up the unfortunate few who commit crimes and depredations and lead lives of infamy and shame, as other races do, as fair specimens of representatives of the entire colored race. And at no time, perhaps, during the Fifty-sixth Congress were these charges and countercharges, containing, as they do, slanderous statements, more persistently magnified and pressed upon the attention of the nation than during the consideration of the recent reapportionment bill, which is now a law . . .

In the catalogue of members of Congress in this House perhaps none have been more persistent in their determination to bring the black man into disrepute and, with a labored effort, to show that he was unworthy of the right of citizenship than my colleague from North Carolina, Mr. [William W.] KITCHIN. During the first session of this Congress, while the Constitutional amendment was pending in North Carolina, he labored long and hard to show that the white race was at all times and under all circumstances superior to the negro by inheritance if not otherwise, and the excuse for his party supporting that amendment, which has since been adopted, was that an illiterate negro was unfit to participate in making the laws of a sovereign State and the administration and execution of them; but an illiterate white man living by his side, with no more or perhaps not as much property, with no more exalted character, no higher thoughts of civilization, no more knowledge of the handicraft of government, had by birth, because he was white, inherited some peculiar qualification, clear, I presume, only in the mind of the gentleman who endeavored to impress it upon others, that entitled him to vote . . .

I might state as a further general fact that the Democrats of North Carolina got possession of the State and local government since my last election in 1898, and that I bid adieu to these historic walls on the 4th day of next March, and that the brother of Mr. KITCHIN will succeed me. Comment is unnecessary . . .

It would be unfair, however, for me to leave the inference upon the minds of those who hear me that all of the white people of the State of North Carolina hold views with Mr. KITCHIN and think as he does. Thank God there are many noble exceptions to the example he sets, that, too, in the Democratic party; men who have never been afraid that one uneducated, poor, depressed negro could put to flight and chase into degradation two educated, wealthy, thrifty white men. There never has been, nor ever will be, any negro domination in that State, and no one knows it any better than the Democratic party. It is a convenient howl, however, often resorted to in order to consummate a diabolical purpose by scaring the weak and gullible whites into support of measures and men suitable to the demagogue and the ambitious office seeker, whose crave for office overshadows and puts to flight all other considerations, fair or unfair . . .

Not content with all that has been done to the black man, not because of any deeds that he has done, Mr. [Oscar W.] UNDERWOOD advances the startling information that these people have been thrust upon the whites of the South, forgetting, perhaps, the horrors of the slave trade, the unspeakable horrors of the transit from the shores of Africa by means of the middle passage to the American clime; the enforced bondage of the blacks and their descendants for two and a half centuries in the United States, now, for the first time perhaps in the history of our lives, the information comes that these poor, helpless, and in the main inoffensive people were thrust upon our Southern brethren . . .

. . . Since [1868] we have reduced the illiteracy of the race at least 45 per cent. We have written and published near 500 books. We have nearly 300 newspapers, 3 of which are dailies. We have now in practice over 2,000 lawyers and a corresponding number of doctors. We have accumulated over $12,000,000 worth of school property and about $40,000,000 worth of church property . . .

We are operating successfully several banks, commercial enterprises among our people in the Southland, including 1 silk mill and 1 cotton factory. We have 32,000 teachers in the schools of the country; we have built, with the aid of our friends, about 20,000 churches, and support 7 colleges, 17 academies, 50 high schools, 5 law schools, 5 medical schools, and 25 theological seminaries. We have over 600,000 acres of land in the South alone. The cotton produced, mainly by black labor, has increased from 4,669,770 bales in 1860 to 11,235,000 in 1899. All this we have done under the most adverse circumstances. We have done it in the face of lynching, burning at the stake, with the humiliation of "Jim Crow" cars, the disfranchisement of our male citizens, slander and degradation of our women, with the factories closed against us, no negro permitted to be conductor on the railway cars, whether run through the streets of our cities or across the prairies of our great country, no negro permitted to run as engineer on a locomotive, most of the mines closed against us. Labor unions—carpenters, painters, brick masons, machinists, hackmen, and those supplying nearly every conceivable avocation for livelihood have banded themselves together to better their condition, but, with few exceptions, the black face has been left out . . . With all these odds against us, we are forging our way ahead, slowly, perhaps, but surely. You may tie us and then taunt us for a lack of bravery, but one day we will break the bonds. You may use our labor for two and a half centuries and then taunt us for our poverty, but let me remind you we will not always remain poor. You may withhold even the knowledge of how to read God's word and learn the way from earth to glory and then taunt us for our ignorance, but we would remind you that there is plenty of room at the top, and we are climbing . . .

Now, Mr. Chairman, before concluding my remarks I want to submit a brief recipe for the solution of the so-called American negro problem. He asks no special favors, but simply demands that he be given the same chance for existence, for earning a livelihood, for raising himself in the scales of manhood and womanhood that are accorded to kindred nationalities. Treat him as a man; go into his home and learn of his social conditions; learn of his cares, his troubles, and his hopes for the future; gain his confidence; open the doors of industry to him; let the word "negro," "colored," and "black" be stricken from all the organizations enumerated in the federation of labor.

Help him to overcome his weaknesses, punish the crime-committing class by the courts of the land, measure the standard of the race by its best material, cease to mold prejudicial and unjust public sentiment against him, and my word for it, he will learn to support, hold up the hands of, and join in with that political party, that institution, whether secular or religious, in every community where he lives, which is destined to do the greatest good for the greatest number. Obliterate race hatred, party prejudice, and help us to achieve nobler ends, greater results, and become more satisfactory citizens to our brother in white.

This, Mr. Chairman, is perhaps the negroes' temporary farewell to the American Congress; but let me say, Phoenix-like he will rise up some day and come again. These parting words are in behalf of an outraged, heart-broken, bruised, and bleeding, but God-fearing people, faithful, industrious, loyal people—rising people, full of potential force . . .

Source: Congressional Record, 56th Cong., 2d sess., January 29, 1901, 1634–1638.

Document 4.11 in Context
"A Friend to the Negro by Action, Utterances and Appointments": Republicans Seek Black Political Support

While Democratic publications such as North Carolina's *Democratic Hand Book* (**Document 4.8**) made blatantly racist appeals to white voters, Republicans worked to retain the loyalty of African American voters—even though most had been disenfranchised by state laws or by threats and intimidation. For example, the GOP published a political pamphlet lauding Republican president William McKinley for proving himself "a friend to the negro by action, utterances and appointments" [39] and lambasting Democrats as "the party engaged in a comprehensive plan of negro degradation." [40] Sections of the *Republican Text-Book for Colored Voters* carried such titles as "Appointments of Colored Men in the Diplomatic and Consular Service by President McKinley" and "Millions Drawn by Colored Men from the Federal Treasury." The president's December 16, 1898, remarks in Tuskegee, Alabama, lauding Booker T. Washington were also included.

The booklet incorporated drawings of—and effusive comments about—black Republican political leaders, including: former representative George H. White of North Carolina, the last African American to serve as a member of Congress until Oscar De Priest, R-Ill., took the oath of office in 1929 (**Document 4.10**), whose "eloquent voice has been frequently raised . . . in defence of his race and in denunciation of the fraud and violence of Democratic political methods";[41] P. B. S. Pinchback, the former interim governor of Louisiana whose claims to Senate and House seats had been rejected (**Document 3.8**), described as "the last of that splendid galaxy of intellectual giants known to Afro-Americans as the 'old guard' "[42]; and former representative Henry P. Cheatham of North Carolina, then recorder of deeds for the District of Columbia and "a strong race man, ever ready to advance the interests of the young men, with whom he is an especial favorite." [43]

The booklet championed McKinley and the Republican Party as the sole allies of political rights for African Americans. When he was a representative from Ohio, McKinley had made a strong floor speech in favor of the 1890 Elections Bill (**Document 4.4**) that passed in the House but died in the Senate. Thus the pamphlet reminded black voters that "a Republican Congress, under the leadership of such men as William McKinley," had "passed a Federal election law through the House of Representatives . . . It was killed in the Senate by the united Democratic party." [44] And given the political reality of Democratic dominance across the South, the Republican booklet made sure to attack Democratic practices in the North as well, where black support could be essential to gaining or retaining power.

▬▬ Document 4.11 ▬▬
A Republican Text-book for Colored Voters, 1901

. . .

Our President and His Administration.

. . . In the fall of 1892 [Democrat] Grover Cleveland was elected President. Six months after his election several prominent failures of old and well-established financial institutions occurred in several large cities. Six months later a panic, which in severity, evil consequences, and in far-reaching malignancy has been without parallel in modern history, had wrecked great banks, closed up thousands of mills and manufacturing plants; thrown millions of laborers idle upon the streets and highways of the land; brought want and starvation to the homes of a great people, and had not yet completed its stupendously ruinous work. The people had called into power a Democratic administration, and had brought themselves financial and economic ruin, an era of suicides and despair. Four weary and hopeless years passed on, which, in their blightful and baneful effects upon the farmer, the mechanic, and the laborer, upon the great body of the American people, who constitute the "bone and sinew" of the land, and no analogy or comparison in all history . . .

President Lincoln was expected to restrict a social evil, not to eradicate it. William McKinley was expected to bring prosperity to 70,000,000 people of every class by a wise and sagacious administration of the great powers which had been conferred upon him.

Has he proved himself equal to the task?

Aye—and more! Prosperity has long been a joyful and an abiding fact. Labor is employed everywhere. The product of the farm finds a ready market in the nation and beyond the seas. American manufactures have received a stimulus and an impetus under this administration never before known, and has out-rivaled foreign competition in many instances for the European, African and Oriental trade . . .

Four years of Republican administration have been accompanied by a return of prosperity. Confidence, so long deferred, has been restored. The people have entered upon a new era of national greatness, and President William McKinley has been the trained and veteran pilot at the helm who has successfully guided the grand old Ship of State through every threatening storm . . .

The Relation of the Republican and Democratic Parties to the Negro.

In the preceding chapter we have discussed briefly the magnificent and indisputable results which have come to the American people as a result of President McKinley's administration. Results by which the negro has profited as well as any other class of citizens; profited in millions of dollars earned; profited in high Federal appointments; profited in a much more liberal recognition in the consular and diplomatic service than ever before in his history as a citizen; profited in high military commands, running through every rank, from that of second lieutenant to colonel; profited by having had a glorious opportunity of elevating his military reputation in the eyes of mankind, and wringing reluctant and eloquent praise from the lips and pens of those who formerly descanted upon his inherent race inferiority; profited by having a President in the White House who placed himself squarely on the side of justice and denounced the infamous barbarity of lynch law in his inaugural address as well as his annual message to the Fifty-sixth Congress.

The negro was invested with popular rights by the Republican party. Those rights have been curtailed and nullified by the Democratic party in many States. Life, liberty and happiness can be enjoyed by every honest and industrious negro in any State where the principles of the Republican party are dominant. Life, liberty and happiness are denied black men in their full meaning in every Southern State dominated by the Democratic party. Law, order and justice reign supreme in every State dominated by the Republican party. Lawlessness and injustice, lynching, murder and incendiarism are practiced on black men in every Southern State dominated by the Democratic party. The republican party, by constitutional amendments, made the negro politically equal to every other citizen. The Democratic party in Louisiana, Mississippi, Alabama, North and South Carolina and other Southern States has adopted State constitutions taking away from the negro practically everything given him by the Republican party in the shape of political rights . . .

The Republican party has never passed a "Jim Crow" law. The Democratic party has passed all such laws. A Republican President has appointed reputable black men to Federal offices. Men of the Democratic party have shot them to pieces . . .

The Negro and the Army under President McKinley's Administration.

In the Spanish-American war there were commissioned 260 colored officers, who drew from the Federal treasury an average amount of $1,450, which, including travel pay to their homes and allowances, would raise the average to $1,700 each.

There were fifteen thousand enlisted men in the service, whose pay and allowances averaged $255 each.

260 officers, $1,700 each	$442,000
15,000 enlisted men, $255 each	3,825,000
Total	$4,267,000

Thus it will be seen that the colored men will have drawn from the Federal treasury, under President McKinley's first administration, the enormous and unprecedented figures of $8,477,000.

Many of the young colored men who served in the Spanish-American war came from the rural districts of the South, saved their money, returned to their homes and bought small farms, paid off mortgages, and have been comfortably started on the road to make themselves prosperous farmers and good American citizens. Others returned to the cities of the nation and have gone into small business enterprises, as a result of their savings while in the Army. the beneficial influence which the military service exerted upon them in teaching lessons of obedience to authority, promptness and individual responsibility is beyond calculation.

Very nearly fifty per cent more money will have been drawn from the treasury of the nation under President McKinley's administration by black men than under any other administration since the Republican party conferred popular rights upon them, in order that under a pop-

ular government they also should be allowed to emphasize their will at the ballot box in the election of law makers and those who execute the law . . .

Speech of President McKinley at [the Tuskegee Normal and Industrial Institute in] Tuskegee, Alabama, December 16, 1898.

. . . To speak of Tuskegee without paying special tribute to Booker T. Washington's genius and perseverance would be impossible. The inception of this noble enterprise was his, and he deserves high credit for it. His was the enthusiasm and enterprise which made its steady progress possible and established in the institution its present high standard of accomplishment. He has won a worthy reputation as one of the great leaders of his race, widely known and much respected at home and abroad as an accomplished educator, a great orator, and a true philanthropist . . .

In North Carolina.

The following, taken from the *Evening Star* of Washington, D.C., an independent paper, of July 25, 1900, is a true index of Republican sentiment in regard to the present attempt of the Democratic party to disfranchise the colored man.

It is remarkable that none of the larger and influential Democratic journals have commented on the North Carolina situation except to apologize for, aid and abet in it.

"The State campaign in North Carolina is approaching a close with demonstrations of force on the part of the Democrats, and threats of personal violence directed at both Populists and Republicans. Terrorizing methods which prevailed in Louisiana and South Carolina twenty or more years ago are in use, and promise to repeat the success of those days. Clubs of armed men wearing flaming red shirts ride the country roads and endeavor to impress upon the opposition in this truculent way the advisability of standing back on election day. 'the Democratic party is going to control this State,' they declare, 'and it prefers to do so without a bloody clash. But if a bloody clash should be necessary to that end, we take occasion to show you that we are ready to go that far' . . ."

Remember These Things.

Of the 397 persons lynched in the United States from January 5, 1897 to January 5, 1898, 391 were colored. They were lynched in the Democratic States of Alabama, Arkansas, Georgia, Louisiana, Missouri, Mississippi, North Carolina, South Carolina, Tennessee, Texas, and Virginia. This state of affairs is sufficient to convince any rational mind of the truth of the statement made by the late Hon. Roscoe Conkling [R-N.Y.] years ago that the Democratic party had made up its mind to exterminate the negro in those States where his numbers were a menace to that party's political supremacy . . .

Source: Thomas H. R. Clarke and Barney McKay, eds., *A Republican Text-book for Colored Voters* (Washington, D.C., 1901), from Library of Congress, http://memory.loc.gov/ammem/aap/aaphome.html.

Document 4.12 in Context
"We . . . Propose a Rebellion, a Revolution, an Uprising, Not by Physical Force, but by the Ballot": George E. Taylor Accepts the National Liberty Party's Presidential Nomination

By the turn of the twentieth century, ongoing hostility from Democrats and a growing sense that Republicans had abandoned both Reconstruction and its broader agenda supporting political and economic rights for blacks fueled a movement to create independent African American political parties. Dissatisfaction with the GOP was not new; in 1883 Frederick Douglass had declared that blacks should "follow no party blindly. If the Republican party cannot stand a demand for justice and fair play it ought to go down." [45]

Some blacks, seeking alternatives, became active in existing white-run minor parties, such as the Populists, although they were rarely welcomed on equal terms. Others founded their own parties, among them the Colored Independent Party in Pennsylvania and the Ohio-based Negro Protective Party that fielded a gubernatorial candidate in 1897.

At the national level, the National Liberty Party was organized in 1904 in St. Louis with representatives from thirty-six states. That year it nominated its first—and only—presidential candidate, George E. Taylor, a journalist and political activist from Iowa. Taylor had served as president of the Negro National Democratic League—endorsing Democratic/Populist candidate William Jennings Bryan (**Document 4.6**) in 1896, based on Bryan's anti-imperialist and economic policies. At the National Liberty Party's July 1904 convention, as his party's presidential candidate, Taylor spoke about his vision for the party in the context of equal rights, especially political rights, for African Americans. His also addressed issues including labor relations, abolition of trusts and veterans' pensions.

Also in 1904, the Socialist party and its presidential candidate, Eugene Debs, attracted some black support as another alternative to the two major parties. A black newspaper in Atlanta, the *Voice of the Negro,* wrote favorably of the candidate and his party:

> The doctrine of Socialism is the doctrine of an industrial State, directed by modern science, with government ownership and control of all public utilities, and based upon the equality of mankind . . . Mr. Debs has said repeatedly that the Socialist party is the black man's hope and friend. There are objections to Socialism in some of its aspects, but it is a splendid field for negotiations for the Negro in these days when the Republican party has forsook him to the persecutions of the Democrats. An examination of the field certainly could do no harm. We must affiliate with a party that will reward our endeavors with friendly co-operation.[46]

These trends toward black political activism outside the two major parties would continue in the 1908 election, when black leaders like W. E. B. DuBois and organizations such as the Negro American Political League would take aim at the GOP and President William H. Taft.

Document 4.12
George E. Taylor Accepts the National Liberty Party's Presidential Nomination, July 1904

The National Liberty Party now confronts the people of the United States claiming their consideration for the first time, but though the organization is in its infancy, the principles for which it stands are fundamental to our republican form of government. In fact, we are struggling to revive the well-nigh deserted principles of the grand old Whig Party (the mother of the Republican party), which declared for "popular rights," government of all the people, for all the people, and by all the people.

When the founders of this republic were called upon to frame the Declaration of Independence and a Constitution for the further guidance, protection and foundation rock of the government, through their inspired wisdom they drafted ordinances declaring their independence, and guaranteeing protection, equal privileges, equal opportunity and equal rights to all citizens of the government. It was at that time clear to them that upon no other premises could the American people hope to secure their freedom and independence, and maintain a popular government. And the history of the past 127 years, proves the correctness of their judgment, that to depart from these fundamental principles is to endanger the very perpetuity of our government.

The National Liberty Party calls the attention of the people of the United States to the bold fact that these fundamental principles are fast being covered up, ignored, disregarded, and practically nullified by the administrative power, the national governing forces of both the Republican and Democratic parties, and the controlling political forces of at least six states of the Union which have recently by state constitutional amendment, actually disfranchised over 2,000,000 American born citizens.

Practically all of these disfranchised people are Negroes, and it is also a fact that, under the Federal Constitution and Laws, we are as emphatically recognized as citizens as are the most aristocratic Caucasians. Why not? . . .

We religiously adhere to the sacredness of our form of government, and subscribe to its every tenet, law and claim. We believe that the tendency of the dominant parties is to dissipate these tenets, laws, and demands, and that it is our duty and the duty of every sober-minded citizen to join us in the arrest of this wholesale dissipation, in the interests of good government, the maintenance of federal power and the perpetuity of our system of government, which the popular statement of the world pronounces the most beneficent the world has ever known.

It must be clear to all unprejudiced students of history that whenever a government fails to secure for all its subjects or citizens at home, as well as abroad, that which it guarantees, that such government is nearing dangerous ground—it matters not whether said neglected citizens belong to or represent a popular or unpopular class. For, in such neglect, a fundamental principle of government is abused, distorted, abandoned, and like a cancer it will continue to grow and spread until finally it gnaws in twain the very vital cords. The Negro who now suffers most directly, by reason of this neglect (disfranchisement) is not in fact the only sufferer, for his immediate calamity is the beginning of the end of the downfall of the producing element of the races who comprise the vast common working classes of this great republic. The Negro of the United States is distinctively a factor in the great and grand army of American working men, and whatever enhances, strengthens, retards or impedes his progress, happiness, manhood, or citizenship rights, proportionately affects all the citizens of his class and standing. Hence, the interest that all common people of every race or nationality in the United States should have in this government. Does the question "Am I my black brother's keeper?" arise in the minds of the common (white) people? If so, I refer to the history of the world from the days of Cain and Abel for your answer. Judas betrayed the Christ only to earn for himself eternal reproach and an ignominious death. Napoleon, through intrigue, captured and starved to death in a dungeon, that gallant statesman and warrior, Toussaint l'Ouverture [a former slave and a leader of the Haitian Revolution], and as a reward, died the death of an exile; the Spaniards, through deception and cunning, assassinated General Maceo, the greatest Negro soldier and general of modern times, and soon afterwards were subjected to banishment and disgraceful defeat as their reward . . .

As to the independence of the National Liberty Party, I do not hesitate to state that, in every sense of the word, we are, and propose to remain, purely independent, for the principles for which we stand are not now germane to the platform of principles of any other political party. If they were, there would be no room or occasion for the existence of this party. The National Liberty Party is purely a creature of necessity.

Never before in the history of American Negro citizenship has the time been so opportune for an independent political movement on the part of the race. And never before has there been a time when such a movement could draw materially from the race. But now in the light of the history of the past four years, with a Republican president in the executive chair, and both branches of Congress and a majority of the Supreme Court of the same political faith, we are confronted with the amazing fact that more than one-fifth of the race are actually disfranchised, robbed of all the rights, powers and benefits of true citizenship, we are forced to lay aside our prejudices, indeed, our personal wishes, and consult with the higher demands of our manhood, the true interests of the country and our posterity, and act while we yet live, ere the time when it shall be too late. No other race of our strength would have quietly submitted to what we have during the past four years without a rebellion, a revolution, or an uprising.

We, too, propose a rebellion, a revolution, an uprising, not by physical force, but by the ballot, through the promulgation of the National Liberty Party. Our education, our civilization and our natural disposition, all incline us to this course as the only rational, consistent, effective method of attaining the desired end, viz.: representation as well as taxation; the full exercise of our constitutional rights as citizens. The only truly effective way for the common people to correct a national evil lies in their power at the ballot box, if they will but exercise it judiciously.

Whenever the race and their co-laborers shall array themselves in one grand independent political phalanx, the very foundations of the two dominant political parties will be shaken and the leaders of both will be brought to a realization of the danger which threatens their organization, and *"the rights of the people"* will again be considered by them instead of that of special classes, as is the present rule.

It is the intention of the committee of the National Liberty Party to perfect all necessary arrangements to have placed upon the ballots of the several states, presidential electors, and in many instances to nominate by petition and otherwise, congressional candidates. Should we fail to complete the organization in all the states this year, we shall continue the work after the election. Our greatest strength, of course, lies in the Southern states, which have not as yet adopted disfranchisement amendments. We expect to make a good showing in Kansas, Indiana, Illinois, Ohio, Pennsylvania, W. Virginia, Tennessee, Iowa, Texas and many other states. It is conservative to estimate that at least sixty per cent of the Negroes of the states in which we secure a place upon the ballot for our candidates will vote for us. It is also fair to presume that a goodly number of the white independents in these states will support the movement. Why not? We stand for the text and the spirit of the Declaration of Independence and the Federal Constitution; for universal suffrage; for the pensioning of all veterans of the war of the rebellion; for the establishment of a National Arbitration Board with power to adjust all differences that may arise between employer and employee; for the abolition of polygamy; for the nullification and repeal of all class legislation; for unsubsidized competition in all lines of commerce, and industry, which means the abolishment of all trusts and combines; for the pensioning of ex-slaves . . . and for a reduction of the tariff. We do not consider the money standard an issue of any merit in this campaign.

. Every Negro who is loyal to his race and the powers that made him a free man, must join with us in heart, if not in action, in this effort to emphasize the fact that the Constitution of the United States is no respecter of persons, but that all American citizens are entitled to exercise all the rights of citizenship regardless of race or color.

Source: George E. Taylor, "A Negro Presidential Candidate's Address, 1904," *Voice of the Negro* (Atlanta, Georgia), July 1904, in *A Documentary History of the Negro People in the United States,* ed. Herbert Aptheker (New York: Citadel Press, 1969), 853–856.

NOTES

1 Robert Smalls, "Election Methods in the South," *North American Review* 151 (1890): 593–600, available from the Secession Era Editorials Project, http://alpha.furman.edu/~benson/docs/smalls.htm.
2 Leon H. Prather, "The Red Shirt Movement in North Carolina, 1898–1900," *Journal of Negro History* 62, no. 2 (April 1977): 175.
3 Quoted in Ibid., 176.
4 "White Beaten to Death by Red Shirts," *Cleveland Gazette,* August 4, 1900.
5 "Negroes Leave the South," *New York Times,* November 24, 1892, in *African American History in the Press, 1851–1899: From the Coming of the Civil War to the Rise of Jim Crow as Reported and Illustrated in Selected Newspapers of the Time,* ed. Schneider Collection, vol. 2, *1870–1899* (Detroit: Gale, 1996), 1184–1185.
6 "Louisiana Negro Convention, 1879," in *A Documentary History of the Negro People in the United States,* ed. Herbert Aptheker (New York: Citadel Press, 1969), 714.
7 "New Orleans Mass Meeting, 1888," *Louisiana Standard,* August 25, 1888, reprinted in *Congressional Record,* 50th Cong., 1st sess., Appendix, 8993–8994, available from the Gilder Lehrman Center, Yale University, www.yale.edu/glc/archive/1151.htm.
8 *Rider to Army Appropriation Act,* 21 Statutes at Large 113, 46th Cong., 2d sess., (May 4, 1880), 81.
9 John T. Morgan, "Shall Negro Majorities Rule?" *Forum* 6 (February 1889): 586–599, in *The Black Experience, 1865–1978: A Documentary Reader,* ed. Anthony J. Cooper (Kent, United Kingdom: Greenwich University Press, 1995), 52–53.
10 Albion W. Tourgée, "Shall White Minorities Rule?" *Forum* 7 (April 1889): 143–155, in Cooper, *The Black Experience 1865–1978,* 56, 59.
11 William L. Clay, *Just Permanent Interests: Black Americans in Congress, 1870–1991* (New York: Amistad, 1992), 44.
12 "The Negro Exodus," *Harper's Weekly,* December 6, 1879, 950, in Schneider Collection, *African American History in the Press, 1851–1899,* vol. 2, 938–939.
13 Quoted in "Douglas and Greener on the Exodus, 2879," in Aptheker, *A Documentary History,* 725.
14 Richard T. Greener, "Defending the 'Negro Exodus,' " *Journal of Social Science* 11 (May 1880): 303–315, http://skyways.lib.ks.us/orgs/schs/ritchie/education/standards/7thgrade/benchmark3/Richard%20Greener.pdf.
15 *Ex parte Yarbrough,* 110 U.S. 651 (1884).
16 Ibid.

17 Henry C. Bannard, "The Oleomargarine Law: A Study of Congressional Politics," *Political Science Quarterly* 2, no. 4 (December 1887): 546.

18 Republican Party Platform of 1892, June 1892, from the American Presidency Project, www.presidency.ucsb.edu/ws/?pid=29628.

19 John M. Langston, *The National Elections Bill: Speech of Hon. John M. Langston, of Virginia, in the House of Representatives,* January 16, 1891, from Library of Congress, http://lcweb2.loc.gov/ammem/aap/aaphome.html.

20 Albion W. Tourgée, "Brief for Homer A. Plessy," October Term 1895, available from San Francisco State University, http://bss.sfsu.edu/waldrep/hist471/brief_for_homer_a_plessy.htm.

21 Penal Code of Alabama (1866), sec. 61, quoted in "Intermarriage between the Races Forbidden (Alabama)," in *Documentary History of Reconstruction: Political, Military, Social, Religious, Educational and Industrial, 1865 to 1906,* ed. Walter L. Fleming (New York: McGraw-Hill, 1966), vol. 1, 274.

22 *Plessy v. Ferguson,* 163 U.S. 537 (1896).

23 "Heated Hot," *Boston Daily Globe,* May 20, 1896, in Schneider Collection, *African American History in the Press,* vol. 2, 1222.

24 Quoted in William M. Brewer, "The Poll Tax and Poll Taxers," *Journal of Negro History* 29, no. 3 (July 1944): 261.

25 Quoted in Paul A. Kunkel, "Modifications in Louisiana Negro Legal Status under Louisiana Constitutions 1812–1957," *Journal of Negro History* 44, no. 1 (January 1959): 17.

26 State Democratic Executive Committee of North Carolina, *The Democratic Hand Book 1898,* (Raleigh, N.C.: Edwards and Broughton, 1898), 2.

27 Ibid., 36.

28 Ibid., 40.

29 Ibid., 43.

30 Reprinted in H. Leon Prather, "The Red Shirt Movement in North Carolina, 1898–1900," *Journal of Negro History* 62, no. 2 (April 1977): 176.

31 "White Beaten to Death by Red Shirts," *Cleveland Gazette,* August 4, 1900.

32 *Congressional Record,* 52d Cong., 1st sess., June 15, 1892, 5272.

33 Ibid.

34 Benjamin Harrison, State of the Union Address, December 9, 1891, from the Amerian Presidency Project, www.presidency.ucsb.edu/ws/index.php?pid=29532.

35 Benjamin Harrison, State of the Union Address, December 6, 1892, from the American Presidency Project, www.presidency.ucsb.edu/ws/index.php?pid=29533.

36 Republican Party Platform, June 16, 1896, from the American Presidency Project, www.presidency.ucsb.edy-ws=?pid=29629.

37 *Congressional Record,* 56th Cong., 2d sess., January 29, 1901, 1637.

38 "The Alpha and Omega of the Negro's Congressional Alphabet," *African Methodist Episcopal Church Review* 17, no. 4 (April 1901): 394–395.

39 Thomas H. R. Clarke and Barney McKay, eds., *A Republican Text-book for Colored Voters* (Washington, D.C., 1901), 9.

40 Ibid., 9.

41 Ibid., 4.

42 Ibid., 29.

43 Ibid., 38.

44 Ibid., 25.

45 Quoted in August Meier, "The Negro and the Democratic Party, 1875–1915," *Phylon* 17, no. 2 (1956): 176.

46 Jesse Max Barber, "The Spread of Socialism," *The Voice of the Negro* (Atlanta, Georgia), June 1904, in Aptheker, *A Documentary History,* 856.

CHAPTER FIVE

The Early Twentieth Century to the Civil Rights Movement

A Slow Return to Washington, 1913–1964

The dawn of the twentieth century may well have seemed like midnight to many African Americans. The great promise of emancipation had been largely negated by the rise of "Jim Crow" systems that segregated and suppressed African Americans legally, socially and politically all across the South. In the North, too, segregation was widespread, though generally the result of common practice rather than official statute. By 1901 the last of the post-Reconstruction black congressmen had left office, and southern states had manipulated their election laws to effectively disfranchise

Rev. Martin Luther King Jr. speaks in front of 250,000 demonstrators at the March on Washington on August 28, 1963. King's "I Have a Dream" speech became a touchstone moment in the civil rights movement. In 1964 President Lyndon Johnson signed the Civil Rights Act, which together with the Voting Rights Act of 1965, eliminated legal justifications for segregation and eventually led to the widespread political enfranchisement of African Americans. Source: The Granger Collection, New York

black voters, even in states like South Carolina, Mississippi and Louisiana, where blacks were a majority or near-majority of the voting-age public. Moreover, the U.S. Supreme Court's decision in *Plessy v. Ferguson* (**Document 4.5**) had established the doctrine of "separate but equal" facilities that was being used not only to authorize separate seating in public transportation—which had been the focus of *Plessy*—but also to justify all manner of segregation practices in hotels, restaurants, theaters and even schools.

Legally enforced social separation and political disfranchisement, however, were not the worst of the circumstances facing African Americans. Mob violence and lynchings aimed at blacks had been common in the South throughout the last third of the nineteenth century. The first quarter of the twentieth century saw repeated race riots: Atlanta in 1906; Springfield, Illinois, in 1908; East St. Louis, Illinois, in 1917; Houston in 1917; Chicago in 1919; Elaine, Arkansas, in 1919; Tulsa, Oklahoma, in 1921; and Rosewood, Florida, in 1923. The riots killed and injured whites as well as blacks, but the majority of victims were African Americans, scores of whom died and hundreds of whom were injured. Untold numbers of black homes, churches and businesses were destroyed.

Sometimes the violence was sparked by allegations of crimes by blacks, particularly accusations that black men had sexually assaulted white women; for example, the 1906 Atlanta riot was fueled by claims—some untrue and others exaggerated—concerning a series of such attacks as reported in white-owned newspapers. Twenty-five black people were killed in the Atlanta riot. On other occasions, riots against blacks were rooted in economic issues and competition for jobs. Both the 1917 East St. Louis riot and the 1919 Chicago riot erupted in an atmosphere of tension exacerbated by the use of black workers to replace striking white workers. The East St. Louis riot left thirty-five blacks dead and hundreds homeless. The Chicago riot killed twenty-three blacks and raged for a week; it took three regiments of National Guard troops and a timely rainstorm to end the violence.

Large-scale rioting was only one way that violence was used to intimidate and suppress blacks. Lynchings of individual blacks in revenge for real or imagined crimes—or simply to terrorize and intimidate—occurred on a regular basis. From about 1890 to 1930, the number of lynching victims declined fairly steadily, but on average at least one African American was lynched each week into the mid-1920s. Scores of churches and schools also were burned as a way of discouraging black organization and self-assertion. These acts of violence took place primarily, but not exclusively, in the South.

In response to the widespread racial violence of the South, severe hardships in the South's agricultural economy and the increasing availability of well-paid, industrial jobs in the North, African Americans began to leave the South. In a swelling human tide that came to be called the Great Migration, African Americans started to move by the tens of thousands to the urban centers of the North during the first decades of the twentieth century. By 1940 more than 1.5 million blacks had left the South. They brought with them enormous social, cultural and political transformation and eventually built a new base of black political power in the northern cities.

That transformation was slow and arduous, however. In the meantime, African Americans struggled to organize in ways that enabled them to exert pressure on the levers of American power. Disenfranchised in the South and still lacking the numbers to be a political force in the North, they sought in the first decades of the century to expand their access to civil and political rights by creating such national organizations as the National Association for the Advancement of Colored People (NAACP), founded in 1909, and the Urban League, founded in 1910, to influence governmental policy and challenge discrimination via legal action.

During the 1912 presidential campaign, for example, such black leaders as W. E. B. DuBois and William Monroe Trotter urged black voters to support Woodrow Wilson, the Democratic candidate, because he promised to deal fairly with African Americans. In an open letter to Wilson published in the *Crisis,* the NAACP's journal, upon Wilson's inauguration in 1913, DuBois called urgently on the new president to fulfill his promises:

> We want to be treated as men. We want to vote. We want our children educated. We want lynching stopped. We want no longer to he herded as cattle on street cars and railroads. We want the right to earn a living, to own our own property and to spend our income unhindered and uncursed . . . In the name then of that common country for which your fathers and ours have bled and toiled, be not untrue, President Wilson, to the highest ideals of American Democracy.[1]

DuBois, Trotter and other blacks were soon dismayed to see Wilson's administration expanding racial segregation in government offices and facilities, ostensibly to avoid friction between black and white employees. In November 1914 a delegation of blacks, led by Trotter, met with Wilson to protest segregation in the Treasury Department and the Post Office buildings in Washington. According to the text of Trotter's remarks published in the Chicago *Defender,* a black newspaper, Trotter told Wilson: "Only two years ago you were heralded as perhaps the second Lincoln, and now the Afro-American leaders who supported you are hounded as false leaders and traitors to their race. What a change segregation has wrought!" [2] Wilson was so irritated by Trotter's statement that he refused to meet further with the group as long as Trotter was its spokesman.

The U.S Supreme Court's landmark May 17, 1954, ruling in Brown v. Board of Education *determined that segregated schools were inherently unequal. Despite a subsequent ruling that school desegregation should proceed with "all deliberate speed," many school systems and parents, especially in the South, resisted. Here, U.S. deputy marshals escort six-year-old Ruby Bridges from William Frantz Elementary School in New Orleans, Louisiana, in November 1960. The first grader was the only black child enrolled in the school; parents of white students boycotted the court-ordered integration by removing their children.* Source: AP Images

Meanwhile, as part of its legal strategy, the NAACP began to file suits attacking a broad range of discriminatory practices used to disenfranchise blacks, including literacy tests, whites-only primaries and poll taxes. The NAACP scored its first big victory in 1915 with the U.S. Supreme Court's decision in *Guinn v. United States,* which threw out Oklahoma's "grandfather clause" regarding literacy tests. The clause stated that illiterate men whose grandfathers had been permitted to vote, could also vote. Most illiterate, black citizens' grandfathers had been slaves; hence few were allowed to vote. Another key success came in the Court's 1927 ruling in *Nixon v. Herndon* (**Document 5.2**), which declared Texas's whites-only Democratic primary election unconstitutional, though legal wrangling over that disenfranchisement technique continued for another seventeen years. The federal government formally outlawed literacy tests and poll taxes with the Civil Rights Act of 1964 (**Document 5.11**) and the Voting Rights Act of 1965 (**Document 6.1**).

The NAACP also carried on a long and determined legal assault against discrimination in education. A series of Supreme Court rulings in the 1930s and 1940s overturned racial discrimination as practiced by the use of separate—but decidedly unequal—programs and facilities in the graduate schools of several southern state universities where the separateness and inequality were very stark. For example, the law school that Texas established for blacks consisted of three rooms in a basement. Those rulings set the stage for what was the NAACP's greatest legal triumph of the twentieth century: the Court's *Brown v. Board of Education* decision in 1954 (**Document 5.9**), which overturned the "separate but equal" doctrine of the *Plessy* ruling as it had been applied to public schools.

Some efforts to fight discrimination, however, were not successful. One longstanding frustration for African Americans in general, and the NAACP in particular, was the inability to win congressional approval for anti-lynching legislation. The organization worked strenuously to keep the issue in the public eye with rallies, articles in the *Crisis,* silent marches and intense lobbying efforts in Washington. In 1918 the NAACP organized a national conference to examine the lynching issue. The governors of eleven states attended, as did U.S. Attorney General Mitchell Palmer and Republican former president William Howard Taft. A statement issued by the conference participants urged Congress to launch a nationwide investigation of lynching and mob murder. A bill to make lynching a federal crime was introduced that fall by Rep. Leonidas C. Dyer, R-Mo., whose constituents included a large number of black victims of the 1917 riot in East St. Louis who had relocated to his district. In 1922 an expanded version of Dyer's bill won approval in the House but was killed in the Senate when southern senators threatened a filibuster. Continuing efforts to pass anti-lynching legislation in Congress over the next thirty-five years were also unsuccessful.

Frustrated by the long-unkept promises of Reconstruction, African Americans slowly transferred their allegiance to the Democratic Party—as evidenced by the willingness of DuBois and Trotter to support Wilson in 1912. By 1928 the growing black population of Chicago enabled Oscar S. De Priest, a Republican, to be elected as the first black member of Congress in nearly three decades (**Document 5.3**). After three terms in Washington, however, he was defeated by Arthur W. Mitchell, a black Democrat (**Document 5.4**). By the time of the De Priest–Mitchell contest in the 1934 election, Americans of many backgrounds and ethnicities had turned against the Republicans, blaming Republican president Herbert Hoover and his policies for the deepening intensity of the Great Depression. "Stubbornly and blindly, the President for three years denied that there was any depression," DuBois wrote in the *Crisis*. "When he was forced to face relief, he went to the rescue of banks, railroads and corporations. Yet, we Negroes were the first and severest sufferers from depression and the last to be relieved." [3]

Dissatisfied black voters helped elect Democrat Franklin D. Roosevelt as president in 1932. Roosevelt's unemployment and poverty relief policies, though more beneficial to whites than blacks, won support from many African Americans. Roosevelt also brought numerous blacks into significant positions in his administration (**Document 5.5**). During World War II, under intense pressure from black leaders, he ordered an end to race-based employment discrimination in the defense industries (**Document 5.6**); this further extended the appeal of the Democratic Party in the black community. In 1948 Roosevelt's Democratic successor, Harry S. Truman, also facing intense pressure, ordered an end to segregation in the military (**Document 5.8**) and was rewarded with electoral support from blacks in key states that helped him win an election that almost everyone thought he would lose.

The growing influence of black voters in the North, the rising sense of confidence and entitlement among black World War II veterans, and the successes of the extended legal assault on Jim Crow segregation helped inspire the civil rights movement that emerged from the Montgomery, Alabama, bus boycott of 1955–1956. Within a decade, the long, slow struggle for political and social equity had borne dramatic and remarkable fruit—the Civil Rights Act of 1964 (**Document 5.11**) and the Voting Rights Act of 1965, which were pushed through Congress by a president who was both a Democrat and a southerner, Lyndon B. Johnson of Texas. The transformation of African Americans from an overwhelmingly Republican to an overwhelmingly Democratic constituency was firmly established, and in the next two decades, African Americans would lay claim to a rapidly growing number of political posts, in state and local governments across the nation and in Congress.

Document 5.1 in Context
"Elected by the People Thereof": Direct Election of Senators Changes the Political Game

On April 8, 1913, the Seventeenth Amendment of the U.S. Constitution was ratified, mandating the direct election of U.S. senators. Previously, they had been selected by state legislatures. Although the direct election movement long predated the twentieth century reappearance of blacks in Congress and was motivated primarily by Progressive-era concerns over the consolidation of economic power, it changed the rules of the political game.

Attempts to amend the Constitution (**Document 1.4**) to require direct election of senators began as early as 1826 and became more insistent after the Civil War, when increasingly powerful railroads and other corporations were perceived to be wielding improper influence on, and causing corruption within, the federal government. The direct election movement, however, was initially stymied because the Senate had to approve any constitutional amendment passed by the House of Representatives.

Faced with roadblocks in Congress, supporters of direct election shifted their attention to promoting an amendment via petition from the states, and by 1905 the idea had won the support of thirty-one states. Under increasing pressure, the Senate finally passed a proposed amendment in 1911. The amendment won final congressional approval in May 1912 and was ratified by the states within a year.

The extent to which the change affected the access of black aspirants to seats in the Senate is not clear. But it is important to note that the first two black senators—Hiram R. Revels (**Document 3.4**) and Blanche K. Bruce—had been appointed during Reconstruction by a coalition of black and white Republicans in the Mississippi legislature. Had the Seventeenth Amendment failed, it is impossible to know whether any legislature would have chosen another black senator.

Under the new system, it was fifty-three years before another African American, Edward W. Brooke III, R-Mass., won a seat in the Senate. Brooke, first elected in 1966, served two terms. While in the Senate, he led efforts to block the nominations of anti–civil rights judges Clement Haynsworth and G. Harrold Carswell to the U.S. Supreme Court and was the first Republican senator to call for President Richard Nixon's resignation after the Watergate scandal was revealed. In 1992, twelve years after Brooke left the Senate, Carol Moseley-Braun, D-Ill., was elected and served a single term; she was the second post–Reconstruction African American, and the first black female, senator. Barack Obama, D-Ill., became only the fifth black senator when he was elected in 2004.

▭ Document 5.1 ▭
Seventeenth Amendment to the U.S. Constitution, Passed by Congress May 13, 1912, Ratified April 8, 1913

. . . The Senate of the United States shall be composed of two Senators from each State, elected by the people thereof, for six years; and each Senator shall have one vote. The electors in each State shall have the qualifications requisite for electors of the most numerous branch of the State legislatures.

When vacancies happen in the representation of any State in the Senate, the executive authority of such State shall issue writs of election to fill such vacancies: *Provided*, That the legislature of any state may empower the executive thereof to make temporary appointments until the people fill the vacancies by election as the legislature may direct.

This amendment shall not be so construed as to affect the election or term of any Senator chosen before it becomes valid as part of the Constitution.

Source: "Seventeenth Amendment to the U.S. Constitution: Direct Election of U.S. Senators," 1913, from the U.S. National Archives and Records Administration, www.ourdocuments.gov.

Document 5.2 in Context
"Color Cannot Be Made the Basis of a Statutory Classification": The NAACP Challenges Texas's Whites-Only Primary

One of the most significant political developments in the United States in the last quarter of the nineteenth century was the systematic disenfranchisement of black voters throughout the South.

Initially, white southern legislators attempted to evade the requirements of the Fourteenth and Fifteenth Amendments (**Documents 3.2** and **3.3**), guaranteeing equal protection and voting rights, by enacting provisions in state constitutions such as grandfather clauses, literacy tests and poll taxes that were designed to prevent blacks from voting. Gradually some of those methods were overturned in court, and even when they were not, literacy tests and poll taxes also kept some whites from voting.

By the 1890s many southern states had discovered a more effective and efficient system of excluding blacks from the political process: the whites-only primary election. The whites-only system sought to evade constitutional requirements by shifting the responsibility for excluding black voters to the political parties, rather than the state. As private associations, supporters of the segregated primaries argued, political parties had the right to determine qualifications for membership and could, therefore, legally exclude blacks.

By the 1920s the Democratic Party in virtually every southern state barred blacks from membership, which meant that blacks could not participate in the party's primary elections. The Republican Party, meanwhile, had almost disappeared in the South because of its role in Reconstruction and past support for black political participation. This meant that victory in the Democratic primary virtually assured a candidate of victory in the general election. As a result, blacks were effectively excluded from the electoral process altogether.

In Texas, however, efforts to exclude black participation by way of the whites-only primary were more overt. The Texas legislature in 1923 enacted a revision of the state's election law, specifically stating that blacks were not eligible to vote in Democratic Party primaries and ordering election officials to invalidate the ballot of any black person who cast a vote in such an election.

The following year, the El Paso branch of the NAACP, with the support of the national organization, filed a lawsuit challenging the Texas law. In 1927 the U.S. Supreme Court ruled, in *Nixon v. Herndon,* that the Texas Democratic primary was unconstitutional because the state had delegated its authority to the Democratic Party.

Texas tried to revise its law to achieve the same effect within the limits of *Nixon v. Herndon,* thereby sparking a twenty-year string of court challenges that eventually opened up the electoral process in Texas. It was not until 1944, in *Smith v. Allwright,* that the Supreme Court did away with whites-only primaries altogether, opening the rest of the South to black political participation. Later, the Civil Rights Act of 1964 (**Document 5.11**) and the Voting Rights Act of 1965 (**Document 6.1**) used the full force of federal law to effectively end southern efforts to disenfranchise black voters.

▬ Document 5.2 ▬
U.S. Supreme Court Decision in *Nixon v. Herndon*, March 7, 1927

Mr. Justice [Oliver Wendell] HOLMES [Jr.] delivered the opinion of the Court.

This is an action against the Judges of Elections for refusing to permit the plaintiff to vote at a primary election in Texas. It lays the damages at five thousand dollars. The petition alleges that the plaintiff is a negro, a citizen of the United States and of Texas and a resident of El Paso, and in every way qualified to vote, as set forth in detail, except that the statute to be mentioned interferes with his right; that on July 26, 1924, a primary election was held at El Paso for the nomination of candidates for a senator and representatives in Congress and State and other offices, upon the Democratic ticket; that the plaintiff, being a member of the Democratic party, sought to vote but was denied the right by defendants; that the denial was based upon a statute of Texas enacted in May, 1923 . . . by the words of which 'in no event shall a negro be eligible to participate in a Democratic party primary election held in the State of Texas,' etc., and that this statute is contrary to the Fourteenth and Fifteenth Amendments to the Constitution of the United States. The defendants moved to dismiss upon the ground that the subject-matter of the suit was political and not within the jurisdiction of the Court and that no violation of the Amendments was shown. The suit was dismissed and a writ of error was taken directly to this Court. Here no argument was made on behalf of the defendants but a brief was allowed to be filed by the Attorney General of the State.

The objection that the subject-matter of the suit is political is little more than a play upon words. Of course the petition concerns political action but it alleges and seeks to recover for private damage. That private damage may be caused by such political action and may be recovered for in suit at law hardly has been doubted for over two hundred years, since Ashby v. White, . . . and has been recognized by this Court . . . If the defendants' conduct was a wrong to the plaintiff the same reasons that allow a recovery for denying the plaintiff a vote at a final election allow it for denying a vote at the primary election that may determine the final result.

The important question is whether the statute can be sustained. But although we state it as a question the answer does not seem to us open to a doubt. We find it unnecessary to consider the Fifteenth Amendment, because it seems to us hard to imagine a more direct and obvious infringement of the Fourteenth. That Amendment, while it applies to all, was passed, as we know, with a special intent to protect the blacks from discrimination against them . . . That Amendment 'not only gave citizenship and the privileges of citizenship to persons of color, but it denied to any State the power to withhold from them the equal protection of the laws . . . What is this but declaring that the law in the States shall be the same for the black as for the white; that all persons, whether colored or white, shall stand equal before the laws of the States, and, in regard to the colored race, for whose protection the amendment was primarily designed, that no discrimination shall be made against them by law because of their color?' . . . The statute of Texas in the teeth of the prohibitions referred to assumes to forbid negroes to take part in a primary election the importance of which we have indicated, discriminating against them by the distinction of color alone. States may do a good deal of classifying that it is difficult to believe rational, but there are limits, and it is too clear for extended argument that color cannot be made the basis of a statutory classification affecting the right set up in this case.

Judgment reversed.

Source: Nixon v. Herndon et al. 273 U.S. 536 (1927), from FindLaw, http://laws.findlaw.com/us/273/536.html.

Document 5.3 in Context
"America Never Will be What It Was Intended to Be until Every Citizen in America Has His Just Rights": Rep. Oscar S. De Priest Returns African Americans to Congress

In January 1929 Oscar S. De Priest, a Republican from Chicago, became the first African American in nearly three decades to take a seat in Congress. As the only black member of Congress throughout his six-year tenure, De Priest carried the aspirations of all African Americans with him to Washington.

"With Mr. De Priest have revived the fervent hopes of twelve million Negro Americans," wrote one analyst of the Chicago political scene. "To them he is a symbol of political progress; the sign, as it were, of a new era in which millions of black Americans will have, at least, a part of their share of federal offices." [4] But De Priest quickly found himself confronting the same racial indignities in Washington that blacks faced all over the country.

De Priest, an effective and forceful machine politician, had claimed the Republican nomination on the strength of his control over Chicago's Third Ward political organization and with the help of Chicago's GOP mayor, William "Big Bill" Thompson. Opponents attempted to derail De Priest's nomination with trumped up corruption charges, but those were dropped two days before he took his seat in Congress.

The first significant controversy De Priest faced in Washington erupted in June 1929, when First Lady Lou Henry Hoover, wife of Republican president Herbert Hoover, invited De Priest's wife to the White House for the annual Congressional Wives Tea (**Document 11.5**). Mrs. Hoover and the White House staff sought to minimize the potential for negative publicity by quietly inviting Mrs. De Priest to the last of five sessions. Only fifteen people, hand picked because of their views on race, were invited to the session; the other four gatherings had guest lists of 180–220 people each. Critics however, were not mollified by the separate session. Southern members of Congress, in particular, railed against the invitation to Mrs. De Priest, and the Texas legislature even passed a resolution denouncing the invitation.

In 1934 De Priest was again the focus of a national controversy when he challenged segregation in a public section of the House restaurant. De Priest had faced no direct opposition in his personal use of the members' restaurant, though some other representatives chose to eat at the Senate restaurant to avoid eating in the same room with a black man. Black members of his staff were able to lunch with him, and on a number of occasions, De Priest's secretary, Morris Lewis, was able to eat there on his own without complaint. On January 23, 1934, however, Lewis and his son were barred from the restaurant. De Priest challenged the policy and introduced a resolution demanding an investigation. On March 21, 1934, De Priest explained his challenge to the restaurant's racial exclusion; his remarks on the House floor are excerpted here.

De Priest's resolution was referred to a committee, where it died after the representative lost his bid for a fourth term in the fall election. The controversy attracted national attention, including coverage by the *New York Times* as well as many black-owned newspapers, but the House restaurant continued to exclude blacks at least until 1948.

▬ Document 5.3 ▬
Rep. Oscar S. De Priest, R-Ill., Challenges Segregation of the Restaurant of the Capitol, March 21, 1934

Mr. DE PRIEST: Mr. Chairman and members of the Committee, I came to Washington as a Representative in Congress on the 15th of April 1929. Up until the 23d day of last January I never heard this question raised which has now been raised by the Chairman of the Committee on Accounts [Lindsay C. Warren, D-N.C.] this year. On that day when my secretary went into the grillroom downstairs he was told by Mr. Johnson that by the orders of the Chairman of the Committee on Accounts he could not be served in that restaurant.

I read in the newspapers an interview where the Chairman of the Committee on Accounts said that no Negro had been served there and would not while he was here. I hope he was not quoted correctly.

I want to say that if the chairman was quoted correctly in that article "that Negroes had not been served there before" he was mistaken. I have seen them there in the grillroom several times. In the last 5 years I think I have seen them there 50 times.

I want to say further, after talking with some Members of the Committee on Accounts, that this question has never been raised in the committee before, and never was raised officially in the committee, if I am correctly informed.

It seems to be an arbitrary ruling on that question.

The restaurant of the Capitol is run for the benefit of the American people, and every American, whether he be black or white, Jew or gentile, Protestant or Catholic, under our constitutional form of Government, is entitled to equal opportunities.

I introduced a resolution on the 24th of January, asking for an investigation of this ruling by the chairman of the committee. That resolution went to the Committee on Rules. The Committee on Rules has not acted as yet. I waited 30 legislative days, and then I filed a petition with the Clerk of this House to discharge the Committee on Rules and to bring the resolution to the floor of the House.

That resolution calls for an investigation only. If the Chairman of the Committee on Accounts has that power, I should like to know it. If the Chairman of the Committee on Accounts has that power, the American people are entitled to know it.

I am going to ask every justice-loving Member in this House to sign that petition, as that seems to be the only way it can be threshed out on the floor of the House.

I come from a group of people—and I am proud of it and make no apology for being a Negro—who have demonstrated their loyalty to the American Government in every respect, making no exception. They have always proved to be good American citizens and have supported the Constitution. I challenge any man to contradict that assertion. If you are going to keep them good American citizens, like I pray they shall always be, it must be done by defending their rights as American citizens.

If we allow segregation and the denial of constitutional rights under the dome of the Capitol, where in God's name will we get them?

I appreciate the conditions that pertain in the territory where the gentleman comes from, and nobody knows that better than I do.

But North Carolina is not the United States of America; it is but a part of it, a one forty-eighth part. Then I expect, too, as long as I am a Member of this House, to contend for every right and every privilege every other American citizen enjoys; and if I did not, I would not be worthy of the trust reposed in me by constituents who have sent me here. [Applause.]

This is not a political problem. Someone said that I was trying to play politics. I did not instigate this; I did not start it; but, so help me God, I am going to stay to see the finish of it . . .

I say to the Members of this House—and I have no feeling in the matter—this is the most dangerous precedent that could be established in the American Government. If we allow this challenge to go without correcting it, it will set an example where people will say Congress itself approves of segregation; Congress itself approves of denying 0.1 [10 percent] of our population equal rights and opportunity; why should not the rest of the American people do likewise? I have been informed that if I insisted on pressing this question it might hurt my usefulness down here. If I did not press it, I would not stay here very long. The people who sent me here would retire me next November, and they would rightly retire me because I should not be here if I did not stand up for a group of people who have always been on the square with this Government. I did not come here from a group of people who have committed treason against the Government; I did not come here from a group of people who are Communists or Socialists; I come here from the most loyal American citizens that we have.

During the World War when emissaries of the enemy were scattering pamphlets over the battlefields of Europe asking the colored people to desert the colors because they received inhuman treatment in America, no colored man deserted, and no man can say and history does not record when a Negro deserted the colors—not one. How do you expect them to go on giving loyal service to America, at a time when there is unrest over the whole world, when the Reds are trying to make inroads amongst my group because they are the lowest in the scale of society, from an economic standpoint, unless we give them something like a square deal in this country? I appreciate all that has been done so far, but the work has not been completed yet. And I say further, ladies and gentlemen of the Congress, that America never will be what is was intended to be until every citizen in America has his just rights under the Constitution . . .

Source: Congressional Record, 73d Cong., 2d sess., March 21, 1934, LXXVIII, 5047–5049.

Document 5.4 in Context
"You Have Had Your Day with the Negro Vote": African Americans Begin to Abandon the Republican Party

One of the most significant developments in American politics during the 1930s was the beginning of a tidal shift in the partisan loyalties of African Americans. From the time of emancipation until the early 1930s, black voters had overwhelmingly supported the Republican

Party. The GOP, after all, had been the party of Lincoln, and the Radical Republicans had pushed through the Thirteenth, Fourteenth and Fifteenth Amendments to the Constitution (**Documents 1.4, 2.8, 3.2** and **3.3**) to outlaw slavery and extend civil rights to the newly freed African Americans at the end of the Civil War.

Republicans' devotion to civil rights issues had waned after the end of Reconstruction, however, and the resurgence of the Democratic Party in the South had brought with it a new wave of segregation, disenfranchisement and brutality for southern blacks. Discrimination in public accommodations and education, meanwhile, had been effectively legitimized by the Supreme Court's "separate but equal" doctrine, laid out in *Plessy v. Ferguson* in 1896 (**Document 4.5**).

As the new century began, blacks started to leave the rural South in huge numbers, driven out by fear and despair over a rising tide of lynchings and other racial violence, and by crop failures that brought on severe economic hardship. They were also drawn north by the appeal of industrial jobs in the nation's urban centers. During the Great Migration, more than 1.5 million black people moved from the southern states to the northern cities between 1910 and 1940.

The black population of New York City jumped by more than 66 percent just between 1910 and 1920, fueling the development of Harlem as a major center of African American life and culture. Philadelphia, too, saw its black population rise by 58 percent in the same period. Major cities in the Midwest saw even larger increases, in terms of percentages: 148 percent in Chicago; 307 percent in Cleveland; 611 percent in Detroit; 749 percent in Akron, Ohio; and 1,283 percent in Gary, Indiana. This concentration of African Americans in cities where they were not barred from voting, as they had been in much of the South, became the foundation of black political power.

When the Great Depression struck, many people blamed the economic collapse on the Republican administration of President Herbert Hoover. When Democrat Franklin D. Roosevelt succeeded Hoover and began implementing relief programs that often helped poor and unemployed blacks—though they generally helped whites more—many African Americans began voting for northern Democrats.

It is emblematic of this nascent, but rapid, political shift that the first African American to serve in Congress since the turn of the century, Oscar S. De Priest of Illinois, was elected as a Republican in 1928, only to be replaced six years later by black Democrat Arthur W. Mitchell, who had started his political career as a Republican. Over the next thirty years, from Mitchell's first election in 1934 through the election of 1964, six more blacks were elected to the House of Representatives—all of them Democrats. It was not until Massachusetts elected Edward W. Brooke III to the Senate in 1966 that another black Republican was seated in Congress.

Mitchell's comments on the House floor regarding declining black support for the Republican Party illustrate the attitudes of many black voters: bitterness at the Republicans' unkept promises, appreciation of Roosevelt's New Deal policies and a determination not to be taken for granted by either of the major political parties.

▬ Document 5.4 ▬
Rep. Arthur W. Mitchell, D-Ill., Addresses Declining Support among Blacks for the Republican Party, June 1, 1936

Mr. MITCHELL of Illinois: . . . For 70 years we followed you blindly; for 70 years we perpetuated you in power; and for 70 long years you promised relief, and forgot your promises the minute you found yourself in office. You have had your day with the Negro vote.

Granting that all you contend is true—and I say it is not—has not the Negro paid you for what you did for him in 1861, 1863 and 1865? Is it your idea that because he was liberated during the administration of a Republican President he must still vote your ticket as a matter of gratitude, with his eyes closed toward his present and future needs? I deny that this should be the requirement of any party. Does not 70 years of unbroken loyalty to you and your party even up the debt, or is it your contention that this party loyalty you are claiming is to be an eternal thing? Can you not cease to talk about what your party did 70 years ago, and tell the aspiring youth of this country what your party proposes to do in 1936 and the years to follow? Do you think we are so blind and so dumb as to be led again to the political slaughter by Republicans seeking to hold office, whose record insofar as we are concerned is a chain of broken promises reaching across three-quarters of a century? . . .

Now, my friends, what is the matter with the gentlemen on this side? I sounded an alarm to you the other day, and whether you believe it or not, you are going to witness not only difficulty but an impossibility in putting the Negro vote in your vest pocket this year. You can no longer fool the Negroes as you have done for 70 years.

You have boasted that you carry us in your vest pocket. That boast, thank God, is no longer true. In 1928, over here in the Barr Building, when Hoover was running for President of the United States, his campaign manager was approached and asked to give some money to maintain Negro headquarters in Chicago, and he said, "We will not give another dime; we have the Negro vote in our vest pocket, and we can win without spending another cent on them."

Now, the Negroes have learned you do not want them . . .

You have said here today that the Democratic Party does not want them. I am inclined to concede that neither party particularly wants us. You, the Republicans, had us for 70 years, and kicked us around like footballs, and showed you have no real respect for us.

It is not a question now of which party wants us; it is a question of which party offers us a better opportunity to rise in this country and live as citizens should live. In other words, the question is this, which party does the Negro want? And I say frankly that the Negro not only wants but he is going to work for that party that assures him of the largest opportunity to enjoy the blessings of freedom, justice, and an opportunity to develop into the fullest degree of manhood. We shall not take either party altogether upon its past record; we shall deal with both parties as they show an interest in us and deal with us in 1936. For my part there is no question in my mind but that the Democratic Party, as constituted today, offers the Negro by far the best opportunity in this country, and I shall use all the influence and all the power that I possess to drive this truth home to the Negroes of this country.

Today the Negro refuses to stand by you simply on 60-year-old promises still unfulfilled. Until you make good the promises that you have made for the last 70 years, we shall try new political fields not marked "G.O.P."

Mr. ROBSION [John M.] of Kentucky: Will the gentleman yield?

Mr. MITCHELL of Illinois: I refuse to yield. The gentleman from Kentucky told you about conditions in Texas and what the Democratic Party would do to you. I come from Alabama and I would like to tell you what the Republican Party will do to you in Alabama . . .

I was a Republican and in a Republican convention in Alabama when the "lily white" Republican Party came into existence. I, with many others, was driven out of the Republican convention in City Hall just across from the big Hilman Hotel in Birmingham. The "lily whites" marched into the hotel. The Negroes were told to go out where they belonged, and no Negro could be admitted to the "lily white" party.

There were a few of us who met the educational qualifications, a few who met the property qualifications, and the Democrats registered us. After we were registered it was left to the Republican Party of Alabama to drive us out, although we were registered voters there. They said they were going to have a real white party. It is high time that you Republicans stopped playing the hypocrite. When the Democratic Party kicked us out they told us they did not want us. You told us that you wanted us and then kicked us out of the party.

The Republican Party has conjured with the name of Lincoln long enough. Lincoln has been dead for 70 years, and his party as the party of human rights died years ago.

Now, I am going to conclude with this story: There were two Irishmen—and I am making no reflections on the Irish; they are my friends—there were two Irishmen walking through the cemetery and reading the inscriptions on the tombstones. They came to one and they read, "Not dead but sleeping." Mike said to Pat, "What does it say there?" Pat says, "Not dead but sleeping." Mike says, "Listen, if I was dead I would confess it and not tell a lie about it, would you?" [Laughter and applause.]

Source: Congressional Record, 74th Cong., 2d sess., June 1, 1936, LXXX, 8551–8552.

Document 5.5 in Context
"Speaking with One Voice for Twelve Million American Negroes": African Americans Demand Political Action from Democrats

By 1937 the movement of black voters from the Republican Party to the Democratic Party was well on its way. African Americans were suffering severely from the economic ravages of the Great Depression, for which Republicans were widely blamed. They were often the first to be fired, and as the economy began to improve and employment increased, they were usually the last to be rehired. The National Recovery Administration (a Democratic program known as the NRA, which had been responsible for establishing wages, prices and codes of employment conduct) did such a poor job of protecting the interests of black workers that many claimed that the agency's initials stood for "Negroes Robbed Again" or "Negro Rights Assassinated."

Still, African Americans had benefited from many of President Franklin D. Roosevelt's New Deal relief programs—though not as much as whites had—and they gave Roosevelt, a Democrat, credit for that. Blacks also rose to new levels of influence and responsibility within the Roosevelt administration. Prodded by his wife, Eleanor, and other liberals, Roosevelt began hiring African Americans for significant positions in the federal bureaucracy. These black leaders included Eugene K. Jones, the first executive secretary of the Urban League; William H. Hastie, a prominent lawyer and law professor at Howard University; Robert Weaver, a scholar who later became the first black cabinet member as secretary of Housing and Urban Development in the Lyndon Johnson administration; and Mary McLeod Bethune, a renowned educator and activist. The president and the Democratic Party also gained African American support based on Eleanor Roosevelt's very public commitment to racial justice, including her open defiance of segregation laws during a 1939 trip to the Conference for Human Welfare in Birmingham, Alabama, where she sat with black attendees.

Many southern white Democrats were not happy about the increasing participation of blacks in the party. At the Democratic National Convention in Philadelphia in 1936—at which thirty-two black delegates were seated—several southern white officials stalked off the convention floor in protest when a black minister was chosen to offer the opening prayer for one session. They walked out again when Rep. Arthur W. Mitchell, the sole black member of Congress, rose to speak. But African Americans were beginning to make their influence felt in the broader political arena. Both Republicans and Democrats began to court the black vote, which was becoming an increasingly pivotal constituency in the northern cities.

Bethune, director of Negro Affairs for the National Youth Administration, was the most influential African American in Roosevelt's administration. She hosted weekly meetings in her home for a group of about thirty black officials—officially called the Federal Council on Negro Affairs, but generally known as the "Black Cabinet"—who discussed how to influence federal policies that affected African Americans. She also used her close personal relationship with Eleanor Roosevelt to gain the president's ear.

In a 1941 letter to the First Lady, for example, she praised the president's executive order banning discrimination in the defense industries, calling it the most important presidential act for the benefit of blacks "since Abraham Lincoln spoke on that memorable day of the emancipation of the slaves." She went on to urge that the president appoint Earl Dickerson of Chicago to the board that would investigate allegations of discrimination. "I think, Mrs. Roosevelt, from many angles, he is the safest man for Negro representation that we can have placed on that Board," Bethune wrote. "I hope you will use your influence in that direction if it can be done." [5]

In early 1937 Bethune sought to influence the administration's policies by using her position in the National Youth Administration to organize and chair a national conference of black leaders. That conference issued wide-ranging recommendations for government action to address the needs of African American citizens. The following document is excerpted from that report and includes Bethune's cover letter to Roosevelt.

▬ Document 5.5 ▬
Mary McLeod Bethune Reports to President Franklin D. Roosevelt on the Problems of the Negro and Negro Youth, January 18, 1937

My dear Mr. President:

I submit to you herewith the recommendations of the National Conference on the Problems of the Negro and Negro Youth held at the Department of Labor, January 6th, 7th and 8th, 1937.

These recommendations are the result of the serious deliberations of 100 representative Negro citizens from all parts of the nation as they considered the fundamental problems facing the Negro and Negro youth of America today.

Our Country opens wide the door of opportunity to the youth of the world but slams it shut in the faces of its Negro citizenry. The great masses of Negro youth are offered only one-fifteenth the educational opportunity of the average American child. The great masses of Negro workers are depressed and unprotected in the lowest levels of agriculture and domestic service while the black workers in industry are generally barred from the unions and grossly discriminated against. Their housing and living conditions are sordid and unhealthy; they live in constant terror of the lynch mob, shorn of their constitutionally guaranteed right of suffrage, and humiliated by the denial of civil liberties.

The conference is mindful of the fact that during the past four years many benefits have come to the Negro that before that time he did not have and we are deeply grateful. However, it is also their opinion that, until now, opportunity has not been offered for Negroes themselves to suggest a comprehensive program for their full integration into the benefits and the responsibilities of the American Democracy.

The conference, speaking with one voice for the twelve million American Negroes, offers these recommendations as the basic outline for a program as a challenge to the social consciousness of the present national administration. We feel now that this is the one time in the history of our race that the Negroes of America have felt free to reduce to writing their problems and their plans for meeting them with the knowledge of sympathetic understanding and interpretation . . .

It is the will of the Conference that I confer with you personally relative to the attached recommendations and to further express their loyalty to you and the leaders of our nation.

Respectfully submitted,

Mary McLeod Bethune

General Chairman, National Conference on the Problems
of the Negro and Negro Youth.

. . . The conference finds that there are four basic problems faced by the Negro and Negro youth in America today . . .

A. *Increased Opportunity for Employment and Economic Security*

1. The conference firmly believes that the employment of capable Negroes on the board and administrative and supervisory staffs of every department of the Federal Government is vitally necessary to . . . the formulation of administrative policies.
2. The conference . . . recommends a $1500 minimum wage for government employees, the five-day, 30-hour week for labor and a $900,000,000 relief fund for the period to June 30th, 1937.

3. The conference favors Federal as against State control of Federal projects and recommends that where projects are turned over to State Committees for management, definite clauses against racial discrimination be written into the plans . . .

4. The conference recommends specifically the following:

   (a) That the Federal Government take increased precaution to prevent the operation of the color bar to employment in all . . . branches of the Government service.

   (b) That the army and navy discontinue their discriminatory practices.

   (c) That the Civil Service Commission discontinue the use of photographs and certify for employment the highest ranking applicant.

   (d) That the United States Employment Service and the National Reemployment Service extend more liberally their facilities to Negro applicants.

   (e) That discrimination against Negroes be prevented on projects employing federal funds . . .

   (f) That immediate Federal action be taken to begin to meet the fundamental problem of farm tenancy . . .

   (g) That the full rights of Negroes as stockholders in Farm Credit Cooperatives be enforced and the benefits of Credit Unions widely extended.

   (h) That domestic workers be protected by minimum labor standards . . .

   (i) That the National Mediation Board and other responsible agencies employ their power and influence to obtain free participation of Negroes in the Twenty-one (21) Standard railroad unions . . .

   (l) That the Federal program of apprenticeship training be extended to Negroes.

   (m)That the National Labor Relations Board be authorized to take necessary steps to protect Negro workers against unfair practices of unions as well as employers.

   (n) That farm workers and domestics be included within the benefits of the Social Security Act.

B. Adequate Educational and Recreational Opportunity

1. The conference recommends that the National Youth Administration and the Civilian Conservation Corps be continued . . .[and] their services be expanded.

2. On matters specifically pertaining to Negroes, the conference recommends:

   (a) That whenever Federal monies are allocated in aid of education to a state or territory which maintains separate educational facilities based on race or color, the amount of such funds expended for Negroes shall not represent a smaller proportion than the ratio which the Negro population bears to the total . . .

   (c) That federally supported or controlled educational institutions or agencies, including the Military Academy and the Naval Academy, be operated without discrimination . . .

   (e) That all facilities, services and privileges in national parks, forests and other centers be made available to Negroes without discrimination . . .

C. Improved Health and Housing Conditions

1. The conference, calling attention to the importance of better health facilities for Negroes in a campaign to make better citizens, lays heavy emphasis on Federal aid to reduce tuberculosis and syphilis among Negroes. It also calls attention to the inadequate facilities for the proper training of Negro nurses.

2. On subjects of Negro Health the conference recommends . . .
   (a) Better medical care and preventive medicine for the colored masses, utilizing fully additional funds made available under the Social Security Act.
   (b) The training and use of competent Negro personnel in health programs
   (c) Internships and residence in hospitals for special training
   (d) Additional Negro public health nurses
   (e) Greater financial support for Freedmen's Hospital and the Medical School of Howard University
   (f) The use of Federal funds for the establishment of health centers in Negro neighborhoods under competent Negro staffs.
   (g) Use of Federal funds in the construction of more hospitals for Negroes
   (h) The opening up of Veterans' Hospitals to Negro Veterans and the inclusion of Negro doctors and nurses on these hospital staffs
   (i) Freer use of Negro personnel in the program for crippled children under the Children's Bureau
3. . . . The conference believes that the Federal Government should continue its program of reducing slums by building low-cost housing projects. It places itself on record as opposing any form of segregation in resettlement developments . . .
4. . . . Specific recommendations bearing on the Negro housing problem include:
   (a) The appointment of a Negro to the Federal Housing Commission . . .
   (b) Contractual clauses providing for employment of skilled Negro workers on all federally sponsored housing projects.
   (c) Guaranteeing to Negroes the right to actual participation in all federal housing projects as tenants and management executives.

D. *Security of Life and Equal Protection under the Law*

1. . . . The ever-present problem of disfranchisement in certain sections of the country, the spectre of mob-rule, the breakdown of local law-enforcing agencies, the humiliation and inconvenience of segregation on public carriers and in public places—all these were emphatically condemned by the conference.
2. Of importance among the resolutions adopted by the conference bearing on these subjects were the following:
   (a) Urging of the passage of Federal Anti-Lynch Law
   (b) Federal intervention of practices which deny to Negro citizens the right to vote
   (c) Federal investigation of police brutality in the District of Columbia.
   (d) Endorsement of the purpose of the La Follette Senate Committee now investigating denial of civil liberties to American citizens.
   (e) Amendment to the Interstate Commerce Act to provide that no interstate carriers shall segregate or in any way discriminate against any interstate passenger on account of race, creed or color.

In offering these recommendations, the spirit of the Conference is not one of complaint or carping criticism but rather of calm and sober analysis of our actual situation. The many difficulties are frankly realized and results are not expected to be achieved at one stroke. In this constructive survey of our needs, the 12,000,000 Negroes in the United States proffer their support to the National Administration in its recognized determination to give to Negroes equality of opportunity with all other loyal American citizens.

Source: Recommendations of the National Conference on the Problems of the Negro and Negro Youth, January 18, 1937. Franklin D. Roosevelt Presidential Papers, Franklin D. Roosevelt Presidential Library, Hyde Park, New York.

Document 5.6 in Context
"To Provide for the Full and Equitable Participation of All Workers": President Franklin D. Roosevelt Bans Employment Discrimination in the Defense Industries

During the summer of 1941, while the world had been at war for nearly two years and the United States was just months away from being thrust into the conflict, President Franklin D. Roosevelt, a Democrat, was working to prepare the nation, psychologically as well as militarily, for the struggle he expected. Though preoccupied by foreign affairs, Roosevelt was also facing domestic pressure from African Americans who were frustrated by the lack of progress in eliminating discrimination in American society.

Roosevelt's New Deal policies and willingness to make the federal government serve the needs of the poor and jobless during the Depression had begun to pull black voters away from their traditional home in the Republican Party, but many black leaders were not satisfied with the pace of change. The sole black member of Congress, Arthur W. Mitchell, D-Ill., had enthusiastically praised Roosevelt, and the president had appointed a significant number of blacks to positions in his administration. But as the nation began to emerge from the Depression, blacks became increasingly angry as they saw themselves left behind by the economic recovery. As employment rebounded, many employers openly advertised for and hired white workers only. Even worse, the government began to cut spending on welfare programs, even though most black workers still had insufficient employment—if they had any employment at all.

After the Republican Party and its presidential candidate, Wendell Wilkie, made a strong appeal to win back black voters in the 1940 campaign, and in reaction to prodding from blacks within his own administration (**Document 5.5**), Roosevelt began to pay closer attention to the concerns of African Americans. He appointed William H. Hastie as a civilian aide to the secretary of war and promoted Benjamin O. Davis Sr. to be the first black brigadier general in the U.S. Army. There appeared to be no progress toward improving the job prospects of black workers, however, as employers and labor unions continued to exclude them.

In the spring of 1941, A. Philip Randolph, president of the Brotherhood of Sleeping Car Porters, announced plans to assemble 10,000 blacks for a march on Washington, D.C., to protest discrimination, a move that threatened to be a major embarrassment for the Roosevelt administration. Randolph and other protest organizers were especially critical of continuing segregation in the U.S. military and workplace discrimination in industries that benefited from large government contracts. When Roosevelt resisted the pressure, Randolph announced plans to increase the size of the march, first to 50,000 and then to 100,000 blacks. A week before the scheduled date of the march, Roosevelt finally acceded to Randolph's demands that he act against racial bias and issued Executive Order 8802, banning employment discrimination in the defense industries.

The executive order was a major victory in the struggle to end employment discrimination in the United States, but the fight was far from over. Complaints of employment discrimination continued steadily throughout World War II, despite the intense wartime need for workers. Historian and African American activist W. E. B. DuBois observed in the spring 1943 issue of the academic journal *Phylon*:

> Employer resistance to this order has been strong and based on the fact that labor groups separated by caste restrictions can be made a very profitable investment. But the chief and continuing resistance has come from the labor unions—from that very movement which has typified and led industrial democracy.[6]

Sustained tensions over workplace discrimination helped fuel the rise of the postwar civil rights movement. In the summer of 1963 Randolph's idea of a march on Washington would be revived with powerful impact.

Document 5.6
Executive Order 8802, Prohibition of Discrimination in the Defense Industry, June 25, 1941

WHEREAS it is the policy of the United States to encourage full participation in the national defense program by all citizens of the United States, regardless of race, creed, color, or national origin, in the firm belief that the democratic way of life within the Nation can be defended successfully only with the help and support of all groups within its borders; and

WHEREAS there is evidence that available and needed workers have been barred from employment in industries engaged in defense production solely because of consideration of race, creed, color, or national origin, to the detriment of workers' morale and of national unity:

NOW, THEREFORE, by virtue of the authority vested in me by the Constitution and the statutes, and as a prerequisite to the successful conduct of our national defense production effort, I do hereby reaffirm the policy of the United States that there shall be no discrimination in the employment of workers in defense industries or government because of race, creed, color, or national origin, and I do hereby declare that it is the duty of employers and of labor organizations, in furtherance of said policy and of this Order, to provide for the full and equitable participation of all workers in defense industries, without discrimination because of race, creed, color, or national origin;

And it is hereby ordered as follows:

1. All departments and agencies of the Government of the United States concerned with vocational and training programs for defense production shall take special measures appropriate to assure that such programs are administered without discrimination because of race, creed, color, or national origin;

2. All contracting agencies of the Government of the United States shall include in all defense contracts hereafter negotiated by them a provision obligating the contractor not to discriminate against any worker because of race, creed, color, or national origin;

3. There is established in the Office of Production Management a Committee on Fair Employment Practice, which shall consist of a Chairman and four other members to be appointed by the President. The Chairman and members of the Committee shall serve

as such without compensation but shall be entitled to actual and necessary transportation, subsistence, and other expenses incidental to performance of their duties. The Committee shall receive and investigate complaints of discrimination in violation of the provisions of this Order and shall take appropriate steps to redress grievances which it finds to be valid. The Committee shall also recommend to the several departments and agencies of the Government of the United States and to the President all measures which may be deemed by it necessary or proper to effectuate the provisions of this Order . . .

Source: "Executive Order 8802," June 25, 1941, from the U.S. National Archives and Records Administration, www.ourdocuments.gov.

Document 5.7 in Context
"The Old Negro of Yesterday Is Dead": Rep. Adam Clayton Powell Jr., D-N.Y., and the Prelude to the Civil Rights Movement

Most discussions of the rise of the civil rights movement start with the Montgomery, Alabama, bus boycott of 1955–1956, or the Supreme Court's 1954 ruling in *Brown v. Board of Education* (**Document 5.9**). While both of those events were enormously influential in shaping the direction of the movement, it is important to remember that they were the result of—and built upon—events that had come before. The civil rights movement did not suddenly materialize from the *Brown* decision or the Montgomery boycott. Civil rights activism by African Americans had been going on for decades and intensified significantly in the decade between the end of World War II and Rosa Parks's arrest for refusing to give up her bus seat to a white passenger in December 1955.

Despite segregation and discrimination in the military, service in World War II infused many black veterans with a new sense of confidence and they returned home with a growing determination that they would no longer accept the old Jim Crow ways. If they could risk their lives in a war for freedom and serve with effectiveness and distinction, they reasoned, they should not have to accept second-class status when they returned home.

However, the power of segregation and white supremacist attitudes, particularly in the South, were a bitter reminder of how little had changed during the war. Upon their return, numerous black veterans in uniform were attacked—and some were killed—by whites. The vivid contrast between the contributions African Americans made to the defense of liberty and the discrimination and restrictions on their own liberties that they faced in their daily lives fueled a growing militancy that erupted with great power and effect in Montgomery and thereafter.

Few African American leaders exemplified the emergence of this new militant attitude with greater charisma and personal style than did Adam Clayton Powell Jr. Powell began his career as assistant pastor under his father at the Abyssinian Baptist Church in Harlem, worked as a newspaper editor and publisher, became a community activist, served on the New York City Council and was elected to the U.S. House of Representatives as a Democrat in 1944. At the time, he was one of just two African Americans in Congress; William L. Dawson, D-Ill., was the other. But Powell was far more outspoken than Dawson or either of their two most recent African American predecessors in Congress—Oscar S. De Priest, R-Ill., and Arthur W. Mitchell,

D-III. Powell's flamboyant, confrontational style made him a controversial figure who was hated by many whites and widely admired by blacks.

In his first book, *Marching Blacks,* which was published in 1945, less than a year after he assumed his seat in Congress, Powell took a provocative approach and articulated the anger and resentment of millions of African Americans over the treatment they received. In this excerpt, Powell describes the volatile attitudes of the war years and urges all blacks to migrate from the southern states.

Powell's call for blacks to abandon the South got a cold reception from reviewers, both white and black. Even Ben Richardson, who was a close associate and was reviewing the book for the *People's Voice*—where Powell was his editor—was sharply critical of Powell's thesis: "[T]he suggestion that Negroes in the South come North in these days of crisis, ill housing, unemployment, labor-capital struggle, and racial tensions, is an invitation to catastrophe for millions of the oppressed." [7] Still, Powell's call to action was part of a growing determination to demand a change in the status quo.

▬▬ Document 5.7 ▬▬
"Civil War II," from *Marching Blacks,* by Rep. Adam Clayton Powell Jr., D-N.Y., 1945

America is in the midst of Civil War II. It began on December 7, 1941, as the result of an irresistible force meeting an immovable object. It must be continued until one or the other triumphs. There can be no compromise.

The irresistible force is the awakened and united new black and new white man determined to build a real democracy for the first time in the history of America. The immovable object is intolerant, antidemocratic, fascist prejudice concentrated in the South but spreading rapidly, especially during the war period, into every section of America. The conflict between these two forces has become so great that the whole future of this nation depends on the outcome. Furthermore, because we live in a compact world, the future of civilization pivots on the result.

When World War II broke out, fifteen million black Americans found themselves politically disinherited, economically exploited, socially ostracized, educationally underprivileged, and confronted with the deepest hypocrisy in the field of religion. Yet they were asked to go forth and die that the world might be safe for democracy. This they did.

In the beginning, the United States Navy offered them no better chance to make the world safe for democracy than to serve either in toilets or kitchens. They could not fly in the Air Force or fight in the Marine Corps and they were Jim-Crowed in the Army. During the days that Bataan was falling and MacArthur was appealing for materiel, black workers were refused employment in the nation's defense industries. It was here that the conflict broke into the open. Blacks were determined to make the world safe for democracy and doubly determined to make America safe as well. They were finished with a dual democracy—one way for white folks and one way for black folks. They knew that there was no way to separate Hitler abroad from Hitlerism at home. A Jew walking down Unter den Linden in Berlin suffered no fewer indignities than a black man on the streets of Tupelo, Mississippi.

The Negro is a born antifascist. Long before Hitler walked across the face of the earth, we knew him. For three centuries, we tasted the bitterness of Nazism under the name of lynchocracy. The Klan Gestapo has burned our homes. The mob of the pogrom has lynched six thousand of us—cutting off parts of our bodies while the breath of God was still in us. We have lived in ghettos, died by the hundreds in concentration camps as sharecroppers, turpentine workers, and peonage victims. We have been denied the vote in poll-tax states and earned an average of six cents a day in sharecropped land—yet we love America.

The old Negro [of] yesterday is dead. The new black has come forward. He has taken this war seriously, refusing to let it remain a white man's war. He believes that the Four Freedoms, the Atlantic Charter, and all the gilt-edged promises of the Century of the Common Man apply to him as well as to the white folks on the other side of the tracks. What's more, he has made up his mind to fight for these promises.

For countless years, dating back to the pre-slavery era in Africa, Negroes were a divided group. As African natives they were divided into a hundred tribes, each selling the other into slavery. Pitted against one another during slavery, the house Negro against the field Negro; wandering for forty years in the wilderness after the Reconstruction Era; lost in a maze of defeatism, frustration, bitterness, divided leadership, and caste system; victimized at the close of World War I in myriad race riots; shot and killed, burned and lynched even in the uniform of this nation; sinking into the very depths of hopelessness during the Depression of the thirties . . . And yet there at the most tragic hour when his leadership had fled to their ivory towers, when Judas within the temple was selling him for thirty pieces, when the crutches upon which he had hobbled for seventy-five years of mythical freedom were taken away from him, there in that terrible hour of complete loneliness, abject poverty, and black misery, the new black was born. For the first time since blacks were brought in chains to America they learned as a group to move under their own power. They found that it is better for a man to crawl than to walk on crutches provided for him by others. If he crawls, one day he will stand and walk.

Blacks today are the most mature minority of this nation. By their side they find new allies in rapidly increasing numbers—the new white men. Throughout the Deep South strong arms are stretching out to lock with theirs. The tide of real American democracy is flooding. It cannot be held back. Marching blacks are going up Freedom Road. If they are defeated, we will have won the war and lost the peace; reaction will triumph over progress. Western culture will have sown the seeds of its own collapse, and fascism will become the political philosophy of these United States. The black is the test-case of America. He cannot be held down and kept in his place if democracy is to live.

Shall this civil war be fought with all the violence and fury of our first civil war? This is a question that only the conscience of white America can answer. The black has discovered the technique of direct nonviolent social action. His resentment is keen, but it is disciplined. His indignation is great, but it is directed. He has lost only when he resorted to violence and has won every time he fought with unity and nonviolence. The question of violence is, therefore, one for white America to decide.

The great friction spot of our American life is the Southland. More than four out of five white persons in the South expect race relations to grow worse after the war. The same opinion is sustained in every other section of America by the majority of white people. These alarming facts are further emphasized by quotations from whites of all classes of all sections, as recorded by the National Opinion Research Center of the University of Denver during the month of August, 1944:

> A county official in Houston, Texas, feels: "The damn-Yankees mingle with the Negroes too much and spoil 'em."

A Berkeley, California, music teacher anticipates post-war trouble stemming from "propaganda and anti-Democratic forces who use the Negro question to 'divide and rule.'"

A radio program director in Tulsa summarizes the problem as follows: "There will be a conflict between the supremacy of the whites and the newly found sense of freedom of the Negro due to the war."

A Southern grocer thinks: "After the war the Negroes are going to demand the equality we preach and don't practice."

A woman old-age pensioner in Chicago answers: "I'm afraid Negroes will have had a taste of equality in the Army and in war jobs, and will demand their rights as citizens. The white people will try to stop them, and there will be trouble."

Other statements expressing the same opinion are as follows: "Some people are now putting Negroes on a basis of equality with whites, and I think after the war there will be trouble with them . . . Negroes have advanced since this war and people will want to push them back, which will cause trouble . . . Negroes will expect wartime privileges in time of peace . . . The present administration has ruined the Negroes—making such an issue of equal rights . . . Negro soldiers coming back from the war will try to force their way in and make their people do the same."

This book will tell the story of the Negro's growth, not in terms of statistics, population, or wealth, but in terms of his increasing mass power. It will record the growing number of whites who are marching up Freedom Road with him, point out proven techniques to bring about a bloodless revolution, and, lastly, urge ten million Negroes now living in the South to migrate North immediately after the end of this war.

A preliminary remark on the subject of migration can be made at this point. While this book will call upon southern Negroes to migrate, it must be understood that urging is unnecessary. Negroes have never been happy in the South. Whenever they had a chance, Negroes of all classes, types, and colors have hit the road. As long as parts of the Bourbon and backward South remain an unfit place for free men to live, black men will march North. Mass migration will therefore do no more than accentuate a natural process—and serve as a warning. A warning to those parts of the South that are still benighted to mend their ways or face ruin, and a warning to the federal government to prepare for great social upheaval and mobility in the very near future and to provide adequate measures—means of transportation, housing, economic opportunities—to prevent human suffering.

Source: Adam Clayton Powell Jr., "Civil War II," in *Marching Blacks*, rev. ed. (1945; New York: Dial Press, 1973), 3–8.

Document 5.8 in Context
"They Will Never Bear Arms Again until All Forms of Bias and Discrimination Are Abolished": President Harry S. Truman Desegregates the Armed Services

Although the United States and the Soviet Union were allies during World War II, it was an uneasy alliance, built upon their common enmity toward Adolf Hitler's Germany rather than friendship or mutual trust. In the war's final months, an intense struggle began to develop among the allies over plans for postwar Europe. As postwar tensions escalated between the two nations, raising the specter of a new war, the issues of discrimination and segregation in the U.S. military surged into the public political debate. President Harry S. Truman's reinstatement of the military draft in March 1948, following a communist takeover of Czechoslovakia, prompted black leaders to demand that the Democratic president end segregation in the military.

Racial bias in the military had been a sore point for African Americans at least as far back as the Civil War when black soldiers were paid less than their white counterparts. Segregation within the military and the discrimination black soldiers often faced in the communities that surrounded military bases, in the North as well as in the South, sparked sometimes-violent confrontations during both World War I and World War II.

In 1943 William H. Hastie, a black civilian aide to the secretary of war, was dismayed to learn that the U.S. Army planned to set up a segregated school to train black officers for ground duty in the Army Air Forces. He decided to resign to protest "reactionary policies and discriminatory practices of the Army Air Forces." Hastie, who would later become the first black federal judge, explained his resignation in a written statement: "The tragedy is that by not wanting the colored man in the first place and by doubting his capacity, the Air Command has committed itself psychologically to courses of action which themselves become major obstacles to the success of colored men in the Air Forces." [8]

In 1948 Truman was engaged in an uphill battle to hang onto the presidency. He had assumed the office after Franklin Delano Roosevelt's death, and many observers doubted he could even win the Democratic nomination, much less the general election in November. Truman struggled to balance an appeal to black voters with his desire not to alienate white Democrats in the South. But a sense of presidential responsibility had been pushing him to act. Shocked by attacks against black soldiers returning from the war, Truman had denounced the violence in his 1947 State of the Union address and set up a commission to examine what could be done to protect the civil rights of African Americans. He also that year became the first president to address the national convention of the National Association for the Advancement of Colored People (NAACP).

Although Truman was sympathetic to the plight of black soldiers, he had to be pressured into desegregating the military. A. Philip Randolph, president of the Brotherhood of Sleeping Car Porters, once again threatened to organize a march on Washington to demand an end to the military's Jim Crow practices; he had made a similar threat in 1941, which had prodded President Franklin D. Roosevelt, D-N.Y., to order an end to discriminatory hiring practices in defense industries (**Document 5.6**). Truman met with Randolph, but stalked out of the meeting after Randolph declared, "I can tell you the mood among Negroes of this country is that they will never bear arms again until all forms of bias and discrimination are abolished." [9]

Randolph worked to keep the issue in the public eye by testifying before Congress and picketing at the White House. Four months after they met, and with the election looming, Truman finally issued Executive Order 9981 on July 26, 1948, officially desegregating the armed services. The order solidified support for Truman among black voters, who in November helped give him desperately needed victories in Ohio, Illinois and California—where most white voters supported his Republican opponent, Thomas E. Dewey—and returned him to office. The impact on the military, however, was gradual. Army combat units in the Korean War were not integrated until 1951, and the last all-black units were not disbanded until 1954.

▬▬ Document 5.8 ▬▬
Executive Order 9981, Desegregation of the Armed Forces, July 26, 1948

Establishing the President's Committee on Equality of Treatment and Opportunity In the Armed Forces.

WHEREAS it is essential that there be maintained in the armed services of the United States the highest standards of democracy, with equality of treatment and opportunity for all those who serve in our country's defense:

NOW THEREFORE, by virtue of the authority vested in me as President of the United States, by the Constitution and the statutes of the United States, and as Commander in Chief of the armed services, it is hereby ordered as follows:

1. It is hereby declared to be the policy of the President that there shall be equality of treatment and opportunity for all persons in the armed services without regard to race, color, religion or national origin. This policy shall be put into effect as rapidly as possible, having due regard to the time required to effectuate any necessary changes without impairing efficiency or morale.

2. There shall be created in the National Military Establishment an advisory committee to be known as the President's Committee on Equality of Treatment and Opportunity in the Armed Services, which shall be composed of seven members to be designated by the President.

3. The Committee is authorized on behalf of the President to examine into the rules, procedures and practices of the Armed Services in order to determine in what respect such rules, procedures and practices may be altered or improved with a view to carrying out the policy of this order. The Committee shall confer and advise the Secretary of Defense, the Secretary of the Army, the Secretary of the Navy, and the Secretary of the Air Force, and shall make such recommendations to the President and to said Secretaries as in the judgment of the Committee will effectuate the policy hereof.

4. All executive departments and agencies of the Federal Government are authorized and directed to cooperate with the Committee in its work, and to furnish the Committee such information or the services of such persons as the Committee may require in the performance of its duties.

5. When requested by the Committee to do so, persons in the armed services or in any of the executive departments and agencies of the Federal Government shall testify before the Committee and shall make available for use of the Committee such documents and other information as the Committee may require.

6. The Committee shall continue to exist until such time as the President shall terminate its existence by Executive order.

Source: "Executive Order 9981," July 26, 1948, from the U.S. National Archives and Records Administration, www.ourdocuments.gov.

Document 5.9 in Context
"In the Field of Public Education, the Doctrine of 'Separate but Equal' Has No Place": *Brown v. Board of Education* Marks a Dramatic Turnaround

The May 17, 1954, ruling of the U.S. Supreme Court in *Brown v. Board of Education* marked a profound and dramatic turnaround by the Court—and the nation—on the issue of racial segregation in America. For more than half a century, public policy had been guided by the Court's 1896 decision in *Plessy v. Ferguson* (**Document 4.5**), which established the doctrine of "separate but equal." Under *Plessy,* segregated facilities for blacks were considered legal and in compliance with the Fourteenth Amendment of the Constitution (**Document 3.2**) if they were substantially equal to the facilities available to whites.

For the first half of the twentieth century, southern states used the *Plessy* decision not only to mandate racially segregated public transportation (which had been the focus of the case) but also to justify all manner of segregated facilities. Schools, in particular, were a focus of segregation, though few people could seriously argue that black students were provided equal facilities.

The National Association for the Advancement of Colored People worked diligently, practically from the time it was founded in 1909, to overturn *Plessy.* Its efforts intensified in the mid-1930s with the hiring of Charles Hamilton Houston to head the NAACP's legal campaign and Houston's subsequent hiring of his former law student, Thurgood Marshall. Houston's strategy was not to challenge segregation directly, but to bring it down by forcing the South to live up to the requirement of *Plessy* that separate facilities be substantially equal. Initial victories resulted from his focus on unequal facilities and programs in state university graduate schools. But the legal questions involved had not forced the Court to confront head-on the "separate but equal" doctrine of *Plessy.*

The *Brown* ruling (which consolidated four separate suits from Kansas, South Carolina, Virginia and Delaware) went to the heart of the matter. Rather than looking merely at the relative equality of physical facilities in particular schools, the Court considered the deeper question of whether there was an essential and irreparable inequality embedded in the very concept of racially segregated schools. In a unanimous opinion, the Court concluded that there was.

Two days later, the NAACP issued a statement hailing the ruling and declaring that "true Americans are grateful for this decision . . . We look upon this memorable decision not as a victory for Negroes alone, but for the whole American people and as a vindication of America's leadership of the free world." [10]

The victory was neither complete nor immediate, but it was enormously important. The *Brown* decision did not specifically overturn *Plessy,* leaving unresolved the application of the "separate but equal" doctrine in public transportation and other public accommodations, but it made clear the direction the Court was heading in its view of segregation. It took the Court a year to produce a second ruling in the case, generally referred to as *Brown II,* explaining how the initial ruling should be implemented. The central language of *Brown II*—that desegregation of schools should proceed with "all deliberate speed" [11]—was interpreted by most African Americans to mean "immediately." But defenders of segregation, especially in the South, used the phrase to justify continued delay.

Despite some resistance, the *Brown* rulings knocked the foundation out from under the Jim Crow system of segregation that had dominated race relations in America since 1896. A decade later, Congress passed the Civil Rights Act of 1964 (**Document 5.11**) and finally put to rest any legal justification for racial segregation in America.

▬ Document 5.9 ▬
U.S. Supreme Court Decision in *Brown v. Board of Education*, May 17, 1954

MR. CHIEF JUSTICE [Earl] WARREN delivered the opinion of the Court.

These cases come to us from the States of Kansas, South Carolina, Virginia, and Delaware. They are premised on different facts and different local conditions, but a common legal question justifies their consideration together in this consolidated opinion.

In each of the cases, minors of the Negro race, through their legal representatives, seek the aid of the courts in obtaining admission to the public schools of their community on a nonsegregated basis. In each instance, they had been denied admission to schools attended by white children under laws requiring or permitting segregation according to race. This segregation was alleged to deprive the plaintiffs of the equal protection of the laws under the Fourteenth Amendment. In each of the cases other than the Delaware case, a three-judge federal district court denied relief to the plaintiffs on the so-called "separate but equal" doctrine announced by this Court in Plessy v. Ferguson, 163 U.S. 537. Under that doctrine, equality of treatment is accorded when the races are provided substantially equal facilities, even though these facilities be separate. In the Delaware case, the Supreme Court of Delaware adhered to that doctrine, but ordered that the plaintiffs be admitted to the white schools because of their superiority to the Negro schools.

The plaintiffs contend that segregated public schools are not "equal" and cannot be made "equal," and that hence they are deprived of the equal protection of the laws. Because of the obvious importance of the question presented, the Court took jurisdiction. Argument was heard in the 1952 Term, and reargument was heard this Term on certain questions propounded by the Court.

Reargument was largely devoted to the circumstances surrounding the adoption of the Fourteenth Amendment in 1868. It covered exhaustively consideration of the Amendment in Congress, ratification by the states, then-existing practices in racial segregation, and the views of proponents and opponents of the Amendment. This discussion and our own investigation convince us that, although these sources cast some light, it is not enough to resolve the problem with which we are faced. At best, they are inconclusive. The most avid proponents of the post-War Amendments undoubtedly intended them to remove all legal distinctions among "all persons born or naturalized in the United States." Their opponents, just as certainly, were antagonistic to both the letter and the spirit of the Amendments and wished them to have the most limited effect. What others in Congress and the state legislatures had in mind cannot be determined with any degree of certainty.

An additional reason for the inconclusive nature of the Amendment's history with respect to segregated schools is the status of public education at that time. In the South, the movement toward free common schools, supported by general taxation, had not yet taken hold. Education of white children was largely in the hands of private groups. Education of Negroes was almost nonexistent, and practically all of the race were illiterate. In fact, any education of Negroes was forbidden by law in some states. Today, in contrast, many Negroes have achieved outstanding success in the arts and sciences, as well as in the business and professional world. It is true that public school education at the time of the Amendment had advanced further in the North, but the effect of the Amendment on Northern States was generally ignored in the congressional debates. Even in the North, the conditions of public education did not approximate those existing today. The curriculum was usually rudimentary; ungraded schools were common in rural areas; the school term was but three months a year in many states, and compulsory school attendance was virtually unknown. As a consequence, it is not surprising that there should be so little in the history of the Fourteenth Amendment relating to its intended effect on public education.

In the first cases in this Court construing the Fourteenth Amendment, decided shortly after its adoption, the Court interpreted it as proscribing all state-imposed discriminations against the Negro race. The doctrine of "separate but equal" did not make its appearance in this Court until 1896 in the case of Plessy v. Ferguson, supra, involving not education but transportation. American courts have since labored with the doctrine for over half a century. In this Court, there have been six cases involving the "separate but equal" doctrine in the field of public education . . . In none of these cases was it necessary to reexamine the doctrine to grant relief to the Negro plaintiff. And in Sweatt v. Painter, supra, the Court expressly reserved decision on the question whether Plessy v. Ferguson should be held inapplicable to public education.

In the instant cases, that question is directly presented. Here, unlike Sweatt v. Painter, there are findings below that the Negro and white schools involved have been equalized, or are being equalized, with respect to buildings, curricula, qualifications and salaries of teachers, and other "tangible" factors. Our decision, therefore, cannot turn on merely a comparison of these tangible factors in the Negro and white schools involved in each of the cases. We must look instead to the effect of segregation itself on public education.

In approaching this problem, we cannot turn the clock back to 1868, when the Amendment was adopted, or even to 1896, when Plessy v. Ferguson was written. We must consider public education in the light of its full development and its present place in American life throughout the Nation. Only in this way can it be determined if segregation in public schools deprives these plaintiffs of the equal protection of the laws.

Today, education is perhaps the most important function of state and local governments. Compulsory school attendance laws and the great expenditures for education both demonstrate our recognition of the importance of education to our democratic society. It is required in the performance of our most basic public responsibilities, even service in the armed forces. It is the very foundation of good citizenship. Today it is a principal instrument in awakening the child to cultural values, in preparing him for later professional training, and in helping him to adjust normally to his environment. In these days, it is doubtful that any child may reasonably be expected to succeed in life if he is denied the opportunity of an education. Such an opportunity, where the state has undertaken to provide it, is a right which must be made available to all on equal terms.

We come then to the question presented: Does segregation of children in public schools solely on the basis of race, even though the physical facilities and other "tangible" factors may be equal, deprive the children of the minority group of equal educational opportunities? We believe that it does.

In Sweatt v. Painter, supra, in finding that a segregated law school for Negroes could not provide them equal educational opportunities, this Court relied in large part on "those qualities which are incapable of objective measurement but which make for greatness in a law school." In McLaurin v. Oklahoma State Regents, supra, the Court, in requiring that a

Negro admitted to a white graduate school be treated like all other students, again resorted to intangible considerations: ". . . his ability to study, to engage in discussions and exchange views with other students, and, in general, to learn his profession." Such considerations apply with added force to children in grade and high schools. To separate them from others of similar age and qualifications solely because of their race generates a feeling of inferiority as to their status in the community that may affect their hearts and minds in a way unlikely ever to be undone. The effect of this separation on their educational opportunities was well stated by a finding in the Kansas case by a court which nevertheless felt compelled to rule against the Negro plaintiffs:

Segregation of white and colored children in public schools has a detrimental effect upon the colored children. The impact is greater when it has the sanction of the law, for the policy of separating the races is usually interpreted as denoting the inferiority of the negro group. A sense of inferiority affects the motivation of a child to learn. Segregation with the sanction of law, therefore, has a tendency to [retard] the educational and mental development of negro children and to deprive them of some of the benefits they would receive in a racial[ly] integrated school system.

Whatever may have been the extent of psychological knowledge at the time of Plessy v. Ferguson, this finding is amply supported by modern authority. Any language in Plessy v. Ferguson contrary to this finding is rejected.

We conclude that, in the field of public education, the doctrine of "separate but equal" has no place. Separate educational facilities are inherently unequal. Therefore, we hold that the plaintiffs and others similarly situated for whom the actions have been brought are, by reason of the segregation complained of, deprived of the equal protection of the laws guaranteed by the Fourteenth Amendment. This disposition makes unnecessary any discussion whether such segregation also violates the Due Process Clause of the Fourteenth Amendment . . .

Source: Brown v. Board of Education of Topeka, 347 U.S. 483 (1954), from FindLaw, http://laws.findlaw.com/us/347/483.html.

Document 5.10 in Context
"We Were Constantly Questioned about the Treatment of Minority Groups and Peoples Here in the United States": Advocacy for Federal Protection of Citizens' Civil Rights

During the 1950s, the number of African Americans in Congress slowly increased to three in 1955 and four in 1957. The election of 1954 brought Charles C. Diggs Jr. of Detroit to Washington to join Adam Clayton Powell Jr. of New York City and William L. Dawson of Chicago in the House of Representatives. All were Democrats. Their small number limited their political power and ability to influence legislation, but the prominence of their position on Capitol Hill gave them a forum to advocate for reforms that would help African Americans.

Nine months after taking office, Diggs traveled to Sumner, Mississippi, to attend the murder trial of two white men accused of killing Emmett Till, a black fourteen-year-old from Chicago who had been kidnapped and brutally murdered while visiting relatives in nearby Money, Mississippi. The killers had been angered by Till's impertinent comment, "Bye, baby," to a white woman in a store. Till was taken from his uncle's home, beaten, shot in the head and thrown in the Tallahatchie River with a heavy metal fan from a cotton gin tied around his neck. He was found three days later.

Diggs went to Mississippi to observe the trial and to help focus national attention on racist violence in the South. Initially, he was barred from the courtroom by the county sheriff, who seemed incredulous at the arrival of what he called "a nigger congressman." The judge eventually let Diggs sit at a small, segregated table with black members of the press corps. "The judge said something about, 'Yeah, have that boy come up here and sit down over here with these news reporters,' " Diggs recalled later.[12]

The two white suspects, who were acquitted during trial by jury, later admitted in a 1956 magazine interview that they had killed Till. Widespread outrage over the murder helped inspire the civil rights movement.

Till's shocking murder and the subsequent trial attracted international media attention. But as remarkable as it was, the Till case was just one instance in a much broader pattern of violence. In the three months preceding Till's murder, two black voting rights activists were murdered in Mississippi: Rev. George Lee of Belzoni was shot in his car after attempting to vote, and Lamar Smith was shot outside the county courthouse in Brookhaven after he had voted. No arrests were made in either case.

After his return to Washington, Diggs introduced a series of civil rights–oriented legislation, none of which passed. One bill called for reorganization of the Justice Department to better protect civil rights, and another called for creation of a commission on civil rights. Diggs also introduced an anti-lynching bill as well as bills to outlaw discrimination in employment, to protect voting rights and to ban the use of the poll tax as a condition for voting. The following selection is excerpted from Diggs's comments during debate on a competing voting rights bill.

▬▬ Document 5.10 ▬▬
Rep. Charles C. Diggs Jr., D-Mich., Argues for Voter Rights Legislation, June 10, 1957

Mr. DIGGS: . . . I am not going to endeavor to elaborate on the significance of this legislation as it relates to our kinship with other people in this world, and especially the darker people of this world, but may I remind you of the statement of the Vice President of the United States when he returned from his historical trip to the continent of Africa; may I remind you of the statements made by our distinguished colleague, the gentlewoman from Ohio [Mrs. Frances P. BOLTON (R-Ohio)], and may I remind you of the statements that are being made by our emissaries and our statesmen and certain other Members of Congress week after week and year after year about the relationship between the treatment of our so-called minority peoples in this country and the prestige of the United States in the Free World. I can certainly attest to the fact that as a member, and a privileged member of the delegation selected from this House to go to Africa, we were constantly questioned about the treatment of minority groups and peoples here in the United States.

I tell you that I have seen stories concerning racial incidents relating to the matter on this floor not only in Africa but also on the European Continent; and if anyone thinks that their provincialism is going to keep these stories from being circulated in these particular areas or keep those stories from affecting the prestige of our country they are mistaken. And certainly these stories are not of the kind of broad concept of democracy that justifies their opposition here in the Congress of the United States.

I would like to take just a few moments, because of the tenor of the discussion up to this time, to give you a little of the background which gave rise to this legislation, to bring this particular measure back into focus on the question whether or not any person anywhere in the United States is permitted to exercise his most important privilege, and that is the privilege of the franchise.

On this floor during this debate the statements has been made: Bring us some evidence of people who have been deprived of their voting privileges here in the United States. We have been challenged to come forth with evidence of this deprivation. Let me say that I am prepared to name you entire counties in these United States where the Negro people are not permitted to vote. I can tell you about counties, for instance, in the State of Florida: Taylor, Madison, Gadsden, and Jefferson Counties, where Negroes are not registered to vote.

I can carry you over into the State of Alabama and refer you to counties in that particular State where Negroes are not registered to vote, and I have the information before me where Negroes in Lowndes County—if I pronounce it correctly—and Wilcox County, Ala., are not permitted to vote.

And I can tell you about the subterfuge that is used in other counties which keeps Negroes' voting privileges down.

I can tell you, for instance, in the State of Alabama about certain additional burdens which are required of Negroes. For instance, there must be present in some of these areas, when a Negro is registering, an elector to sign the application of the Negro, but this is not required of the other people. The Negro, consequently, must have a white person sign his application in certain areas of this State. A Negro cannot do this in many counties in Alabama, as many whites will not sign the application of Negroes.

We have a situation in Alabama where in a couple of counties the members of the board of registrars have resigned rather than register Negroes. This has been the case in Bullock and Macon Counties in Alabama.

With relation to the processing of applications, many who fail to receive their certificates have been told that the applications have not been processed; but the white applicants in most instances receive their certificates immediately upon registering.

Many boards discourage Negroes from voting in Alabama by pretending to be busy when they come in to register, failing to recognize their presence, or that a Negro is applying for registration. In some instances when they finally recognize him he is told that there is not a quorum of the registrars present and the Negro's application cannot be registered.

In some instances the place used for Negroes will accommodate only one person and therefore, there is a long line where only one person can fill out the questionnaire required at a time, and the long wait discourages some; others must go back to work.

We have a situation where some boards make no pretense whatsoever but tell Negroes they are not registering Negroes while others may be considerate and pretend that there are just no blanks available. Still others are told to come back at some future date and are continually told to come back at some future date . . .

. . . Many times boards will show by their obvious resentment that they do not want to be bothered.

I could go on and on and cite these subterfuges which are being used in this particular State.

I could also swing over to the State of Mississippi and point out to you 13 counties in the State of Mississippi that do not have one Negro registered on their books. I invite any Representative from that State to explain why a Negro in any of these 13 counties is not registered. I am talking about counties whose population ranges from 12 percent all the way up to 74 percent in Jefferson County, and there are no Negroes registered to vote. I invite the distinguished Representatives from that State to explain why there are no Negroes registered in those particular counties.

Mr. Chairman, on the basis of the testimony that was given in the hearings from the people living in these various sections, who have pointed out that through intimidation, coercion, and subterfuge, they are kept from the polls, this is ample testimony why this legislation is sorely needed. I have not heard on this floor during the entire debate anyone come up with a solution of this particular problem, other than the solution which is incorporated in this legislation.

The reason that we are here today seeking relief on the Federal level is because the offending States are not protecting the right to vote on the part of these people to whom I have referred. They do not want that kind of States rights because they know that once full participation of the ballot is in the hands of all the people they will have to, of course, answer to all of the people as it relates to matters in which they express an interest here in Washington.

Mr. [James] FULTON [R-Pa.]: Mr. Chairman, will the gentleman yield?

Mr. DIGGS: I yield to the gentleman from Pennsylvania.

Mr. FULTON: A statement has been made to me on the floor that the Negroes who are not registered were not interested in voting. I doubted that because I come from a Northern State. I would like to have the gentleman, as he knows so many of them, tell us whether these Negroes really want to vote and take an interest in the civic affairs of their communities, because there are many of us on the floor, regardless of color or religion, who want them to have that right and who want to find out how to get them the right to do so.

Mr. DIGGS: In all fairness to the gentleman, the question of voter participation is approximately the same in all areas, at least in the northern areas among a particular group as in any other particular group. You do not find a marked lag between the participation of people in the voting processes, whether they are Negro or white, when they have the opportunity to vote.

I want you to look at the statistics. For instance, let me cite these 13 particular counties. In Carroll County, Miss., which has a Negro population of 57 percent, not one Negro is registered in the entire county.

In Chickasaw, 44.5 percent Negroes, not one Negro registered; Clarke County, 40.7 percent Negroes, not one Negro registered; Issaquena, 67.4 percent. Incidentally Issaquena County is the birthplace of my father. Jefferson County, 74.5 percent Negroes, not one registered. Lamar County, 15.9 percent Negroes; Noxubee, 74.4 percent; Pearl River, 21.8 percent; Tallahatchie, 63.7 percent.

And may I remind you that Tallahatchie County is the county where the Till trial was held.

When you consider the fact that you have to be a registered voter in Mississippi as a condition precedent to serving on juries, you can see how this can become compounded so far as the Negro people are concerned, not only as it relates to voting but as it relates to all rights in those particular States. I could go on and on to point that out . . .

Source: Congressional Record, 85th Cong., 1st sess., June 10, 1957, vol. 103, part 7, 8704–8705.

Document 5.11 in Context
"To Enforce the Constitutional Right to Vote": The Civil Rights Act Culminates a Decade of Protest

The Civil Rights Act of 1964 was the culmination of a decade of protest, confrontation and escalating racial violence. The Supreme Court's 1954 school desegregation ruling, *Brown v. Board of Education* (**Document 5.9**), was followed by the murder of Emmett Till, the Montgomery, Alabama, bus boycott, the emergence of Rev. Martin Luther King Jr. and the civil rights movement, Freedom Rides and confrontations over school integration that required intervention by federal marshals and troops.

The turmoil seemed to be spinning almost out of control. President John F. Kennedy, a Democrat, had to send federal troops to Oxford, Mississippi, in October 1962 to enforce a federal court ruling ordering that James Meredith, a black student, be admitted to the University of Mississippi. The violence surrounding Meredith's enrollment left two people dead and more than seventy soldiers and federal marshals injured.

In early May 1963 the nation was shocked by television news coverage of protest marches in Birmingham, Alabama, where some of the city's white police officers attacked black marchers—mostly children and teens—with batons, water blasted from fire hoses and dogs. Barely a month later, Alabama National Guard troops had to be used to enforce a federal court order to admit two black students to the University of Alabama.

Kennedy addressed the nation on June 11, announcing that he would propose legislation to Congress that would increase the pace of school desegregation, protect the rights of black voters and end discrimination in public facilities—such as hotels, restaurants and stores. He explained:

> We face . . . a moral crisis as a country and a people. It cannot be met by repressive police action. It cannot be left to increased demonstrations in the streets. It cannot be quieted by token moves or talk. It is a time to act in the Congress, in your State and local legislative body and, above all, in all of our daily lives. [13]

Civil rights groups decided to support Kennedy's proposal by reviving A. Philip Randolph's 1941 idea of a march on Washington. Randolph's threats of such a march had prompted President Franklin D. Roosevelt to issue an order banning discrimination in hiring in the defense industries (**Document 5.6**) and President Harry S. Truman to order an end to segregation in the armed forces (**Document 5.8**). This time organizers made no threats, but went through with the "March on Washington," which brought nearly 250,000 demonstrators to the Lincoln Memorial in August 1963. It also produced perhaps the most recognized moment of the civil rights movement: King's "I Have a Dream" speech.

Despite the president's and civil rights leaders' calls for change, the violence continued. On September 15, 1963, four young black girls were killed in the bombing of a Birmingham church by white supremacists, and on November 22, Kennedy was assassinated in Dallas, Texas. Kennedy's successor, Democrat Lyndon B. Johnson of Texas, soon announced that he would push aggressively for congressional approval of the civil rights legislation Kennedy had proposed. By July 1964, the Civil Rights Act had been passed by Congress and signed by Johnson, finally putting an end to legally mandated segregation in public accommodations. The law also prohibited discrimination by labor unions and employers, and included strict enforcement provisions.

The Civil Rights Act of 1964 and the Voting Rights Act of 1965 (**Document 6.1**) dramatically altered the structure of American society by eliminating legal justifications for segregation and increasing the access of African Americans not just to public facilities, but also to the political process. One important result would be a rapid and significant increase in African American representation in Congress.

▄▄▄ Document 5.11 ▄▄▄
Civil Rights Act of 1964, July 2, 1964

AN ACT To enforce the constitutional right to vote, to confer jurisdiction upon the district courts of the United States to provide injunctive relief against discrimination in public accommodations, to authorize the Attorney General to institute suits to protect constitutional rights in public facilities and public education, to extend the Commission on Civil Rights, to prevent discrimination in federally assisted programs, to establish a Commission on Equal Employment Opportunity, and for other purposes.

Be it enacted by the Senate and House of Representatives of the United States of America in Congress assembled, That this Act may be cited as the "Civil Rights Act of 1964".

TITLE I—VOTING RIGHTS
SECTION 101 . . .

"(2) No person acting under color of law shall—

"(A) in determining whether any individual is qualified under State law or laws to vote in any Federal election, apply any standard, practice, or procedure different from the standards, practices, or procedures applied under such law or laws to other individuals within the same county, parish, or similar political subdivision who have been found by State officials to be qualified to vote; . . .

TITLE II—INJUNCTIVE RELIEF AGAINST DISCRIMINATION IN PLACES OF PUBLIC ACCOMMODATION
SEC. 201. (a) All persons shall be entitled to the full and equal enjoyment of the goods, services, facilities, and privileges, advantages, and accommodations of any place of public accommodation, as defined in this section, without discrimination or segregation on the ground of race, color, religion, or national origin . . .

TITLE III—DESEGREGATION OF PUBLIC FACILITIES

SEC. 301. (a) Whenever the Attorney General receives a complaint in writing signed by an individual to the effect that he is being deprived of or threatened with the loss of his right to the equal protection of the laws, on account of his race, color, religion, or national origin, by being denied equal utilization of any public facility which is owned, operated, or managed by or on behalf of any State or subdivision thereof, other than a public school or public college as defined in section 401 of title IV hereof, and the Attorney General believes the complaint is meritorious and certifies that the signer or signers of such complaint are unable, in his judgment, to initiate and maintain appropriate legal proceedings for relief and that the institution of an action will materially further the orderly progress of desegregation in public facilities, the Attorney General is authorized to institute for or in the name of the United States a civil action in any appropriate district court of the United States against such parties and for such relief as may be appropriate, and such court shall have and shall exercise jurisdiction of proceedings instituted pursuant to this section. The Attorney General may implead as defendants such additional parties as are or become necessary to the grant of effective relief hereunder . . .

TITLE IV—DESEGREGATION OF PUBLIC EDUCATION DEFINITIONS

SEC. 401. As used in this title—

(a) "Commissioner" means the Commissioner of Education.

(b) "Desegregation" means the assignment of students to public schools and within such schools without regard to their race, color, religion, or national origin, but "desegregation" shall not mean the assignment of students to public schools in order to overcome racial imbalance.

(c) "Public school" means any elementary or secondary educational institution, and "public college" means any institution of higher education or any technical or vocational school above the secondary school level, provided that such public school or public college is operated by a State, subdivision of a State, or governmental agency within a State, or operated wholly or predominantly from or through the use of governmental funds or property, or funds or property derived from a governmental source.

(d) "School board" means any agency or agencies which administer a system of one or more public schools and any other agency which is responsible for the assignment of students to or within such system . . .

TITLE V—COMMISSION ON CIVIL RIGHTS

. . .

"Duties of the Commission

"SEC. 104. (a) The Commission shall—

"(1) investigate allegations in writing under oath or affirmation that certain citizens of the United States are being deprived of their right to vote and have that vote counted by reason of their color, race, religion, or national origin; which writing, under oath or affirmation, shall set forth the facts upon which such belief or beliefs are based;

"(2) study and collect information concerning legal developments constituting a denial of equal protection of the laws under the Constitution because of race, color, religion or national origin or in the administration of justice;

"(3) appraise the laws and policies of the Federal Government with respect to denials of equal protection of the laws under the Constitution because of race, color, religion or national origin or in the administration of justice;

"(4) serve as a national clearinghouse for information in respect to denials of equal protection of the laws because of race, color, religion or national origin, including but not limited to the fields of voting, education, housing, employment, the use of public facilities, and transportation, or in the administration of justice;

"(5) investigate allegations, made in writing and under oath or affirmation, that citizens of the United States are unlawfully being accorded or denied the right to vote, or to have their votes properly counted, in any election of presidential electors, Members of the United States Senate, or of the House of Representatives, as a result of any patterns or practice of fraud or discrimination in the conduct of such election . . .

TITLE VI—NONDISCRIMINATION IN FEDERALLY ASSISTED PROGRAMS

SEC. 601. No person in the United States shall, on the ground of race, color, or national origin, be excluded from participation in, be denied the benefits of, or be subjected to discrimination under any program or activity receiving Federal financial assistance . . .

TITLE VII—EQUAL EMPLOYMENT OPPORTUNITY

. . .

Discrimination Because of Race, Color, Religion, Sex, or National Origin

SEC. 703. (a) It shall be an unlawful employment practice for an employer—

(1) to fail or refuse to hire or to discharge any individual, or otherwise to discriminate against any individual with respect to his compensation, terms, conditions, or privileges of employment, because of such individual's race, color, religion, sex, or national origin; or

(2) to limit, segregate, or classify his employees in any way which would deprive or tend to deprive any individual of employment opportunities or otherwise adversely affect his status as an employee, because of such individual's race, color, religion, sex, or national origin . . .

Equal Employment Opportunity Commission

SEC. 705. (a) There is hereby created a Commission to be known as the Equal Employment Opportunity Commission, which shall be composed of five members, not more than three of whom shall be members of the same political party, who shall be appointed by the President by and with the advice and consent of the Senate . . . (g) The Commission shall have power—

(1) to cooperate with and, with their consent, utilize regional, State, local, and other agencies, both public and private, and individuals;

(2) to pay to witnesses whose depositions are taken or who are summoned before the Commission or any of its agents the same witness and mileage fees as are paid to witnesses in the courts of the United States;

(3) to furnish to persons subject to this title such technical assistance as they may request to further their compliance with this title or an order issued thereunder;

(4) upon the request of (i) any employer, whose employees or some of them, or (ii) any labor organization, whose members or some of them, refuse or threaten to refuse to cooperate in effectuating the provisions of this title, to assist in such effectuation by conciliation or such other remedial action as is provided by this title;

(5) to make such technical studies as are appropriate to effectuate the purposes and policies of this title and to make the results of such studies available to the public;

(6) to refer matters to the Attorney General with recommendations for intervention in a civil action brought by an aggrieved party under section 706, or for the institution of a civil action by the Attorney General under section 707, and to advise, consult, and assist the Attorney General on such matters . . .

Source: "Civil Rights Act," July 2, 1964, from the U.S. National Archives and Records Administration, www.ourdocuments.gov.

NOTES

1 W. E. B. DuBois, "An Open Letter to Woodrow Wilson," in *A Documentary History of the Negro People in the United States, 1910–1932*, ed. Herbert Aptheker (Secaucus, N.J.: The Citadel Press, 1973), 60–62.

2 "The Trotter Encounter with President Wilson," in Aptheker, *A Documentary History*, 70–78.

3 "Herbert Hoover, by W. E. B. DuBois," in Aptheker, *A Documentary History*, 739–743.

4 George F. Robinson Jr., "The Negro in Politics in Chicago," *Journal of Negro History* 17, no. 2 (April 1932): 226.

5 Mary McLeod Bethune, "Letter to Eleanor Roosevelt," July 10, 1941, in *Mary McLeod Bethune: Building a Better World: Essays and Selected Documents*, ed. Audrey Thomas McCluskey and Elaine M. Smith (Bloomington, Ind.: Indiana University Press, 1999), 240–241.

6 W. E. B. DuBois, "A Chronicle of Race Relations," *Phylon* 4, no. 1 (1st Quarter 1943): 80.

7 Quoted in Wil Haygood, *King of the Cats: The Life and Times of Adam Clayton Powell Jr.* (New York: Houghton Mifflin, 1993), 133.

8 John H. Bracey Jr., August Meier and Elliott Rudwick, eds., *The Afro-Americans: Selected Documents* (Boston: Allyn and Bacon, 1972), 614–618.

9 "The Transformation of the Racial Views of Harry Truman," *Journal of Blacks in Higher Education* no. 26 (Winter 1999–2000): 28–30.

10 Clayborne Carson, David J. Garrow, Gerald Gill, Vincent Harding and Darlene Clark Hine, eds., *The Eyes on the Prize Civil Rights Reader* (New York: Penguin Books, 1991).

11 *Brown v. Board of Education of Topeka*, Implementation Decree, May 31, 1955, Records of the Supreme Court of the United States; Record Group 267, U.S. National Archives.

12 PBS, *Eyes on the Prize: Awakenings (1954–1956)*, produced by Blackside Inc., 1987.

13 John F. Kennedy Speech, "Radio and Television Report to the American People on Civil Rights," June 11, 1963, in *Public Papers of the Presidents of the United States: John F. Kennedy, 1963*, from the American Presidency Project, www.presidency.ucsb.edu/ws/?pid=9271.

CHAPTER SIX

The Civil Rights Movement and Beyond
Equal Rights and Political Empowerment, 1965–1993

S tarting in the mid-1960s, the number of African Americans in Congress and the influence they wielded, both individually and collectively, increased steadily. One major contributing factor was the Voting Rights Act of 1965 (**Document 6.1**), which triggered a significant increase in black voters and office-holders from seven southern states; none of those states had elected a black representative since the end of the 1800s. In 1966 the U.S. Supreme Court unanimously upheld the law's constitutionality, rejecting South Carolina's argument that it exceeded congressional authority under the Fifteenth Amendment (**Document 3.3**). Even so, the Voting Rights Act proved imperfect. In a January 1975 report to Congress and the president, the U.S. Civil Rights Commission concluded that the law "has contributed substantially to the marked increase in all forms of minority political participation in the last 10 years" but observed that "detailed examination of recent events reveals that discrimination persists in the political process. The promise of the 15th amendment and the potential of the Voting Rights Act have not been fully realized." [1] African American members were among those who successfully pressed for its extension that year.

Rev. Martin Luther King Jr. led civil rights marchers, eight abreast, across the Alabama River on the Edmund Pettus Bridge at Selma on March 21, 1965. The marchers were at the start of a fifty-mile march to the Alabama state capital in their fight for voter registration rights for African Americans, who were being discouraged from registering, particularly in small towns in the South. After they crossed the bridge, the marchers were teargassed and beaten by police. Five months later, President Lyndon B. Johnson signed the Voting Rights Act of 1965.
Source: AP Images

Another significant factor contributing to increased African American political participation was congressional reapportionment after the 1970 and 1980 censuses. These remapping processes created more "majority-minority" congressional districts, where African Americans constituted a majority of residents and therefore wielded greater political power. Ironically, the concentration of black residents in such districts had occurred as a result of residential segregation that had long prevented many African Americans from moving to majority-white neighborhoods.

Still another factor contributing to black political empowerment was the Republican Party's continuing failure to effectively address the domestic policy concerns of black Americans, a trend that had been evident throughout the post–World War II era (**Document 8.4**). That kept the door open for Democrats to mobilize black voters and promote black candidates, principally in urban districts, without significant Republican opposition. Building the black political base provided a counterbalance to the large-scale defection of conservative Democrats to the GOP in the South, a region that Democratic presidential candidates and congressional leaders had relied upon before the national party embraced civil rights.

Reflecting the increasing number of black representatives in Congress, the Congressional Black Caucus was established in 1971 (**Document 6.2**) to provide a mechanism for leveraging black members' political influence within Congress and, more importantly, with the executive branch, the Democratic party and the public. As the number of Caucus members grew, so did their clout in Congress.

In 1965 only two members—both from overwhelmingly black and Democratic districts—chaired major committees: William L. Dawson of Illinois (Government Operations) and Adam Clayton Powell Jr. of New York (Education and Labor). Historically, Congress's seniority system, which rewarded longevity in office with subcommittee and committee chairs, had benefited white, usually conservative southern Democrats who easily won reelection in one-party districts.

Ronald V. Dellums of California, one of the new wave of Democratic African American representatives, described the political realities he faced after his election in 1970: "As a 'left-wing radical' elected to a Democrat-controlled Congress—a Congress significantly influenced by its 'Southern Barons' and one that shared power with Richard Nixon's White House—I found the challenge even more daunting." [2] Dellums was among those who successfully fought the authoritarianism of such entrenched barons to win prize committee assignments (**Document 6.4**). However, through the 1970s and 1980s, the same seniority system pushed more liberal blacks, who were safely ensconced in their own one-party urban districts, to the top of the ladder. By 1979–1980 nine of the Caucus's sixteen members chaired subcommittees. Dellums observed:

> Like the Southern Barons of an earlier era, I and other like-minded legislators became a group—in our case a group of urban progressives—who ultimately benefited from seniority, and whose ideas and ideals would begin to find their way more prominently into the debate and into the legislative product. By staying engaged, and by learning the legislative process and demanding that it accord our ideas the dignity granted to those of other coalitions, we began more and more to influence legislative outcomes. However, seniority alone does not account for our success. We depended very much on the presence of what the Reverend Jesse Jackson would later come to refer to as "street heat"—people mobilized to command the attention of the organs of power. Their activism always enhanced our ability to achieve success legislatively on behalf of their idealism and ideas.[3]

Bolstering their seniority was the fact that in most congressional elections, incumbency and its accompanying resources—among them staff, media access, fund-raising ability, free mailing privileges and district offices—provide a powerful advantage over potential challengers. Also, many African Americans chose to retain their safe seats in the House rather than run for higher office.

Relations between the Caucus and presidents varied largely, but not exclusively, on partisan lines. There was hostility toward Republican Richard M. Nixon on personal, political and policy grounds, and African Americans were among the leaders of the impeachment movement (**Document 6.5**). However, Caucus members found Republican Gerald R. Ford, their former House colleague, still ideologically distant but more congenial (**Document 6.6**). For example, it took more than a year for Nixon to agree to sit down with them (**Document 6.3**). But when the Caucus sent Ford,

President Richard M. Nixon's first meeting with members of the Congressional Black Caucus occurred on March 25, 1971, more than one year after the caucus was organized. Relations between the White House and the Caucus remained tense throughout Nixon's presidency. Clockwise from lower right are: Reps. Parren J. Mitchell of Maryland; Shirley A. Chisholm of New York; Charles C. Diggs Jr. of Michigan; Nixon; Reps. Augustus F. Hawkins of California; William L. Clay of Missouri; Ronald V. Dellums of California; Nixon adviser Robert Finch; HUD Secretary George Romney; Del. Walter E. Fauntroy, Washington, D.C.; Reps. Ralph H. Metcalfe of Illinois; George W. Collins of Illinois; Robert N. C. Nix of Pennsylvania; Nixon adviser Clark MacGregor; Reps. John Conyers Jr. of Michgan; Louis Stokes of Ohio; and Charles B. Rangel of New York. Source: AP Images

then the House minority leader, the recommendations it had sent to Nixon, Ford replied in only two days. He wrote to Caucus chair Charles C. Diggs Jr., D-Mich.: "I will be very pleased to meet with you and your associates . . . My initial reaction is that such a meeting should include our House Republican Leadership as whole." [4] Rep. Louis Stokes, D-Ohio, described Ford's subsequent presidential administration as less cold and calculating than Nixon's, although Stokes found little difference in the two Republicans' attitudes toward urban America. The 1976 election of Democrat Jimmy Carter dramatically improved Caucus access to the White House and Cabinet officials (**Document 6.8**). Cooler relations with Republicans Ronald Reagan and George H. W. Bush followed. The group's closest relationship with any president to date came with the election of Democrat Bill Clinton.

During the three decades discussed in this chapter, the Caucus issued reactions to presidential State of the Union addresses and offered its own legislative agendas (**Document 6.7**). It also proposed comprehensive alternatives to presidential budget plans (**Document 6.12**).

Even a close relationship between the Caucus and a president did not ensure unquestioning support for a president's position or policy. In 1993 the Caucus sharply criticized the newly elected Clinton for withdrawing the nomination of African American law professor Lani Guinier to be assistant attorney general for civil rights; the Caucus chair, Rep. Kweisi Mfume, D-Md., rebuffed White House overtures to discuss alternative candidates for the position. Three months later, Clinton attended the annual Congressional Black Caucus Foundation dinner for the first time in his presidency. There he praised the Caucus for its leadership and commitment, reminded the audience of some of his appointments—including those of former representatives Mike Espy, D-Miss., as secretary of Agriculture and Shirley A. Chisholm, D-N.Y., as ambassador to Jamaica (she withdrew for health reasons)—then, without mentioning Guinier, said, "Thank you for your support. Thank you for your constructive criticism." [5] Nor did a generally distant or hostile relationship mean Caucus members opposed a president's position on every issue, as demonstrated by their backing for Nixon's revenue sharing initiative that allocated part of federal tax revenues to states and localities. And Reagan ultimately signed legislation he had long opposed to make Rev. Martin Luther King Jr.'s birthday a national holiday (**Document 6.10**).

During this period, the Caucus had mixed success in seeing its priorities enacted. Major victories included the Humphrey-Hawkins Full Employment and Balanced Growth Act of 1978 (**Document 6.9**) and the Comprehensive Anti-Apartheid Act of 1986 (**Document 6.11**), which was aimed at weakening the white supremacist government of South Africa. Other proposals failed to come to fruition, including full voting representation for the District of Columbia and rechanneling part of the Pentagon's growing budget to domestic programs.

Even when their numbers were small in proportion to total House membership and to the country's African American population, Caucus members' general solidarity in floor votes—bloc voting—helped maximize their leverage and bargaining power with their colleagues, and especially with the leadership. In the late 1970s members voted together 76 percent of the time on defense and foreign affairs, and 94 percent of the time on social issues like education, health, housing and crime. They displayed greater unity in floor votes with each other than with their regional or state party delegations. While there was a high degree of cohesion on legislative votes, the Caucus was not monolithic, nor was unanimity guaranteed in light of differences in personal ideology such as over the death penalty and economic priorities. Other factors that led to disagreement on legislation included political realities or voter sentiment in a member's district or state, committee assignments and depth of partisan allegiance. There also were well-publicized disagreements on nonlegislative matters, as when members split over participating in a 1972 national black political convention in Gary, Indiana, and over whether to endorse presidential candidates in Democratic primaries and nominating conventions.

Document 6.1 in Context
"To Enforce the Fifteenth Amendment to the Constitution of the United States": President Johnson Signs the Voting Rights Act of 1965

That African Americans still lacked equal access to the ballot by the 1960s was no surprise, given the history of disenfranchisement in both the North and South following the Reconstruction era. A federal voting rights act had long been a major goal of the civil rights movement, and President Lyndon B. Johnson supported the measure based on his genuine belief in equal rights and an astute understanding of Democrats' need to retain black political support. His landslide election victory in November 1964 created a political climate in Congress that made that goal achievable.

Earlier in the year, a delegation that included Reps. Charles C. Diggs Jr., D-Mich., Augustus F. Hawkins, D-Calif., John Conyers Jr., D-Mich., Robert N. C. Nix, D-Pa., and Adam

Clayton Powell Jr., D-N.Y., visited Selma, Alabama, to investigate problems confronting blacks who wanted to register to vote. In a telegram to Johnson, who was then serving the rest of assassinated president John F. Kennedy's term, they reported:

> We have significant evidence that present statutes are permissive of abuses by local authorities who will not act in good faith to protect the right of franchise . . . It is the consensus of our group that further legislation is necessary to insure the right of vote of these and all citizens . . .
>
> Further, such legislation should provide for the elimination of so-called literacy tests, whose real objective is to provide another tool to be used by a racially prejudiced registrar. [6]

Congressional consideration came amid the turbulence and civil disobedience of freedom marches, demonstrations and sit-ins. The resulting Voting Rights Act of 1965 prohibited discrimination in voting—enforceable in federal court—and banned literacy tests as a qualification for voting. Further, the law required Justice Department approval for changes in voting laws in states where fewer than 50 percent of the voting-age population had taken part in the elections of 1960, 1964 or both.

Even before Johnson signed the legislation, the Justice Department and the U.S. Commission on Civil Rights geared up to implement the new law. A Justice Department memo listed counties where federal examiners—essentially inspectors—would be assigned; among them were Hale County, Alabama, where 94.5 percent of whites and only 5.5 percent of blacks were registered, and Madison County, Mississippi, where the number of white voters registered exceeded the number of white voting-age residents while only 2 percent of blacks were registered. Many of the counties under scrutiny had more black than white adult residents.

On the day the Voting Rights Act was signed, John R. Lewis, who then headed a major civil rights advocacy group called the Student Nonviolent Coordinating Committee, wrote to Johnson in appreciation: "There can be no doubt that legislation of the range and thoroughness of this Bill could not have been possible without the approval and strong support of the President." Lewis, a future representative from Georgia, went on to remind Johnson about related issues: the jailing of blacks who attempted to register to vote in Georgia and Alabama, the desire for home rule in the District of Columbia and pending challenges to 1964 congressional elections in Mississippi, where blacks had been denied the right to vote. Lewis's letter also called for extending the minimum wage and surplus food programs and eliminating "de facto racial segregation" in federal courts in the South.[7]

Johnson signed the Voting Rights Act five months after African Americans were beaten and tear-gassed by police for marching across the Edmund Pettus Bridge in Selma, Alabama, in protest of the unfair practices that had prevented them from voting. In 2006 President George W. Bush signed legislation extending the measure another twenty-five years (**Document 7.10**).

Document 6.1
Voting Rights Act of 1965, August 6, 1965

AN ACT To enforce the fifteenth amendment to the Constitution of the United States, and for other purposes . . .

SECTION 2. No voting qualification or prerequisite to voting, or standard, practice, or procedure shall be imposed or applied by any State or political subdivision to deny or abridge the right of any citizen of the United States to vote on account of race or color.

SEC. 3. (a) Whenever the Attorney General institutes a proceeding . . . to enforce the guarantees of the fifteenth amendment in any State or political subdivision the court shall authorize the appointment of Federal examiners by the United States Civil Service Commission . . . to enforce the guarantees of the fifteenth amendment . . . *Provided,* That the court need not authorize the appointment of examiners if any incidents of denial or abridgement of the right to vote on account of race or color (1) have been few in number and have been promptly and effectively corrected by State or local action, (2) the continuing effect of such incidents has been eliminated, and (3) there is no reasonable probability of their recurrence in the future.

(b) If in a proceeding instituted by the Attorney General under any statute to enforce the guarantees of the fifteenth amendment in any State or political subdivision the court finds that a test or device has been used for the purpose or with the effect of denying or abridging the right of any citizen of the United States to vote on account of race or color, it shall suspend the use of tests and devices in such State or political subdivisions as the court shall determine is appropriate and for such period as it deems necessary.

(c) If in any proceeding instituted by the Attorney General under any statute to enforce the guarantees of the fifteenth amendment in any State or political subdivision the court finds that violations of the fifteenth amendment justifying equitable relief have occurred . . . the court, in addition to such relief as it may grant, shall retain jurisdiction for such period as it may deem appropriate and during such period no voting qualification or prerequisite to voting, or standard, practice, or procedure with respect to voting different from that in force or effect at the time the proceeding was commenced shall be enforced unless and until the court finds that such qualification, prerequisite, standard, practice, or procedure does not have the purpose and will not have the effect of denying or abridging the right to vote on account of race or color . . .

SEC. 4. (a) To assure that the right of citizens of the United States to vote is not denied or abridged on account of race or color, no citizen shall be denied the right to vote in any Federal, State, or local election because of his failure to comply with any test or device in any State with respect to which the determinations have been made . . . unless the United States District Court for the District of Columbia . . . has determined that no such test or device has been used during the five years preceding the filing of the action for the purpose or with the effect of denying or abridging the right to vote on account of race or color . . .

(c) The phrase "test or device" shall mean any requirement that a person as a prerequisite for voting or registration for voting (1) demonstrate the ability to read, write, understand, or interpret any matter, (2) demonstrate any educational achievement or his knowledge of any particular subject, (3) possess good moral character, or (4) prove his qualifications by the voucher of registered voters or members of any other class . . .

SEC. 7. (a) The examiners for each political subdivision shall, at such places as the Civil Service Commission shall by regulation designate, examine applicants concerning their qualifications for voting . . .

SEC. 8. Whenever an examiner is serving under this Act in any political subdivision, the Civil Service Commission may assign, at the request of the Attorney General, one or more persons, who may be officers of the United States, (1) to enter and attend at any place for holding an election in such subdivision for the purpose of observing whether persons who are entitled to vote are being permitted to vote, and (2) to enter and attend at any place for tabulating the votes cast at any election held in such subdivision for the purpose of observing whether votes cast by persons entitled to vote are being properly tabulated . . .

SEC. 10. (a) The Congress finds that the requirement of the payment of a poll tax as a precondition to voting (i) precludes persons of limited means from voting or imposes unreasonable financial hardship upon such persons as a precondition to their exercise of the franchise, (ii) does not bear a reasonable relationship to any legitimate State interest in the conduct of elections, and (iii) in some areas has the purpose or effect of denying persons the right to vote because of race or color. Upon the basis of these findings, Congress declares that the constitutional right of citizens to vote is denied or abridged in some areas by the requirement of the payment of a poll tax as a precondition to voting.

(b) In the exercise of the powers of Congress under section 5 of the fourteenth amendment and section 2 of the fifteenth amendment, the Attorney General is authorized and directed to institute forthwith in the name of the United States such actions, including actions against States or political subdivisions, for declaratory judgment or injunctive relief against the enforcement of any requirement of the payment of a poll tax as a precondition to voting, or substitute therefor enacted after November 1, 1964 . . .

SEC. 11. (a) No person acting under color of law shall fail or refuse to permit any person to vote who is entitled to vote under any provision of this Act or is otherwise qualified to vote, or willfully fail or refuse to tabulate, count, and report such person's vote.

(b) No person, whether acting under color of law or otherwise, shall intimidate, threaten, or coerce, or attempt to intimidate, threaten, or coerce any person for voting or attempting to vote, or intimidate, threaten, or coerce, or attempt to intimidate, threaten, or coerce any person for urging or aiding any person to vote or attempt to vote, or intimidate, threaten, or coerce any person for exercising any powers or duties . . .

(d) Whoever, in any matter within the jurisdiction of an examiner or hearing officer knowingly and willfully falsifies or conceals a material fact, or makes any false, fictitious, or fraudulent statements or representations, or makes or uses any false writing or document knowing the same to contain any false, fictitious, or fraudulent statement or entry, shall be fined not more than $10,000 or imprisoned not more than five years, or both.

SEC. 12 . . . (c) Whoever conspires to violate the provisions . . . or interferes with any right secured . . . shall be fined not more than $5,000, or imprisoned not more than five years, or both.

(d) Whenever any person has engaged or there are reasonable grounds to believe that any person is about to engage in any act or practice prohibited . . . the Attorney General may institute for the United States, or in the name of the United States, an action for preventive relief, including an application for a temporary or permanent injunction, restraining order, or other order, and including an order directed to the State and State or local election officials to require them (1) to permit persons listed under this Act to vote and (2) to count such votes . . .

SEC. 13 . . . (c)(1) The terms "vote" or "voting" shall include all action necessary to make a vote effective in any primary, special, or general election, including, but not limited to, registration, listing pursuant to this Act, or other action required by law prerequisite to voting, casting a ballot, and having such ballot counted properly and included in the appropriate totals of votes cast with respect to candidates for public or party office and propositions for which votes are received in an election . . .

SEC. 17. Nothing in this Act shall be construed to deny, impair, or otherwise adversely affect the right to vote of any person registered to vote under the law of any State or political subdivision . . .

Source: Voting Rights Act of 1965, August 6, 1965, Public Law 89-110, *U.S. Statutes at Large* 79: 437–446.

Document 6.2 in Context
"Part of the Black Leadership, but Not *the* Black Leadership": The Founding of the Congressional Black Caucus

The Congressional Black Caucus, founded to give black lawmakers increased visibility and political influence by working together, has its roots in the Democratic Select Committee that Rep. Charles C. Diggs Jr., D-Mich., organized in 1969. That committee held hearings on controversial issues, including an inquiry into the December 1969 killing of two Black Panther leaders by Chicago police. Three witnesses at those hearings would later serve in Congress— Illinois Democrats Ralph H. Metcalfe, Harold Washington and Gus Savage—and the hearings spurred a federal grand jury investigation. The committee also addressed racial discrimination in the armed services and the 1970 police shooting of students at predominately black Jackson State College in Mississippi.

Then in 1971, amid growing black political awareness and with thirteen members in the House, the Caucus was incorporated as a nonpartisan organization to "promote the public welfare through legislation designed to meet the needs of millions of neglected citizens." [8] As the Caucus explained:

> Our concerns and obligations as members of Congress do not stop at the boundaries of our districts, our concerns are national and international in scope. We are petitioned daily by citizens living hundreds of miles from our districts who look on us as Congressmen-at-large for black people and poor people in the United States.[9]

The Caucus's members boycotted President Richard M. Nixon's 1971 State of the Union address to protest his policies, and the group gained its first national recognition later that year when it presented sixty domestic and foreign policy proposals to Nixon at a White House meeting (**Document 6.3**).

The Caucus encountered skepticism in its early years, on and off Capitol Hill. Some conservative Republicans, such as Vice President Spiro T. Agnew, expressed doubts about the organization, and even some liberal Democrats and civil rights activists questioned its viability and motives. Through the years, critics have also attacked it as unduly partisan because its membership has been overwhelmingly Democratic. Rep. Gary A. Franks, R-Conn., did join, but Sen. Edward W. Brooke III, R-Mass., and Rep. J. C. Watts Jr., R-Okla., declined to do so (**Documents 8.4** and **8.7**). In 1975 Rep. Fortney H. Stark Jr., a white Democrat from California, formally applied for membership but acknowledged that "I lack an implicit qualification." [10] The Caucus turned him down.

As time passed and its membership grew in numbers and seniority, the Caucus led legislative efforts on issues as diverse as urban development, drug abuse, South African apartheid and civil rights. It successfully advocated key committee assignments for its members, such as securing an Armed Services Committee seat for Rep. Ronald V. Dellums, D-Calif. (**Document 6.4**). The Caucus also provided a vehicle for collective public outreach and communications on a scale that individual members could not achieve by themselves. In its early years, for example, members regularly wrote op-ed columns for the *Boston Globe,* and the Caucus later launched a weekly "Message to America" radio broadcast aired on stations affiliated with the American Urban Radio Network.

In 1976 it established the nonprofit Congressional Black Caucus Foundation Inc. as a public policy, educational and research institute that also sponsors an annual legislative conference and regional public policy symposiums on topics including economic development, health, education and Africa.

The Caucus has adopted the motto "Black people have no permanent friends, no permanent enemies . . . just permanent interests," and it describes itself as "the conscience of Congress since 1969."

In these excerpts from his autobiography, cofounder Charles B. Rangel, D-N.Y., discussed expectations and limitations that he and his colleagues had when forming the Caucus, as well as the need for its members to balance their individual political and district needs with the nation's broader racial concerns.

▬▬ Document 6.2 ▬▬
Rep. Charles B. Rangel, D-N.Y., Describes the Founding of the Congressional Black Caucus in 1971

. . . Our biggest fear was that, by virtue of holding office in the national government, we would mislead people into thinking that we were the nation's black leaders in every area—from civil rights to economics to local politics. Our formation, two years after the death of Martin Luther King Jr., received an unprecedented amount of national and international publicity. All Americans concerned with continuing the advancement of African Americans beyond the triumphs of King's nonviolent, nonpartisan movement were searching for the next center of leadership. Our struggle had profound implications for majority-minority power relationships worldwide, and people all over the world were actively looking for the next chapter in our story.

We didn't want to become the custodians of all black American aspirations, because we knew that meant being responsible for all of black America's problems. We didn't want to create expectations that would far exceed our ability to perform. It was also important not to be seen as usurping the surviving civil rights leadership organizations like the NAACP, the Southern Christian Leadership Council, and the Urban League. My vision was that we were part of the black leadership, but not *the* leadership . . .

From the beginnings of the Congressional Black Caucus, black leadership in the post–civil rights era, which coincides with my time in Congress, has run on two tracks, the group and the individual. I run for Congress as an individual, but I'm elected by a group that can variously expect me to represent the interests of the individual district and the interests of the race. Quite frequently they expect me to represent both interests simultaneously, cutting down my room to maneuver as an individual, and sometimes threatening to put me in political hot water.

Source: Charles B. Rangel with Leon Wynter, *And I Haven't Had a Bad Day Since: From the Streets of Harlem to the Halls of Congress* (New York: St. Martin's Press, 2007), 185–186, 221.

Document 6.3 in Context
"A View Widely Shared among a Majority of the Citizens We Represent": President Richard M. Nixon and the Congressional Black Caucus

Black Democrats in the U.S. House of Representatives had a high level of mistrust in President Richard M. Nixon, who took office in January 1969. It did not help relations when it took Nixon until March 1971 to meet formally with the Congressional Black Caucus to discuss its legislative and policy priorities. In their opening statement, the Caucus told Nixon:

> We would be less than honest, Mr. President, if we do not reflect a view widely shared among a majority of the citizens we represent. That view is that the representatives of this administration, by word and deed, have at crucial points retreated from the national commitment to make Americans of all races and cultures equal in the eyes of their government, to make equal the poor as well as the rich, urban and rural dwellers as well as those who live in suburbs . . . If we are in fact to be equal in this country, then the government must help us achieve these results. [11]

Two months after their initial White House meeting, Nixon sent to each Caucus member the letter that follows. While he did not address most of the issues the Caucus had raised, his letter underscored a shared concern about welfare reform and revenue sharing, the program that annually allocated a share of federal taxes among state and local governments. However, soon after receiving this letter, Rep. Augustus F. Hawkins, D-Calif., appeared on the news show *Meet the Press,* where he was critical of the president's response to the Caucus's proposals:

> I recall that the president said he should be judged not by his words but by his deeds. I can now understand, because his words have very little meaning, and I think the enumeration of his deeds in terms of the accomplishments that he attempted to justify was certainly very faulted. [12]

Not only were there ongoing, sharp disagreements over policies—in the areas of urban affairs, the economy and the Vietnam War (**Document 12.3**), among others—but there were also sharp political disagreements. For example, prior to the 1972 presidential and congressional elections, the Caucus attacked Nixon for what Rep. Louis Stokes, D-Ohio, called "blatant exploitation of politically naive" black entertainers such as Sammy Davis Jr., James Brown and Lionel Hampton, who had endorsed the Republican president's reelection. Such performers, Stokes said, "are all dancing to the tune of 'benign neglect.' It's a tune being orchestrated by the White House—by the same Administration that, in four short years, has begun to strip away the constitutional and human rights of minority, poor and disadvantaged Americans." [13] At the same time, Rep. Ralph H. Metcalfe, D-Ill., asserted that Nixon's solicitation of endorsements from African American entertainers and athletes "underestimates the political sophistication of our black citizens." [14]

Near the end of the campaign, one of the White House's most visible African American staffers, Stanley S. Scott, assistant to the director of communications for the executive branch, responded to the criticism. He defended Nixon's achievements in civil rights and minority hiring, attacked Democratic presidential nominee George S. McGovern's record on civil rights and lambasted the Caucus:

> Unfortunately, even the Black Caucus cannot come up with anything but tired old phrases and bitter personal attacks. Challenged for the first time in years, and seeing

their personal political machines in danger of eroding, the Caucus stooped to the 'Uncle Tom' label on a scare campaign which does not credit the Caucus' ability to argue its case. [15]

When Nixon faced impeachment in 1974 (**Document 6.5**), three African American members of the House Judiciary Committee participated in the hearings on whether he should be removed from office.

▬ Document 6.3 ▬
President Richard M. Nixon's Letter to Members of the Congressional Black Caucus, May 18, 1971

THE WHITE HOUSE
WASHINGTON
May 18, 1971

Dear Congressman Diggs:

I valued the opportunity to meet with you and your colleagues of the Congressional Black Caucus on March 25. The sixty recommendations for governmental action which you presented to me at that meeting have served as a framework for review of the matters we discussed.

The Administration has examined these recommendations in depth over the past seven weeks. A fresh assessment of all the alternatives in each area characterized this review process, both at the operating department level and then at the White House. Present policies served as a starting point, but we went beyond these in attempting to draw our conclusions of the merits in each case. We found that your broad goals are largely the same as those of the Administration, and we used this review as an occasion for measuring actual results against these goals and for considering appropriate changes where results seemed inadequate.

This review, culminating in the preparation of detailed responses to each of your proposals, was conducted under the overall supervision of the Domestic Council and the Office of Management and Budget. At the same time, George Shultz, Director of OMB, prepared at my request a summary report of this Administration's major programs and activities in the field of civil rights and related social and economic programs. Having reviewed and concurred in this report and the sixty responses, I am pleased to transmit them to you and your colleagues herewith.

These documents constitute a progress report on our efforts to achieve equality, justice, and full opportunity for all Americans. We have tried to make them candid and factual. They measure both successes and shortcomings. In those instances in which we have found ourselves in disagreement with your recommendations, we have acknowledged the disagreement but also spelled out our alternative approaches. In many cases, we have found a basic accord between your recommendations and our policies.

I am encouraged to note that there is such accord in three especially critical areas: We share a determination to reform the welfare system so that it will help solve, rather than aggravate, the problems of those who lack a minimum income. You attach high priority, as I do, to a program of revenue sharing that will enable our cities and States to serve the people better. And you are committed, as I am, to a concerted drive for expanded economic opportunities for minorities and all other Americans—a drive to validate with jobs, income, and tangible benefits the pledges this society has made to the disadvantaged in the past decade.

This is the building work of the Seventies, and it is bound to be more difficult than the legislative efforts of the Sixties. Equality of opportunity has been affirmed in American law; conscience and public resolve brought that much to pass. But now we have entered a new and much harder phase. The steady gains of the years ahead will inevitably be less dramatic than the bright hopes raised a few years ago. We continue to honor those hopes. At issue now is whether all of us have the realism and stamina to persist in the long, hard task of realizing them in American life, of translating rhetorical promise into concrete results.

We are already making significant progress as noted in the attached report and the detailed responses. Much more remains to be done to realize our shared goals. I am determined to press forward vigorously—believing as I do that full opportunity and equal justice for all are basic to the American ideal.

I have directed that the process of monitoring and evaluation reflected by the report and responses be continued, and my Administration will remain receptive to your views and those of your Congressional colleagues as we continue to search for the best ways of achieving progress on matters of common concern.

Sincerely,
RICHARD NIXON [signature]

Honorable Charles C. Diggs, Jr.
House of Representatives
Washington, D.C. 20515

Source: Richard M. Nixon to Charles C. Diggs Jr., letter, May 18, 1971, Gerald R. Ford Presidential Library, Ann Arbor, Michigan.

Document 6.4 in Context
"Real Influence in the Process of Determining National Priorities": Rep. Ronald V. Dellums, D-Calif., Fights for a Seat on the House Armed Services Committee

Committees do most of the work in Congress and have the power to oversee and investigate executive branch activities. At the time the number of African American members was increasing in the late 1960s and early 1970s, new representatives were often assigned to committees with little regard to their personal interests or the priorities of their districts. Only as they built seniority could they move to more powerful, prestigious or relevant panels—if they had the blessing of their party leaders. The seniority system eventually made it possible for Reps. William L. Dawson, D-Ill., and Adam Clayton Powell Jr., D-N.Y., to become committee chairs.

Rep. Shirley A. Chisholm, D-N.Y., encountered the rigidity of the system after her election in 1968. She asked for a seat on the Education and Labor Committee based on her twenty years of experience as an educator and prior service on a state legislative education committee. Her alternative preferences were the Banking and Currency Committee, which handled federal funding for housing, or the Post Office and Civil Service Committee because African Americans comprised a large proportion of postal workers. To her dismay, she was assigned to the Agriculture Committee and its subcommittees on rural development and forestry.

Chisholm reacted in a way that newcomers were warned against. First she protested unsuccessfully to Speaker John W. McCormack, D-Mass., who told her to be a good soldier. She described her reply in her autobiography, in a chapter called "Breaking the Rules": "The time is growing late, and I can't be a good soldier any longer. It does not make sense to put a black woman representative on a subcommittee dealing with forestry. If you do not assist me, I will have to do my own thing." [16] She then complained to the Democratic caucus, arguing, "I think it would be hard to imagine an assignment that is less relevant to my background or to the needs of the predominantly black and Puerto Rican people who elected me, many of whom are unemployed, hungry, and badly housed, than the one I was given." [17] Ultimately, she accepted a seat on the Veterans' Affairs Committee and its education and training subcommittees: "It was an improvement; as I told people, 'There are a lot more veterans in my district than there are trees.' " [18]

Ronald V. Dellums was elected in 1970 as a Democratic anti–Vietnam War candidate from California; during his campaign, he was attacked by Vice President Spiro T. Agnew, who labeled him "an out-and-out radical" who needed to be "purged from the body politic." [19] Dellums hoped for a spot on the Education and Labor Committee, with its responsibility for many War on Poverty programs. Instead, he got assigned to the Foreign Affairs and District of Columbia committees. After Dellums's 1972 reelection, he pursued an Armed Services Committee seat. The Congressional Black Caucus intervened on his behalf with the Democratic Party leadership, especially Speaker Carl B. Albert, D-Okla. Albert later recalled how the committee chair, F. Edward Hébert, D-La., "long had refused to add a black to his Armed Services Committee. In 1973, he begrudgingly agreed to accept a black member, any black member except . . . Dellums." [20] The following excerpt from Dellums's memoir describes his experience.

▬ Document 6.4 ▬
Rep. Ronald V. Dellums, D-Calif., Recalls the Fight for a Prized Committee Assignment in January 1973

. . . I saw that the big money in the sphere of national security and international affairs was in the defense bills that were the concern of the House Armed Services Committee (HASC).

In my first two years in the House I had taken the floor many times to argue that we needed to free dollars from the military budget to fund social priorities. On more than one occasion a fellow member had come to me to say, "Ron, you speak eloquently about priorities; but you're talking about a world that doesn't exist. You're naïve. You don't seem to fully grasp the danger of the communist menace in the world. The East-West split poses a danger to our way of life. I may agree with you that we need to address these problems, but you're arguing naively that we can cut the defense budget. We need to maintain our ability to contain the Soviet threat."

I resented the fact that my colleagues perceived me as naïve, or worse, rhetorical, or even worse, uninformed. The only way to overcome this perception was to go into the heart of the matter and become a knowledgeable and credible analyst of the issues, strategies, and programs in question. I needed to learn how to argue from the vantage point of military requirements, in order to demonstrate that money existed in those accounts that could be redirected to meet our urgent domestic priorities without damaging our national security. I needed to challenge the assumptions and the policies that underpinned the military budget. I needed to learn their language, their argument, their assumptions, and their way of thinking.

In part because I thought of myself as a peace advocate, I had not learned enough about "forward deployment," "missile throw weights," "strategic defense," and the myriad other concepts (and buzzwords) that dominated the debate when it came to military policy and budgets. By not being "expert," I and other peace movement activists had lessened the chances that our ideas would be taken seriously. As far as many were concerned, our relative ignorance had become just one more reason for not listening, not hearing, or not supporting the ideas we advanced. That excuse, in my opinion, had to be eliminated . . .

I went to our next meeting and discussed my interest in a seat on the House Armed Services Committee. None of the other caucus members expressed an interest or felt inclined to seek an assignment to that committee, so the group as a whole agreed to send a letter to the Democratic leadership in behalf of my appointment even though we understood that this [was] going to be a difficult, uphill battle. In fact, nobody in the CBC [Congressional Black Caucus] really believed I had a chance of securing the appointment to the Armed Services Committee, because of my high-profile activities in opposition to the Vietnam War and in favor of reducing military spending . . .

The next step on the pathway to membership on a committee was to make a request through one's "zone representative" to the Ways and Means Committee's senior members sitting as the "Committee on Committees" of the Democratic Caucus . . .

"Ron," [Rep. James C.] Corman [D-Calif.] said when I came on the line, "they've turned down your request for HASC . . ."

Although disappointed, I was not surprised. "Why did they turn me down?"

Corman told me that the night before, HASC chairman F. Edward Hébert had called each member of the Committee on Committees to inform them that he did not want me on the HASC "under any circumstances." Corman had learned that Hébert's pitch had been that "Dellums is a radical from Berkeley" and placing me on "his" committee would be a "significant security breach." Hébert, a conservative Democrat from Louisiana, had argued that the HASC could never have a closed, classified session and be confident that the classified information would stay in that room . . .

. . . Determined to make good on my pledge to take the voice of the peace movement inside the system; it was not enough to be in the House, I needed to secure a committee assignment that would give me real influence in the process of determining national priorities, and I'd committed to HASC . . .

. . . I had argued to the CBC that the day was over for allowing the leadership to pick who were "good blacks" or "bad blacks." We had to be able to choose our own leaders and to determine who among us would serve on which committees. We needed to inform the Democratic leadership that they should be responsive to our request, that this was a matter of principle . . .

As we entered the Speaker's personal office he was very friendly. "We did well for you fellas. We got your people on all the committees they wanted, except for Ron. The chairman weighed in strongly and objected. The committee didn't want to overrule him." . . .

[Rep. Louis] Stokes [D-Ohio], in his erudite and dignified fashion, laid out our argument. "Mr. Speaker, this is a matter of principle to us, that a black person serve on the Armed Services Committee. The CBC has made a collective decision to have Ron serve. Ron is the one person among us with experience, expertise, and interest in these matters." He reminded the three leaders of my ad hoc hearings on war crimes, of my leadership in the CBC hearings on racism in the military, and that I had taken up many issues regarding the military budget during floor debate in the House. He concluded his opening argument by noting that "black people throughout the country, both in the military and out of the military, recognize Ron Dellums for his leadership in this area. There is no reason to exclude him just because he's Ron Dellums. This is a matter of principle."

Throughout the discussion that followed, Clay provided the refrain, "There is no reason other than racism that Ron would not be allowed to serve on the committee. We want him to serve and he will serve!" . . .

The Speaker indicated that "the chairman believes that you would be a security risk," confirming the information that Corman had relayed to me earlier. The whole basis of the effort to keep me off the committee was the characterization of me as a "commie" threat to the nation.

Trying to keep my anger in check, I challenged Hébert's assumption. "I am a member of the Foreign Affairs Committee and have dealt with classified information before . . ."

"How can I be considered professional on one committee but not another?" I asked. "I raised my hand and swore to uphold the Constitution and the laws, just like four hundred and thirty-four other members did. What makes anybody think I'm not prepared to deal honorably with my oath?"

Clay said, "If you don't put Ron on the committee, the CBC will call a press conference and denounce the party and the Congress as racist. There's no other possible explanation for excluding this brother from service on the committee." . . .

Looking back and forth between us, Speaker Albert said, "I'll go back in and see if we can't get the committee to reconsider." . . .

At that moment I knew we had won . . .

Source: Ronald V. Dellums and H. Lee Halterman, *Lying Down with the Lions: A Public Life from the Streets of Oakland to the Halls of Power* (Boston: Beacon Press, 2000), 97–103.

Document 6.5 in Context
"The Diminution, the Subversion, the Destruction of the Constitution": House Judiciary Committee Hearings on the Impeachment of President Richard M. Nixon

Republican President Richard M. Nixon had narrowly defeated Democrat Hubert H. Humphrey in 1968, but he trounced Democrat George S. McGovern for reelection in 1972. McGovern captured only 17 electoral votes from the District of Columbia and Massachusetts, compared with Nixon's forty-nine-state sweep of 520 electoral votes. But Nixon's 1972 reelection was tainted by the Watergate scandal—a break-in at the Democratic National Committee headquarters in Washington, D.C., that was engineered by his political operatives—and a conspiracy by the president and his top aides to cover up the scandal. That conspiracy included bribery, perjury and defiance of congressional demands for access to White House documents and files. Ultimately, the U.S. Supreme Court rejected Nixon's claims of executive privilege and ordered him to release audiotapes of White House conversations.

The Watergate scandal also fueled a highly organized movement to impeach a president for the first time since Andrew Johnson in 1868 (**Document 3.1**). The only sitting black senator in 1972, Edward W. Brooke III of Massachusetts, came out early in favor of removing fellow Republican Nixon from office.

The House Judiciary Committee, which had three African American members—John Conyers Jr., D-Mich., Charles B. Rangel, D-N.Y., and Barbara C. Jordan, D-Texas—conducted nationally televised hearings on the impeachment resolutions. The following document contains excerpts from each of their opening statements.

The Judiciary Committee approved three articles of impeachment. The first article accused the president of obstruction of justice for his role in the Watergate cover-up, including impeding the Justice Department, the Federal Bureau of Investigation and the Watergate special prosecutor. The second article addressed misuse of the Internal Revenue Service, the Central Intelligence Agency, the Secret Service and the FBI for political purposes and in violation of individual rights. The third article dealt with disobeying committee subpoenas.

Some committee members were not satisfied with the articles that were approved. For example, Conyers criticized the committee's failure to adopt an article about the unauthorized bombing of neutral Cambodia in Southeast Asia, arguing that Nixon's rationale for the secret air strikes was a subterfuge that hid the president's true motives under the guise of national security. He later wrote that the president's Vietnamization policy

> required the bombing of Cambodia, which in turn required secrecy at all costs. The pressures of concealment led in turn to a spirit of distrust within the administration as the President and his aides became increasingly enmeshed in the snare of lies and half-truths they had themselves created . . .
>
> President Nixon . . . usurped the power of the Congress to declare war . . . In so doing, he also denied the people of the United States their right to be fully informed about the actions and policies of their elected officials . . .
>
> The question we must ponder is, *why the Congress has not called Mr. Nixon to judgment for the bombing of Cambodia?* [21]

Rangel, in his supplemental remarks in the committee report, agreed with Conyers on the bombing-related article of impeachment and argued that the committee should also have approved an article based on Nixon's misuse of government funds to improve two homes that he owned in Florida and California.

Nixon resigned on August 9, 1974, before the full House could vote on impeachment and before the matter could proceed to a Senate trial. Vice President Gerald R. Ford pardoned him the following month. Conyers later rose to become chair of the Judiciary Committee.

▬▬ Document 6.5 ▬▬
Opening Statements of House Judiciary Committee Members John Conyers Jr., D-Mich., Charles B. Rangel, D-N.Y., and Barbara C. Jordan, D-Texas, on the Impeachment of President Richard M. Nixon, July 1974

Mr. CONYERS: . . . The search for what we individually regard as truth in a matter so momentous as this is always most difficult, and so as we proceed here, we are in effect expounding the Constitution as one early juror said, giving it life and meaning and in the process we are also necessarily reviewing what kind of leaders we are. I suppose finally, we are determining what kind of government this Nation is going to have . . .

Certainly no one can accuse us of having rushed to judgment. This marks the third consecutive year that resolutions of impeachment have been filed against the President of the United States. I suppose that we should admit that we sit here not because we want to but because we have to, and we have to because for the first time in the history of this country, millions of citizens are genuinely afraid that they may have in office a person who might entertain the notion of taking over the Government of this country, a politician who has more effectively employed the politics of fear and division than any other in our time . . .

Richard Nixon, like the President before him, is in a real sense a casualty of the Vietnam war, a war which I am ashamed to say was never declared . . . The study of the 42 volumes of carefully compiled documents and papers and testimony revealed clearly the pressures of an administration so trapped by its own war policies and the desire to stay in office it was forced to enter into an almost unending series of plans for spying and burglary and wiretapping inside this country and against its own citizens without precedent in American history.

The President took the power of his office and under the guise of protecting and executing the laws the he swore to uphold, he abused them and in so doing he has jeopardized the strength and integrity of the Constitution and the laws of the land and the protections that they ought to afford all of the people . . .

Witness the deception that the President practiced on the Congress and the American people when from May 17, 1969, he approved a secret bombing campaign personally that as a result caused more than 150,000 air strikes to take place and more than 500,000 tons of bombs dropped on a neutral nation. And yet 2 months after that date in which he had personally authorized this conduct, the President said, "I have tried to present the facts about Vietnam with complete honesty and I shall continue to do so . . .

And so, my friends, it seems to me that marked the beginning of the intelligence-gathering activity which under his direction or on his authority is unparalleled. These activities involved widespread and repeated abuses of power and illegal and improper activities by the executive agencies and, of course, wholesale violations of the constitutional rights of citizens.

Mr. RANGEL: . . . Some say this is a sad day in America's history. I think it could perhaps be one of our brightest days. It could be really a test of the strength of our Constitution, because what I think it means to most Americans is that when this or any other President violates his sacred oath of office, the people are not left helpless, that they can, through the House of Representatives charge him, and his guilt will finally be decided in the hall of the U.S. Senate.

What is really sad about this thing is that morality is no longer expected in Government. Indeed, it would not have been sensational news that my President, the President of the United States, decided to obey an order of the U.S. Supreme Court. That should not have been news, because I can't consider that any other citizen of the United States would even have thought about defying such an order from the highest Court in the land . . .

On November 7, 1972, Richard Milhous Nixon won reelection in a campaign that was dedicated to the restoration of law and order in our streets. And shortly thereafter, he was sworn in as 36 Presidents before him and said that he would faithfully execute the laws of our land. One wonders what was going on through President Nixon's mind as this solemn oath was being administered. Was he thinking about the opportunity he would have in the next 4 years of his administration to heal the wounds of the people in this Nation, to bring together at least in some small part the hopes and dreams of millions of Americans? Was he thinking about the aspirations of our young and our aged and the needs of our poor people, white, black, other minorities? I think not, because this President held secret the knowledge that he had participated in the most bizarre criminal conspiracy ever recorded in the history of the United States . . .

Ms. JORDAN: . . . Earlier today we heard the beginning of the Preamble to the Constitution of the United States, We, the people. It is a very eloquent beginning. But when that document was completed on the 17th of September in 1787 I was not included in that "We, the people." I felt somehow for many years that George Washington and Alexander Hamilton just left me out by mistake. But through the process of amendment, interpretation and court decision, I have finally been included in "We, the people."

Today, I am an inquisitor, I believe hyperbole would not be fictional and would not overstate the solemness that I feel right now. My faith in the Constitution is whole, it is complete, it is total. I am not going to sit here and be an idle spectator to the diminution, the subversion, the destruction of the Constitution . . .

We know the nature of impeachment. We have been talking about it awhile now . . .

At this point I would like to juxtapose a few of the impeachment criteria with the President's actions.

Impeachment criteria: James Madison, from the Virginia Ratification Convention: If the President be connected in any suspicious manner with any person and there be grounds to believe that he will shelter him, he may be impeached."

We have heard time and time again that the evidence reflects payment to the defendants of money. The President had knowledge that these funds were being paid and these were funds collected for the 1972 Presidential campaign . . .

The South Carolina Ratification Convention impeachment criteria: Those are impeachable who "behave amiss or betray their public trust."

Beginning shortly after the Watergate break-in and continuing to the present time the President has engaged in a series of public statements and actions designed to thwart the lawful investigation by Government prosecutors. Moreover, the President has made public announcements and assertions bearing on the Watergate case which the evidence will show he knew to be false.

These assertions, false assertions, impeachable, those who misbehave. Those who "behave amiss or betray their public trust."

James Madison again at the Constitutional Convention: "A President is impeachable if he attempts to subvert the Constitution."

The Constitution charges the President with the task of taking care that the laws be faithfully executed, and yet the President has counseled his aides to commit perjury, willfully disregarded the secrecy of grand jury proceedings, concealed surreptitious entry, attempted to compromise a Federal judge while publicly displaying his cooperation with the processes of criminal justice . . .

Source: House Committee on the Judiciary, *Debate on Articles of Impeachment: Hearing of the Committee on the Judiciary, House of Representatives,* July 24, 25, 26, 27, 29, and 30, 1974 (Washington, D.C.: U.S. Government Printing Office, 1974), 37–39, 103–107, 110–113.

Document 6.6 in Context
"In General, the Proposals by the Caucus Are Do-able": The Congressional Black Caucus and President Gerald R. Ford

The Congressional Black Caucus's relationship with President Gerald R. Ford, a Republican, was wary but warmer than with his predecessor, Richard M. Nixon (**Document 6.3**). Caucus members had served with Ford, who was House minority leader until he became vice president in 1973; as president, Ford was more open to listening to the Caucus and to inviting its members to White House social events.

William Raspberry, a black *Washington Post* columnist, noted that it took Ford less than a week after his swearing-in to seek a meeting with the Caucus—in contrast to the fourteen months it took the Caucus to obtain a meeting with Nixon. Raspberry wrote shortly before that meeting:

> Well, political gesture or not, the invitation—which President Ford personally telephoned to [Rep. Charles B.] Rangel [D-N.Y.]—suggests the prospect of a far different relationship than existed between the former President and the Caucus. It could be an important gesture. By extending the invitation himself, and at the very beginning of his administration, he was saying: Forget the Nixon episode; forget my own legislative record. Let's see if we can't work together, starting now.[22]

At the meeting on August 21, 1974, Caucus members presented position papers to Ford on such issues as poverty and full employment, crime and criminal justice, the status of black women, narcotics, the military budget, voting rights, relations with and foreign aid to Africa, mass transit and minority economic development. Rather than submit an issue-focused policy paper, Rep. Robert N. C. Nix Sr., D-Pa., submitted a formal statement that questioned Ford's willingness to endorse Caucus-backed policies. Noting that he had voted against Ford's confirmation as vice president, Nix wrote:

> Mr. Ford's record during his twenty-five years in Congress leaves me with grave doubts as to whether he will pursue policies and programs that will meet the needs of the American people as I see them . . . I believe him to be a decent and honorable man. But the nation needs more than decency and honor—it needs strong and progressive leadership.
>
> When President Ford was in Congress he voted against progressive measures and for special interests . . . He favored the welfare of big business over the welfare of working men and women.[23]

At a news conference immediately after the meeting, Rangel reported:

> The President has advised the caucus collectively and individually that not only is his door open to us to discuss these major problems, but more importantly, that each one of us could call and only if he was out of the country or was engaged in some meeting that . . . he would be certain to return that call to find out what our concerns were.[24]

But the news conference made it clear that the Caucus and Ford didn't see eye to eye on everything. Rep. Ronald V. Dellums, D-Calif., told reporters

> that we viewed with concern the statements that the President made that one of his efforts toward dealing with inflation would be restraint on Federal funds and that if

he saw the defense budget as sacrosanct it would mean that we would be back in the same ball game we have been in and that would be cuts in important human domestic programs.[25]

The following excerpts are from Office of Management and Budget analyses used to help craft Ford's formal response to the Caucus position papers. In a September 26, 1974, cover memo submitting the analyses to higher-level White House staffers, Stanley S. Scott, special assistant to the president for minority affairs and one of Ford's top black advisors, wrote, "You'll also note that, in general, the proposals by the Caucus are do-able, and many can achieve short-run payoffs for the President." [26] Scott, a former Nixon aide, served as Ford's liaison with minorities.

Relations between Ford and the Caucus would prove to be what one observer called a "short caucus honeymoon." [27] The conservative president did not endorse many of the Caucus's proposals during the remainder of his term, and African American lawmakers were angered by his pardon of Nixon. Even so, most Caucus members sided more often with Ford on legislation during his first year in office than they had with Nixon.

▬▬ Document 6.6 ▬▬
Office of Management and Budget Analyzes Congressional Black Caucus Proposals, September 1974

MILITARY BUDGET, TAX SYSTEM, AND PRICING POLICIES
Congressman Ronald V. Dellums
(and on MILITARY BUDGET by Congressman Andrew Young)

Summary of Principal Assertions and Recommendations

The country is suffering from faulty national priorities which have dominated its resource allocation decisions since the beginning of Vietnam. The size of the Defense budget is the basic problem of which inflation and "extremely high" unemployment are just two of several symptoms. It follows, then, that the President's intention to apply fiscal restraints to the civilian sector while holding the Defense budget "sacrosanct" is a very bad idea.

This is especially true since (1) there is fat in the Defense budget, (2) social programs are not inflationary while Defense expenditures are, (3) education suffers most in the guns vs. butter trade off, (4) sufficient sums have never been allocated to human needs and societal returns are greater from dollars spent on human resources.

The proper course, therefore, is (1) to cut the Defense budget, (2) increase revenues up to $50 billion by closing tax loopholes and curtailing subsidies to inefficient business interests, (3) restoring economic competition while (4) reintroducing PEP [the Public Employment Program, created in 1971 to subsidize employment in public sector jobs for two years] in a more problem-oriented form, and (5) "scrutinizing" the possibility of wage-price controls in a form which would cover interest and profits while allowing labor a certain amount of catch up.

Analysis of Assertions

Verified: It is true that inflation is high enough to be worth fighting; that reductions in private and public spending will help fight it while simultaneously causing more unemployment; that since Parkinson's law has not been repealed there is fat in the Defense budget; that tax "loopholes" do exist in the amount of some $60 billion; that the restoration of competition would be anti-inflationary notwithstanding unpredictable adjustment problems; that Black employees are, nearly always, last on/first off; that today's minority unemployment rate may be accurately described as "extremely high" since it is over 9%.

Modifications should be made to the assertions that the military budget is or has been "sacrosanct" and that PEP was mostly beneficial to "highly skilled technical people."

In 1975 dollars, the military budget is down from $124.6 B [billion] in 1969 to $85.8 B in 1974. This is lower even than 1963 when it was $93.7 B. Further, the President says it isn't sacrosanct.

It is *inaccurate* to assert that social programs are not inflationary while military ones are. In fact, there are more similarities than differences and it is the means of financing which is the crucial determinant for both.

Reasonable men *disagree* about the assertions that human resource programs have always been underfunded (if they don't work, they have been overfunded), that wage and price controls are desirable, and that the size of the Defense budget is directly related to the quality of our Defense (neither side can "prove" its case, since all contention can only rest on the speculated intentions of other countries) . . .

Proposed Response

- Cut the Defense budget: A cut in this particular area would constitute the same sort of "signal" as the delayed Federal pay raises. It sets an even more compelling example because of the controversial nature of the subject matter. A cut of $6 B should be made with the understanding that it does not effect the "bone and muscle" of national defense.
- Increase revenue by closing loopholes. This recommendation combines two worthwhile ends. It promotes reform while at the same time collecting anti-inflationary tax revenues. With $60 B of items to choose among, this should be undertaken.
- Restore economic competition: This should be tried, even though the country may be expected to have a very low tolerance for the inevitable adjustment casualties of deregularization. If, however, the leadership presents this approach as a foundational anti-inflationary reform, it might be accepted.

FULL VOTING REPRESENTATION FOR THE DISTRICT OF COLUMBIA
Congressman Walter E. Fauntroy

Summary of Principal Assertions and Recommendations

Basically, the paper asserts that the nearly 800,000 residents of the District of Columbia are being denied the right of true representation at the national level and adopts the position that the lack of voting representation is a mockery of the democratic process and a monumental injustice. Further, the paper asserts that the only way to correct this lack of franchise is by constitutional amendment.

The single recommendation is for the Ford Administration to be closely associated with the passage and ultimate adoption of a constitutional amendment permitting D.C. residents to elect two senators and as many representatives as the District would be entitled to have if it were a state.

Analysis of Assertions

The assertion that District residents lack national franchise is factual. The supporting data, i.e., the identification of states with lesser populations is accurate. The assertion that the only way to correct the injustice is through constitutional amendment is not technically correct.

The pros and cons of the District of Columbia representation issue are numerous and historically enchanting. However, in 1974, very few people argue against the moral and democratic basis for granting the franchise to the District's residents. The problem now centers around the appropriate mechanism for accomplishing this objective in view of the many complexities involved. In simple terms, the alternatives are full statehood at one extreme and retrocession to Maryland at the other. Neither of these alternatives involve a constitutional amendment, both provide full representation for individual residents, and both require some provisions for a Federal enclave to protect the Constitutional requirement for a neutral seat of Government. In addition, both raise a host of questions in the areas of Federal payments and revenue sources, the proper role and function of existing administrative structures, and the will of the residents themselves. Discussions of statehood generate even more emotional and political issues concerning the ability of the residents to accomplish self-government and the creation of a political entity which is almost certain to be controlled by a racial minority. Proposals for a constitutional amendment tend to fall somewhere in the middle of the spectrum and generally deal with the *prima-facie* entitlement to representation based on fundamental principles of democracy . . .

Specifically, the paper does not argue for statement or retrocession—which would automatically accomplish full voting representation, nor does it address the unique relationship existing between the District of Columbia and the Federal Government—which could be used to support the case for limited representation. The argument as put forth in the paper to justify representation solely on population size has no validity in the United States Senate . . .

Assessment of Recommendations

The budget impact of the recommendation would be minimal with major costs related to salaries and operating expenses of the increased Senators and Representatives. The recommendation in its present form would, if adopted, unquestionably rectify the specific problem of lack of franchise. However, there remains the question of do-ability . . .

Proposed Response

In the near term, it is recommended that there be presidential affirmation for the principle of national representation for all Americans.

Longer range, support for national representation can be reiterated by pertinent remarks in messages to the Congress or other public statements.

Source: Office of Management and Budget, Gerald R. Ford Presidential Library, Ann Arbor, Michigan.

Document 6.7 in Context
"Economic and Political Problems Common to the Nation and the Black Community": The Congressional Black Caucus Forwards a Legislative Agenda

Gerald R. Ford had been in the White House for only six months when the Congressional Black Caucus wrote him a letter commending him for endorsing the extension of the 1965 Voting Rights Act (**Document 6.1**) and the reduction of tax rates for low-income Americans in his January 1975 State of the Union address. But the Caucus expressed disappointment "in major aspects of your economic proposals . . . Once again, your Administration appears pre-occupied with current symptoms of economic unrest" instead of the "basic systemic causes which have brought about this period of continuing economic dislocation." While reiterating concern "about the scope and direction of your overall economic proposals," the Caucus expressed its willingness "to assist you in the development of creative approaches to critical issues facing us all." [28]

As an alternative to the White House proposals, the Caucus offered its own comprehensive legislative agenda—what it called its "first formal statement of legislative goals and activities for an upcoming session of Congress" [29]—unveiled in early 1975. In a February press release, the group explained that "the political context is fresh for new discussion and action on these issues" and said that the organization's aim was to build on the relationship that Ford seemed interested in developing and to push the administration to act on its recommendations on some of the issues the Caucus had laid out in its meeting with the new president (**Document 6.6**).

The legislative agenda presented in March 1975 by Rep. Charles B. Rangel, D-N.Y., on domestic policy, highlighted such issues as education and employment, crime and political rights, and housing and health. At the same time, the Caucus addressed the domestic ramifications of several aspects of U.S. foreign policy. One was military spending and the post–Vietnam War dilemma of guns versus butter. Here, the Caucus stressed its commitment to a strong defense but laid out a menu of military projects it argued should be cut to provide funding for domestic programs. Also on the foreign affairs front, the agenda addressed U.S. companies doing business in South Africa, long a topic of concern to Caucus members (**Document 6.11**); the importation of chrome from the white supremacist-governed African country of Rhodesia; international drug trafficking; and elimination of tax incentives for foreign investments that the group believed were draining jobs and businesses out of the United States.

In addition to the excerpts that follow from the broad, overall agenda, the Caucus called for a restructuring of capital gains tax rules, a national holiday honoring Rev. Martin Luther King Jr. (**Document 6.10**), universal voter registration and full employment legislation (**Document 6.9**), among other topics. The agenda also included dozens of proposals sponsored by individual members, including recognition of Mexican American land rights, grand jury reform, item pricing on consumer products, low-interest loans for housing rehabilitation projects, creation of a cabinet-level minority enterprise agency and Medicare coverage for Pap smears. Some Caucus proposals would become law, such as sanctions against U.S. business involvement in South Africa and tougher laws against narcotics traffic.

====== **Document 6.7** ======
Excerpts from the 1975 Congressional Black Caucus Legislative Agenda, March 5, 1975

. . . For too long, we have seen no fundamental change in our national policies and priorities in response to domestic needs. In the 1930's, the Great Depression led to a system of Social Security. Following the War, the Employment Act of 1946 was passed. In the 1960's major civil rights laws were passed. And in the mid-'60's, a belated and only partial response to the problems of poverty was begun.

Today, we face a period of economic turmoil following closely an era of tragic international and American political turmoil. Yet, as in the '30's, these great events have served to create a common understanding among most Americans as to our common dilemma. It is not the rich against the poor, black against white. Instead, there is a mutual recognition that any of us may be the next victim of unemployment, and that all of us will most certainly be the next victims of inflation.

The Congressional Black Caucus has as its motto that "we have no permanent friends and no permanent enemies, only permanent interests." At this time of economic distress, we feel we have many more friends than enemies, as our interests are even more clearly those of the nation. While our foremost concerns are those of blacks, those concerns and their remedies are inextricably intertwined with those of all Americans.

This legislative agenda begins to address both economic and political problems common to the nation and the black community. In this agenda, there are no instant solutions; there are specific remedies. As legislators, we operate in the legislative context, and our agenda consists of bills and resolution which will come before Congress this year . . . Some will pass; some will not . . .

Federal Domestic Assistance Programs

Our third major priority will involve federal domestic assistance programs. Four broad and timely issues here are revenue sharing, health care, social insurance, and education.

(a) Prior to endorsing continuation of general revenue sharing, we will be making a searching review of that program and its impact on minority and lower-income persons.

(b) Health care and (c) Income security, two other program priorities, involve the most basic security and well-being of a very large number of our citizens.

(d) Two major existing education programs, the Higher Education and Vocational Education Acts, will be up for renewal this year and important questions involving aid to education will be debated.

(e) Other major issues will come before this Congress, such as energy, the environment and assistance to nations of the Third World. It is those with lower incomes who suffer most from massive cost rises for energy. The Caucus supports passage of an energy rebate system, the F.U.E.L. plan . . . to keep energy costs within the means of lower-income persons. It is those in the central cities, and in many rural areas, who suffer these effects of our worst environments. And it is those in developing nations who suffer the effects of a turn from our long-term commitment of economic aid and equity to the developing Third World nations to an over-reliance on military aid . . .

AREAS OF MAJOR LEGISLATIVE FOCUS

THE BUDGET AND APPROPRIATIONS PROCESS

. . . The Congressional Black Caucus will make a major effort this year to have federal appropriations more nearly reflect real national priorities. We are especially concerned over plans for fiscal restraints coming at a time that the Administration budget calls for defense budget authority of over $100 billion . . . We are neither anti-military, nor do we advocate a weak defense posture. But we cannot see any valid relationship between the absolute size of the military budget and the quality of America's defense . . .

There are numerous budget areas which deserve paring. These include:

The B-1 Bomber.
The Trident Submarine.
Overseas troop level, by 100,000 troops.
AWACS [Airborne Warning and Control System] Air Warning System . . .
Additional military aid to Southeast Asia.
$2.3 billion for inflationary costs for ship-building . . .

VOTING RIGHTS ACT OF 1965

Key to the maintenance of a free and open democratic society are the rights of individuals to exercise their franchise to vote. The Voting Rights Act of 1965 has been perhaps the most effective piece of civil rights legislation ever passed. Focusing on areas where the exclusion of black voters was greatest, largely in the South, the Voting Rights Act has resulted in the registration of over 1 million persons since 1965 . . . Yet there is considerable evidence, such as in the recent U.S. Civil Rights Commission Study, that the problems persist, and that without the Act, there would be serious regression in black voting rights . . .

HEALTH CARE

The United States is the only industrialized nation in the world that does not have a comprehensive health care system. Medicaid and Medicare reach only a minimal number of people and with a relatively low level of benefits. A large number of persons have no medical plan at all, and even those with medical plans frequently do not have regular preventive care . . .

Legislation will be introduced in this session of Congress, as it was in the last, to create national health care . . .

SOCIAL INSURANCE

For a number of years, there has been a great deal of discussion about welfare abuse, welfare reform and welfare replacement. Welfare or income security must be addressed this year both in terms of the amount of money and resources consumed by the program.

More importantly, it must be discussed in human terms. Welfare recipients are citizens who have a right to be treated with dignity.

The Caucus will explore and discuss the various alternatives to the present social insurance system which are presented. In particular, we will take a close look at the concept of a negative income tax . . .

Any welfare replacement or income supplement program is doomed to failure unless it is tied to job development, job training, a vastly expanded child care program, and a thorough and far-reaching program to eradicate sex and racial discrimination in education, job training and unemployment . . .

EDUCATION
. . . A renewed Vocational Education Act must contain provisions to ensure that handicapped and disadvantaged students receive substantial benefits from the program . . .

INDIVIDUAL LEGISLATIVE INITIATIVES
In addition to the preceding areas of major focus, following are some forty pieces of legislation in ten major categories which are being introduced by members of the Congressional Black Caucus. In different ways, each affects substantial segments of the nation.

1. Child Care ([Shirley A.] Chisholm [D-N.Y.]).—A child care bill to be introduced would establish federally aided child development programs to provide comprehensive services to children under the age of six . . .

2. Civil and Political Rights and Liberties: Voting Representation for the District of Columbia ([Walter E.] Fauntroy [D-D.C.], [Charles C.] Diggs [Jr., D-Mich.]).— . . . A bill to be introduced later this year will provide for full voting members of the Senate and House from Washington, D.C. . . .

Amnesty ([Ronald V.] Dellums [, D-Calif.]).—A bill introduced provides automatic general amnesty for failing to comply with any requirement of, or relating to service in the Armed forces during our Indochina involvement . . .

3. Criminal Justice: Gun Control (Dellums, Fauntroy, [Ralph H.] Metcalfe [D-Ill.], [Robert N. C.] Nix [D-Pa.]).— . . . Black on black crime is an especially prevalent problem. Several bills offered by Caucus members and by others would ban the importation, manufacture, sale, purchase, transfer, transportation, receipt, possession and ownership of handguns, except in certain circumstances . . .

Office of Federal Correctional Ombudsman (Metcalfe).—An independent third party system for investigating and arbitrating complaints of both inmates and the staffs of the federal prison system and those who are under the direction of the federal parole board should be established . . .

4. Consumer Protection: . . . Antitrust ([Barbara C.] Jordan [D-Texas]).—Efforts must be made to increase the effectiveness of antitrust laws by such means as permitting state Attorneys General the authority to file class action antitrust suits in federal courts, repealing state fair trade laws, and by preventing leading conglomerates from controlling alternative sources of energy . . .

5. Foreign Affairs: . . . African Development Funding Act ([Andrew J.] Young [D-Ga.]).—Would provide for multilateral trade and technical assistance commitments based on the development priorities of African nations . . .

7. Health: Narcotics ([Charles B.] Rangel [D-N.Y.]). The Congressional Black Caucus supports legislative and appropriations efforts to (1) increase the Drug Enforcement Agency's budget, (2) provide funding for supportive services such as education and employment counseling to permit treated addicts to return to the economic mainstream . . .

10. Women's Rights: Rape Prevention and Control ([Yvonne Brathwaite] Burke [D-Calif.]).—A National Center for the Prevention and Control of Rape within the National Institute of Mental Health should be established . . .

Social Security Coverage for Homemakers (Jordan).—A bill has been introduced which recognizes household employees as self-employed workers and provides them with all the social security benefits available to other workers.

Source: Remarks of Charles B. Rangel in *Congressional Record*, 94th Cong., 1st sess., March 5, 6, and 10, 1975, 5413–5414, 5588–5590, 5958–5960.

Document 6.8 in Context
"Of All the People I Have Ever Known in Public Service, Andy Young Is the Best": Rep. Andrew J. Young Jr., D-Ga., Becomes U.S. Ambassador to the United Nations

Andrew J. Young Jr. was a close ally of Rev. Martin Luther King Jr. and first marched in the District of Columbia at the 1957 Prayer Pilgrimage seeking the right to vote. He marched in Washington again in 1963 with King and in 1968's Poor People's Campaign. Young was elected to the House of Representatives in 1972. During the 1976 presidential campaign, in which President Gerald R. Ford was the Republican nominee, Young played a major role in advising his fellow Georgia Democrat, former governor Jimmy Carter.

After Carter's victory, the president-elect named Young U.S. ambassador to the United Nations. While important symbolically, the appointment also signaled Carter's specific foreign policy interest in Africa and general interest in international human rights, both topics of longtime concern to the Congressional Black Caucus. A few days after being sworn in, Young was sent on his first official trip to Africa, as Carter explained in a national broadcast, "to demonstrate our friendship for its peoples and our commitment to peaceful change toward majority rule in southern Africa." [30]

From the start of his administration, Carter confronted a series of significant issues on that continent, including the racist regime and apartheid policies of South Africa (**Document 6.11**) and the presence of communist Cuban troops in Angola. At a news conference in February 1977, he discussed mass murders and human rights abuses that "have disgusted the entire civilized world" under Ugandan dictator Idi Amin.

By the end of his administration, Carter could report advances in Africa—the doubling of U.S. aid and Zimbabwe's independence—and would acknowledge the challenges that had confronted him during his four years in the White House, including independence for Namibia and a Liberian coup.

Young later wrote about the start of his thirty-three month tenure at the United Nations:

> In the Congress, I was viewed as moderate because I refused to vote a strict party line with the Congressional Black Caucus and the liberal democrats who were my best friends.
>
> Now I found myself in New York being branded by the so-called liberal New York media as a radical—even a fanatic—because I emerged as the Carter Administration's most visible proponent of human rights . . .
>
> The world was not an alien environment against which we had to defend ourselves as much as it was a place that was attempting to solve many of the same problems of human survival and development. We had been aspiring toward mutual

goals with a great deal of success. I saw our role in the U.S. as providing vision and leadership.[31]

As for the thorny Middle East situation that Carter and Young tackled, including the historic Camp David Accords between Israel and Egypt signed in 1978, Young observed:

> There is an acceptable risk for war that is considered one's patriotic duty. Few men and women are able to see the risk for peace as a more powerful patriotic responsibility . . . And we can only have peace when the peacemakers of a society are encouraged to act as courageously as the warriors.[32]

Here are Carter's remarks at Young's swearing-in ceremony as UN ambassador. Supreme Court Justice Thurgood Marshall administered the oath of office.

▬ Document 6.8 ▬
President Jimmy Carter's Remarks at the Swearing-in of Rep. Andrew J. Young Jr., D-Ga., as U.S. Ambassador to the United Nations, January 30, 1977

I can see that I may have made the wrong choice. Andy is the first Cabinet-level officer who has gotten more applause than the President. [*Laughter*] But I'm not surprised, nor disappointed. I think that is an indication that all of you recognize, along with me, the superb qualities that come to major government service with Andrew Young. Andy has heard me say this many times, and I have never said it about anyone else—of all the people I have ever known in public service, Andy Young is the best.

He exemplifies to me a very rare combination of inner strength and quiet self-assurance, deep religious faith, superb personal courage, sensitivity to other people's needs who are not so influential or well known or powerful as he is, an ability to work with others, a way to assess a complicated question and divulge his accurate but sensitive and simple analysis to other people, an ability to work with his own peer group. That is really a combination that is rare.

I think all of you know Andrew Young's background. Some of you in the audience were there with him when he saw what was wrong with our Nation and knew what was right and had the courage to suffer personally—and in many instances in a subordinate position, with Martin Luther King and others—and change the consciousness, I think, not only of our own country but the whole world. And he did this in a way that made us all proud of him.

He did not want or ask for this job. I wanted Andy to be the Ambassador of our country to the United Nations for a long time. And it was only with the greatest reluctance on his part that he finally agreed to do it for me and for our country. But his reluctance was not an unwillingness to serve the United States. It was a belief, because of humility, that he wasn't quite ready for it. He said that when he was quite a young man that he wanted to be Ambassador to the United Nations because of the unique contribution that could be made there. But he thought that the time might be 4 years or 8 years in the future. So, our Nation's gain is Georgia's loss. And Andrew Young has agreed to occupy this very important position.

Yesterday morning, in the privacy of my own little office adjacent to the Oval Office, Andrew Young and [Secretary of State] Cyrus Vance and [National Security Adviser] Zbigniew Brzezinski and I spent 2 full hours talking about the most difficult and challenging international questions that face our country. And on the basis of equality of exchange, and so forth, we tried to evolve what our Nation ought to do. And it was a reassuring thing to have Andrew Young there. And I am very grateful this afternoon that he is willing to serve. I look forward to greater things from him in the future.

I hope to measure up as President to the standards that he sets as Ambassador to the United Nations. His status will be equal to that of the Secretary of State or the Secretary of the Treasury or anyone else. And his closeness to me personally will ensure that there is never a division of sense of purpose or a need for action between him, as he deals with almost 150 other nations' leaders in New York and around the world, and I and Cyrus Vance, who is here, as we deal from Washington with those same countries on a different leadership basis. So that compatibility will greatly magnify his own good influence . . .

Source: Jimmy Carter, *Public Papers of the Presidents of the United States: Jimmy Carter, 1977* (Washington, D.C.: U.S. Government Printing Office, 1977), 46–47.

Document 6.9 in Context
"Rethinking the Operations and Purposes of Our Economic System": Humphrey-Hawkins Full Employment Legislation of 1978

In the aftermath of World War II amid an economic boom in the United States, which had become the world's dominant economic power, Congress made a commitment in the Employment Act of 1946 to "promote maximum employment." That commitment was never fulfilled, however, in part because of political opposition to what critics claimed was government meddling in the private sector. In 1975, recognizing the country's rising jobless rate, African American representative Augustus F. Hawkins, D-Calif., and white senator Hubert H. Humphrey, D-Minn., sponsored legislation based on the philosophical foundation that full employment is good national policy.

In explaining the principles behind the legislation, Hawkins articulated the concept of linking human rights, equal opportunity and full employment at a time of rising unemployment in the United States. At the same time, he acknowledged that such an approach would require a "profound change in the American way of life, and it would commit the entire society to rethinking the operations and purposes of our economic system." He stressed that

> this is not simply a bill proposing further creation of public service employment jobs . . . This would involve providing opportunities for the millions of people currently disclosed by the official data—the unemployed, involuntary part-timers, and job seekers not in the labor force—and the millions of other persons who are not considered in the official data but who nevertheless are able and willing to work.[33]

At an October 1977 press conference, President Jimmy Carter responded to a reporter who asked him whether he had decided to support the legislation:

> During the campaign I promised to support the Humphrey-Hawkins bill, but expressed some concern about the detailed factors included in the Humphrey-Hawkins bill at that time and did not approve the version as it then existed. It's been constantly amended over the last 2 or 3 years since introduction.

My staff have recently been working with Congressman Hawkins, with Senator Humphrey on the telephone, with their staffs, and others, to evolve a full employment bill that we could indeed support without equivocation or hesitancy. We are making good progress about that. And I would guess that within the next few days we would be prepared, if things go well, to announce our support of the Humphrey-Hawkins bill.[34]

As enacted, what became known as the Humphrey-Hawkins Full Employment and Balanced Growth Act of 1978 outlined a comprehensive national policy and steps to implement long-term, medium-term and short-term goals regarding national priorities, monetary policy, overcoming inflation, countercyclical employment policies, youth employment, coordination with state and local government and private sector economic activity, regional employment problems, and job training and counseling.

In his January 1981 State of the Union address, a few days before turning the presidency over to Republican Ronald Reagan, Carter cited the bill as a significant accomplishment during his administration. Ultimately, however, economic and political forces and realities prevented the well-meaning goals set out in the law from being reached. For example, the United States failed to achieve such specified benchmarks as a maximum 3 percent unemployment rate for workers aged twenty or older by 1983 or a 0 percent inflation rate by 1988. While the law remains on the books as of 2007, the ramifications of globalization, deindustrialization of the United States, the shift of manufacturing and service jobs overseas, demographic changes and other macro-level economic factors make the prospects for reaching its targets increasingly unlikely.

▬▬ Document 6.9 ▬▬
Humphrey-Hawkins Full Employment and Balanced Growth Act, October 27, 1978

AN ACT To translate into practical reality the right of all Americans who are able, willing, and seeking to work to full opportunity for useful paid employment at fair rates of compensation; to assert the responsibility of the Federal Government to use all practicable programs and policies to promote full employment, production, and real income, balanced growth, adequate productivity growth, proper attention to national priorities, and reasonable price stability; to require the President each year to set forth explicit short-term and medium-term economic goals; to achieve a better integration of general and structural economic policies; and to improve the coordination of economic policymaking within the Federal Government.

Be it enacted by the Senate and House of Representatives of the United States of America in Congress assembled,

SECTION 1. This Act and the following table of contents may be cited as the "Full Employment and Balanced Growth Act of 1978" . . .

GENERAL FINDINGS

SEC. 2. (a) The Congress finds that the Nation has suffered substantial unemployment and underemployment, idleness of other productive resources, high rates of inflation, and inadequate productivity growth, over prolonged periods of time, imposing numerous economic and social costs on the Nation. Such costs include the following:

(1) The Nation is deprived of the full supply of goods and services, the full utilization of labor and capital resources, and the related increases in economic well-being that would occur under conditions of genuine full employment, production, and real income, balanced growth, a balanced Federal budget, and the effective control of inflation.

(2) The output of goods and services is insufficient to meet pressing national priorities.

(3) Workers are deprived of the job security, income, skill development, and productivity necessary to maintain and advance their standards of living.

(4) Business and industry are deprived of the production, sales, capital flow, and productivity necessary to maintain adequate profits, undertake new investment, create jobs, compete internationally, and contribute to meeting society's economic needs. These problems are especially acute for smaller businesses. Variations in the business cycle and low-level operations of the economy are far more damaging to smaller businesses than to larger business concerns because smaller businesses have fewer available resources, and less access to resources, to withstand nationwide economic adversity. A decline in small business enterprises contributes to unemployment by reducing employment opportunities and contributes to inflation by reducing competition.

(5) Unemployment exposes many families to social, psychological, and physiological costs, including disruption of family life, loss of individual dignity and self-respect, and the aggravation of physical and psychological illnesses, alcoholism and drug abuse, crime, and social conflicts.

(6) Federal, State, and local government budgets are undermined by deficits due to shortfalls in tax revenues and in increases in expenditures for unemployment compensation, public assistance, and other recession-related services in the areas of criminal justice, alcoholism and drug abuse, and physical and mental health.

(b) The Congress further finds that:

(1) High unemployment may contribute to inflation by diminishing labor training and skills, underutilizing capital resources, reducing the rate of productivity advance, increasing unit labor costs, and reducing the general supply of goods and services.

(2) Aggregate monetary and fiscal policies alone have been unable to achieve full employment and production, increased real income, balanced growth, a balanced Federal budget, adequate productivity growth, proper attention to national priorities, achievement of an improved trade balance, and reasonable price stability, and therefore must be supplemental by other measures designed to serve these ends . . .

(4) Increasing job opportunities and full employment would greatly contribute to the elimination of discrimination based upon sex, age, race, color, religion, national origin, handicap, or other improper factors.

(c) The Congress further finds that an effective policy to promote full employment and production, increased real income, balanced growth, a balanced Federal budget, adequate productivity growth, proper attention to national priorities, achievement of an improved trade balance, and reasonable price stability should (1) be based on the development of explicit economic goals and policies involving the President, the Congress, and the Board of Governors of the Federal Reserve System, with maximum reliance on the resources and ingenuity of the private sector of the economy, (2) include programs specifically designed to reduce high unemployment due to recessions, and to reduce structural unemployment within regional areas and among particular labor force groups, and (3) give proper attention to the role of increased exports and improvement in the international competitiveness of agriculture, business, and industry in providing productive employment opportunities and achieving an improved trade balance.

(d) The Congress further finds that full employment and production, increased real income, balanced growth, a balanced Federal budget, adequate productivity growth, proper attention to national priorities, achievement of an improved trade balance through increased exports and improvement in the international competitiveness of agriculture, business, and industry, and reasonable price stability are important national requirements and will promote the economic security and well-being of all citizens of the Nation . . .

COUNTERCYCLICAL EMPLOYMENT POLICIES

SEC. 202. (a) Any countercyclical efforts undertaken to aid in achieving the purposes of section 201 shall consider for inclusion the following programmatic entities:

(1) accelerated public works, including the development of standby public works projects;
(2) public service employment;
(3) State and local grant programs;
(4) the levels and duration of unemployment insurance;
(5) skill training in both the private and public sectors, both as a general remedy and as a supplement to unemployment insurance;
(6) youth employment programs as specified in section 205;
(7) community development programs to provide employment in activities of value to the States, local communities (including rural areas), and the Nation;
(8) Federal procurement programs which are targeted on labor surplus areas; and
(9) augmentation of other employment and training programs which would help to reduce high levels of unemployment arising from cyclical causes . . .

YOUTH EMPLOYMENT POLICIES

SEC. 205. (a) The Congress finds and declares—,

(1) That serious unemployment and economic disadvantage of a unique nature exist among youths even under generally favorable economic conditions;
(2) that this group constitutes a substantial portion of the Nation's unemployment, and that this significantly contributes to crime, alcoholism and drug abuse, and other social and economic problems; and
(3) that many youths have special employment needs and problems which, if not promptly addressed, will substantially contribute to more severe unemployment problems in the long run.

(b) To the extent deemed necessary in fulfillment of the purposes of this Act, the President shall improve and expand existing youth employment programs, recommending legislation where required. In formulating any such program, the President shall—,

(1) include provisions designed to fully coordinate youth employment activities with other employment and training programs;
(2) develop a smoother transition from school to work;

(3) prepare disadvantaged and other youths with employability handicaps for regular self-sustaining employment;

(4) develop realistic methods for combining training with work; and

(5) develop provisions designed to attract structurally unemployed youth into productive full-time employment through incentives to private and independent sector businesses . . .

Source: Full Employment and Balanced Growth Act of 1978, October 27, 1978, Public Law 95-523, *U.S. Statutes at Large* 92: 1887.

Document 6.10 in Context
"All Right-Thinking People, All Right-Thinking Americans Are Joined in Spirit with Us This Day": A Holiday to Honor Rev. Martin Luther King Jr.

Rev. Martin Luther King Jr. was assassinated on April 4, 1968. Four days later, Rep. John Conyers Jr., D-Mich., first sponsored legislation to make the slain civil rights leader's birthday a national holiday. Conyers and Rep. Shirley A. Chisholm, D-N.Y., continued to reintroduce the bill for fifteen years before it became law.

Over the years, opponents criticized the proposed holiday on a variety of grounds—citing the cost of paying governmental employees for another day off, arguing that the holiday would mainly target minorities and asserting that King was a rabble-rouser who provoked civil violence and was unworthy of such an honor. Some opponents believed that King should be honored only on the same day as other famous Americans, such as Thomas Jefferson, who did not already have a day of their own.

The House finally passed the bill on August 2, 1983. During the Senate debate that followed, Sen. Jesse Helms, R-N.C., claimed that King had been a communist sympathizer. Helms led an unsuccessful filibuster to block the measure, which the Senate approved on October 19.

At a Rose Garden ceremony, President Ronald Reagan—who had criticized the legislation only weeks earlier as "based on an image not a reality"—signed the bill. He spoke about some of King's activities, including the 1955–1956 bus boycott in Montgomery, Alabama, and King's August 1963 "I Have a Dream" speech, delivered before a quarter million listeners in front of the Lincoln Memorial in Washington, D.C. The president stated, "But traces of bigotry still mar America. So, each year on Martin Luther King Day, let us not only recall Dr. King but rededicate ourselves to the Commandments he believed in and sought to live every day." [35] He made no mention of his previous opposition to the measure. After Reagan's remarks, King's widow, Coretta Scott King, told the president and the guests, "All right-thinking people, all right-thinking Americans are joined in spirit with us this day." [36]

Document 6.10
Legislation Creating the Martin Luther King Jr. Holiday, November 2, 1983

AN ACT To amend title 5, United States Code, to make the birthday of Martin Luther King, Jr., a legal public holiday.

Be it enacted by the Senate and House of Representatives of the United States of America in Congress assembled, That section 6103(a) of title 5, United States Code, is amended by inserting immediately below the item relating to New Year's Day the following:

"Birthday of Martin Luther King, Jr., the third Monday in January."

SEC. 2. The amendment made by the first section of this Act shall take effect on the first January 1 that occurs after the two-year period following the date of the enactment of this Act.

Source: An Act to Establish the Martin Luther King, Junior, Federal Holiday, November 2, 1983, Public Law 98-144, *U.S. Statutes at Large* 97: 917.

Document 6.11 in Context
"Reforms . . . That Will Lead to the Establishment of a Nonracial Democracy": Congress Overrides President Reagan's Veto of Economic Sanctions against South Africa

For years, black members of Congress and their allies advocated U.S. economic sanctions against the white-supremacist, apartheid government in South Africa; the first congressional anti-apartheid bill was introduced in 1972, and similar legislation failed to pass until 1986.

President Ronald Reagan's administration opposed sanctions, abstaining from a 1984 United Nations Security Council resolution condemning apartheid and favoring instead what it called "constructive engagement" with the South African government to persuade it to moderate its apartheid policies. In addition to the multinational approach taken by the United Nations, sanctions advocates intended to use congressionally mandated restrictions on U.S. exports and investments to pressure the South African government to eliminate racially discriminatory policies. Finally, the Comprehensive Anti-Apartheid Act, introduced by Rep. William H. Gray III, D-Pa., with 106 cosponsors, passed Congress, only to be vetoed by Reagan on September 26, 1986.

Reagan explained in his veto message that his administration opposed apartheid but believed that the sanctions in the legislation would harm those it was designed to assist:

> This Administration has no quarrel with the declared purpose of this measure. Indeed, we share that purpose: To send a clear signal to the South African Government that the American people view with abhorrence its codified system of racial segregation. Apartheid is an affront to human rights and human dignity. Normal and friendly relations cannot exist between the United States and South Africa until it becomes a dead policy. Americans are of one mind and one heart on this issue.
>
> But while we vigorously support the purpose of this legislation, declaring economic warfare against the people of South Africa would be destructive not only of their efforts to peacefully end apartheid, but also of the opportunity to replace it with a free society.
>
> The sweeping and punitive sanctions adopted by the Congress are targeted directly at the labor intensive industries upon which the victimized peoples of South Africa depend for their very survival. Black workers—the first victims of apartheid—would become the first victims of American sanctions.[37]

Congress reacted swiftly and overrode the veto on October 2, 1986, making the policy law. Reagan then issued an executive order directing that "all affected Executive departments and agencies shall take all steps necessary, consistent with the Constitution, to implement the requirements of the Act." [38]

After the law took effect, Congressional Black Caucus members advocated even tighter sanctions. For example, Rep. George T. "Mickey" Leland, D-Texas, introduced a bill in 1989 to prohibit South African residents and businesses from acquiring or owning 5 percent or more of the stock of U.S. corporations, saying, "Our past actions suggest that Americans find apartheid so morally abhorrent that we chose not to associate with such a racist system . . . If we seek to send a clear message to South Africa, we must end South African investment in the United States." [39]

When South African anti-apartheid activist Nelson Mandela was released on February 11, 1990, after twenty-seven years in prison, the Caucus increased its resolve to maintain pressure on the apartheid government. Mandela's African National Congress political party swept the 1994 elections, the first democratic elections in that country's history, signaling an end to apartheid. At a Caucus luncheon honoring President Mandela later that year, President Bill Clinton lauded the Caucus for raising public consciousness about "the terrible injustice of apartheid," consistently acting on "a deep-rooted commitment to South Africa's freedom" and its "unbending will." [40] Clinton called on the United States to help South Africa with problems encompassing jobs, education, housing, health and poverty.

▬ Document 6.11 ▬
Comprehensive Anti-Apartheid Act of 1986, October 2, 1986

AN ACT To prohibit loans to, other investments in, and certain other activities with respect to, South Africa, and for other purposes

Be it enacted by the Senate and House of Representatives of the United States of America in Congress assembled,

SHORT TITLE
SECTION 1. This Act may be cited as the "Comprehensive Anti-Apartheid Act of 1986". . .

TITLE I—POLICY OF THE UNITED STATES WITH RESPECT TO ENDING
    APARTHEID

Policy toward the Government of South Africa
SEC. 101. (a) United States policy toward the Government of South Africa shall be designed to bring about reforms in that system of government that will lead to the establishment of a nonracial democracy.

(b) The United States will work toward this goal by encouraging the Government of South Africa to—

(1) repeal the present state of emergency and respect the principle of equal justice under law for citizens of all races;

(2) release Nelson Mandela, Govan Mbeki, Walter Sisulu, black trade union leaders, and all political prisoners;

(3) permit the free exercise by South Africans of all races of the right to form political parties, express political opinions, and otherwise participate in the political process;

(4) establish a timetable for the elimination of all apartheid laws;

(5) negotiate with representatives of all racial groups in South Africa the future political systems in South Africa; and

(6) end military and paramilitary activities aimed at neighboring states . . .

TITLE III—MEASURES BY THE UNITED STATES TO UNDERMINE APARTHEID

Prohibition on the Importation of Krugerrands

SEC. 301. No person, including a bank, may import into the United States any South African krugerrand or any other gold coins minted in South Africa or offered for sale by the Government of South Africa.

Prohibition on the Importation of Military Articles

SEC. 302. No arms, ammunition, or military vehicles produced in South Africa or any manufacturing data for such articles may be imported into the United States . . .

Prohibition on Computer Exports to South Africa

SEC. 304. (a) No computers, computer software, or goods or technology intended to manufacture or service computers may be exported to or for use by any of the following entities of the Government of South Africa:

(1) The military.

(2) The police.

(3) The prison system.

(4) The national security agencies.

(5) ARMSCOR [Armaments Corporation of South Africa] and its subsidiaries or the weapons research activities of the Council for Scientific and Industrial Research.

(6) The administering authorities for controlling the movements of the victims of apartheid.

(7) Any apartheid enforcing agency . . .

Prohibition on Loans to the Government of South Africa

SEC. 305. (a) No national of the United States may make or approve any loan or other extension of credit, directly or indirectly, to the Government of South Africa or to any corporation, partnership or other organization which is owned or controlled by the Government of South Africa . . .

Prohibitions on Nuclear Trade with South Africa

SEC. 307. (a) Notwithstanding any other provision of law—

(1)   The Nuclear Regulatory Commission shall not issue any license for the export to South Africa of production or utilization facilities, any source or special nuclear material or sensitive nuclear technology, or any component parts, items, or substances which the Commission has determined . . . to be especially relevant from the standpoint of export control because of their significance for nuclear explosive purposes . . .

Government of South Africa Bank Accounts

SEC. 308. (a) A United States depository institution may not accept, receive, or hold a deposit account from the Government of South Africa or from any agency or entity owned or controlled by the Government of South Africa except for such accounts which may be authorized by the President for diplomatic or consular purposes . . .

Prohibition on Importation of Uranium and Coal from South Africa

SEC. 309. (a) Notwithstanding any other provision of law, no-

(1) uranium ore,
(2) uranium oxide,
(3) coal, or
(4) textiles,
that is produced or manufactured in South Africa may be imported into the United States . . .

Prohibition on New Investment in South Africa

SEC. 310. (a) No national of the United States may, directly or through another person, make any new investment in South Africa . . .

Policy toward Violence or Terrorism

SEC. 312. (a) United States policy toward violence in South Africa shall be designed to bring about an immediate end to such violence and to promote negotiations concluding with a removal of the system of apartheid and the establishment of a non-racial democracy in South Africa . . .

Prohibition on United States Government Procurement from South Africa

SEC. 314. On or after the date of enactment of this Act, no department, agency or any other entity of the United States Government may enter into a contract for the procurement of goods or services from parastatal organizations except for items necessary for diplomatic and consular purposes.

Prohibition on the Promotion of United States Tourism in South Africa

SEC. 315. None of the funds appropriated or otherwise made available by any provision of law may be available to promote United States tourism in South Africa.

Prohibition of United States Government Assistance to, Investment in, or Subsidy for Trade with, South Africa

SEC. 316. None of the funds appropriated or otherwise made available by any provision of law may be available for any assistance to investment in, or any subsidy for trade with, South Africa, including but not limited to funding for trade missions in South Africa and for participation in exhibitions and trade fairs in South Africa . . .

Prohibition on Cooperation with the Armed Forces of South Africa

SEC. 322. No agency or entity of the United States may engage in any form of cooperation, direct or indirect, with the armed forces of the Government of South Africa, except activities which are reasonably designed to facilitate the collection of necessary intelligence . . .

TITLE IV—MULTILATERAL MEASURES TO UNDERMINE APARTHEID

Negotiating Authority

SEC. 401. (a) It is the policy of the United States to seek international cooperative agreements with the other industrialized democracies to bring about the complete dismantling of apartheid. Sanctions imposed under such agreements should be both direct and official executive or legislative acts of governments . . .

Limitation on Imports from Other Countries

SEC. 402. The President is authorized to limit the importation into the United States of any product or service of a foreign country to the extent to which such foreign country benefits from, or otherwise takes commercial advantage of, any sanction or prohibition against any national of the United States imposed by or under this Act . . .

TITLE V—FUTURE POLICY TOWARD SOUTH AFRICA

Additional Measures

SEC. 501. It shall be the policy of the United States to impose additional measures against the Government of South Africa if substantial progress has not been made within twelve months of the date of enactment of this Act in ending the system of apartheid and establishing a nonracial democracy . . .

Study of Health Conditions in the "Homelands" Areas of South Africa

SEC. 503. The Secretary of State shall conduct a study to examine the state of health conditions and to determine the extent of starvation and malnutrition now prevalent in the "homelands" areas of South Africa . . .

TITLE VI—ENFORCEMENT AND ADMINISTRATIVE PROVISIONS

Regulatory Authority

SEC. 601. The President shall issue such rules, regulations, licenses and orders as are necessary to carry out the provisions of this Act . . .

Source: Comprehensive Anti-Apartheid Act of 1986, Public Law 99-440, *U.S. Statutes at Large* 100: 1086

Document 6.12 in Context
"Human Conditions . . . Which Demand a Responsible Fiscal Response from Our Nation": The Congressional Black Caucus Offers Alternative Budget Proposals

After Republican president Ronald Reagan took office in 1981, he challenged critics of his administration's budget plans to propose alternatives of their own. The Congressional Black Caucus did so in March of that year. The Caucus's response would become an annual ritual, regardless of whether a Republican or Democrat sat in the Oval Office. Through these alternative budgets, the Caucus could explain to the public how the nation could finance its priorities. For example, the Caucus's proposed "Quality of Life" budget for fiscal year 1991 did not merely call for reduced Defense Department spending but also detailed which weapons systems it believed could be eliminated, such as the Trident II missile and the B-2 bomber, or reduced, as through the purchase of fewer F-16 jet fighters. In the proposal, Caucus Chair Ronald V. Dellums, a California Democrat, wrote, "We have thus focused the attention of the American people and this Congress on human conditions here in this country and around the globe which demand a responsible fiscal response from our nation." [41]

Although the Caucus was unsuccessful in its annual efforts to persuade Congress to adopt its budget instead of the White House's, it continued to proffer comprehensive alternatives. Its fiscal year 1993 proposal, prepared in 1992 and self-described as "a budget for new world realities," criticized Reagan's Republican successor, President George H. W. Bush, for failing to "take advantage of the window of opportunity that new world conditions offer for serious cuts in military spending. In so doing, he squanders resources that could be used to correct the many problems created by the 1980's misplaced budget priorities."[42] It also urged an end to "straightjacket" agreements that precluded Congress from transferring military savings to domestic programs, advocated reinvestment of military savings into education, economic development, veterans' services and health, and called for redistributing tax breaks for the wealthy to "working- and middle-class taxpayers." [43]

For fiscal year 1994, the Caucus teamed with the House Progressive Caucus to jointly offer an alternative plan, "A Budget to Rebuild America," as a counterproposal to the budget submitted to Congress by their fellow Democrat, President Bill Clinton. The coalition of the two caucuses titled its fiscal year 1996 plan "A Budget for the Caring Majority and for Rebuilding America," and in announcing it, Congressional Black Caucus Chair Major R. O. Owens, D-N.Y., said:

> We are in compliance with the ill conceived mandate to balance the budget by the year 2002 . . . But we don't persecute senior citizens, working families and the poor. We cut the giant abusers. We cut greedy freeloading corporations like McDonalds; Lockheed; Archer Daniels Midland and the mob of agribusiness monsters. [44]

Thus the annual alternative budget proposals also served as vehicles to present an alternative vision of national priorities and political philosophy, as well as an outline of how to afford those priorities. Excerpts of the proposal for the 1991 fiscal year follow and are representative of how the Caucus balanced competing national interests and economic assumptions. The figures are given in billions of dollars.

═══ Document 6.12 ═══
Congressional Black Caucus Fiscal Year 1991 Alternative Budget, April 1990

EXECUTIVE SUMMARY
. . . The CBC has shown that we can provide for our national security, increase spending for crucial social programs, reduce budget deficits, and generate requisite revenues without increasing taxes for the vast majority of taxpayers. For FY 91, we have crafted a budget that seeks to capitalize on the dramatic changes occurring in our world. Changes in Southern Africa, Central America, Eastern Europe, and around the globe represent a dramatic opportunity to reprogram tens of billions of dollars that would be spent on armaments and to reinvest them in the human and physical resources of our nation . . .

FUNCTIONS IN BRIEF
In the section below, the $ figures are Budget Authority/Outlays

National Defense (Function 050)

Current Services:	$310.4/$306.4
President Bush:	$306.9/$303.3
CBC:	$259.4/$279.5

. . . The CBC plan is based on seven principles:

- reduce the threat of nuclear war through arms control negotiations and restrictions on new nuclear weapons funding; this instead of the administration emphasis on the continued development of a first-strike and nuclear war-fighting capability . . .
- reduce the one-half to two-thirds of the military budget directed at preparing to fight a protracted World War II-style land war in Europe.
- reduce active force levels by 10 percent this year . . .
- redefine the U.S. relationship with the Third World and move away from the present emphasis on intervention and intimidation.
- eliminate overlapping and unnecessary weapons and procurement inefficiencies, and abuse;
- fully support military personnel and their families; and

- establish programs for economic conversion and military toxic waste clean-up . . .

International Affairs (Function 150)

Current Services:	$39.0/ $17.9
President Bush:	$19.0/ $18.2
CBC:	$20.4/ $19.9

The CBC proposes substantial increases in humanitarian and economic assistance while reducing spending on foreign military sales. The principal CBC proposals include:

- increased funding for African and Caribbean development assistance and sub-Saharan famine relief . . .
- reductions in foreign military sales
- expansion of PL480 program and increased funding for addressing world hunger
- increased funding for refugee assistance programs
- support for emerging democracies, including Namibia
- expansion of minority agencies engaged in humanitarian and relief assistance
- increased assistance to victims of human rights violations
- full support for UN, and for U.S. participation in UN specialized agencies and peace-keeping forces . . .

Natural Resources and Environment (Function 300)

Current Services:	$18.2/ $18.1
President Bush:	$17.6/ $18.2
CBC:	$19.2/ $18.8

The CBC strongly supports environmental protection and national resource management and preservation programs. The CBC alternative includes support for:

- full enforcement and implementation of EPA regulations
- full funding for Superfund and other toxic waste disposal initiatives
- full funding for all Clean Air Act programs
- creation of a new program in community and urban forestry
- creation of an African-American Heritage Museum on the Federal mall and full funding for cultural history programs

Agriculture (Function 350)

Current Services:	$22.2/ $17.6
President Bush:	$20.1/ $14.9
CBC:	$20.7/ $16.5

The CBC proposes increasing federal financial assistance to small- and mid-sized farms, loans to minority farmers, and food assistance and nutrition programs for low-income families. The principal recommendations include:

- reducing Bush cuts in CCC crop subsidy provisions

- rejection of Administration proposal to shift FmHA from direct lending to loan guarantor role
- increased funding to address the global food crises
- implementation of the Minority Farm Act
- expansion of Limited Resources Operating Loan Program for beginning low-equity producers
- funding new research and extension positions . . .

Medicare (Function 570)

Current Services:	$125.1/$104.2
President Bush:	$125.2/ $98.6
CBC:	$125.1/$104.2

The CBC supports full health coverage for the nation's senior citizens. It rejects the continued deterioration in the coverage offered by Medicare. In particular the CBC:

- eliminates all proposed cuts in Medicare funding
- opposes increases in Part A deductibles and Part B premiums . . .

Income Security (Function 600)

Current Services:	$165.7/$140.8
President Bush:	$198.9/$153.7
CBC:	$200.5/$159.0

The CBC budget reflects the belief that the Federal government has the responsibility to provide income, housing, and food for low-income Americans, especially families with children, the elderly, the disabled, and the working poor. The CBC alternative:

- supports McKinney Act homeless assistance programs
- expansion of the WIC Supplemental Feeding Program
- increases School Breakfast & Child Care Food Programs and maintains Snack to Child Care
- restores Private Non-Profit Sponsorship of Summer Food Program and revises Service Area Flexibility
- enhances AFDC Assistance and Community Food Nutrition
- supports new appropriations to states for AFDC Work Activities and Job Opportunities and Basic Skills (JOBS) Training
- implements emergency child protective service grants targeted for children of substance abusers . . .

Administration of Justice (Function 750)

Current Services:	$13.7/$12.8
President Bush:	$12.6/$12.6
CBC:	$14.6/$13.6

The CBC provides for the full implementation of the Anti-Drug Abuse Act and rejects Administration proposals to underfund drug enforcement. The CBC rejects Administration efforts to reduce funding for the Legal Services Corporation and the Juvenile Justice and Delinquency programs. The CBC Alternative proposes:

- full funding for the Anti-Drug Abuse Act for the war on drugs
- increased funding for federal, state, and local drug enforcement and anti-drug programs
- expanded joint interdiction by DEA, FBI and Organized Crime Drug Enforcement Task Forces
- increased resources for federal correctional, litigative and judicial activity
- increased Criminal Justice Assistance and increased death benefits
- full funding for the Legal Services Corporation . . .

Source: Congressional Black Caucus, *Congressional Black Caucus Quality of Life Budget, FY 1991,* April 30, 1990.

NOTES

1 U.S. Commission on Civil Rights, "The Voting Rights Act: Ten Years After," letter of transmittal, January 1995.
2 Ronald V. Dellums and H. Lee Halterman, *Lying Down with the Lions: A Public Life from the Streets of Oakland to the Halls of Power* (Boston: Beacon Press, 2000), 4.
3 Ibid., 5.
4 Gerald R Ford to Charles C. Diggs Jr., letter, April 7, 1971, Gerald R. Ford Presidential Library, Ann Arbor, Michigan.
5 William J. Clinton, "Remarks at the Congressional Black Caucus Foundation Dinner," September 18, 1993, in *Public Papers of the Presidents of the United States: William J. Clinton—1993* (Washington, D.C.: U.S. Government Printing Office, 1995), vol. 2, 1535–1539.
6 Charles C Diggs Jr. et al. to Lyndon Baines Johnson, telegram, February 10, 1965, Lyndon Baines Johnson Presidential Library, Austin, Texas.
7 John Lewis to Lyndon Baines Johnson, letter, August 6, 1965, Lyndon Baines Johnson Presidential Library.
8 Congressional Black Caucus, "CBC History," www.congressionalblackcaucus.net.
9 Charles C. Diggs Jr., in the *Congressional Record,* 92d Cong., 1st sess., March 30, 1971.
10 "Blockbusting the Black Caucus," *Time,* June 9, 1975, www.time.com/time/magazine/article/0,9171,913115,00.html.
11 Congressional Black Caucus, "Statement to the President of the United States by the Congressional Black Caucus," U.S. House of Representatives, March 25, 1971, Gerald R. Ford Presidential Library.
12 William L. Clay, *Just Permanent Interests: Black Americans in Congress, 1870–1991* (New York: Amistad Press, 1992), 151.
13 Congressional Black Caucus, "Congressional Black Caucus Blasts President Nixon for Exploiting Black Entertainers," press release, October 16, 1972, Gerald R. Ford Presidential Library.
14 Ibid.
15 Stanley S. Scott, "Response to Black Caucus Statement," October 1972, Gerald R. Ford Presidential Library.
16 Shirley Chisholm, *Unbought and Unbossed* (Boston: Houghton Mifflin, 1970), 83.
17 Ibid., 84.
18 Ibid., 86.
19 Dellums and Halterman, *Lying Down with the Lions,* 4.

20 Carl Bert Albert, *Little Giant: The Life and Times of Speaker Carl Albert* (Norman, Okla.: University of Oklahoma Press, 1990), 343.

21 John Conyers Jr., "Why Nixon Should Have Been Impeached," *Black Scholar* 6, no. 2 (October 1974): 2–8; 3, 5, 7.

22 William Raspberry, "President Ford's Overture to the Black Caucus," *Washington Post,* August 16, 1974.

23 Robert N. C. Nix, "Statement of Hon. Robert N. C. Nix on the Ford Administration," August 21, 1974, Gerald R. Ford Presidential Library.

24 "Press Conference of Charles B. Rangel, Congressman from the State of New York, Ronald V. Dellums, Congressman from the State of California, and Charles C. Diggs, Congressman from the State of Michigan," August 21, 1974, Office of the White House Press Secretary, Gerald R. Ford Presidential Library.

25 Ibid.

26 Stan Scott, "Analysis of Congressional Black Caucus Position Papers," memorandum to Jim Cavanaugh and Warren Hendricks, September 26, 1974, Gerald R. Ford Presidential Library.

27 Marguerite Ross Barnett, "The Congressional Black Caucus," *Proceedings of the Academy of Political Science* 32, no. 1 (1975): 48.

28 Congressional Black Caucus to President Gerald R. Ford, letter, January 16, 1975, Gerald R. Ford Presidential Library.

29 Congressional Black Caucus, "Congressional Black Caucus Announces Its Legislative Agenda," press release, February 27, 1975, Gerald R. Ford Presidential Library.

30 Jimmy Carter, "Report to the American People: Remarks from the White House Library," February 23, 1977, in *Public Papers of the Presidents of the United States: Jimmy Carter, 1977* (Washington, D.C.: U.S. Government Printing Office, Washington, 1977), 220.

31 Andrew Young, *A Way Out of No Way: The Spiritual Memoirs of Andrew Young* (Nashville, Tenn.: Thomas Nelson Publishers, 1994), 127–128.

32 Ibid., 137–138.

33 Augustus F. Hawkins, "Planning for Personal Choice: The Equal Opportunity and Full Employment Act," *Annals of the American Academy of Political and Social Science* 418 (March 1975): 14.

34 Jimmy Carter, News Conference, October 13, 1977, from the American Presidency Project, www.presidency.ucsb.edu/ws/index.php?pid=6791.

35 Ronald Reagan, "Remarks on Signing the Bill Making the Birthday of Martin Luther King Jr. a National Holiday," November 2, 1983, from the Ronald Reagan Presidential Library, www.reagan.utexas.edu/archives/speeches/1983/110283a.htm.

36 Ibid.

37 Ronald Reagan, "Message to the House of Representatives Returning without Approval a Bill Concerning Apartheid in South Africa," September 26, 1986, from the Ronald Reagan Presidential Library, www.reagan.utexas.edu/archives/speeches/1986/092686b.htm.

38 Ronald Reagan, Executive Order 12571, "Implementation of the Comprehensive Anti-Apartheid Act," October 27, 1986, Section 1, from the Ronald Reagan Presidential Library, www.reagan.utexas.edu/archives/speeches/1986/102786d.htm.

39 *Congressional Record,* 101st Congress, 1st sess., January 24, 1989, E157.

40 William J. Clinton, "Remarks at a Congressional Black Caucus Luncheon for President Nelson Mandela," October 5, 1994, in *Public Papers of the Presidents: William J. Clinton, 1994* (Washington, D.C.: U.S. Government Printing Office, 1996), vol. 2, 207.

41 Congressional Black Caucus, *Congressional Black Caucus Quality of Life Budget, FY 1991,* April 30, 1990, 20.

42 Congressional Black Caucus, *The FY 1993 Alternative Budget,* 1992, 3.

43 Congressional Black Caucus, *The FY 1993 Alternative Budget,* 1992, 6–7.

44 Congressional Black Caucus, "Congressional Black Caucus Cuts Corporate Welfare to Balance U.S. Budget," press release, May 1995.

CHAPTER SEVEN

The Modern Era

The Congressional Black Caucus and the "Republican Revolution," 1994–2007

The closing decade of the twentieth century and the opening years of the twenty-first were a difficult time for members of the Congressional Black Caucus. Though the African American congressional delegation hovered consistently around forty members and it remained—as it had been since the 1930s—overwhelmingly Democratic, a shifting national political mood often left its members in the political minority and on the defensive. The Republican advance that had begun after Barry Goldwater's presidential candidacy in 1964 took a dramatic leap forward

Rep. J. C. Watts Jr., R-Okla., speaks in support of the Republican Contract with America at the National Press Club in Washington, D.C., on January 12, 1995. In 1997 Watts was selected to deliver the televised Republican response to President Bill Clinton's State of the Union address. By his third term in Congress, Watts had become chair of the GOP House Conference, the number four party leadership post. Source: AP Images/Charles Tasnadi

with the administration of President Ronald Reagan in the 1980s. In 1994, although Democrat Bill Clinton was in the White House, the GOP captured a majority in both houses of Congress for the first time in forty years. When Republican George W. Bush was elected president in 2000, his party controlled both the legislative and executive branches for the first time since President Dwight D. Eisenhower's first term (1953–1957).

As the Republican Party consolidated its political power, many members aggressively advanced an agenda that emphasized cutting taxes and federal programs to reduce the size of the federal government. These cuts threatened some of the social programs that African American members of Congress had long supported. The federal government's commitment to affirmative action—an approach to employment and college admissions that was launched in the 1960s during the Democratic administration of President Lyndon B. Johnson to help offset the inequities of segregation and persistent racial discrimination—also came under fire.

Republican presidents George H. W. Bush and George W. Bush, continuing the efforts of President Reagan, worked to appoint conservatives to the federal courts, including the Supreme Court. Conservative political activists pressured George W. Bush in particular to combat what they saw as the improper—and liberal—activism of some federal judges.

Indeed, the battle over court appointments was a continuing source of tension. George H. W. Bush's nomination of Clarence Thomas to the Supreme Court in 1991 (**Document 7.1**) resulted in bipartisan antagonism that set the tone for the consideration of many future judicial appointments. Although Thomas was African American, his intensely conservative legal philosophy and concerns about his record as head of the Equal Employment Opportunity Commission prompted the Congressional Black Caucus to oppose his nomination. The fight over Thomas's appointment became exceptionally bitter after allegations emerged that he had sexually harassed a female subordinate at the EEOC. Both Thomas and his accuser, then-law professor Anita Hill, testified during nationally televised Senate hearings that polarized public opinion and left a residue of lingering partisan animosity.

The next two Supreme Court appointments—Ruth Bader Ginsburg and Stephen Breyer—were confirmed with relatively little conflict, but they were nominated by Democrat Clinton while the Democrats held a majority in Congress. After the Republicans won control of Congress in the midterm elections of 1994, the new majority began to resist some of Clinton's appointments to federal district and appeals courts by blocking action on the more liberal appointees. When Republican George W. Bush took office in January 2001, Democrats in Congress attempted to block some of Bush's appointments. The Democrats' minority status in the Senate forced them to rely on parliamentary maneuvers, particularly the filibuster, which precipitated a nasty battle in 2005 when Republicans threatened to resort to the "constitutional option"—or the "nuclear option" as the Democrats dubbed it—of banning the filibuster altogether. A bipartisan group of senators, including John S. McCain, R-Ariz., and Ben E. Nelson, D-Neb., calling themselves the "Gang of 14" eventually forged a compromise that defused the crisis, but bitterness over the process of judicial appointments remained.

Ideological concerns over the pivotal role of the judiciary were at the core of the disputes. Conservative Republicans were angry over what they saw as a pattern of "liberal activism" by judges stretching back to the Supreme Court led by Chief Justice Earl Warren in the 1950s and 1960s. Liberal Democrats, conversely, were fearful that extremely conservative judicial appointments—especially to the Supreme Court—could roll back what they saw as key advances that had been achieved by court action. Of greatest concern for Congressional Black Caucus was the possibility of the erosion of principles grounded in decisions such as *Brown v. Board of Education* (**Document 5.9**), which banned racial segregation in public schools, and *Regents of the University of California v. Bakke,* which allowed public colleges and universities to consider race as they attempted to promote diversity in selecting students for admission.

In recent years, Caucus members have sought to hold their ground in the face of growing conservative criticism that the courts have gone too far in their efforts to guarantee civil rights. Most Caucus members have been forced into the role of spectator since confirmation of judicial appointments is the prerogative of the Senate, and only two African Americans have served in the Senate since 1993. One of the two—Carol Moseley-Braun, D-Ill.—was inspired to run for the Senate in 1992 against an incumbent of her own political party, Sen. Alan J. Dixon, because he had voted to confirm Clarence Thomas's appointment to the Supreme Court. Moseley-Braun served one term in the Senate. The other African American senator, Barack Obama, D-Ill., was elected in 2004. He opposed President Bush's two Supreme Court nominations the next year.

Both of George W. Bush's nominees—John G. Roberts Jr., who was nominated as chief justice, and Samuel Alito, who was nominated as an associate justice—declined requests by the Congressional Black Caucus for meetings to discuss their judicial philosophies. The Caucus opposed Roberts (**Document 7.8**) because of concerns about his position on civil rights and later recommended against confirming Alito for the same reason. During the Senate debate, Obama cited similar concerns in voting against confirmation of both Roberts and Alito:

> I want to take Judge Roberts at his word that he doesn't like bullies and he sees the law and the Court as a means of evening the playing field between the strong and the weak. But given the gravity of the position to which he will undoubtedly ascend and the gravity of the decisions in which he will undoubtedly participate during his tenure on the Court, I ultimately have to give more weight to his deeds and the overarching political philosophy that he appears to have shared with those in power than to the assuring words that he provided me in our meeting. [1]

While judicial appointments, with their potential for long-term impact, were a focal point in the ideological battles of the late twentieth and early twenty-first centuries, they were not the only issue with which African Americans in Congress struggled. The Republicans' Contract with America (**Document 7.2**) was the central policy statement behind the 1994 GOP campaign that produced the twelve-year Republican majority in both chambers of Congress. House Republicans, under the leadership of Speaker Newt Gingrich, R-Ga., moved quickly to enact a range of reforms called for by that contract. This meant that not only did high-seniority black Democrats like Reps. John Conyers Jr. of Michigan and William L. Clay of Missouri lose control of the House committees they had chaired, but serving in the new congressional minority, they were confronted with an ambitious GOP legislative agenda that ran strongly counter to their own priorities. In particular, welfare reform became a heated issue, and many African American legislators attacked the GOP plan as unfair and punitive toward the poor.

Black Democrats were in turn attacked by conservatives who charged that they were increasingly out of touch with the mainstream views of America—even mainstream African American opinion. The 1990s saw a growth in the prominence of black conservatives, both as political and social commentators and as officeholders. Two black Republicans—Gary A. Franks of Connecticut and J. C. Watts Jr. of Oklahoma—were elected to the House, and Watts rose quickly in the GOP House leadership. In 1997 Watts played a highly visible role when he delivered the Republicans' broadcast response to President Clinton's State of the Union address (**Document 7.4**). Other African American Republicans, such as Condoleezza Rice, Colin Powell and Rodney Paige, were appointed to prominent cabinet positions in the administrations of George H. W. Bush and George W. Bush. Nationally, the GOP made a concerted effort in the late 1980s and 1990s to challenge the Democratic Party's long-standing claim on the political loyalties of African Americans.

To some extent, members of the Caucus also found themselves struggling against the efforts of some more conservative Democratic leaders to move the party toward the center of the political spectrum as a way of countering Republican gains. Caucus members were incensed in 1993 when President Clinton withdrew his nomination of an African American law professor, Lani Guinier, to head the civil rights division of the Justice Department. Conservatives criticized some of Guinier's academic writings, labeling her a "quota queen" who had a much too liberal view of affirmative action.[2] Black Caucus members also confronted Clinton over some of his federal budget proposals, which they felt cut too deeply into crucial social services (**Document 7.3**).

Despite their occasional differences, however, members of the Caucus were remarkably close to Clinton, joking at a Caucus-sponsored dinner after Clinton left office that he had been America's "first black president." [3] Caucus members also were among Clinton's most loyal and vocal supporters when the president's sexual relationship with intern Monica Lewinsky became a scandal that evolved into impeachment proceedings in Congress. Several Caucus members helped draft a minority report in the House Judiciary Committee (**Document 7.5**) that argued

Vice President Al Gore delivers remarks at the Congressional Black Caucus's swearing-in ceremony in Washington, D.C., on January 3, 2001. Three days later Gore presided over a joint session of Congress called to ratify the electoral college votes in the 2000 presidential election. As the Senate president, he was forced to repeatedly rule out of order the efforts of Caucus members who sought to challenge the Florida results with the goal of making him president. First row, from left: Gore and Reps. Gregory W. Meeks, D-N.Y., Bobby L. Rush, D-Ill., and Sheila Jackson-Lee, D-Texas. Second row, from left: Reps. Juanita Millender-McDonald, D-Calif., Charles B. Rangel, D-N.Y., Major R. O. Owens, D-N.Y., and Edolphus Towns, D-N.Y. Third row, from left: Del. Eleanor Holmes Norton, D-D.C., and Reps. Maxine Waters, D-Calif., Eva M. Clayton, D-N.C., Sanford D. Bishop Jr., D-Ga., and Corrine Brown, D-Fla.
Source: AP Images/Kamenko Pajic

strenuously against adoption of the proposed articles of impeachment, and some of them also appended their own personal statements to the report. Still others made their opposition known during the floor debate over the articles that were eventually approved by the House.

Caucus members also were stalwarts in the campaign to get Clinton's vice president, Al Gore, nominated as the Democratic presidential candidate in 2000. Later, in that year's post-election maneuvering, their support for Gore merged with their anger over what they alleged were illegal efforts to suppress the black vote in Florida and elsewhere on election day. The battle over voting procedures and vote tallies in Florida became one of the most heated in American political history, and it took a ruling from a sharply divided U.S. Supreme Court to halt the Florida vote recounts, effectively giving Republican George W. Bush the presidency. Even then, however, the Caucus did not give up the fight. In early January 2001, when Congress met to certify the votes of the electoral college, some Caucus members tried repeatedly—but unsuccessfully—to challenge the votes from Florida (**Document 7.6**).

Between 1991 and 2007, African Americans in Congress sought to advance social issues of concern to their constituents, such as education (**Documents 7.7 and 7.9**), domestic abuse, and protection from racially motivated violence. But the battle over the 2000 Florida election underscored in the minds of many that the gains of African Americans in previous decades could not be taken for granted. The Caucus played a major role in the effort that led, in mid-2006, to a twenty-five-year renewal of the Voting Rights Act of 1965 (**Document 7.10**). The bill as passed did face opposition from some who argued that a renewed act should be amended to apply to all states, and not simply southern ones that had a past history of voting irregularities. Some legislators also opposed provisions for multilingual ballots. To some Caucus members, the debate echoed strongly the original resistance to the law forty years earlier. In an interview, Rep. John R. Lewis, D-Ga., said:

> I'm shocked, I'm surprised, and I'm also very saddened, to relive some of these issues over again, using some of the same language that was used in the 1950s and 1960s . . . I do believe there is a deliberate, systematic attempt to deny certain groups in our population access to the ballot, to limit the participation of more people in the political process.[4]

Opposed by only a handful of legislators, the renewal bill passed with overwhelming bipartisan support in both houses of Congress, giving new life to a landmark accomplishment. President George W. Bush signed it into law on July 27, 2006.

Document 7.1 in Context
"Chairman Thomas 'Demonstrated an Overall Disdain for the Rule of Law' ": Opposition to the Supreme Court Nomination of Clarence Thomas

In 1991 Republican president George H. W. Bush nominated Clarence Thomas, an African American, to a seat on the U.S. Supreme Court, setting off a controversy that became one of the most heated and racially charged in the history of federal judicial appointments. The conflict pitted the Congressional Black Caucus and a variety of African American organizations identified with the civil rights movement of the 1950s and 1960s against the conservative Republicans who had held the White House for nearly twelve years and who would, within three years, claim control of Congress.

The televised Senate confirmation hearings on the Thomas nomination captivated public attention—and were etched in the public memory—when Anita Hill, a law professor who was a former subordinate of Thomas's at the Equal Employment Opportunity Commission, testified that Thomas had sexually harassed her while working at the EEOC. Hill's testimony, which came very late in the confirmation process, quickly transformed the hearings into a morality play with Hill's allegations that Thomas had used crude sexual innuendo in his conversations with her, had told dirty jokes in her presence, and had discussed pornographic videos he had rented. Thomas passionately denied the allegations and denounced the attack on his nomination as a "high-tech lynching." His supporters launched their own energetic assault on Hill's credibility.

The high-intensity coverage of he-said-she-said sexual politics obscured the more profound battle that had been raging for months over deep-seated political and racial issues. Democrats did not view Thomas as merely a Republican federal appeals court judge being recommended for a promotion; they also considered him to be intensely conservative. Many expected him to become a key vote against abortion rights if confirmed, and before becoming a judge he had been critical of welfare, affirmative action and a wide range of other programs supported by many African American civil rights leaders and organizations. Moreover, he would not fill just any seat: the vacancy had been left by the resignation of Justice Thurgood Marshall, the first African American Supreme Court justice and an almost mythic figure in the civil rights movement. Marshall had led the legal team for the National Association for the Advancement of Colored People to victory in the landmark 1954 case,

Brown v. Board of Education (**Document 5.9**), in which the Supreme Court had ruled racial segregation in public schools unconstitutional. The fact that Thomas had criticized that ruling rankled many civil rights activists.

The letter below, signed by the chairs of a dozen House committees and subcommittees, including four members of the Caucus, was written before Hill's testimony became the focal point of the confirmation hearings and challenges Thomas's suitability for the Court on the basis of his record on civil rights issues.

▬ Document 7.1 ▬
Letter by House Committee Chairs Opposing the Appointment of Clarence Thomas to the U.S. Supreme Court

Washington, D.C.
September 11, 1991

Hon. Joseph R. Biden Jr.,
Chairman, Committee on the Judiciary,
Dirksen Senate Office Building,
Washington, D.C.

Dear Senator Biden:

In 1989, we wrote to President Bush urging him not to appoint Clarence Thomas to the U.S. Court of Appeals for the District of Columbia. We made this recommendation as chairpersons of the congressional committees and subcommittees overseeing the Equal Employment Opportunity Commission (EEOC). We were troubled by his record as Chair of that agency—a record which we believed raised serious questions about his judgment, respect for the law and general suitability to serve as a member of the Federal judiciary. We now write to express our strong opposition to his nomination to the United States Supreme Court.

In our letter to the President, we said we believed Chairman Thomas developed policy directives and enforcement strategies which undermined Title VII of the 1964 Civil Rights Act and the Age Discrimination in Employment Act (ADEA). A copy of that letter is enclosed for your review.

Since being nominated several weeks ago, a number of reports on Judge Thomas have been released by civil rights organizations and the press. These reports have analyzed his opinions on issues critical to the elimination of discrimination against minorities, women and the elderly, and his tenure at EEOC and the Department of Education's civil rights office. Our comments are confined to the nominee's conduct as a high-ranking federal official.

The reports show a radical switch in his views on Supreme Court affirmative action decisions, including court ordered affirmative action to remedy past discrimination. Judge Thomas supported a majority of these decisions in his early tenure at EEOC. But in 1985, he challenged the holding in *Griggs v. Duke Power* (barring employer use of discriminatory practices that are unrelated to job performance). By 1987, he denounced *Bakke v. Regents of University of California* (permitting colleges and universities to consider race to insure diversity in admissions, but prohibiting rigid admission quotas). If a majority of the Court were to join Judge Thomas in rejecting these fundamental principles it would greatly damage the hard fought guarantee of equal opportunity embodied in our Constitution and federal civil rights laws.

Our previous letter offered the following criticisms: "his public statements supporting equal employment opportunity conflict(ed) with his directives to agency staff" and he "resisted congressional oversight and (was) less than candid with legislators about agency enforcement policies."

We urge you to review in more detail his record of resistance at the EEOC. And, we encourage you to consider his defiance of the *Adams* order while Assistant Secretary for Civil Rights at the Department of Education (Legal Times, Week of August 19, 1991).

Two years ago, we concluded Chairman Thomas "demonstrated an overall disdain for the rule of law." More recent, detailed reports reaffirm that conclusion. For that reason we conclude Judge Thomas should not be confirmed as Associate Justice of the United States Supreme Court. His confirmation would be harmful to that court and to the nation.

Sincerely,

Don Edwards, Chairman, Subcommittee on Civil and Constitutional Rights; Edward R. Roybal, Chairman, Select Committee on Aging; John Conyers, Chairman, Committee on Government Operations; William (Bill) Clay, Chairman, Committee on Post Office and Civil Service; Patricia Schroeder, Chairwoman, Armed Services Subcommittee on Military Installations and Facilities; Gerry Sikorski, Chairman, Post Office and Civil Service Subcommittee on Civil Service; Cardiss Collins, Chairwoman, Energy and Commerce Subcommittee on Commerce, Consumer Protection and Competitiveness; Matthew G. Martinez, Chairman, Education and Labor Subcommittee on Human Resources; Tom Lantos, Chairman, Government Operations Subcommittee on Employment and Housing; Barbara Boxer, Chairwoman, Government Operations Subcommittee on Government Activities and Transportation; Pat Williams, Chairman, Education and Labor Subcommittee on Labor-Management Relations; Charles A. Hayes, Chairman, Post Office and Civil Service, Subcommittee on Postal Personnel and Modernization.

Source: Congressional Record, 102d Cong., 1st sess., October 7, 1991, vol. 137, pt. 18, 25668.

Document 7.2 in Context
"A Detailed Agenda for National Renewal": The Republican Contract with America Reshapes Congress

Three hundred Republican members of and candidates for the House of Representatives running in the election that was just six weeks away gathered on September 27, 1994, on the steps of the U.S. Capitol to sign the Republican Contract with America. The document pledged the Republican House members and would-be members to support a ten-point legislative plan for a constitutional amendment requiring a balanced federal budget as well as tax cuts, welfare reform, anticrime legislation and term limits on legislators, among other things.

How much impact the signing ceremony and the Contract with America actually had on the 1994 election is debatable. The announcement came relatively late in the campaign, and polls conducted shortly before and after the election indicated that relatively few voters were even aware of the document. But whatever its influence, the Republicans did capture both chambers of Congress for the first time in forty years, and the Contract with America became the blueprint for a sweeping legislative program launched by the new Speaker of the House, Newt Gingrich, R-Ga.

In the first 100 days of its opening 1995 session, the House voted on all ten pieces of legislation called for in the contract, and nine were passed. Only the proposal for a constitutional amendment establishing term limits for members of Congress was rejected. Senate Republicans, however, were less supportive of the legislation, and many Democrats in both chambers strenuously resisted proposals that threatened to undo certain social programs. President Bill Clinton also threatened to veto some of the legislation if it passed both the House and Senate.

Members of the Congressional Black Caucus, meanwhile, found themselves fighting to protect gains that had been made since the mid-1960s. In particular, Caucus members worried that welfare reforms and budget balancing measures called for in the GOP legislation would undercut programs that had been particularly beneficial to poor African Americans. Not only were Caucus members in the minority party in Congress, but some of their more conservative Democratic colleagues were willing to compromise with the Republican proposals. Rep. John R. Lewis, D-Ga., outlined for *Ebony* magazine the effects of the power shift from the perspective of the Caucus:

> The Republican victory is a major setback for Black Americans because as a whole, the leaders who are taking over have been insensitive to the problems, the needs and concerns of African-Americans. Our progress toward full political participation has been sidetracked or derailed, maybe for at least two years. We're losing three to four chairmanships. There would have been more than 16 subcommittee chairs. I will no longer be chief majority whip in the leadership of the House, although I may play some other role in the minority. But we really become a minority within a minority.[5]

On the other side of the aisle, however, the two African American Republican members of the House, J. C. Watts Jr. of Oklahoma and Gary A. Franks of Connecticut, supported the Contract with America and the legislative agenda it laid out.

For more than a decade, the Republican Contract with America defined the social and economic agendas of Congress. It opened the way for legislation that challenged the Democrats in general and the members of the Congressional Black Caucus in particular.

▬ Document 7.2 ▬
Republican Contract with America, September 27, 1994

As Republican Members of the House of Representatives and as citizens seeking to join that body we propose not just to change its policies, but even more important, to restore the bonds of trust between the people and their elected representatives.

That is why, in this era of official evasion and posturing, we offer instead a detailed agenda for national renewal, a written commitment with no fine print.

This year's election offers the chance, after four decades of one-party control, to bring to the House a new majority that will transform the way Congress works. That historic change would be the end of government that is too big, too intrusive, and too easy with the public's money. It can be the beginning of a Congress that respects the values and shares the faith of the American family.

Like Lincoln, our first Republican president, we intend to act "with firmness in the right, as God gives us to see the right." To restore accountability to Congress. To end its cycle of scandal and disgrace. To make us all proud again of the way free people govern themselves.

On the first day of the 104th Congress, the new Republican majority will immediately pass the following major reforms, aimed at restoring the faith and trust of the American people in their government:

- FIRST, require all laws that apply to the rest of the country also apply equally to the Congress;
- SECOND, select a major, independent auditing firm to conduct a comprehensive audit of Congress for waste, fraud or abuse;
- THIRD, cut the number of House committees, and cut committee staff by one-third;
- FOURTH, limit the terms of all committee chairs;
- FIFTH, ban the casting of proxy votes in committee;
- SIXTH, require committee meetings to be open to the public;
- SEVENTH, require a three-fifths majority vote to pass a tax increase;
- EIGHTH, guarantee an honest accounting of our Federal Budget by implementing zero base-line budgeting.

Thereafter, within the first 100 days of the 104th Congress, we shall bring to the House Floor the following bills, each to be given full and open debate, each to be given a clear and fair vote and each to be immediately available this day for public inspection and scrutiny.

1. THE FISCAL RESPONSIBILITY ACT: A balanced budget/tax limitation amendment and a legislative line-item veto to restore fiscal responsibility to an out-of-control Congress, requiring them to live under the same budget constraints as families and businesses.
2. THE TAKING BACK OUR STREETS ACT: An anti-crime package including stronger truth-in-sentencing, "good faith" exclusionary rule exemptions, effective death penalty provisions, and cuts in social spending from this summer's "crime" bill to fund prison construction and additional law enforcement to keep people secure in their neighborhoods and kids safe in their schools.
3. THE PERSONAL RESPONSIBILITY ACT: Discourage illegitimacy and teen pregnancy by prohibiting welfare to minor mothers and denying increased AFDC [Aid to Families With Dependent Children] for additional children while on welfare, cut spending for welfare programs, and enact a tough two-years-and-out provision with work requirements to promote individual responsibility.
4. THE FAMILY REINFORCEMENT ACT: Child support enforcement, tax incentives for adoption, strengthening rights of parents in their children's education, stronger child pornography laws, and an elderly dependent care tax credit to reinforce the central role of families in American society.
5. THE AMERICAN DREAM RESTORATION ACT: A $500 per child tax credit, begin repeal of the marriage tax penalty, and creation of American Dream Savings Accounts to provide middle class tax relief.

6. THE NATIONAL SECURITY RESTORATION ACT: No U.S. troops under U.N. command and restoration of the essential parts of our national security funding to strengthen our national defense and maintain our credibility around the world.

7. THE SENIOR CITIZENS FAIRNESS ACT: Raise the Social Security earnings limit which currently forces seniors out of the work force, repeal the 1993 tax hikes on Social Security benefits and provide tax incentives for private long-term care insurance to let Older Americans keep more of what they have earned over the years.

8. THE JOB CREATION AND WAGE ENHANCEMENT ACT: Small business incentives, capital gains cut and indexation, neutral cost recovery, risk assessment/cost-benefit analysis, strengthening the Regulatory Flexibility Act and unfunded mandate reform to create jobs and raise worker wages.

9. THE COMMON SENSE LEGAL REFORM ACT: "Loser pays" laws, reasonable limits on punitive damages and reform of product liability laws to stem the endless tide of litigation.

10. THE CITIZEN LEGISLATURE ACT: A first-ever vote on term limits to replace career politicians with citizen legislators.

Further, we will instruct the House Budget Committee to report to the floor and we will work to enact additional budget savings, beyond the budget cuts specifically included in the legislation described above, to ensure that the Federal budget deficit will be less than it would have been without the enactment of these bills.

Respecting the judgment of our fellow citizens as we seek their mandate for reform, we hereby pledge our names to this Contract with America.

Source: "Republican Contract with America," from the U.S. House of Representatives, www.house. gov/house/Contract/CONTRACT.html.

Document 7.3 in Context
"The Essential Tools Recipients Need to Move from Welfare to Work": The Battle over Welfare Reform

In his first State of the Union address in 1993, Democratic president Bill Clinton received a loud round of bipartisan applause when he pledged to "end welfare as we know it." It was a campaign promise he had made as he sought to change the image of the Democratic Party and appeal to centrist and conservative voters. Democrats had long been attacked by Republicans generally, and conservatives in particular, as the party of big-spending programs, and welfare was one of the prime pieces of evidence to which critics pointed. Republicans were critical of welfare because they believed that the existing system bred dependency on the part of welfare recipients and actually encouraged them to remain unemployed. "We have to end welfare as a way of life and make it a path to independence and dignity," Clinton said in his speech.[6]

But the Clinton administration did not press the issue of welfare reform during the president's first two years in office, emphasizing health care and deficit reduction issues instead. So in 1994, Republican congressional candidates took the initiative, making welfare reform a central feature of their proposed legislative agenda, the Republican Contract with America

(**Document 7.2**). When the 1994 elections resulted in a Republican majority in Congress for the first time in forty years, House GOP members moved aggressively to enact the contract.

The welfare legislation sparked heated debate. The GOP proposal called for sharp cuts in welfare spending, prohibited welfare payments to mothers younger than eighteen or increases in payments to mothers who had additional children while already receiving welfare, required welfare recipients to work or lose benefits, and barred anyone from receiving benefits for more than two years. Critics called the proposal cruel and unfairly punitive, and Clinton vetoed two bills before Congress passed a compromise that softened some elements of the Republicans' plan.

The document that follows is a statement by Rep. Sanford D. Bishop Jr., D-Ga., the conservative "Blue Dog" Congressional Black Caucus member, in support of the compromise legislation that was signed several weeks later.

Document 7.3
Rep. Sanford D. Bishop Jr., D-Ga., Supports the Personal Responsibility and Work Opportunity Act, July 31, 1996

Mr. BISHOP: Mr. Speaker, I rise today in support of H.R. 3734, the Balanced Budget Reconciliation/Welfare Reform Act. We must set forth a vision for our country. We want an America that gives all Americans the chance to live out their dreams and achieve their God-given potential. We want an America that is still the world's strongest force for peace and freedom. And we want an America that comes together around our enduring values instead of drifting apart.

For the past 4 years, President Clinton and the Democrats in Congress have worked for a responsible, commonsense agenda to revitalize core American values: work, personal responsibility, opportunity, and a stronger family and community life for everyone. We are on the right track, and we must make sure the country continues moving toward an economically secure, militarily strong, more compassionate, and a more fiscally responsible future.

Our country is at a historic crossroads. We can go to the left and return to an irresponsible non-sense agenda that is antiwork, antiopportuntiy, antifamily and that breeds insecurity, dependency, and despair. We can go to the right and abruptly and cynically abandon our commitment to a safety net for children, seniors, and the disabled. Or we can go straight ahead, following the leadership of President Clinton—each of us, individually and all of us collectively as a Nation—in the direction of prudence and responsibility.

Welfare reform is a monumental example. While there are those who fear that going forward to implement welfare reform will destroy the safety net of security for poor children, seniors, and the disabled, I believe that not to go forward would cause us to aimlessly drift farther away from the core American values of work, personal responsibility, opportunity, stronger families and communities. By going forward with welfare reform, we are ridding ourselves of a system that does not conform to our Nation's guiding principles and replacing it with a new system which will provide the essential tools recipients need to move from welfare to work.

This is the beginning of a process that can transform welfare into an opportunity rather than a way of life.

It is about giving a hand-up rather than a hand-out.

It is about requiring and rewarding work while providing access to job skills and expanded job opportunities.

It is about providing essential child care and health care to give working families a sense of security about the well-being of their children.

It is about cracking down on deadbeat parents and those who abuse the system—but not on innocent children.

It is about creating a welfare system that makes sense.

This means a system that maintains a fair, efficient, and responsible safety net for individuals and families in critical need and one which empowers people to move out of the shadows of poverty and into a bright new day of productivity and hope.

As one who has worked on welfare reform for many years—first in the Georgia General Assembly, where I helped write the PEACH (Positive Employment and Community Help) program, our State's innovative welfare-to-work plan. And now in Congress—I know how challenging the status quo can be.

The proposals originally pushed by Republicans were too weak on work and too tough on children and families. They would have block granted and drastically underfunded the food stamp and school lunch programs; denied Medicaid to our most vulnerable citizens; and would have failed to provide adequate funding for work programs and child care.

With the strong leadership and perseverance of President Clinton and congressional Democrats, we fought them. And we succeeded. When faced with the realization that Americans want a system that promotes work and responsibility but not the mean-spirited proposals they were pushing, the Republicans conceded.

The law we finally enacted is certainly not perfect. It goes too far in cutting nutritional assistance and cuts off aid to legal immigrants who have worked hard and paid taxes. It has its shortcomings and uncertainties. These we must resolve and correct. I plan to work with the President and the Members of this body to do just that.

Passing this legislation is not enough. We must now make sure all Americans have the skills they need to get jobs. We must now make sure that jobs are available so all Americans can go to work. We must now make sure that all Americans are empowered with the tools they need to help themselves to realize their dreams and achieve their God-given potential. We must ensure that the American value of personal responsibility as embodied in this bill will not be a stumbling block but a stepping-stone to a better quality of life for all Americans.

Again, I urge my colleagues to support this bill.

Source: Congressional Record, 104th Cong., 2d sess., July 31, 1996, E1539.

Document 7.4 in Context
"To Limit the Claims and Demands of Washington": Rep. J. C. Watts Jr. Speaks for the Republican Party

Every African American elected to Congress during the nineteenth century was a Republican, as was the first African American elected in the twentieth century, Oscar S. De Priest of Illinois. After De Priest left office in January 1935, however, only four more black Republicans served as members of Congress during the century—one in the Senate and three in the House. Even after the Voting Rights Act of 1965 (**Document 6.1**) sparked a dramatic upsurge in black representation, there was never more than one African American Republican in Congress at one time until Republican J. C. Watts Jr. of Oklahoma was elected in 1994: Watts, who began the first of his four terms in January 1995, joined Rep. Gary A. Franks, R-Conn., who was in his third term. The other forty-two African Americans in Congress were all Democrats, and Watts pointedly declined to join the Congressional Black Caucus because he saw no point in being consistently outvoted; Franks, though, was a member.

Watts and Franks reflected a growing African American presence in the GOP. Conservative African Americans—commentators such as Shelby Steele, activists like Ward Connerly, jurists like Clarence Thomas and high-level appointees such as Colin Powell and Condoleezza Rice—were increasingly prominent in Republican circles as the party's conservative agenda became a force in national politics during the 1980s and early 1990s. Watts was among the 300 GOP candidates who signed the Republican Contract with America (**Document 7.2**) that became a focal point of the GOP campaign in 1994 and helped his party capture a majority of the seats in Congress for the first time in forty years.

A charismatic and articulate former college football star, Watts represented a predominantly white district, and his political skills and voter appeal helped him rise rapidly into the party leadership. By his third term in the House, he was elected chair of the GOP House Conference, the number four party leadership post. He was selected by the Republicans to deliver the GOP's broadcast response, excerpted here, to Democratic President Bill Clinton's February 4, 1997, State of the Union address.

▬ Document 7.4 ▬
Rep. J. C. Watts Jr., R-Okla., Delivers the GOP Reply to President Bill Clinton's State of the Union Address, February 4, 1997

Good evening.

My name is J. C. Watts Jr. I'm the Republican Congressman from the Fourth District of Oklahoma, and I've been asked to speak to the American people in response to the president's address this evening . . .

I grew up in Oklahoma. My district includes the towns of Midwest City, Norman, Lawton, Walters, Waurika and Duncan, just to name a few. We raise cattle back home, we grow some cotton and wheat, peanuts, and we drill for oil.

We've got Tinker and Altus Air Force Bases nearby, and we have the Army post at Fort Sill. The University of Oklahoma is there. That's where I went to school. I played a little football and graduated with a degree in journalism. I tell you all this because I want you to know that the district I'm blessed to represent is as diverse as America itself.

It's the kind of place reporters usually call the heartland, and they're right—in so many ways, it is America's heart.

I'm going to try to use my words tonight, and my time, not to confuse issues but to clarify them, not to obscure my philosophy and my party's but to illuminate it. Because the way I see it, the purpose of politics is to lead, not to mislead.

Those of us who have been sent to Washington have a moral responsibility to offer more than poll-tested phrases and winning smiles. We must offer a serious vision. We must share our intentions. We must make our plans clear. That's my job tonight: to tell you what we believe—what the Republican Party believes, and what we will work for.

We believe first of all that the state of this union really isn't determined in Washington, D.C. It never has been, and it never will be. But for a long time the Federal Government has been grabbing too much power and too much authority over all of the people. And it is those people, it is all of us, who decide the real state of the Union.

Doc Benson in Oklahoma City decides the state of the union. He runs a nonprofit called the Education and Employment Ministry, where he believes that you restore men and women by restoring their dreams and finding them a job.

Freddy Garcia is the state of the union, also. Freddy was a drug addict in San Antonio, Tex. Now he has a ministry helping people get off drugs. His Victory Fellowship has success rates that the social scientists can only dream of.

I saw the state of the union last week in Marlow, Okla. A bunch of us met at the elementary school, where we ate beef brisket and baked beans, and the Chamber of Commerce recognized the Farm Family of the Year. The McCarleys won and their kids were oh so proud.

The strength of America is not in Washington. The strength of America is at home in lives well lived in the land of faith and family. The strength of America is not on Wall Street but on Main Street, not in big business but in small businesses with local owners and workers. It's not in Congress, it's in the city hall. And I pray Republicans and Democrats both understand this. We shouldn't just say it—we should live it.

And so we have made it our mission to limit the claims and demands of Washington, to limit its call for more power, more authority and more taxes. Our mission is to return power to your home, to where mothers and fathers can exercise it according to their beliefs.

So let me tell you three actions the Republicans will take in the coming year.

First, we can help our country by bringing back the knowledge, the ancient wisdom, that we're nothing without our spiritual, traditional and family values. The Republicans will take action to give those values a bigger place in solving America's problems. After all, our values are more important to our future than any so-called bureaucratic breakthrough . . .

I wasn't raised to be Republican or Democrat. My parents just taught by example. They taught me and my brothers and sisters that if you lived under their roof, you were going to work. They taught us if you made a mistake, as we all do, you've got to own up to it, you call it what it is and you try to turn it around. They taught us if you spend more money than you make, you're on a sure road to disaster.

I was taught to respect everyone for the simple reason that we're all God's children. I was taught, in the words of Dr. Martin Luther King Jr. and from my uncle Wade Watts, to judge a man not by the color of his skin but by the content of his character. And I was taught that character does count and that character is simply doing what's right when nobody's looking . . .

So our first priority is to bring values back, and give them pride of place in our moral and economic renewal, and in the next few weeks we will be visiting a number of communities to highlight the accomplishments of active faith-based organizations.

The second thing Republicans will do is face a problem that demands immediate attention. We must get our Government's financial affairs in order. The biggest step in that direction is an amendment to the U.S. Constitution that demands that the federal government balance its books.

We are more than $5 trillion in debt. This year we will spend $330 billion on interest payments alone on the national debt. And you know what? Not one dime of that $330 billion will go to strengthen Medicare, Medicaid. Not one dime of it will go to find a cure for cancer or fight drugs and crime. And worse yet, not one dime will go toward learning, making the classrooms a centerpiece of our education.

Over $5 trillion worth of national debt is more than financially irresponsible. Friends, it's immoral, because someone is going to have to pay the piper. And you know who it's going to be? It's going to be our kids and our grandkids . . .

The balanced budget amendment will force the government to change its ways—permanently.

No longer will the president or Congress be able to spend money we don't have on benefits our children will never see . . .

Third and finally, I want to say a few words about the Republican vision of how we can continue to make this "one nation under God, indivisible, with liberty and justice for all."

You know, I'm just old enough to remember the Jim Crow brand of discrimination. I've seen issues of race hurt human beings and hurt our entire nation. Too often when we talk about racial healing, we make the old assumption that government can heal the racial divide.

In my lifetime there have been some great and good laws that took some evil and ignorant laws off the books. So legislation has its place. But friends, we're at a point now where we have to ask ourselves some questions, and I ask you—if legislation is the answer to the racial divide in our nation, then why in God's name in our time has the division grown? Why is the healing we long for so far from reality? Why does it seem that the more laws we pass, the less love we have?

The fact is, our problems can't be solved by legislation alone. Surely we have learned from our long, difficult journey a great truth: government can't ease all the pain. We must deal with the heart of man.

Republicans and Democrats—red, yellow, black and white—have to understand that we must individually, all of us, accept our share of responsibility. We must decide, as we stand on the edge of the new age, if we will be a captive of the past. America must be a place where all of us—red, yellow, black and white—in some way feel a part of the American dream. It does not happen by dividing us into racial groups. It does not happen by trying to turn rich against poor or by using the politics of fear. It does not happen by reducing our values to the lowest common denominator. And friends, it does not happen by asking Americans to accept what's immoral and wrong in the name of tolerance . . .

I am reminded of the final words of President John Kennedy's inaugural address. He said this: "Let us go forth to lead the land we love, knowing that here on earth, God's work must truly be our own." I say amen to that.

Thank you for your graciousness in listening to me so late in the evening. God bless you, and God bless our children. And thank you very much.

Source: J. C. Watts Jr., "Republican Response: Watts Asks Voters to Demand Balanced-Budget Amendment," February 4, 1997, transcript, *CQ Weekly Online*, February 8, 1997, 385–386, http://library.cq press.com/cqweekly.

Document 7.5 in Context
"History Will Judge Not Only the Conduct of the President but the Conduct of This Committee": Black Democrats Defend President Clinton against Impeachment

Nothing inflamed American politics in the 1990s—an era of intense partisanship and ideological tidal shifts—like the impeachment of President Bill Clinton. Clinton had sought to carve out a new centrist position for the Democratic Party by blending fiscal conservatism with social progressivism. But midway through his second term, his hold on the White House was threatened when the allegations of extramarital affairs that had dogged him since his first campaign for the presidency in 1992 erupted first into a full-fledged scandal and then into a constitutional crisis.

Clinton was accused of having an affair with a young White House intern named Monica Lewinsky and then lying about it under oath. Although media reports often focused on sensational and tawdry aspects of the president's alleged sexual activities, the debate over impeachment turned on much more complex issues of legal process: whether he had committed perjury and obstructed justice. In 1994 Clinton was sued by a former Arkansas state employee named Paula Jones, who alleged he had sexually harassed her while he was governor of the state. During his deposition for the Jones case, Clinton denied having "sexual relations" with Lewinsky. Jones's suit was eventually dismissed—then settled while the dismissal was being appealed—but Clinton's testimony became a key focus of Independent Counsel Kenneth Starr's investigation and the grand jury that was impaneled to look into the matter. When evidence surfaced that Clinton had, in fact, had sexual contact with Lewinsky, Republicans in Congress accused Clinton of perjury and obstruction of justice.

In September 1998 Starr turned in his report, referring the matter to the House of Representatives; in November House Republicans launched hearings. The president's behavior, the Republicans argued, amounted to an obstruction of justice so serious that impeachment and removal from office were warranted and necessary. Democrats expressed shock and disapproval over Clinton's behavior, but contended that it did not rise to the level of "high crimes and misdemeanors" set out as the standard for impeachment by the Constitution.

In the House debate over articles of impeachment, members of the Congressional Black Caucus were among Clinton's most ardent supporters. Clinton was popular among African Americans because of his attentiveness to their economic and social concerns and his appointment of more blacks and other minorities to high-level administration positions than any previous president. At a Caucus awards dinner in 2001, after Clinton had left office, the Caucus chair, Rep. Eddie Bernice Johnson, D-Texas, lauded Clinton's presidency. She said Clinton "took so many initiatives he made us think for a while we had elected the first black president." [7]

Caucus members were steadfast in their support for Clinton during the impeachment debate. Rep. Barbara Lee, D-Calif., argued that the impeachment and the process that led to it "are the real crimes against the American people and our democracy." [8] However, the sole African American Republican in Congress, J. C. Watts Jr. of Oklahoma, voted with his party in favor of impeachment. He said a decent respect for honesty and the law, and a concern for the future of America's children required impeachment: "If we do not label lawlessness, our children cannot recognize it. And if we do not punish lawlessness, our children will not believe it." [9]

The following document includes excerpts from the minority report issued by Democratic members of the House Judiciary Committee opposing the articles of impeachment recommended to the full House by the committee's Republican majority. Six members of the Congressional Black Caucus served on the committee and all signed the minority report.

▓▓ Document 7.5 ▓▓
Minority Report of the House Committee on the Judiciary on the Impeachment of President Bill Clinton, December 16, 1998

VIII. MINORITY VIEWS

For only the second time in the history of our Nation, the House is poised to impeach a sitting President. The Judiciary Committee Democrats uniformly and resoundingly dissent.

We believe that the President's conduct was wrongful in attempting to conceal an extramarital relationship. But we do not believe that the allegations that the President violated criminal laws in attempting to conceal that relationship—even if proven true—amount to the abuse of official power which is an historically rooted prerequisite for impeaching a President. Nor do we believe that the Majority has come anywhere close to establishing the impeachable misconduct alleged by the required clear and convincing evidence.

Historian Arthur Schlesinger, appearing before the Committee on November 9, 1998, explained the grave dangers of "dumbing-down" the impeachment process for largely private misconduct:

> Lowering the bar to impeachment creates a novel, indeed revolutionary theory of impeachment, a theory that would send us on an adventure with ominous implications for the separation of powers that the Constitution established as the basis of our political order.

Impeachment is like a wall around the fort of the separation of powers fundamental to our constitution; the crack we put in the wall today becomes the fissure tomorrow, which ultimately destroys the wall entirely. This process is that serious. It is so serious the wall was not even approached when President Lincoln suspended the *writ of habeas corpus,* nor when President Roosevelt misled the public in the lend-lease program, nor when there was evidence that Presidents Reagan and Bush gave misleading evidence in the Iran-contra affair.

We also note at the outset our profound disagreement with the process that the Judiciary Committee undertook to report this resolution. Without any independent examination of fact witnesses, this Committee essentially rubber-stamped a September 9th Referral from the Office of Independent Counsel (OIC). That Referral contained largely unproven allegations based on grand jury testimony—often inadmissable hearsay evidence—which was never subject to cross examination. Indeed the Committee's investigation of this material amounted to nothing more than simply releasing to the public the Referral and tens of thousands of accompanying pages of confidential grand jury material. In this regard, we decry the partisanship that accompanied this sad three month process at nearly every turn, and point out its unfortunate departure from the experience of Watergate in 1974.

There is no question that the President's actions were wrong, and that he has suffered profound and untold humiliation and pain for his actions. But it is also undeniable that, when asked squarely about his relationship with Ms. Lewinsky before the grand jury, the

President directly admitted to the improper physical relationship. The core of the charges against the President, thus, is that he did not adequately describe the intimate details of the relationship, and that his attempts to conceal his relationship amounted to a criminal conspiracy. Our review of the evidence, however, convinces us of one central fact—there is no persuasive support for the suggestion that the President perjured himself in his civil deposition or before the grand jury in any manner nearing an impeachable offense, obstructed justice, or abused the powers of his office. A few examples will make the point.

The President's statements under oath in the dismissed *Jones* case were in all likelihood immaterial to that case and would never have formed the legal basis for any investigation. The alleged perjury before the grand jury also involves petty factual disputes which have no standing as impeachment counts. The Majority further alleges that the President attempted to find Ms. Lewinsky a job in order to buy her silence. But the evidence makes clear that efforts to help Ms. Lewinsky find a job began in April 1996, long before she ever was identified as a witness in the *Jones* case. Ms. Lewinsky herself testified that "no one ever asked me to lie and I was never promised a job for my silence." Likewise, while the Majority contends that the President tried to hide gifts he had given Ms. Lewinsky, the evidence makes clear that Ms. Lewinsky—and not the President—initiated the transfer of those items to the President's secretary, Ms. Currie. Finally, while the Committee wisely rejected the abuse of power allegations brought by the OIC, it then improvidently substituted a spurious new charge of abuse largely because they did not like the President's tone in responding to the 81 questions posed by Chairman Hyde.

In this context, we also point out, that since the election of President Clinton in 1992, Congressional Republicans and the OIC have spent tens of millions of dollars of taxpayers' monies on investigations of the President—investigations which have been discredited in the eyes of the public. In the process, Congressional Republicans have perverted the powers of Congressional investigation into a political weapon, setting a dangerous precedent for future generations.

Finally, we note that there is virtual unanimity among Democrats and Republicans that the Senate will not convict President Clinton, and, thus, that the House is merely using the extraordinary powers of impeachment to express its displeasure for presidential actions. We regard this use of the impeachment sword as a perversion of our Constitutional form of government and as a dangerous arrogation of power by the Majority . . .

VI. Conclusion [of Minority Views]

After considering thousands of pages of constitutional history, evidentiary findings, and testimony of witnesses, this Committee should now be in a position to recognize not only what impeachment is, but also what it is not. Impeachment is not a means to express punitive judgements; it is not a vehicle for policing civil litigation or grand jury proceedings; and it is not a means for censuring immoral conduct. Other criminal and judicial sanctions are available for that purpose. Impeachment serves to protect the nation, not punish offenders. As the preceding dissenting views makes clear, removing the President on the basis of the record before us ill serves that national interest.

Both Majority and Minority Members agree that removal from office is appropriate only for conduct that falls within the Constitutional standards of "Treason, Bribery, or Other High Crimes and Misdemeanors." By that standard, the evidence before the Committee falls far short. Some four hundred of the nation's leading historians, and a like number of constitutional law scholars took the trouble to write to the Committee expressing their view that the President's misconduct, even if proven, would not satisfy constitutional require- ments for removal from office. As Harvard Law Professor Lawrence Tribe's statement at the November 9 hearings made clear, "weakening the presidency through watering down the basic meaning of "high Crimes and Misdemeanors seems a singularly ill conceived . . . way of backing into a new—and for us untested—form of government."

Majority members of the Committee repeatedly insisted that their role in impeachment proceedings was to protect "the Rule of Law." If so, the appropriate means would be adher- ence to constitutional standards and basic requirements of procedural fairness and due process. The Committee's own inquiry, and the Independent Counsel's Referral, all far short of those requirements.

As Minority Members of the Committee recognized, the President is not above the law. But neither is he beneath its protections. He is entitled to fair notice of the charges and an unbiased investigation as to their support. The Independent Counsel's Referral and the resulting Articles of Impeachment provide neither. The ethical violations by OIC prosecu- tors and their failure to provide the Committee with exculpatory materials calls into ques- tion the quality and credibility of the information they provided. Since the Committee itself called no fact witnesses and conducted no independent investigation, its record fails to sup- ply the clear and convincing evidence necessary to support impeachment.

In the long run, history will judge not only the conduct of the President but the conduct of this Committee. Because its proceedings fail to conform to fundamental constitutional standards, Minority Members respectfully dissent . . .

Source: House Committee on the Judiciary, *Impeachment of William Jefferson Clinton, President of the United States,* 105th Cong., 2d sess., December 16, 1998, H. Rep. 105-830, 200–201, 277–278, from the U.S. Government Printing Office, www.gpoaccess.gov/serialset/creports/index.html.

Document 7.6 in Context
"I Rise on Behalf of the Congressional Black Caucus to Object": Congressional Black Caucus Members Challenge the 2000 Presidential Election Results

The presidential election of 2000 was one of the tightest and most controversial in U.S. his- tory. For more than a month after election day, the result was in doubt because of voting irregularities and challenges to the vote tallies in Florida. Recounts were begun and halted as Texas governor George W. Bush and his Democratic opponent, Vice President Al Gore, turned to the courts. Eventually, on December 12, a sharply divided U.S. Supreme Court ruled 5–4 that recounts of the Florida votes should stop, essentially making Bush the winner. The legal proceedings had focused on inconsistencies in the standards used by different Florida counties to conduct their vote recounts, and the Court ruled that there was not enough time to establish consistent standards before the state's deadline for certifying presidential elec- tors. Gore conceded defeat the following day, and for the first time since Benjamin Harrison was elected in 1888, a candidate captured the electoral votes necessary to become president without winning the popular vote.

The Supreme Court's decision and Gore's concession did not end the matter for mem- bers of the Congressional Black Caucus. Many African Americans were outraged by what they contended was election fraud in Florida, which they argued had disenfranchised thousands of black voters. Caucus members accused Republican elections officials in the state—where Bush's brother Jeb was governor—of manipulating election laws, improperly removing the names of voters from registration lists, producing unnecessarily complex ballots and even enlisting police to intimidate potential voters near polling places in an effort to suppress turnout in the largely black—and strongly Democratic—precincts of south Florida. Republican officials denied the charges.

Black members of Congress said the voting problems in Florida negated 135 years of work to ensure that African Americans' voices were heard and their votes counted. Rep. Eddie Bernice Johnson, D-Texas, asked,

> How long will we settle for injustice in America? How long will we have to fight to perfect the 15th Amendment? How long will we have to struggle for something that should be every American's birthright? . . . There is overwhelming evidence that George W. Bush did not win this election, either by national popular vote or the Florida popular vote. As members of Congress charged with defending the constitutional principles of this country, it is our duty to challenge this vote.[10]

The focus of the Caucus's challenge was Florida's twenty-five electoral votes, which gave Bush a slender, one-vote victory in the electoral college. When a joint session of Congress convened on January 6, 2001, for the official count and ratification of the electoral college vote, Caucus members made a strenuous effort to overturn the Florida result. The moment was steeped in irony as Gore, in his role as vice president, presided over the session and found himself repeatedly forced to gavel down and rule out of order Caucus members who were trying to make him president. Democratic senators refused to sign the representatives' objections—considering the maneuver too divisive—so the objections failed to win recognition from the chair. But the repeated efforts of Caucus members to voice their outrage produced a remarkable example of political theater.

▬ Document 7.6 ▬
Black Caucus Members Challenge Florida Electoral College Votes in the 2000 Election, January 6, 2001

The VICE PRESIDENT [Al Gore]. The Chair now hands to the tellers the certificate of the electors for President and Vice President of the State of Florida, and they will read the certificate and will count and make a list of the votes cast by that State.

Mr. [Chaka] FATTAH [D-Pa.] (one of the tellers): This is the one we have all been waiting for.

We, the undersigned duly elected and serving Electors for President and Vice-President hereby certify that we have this day met in the Executive Offices of the Capitol at Tallahassee, Florida, and cast our votes for President of the United States and our votes for Vice-President of the United States and that the results are as follows: Those receiving votes for President of the United States and the number of such votes were: George W. Bush, 25. Those receiving votes for Vice-President of the United States and the number of such votes were: Dick Cheney, 25. Done at Tallahassee, the Capitol, this 18th day of December, A.D., 2000.

Signed by the pertinent electors and duly attested.

Mr. President, the certificate of the electoral vote of the State of Florida seems to be regular in form and authentic, and it appears therefrom that George W. Bush of the State of Texas received 25 votes for President and Dick Cheney of the State of Wyoming received 25 votes for Vice President.

The VICE PRESIDENT: Is there objection?

Mr. [Alcee L.] HASTINGS [D] of Florida: Mr. President, I object to the certificate from Florida.

The VICE PRESIDENT: The gentleman from Florida (Mr. HASTINGS) will present his objection. Is the gentleman's objection in writing and signed by a Member of the House of Representatives and by a Senator?

Mr. HASTINGS of Florida: Mr. President, and I take great pride in calling you that, I must object because of the overwhelming evidence of official misconduct, deliberate fraud, and an attempt to suppress voter turnout.

The VICE PRESIDENT: The Chair must remind Members that under section 18, title 3, United States Code, no debate is allowed in the joint session.

Mr. HASTINGS of Florida: Thank you, Mr. President. To answer your question, Mr. President, the objection is in writing, signed by a number of Members of the House of Representatives, but not by a Member of the Senate.

Thank you, Mr. President.

The VICE PRESIDENT: The Chair thanks the gentleman from Florida for his courtesy. Since the present objection lacks the signature of a Senator, accordingly, the objection may not be received . . .

Mrs. [Carrie P.] MEEK [D] of Florida: Mr. President, I have an objection.

The VICE PRESIDENT: Is the objection in writing and signed by a Member of the House and by a Senator?

Mrs. MEEK of Florida: Mr. President, it is in writing and signed by myself and several of my constituents from Florida. A Senator is needed, but missing.

The VICE PRESIDENT: On the basis previously stated, the objection may not be received . . .

Ms. [Corrine] BROWN [D] of Florida: Mr. President, I stand for the purpose of objecting to the counting of the vote from the State of Florida as read.

The VICE PRESIDENT: Is the objection in writing and signed by a Member of the House of Representatives and a Senator?

Ms. BROWN of Florida: Mr. President, it is in writing and signed by several House colleagues on behalf of, and myself, the 27,000 voters of Duval County, of which 16,000 of them are African Americans that were disenfranchised in this last election.

The VICE PRESIDENT: The gentlewoman will suspend . . .

Ms. EDDIE BERNICE JOHNSON [D] of Texas: Mr. President, I rise on behalf of the Congressional Black Caucus to object to the 25 electoral votes from Florida.

The VICE PRESIDENT: Does the gentlewoman state an objection, and is it in writing and signed by a Member of the House of Representatives and a Senator?

Ms. EDDIE BERNICE JOHNSON of Texas: It is in writing, signed by a number of Members of Congress, and because we received hundreds of thousands of telegrams and e-mails and telephone calls, but we do not have a Senator . . .

The VICE PRESIDENT: The Chair thanks the gentlewoman from Texas. On the previous basis stated, the objection may not be received . . .

Ms. [Maxine] WATERS [D-Calif.]: Mr. Vice President, I rise to object to the fraudulent 25 Florida electoral votes.

The VICE PRESIDENT: Is the objection in writing and signed by a Member of the House and a Senator?

Ms. WATERS: The objection is in writing, and I do not care that it is not signed by a Member of the Senate.

The VICE PRESIDENT: The Chair will advise that the rules do care, and the signature of a Senator is required . . .

Ms. [Barbara] LEE [D-Calif.]: Mr. President, I have an objection.

The VICE PRESIDENT: Is the objection in writing and signed by a Member of the House of Representatives and a Senator?

Ms. LEE: Mr. President, it is in writing and signed by myself on behalf of many of the diverse constituents in our country, especially those in the Ninth Congressional District and all American voters who recognize that the Supreme Court, not the people of the United States, decided this election.

The VICE PRESIDENT: Is the objection signed by a Senator?

Ms. LEE: Unfortunately, Mr. President, it is not signed by one single Senator . . .

Ms. [Cynthia A.] MCKINNEY [D-Ga.]: Mr. President, I object to Florida's electors, and in view of the fact that debate is not permitted in joint session and pursuant to title 3, I move that the House withdraw from the joint session in order to allow consideration of the facts surrounding the slate of electors from Florida.

The VICE PRESIDENT: The Chair will remind the Members of the joint session that even though a Member's motion may affect only one House, the statutory principle of bicameral signatures must, nevertheless, be applied . . .

Ms. WATERS: I have a motion of objection.

The VICE PRESIDENT: Is the motion in writing, and is it signed by a Member of the House of Representatives and Member of the Senate?

Ms. WATERS: The motion is in writing, Mr. President, and I rise to offer a motion to withdraw from the joint session. There is no reference to the section that you have referenced to quorum or withdrawal.

The VICE PRESIDENT: The Chair will respectfully advise the gentlewoman from California that sections 15 through 18 of title 3, as previously stated, in the opinion of the Chair and the Parliamentarians require the Chair to rule that no procedural question is to be recognized by the Presiding Officer in the joint session, even if it applies to only one House, unless presented in writing and signed by both a Representative and a Senator.

Since the Chair has been advised that the gentlewoman's motion is not signed by a Senator, on the basis previously stated, the motion may not be received . . .

Ms. [Sheila] JACKSON-LEE [D] of Texas: Mr. President, I rise to make a point of order.

The VICE PRESIDENT: Is the point of order in writing, and is it signed by a Member of the House of Representatives and a Senator?

Ms. JACKSON-LEE of Texas: Mr. President, being that this is a solemn day and a day that we are affirming the voices of the American people, we wish to delay this until a quorum has been maintained.

The VICE PRESIDENT: The gentlewoman will be advised, as all Members of the joint session will be advised, that a motion for the presence of a quorum is not in order unless it is signed by a Member of the House of Representatives and a Senator.

Since the Chair is advised that the gentlewoman's motion is not signed by a Senator, it is not received.

Ms. JACKSON-LEE of Texas: Thank you, Mr. President. It is signed by me but I do not have a Senator.

The VICE PRESIDENT: The Chair thanks the gentlewoman from Texas.

For what purpose does the gentleman from Illinois (Mr. JACKSON) rise?

Mr. [Jesse L.] JACKSON [Jr., D] of Illinois: Mr. President, I have an objection.

The VICE PRESIDENT: Is the gentleman's objection in writing and signed by a Member of the House of Representatives and a Senator?

Mr. JACKSON of Illinois: Yes, sir, I have signed it.

The VICE PRESIDENT: Is the objection signed by a Senator?

Mr. JACKSON of Illinois: Mr. President, I am objecting to the idea that votes in Florida were not counted; and it is a sad day in America, Mr. President, when we cannot find a Senator to sign these objections. New Democratic Senators will not sign the objection, Mr. President. I object.

The VICE PRESIDENT: The gentleman will suspend . . .

Mr. HASTINGS of Florida: Mr. President, point of order. Would the President advise whether or not there is an opportunity to appeal the ruling of the Chair?

The VICE PRESIDENT: This is going to sound familiar to you, to all of us . . .

Mr. HASTINGS of Florida: We did all we could, Mr. President.

The VICE PRESIDENT: The Chair thanks the gentleman from Florida . . .

Mr. JACKSON of Illinois: Mr. President, is it possible to ask at this hour for a Democratic Senator to sign one of these Democratic objections by unanimous consent? Is that within the House rules?

The VICE PRESIDENT: The Chair will advise the gentleman from Illinois that any Member of either Chamber may do as he or she wishes, so long as it is within the rules of the joint session. So it is possible, as long as it does not violate the rules, but the Chair will not entertain debate, because that is a violation of the rules of the joint session.

If there is no further objection, the Chair hands the tellers the certificates of the electors for President and Vice President of the State of Georgia, and they will read the certificate and will count and make a list of the votes cast by that State . . .

Source: Congressional Record, 107th Cong., 1st sess., January 6, 2001, H34–H36.

Document 7.7 in Context
"A *Plessy v. Ferguson* Moment": Rep. John Conyers Jr., D-Mich., Defends Affirmative Action

One of the biggest concerns facing African American public officials during the 1990s and first decade of the next century was the preservation of an important product of the civil rights movement: affirmative action. The concept goes at least as far back as Democratic president Franklin D. Roosevelt's Executive Order 8802 in 1941 (**Document 5.6**), which mandated fair employment practices in the defense industry. The term is commonly traced to Executive Order 11246, issued by Democratic president Lyndon B. Johnson on September 24, 1965, requiring that companies doing business with the federal government provide equal employment opportunities for African Americans and others who had faced discrimination in the workplace. In conjunction with the Civil Rights Act of 1964 (**Document 5.11**) and the Voting Rights Act of 1965 (**Document 6.1**), Johnson's order sought to end the century of discrimination following emancipation that had denied blacks their civil rights and had blocked them from political and economic advancement.

Johnson's order required federal contractors to "take affirmative action to ensure that applicants are employed, and that employees are treated during employment, without regard to their race, color, religion, sex or national origin." [11] The idea was to make employers consider and hire qualified workers who might otherwise have been rejected for employment because of discriminatory practices. But by the mid-1970s, lawsuits began to arise, attacking affirmative action programs as reverse bias that discriminated against whites in general, and white men in particular.

The most prominent of those cases, *Regents of the University of California v. Bakke,* reached the Supreme Court in 1978. Allan Bakke, a white applicant, sued because he was denied admission to the University of California–Davis Medical School; his suit accused the university of using a quota system that gave preference to less qualified minority students. A divided Court ultimately ordered that Bakke be admitted to the medical school but also ruled that race could be considered as one factor in university admissions.

Affirmative action programs continued to come under fire throughout the 1980s and 1990s as conservative Republicans gained increasing political power to set the nation's political agenda. But not until 2003—twenty-five years after *Bakke*—did the Supreme Court again consider a major challenge to affirmative action. A pair of cases, *Grutter v. Bollinger* and *Gratz v. Bollinger,* challenged the affirmative action procedures of the University of Michigan in its undergraduate and law school admissions programs. In its ruling, the Court reaffirmed its position in *Bakke* that race could be considered but insisted that the use of race be "narrowly tailored."

The document that follows is a statement issued by Rep. John Conyers Jr., D-Mich., as the Supreme Court prepared to hear arguments in the University of Michigan cases. Conyers shared with other Congressional Black Caucus members: the view that erosion of affirmative action programs threatened to undermine the progress that had been made since the 1950s in eliminating segregation and racial discrimination.

▬▬ Document 7.7 ▬▬
Rep. John Conyers Jr., D-Mich., Attacks Challenge to Affirmative Action, April 1, 2003

Conyers Calls Michigan Affirmative Action Argument a Plessy v. Ferguson *Moment*

Congressman John Conyers, Jr., Ranking Member of the House Judiciary Committee issued the following statement regarding this morning's Supreme Court arguments about the University of Michigan's undergraduate and law school admission programs:

"Today, we stand on the threshold of a Plessy v. Ferguson moment; a time when the position of the Supreme Court can influence the movement of this nation toward the continuing commitment of full participation for all its citizens. Or the Court can abandon the progress of 30 years in the name of a distorted equal protection claim—one that is out of touch with the social reality of our nation.

This morning's Supreme Court arguments about the University of Michigan's undergraduate and law school admission programs is by far the most important civil rights case on higher education to be considered by the Supreme Court since Regents of the University of California v. Bakke first upheld the notion of affirmative action in 1978.

Instead of supporting our affirmative action programs, the Bush administration abandoned the vision of diversity articulated by Justice Powell in favor of so-called "race-neutral" percentage plans that are now in effect in Texas, California and Florida, knowing full well that these percentage plans do not really work. This administration even rejected the argument for affirmative action made in the military's amicus brief about the importance of a fully integrated officer corp, while we are at war, with black and brown soldiers on the front line.

While minority enrollment has begun to recover from the drastic declines following the abolition of affirmative action on these campuses, it is precisely because of an increase in race conscious recruitment and financial aid—not the percentage plans. Campuses have doubled their recruitment and need-based aid just to make modest gains towards affirmative action based numbers. If anything, these percentage plans have diverted white students to the flagship campuses and minorities to the rest, attesting to the fact that this administration not only tolerates segregation, but encourages it.

Affirmative action has a special place in our colleges and universities, ensuring that future generations learn to respect and appreciate their differences and similarities. Diversity gives all students the advantage of new perspectives in the classroom and is a critical factor in building an elite university like the University of Michigan. For more than two decades, Bakke has been the law of the land and seeking diversity in education admissions has been constitutional as serving a compelling state interest.

The notion that the compelling social need for a diverse student body should be jettisoned in the name of equal protection—in a social context where discrimination exists on many planes, where funding for public schools is disparate, and where a complex interplay of social and historical conditions often perpetuate segregation—simply ignores the reality of minority America.

We as a nation are at the crossroad of continued progress in the area of civil rights. We need to ask ourselves if we are willing to backtrack to the pre-Brown [v. Board of Education] era when the races faced starkly different, and unequal worlds. Despite our increasingly diverse society, data shows that Americans of different racial and ethnic groups live largely separate lives. They live in separate neighborhoods, reside in separate communities, worship separately and attend separate elementary and secondary schools. In fact, Americans establish very few meaningful relationships across racial and ethnic lines.

The most important social issue we face in this new century is how a highly diverse social people—a people that will have no majority race by the middle of the century—can coexist and prosper together. Our diversity should be seen as our strength, not weakness. If we fall victim to backward-looking 19th Century legalistic formulas that result in the de facto segregation of American life, we will all be the worse for it."

Source: Rep. John Conyers Jr., D-Mich., "Conyers Calls Michigan Affirmative Action Argument a Plessy v. Ferguson Moment," news release, April 1, 2003, http://www.house.gov/list/press.

Document 7.8 in Context
"Judge Roberts Failed to Answer Any of Our Major Concerns":
The Congressional Black Caucus Opposes the Nomination of
John G. Roberts Jr. as Chief Justice

Fourteen years after opposing Clarence Thomas's nomination to the U.S. Supreme Court, the Congressional Black Caucus again opposed another Republican president's choice: George W. Bush's nomination of conservative federal judge John G. Roberts Jr. to serve as chief justice. While the Roberts confirmation debate lacked the controversies of the Thomas appointment, Democrats' concerns over Roberts's record on civil rights and the direction in which he would take the Court were central to the debate.

African Americans in Congress were worried when Roberts was initially nominated to replace moderate justice Sandra Day O'Connor, who had announced her retirement. But before Roberts could be confirmed to fill the O'Connor vacancy, Chief Justice William Rehnquist died and Roberts was tapped instead as the next chief justice. Opponents feared that Roberts's relative youth—he was fifty years old—would enable him to lead the Court in an increasingly conservative direction for many years. The Congressional Black Caucus worried that a Roberts-led Court might erode or reverse decades of civil rights-related gains that had been made via decisions on voting rights, school desegregation, affirmative action and the death penalty.

Rep. Melvin L. Watt, D-N.C., who was chair of the Caucus, and Delegate Eleanor Holmes Norton, D-D.C., who was chair of the Caucus's Judicial Nominations Task Force, wrote to Roberts to request a meeting so they could make their own evaluation and make their views known to the Senate "because the federal judiciary, and most especially the U.S. Supreme Court, has played an indispensable role in the continuing stride of African Americans toward full equality and equal justice under the constitution and laws of our country." [12]

When Roberts declined to meet with them, Watt issued a statement expressing Caucus members' displeasure: "We especially wanted to hear from him firsthand about the stance he has taken on affirmative action and about his efforts to limit the effectiveness of the Voting Rights Act when the Act was last renewed." [13]

Roberts did meet individually with one Caucus member, Sen. Barack Obama, D-Ill., the only African American senator. Obama voted against Roberts's confirmation. Despite the opposition of Obama and the Congressional Black Caucus, the Senate confirmed Roberts with a 78–22 vote. The document that follows is the Caucus's statement of opposition issued a few days before the confirmation vote.

▰▰▰ Document 7.8 ▰▰▰
Congressional Black Caucus Opposes Nomination of John G. Roberts Jr. as Chief Justice, September 20, 2005

(Washington, D.C.)—U.S. Representative Melvin L. Watt, Chairman of the Congressional Black Caucus (CBC), and Congresswoman Eleanor Holmes Norton, Chair of the CBC's

Judicial Task Force, issued the following statement on behalf of the CBC opposing the confirmation of Judge John Roberts, Jr. to be Chief Justice of the United States Supreme Court:

"After doing our own study of the complete record of Judge John Roberts, Jr. and of his testimony before the Senate Judiciary Committee, the CBC strongly opposes the confirmation of Judge Roberts as Chief Justice of the Supreme Court and encourages the Senate to defeat his nomination for the following reasons:

"Our review of his papers before the Senate hearing showed that the most controversial part of Judge Roberts' record was his civil rights record and views.

"The CBC requested that Judge Roberts meet with representatives of the CBC to explore the CBC's concerns about his civil rights record and views. Unfortunately, Judge Roberts and the White House rejected this request.

"Important documents that would have given a fuller picture of Judge Roberts' civil rights record and views during his federal government tenure were withheld from the Judiciary Committee and the public by the White House. Withholding documents about civil rights, an immensely important issue to the nation deeply implicating the Court, leaves the strong impression that the records would reveal positions concerning civil rights that the Senate and many Americans would find unacceptable today.

"Because of our serious concern about those parts of Judge Roberts' record and about the substantial gap left by the refusal to release other pertinent documents, the CBC submitted a list of questions concerning his civil rights record and views to the 18 members of the Senate Judiciary Committee, and requested that Judge Roberts be asked to respond to these or similar questions. We especially need clarification concerning John Roberts' repeated attempts to narrow and limit the effectiveness of the 1965 Voting Rights Act when the Act was last renewed, and an explanation concerning whether he still opposes affirmative action.

"We are pleased that most of the questions we submitted were asked by various members of the Senate Judiciary Committee. However, we were very disappointed that Judge Roberts' chose to avoid responding to the questions concerning civil rights. Instead of explaining his views on civil rights or indicating any changes, Judge Roberts chose to avoid answering these questions. His evasive responses mainly focused on his youth as a lawyer at the time and his claim to have been only a staff lawyer, when in fact throughout his service, Judge Roberts often advised and recommended Presidents Ronald Reagan and George H. W. Bush on administration policy and strategic approaches to civil rights matters, not legal issues or language. His responses only heightened our concerns.

"Judge Roberts' civil rights record and views remained the most controversial and unexplained part of his record when the Judiciary Committee hearing concluded, just as his civil rights record and views had been the most controversial part of his record when the hearing began. Judge Roberts failed to answer any of our major concerns. Service as Chief Justice of the Supreme Court is far too critical to people of color to leave these critical concerns unanswered. Therefore, the CBC strongly opposes the confirmation of Judge Roberts and urges all Senators to oppose his nomination."

Source: Congressional Black Caucus, "The Congressional Black Caucus Opposes Roberts Nomination," news release, September 20, 2005, www.house.gov/list/press/nc12_watt/pr_cbc_ 092005_ robnom.html.

Document 7.9 in Context
"A World Class Education for Every American Child": Congressional Black Caucus Members Emphasize Education Policy

Even before emancipation (**Document 2.3**), education was a high priority among African Americans. Scores of slave narratives and interviews with former slaves testify to the risks black people were willing to take to learn to read and write at a time when their learning those skills was often harshly punished. In most southern states it was illegal to teach slaves to read and write, though some slave owners occasionally ignored the law if those skills made slaves more useful in helping to operate a farm or a business. But slaves who sought to learn against their owners' wishes—or who sought to share reading and writing skills they already had with other slaves—might be beaten, maimed or even killed. Later, legal efforts to ensure education quality for black children led to the landmark Supreme Court decision in *Brown v. Board of Education* (**Document 5.9**), which declared racial segregation in public schools unconstitutional—a triumph of the civil rights movement. And at the end of the twentieth century and start of the twenty-first, education remained a top concern for African American members of Congress.

Increasing global economic competition sharpened public awareness of the need for education, and growing dissatisfaction with America's schools—particularly those in urban areas—prompted numerous education reform proposals. Heightened standards, charter schools, tax-funded private school vouchers and increased emphasis on standardized testing all were proposed and tried in various forms and at various levels of government. Members of the Congressional Black Caucus, many of whom represented urban areas with struggling school districts, regularly sought to increase the federal government's commitment to education, particularly to urban schools. In December 2001 both chambers of Congress passed a bipartisan, sweeping education reform bill known as the No Child Left Behind Act, which was intended to improve America's schools by requiring greater accountability from teachers and school administrators, and by establishing rigorous testing standards for students to ensure education goals were being met. But as the legislation was put into action across the country, African American legislators expressed dismay and anger, contending that the federal government had failed to provide sufficient funding to enable schools to meet the demanding new standards.

In a June 2005 radio address sponsored by the Caucus, Rep. Elijah E. Cummings, D-Md., criticized the Republicans' insufficient funding of the program:

> Despite Democratic efforts to keep our promise by increasing federal funding for local public schools, the Republicans have under funded "No Child Left Behind" by $27 billion dollars. The consequences have been tragic:
>
> - Nearly 5 million children are not receiving the help they need in reading and math;
> - Almost 15,000 teachers are being denied the further training that will make them even better in the classroom; and
> - More than 1.4 million children are being denied the after-school programs that can make a big difference in their lives.

> "We, in the Congressional Black Caucus, believe that this failure to assure a quality education for every American child is the greatest threat that our nation faces today.[14]

In a variety of radio broadcasts and policy statements, Caucus members demanded adequate federal funding and also called for expanding the highly successful Head Start program to ensure that low-income children had access to preschool education. They also proposed increased spending on Pell Grants, scholarships and other financial assistance programs to enable more black students to attend college and pursue graduate studies. In addition, they recommended increased support for historically black colleges and universities.[15]

The speech excerpted here, prepared by Sen. Barack Obama, D-Ill., for delivery at the Center for American Progress in October 2005, is representative of the concerns felt by many members of the Caucus.

Document 7.9
Sen. Barack Obama, D-Ill., on "Teaching Our Kids in a 21st Century Economy," October 25, 2005

The other day, I was reading through Jonathan Kozol's new book, Shame of a Nation. In it, he talks about his recent travels to schools across America, and how fifty years after Brown v. Board of Education, we have an education system in this country that is still visibly separate and painfully unequal.

At one point, Kozol tells about his trip to Fremont High School in Los Angeles, where he meets some children who explain with heart-wrenching honesty what living in this system is like. One girl told him that she'd taken hairdressing twice, because there were actually two different levels offered by the high school. The first was in hairstyling; the other in braiding.

Another girl, Mireya, listened as her friend told this story. And she began to cry. When asked what was wrong, she said, "I don't want to take hairdressing. I did not need sewing either. I knew how to sew. My mother is a seamstress in a factory. I'm trying to go to college. I don't need to sew to go to college. My mother sews. I hoped for something else."

I hoped for something else.

It's a simple dream, but it speaks to us so powerfully because it is our dream—one that exists at the very center of the American experience. One that says if you're willing to work hard and take responsibility, then you'll have the chance to reach for something else; for something better.

The ideal of public education has always been at the heart of this bargain. From the moment the earliest Americans stepped out from the shadows of tyranny and built the first free schools in the towns of New England and across the Southern plains, it was the driving force behind Thomas Jefferson's declaration that ". . . talent and virtue, needed in a free society, should be educated regardless of wealth, birth or other accidental condition."

It's a bargain our government kept as we moved from a nation of farms to a nation of factories, setting up a system of free public high schools to give every American the chance to participate in the new economy. It's a bargain we expanded after World War II, when we sent over two million returning heroes to college on the GI Bill, creating the largest middle class in history.

And even when our government refused to hold up its end of this bargain; when America fell short of its promise and forced Linda Brown to walk miles to a dilapidated Topeka school because she wasn't allowed in the well-off, white-only school near her house; even then, ordinary people marched and bled, they took to the streets and fought in the courts, they stood up and spoke out until the day when the arrival of nine little children at a school in Little Rock made real the decision that in America, separate could never be equal. Because in America, it's the promise of a good education for all that makes it possible for any child to transcend the barriers of race or class or background and achieve their God-given potential.

In this country, it is education that allows our children to hope for something else.

And as the twenty-first century unfolds, we are called once again to make real this hope—to meet the new challenges of a global economy by carrying forth the ideals of progress and opportunity through public education in America.

We now live in a world where the most valuable skill you can sell is knowledge. Revolutions in technology and communication have created an entire economy of high-tech, high-wage jobs that can be located anywhere there's an internet connection. And today, a child in Chicago is not only competing for jobs with one in Boston, but thousands more in Bangalore and Beijing who are being educated longer and better than ever before.

America is in danger of losing this competition. We now have one of the highest high school dropout rates of any industrialized country. By 12th grade, our children score lower on their math and science tests than most other kids in the world. And today, countries like China are graduating eight times as many engineers as we do.

And yet, as these fundamental changes are occurring all around this, we still hear about schools that are giving students the choice between hairstyling and braiding.

Let's be clear—we are failing too many of our children. We're sending them out into a 21st century economy by sending them through the doors of 20th century schools . . .

If we do nothing about this, if we accept this kind of economy; this kind of society, we face a future where the ideal of American meritocracy could turn into an American myth. A future that's not only morally unacceptable for our children; but economically untenable for a nation that finds itself in a globalized world, as countries who are out-educating us today out-compete our workers tomorrow.

Now, the American people understand that government alone can't meet this challenge. They understand that we need to transform our educational culture, from one of complacency to one that constantly strives for excellence. And they understand that government cannot replace parents as the primary motivator for the hard work and commitment that excellence requires.

But they also know that government, through the public schools, plays a critical role. And what they've seen from government for close to two decades is not innovation or bold calls to action. Instead, what they've seen is inaction and tinkering around the edges of our education system—a paralysis that is fueled by ideological battles that are as outdated as they are predictable . . .

Like most ideological debates, this one assumes that there's an "either-or" answer to our education problems. Either we need to pour more money into the system, or we need to reform it with more tests and standards . . .

If we truly believe in our public schools, then we have a moral responsibility to do better—to break the either-or mentality around school reform, and embrace a both-and mentality. Good schools will require both the structural reform and the resources necessary to prepare our kids for the future . . .

It's not as if innovation isn't taking place around the country. It's taking place in wealthier schools, like Illinois' Adlai Stevenson High School, which has one of the highest percentages of students taking AP exams in the country, and California's New Tech High, which puts a computer in front of every child. But it's also taking place in schools where large majorities of children find themselves below the poverty line yet above the national average in achievement—places like Newark's Branch Book Elementary and Chicago's Carson Elementary School.

The problem is that we are not applying what we've learned from these successes to inform national policy. We need new vision for education in America—one where we move past ideology to experiment with the latest reforms, measure the results, and make policy decisions based on what works and what doesn't . . .

So here's what I'm proposing: the creation of what I call Innovation Districts. School districts from around the country that want to become seedbeds of reform would apply and we'd select the twenty with the best plans to put effective, supported teachers in all classrooms and increase achievement for all students. We'd offer these districts substantial new resources to do this, but in return, we'd ask them to try systemic new reforms. Above all, we'd require results.

In Innovation Districts, we'd ask for reforms in four broad areas: teaching, most importantly, but also how teachers use their time, what they teach, and what we can do to hold our schools accountable for achievement . . .

In the end, children succeed because somewhere along the way, a parent or teacher instills in them the belief that they can. That they're able to. That they're worth it.

At Earhart Elementary in Chicago, one little girl, raised by a single mom from a poor background, was asked the secret to her academic success.

She said, "I just study hard every night because I like learning. My teacher wants me to be a good student, and so does my mother. I don't want to let them down."

In the months and years to come, it's time for this nation to rededicate itself to the ideal of a world class education for every American child. It's time to let our kids hope for something else. It's time to instill the belief in every child that they can succeed—and then make sure we make good on the promise to never let them down. Thank you.

Source: Barack Obama, "Teaching Our Kids in a 21st Century Economy," October 25, 2005, http://obama.senate.gov/speech.

Document 7.10 in Context
"To Ensure that the Right of All Citizens to Vote . . . Is Preserved and Protected as Guaranteed by the Constitution": New Life for the Voting Rights Act

On July 27, 2006, President George W. Bush signed into law a bill extending for twenty-five years one of the crowning achievements of the civil rights movement— the Voting Rights Act of 1965 (**Document 6.1**). Key provisions of the law were scheduled to expire in 2007, and while the final renewal bill passed by an overwhelming margin in the House and without opposition in the Senate, preservation of all those provisions was not a foregone conclusion. For more than a year, civil rights activists and members of the Congressional Black Caucus had been rallying support for extending the provisions, and final action by the House was delayed at least once by opposition from southern conservatives who resented restrictions placed on southern states.

At the heart of the debate were provisions of the original law that required nine, mostly southern, states to obtain federal approval for any changes in voting procedures; set the process for determining which states and jurisdictions must obtain that approval; set criteria for the monitoring of elections by the U.S. Justice Department; and required that voting materials in areas with large numbers of non-English-speaking citizens be produced in languages in addition to English. Supporters of the renewal argued that extending the provisions were necessary to protect the voting rights of minority groups. Opponents argued that the renewal bill ignored the progress that many states had made in the forty years since the law was originally passed.

"By passing this rewrite of the Voting Rights Act, Congress is declaring from on high that states with voting problems 40 years ago can simply never be forgiven," said Rep. Lynn A. Westmoreland, a white Republican from Georgia.[16] Amendments were offered to reduce the length of the renewal from twenty-five years to ten and to remove the requirement for bilingual voting materials in some jurisdictions.

Members of the Caucus led the fight for the renewal with passionate reminders of the civil rights struggle of the 1950s and 1960s that led to the original law. During the debate in the House, Rep. John R. Lewis, D-Ga., showed photographs of himself and other civil rights activists beaten by police during a 1965 march across the Edmund Pettus Bridge in Selma, Alabama to support voting rights for blacks. He said:

> Yes, we have made some progress. We have come a distance. We are no longer met with bullwhips, fire hoses, and violence when we attempt to register and vote. But the sad fact is, the sad truth is discrimination still exists, and that is why we still need the Voting Rights Act. And we must not go back to the dark path . . . When we marched from Selma to Montgomery in 1965, it was dangerous. It was a matter of life and death. I was beaten, I had a concussion at the bridge. I almost died. I gave blood, but some of my colleagues gave their very lives.[17]

Document 7.10
Renewal of the Voting Rights Act of 1965, July 27, 2006

AN ACT To amend the Voting Rights Act of 1965.

Be it enacted by the Senate and House of Representatives of the United States of America in Congress assembled,

SECTION 1. SHORT TITLE.

This Act may be cited as the 'Fannie Lou Hamer, Rosa Parks, and Coretta Scott King Voting Rights Act Reauthorization and Amendments Act of 2006'.

SEC. 2. CONGRESSIONAL PURPOSE AND FINDINGS.

(a) PURPOSE-The purpose of this Act is to ensure that the right of all citizens to vote, including the right to register to vote and cast meaningful votes, is preserved and protected as guaranteed by the Constitution.

(b) FINDINGS-The Congress finds the following:

(1) Significant progress has been made in eliminating first generation barriers experienced by minority voters, including increased numbers of registered minority voters, minority voter turnout, and minority representation in Congress, State legislatures, and local elected offices. This progress is the direct result of the Voting Rights Act of 1965.

(2) However, vestiges of discrimination in voting continue to exist as demonstrated by second generation barriers constructed to prevent minority voters from fully participating in the electoral process.

(3) The continued evidence of racially polarized voting in each of the jurisdictions covered by the expiring provisions of the Voting Rights Act of 1965 demonstrates that racial and language minorities remain politically vulnerable, warranting the continued protection of the Voting Rights Act of 1965.

(4) Evidence of continued discrimination includes—

  (A)   the hundreds of objections interposed, requests for more information submitted followed by voting changes withdrawn from consideration by jurisdictions covered by the Voting Rights Act of 1965, and section 5 enforcement actions undertaken by the Department of Justice in covered jurisdictions since 1982 that prevented election practices, such as annexation, at-large voting, and the use of multi-member districts, from being enacted to dilute minority voting strength;

  (B)   the number of requests for declaratory judgments denied by the United States District Court for the District of Columbia;

  (C)   the continued filing of section 2 cases that originated in covered jurisdictions; and

  (D)   the litigation pursued by the Department of Justice since 1982 to enforce sections 4(e), 4(f)(4), and 203 of such Act to ensure that all language minority citizens have full access to the political process.

(5) The evidence clearly shows the continued need for Federal oversight in jurisdictions covered by the Voting Rights Act of 1965 since 1982, as demonstrated in the counties certified by the Attorney General for Federal examiner and observer coverage and the tens of thousands of Federal observers that have been dispatched to observe elections in covered jurisdictions.

(6) The effectiveness of the Voting Rights Act of 1965 has been significantly weakened by the United States Supreme Court decisions in Reno v. Bossier Parish II and Georgia v. Ashcroft, which have misconstrued Congress' original intent in enacting the Voting Rights Act of 1965 and narrowed the protections afforded by section 5 of such Act.

(7) Despite the progress made by minorities under the Voting Rights Act of 1965, the evidence before Congress reveals that 40 years has not been a sufficient amount of time to eliminate the vestiges of discrimination following nearly 100 years of disregard for the dictates of the 15th amendment and to ensure that the right of all citizens to vote is protected as guaranteed by the Constitution.

(8) Present day discrimination experienced by racial and language minority voters is contained in evidence, including the objections interposed by the Department of Justice in covered jurisdictions; the section 2 litigation filed to prevent dilutive techniques from adversely affecting minority voters; the enforcement actions filed to protect language minorities; and the tens of thousands of Federal observers dispatched to monitor polls in jurisdictions covered by the Voting Rights Act of 1965.

(9) The record compiled by Congress demonstrates that, without the continuation of the Voting Rights Act of 1965 protections, racial and language minority citizens will be deprived of the opportunity to exercise their right to vote, or will have their votes diluted, undermining the significant gains made by minorities in the last 40 years . . .

Source: U.S. Congress, *Fannie Lou Hamer, Rosa Parks, and Coretta Scott King Voting Rights Act Reauthorization and Amendments Act of 2006,* from U.S. Department of Justice, Civil Rights Division, www.usdoj.gov/crt/voting/vra06.htm.

NOTES

1 *Congressional Record,* 109th Cong., 1st sess., September 22, 2005, S10366.
2 Laurel Leff, "From Legal Scholar to Quota Queen," *Columbia Journalism Review,* September/October 1993, http://backissues.cjrarchives.org/year/93/5/quota.asp.
3 Marc Morano, "Clinton Honored as 'First Black President' at Black Caucus Dinner," Cybercast News Service, October 1, 2001, www.cnsnews.com.
4 Matthew Cardinale, "APN Chat with Rep. John Lewis on the Voting Rights Act Renewal," *Atlanta Progressive News,* June 29, 2006, www.atlantaprogressivenews.com/news/0064.html.
5 Hans J. Massaquoi, "What the Republican Sweep of Congress Means to Blacks," *Ebony,* February 1995.
6 William J. Clinton, "Address Before a Joint Session of Congress on Administration Goals," February 17, 1993, from the American Presidency Project, www.presidency.ucsb.edu/ ws/ ?pid=47232.
7 Marc Morano, "Clinton Honored as 'First Black President' at Black Caucus Dinner," Cybercast News Service, October 1, 2001, www.cnsnews.com/ViewNation.asp?Page=/Nation/archive/ 200110/NAT20011001e.html.
8 "Government of Men, Not Angels," *Washington Post,* December 20, 1998.
9 Ibid.
10 CNN, "Congressional Black Caucus Protests Electoral Vote Count," news conference transcript, January 6, 2001, http://transcripts.cnn.com/TRANSCRIPTS/0101/06/se.02.html.
11 President Lyndon B. Johnson, "Executive Order 11246, as Amended," September 24, 1965, from the U.S. Department of Labor Employment Standards Administration, www.dol.gov/esa/ regs/statutes/ofccp/eo11246.htm.
12 Congressional Black Caucus, "CBC Concern about Roberts' Racial Record Stimulates Unprecedented Submission of Questions for Senators to Ask Nominee," news release, September 10, 2005, www.house.gov/list/press/nc12_watt/cbc_pr_9102005.html.
13 Congressional Black Caucus, "John Roberts Rejects Meeting with Congressional Black Caucus Leaders," news release, September 9, 2005, http://www.house.gov/list/press/nc12_watt/ cbc_pr_johnrobertsrejects09092005.htm.
14 Congressional Black Caucus, "U.S. Rep. Elijah Cummings to Deliver Weekly CBC 'Message To America,' " news release, June 4, 2005, www.house.gov/list/press/nc12_watt/ cbcpr_642005.html
15 Congressional Black Caucus, "The Congressional Black Caucus Agenda for the 109th Congress," from the Black Leadership Forum, www.blackleadershipforum.org.
16 *Congressional Record,* 109th Cong., 2d sess., July 13, 2006. H5150.
17 Ibid., H5164.

CHAPTER EIGHT

African Americans Run for Office
Campaigns and Elections

When African Americans first ran for Congress during Reconstruction, as early as 1868 in the immediate aftermath of the Civil War, the tumultuous political conditions in parts of the South made many of them credible candidates. Indeed, under the Radical Republican–controlled Congress, large numbers of white southerners, mostly Democrats, had temporarily lost the right to vote because of their allegiance to the Confederacy; this briefly created a more friendly environment for black candidates. As the former Confederate states were readmitted to the Union—starting in July 1866 with Tennessee and ending

Republican Massachusetts attorney general Edward W. Brooke III, shown here after winning his party's nomination for the U.S. Senate, defeated former Democratic governor Endicott Peabody in 1966 to become the first popularly elected African American senator in U.S. history and the first black senator since Blanche K. Bruce left office in 1881. Brooke declined to join the overwhelmingly Democratic Congressional Black Caucus in 1971 and spent much of his career trying to open the Republican Party to African American voters.
Source: AP Images/Frank C. Curtin

in July 1870 with Georgia—and most white voters again were enfranchised, the Republican Party was eager to maintain its majority hold on Congress. Black voters were essential to that effort, and Republicans worked both to register them to vote and to nominate them for office, although sometimes only as token candidates to fill partial terms.

In some majority-black districts, however, multiple black candidates split the African American vote enough that a white candidate still won. That happened in 1876, after the Democrats regained control of Congress. The Alabama legislature gerrymandered a majority-black district, forcing two African American Republicans into the same district. Incumbent Jeremiah Haralson lost his renomination bid to former representative James T. Rapier, but chose to run as an independent. In the general election, Rapier and Haralson split the black vote, and their white opponent, Democrat Charles M. Shelley, won.

Successful campaigning during the nineteenth century often required many of the same trappings as elections today. For example, while running in Virginia for a Republican nomination for Congress in 1888, African American candidate John M. Langston sent voters a biographical sketch with his picture, formed Langston clubs in every county in the district, bought a building for campaign headquarters and political rallies, and contributed to a newspaper edited by two supporters. Although Langston failed to secure the Republican nomination, he poured $15,000 of his own money into the campaign as an independent. Despite this, he fell 643 votes short of white Democrat Edward C. Venable, who was elected. Unwilling to give up, Langston spent an additional $10,000 to challenge his defeat. His formal notice of contest to Venable stated in part:

> I claim in each and all of the election districts and wards of the Congressional District, and at the polls on election day of all the said election districts and wards, that undue influence was used by your party friends and supporters and my opponents upon the duly qualified electors.[1]

Ultimately, after finding evidence of fraud committed on Venable's behalf, the House seated Langston, who served as a Republican for the final five-and-a-half months of the two-year term.

Indeed, electoral fraud and corruption led to a series of contested congressional elections during Reconstruction, in both the South and the North. Many, like that of J. Willis Menard, R-La.—the first African American to claim a House seat, albeit unsuccessfully—involved black candidates (**Document 8.1**). Those cases often involved allegations of bribery, harassment of black and white voters alike, ballot-tampering and illegal rejection of returns. A dispute over one South Carolina seat dragged on for almost the full two-year term before the House declared the seat vacant, ousting African American Robert C. De Large, because the irregularities by both sides were so pervasive. Rep. Josiah T. Walls, R-Fla., won three House elections, but was twice removed partway through his terms and replaced by Democrats because of voting irregularities.

As Reconstruction and the power of Radical Republicans faded, white Democrats in Virginia and Tennessee began in October 1869 to regain political power in the South. They disenfranchised black voters (**Document 4.6**) and redrew congressional districts to minimize the possibility of Republican victors, black or white. Meanwhile, the withdrawal of federal troops from the South in 1877 and Congress's failure to enact new voting rights laws and enforce existing ones (**Document 4.4**) signaled a further decline in the possibility of black candidates winning House seats. George H. White, R-N.C., who left Congress in March 1901 (**Document 4.10**), would be the last African American representative until Oscar S. De Priest, R-Ill., won an election in 1928 (**Document 5.3**).

During the second half of the twentieth century, the civil rights movement—particularly passage of the Voting Rights Act of 1965 (**Document 6.1**)—and reapportionment that created more majority-black districts—spurred growth in the number of African American candidates, who had become predominantly Democratic as the Democrats increasingly championed civil rights. Urban political machines were the avenue to electoral success for some candidates, such as Chicago's William L. Dawson and Ralph H. Metcalfe, who could count on their party organization to raise necessary funds, get out the vote and provide patronage for political supporters. The real decisions in such districts were not made in the November elections, but in the Democratic primaries, such as the 1970 contest in New York between Rep. Adam Clayton Powell Jr. and Charles B. Rangel, and the 1972 contest between Rangel and Livingston L. Wingate (**Document 8.5**). A number of black Democrats won in predominantly white districts, including Ronald V. Dellums of California in 1970 (**Document 6.4**), Katie B. Hall of Indiana in 1982 (although Hall failed to win renomination in 1984) and Keith Ellison of Minnesota in 2006 (**Document 8.9**). When the Democrats recaptured

Democrat Barack Obama, left, and Republican Alan Keyes, right, squared off in the second of three debates in the race for the open U.S. Senate seat from Illinois on October 21, 2004, in Chicago. Source: AP Images/Jeff Roberson

both chambers of Congress in 2006, three African Americans were newly elected: Ellison, Yvette D. Clarke of New York and Hank Johnson of Georgia. Ellison replaced a retiring white Democrat, Clarke replaced a retiring black Democrat and Johnson defeated black incumbent Cynthia A. McKinney in the Democratic primary. In addition, a few black Republicans have won in overwhelmingly white districts or states: Sen. Edward W. Brooke III of Massachusetts in 1966 (**Document 8.4**) and Reps. Gary A. Franks of Connecticut in 1990 and J. C. Watts Jr. of Oklahoma in 1994 (**Document 8.7**).

Many factors beyond demographics and the drawing of district lines affect the viability of candidates, including national and local political trends and the ability to raise money for campaigns. The power of incumbency is considerable: it provides staff, as well as access to media coverage and government-funded mailing privileges. Some African American incumbents who face minimal reelection opposition redistribute surplus campaign cash to assist other black or white candidates with similar political views, thus developing additional political leverage if the candidates they underwrite win. Despite the advantages of incumbency, winning a seat has been no guarantee of longevity on Capitol Hill during any era. Among those defeated after a single term were Sen. Carol Moseley-Braun, D-Ill., defeated in 1998; Rep. Benjamin S. Turner, R-Ala., defeated in 1872; Rep. James T. Rapier, R-Ala., defeated in 1874; Rep. Charles E. Nash, R-La., defeated in 1876; Del. Melvin H. Evans, R-Virgin Islands, defeated in 1980; Rep. Bennett M. Stewart, D-Ill., defeated in 1980; Rep. Alton R. Waldon Jr., D-N.Y., defeated in 1986; and Del. Victor O. Frazer, I-V. I., defeated in 1996.

This chapter explores aspects of campaigns, including candidate campaign styles; primaries and noteworthy contests, such as Brooke's first Senate campaign; John R. Lynch's string of wins and losses in Reconstruction Mississippi (**Document 8.2**); the first Senate election between two black major party nominees, Barack Obama and Alan Keyes in Illinois (**Document 8.8**); and Ellison's victory as the first Muslim elected to Congress (**Document 8.9**). It also looks at how Congress handles challenges to election results. The chapter examines Rep. Harold Washington's election as mayor of Chicago (**Document 8.6**) as an example of how some African Americans seek other offices after leaving Congress. In addition, it documents the vice presidential and congressional candidacies of a black communist, James W. Ford (**Document 8.3**), to consider political avenues outside the Democratic and Republican parties. Finally, the unsuccessful 2006 contests of black Senate candidates Harold E. Ford Jr. of Tennessee and Michael S. Steele of Maryland (**Document 8.10**) illustrate that race was still a visible factor in elections into the twenty-first century.

Document 8.1 in Context
"I Wish the Case to Be Decided on Its Own Merits and Nothing Else":
Louisiana Republican J. Willis Menard Fails to Secure a House Seat

When Louisiana Republican J. Willis Menard appeared in the U.S. House of Representatives on February 27, 1869, to defend his claim to a seat, he hoped to make history—but he ended up as only a footnote. The writer and newspaper editor, who stood on the brink of becoming the first African American in Congress, merely became the first to speak on the House floor.

The House confronted a dual dilemma concerning Louisiana's Second District. After the April 1868 election, it seated Democrat James Mann, whose opponent, Simon Jones, contested the results. Before Jones's challenge could be decided, "death had closed the eyes and lips" of Mann, as a colleague put it.[2] Meanwhile, the Louisiana legislature redistricted the state and in November 1869 held a special election in the remapped district to fill the vacancy for the remainder of the term. That contest pitted Menard against Caleb Hunt, who was a white Democrat. The election was marred by intimidation by Democrats who "sacked Republican churches, school-houses, club rooms, and residences, dispersed Republican meetings . . . and established a reign of terror," as *Harper's Weekly* reported.[3] Hunt received the most votes, but Gov. Henry Clay Warmoth, a Republican, concluded that black voters had been illegally disenfranchised and gave Menard the official election certificate.

When the full House rejected Jones's claim to the seat based on the 1868 election, the question became whether Menard or Hunt—or neither—had won the 1869 special election and should be sworn in for the remaining week of the term. The House Committee on Elections ultimately recommended against seating either Menard or Hunt, and its report went to the full House for debate. Menard spoke from the House floor about procedural aspects of Hunt's challenge, actions by the governor and legislature of Louisiana, fraud and how Congress had handled earlier redistricting disputes. He asked for no favor based on his race but noted that most of the voters who had been deprived of their rights were black Republicans. He contrasted his treatment with that of white Republican Lionel A. Sheldon, who defeated Hunt on the same election day for the new, full term.

The House debate focused on technicalities of Louisiana election law, the governor's actions and the effects of redistricting, but race was an undercurrent. Democrats made political capital of some Republicans' unwillingness to seat Menard. For example, Rep. Lewis W. Ross, D-Ill., said, "I understand Mr. Menard, a colored man, holds the regular certificate, and that the other side who belong to his party are keeping him out of his seat. Do they say that he shall not have his rights like any other citizen because of his race or color?" Charles Upson, R-Mich., retorted, "You and your friends who voted against the constitutional amendment"—the Thirteenth Amendment (**Document 2.8**)—"will have the opportunity to vote to give Mr. Menard a seat upon this floor." [4] Citing election irregularities, Republican Samuel M. Arnell of Tennessee, lamented, "I regret profoundly that on this occasion, the first in the history of this country where a colored man has presented himself in this Hall and claimed a seat, I cannot vote for his admission. All my sympathies are with him and his race." [5]

The House declined to seat either Menard or Hunt. Some critics blamed other Republicans, who were in the majority, for overscrutinizing Menard's credentials to avoid openly opposing him based on race. The debate foreshadowed difficulties other African Americans, including P. B. S. Pinchback (**Document 3.8.**), would have in convincing Congress to seat them.

▬ Document 8.1 ▬
J. Willis Menard, R-La., Tries to Claim a Seat, February 27, 1869

Mr. MENARD, (the contestant.): Mr. Speaker, I appear here more to acknowledge this high privilege than to make an argument before this House. It was certainly not my intention at first to take any part in this case at all; but as I have been sent here by the votes of nearly nine thousand electors I would feel myself recreant to the duty imposed upon me if I did not defend their rights on this floor. I wish it to be well understood before I go any further that in the disposition of this case I do not expect nor do I ask that there shall be any favor shown me on account of my race or the former condition of that race. I wish the case to be decided on its own merits and nothing else. As I said before the Committee of Elections, Mr. [Caleb] Hunt who contests my seat is not properly a contestant before this House, for the reason that he has not complied with the law of Congress in serving notice upon me of his intention to contest my seat. The returns of the board of canvassers of the State of Louisiana were published officially on the 25th of November, and the gentleman had sufficient time to comply with the law of Congress if he had chosen to do so. When Congress convened on the 7th of December he presented to the Speaker of this House a protest against my taking my seat. I did not know the nature of that protest until about the middle of January, when the case was called up before the committee.

Upon this point of notice I desire to call the attention of the House to this fact: that General [Lionel A.] Sheldon [R-La.], who ran on the same ticket that I did as a candidate for the Forty-First Congress, was declared to be elected upon the same grounds that I was, and he wrote to the chairman of the Committee of Elections to find out his opinion with regard to this question of notice. Mr. Hunt, it seems, failed to give him notice also; and I understood when I was last in New Orleans that it is the opinion of the chairman of the Committee of Elections that the case of Mr. Sheldon is a very clear one. I am very sorry that the chairman of the Committee of Elections did not give me the benefit of that opinion.

I am of opinion that when Congress enacted that law it certainly intended that every contestant should comply with its requirements, and I can see no reason why the law should be set aside in this case any more than in any other, and I think that if Mr. Hunt did not know the law of Congress he was a very poor subject to be sent to Congress. [Laughter.]

Now, sir, the Committee of Elections, in their report, have cited the New Hampshire case of *Perkins vs. Morrison*, but they take as a precedent the action of the minority of the committee in that case, which is very strange indeed, and they give us no benefit from the report of the majority of that committee . . .

Mr. Speaker, in the matter of redistricting the State of Louisiana the Governor had no authority of law whatever to send his precept for an election to fill this vacancy to any other district than the new one made by the Legislature on the 22d of August, 1868. He could not have ordered an election to fill this vacancy under a law which had been repealed.

There is another point to which I wish to call the attention of this House. The State was redistricted before Colonel [James] Mann died. Therefore, at the time when he died his district was intact, and no change was made in it after his death. And the voters in that portion of the new district which were formerly within the districts that elected Mr.

[Joseph P.] NEWSHAM [R-La.] and Mr. [Michel] VIDAL [R-La.] to this House were no longer constituents of those gentlemen, but had become the constituents of Mr. Mann. So far as the law is concerned Mr. Mann represented the new district as it now stands. And when he died, and there was a vacancy in that new district, the Governor of the State had no power whatever to order an election in the old district to fill the vacancy, but the election had to be held by law within the territorial limits of the new district. The Legislature of Louisiana, according to the Constitution of the United States, had the power to change the districts. Therefore the Governor was by the new redistricting act to order an election to fill the vacancy within the new district.

Now, I would call attention to another point. If it be admitted that the election was legal, and that the Legislature had full power to create new districts, I ask a moment's attention while I compare the vote on the 3d of November with the vote cast in the preceding April election on the ratification of the constitution. In the first, second, third, tenth, and eleventh wards of the city of New Orleans, which are included in the new second congressional district, the vote for the constitution in April was 7,373. In the same wards on the 3d of November there were only 125 votes, showing a falling off of 7,248 votes in the space of six months. In the parish of Jefferson, on the 17th and 18th days of April, 1868, the votes for the constitution were 3,133. On the 3d of November following the Republican votes in that parish were only 662; showing a falling off in six months of 2,470 votes. This is sufficient to show to any reasonable person that the loyal voters in this portion of the district were deprived of the right to go to the polls and cast their ballots. Now, this falling off was caused by the intimidations and threats made and the frauds practiced in those parishes. And I now ask Congress on behalf of the loyal people of my district to set aside the returns of votes from those parishes, so as to give the rebels there no more encouragement for their systematic plan of fraud and intimidation, And if the votes of those two parishes are thrown out I will then have, in the remainder of the district, a majority over Mr. Hunt, my contestant, of 3,341 votes. And as I hold the certificate of election from the Governor, I hold that I should be recognized and admitted to this body as the legal Representative of the district in which a vacancy was created by the death of my predecessor, Mr. Mann. There is no evidence whatever that there was any fraud in the election in the remaining five parishes of the district. Our vote in November compares favorably with the vote cast in April for the constitution. And I think that Congress should recognize the right of the voters of those parishes to be represented here. Had the same Republican vote been cast in November that was cast in April in the parishes of Orleans and Jefferson I would still have a majority over Mr. Hunt of several hundred votes.

It will be noticed that under the new registration for the election of November there were 20,314 voters registered in the five wards of the city of New Orleans comprised in the second congressional district of Louisiana. The total votes in those wards cast at the election, admitting all of them to have been legal, were 11,660, showing that over 8,500 legal voters were deprived of the right to vote in consequence of the condition of things then existing in Louisiana, and I have every reason to believe, judging from the election in April previous, that those 8,500 were Republican voters. I ask this House to give these men—most of whom were colored—some consideration, and not allow the rebel votes to be counted against them. If this is done, it is possible that at the next election loyal men will have a chance to express their will through the ballot-box. And according to the

registration for the parish of Jefferson there were then 5,969 voters, while the total number of votes cast on the 3d of November was 2,886, showing that in that parish alone there
were 3,083 loyal voters who were deprived of their right to vote in consequence of the
intimidation and lawlessness there.

[Here the hammer fell.]

The SPEAKER: The fifteen minutes have expired. The other claimant, Mr. Hunt, is now entitled to the floor for fifteen minutes.

Mr. [Michael] KERR [D-Ind.]: Mr. Hunt desires me to say that he does not wish to occupy
any part of his fifteen minutes. He leaves the question to be discussed by other gentlemen . . .

Source: Congressional Globe, 40th Cong., 3d sess., February 27, 1869, 1684.

Document 8.2 in Context
"A Living Monument of Rifled Ballot Boxes, Stifled Public Justice, and a Prostituted Suffrage": The Electoral Fortunes of Rep. John R. Lynch, R-Miss.

Mississippi State House Speaker John R. Lynch, an African American, defeated Republican
incumbent Legrand W. Perce in the 1872 Republican congressional primary and beat Democrat Hiram Cassidy in the general election, becoming the youngest member of Congress
when he took his seat in March 1873. His legislative interests in Washington included voting rights, civil rights, navigation on the Mississippi River and projects that benefited his
home state.

From there, Lynch's political career traveled up and down. With Congress's approval, the
Mississippi legislature postponed the 1874 election "in the interest of economy" to coincide
with a special election for state treasurer.[6] Lynch won reelection in 1875 against Democrat
Roderick Seal in an election cycle that was later investigated by the Senate due to allegations of widespread violence, fraud and intimidation of black voters in that state (**Document
3.10**). A local newspaper covered a campaign appearance in Biloxi, where Lynch's "deportment and bearing were respectful and polite . . . He at some length alluded to his record in
Congress and gave his reasons for voting for several obnoxious measures, but felt no regret
for what he had done." [7] Seal, as Lynch later wrote, had "threatened to contest the election,
but the party organization, through its leaders caused him to desist. They evidently did not
desire to have their election methods ventilated upon the floor of the house of representatives, hence there was no contest." [8]

However, in 1876 Lynch lost to Democrat James R. Chalmers, a former Confederate general, and tried unsuccessfully to contest the results. In 1880 Lynch took on Chalmers again
and lost a fraud-riddled election in a strangely shaped and predominantly African American
"shoestring" district, but the GOP-controlled House of Representatives upheld Lynch's challenge and seated him. Finally, when the Mississippi legislature reapportioned the state to favor
Democrats, Lynch found himself running for reelection in 1882 from a district where he was
not well known, and he lost to Democrat Henry S. Van Eaton by about 800 votes.

After leaving Congress, Lynch remained active in Republican politics, became the first black
keynote speaker at a major party's national convention in 1884, accepted an appointment

from President Benjamin Harrison as an auditor in the Treasury Department and served as a U.S. Army officer during the Spanish-American War.

Lynch's autobiography describes his campaigns and political challenges. The following excerpts contrast what he considered the fairness and qualifications of his opponents in 1872 and 1882—elections that he won and lost, respectively—with the rancorous and corrupt election of 1880, when he lost to Chalmers at the polls but was nonetheless seated by the House.

▬ Document 8.2 ▬
Rep. John R. Lynch, R-Miss., Recollects His Election Campaigns, 1872–1882

1872: Election to Congress

. . . After a warm and exciting campaign, extending over a period of about one month, the primaries in the different voting precincts were held which resulted in a sweeping victory for the Lynch ticket, which enabled that faction to send a solid delegation to the congressional district convention. This made John R. Lynch the nominee of the party for Congress in that district, without further serious opposition. The Perce men gracefully acquiesced in the decision and gave the ticket their loyal support . . .

The Democrats nominated a very able and popular man in the person of Judge Hiram Cassidy of Franklin County. Both candidates made a thorough canvass of the district, joint debates having been held at several important points. Of the sixteen counties of which the district was composed, only four, Adams, Claiborne, Jefferson, and Wilkinson, were safely and reliably Republican, while four others, Copiah, Lincoln, Pike, and Amite, were close and doubtful. The other eight counties were reliably Democratic, but the normal Republican majority in the four Republican counties was believed to be large enough to overcome the Democratic majority in the other twelve counties, assuming that the Democrats would carry all of them, which, however, they did not do.

When the returns were all in, the result was not only a Republican majority of more than five thousand, but the same party had carried nearly every one of the doubtful counties . . .

1875: Gloomy Prospects for Reelection

. . . My own renomination for Congress from the Sixth, or Natchez, District was a foregone conclusion, since I had no opposition in my own party . . .

When the polls closed on the day of the election, the Democrats, of course, had carried the state by a large majority . . . Of the six members of Congress, I was the only one of the regular Republican candidates that pulled through and that by a greatly reduced majority . . .

1880: The Battle for Reelection

. . . I decided to measure arms with General Chalmers in 1880 for representative in Congress from the Sixth, or "shoestring," District. The fact was soon made plain to me, however, that I had on my hands the fight of my life, not only for the election but for the nomination. There were three candidates for the nomination besides myself—Judge E. Jeffords of Issaquena County, General W. F. Fitzgerald of Warren County, and my personal friend, Captain Thomas W. Hunt of Jefferson County. Captain Hunt was the man that placed my name in nomination for Congress in 1876. Chiefly through my efforts and influence he had been made United States marshal for the southern judicial district of the state, with headquarters at Jackson, the state capital.

To my great surprise, I found out that my personal friend and political ally, James Hill, was responsible for the candidacy of Captain Hunt. This meant that the political alliance and combination composed of [former Republican Sen. Blanche K.] Bruce, Lynch, and Hill was at last to be dissolved. This made the fight on my part much harder and more doubtful than it otherwise would have been, since it meant a division in the ranks of those upon whom I relied for support. It was at first denied that Hill was responsible for the candidacy of Hunt, but when I made known to Hunt the source of my information, the authenticity of which could not be questioned, he frankly confessed that it was true . . .

Shortly after the nomination, I entered upon an active and aggressive canvass of the district. One of the greatest difficulties I encountered was to get the Republican voters to turn out on election day. This was not due to indifference or lack of interest on their part, but on account of the way they had been treated at previous elections. They had turned out in large numbers on such occasions only to find that all sort of tricks and devices, sometimes violence, were resorted to, to prevent them from voting; and if they were allowed to vote, their votes had been counted and returned against the candidates for whom they had voted and for the candidates against whom they had voted. In other words, a Republican vote polled in some counties meant a Democratic vote counted and returned . . .

Consternation was created in the ranks of the Democracy. Something had to be done to save Chalmers. The discovery was finally made that the tickets used by the Republicans had a printer's dash to separate the different groups of candidates. This innocent and harmless little dash, it was claimed, was a violation of the state law which provided that no ticket should have any distinguishing mark or device by which one ticket could be distinguished from another . . . But fortunately for the disenfranchised Republicans of that district, the Republican party had not only elected the president, but had a small but safe majority in the lower house of Congress. I therefore carried the case to the House through the medium of a contest . . .

1882: Party and Election Disputes

The contested-election case of Lynch against Chalmers was finally disposed of by the House of Representatives in the spring of 1882. The Committee on Elections . . . gave the case a thorough, careful, and patient investigation . . .

The case was strongly and ably presented to the House by the chairman and several other members of the committee, and in accordance with the custom and practice in such cases, I was allowed one hour to present the case from my own standpoint and in my own way . . . The contestee paid strict and close attention to my remarks. The sentence that seemed to affect him more than any other was this: "In the official person of the contestee in this case the country is presented with a living monument of rifled ballot boxes, stifled public justice, and a prostituted suffrage." . . . When the vote was taken, every Republican and Independent member voted for the resolution which declared that I had been legally elected and entitled to the seat . . . while a large number of Democratic members refrained from voting, their action in so doing being intended no doubt to be construed as a silent but effective protest against retaining a man in a seat to which they knew he had not been and could not be fairly elected, but whose conduct and influence had been the occasion of much embarrassment to them as well as injury to the good name of the Democratic party.

As a result of the Lynch-Chalmers contest, the Democratic legislature of Mississippi decided to put an end to such contests in the future by reorganizing the congressional districts . . .

. . . The Democrats nominated one of their strongest and best men, in the person of Judge Henry S. Van Eaton of Wilkinson. I was nominated by the unanimous vote of the Republican convention and shortly thereafter I entered upon an active and aggressive canvass of the district. Judge Van Eaton and I met in joint debate at several places. The canvass was entirely free from bitterness and excitement, and I was treated with marked courtesy and respect at every point.

The absolute fairness with which the election was conducted took the Republicans very much by surprise . . .

Source: John R. Lynch, *Reminiscences of an Active Life: The Autobiography of John Roy Lynch,* ed. John Hope Franklin (Chicago: University of Chicago Press, 1970), 102–103, 165, 167, 217–218, 224, 232–233, 261, 264–265.

Document 8.3 in Context
"It Is Only the Communist Party Which . . . Fights for Every Demand and Need of the Negroes": James W. Ford Runs for Congress and Vice President on the Communist Party Ticket

After Reconstruction, it was not unusual for African Americans to feel disconnected from the two major political parties. One response was to turn to new parties, such as the African American–oriented National Liberty Party (**Document 4.11**). Another option was to seek political clout through alternative, sometimes radical, parties. In 1918, for example, George F. Miller, the president of the National Equal Rights League, ran for Congress in New York as a Socialist. He was the first black House nominee of the twentieth century.

In the aftermath of the Depression, the Communists made serious efforts to recruit black voters and candidates. The Communist Party's 1930 "Communist International Resolution of the Negro Question in the United States" argued that the "Negro working class" could "play a considerable role in the class struggle against American imperialism" and said the party "must come out as the champion of the right of the oppressed Negro race for full emancipation" and make "the Negro problem . . . part and parcel of all and every campaign conducted by the Party," including election campaigns.[9]

One recruit was party organizer James W. Ford, a World War I veteran who was named leader of the party's section in Harlem in 1933. He was the unsuccessful Communist candidate for a House seat from New York City in 1930 and 1934. Both times, the victor was Democrat Joseph A. Gavagan.

When the Communist Party nominated Ford in 1932 as its vice presidential candidate, he became the first black candidate to be named on a presidential ticket since George Taylor of the National Liberty Party in 1904. Ford ran with William Z. Foster; their ticket drew 103,307 votes, or 0.3 percent of the total cast, putting them behind the Socialists but ahead of the Prohibitionists. Ford appeared on the ballot again in 1936 and 1940 as Earl Browder's running mate, but the ticket pulled fewer votes in each successive election.

Ford's 1936 speech, accepting the vice presidential nomination at the party's New York City convention, came when President Franklin D. Roosevelt's New Deal was four years old and the Depression had been ongoing for seven years. Ford sharply criticizes the only black member of Congress, Rep. Oscar S. De Priest, R-Ill., as part of a corrupt political machine, and he accuses the Democrats of moving too slowly to address racial issues, especially in the South. The speech also sounds common themes of the Communist Party—racial unity and the evils of capitalism—and emphasizes the party's active role in pressing for the freedom of the Scottsboro boys, nine black teenagers falsely accused in 1931 of gang-raping two white women in Tennessee.

▬▬ Document 8.3 ▬▬
James W. Ford Accepts the 1936 Communist Party Nomination for Vice President, June 1936

Comrades and Friends:

This is indeed an honor that the Communist Party has conferred upon me. But I do not take it as an individual tribute. It is a tribute to the entire Negro people; it is another proof that the Communist Party is the outstanding fighter for their freedom from segregation and oppression of every kind. The other parties lavish sweet words on the Negro people; but it is only the Communist Party which, day in and day out, fights for every demand and need of the Negroes—in the terror- and lynch-ridden South and the poverty-stricken slums of Harlem and the South Side of Chicago.

The American people face their greatest crisis since the Civil War. This recalls the heroic part played by Negro regiments in turning the tide towards victory, and the role played by that great Negro liberation leader—Frederick Douglass. His close associate was John Brown, who saved Kansas from slavery and who died that the Negro people might be freed.

John Brown died in a brave but individualist attempt to free the slaves. *Earl Browder symbolizes an invincible international movement dedicated to the liberation, not only of the Negro people but of all oppressed races and nationalities.* Earl Browder and the Communist Party are the inheritors of the tradition of Frederick Douglass, Abraham Lincoln and John Brown. We Communists, Negro and white together, will carry out what they dreamed of.

The Republican Party has always posed as the friend of the Negro people. It even sent a Negro Congressman to Washington. But Mr. [Oscar S.] De Priest was part and parcel of the corrupt machine which brutally suppresses the Negroes in Chicago. The Republicans have not fought against segregation, against discrimination on jobs and relief. Today, the Republicans, sponsored by the Liberty Leaguers, are in alliance with the worst enemies of the Negro people. It was they who subsidized the infamous Grass Roots-Ku Klux Klan convention of hate, led by Governor [Eugene] Talmadge of Georgia.

The Democratic administration has been a little more favorable to Negroes. But in the South, the reactionary Democrats have openly countenanced lynchings and tortures, are responsible for the continued imprisonment of the Scottsboro boys . . .

I urge the Negro people in their own interest, in the interest of freedom and equal rights, to support the Communist Party, which saved the Scottsboro boys, which stands for every Negro demand, which is the party of the Negro people.

I appeal to the white workers, Communists and non-Communists, to remember that the Negro people must not be left to fight alone. The responsibility lies with the white workers to help free their brothers in a black skin. Unless the Negro people are freed there can be no freedom for the white workers. Both must fight shoulder to shoulder against their common enemy, Wall Street, which waxes fat on their misery and suffering. Both must defeat the sinister forces of reaction which plan to enslave, not only the Negro workers, but the white workers as well. Let us unite to defeat reaction. Let us go forward to freedom and equality for the Negro people in a free, happy and prosperous America.

Source: James W. Ford, *The Negro and the Democratic Front* (New York: International Publishers, 1938), 211–212.

Document 8.4 in Context
"Genuine Conservatism in the Republican Party Has Been Shunted Aside": Edward W. Brooke III of Massachusetts Runs for the Senate, 1966

Republicans suffered a shattering defeat in the 1964 elections. Their conservative presidential candidate, Sen. Barry M. Goldwater of Arizona, lost to Democratic incumbent Lyndon B. Johnson in a landslide, and GOP numbers in Congress shrank dramatically. Two years later, the African American attorney general of Massachusetts, Republican Edward W. Brooke III, sought an open Senate seat.

For Brooke in 1966, his party's rightward swing posed a political dilemma. Although he had not supported Goldwater—he had favored the more liberal Republican contender, New York governor Nelson A. Rockefeller—Brooke had to distance himself from the GOP's 1964 electoral disaster without alienating the Republican voting base. He considered himself a conservative, but he wanted the federal government to address racial bias, poverty and urban decay, problems he contended were being ignored by his party's leadership. Brooke had twice won statewide office in the state that had sent Democrat John F. Kennedy to the Senate, and he was seeking to replace a popular Republican senator, Leverett Saltonstall, who was retiring. Another Republican, John A. Volpe had been elected governor in 1964 and would win reelection in 1966.

Brooke tackled the dilemma in a book published shortly before the election, *The Challenge of Change: Crisis in Our Two-Party System.* In it, he frankly discussed the problems he believed the Republicans faced, including a penchant for offering slogans rather than solutions, as well as the flaws he perceived in the Democratic party. He also recognized the long-term stakes in reversing the decline of GOP loyalists:

> Voters who had once considered themselves Republican by instinct and who remained faithful to the party from their earliest voting years are now voting Democratic. Once allegiance of this kind is shattered, it is virtually impossible to restore a sense of permanent personal identification with the party. And most disheartening of all is the Republican showing among the youngest generation of voters ... To an entire new generation of voters, "Republicanism" means something obscure but negative.[10]

Brooke's 61–39 percent victory over former Democratic governor Endicott Peabody made him the first popularly elected black senator in U.S. history, and the first African American senator since Blanche K. Bruce left office in 1881. He was reelected in 1972 by a 64–35 percent margin.

When the Congressional Black Caucus was formed in 1971 (**Document 6.2**), Brooke declined to join because of its overwhelmingly Democratic orientation, and he was the only African American in Congress who did not boycott President Richard M. Nixon's State of the Union address that year. Rep. Augustus F. Hawkins, D-Calif., once described a major political distinction between Brooke, as a senator from an overwhelmingly white state, and Caucus members, who represented predominantly black House districts:

> It would be nice to have a Republican to remove any suspicion that we are a partisan group. But Senator Brooke's problems are somewhat different from ours. We represent ghettos. Our problems are the problems of the ghettos. He represents a state, and a state with a small black population.[11]

Brooke lost his 1978 reelection bid to Democrat Paul E. Tsongas by 10 percentage points. Several factors contributed to his defeat. Tsongas's liberalism attracted independents and Democrats who had voted for Brooke in prior elections. Also, Brooke's recent divorce had been rancorous, and he had been accused of omitting a loan from his financial report to the Secretary of the Senate.

In 2004, more than a quarter-century later, Brooke recalled how he had spent much of his career attempting to open the Republican Party to more black voters. With the Republican National Convention coming up and President George W. Bush seeking reelection, Brooke wrote of his fear that there would be

> far too few black delegates at our convention. One reason Barry Goldwater failed so totally was that he and his advisors hoped that by opposing the civil rights movement—or, less gently put, supporting racism—they would sweep to victory both in the South and elsewhere in America. This strategy failed because it underestimated the decency of the American people. If our party writes off black votes in a cynical appeal to votes based on prejudice, it too will fail, both politically and morally.[12]

In this excerpt from his book, Brooke interprets the role of conservatism in U.S. history and conveys his belief that conservatism is compatible with action on contemporary social issues, including education, health care and the environment.

▬ Document 8.4 ▬
Edward W. Brooke III of Massachusetts Discusses Republican Conservatism, 1966

A profound respect for stability and respectability, for orderly and traditional patterns of government lies near the center of the American political soul. The Republican Party should be able to turn that respect to good account. Senator Goldwater has said repeatedly that of the two major parties, ours logically must represent conservative sentiment in America. I agree. But what is conservatism? How ought it to be interpreted and applied? Here is where we have gone astray. Not conservatism is responsible for the Republican decline, but a severe distortion of conservatism which has robbed it of its potentially great appeal . . .

Genuine conservatism in the Republican Party has been shunted aside by a jumble of oversimplified, misleading articles of faith which trade wishful thinking for economic and social reality, and appeals to ancient virtues for rational planning about what to do next. There has always been a danger of misrepresenting conservatism in this way, but Senator Goldwater has, alas, made the danger a clear and present reality . . .

First, it should be pointed out that not ancient or tested truths guided our Republic through its early days, but new—and in those days, radical—propositions. That men were born free and created equal, that human rights are inviolable, that government was established in order to insure all citizens Life, Liberty and the Pursuit of Happiness—these were brilliant new theories, consciously instituted as the foundation of government for the first time in history. The United States was a new nation offering new hope based on new theories of man, society and government. The very word "republic" was synonymous with "radicalism" in that age of monarchies. No doubt "conservatives" of Senator Goldwater's leaning would have denounced constitutional republicanism in those days as wildly irresponsible.

Most of the Founding Fathers were men of property and conservative by temperament. Yet in the work of establishing the Republic's new political institutions, they were nothing if not innovators. All that the Founding Fathers created—the Constitution, Federalism, the Supreme Court, the Bill of Rights, the separation of legislative, executive and judicial powers—was either totally original, or originally applied to the workings of a national government. The conventional slogans about the Founding Fathers suggest that it was their will to change nothing but to make the old order permanent. In fact, their experience suggests precisely the opposite.

It is perfectly true, however, that many of the "truths" arrived at during the early days of the Republic *will* do equally well for us. The question is, which truths? What should we take from our progenitors, use to solve our problems, and pass to our progeny? *What do we want to conserve?* Obviously not a set of legislative truths. If the legislative work of the early days of the Republic would do equally well for us, we would now be crippled with laws regulating the use of slaves, horses and craft guilds—and unable to deal with automobiles, railroads, wonder drugs, and everything else which has been introduced into American life since the eighteenth century. If the Founding Fathers thought they could solve the problems of succeeding ages, they would have simply enacted a set of permanent laws, and dispensed with legislatures of the future. A Republic of this sort would not have endured a year
. . .

Conservatism must be founded on deep respect and interests in individual men—in their freedom, their security, their opportunity for development, their overall well-being. It is absurd to believe that conservatives by definition are uninterested in such problems as water pollution or medical care for the aged or the fate of America's underprivileged minorities. It is nonsensical to assume that conservati[ves] must by nature oppose all poverty programs, medical programs, educational programs. Unfortunately, most Americans still make these assumptions. And, unfortunately, conservatism has come to be associated with the protection of institutions, especially of management and industry—not the protection of men . . .

Genuine conservatives want to profit from the past, not live in it. They are skeptical about reforms, but willing to accept them—indeed, to propose and engineer them—when they are required. They treasure the past not as a Utopia, but for its insights into the problems of the present and the future. They understand that new problems require new thought and new solutions, and that few problems of a complex, industrialized society can be simply and easily solved. They appreciate that social progress is essential to a society's stability, and that unless changes are made in the superstructure of society, the pressures for change will undermine the foundation of that society. They look forward to the future as a time of opportunity, not a time of trouble . . .

Source: Edward W. Brooke III., *The Challenge of Change: Crisis in Our Two-Party System* (Boston: Little, Brown, 1966), 244–245, 247–249, 252, 253.

Document 8.5 in Context
"What He Will Fight for in Washington": Livingston L. Wingate Challenges Rep. Charles B. Rangel, D-N.Y., in the June 1972 Democratic Primary

Historically, congressional incumbents are most vulnerable when they first seek reelection. They have had only one term—two years in the House or six in the Senate—to establish themselves and to demonstrate their legislative effectiveness to their constituents. Meanwhile, they generally have drained their campaign coffers and, upon arrival in Washington, rank at the bottom of the seniority ladder and are often placed on low-profile committees.

In 1970 Charles B. Rangel of New York narrowly won a five-way Democratic primary with 33 percent of the vote, edging out the well-known and outspoken incumbent, Rep. Adam Clayton Powell Jr., by 150 votes. Rangel benefited from both voters' dissatisfaction with Powell and reapportionment that had added more liberal, white neighborhoods to the Harlem-centered district. With the cross-endorsement of the Republicans, he won the election that November with 89 percent of the vote; the rest went to minor-party candidates.

Then in the 1972 primary, challenger Livingston L. Wingate, a former Powell aide, sought to oust first-term Rangel. Powell supporters saw a Wingate victory as a way to vindicate Powell. Yet both Wingate and Rangel portrayed themselves as heir to the Powell legacy, and both temporarily suspended campaigning when Powell died a few months before the primary.

Rangel, a high school dropout who went to college and law school after army service in the Korean War, had been a state legislator and unsuccessful candidate for city council president before defeating Powell. Wingate was a lawyer, union leader and former president of the New York Urban League. Both men were liberals with government experience and civil rights records, and both strongly opposed the war in Vietnam. One challenge for the two candidates was securing support from three distinctive groups of voters within the district: African Americans, who accounted for most residents of Harlem; Hispanics, who were the dominant ethnic group in East Harlem; and white liberals, who largely populated the Upper West Side.

Rangel won the primary 77–23 percent and took 96 percent of the vote in the November general election. Wingate later became a state court judge; when he died in 1995, Rangel attended the funeral.

Here are excerpts from Rangel's campaign flyer on public housing and from Wingate's general campaign flyer.

▬ Document 8.5a ▬
Campaign Flyer for Charles B. Rangel in New York's Nineteenth Congressional District, June 1972

CONGRESSMAN CHARLES RANGEL FIGHTS FOR BETTER
PUBLIC HOUSING!

7 1/2% Rent Increase—Rangel Says "No!"

Congressman CHARLES B. RANGEL opposes *any* increase in the rent for tenants of public housing. He has asked the Department of Housing and Urban Development to increase the Federal subsidy to the Housing Authority to avoid a rent hike.

RANGEL says, "Rents must not go up while maintenance and heating get worse. All people have a right to decent housing at a price they can afford."

Day Care Services for All Housing Projects—Rangel Says "Yes!"

Congressman RANGEL is fighting to make available day care facilities for all tenants of public housing who seek them. Day care services with professional and parental staff and with health and nutritional services are vital to insure that our children develop to their full potential. That is why Congressman RANGEL has introduced legislation to put day care facilities in all projects.

Rangel Works to Improve Housing Security and Police Protection

CHARLIE RANGEL has been fighting alongside concerned tenants to guarantee all residents of public housing a safe place to live. RANGEL has called for 1 Housing Authority policeman for each 75 apartments, not the inadequate 1 officer for 125 units. He is working for improved Federal-local cooperation to increase funding for security and safety. Congressman RANGEL supports the creation of a separate auxiliary Housing Authority police force of concerned citizens who would volunteer one evening a week in their own building.

Why We Need Public Housing

CHARLES B. RANGEL believes that the government has a moral duty to see that all our people are given decent housing. There should be no stigma placed on those who live in subsidized housing. Public housing tenants should have the same rights as residents of private buildings: the right to apartments without rats or roaches, to heat and hot water, to well-lit and clean hallways, to good maintenance services. Families which live in the projects should not be treated as second-class citizens.

RE-ELECT CONGRESSMAN CHARLES RANGEL

Source: Flyer from the personal collection of Eric Freedman.

Campaign Flyer for Livingston L. Wingate in New York's Nineteenth Congressional District, June 1972

WHAT HE BELIEVES, WHAT HE WILL FIGHT FOR IN WASHINGTON: LIVINGSTON L. WINGATE FOR CONGRESS

. . .

WINGATE'S STAND

Busing

We cannot permit yet another generation of minority group children in the urban ghettos to be crippled by inferior education. Widespread busing is not the answer insofar as it further polarizes, further victimizes the ghetto youngster and swallows up educational funds desperately needed in the ghetto community. But neither is it an answer to buy President Nixon's "anti-busing" stance which would wall Blacks and Puerto Ricans into their ghettos and barrios, and abridge our rights to live and learn where we please . . .

Narcotics & Crime

Methadone and other types of maintenance programs may have provided a partial short-term emergency relief to what is a national crisis and disgrace. But we must not forget that this type of remedy helps only the victims of drug inspired crimes by, in theory, reducing the addict's need to steal. What about the addicts themselves? In humanity's name they cannot be dismissed or banished . . .

Housing

Urban renewal, sadly, has proved a chaotic disgrace. We must ensure that all current or future projects in New York do not end up obliterating basically sound buildings and driving away the poor and working middle class. Naturally, I support improved housing in the ghetto, but my attack on The Albany Republican leaders' repeal of rent control last summer, shows my equal concern that the costs of middle class housing be kept in line . . .

Women's Rights

Equal pay for equal work is a well known and long desired objective for minority groups in this country. It goes without saying that America's women, of whatever race, are entitled to the same thing. In addition, I actively supported the original liberalized abortion bill and will support all those measures which give women, as individuals, full equality before the law and the right to determine their own destiny . . .

The War

The Indochina conflict undoubtedly has contributed substantially to the gravest American crisis since the Civil War. Although I do not advocate a total abandonment of U.S. responsibilities in the world community, absolute priority must be given to domestic problems.

President Nixon's current re-escalation of the war against North Vietnam is sheer folly. I advocate a unilateral statement that our troops will be withdrawn within a specified time, six months at latest, coupled with a re-intensified effort, conducted separately, for the return of our P.O.W's . . .

Source: Flyer from the personal collection of Eric Freedman.

Document 8.6 in Context
"A Very Serious Vow . . . to Do Everything in My Power to Protect This City": Rep. Harold Washington, D-Ill., Is Elected Mayor of Chicago

Since the earliest days of the Republic, it has been common for white members of the U.S. House of Representatives to parlay their positions into higher elective office, either statewide or national—governor, vice president, even president, and, after the Seventeenth Amendment (**Document 5.1**), senator. That has not generally been the case for African American representatives, none of whom had been elected to the Senate or a governor's office by 2007. A few representatives have run for those offices, including Shirley A. Chisholm, D-N.Y., who sought the Democratic nomination for president in 1972; Gary A. Franks, R-Conn., who lost a 1998 Senate campaign; and Denise L. Majette, D-Ga., who gave up her House seat after one term to become her party's unsuccessful Senate nominee in 2004.

More commonly, black former representatives have won lower state offices or local offices after leaving the Capitol. For example, in the Reconstruction era, Robert B. Elliott, R-S.C., resigned from Congress to rejoin the South Carolina House of Representatives, where he became speaker, although his subsequent statewide race for attorney general fell short. More recently, Andrew J. Young Jr., D-Ga., became mayor of Atlanta after serving as U.S. ambassador to the United Nations (**Document 6.8**), but he lost a campaign for governor. Barbara-Rose Collins, D-Mich., won a Detroit City Council seat after losing renomination for Congress, and Yvonne Brathwaite Burke, D-Calif., became a Los Angeles County supervisor after losing a race for state attorney general. In 2006 Ronald V. Dellums, D-Calif., who had chaired the House Armed Services Committee (**Document 6.4**), was elected mayor of Oakland, California.

One of the most significant such transitions came in 1983, when Rep. Harold Washington, D-Ill., defeated the candidate of the well-entrenched Chicago Democratic machine to win the mayoral primary and then the general election. As Washington candidly acknowledged in his first inaugural address, which is excerpted here, he inherited a city government drowning in red ink, patronage appointments and struggling public schools. Solving these problems inevitably would mean layoffs of city workers, spending cuts and tough negotiations with public employee unions.

Later, in an October 13, 1987, speech during his second term, he told the audience:

We didn't get here the easy way. We got here by making the hard choices . . .
    We made the hard choice to resist the counsel of phony compromise and false accommodation, we refused to give up and give in to the cronyism and corruption that had brought Chicago to the brink of disaster . . . We said a city of free citizens working together with an open government is stronger than a smoke-filled room of corrupt politicians.

We made the hard choice for affirmative action . . . We said that jobs and contracts were going to be spread around.

We made the hard choice for financial responsibility . . . it cost us 8,000 layoffs and many hardships, but we wiped out Chicago's $168 million deficit . . . we gave you four years of balanced budgets.[13]

Washington died in office of a heart attack less than two months later.

▬▬ Document 8.6 ▬▬
Harold Washington Delivers His First Inaugural Address as Mayor of Chicago, April 29, 1983

. . . This is a very serious vow that I've just taken before God and man, to do everything in my power to protect this city and every person who lives in it.

I do not take this duty lightly. I was up late last night thinking about this moment. It went through my head hundreds and hundreds of times, and words that I was reading put me in a reflective and a somber, somber mood.

On my right hand last night was a Bible, which is a very good book for a new mayor to pay attention to. And, in front of me was a report of the city's finances which my transition team had prepared, and it did not contain very good news. To my left there was no book, because the one I wanted the most does not exist. It's the one that I wish had been written by my tribesman, Jean Pointe Baptiste Du Sable, who settled Chicago over 200 years ago.

And, as I reflected last night for a brief period of time, I wish he had written a book about how to be a mayor of a vast city like ours, a repository of wisdom that had been handed down from mayor to mayor for all these years.

Because, after reading the report about the actual state of the city's finances, I wanted some good solid, sound advice . . .

So I made a list of some of the things you told me during the election campaign, and I found out that you had given me the best and most solid advice.

The first thing you told me is to do no harm. You told me that the guiding principle of government is to do the greatest good. Your instructions which I heard from neighborhood after neighborhood, said to be patient and be fair, be candid and, in short, to continue to tell the truth . . .

All during the campaign I knew that the city had financial problems and I talked about them repeatedly, incessantly. A majority of the voters believed me and embarked on what can only be described as a great movement and revitalization labeled reform . . .

My election was made possible by thousands and thousands of people who demanded that the burdens of mismanagement, unfairness and inequity be lifted so that the city could be saved.

One of the ideas that held us all together said that neighborhood involvement has to take the place of the ancient, decrepit and creaking machine. City government for once in our lifetime must be made equitable and fair. The people of Chicago have asked for more responsibility and more representation at every city level . . .

Reluctantly, I must tell you that because of circumstances thrust upon us, each and every one of us, we must immediately cut back on how much money the city can spend.

Monday I will issue an order to freeze all city hiring and raises, in order to reduce the city expenses by millions of dollars. We will have no choice but to release several hundred new city employees who were added because of political considerations . . .

Beginning Monday, executive salaries will be cut . . .

Unnecessary city programs are going to have to be ended, and the fat removed from all departments until there is sinew and bone left.

So that there's no confusion, these cuts will begin in the mayor's office.

But these measures are not enough to make up the enormous deficits we have inherited. Like other cities across the state, we simply cannot provide adequate public service without additional sources of revenue. During the election, I said that there was no alternative to a higher state income tax . . .

In the months ahead, we will be instituting some new fiscal methods and controls and I shall certainly keep you informed, if necessary on a day-to-day basis, as to our progress . . .

Business as usual will not be accepted by the people of this city. Business as usual will not be accepted by any part of this city. Business as usual will not be accepted by this chief executive of this great city.

The only greater challenge in our history in Chicago was 110 years ago when Mayor Joseph Medill looked over a city burned to the ground and called for an enormous outpouring of civic spirit and resources to make the city new . . .

I'm calling for more leadership and more personal involvement in what goes on. We know the strength of the grass roots leadership because our election was based on it. We want this powerful infrastructure to grow because the success of tomorrow's city depends upon it, and the world and country look for an example as to how we can find the way out.

Information must flow freely from the administration to the people and back again. The city's books will be open to the public because we don't have a chance to institute fiscal reform unless we all know the hard facts. I believe in the process of collective bargaining when all the numbers are on the table and the city and its unions sit down and hammer out an agreement together. The only contracts in life are those that work and work because they are essentially fair.

Having said all this, I want you to know that the situation is serious but not desperate. I am optimistic about our future. I'm optimistic not just because I have a positive view of life, and I do, but because there is so much about this city that promises achievement.

We are a multi-ethnic, multi-racial, multi-language city and that is not a source to negate but really a source of pride, because it adds stability and strength to a metropolitan city as large as ours.

Our minorities are ambitious, and that is a sign of a prosperous city on the move. Racial fears and divisiveness have hurt us in the past. But I believe this is a situation that will and must be overcome.

Our schools must be improved. They're going to get a lot better because we're calling on students, teachers and administrators to study longer and achieve more . . .

Last night I saw the dark problems and today I see the bright promise of where we stand, Chicago has all the resources necessary for prosperity. We are at the crossroads of America— a vital transportation, economic, and business center. We are the heartland . . .

. . . I hope someday to be remembered by history as the mayor who cared about people and who was, above all, fair. A mayor who helped, who really helped, heal our wounds and stood the watch while the city and its people answered the greatest challenge in more than a century. Who saw that city renewed . . .

Source: Harold Washington, *Climbing a Great Mountain: Selected Speeches of Mayor Harold Washington* (Chicago: Bonus Books, 1988), 1–7.

Document 8.7 in Context
"The Innate Goodness in People Came Forth": Black Republicans Return to the U.S. House of Representatives

In 1978 Melvin H. Evans won a single term as the nonvoting delegate from the Virgin Islands, the first black Republican in the House of Representatives since 1901. On January 3, 1991, Gary A. Franks of Connecticut became the first voting black Republican representative since Oscar S. De Priest of Illinois failed to win reelection in 1934. Then in January 1995, Franks was joined by Oklahoma Republican J. C. Watts Jr. as the GOP took control of the House during the 1994 election. Both Franks and Watts defeated white candidates in largely white districts.

In 1990 Franks won a heated battle for the GOP nomination at a party caucus, then in the general election beat Democrat Toby Moffett, a former representative seeking a return to Congress. In the excerpts from his autobiography that follow, Franks discusses the role of race in that campaign.

In 1994 Watts weighed a possible run for the Senate but opted instead for an open House seat being vacated by a Democrat in a politically moderate-to-conservative district. He won a runoff GOP primary. The following excerpt from his autobiography describes racial aspects of his successful campaign against David Perryman.

Although Franks and Watts both espoused conservative political philosophies, there was a sharp difference in their approaches to some issues and in their relationship with their black Democratic colleagues. For example, Watts opposed Franks's legislative proposal to restrict or prohibit affirmative action in the federal government. Also, Franks joined the Congressional Black Caucus. Watts did not, saying that although he and Caucus members shared many concerns and goals, "I feared the increasing demands put on blacks to toe a particular ideological line would manifest itself tenfold in this particular caucus. I wanted to remain a free agent." [14]

Franks did have his conflicts with Caucus Democrats, and he recalled tensions at some of their early meetings. On one occasion, he told them that his district was not drawn to represent blacks only but was nearly a cross-section of American demographics. In 1995 he introduced legislation—which died in the Democratic-controlled House—to prohibit set-asides based on race or gender in federal contracts.

Both men served three terms. Watts quickly rose to a leadership position as House Republican Conference chair before he decided not to seek reelection in 2002. Franks lost his seat in 1996 and made an unsuccessful Senate bid in 1998.

▬▬ Document 8.7 ▬▬
Republican Reps. Gary A. Franks of Connecticut and J. C. Watts Jr. of Oklahoma Describe Their First Campaigns in 1990 and 1994

Rep. Gary A. Franks on His First Campaign in 1990

. . . Then the dirty tricks started. At several nearby all-white functions in the Naugatuck Valley, I suddenly found myself surrounded by a small gaggle of black boys. They were much more bedraggled than any child I had ever seen in Waterbury, yet they swarmed around and greeted me as if I were a long-lost father. The same group of boys showed up at two events. We were suspicious and passed word over to the [Toby] Moffett campaign that there had better not be any more of this. The boys never showed up again.

Our first debate took place at Wilton High School. When we entered, Moffett was shocked to discover that one-third of the audience was black and almost two-thirds were solidly in my favor . . .

We could see the uglier side of this campaign in the many FRANKS FOR CONGRESS lawn signs that ended up with "nigger" scrawled across them, or the late-night phone calls in which our supporters were asked, "You're not really going to vote for that nigger, are you?" . . .

. . . I ended up winning seventeen of the twenty-five towns and cities in the district . . .

. . . The president was on the phone.

"How are you doing?" I heard George Bush's voice at the other end of the line.

"Very well, Mr. President. We won." . . .

That night was the culmination of a dream everyone once thought impossible—that a black man could win an election by running on the issues in a predominantly white congressional district. Ours may not yet be a truly color-blind society, but there is no question we are steadily moving in the right direction . . .

Rep. J. C. Watts Jr. on His First Campaign in 1994

. . . With my primary behind me, my focus now turned to my Democratic opponent, David Perryman, a lawyer and former county chairman. The campaign settled down around several issues—defense, term limits, gun control, abortion, taxes, and, of course, the Contract with America . . .

. . . I have to say that I was as surprised as the next guy to see my opponent decide to play the race card . . .

. . . Perryman began running TV ads with a picture of me from the days when I wore my hair in a full-blown Afro, the style my father always hated.

For many people, the hairstyle still conjured up visions of Black Panthers and black power, radicals and revolution . . . It didn't take a political scientist to see my opponent's use of this outdated image was a not-too-subtle appeal to racial fears. The underlying message was clear: "Do you want some bushy-headed troublemaker representing you in Washington?" . . .

. . . The Democrats' decision to use racism backfired when people rejected this kind of politics.

Even though only 9 percent of the Fourth District is black, and 68 percent Democrat, on election day, my opponent limped in 9 percentage points behind me in a three-way race.

There was more stress to come in my political life, but when the flag of racism was flown, the innate goodness in people came forth . . .

Sources: Gary Franks, *Searching for the Promised Land: An African American's Optimistic Odyssey* (New York: ReganBooks, 1996), 66–67, 71. J. C. Watts Jr., *What Color Is a Conservative? My Life and My Politics* (New York: HarperCollins, 2002), 179–181.

Document 8.8 in Context
"The Most Important Principle of Our Nation's Life . . . Is at Stake in This Election": The First U.S. Senate Race Featuring Two Black Major Party Nominees

The 2004 Senate campaign in Illinois was the nation's first in which two African American candidates faced each other as major party nominees—and created one of the sharpest philosophical demarcations in that year's elections. State senator Barack Obama, who had once been an unsuccessful U.S. House candidate, won a seven-way Democratic primary to secure the nomination for the seat being vacated by retiring GOP senator Peter G. Fitzgerald.

On the Republican side, the candidate originally nominated to replace Fitzgerald withdrew after embarrassing claims his ex-wife made about their sex life appeared in the press. With only three months to the election, Republicans scrambled to find a replacement. Unable to recruit a credible contender from Illinois, party leaders recruited conservative talk show host Alan Keyes. Keyes, a Maryland resident and former U.S. ambassador to the United Nations Economic and Social Council, had made one unsuccessful Senate attempt in Maryland and had twice sought the Republican presidential nomination.

The chasm between the candidates' positions on high-profile issues was vast. Keyes emphasized morality themes and promised to

> labor to abolish the income tax; liberate entrepreneurial and charitable initiative; honor marriage and the family; respect the equal dignity of all human beings, born and unborn; reclaim American sovereignty from global bureaucracy; and show, by word and deed, the role of statesmanship in a free republic.[15]

Obama focused more on the war in Iraq; in his keynote address to that summer's Democratic National Convention, he said:

> When we send our young men and women into harm's way, we have a solemn obligation not to fudge the numbers or shade the truth about why they're going, to care for their families while they're gone, to tend to the soldiers upon their return, and to never ever go to war without enough troops to win the war, secure the peace, and earn the respect of the world.[16]

On the domestic front, Obama called for a continuation of affirmative action, universal pre-school education, retooling the North American Free Trade Agreement to better protect U.S. jobs and the environment, and improved access to health care.

A debate sponsored by the League of Women Voters opened with mutual verbal assaults that never let up. Obama blasted Keyes as a carpetbagger who "doesn't have a track record of service in Illinois. Instead, he talks about a moral crusade, and labels those who disagree with him as sinners." [17] Keyes, in turn, accused Obama of a total lack of understanding of what is at stake for the people of this state and, indeed, of our nation in issues like abortion, in issues like the defense of traditional marriage. In point of fact, the most important principle of our nation's life—that we are all created equal and endowed by our Creator, not by human choice, with our unalienable rights—is at stake in this election, as it was in the great election that was the dividing line between Lincoln and Douglas in 1858.[18]

The following excerpts focus on the candidates' views on abortion, gun control, gay rights, the war in Iraq and the death penalty. The questions are posed by ABC Channel 7 news anchor Ron Magers, Channel 7 reporter Andy Shaw, Chicago Public Radio correspondent Carlos Hernandez-Gomez and *Chicago Sun-Times* columnist Laura Washington.

Obama defeated Keyes in the general election, winning 70 percent of the vote. He announced on February 10, 2007, that he would seek the 2008 Democratic presidential nomination.

▬ Document 8.8 ▬
Republican Alan Keyes and Democrat Barack Obama Debate the Issues in the Illinois Election for U.S. Senate, October 21, 2004

RON MAGERS, ABC 7 NEWS ANCHOR: Good evening, and welcome to the first televised debate between the candidates for the U. S. Senate, from the state of Illinois . . .

The war in Iraq. Is it the right war at the right time, and where and how does it end?

[ALAN] KEYES: Well, the truth is, the question is raised as if we have a choice. We either fight the war against terror, or the terrorists kill us. We must fight that war by carrying the war to the enemy.

What President Bush did, in going into Iraq, was take a situation where there was a probability that we were going to be attacked with weapons of mass destruction developed by Saddam Hussein, handed off to the terrorist network that he was part of, for he had provided payments, for instance, to Hamas—they work with Al Qaeda in the training camps, and so forth—all of this, he understood . . .

[BARACK] OBAMA: The fact of the matter is, is that there were no weapons of mass destruction. There was no connection between Saddam Hussein and Al Qaeda. This has cost us billions of dollars, thousands of lives, and has in fact made us less secure, because it has frayed a set of international norms and rules and institutions that were in place, that could have helped us defeat terrorism.

Mr. Keyes referred to the notion that, somehow, by fighting this war in Iraq, we reduced the probability of attack to zero. That obviously cannot be the case, particularly when we have nuclear fuel that's lying around in the former Soviet Union, and we have not advanced bills in the Senate that would accelerate our securing that nuclear fuel. There are all sorts of holes in our homeland defense, that have not been attended to. We still have ports that are unsecure. We still have nuclear plants and chemical plants that are unsecure. The fact of the matter is, this has not been a well-fought, or well-thought-out war . . .

KEYES: As is often the case, a willful misunderstanding of what I made clear. We reduced the probability of an attack from Saddam Hussein to zero. I think all of us can agree on that. The breathtaking naïveté of the assertion that there are no connections between Al Qaeda and Saddam Hussein, when Saddam Hussein was providing payments to the families of suicide bombers sponsored by Hamas, when Hamas and Al Qaeda have intimate ties—I worked on the problem of terrorism on the National Security Council staff. Maybe that's why I understand it a little better than Senator Obama, and know that, in point of fact, those ties are real, and we can't afford to let them operate . . .

ANDY SHAW, ABC-CHANNEL 7 REPORTER: Mr. Keyes, you shocked a lot of people a month ago when you said that law-abiding citizens trained in gun safety should be allowed to carry machine guns on the streets of cities like Chicago. Explain that, if you will.

KEYES: Well, actually, as you know, Andy, I never said that. I was asked a question about whether or not people should have access, under our Constitution and laws, to automatic weapons, and I referred the reporter to the factual situation—that, in fact, under our Constitution and laws, such access is allowed . . .

The gun control mentality is ruthlessly absurd. It suggests that you pass a law which will bind law-abiding citizens. They won't have access to weapons. Now, we know that criminals, by definition, are people who don't obey laws. Therefore, you can pass all the laws that you want. They will still have access to these weapons, just as they have access to illegal drugs and other things right now. That means you end up with a situation in which the law-abiding folks can't defend themselves, and the crooks have all the guns . . .

OBAMA: Well, let's be clear. Mr. Keyes, for example, does not believe in common gun safety laws like the assault weapons bill. I have, as one of my guests today, the head of the Fraternal Order of Police. I'm proud of the support that I've received from that organization, in part, because they are concerned precisely about what Mr. Keyes referred to—getting shot by assault weapons, when they go in, in an attempt to do a drug bust . . .

And the fact of the matter is, is that Mr. Keyes does not believe in any limits, that I can tell, with respect to the possession of guns, including assault weapons that have only one purpose, and that is to kill people, unless you're seeing a lot of deer out there wearing bullet-proof vests, then there is no purpose for many of the guns . . .

[CARLOS] HERNANDEZ-GOMEZ [CHICAGO PUBLIC RADIO CORRESPONDENT]: Ambassador Keyes, you're a Roman Catholic who often touts your pro-life position as an opponent of abortion. You've also said there are certain circumstances in which the death penalty is essential. But the Pope has said, "The dignity of human life must never be taken." The Pope also says that the death penalty is both cruel and unnecessary.

Doesn't that mean you're not completely pro-life? How does your support of capital punishment, and opposition to abortion, conflict with your Roman Catholic faith?

KEYES: It doesn't conflict at all . . .

Abortion is intrinsically, objectively, wrong and sinful, whereas capital punishment is a matter of prudential judgment which is not, in and of itself, a violation of moral right. And that has been made clear in every pronouncement . . .

The question of whether or not you should apply capital punishment, in an instance where someone has been found to be guilty, is something that depends on circumstances, that depends on judgments about efficacy and balancing the results against what is, in fact, to be effected in capital punishment. And that is an area where Catholics, as others, have the right to debate, to disagree, and to exercise their judgment and common sense . . .

OBAMA: Well, I believe that the death penalty is appropriate in certain circumstances. There are extraordinarily heinous crimes—terrorism, the harm of children—in which it may be appropriate. Obviously, we've had some problems in this state in the application of the death penalty, and that's why a moratorium was put in place, and that's why I was so proud to be one of the leaders in making sure that we overhauled a death penalty system that was broken . . .

We have to have this ultimate sanction for certain circumstances in which the entire community says, "This is beyond the pale." . . . But I also think that it's gotta be fair and uniformly applied, and that's something that has not always happened in this state, and I'm glad that we've made some improvements on this score.

Now, I agree with, actually, Mr. Keyes that the issue of abortion and the death penalty are separate questions. It's unfortunate that, I think, whereas, with respect to the death penalty, Mr. Keyes respects the possibility that other people may have a differing point of view, that in this area, he has labeled them everything from "terrorists," to people promoting a "slaveholder position," to suggesting that they are consistent with Nazism . . .

[LAURA] WASHINGTON[SUN-TIMES COLUMNIST]: Ambassador Keyes, you've criticized gays and lesbians throughout much of your political career. You called homosexuality an abomination. In response to a reporter's question, you said that Vice President Dick Cheney's daughter was a selfish hedonist, and you said that the children raised by gay couples could be the victims of incest . . .

KEYES: . . . I do not say that homosexual relations is an abomination, the Bible says so. And many people in this state believe the Bible when it says so.

And for others to imply that that belief shall now be subject to penalties of law means that we are bringing freedom of religion in this society to an end, and beginning the persecution of our Christian citizens under the law, for believing in what the Scripture tells them is true . . .

Second, I have not called people names. I simply describe a situation. Marriage—traditional marriage—is based upon heterosexual relations, because they are connected to procreation. In every society and civilization, marriage is connected to the business of regulating the consequences of procreation, understanding what shall be the authority of the parents, their responsibility to their children, children's responsibility to their parents, inheritance laws . . .

OBAMA: . . . This is obviously an issue that Mr. Keyes has based, in premise, a lot of his campaign on. I believe that marriage is between a man and a woman, but I also detest the sort of bashing and vilifying of gays and lesbians, because I think it's unduly divisive. It's unnecessary.

Most gays and lesbians are simply seeking basic recognition of their rights, so that they're not discriminated against in employment, that they're not discriminated against with respect to renting a house, that they are able to visit their partner in a hospital, that they can transfer property . . .

Source: Reprinted with permission of ABC-7. Transcript available at Renew America, www.renewamerica.us/archives/media/debates/04_10_21debate2.htmChicago.

Document 8.9 in Context
"A Moderate Muslim Who Extends His Hand in Friendship": Keith Ellison, D-Minn., Becomes the First Muslim Elected to Congress

Keith Ellison, a Minnesota state legislator, made history in January 2007 by becoming both the first Muslim in Congress and the first African American representative from Minnesota. He won a seven-way Democratic primary for an open seat, then defeated the white Republican nominee in November 2006.

During the election, religion became more of an issue than race, and it involved Ellison's former support of Louis Farrakhan, leader of the Nation of Islam. Ellison had converted to Islam in college, where he used a pseudonym to write a newspaper column rejecting criticisms that Farrakhan was racist. In addition, Ellison's Republican opponent, Alan Fine, claimed that Ellison received support from a pro-terrorism Muslim lobbying group.

In discussing his faith, Ellison said:

> People draw strength and moral courage from a variety of religious traditions. Mine have come from both Catholicism and Islam. I was raised Catholic and later became a Muslim while attending Wayne State University. I am inspired by the Quran's message of an encompassing divine love, and a deep faith guides my life every day.[19]

In a year when many Democrats portrayed themselves as moderates in hopes of victory, Ellison articulated traditional liberal stances on gun control, the environment, stem cell research and abortion rights. He called for an immediate withdrawal of U.S. troops from Iraq, advocated universal single-payer health coverage, opposed a proposed constitutional ban on gay marriage and criticized "so-called 'fair trade' deals" such as the North American Free Trade Agreement for draining jobs from Minnesota to countries where workers toil under "sweatshop conditions." He endorsed peace movements in Israel and elsewhere in the Middle East and criticized "a system of educational apartheid" in public schools.[20]

Addressing widespread concerns over illegal immigration, Ellison said, "There are forces in this country who are rabidly anti-immigrant, and politicians who use immigrants as pawns in their political games. These regressive forces have coalesced into a political movement that must be stopped." Praising immigrants' contributions to economic growth, he advocated "a clear path to citizenship for the 11 million people who are already in the United States working and paying taxes" and an expedited process to reunite families.[21]

The *Minneapolis Star-Tribune* endorsed him. Its editors wrote:

> We are mindful that Ellison has a history of carelessness that is more than personal peccadillo—unpaid parking tickets, late taxes, missed deadlines for campaign finance documents. He has promised to run a tighter ship, and he will have to if he wants to secure the confidence of Fifth District constituents and survive the brutal politics of Washington. But his talent, legislative track record and passion for a better society justify the voter's gamble on his future.[22]

Ellison's Republican opponent, Fine, characterized himself as "fiscally prudent, socially responsible" and "proud to be an American." Fine listed his own priorities as deficit reduction, safer neighborhoods, improved U.S. diplomacy, reduced dependence on fossil fuels, strengthened social security, environmental protection and "a return to fiscal prudence." He opposed an immediate withdrawal of U.S. forces from Iraq, calling instead for a "multinational approach" to leave Iraq "as soon as possible." [23]

The following excerpts are from endorsements by Spanish-language and Jewish newspapers as well as pro-choice and environmental organizations. Ellison also won endorsements from African American, labor and other groups. In the general election, he outpolled Fine by 56 percent to 21 percent; independent and Green Party candidates received the rest of the votes.

▬ Document 8.9 ▬
Political Endorsements for Democratic House Candidate Keith Ellison of Minnesota, 2006

NARAL Pro-Choice America

. . . He is a strong pro-choice candidate who supports the values of freedom, privacy, and personal responsibility . . . Americans are tired of the divisive attacks on a woman's right to choose by anti-choice politicians in Congress. The same lawmakers who oppose a woman's right to choose do nothing to prevent the need for abortion, only making it more dangerous. Not only are they pushing extreme and divisive bans to criminalize abortion, but they have even attacked women's access to birth control and blocked votes on legislation that would actually make abortion less necessary . . .

American Jewish World

. . . Voters could make an emphatic statement—one that would gain national and international attention—by casting their ballots for Keith Ellison. The 43-year-old state representative would bring a singular passion and intelligence to the job of representing citizens of Minnesota Fifth District; in many ways, Ellison represents the progressive populist vision that Minnesota lost with the untimely passing of [Democratic Sen.] Paul Wellstone in 2002.

Ellison acted as the lawyer for the House DFL [the Democratic-Farmer-Labor party in the Minnesota House of Representatives] caucus in an ethics proceeding against former representative Arlon Lindner, who contended that gays were not victims of Nazi oppression in the Holocaust. Ellison understands the importance of guarding against Holocaust denial and revisionism, and links the lessons of the Shoah to more recent cases of genocide in Rwanda and Darfur. Further, he supports the State of Israel and the continuation of U.S. aid to Israel. He holds to the mainstream position of a negotiated two-state solution regarding the long-standing Israeli-Palestinian conflict.

We all know that nobody is perfect and no political candidate is without shortcomings . . . We cannot take our civil liberties for granted, especially in the face of well-reported government actions to curb our constitutional rights and consolidate political power. In the trying times ahead, we will need courageous political leadership and we must hold our elected representatives accountable . . .

. . . In Ellison, we have a moderate Muslim who extends his hand in friendship to the Jewish community and supports the security of the State of Israel . . .

Gente de Minnesota

. . . The main reason we endorsed Ellison is because he has been there for the Latino community over and over again . . . He spoke out against Governor [Tim] Pawlenty's statements attributing increased crime rates to immigration . . .

He lobbied very hard for our endorsement and showed the most interest in it . . . Some in our editorial committee had problems with what we perceived as answers that opposed increased commercial trade with Latin America. Many Latino small business owners in the US and Latin America would benefit with increased trade. We agree with some of his concerns and the concerns of the other candidates about labor and environmental consequences to some of the free trade agreements in the past with Mexico, Chile and Central America. But the future prosperity in Latin America is tied to more future trade between the United States and Latin America. There can be disagreements between friends . . .

We had some concerns about mainstream media reports on Ellison's past. We asked him about his reported previous affiliation with Louis Farrakhan, political statements he made as a young man, and his past problems in paying fines and reporting his campaign expenses. But we believe he is working hard to address his organizational problems and he has rejected the teachings of Farrakhan now that he understands them better.

There isn't a biased bone in the Keith Ellison we met and we feel very comfortable that the problems addressed by the mainstream media have been blown out of proportion . . .

Clean Water Action

. . . Keith will be a champion for the environment in Congress as evidenced by his legislative career, in particular his leadership on controversial legislative issues that are really important to public health such as the pesticide atrazine; as well as his successful work on legislation to reduce the presence of lead and mercury in the environment. And before his legislative career, his success [as] an advocate for environmental justice, his effort to create Environmental Justice Advocates Minnesota . . . All these aspects of Keith's record tell us that he won't just vote right on environmental issues, but champion the environment in Congress . . .

Sources, in order of appearance: Keith Ellison for Congress, "NARAL Pro-Choice America Endorses Keith Ellison," press release, October 12, 2006, www.keithellison.org; "Choices in the DFL Fifth District Primary," *American Jewish World,* September 1, 2006; "*Gente de Minnesota* Endorsements for September 12th, 2006, Primary Congress, 5th Congressional District and Legislative Races," *Gente de Minnesota,* August 18, 2006, www.gentedeminnesota.com; Keith Ellison for Congress, "Minnesota's Two Premiere Environmental Groups Endorse Ellison for Congress: Sierra Club and Clean Water Action Call Ellison 'A champion for the environment,' " press release, www.keithellison.org.

Document 8.10 in Context
"Slavishly Supporting the Republican Party" and "Harold—Call Me": Michael S. Steele, R-Md., and Harold E. Ford Jr., D-Tenn., Run for the Senate Unsuccessfully

As of late 2007, there has never been more than one African American in the Senate at the same time. During Reconstruction, the Mississippi legislature elected Republicans Hiram R.

Revels (**Document 3.4**) and Blanche K. Bruce (**Document 3.11**), but they did not serve together. In 1966 Massachusetts voters elected Republican Edward W. Brooke III (**Document 8.4**), making him the first black senator since Bruce left office in 1881. Carol Moseley-Braun, D-Ill., won a single term in 1992, and in 2004 Barack Obama, another Illinois Democrat, was elected (**Document 8.8**).

The 2006 election made two or even three simultaneously serving black senators a realistic prospect. In Maryland, former Congressional Black Caucus chair Kweisi Mfume, who had left Congress to become chief executive officer of the National Association for the Advancement of Colored People, placed second in a crowded Democratic primary for an open Senate seat. While Rep. Benjamin L. Cardin, who is white, won that primary, Maryland Republicans nominated the state's black lieutenant governor, former state GOP chair Michael S. Steele. In Tennessee, Democrat Harold E. Ford Jr. gave up his safe House seat to run for the Senate against white Republican Bob Corker.

Although their parties and issue positions differed, Steele and Ford shared similar, formidable challenges. Steele was a Republican in an overwhelmingly Democratic state running for an open seat long held by a retiring Democrat. Ford was a Democrat in an increasingly Republican state running for an open seat long held by a retiring Republican.

Also, controversies emerged in both campaigns over comments that critics deemed racially insensitive. The Maryland GOP decried as "racist" Democratic representative Steny H. Hoyer's comment that Steele had a history of "slavishly supporting the Republican party," a statement the Maryland lawmaker made while introducing Steele's opponent, Cardin, to a group of black businesspeople. But the most publicized incident was a television attack ad against Ford in which a white woman recalled meeting Ford "at the Playboy party," then winked and said, "Harold—call me." Critics felt the advertisement played to historic southern prejudices regarding relationships between black men and white women. The ad, paid for by the Republican National Committee, stirred up so much controversy that even Ford's Republican opponent publicly denounced it and asked that it be pulled from the air.

Both contests had national implications because Democrats believed they had a chance of securing a Senate majority for the first time in twelve years, while Republicans were desperate to keep the Senate as a bulwark for President George W. Bush, who was beleaguered by growing opposition to the war in Iraq. As a result, Democrats pumped millions of dollars into Ford's campaign, while Republicans did the same for Steele's. Even so Ford's and Steele's opponents heavily outspent them.

On November 5, the chairs of the Senate campaign committees, Elizabeth H. Dole, R-N.C., and Charles E. Schumer, D-N.Y. faced off on the NBC Sunday morning political talk show *Meet the Press,* hosted by Tim Russert. With only forty-eight hours before the election, the participants highlighted the Steele and Ford candidacies as they stumped for their respective parties. Their debate is excerpted here.

Ultimately, Ford lost to Corker 48–51 percent, while Steele lost to Cardin by a wider margin, 43.7–54.7 percent.

▬ Document 8.10 ▬
Sen. Elizabeth H. Dole, R-N.C., and Sen. Charles E. Schumer, D-N.Y., Discuss the Ford and Steele Campaigns with Tim Russert on *Meet the Press,* November 5, 2006

MR. [Tim] RUSSERT: And let me turn to the U.S. Senate.

Senator Schumer, two states that you must hold that currently have Democratic senators, are New Jersey and Maryland. Here is our latest poll on New Jersey:

Menendez, the Democratic candidate, 48; Tom Kean Jr., 41. In Maryland, the Democrat, Ben Cardin 47; Michael Steele, the Republican, 44. How concerned are you that in those two Democratic states you may get upset?

SEN. [Charles E.] SCHUMER: Well, we think we're going to win both of those states. I think in blue states in particular, the wind is strongly at our back. Democrats, independents, even Republicans in those states want change. And when they find out, as they have, that candidates like these are going to continue a rubber-stamp Congress—both have said—both Tom Kean Jr. and Michael Steele have said "stay the course in Iraq," people of their states don't like it. Both have supported—or both are against stem cell research, the people in their states don't like it. Kean has talked about privatizing Social Security. Michael Steele is against stem cell research. They are so against what the people in the states want that I believe we're going to keep both of those states.

MR. RUSSERT: Senator Dole, there are seven key battleground states for the Republicans . . . In six of those seven, the Republican is either behind or tied . . .

SEN. [Elizabeth H.] DOLE: You know, we've got . . .

MR. RUSSERT: What do you think?

SEN. DOLE: We've got some internal polls that certainly differ from some of the ones that you just read.

MR. RUSSERT: So you're going to sweep them all?

SEN. DOLE: You know, let's—let me, let me talk about what is normally regarded, as you guys talk about the firewall with Virginia and Tennessee and Missouri. And we're winning in all those states. Now, I wanted to expand that firewall, because I have a much broader firewall. You look at, at, at Rhode Island, the state of Montana, these are very, very tight races. And then we've been putting money into three blue states. Chuck has had to put millions of dollars into New Jersey, into Maryland, into Michigan. You've put a lot of money into the state of Washington. That's millions that doesn't go against our incumbents. So as I look at the situation at this point, sure, this is a very tough cycle, no question.

MR. RUSSERT: Why? Why?

SEN. DOLE: When a president has been—when a president has been re-elected, you look through history, and there's no question it's a very tough cycle. But you know, we've got some X factors that really enable us to have an opportunity to break through, to weather the storm . . . You look in Maryland and you've got a fresh leadership here in Michael Steele in terms of wanting to really shake up Washington. And his opponent, Ben Cardin, has been in government for 40 years. You know, Michael has just gotten the endorsements of some key African-American leaders in Prince Georges County, great leader . . .

MR. RUSSERT: Do you believe the voters are turned off by this negativity?

SEN. DOLE: I think that, at this point, there's a lot of, a lot of negativity out there, but nevertheless, it does carry messages. It's based on research. And I think that—you know, I think of one particular situation where—and this was a Harold Ford ad, and it was, it, it has run its course, but basically, what that ad did was to point out his views on certain issues, and that's the last thing he wanted to do was to talk about his record.

MR. RUSSERT: There was also an ad paid for by the Republican National Committee . . .

SEN. DOLE: Because it was an absolute . . .

MR. RUSSERT: . . . which had a blonde, white woman winking in the camera saying "Call me, Harold," and many African-Americans, including former Republican Senator Bill Cohen [of Maine], said that ad was racist.

SEN. DOLE: I did not see it as racist. I respect those who saw it otherwise. But let me tell you what that ad did: It pointed out his views on, on his record, that he is, he's on the wrong side of the abortion issues, that he's protected gay marriage, that he has an F from . . .

SEN. SCHUMER: He's voted against gay marriage every time.

SEN. DOLE: . . . an F for the—from the National Rifle Association . . .

MR. RUSSERT: OK.

SEN. DOLE: . . . that he's a tax increaser. This is one of the biggest political frauds in history, his trying to, to, re—redefine himself. And that ad pointed out particular matters that he didn't want to, to step up to, in terms of . . .

MR. RUSSERT: So that's not a negative ad?

SEN. DOLE: . . . in terms of the—it, it pointed out facts there, in terms of . . .

MR. RUSSERT: OK, we . . .

SEN. DOLE: . . . Harold Ford's true record. So . . .

MR. RUSSERT: We have to take a break . . .

Source: Meet the Press, November 5, 2006, transcript from MSNBC.com, www.msnbc.msn.com/id/ 15488330/.

NOTES

1 "Notice of Contest, John M. Langston, Contestant, vs. E. C. Venable, Contestee," December 22, 1888, Library of Congress, Frederick Douglas Papers, http://memory.loc.gov/ammem/ doughtml/doughome.html.

2 *Congressional Globe,* 40th Cong., 3d sess., February 27, 1869, 1682.

3 "Louisiana," *Harper's Weekly,* December 5, 1868, in *African American History in the Press 1851–1899,* ed. Schneider Collection, vol. 1, *1851–1869* (Detroit: Gale, 1996), 588.

4 *Congressional Globe,* 40th Cong., 3d sess., February 27, 1869, 1683.

5 Ibid., 1695.

6 John R. Lynch, "Communications," *Journal of Negro History* 16, no. 1 (January 1931): 112.

7 John R. Lynch, *Reminiscences of an Active Life: The Autobiography of John Roy Lynch,* ed. John Hope Franklin (Chicago: University of Chicago Press, 1970), xix.

8 Lynch, "Communications," 113.

9 "Resolution of the Communist International, 1930: The Communist Position on the Negro Question in the United States," *Communist International* no. 2 (February 1, 1931), available at From Marx to Mao, www.marx2mao.com/Other/CR75.html#s2.

10 Edward W. Brooke, *The Challenge of Change: Crisis in Our Two-Party System* (Boston: Little, Brown, 1966), 7.

11 William L. Clay, *Just Permanent Interests: Black Americans in Congress, 1870–1991* (New York: Amistad, 1992), 143.

12 Edward W. Brooke, "A Party for All of Us," *New York Times,* August 30, 2004.

13 Harold Washington, *Climbing a Great Mountain. Selected Speeches of Mayor Harold Washington* (Chicago: Bonus Books, 1988), 215.

14 J. C. Watts Jr., *What Color Is a Conservative? My Life and My Politics* (New York: HarperCollins, 2002), 186.

15 Alan Keyes and Barack Obama, U.S. Senate Debate Sponsored by the League of Women Voters in Illinois, October 21, 2004, transcript, from Renew America, www.renewamerica.us/archives/media/debates/04_10_21debate2.htm

16 Illinois Senate Candidate Barack Obama, Keynote Address at Democratic National Convention, July 27, 2004, transcript, from the *Washington Post*, www.washingtonpost.com/wp-dyn/articles/A19751-2004Jul27.html.

17 Keyes and Obama, U.S. Senate Debate transcript.

18 Ibid.

19 "Minnesota Voters Send First Muslim to Capitol Hill," CNN.com, November 8, 2006, www.cnn.com/2006/POLITICS/11/08/muslim.elect/index.html.

20 Keith Ellison for U.S. Congress, www.keithellison.org.

21 Ibid.

22 "Ellison, Wetterling, Peterson, Oberstar: Two Newcomers and Two Incumbents," *Minneapolis Star-Tribune*, October 25, 2006.

23 Alan Fine for U.S. Congress, www.fineforcongress.org.

CHAPTER NINE

African Americans Face a Political Reality
Ethics and Corruption Investigations

Congress has had ethics, conflict of interest and corruption scandals since the early days of the Republic, and has the authority to take a range of disciplinary measures against members who violate ethics standards, including expulsion, censure and reprimand. In addition, representatives and senators are not immune from criminal prosecutions in state and federal courts or from civil lawsuits.

Rep. Adam Clayton Powell Jr., D-N.Y., is shown here on January 21, 1970. In 1967 the House of Representatives voted 307–116 to refuse to seat the flamboyant congressman amidst allegations of impropriety. Powell sued and in 1969 the U.S. Supreme Court ruled the House had improperly excluded an elected member who met constitutional requirements for membership. Source: AP Images

Allegations of campaign irregularities and fraud involving African American members extend back to the Reconstruction era. For example, John A. Hyman, R-N.C., arrived in Congress in 1875 with a reputation for dishonesty as a state legislator, and he was accused of criminal misconduct after his single term ended. In 1878 the House Judiciary Committee investigated the circumstances of the 1872 state court bribery conviction and sentence of Robert Smalls, R-S.C. (**Document 2.4**) and determined that his conduct did not violate any privilege or right of the House; the governor of South Carolina pardoned Smalls the next year.

Since 1798 the House has investigated more than 100 members; the African Americans among them include Adam Clayton Powell Jr., D-N.Y., who was excluded—denied his seat—for misuse of office and obstruction of the legislative process (**Document 9.2**), and Charles C. Diggs Jr., D-Mich., who was censured for misuse of funds (**Document 9.3**). Convicted felon Melvin J. Reynolds, D-Ill. (**Document 9.7**) resigned before an ethics investigation was complete, and convicted felon Walter R. Tucker III, D-Calif. (**Document 9.8**), announced his resignation the day an expulsion resolution was introduced. After the House unanimously voted to reprove Earl F. Hilliard, D-Ala., in 2001 for improper use of campaign funds, he was defeated in the 2002 primary. In other instances where the House has taken no official action, its Committee on Standards of Official Conduct—informally known as the Ethics Committee—has not recommended action. One such case involved a complaint that Barbara-Rose Collins, D-Mich., misused government and campaign funds and staff

(**Document 9.10**). In another case, the committee decided that a public apology and adverse publicity were sufficient to resolve a sexual harassment case against Gus Savage, D-Ill. (**Document 9.5**).

In 1983 a special counsel investigated alleged cocaine and marijuana use by Rep. Ronald V. Dellums, D-Calif., and one of his aides but found no basis for ethics committee action. In 2000, after a yearlong inquiry into whether Rep. Corrine Brown, D-Fla., had allegedly accepted improper benefits, including a car given as a gift to her daughter, the committee issued a press statement but took no further action against Brown for demonstrating "at the least, poor judgment" and creating "substantial concerns regarding both the appearance of impropriety and the reputation of the House of Representatives." [1]

Former delegate Walter E. Fauntroy, D-D.C., faced criminal charges after he left Congress to seek another office. In 1995 he was charged with filing a false House financial disclosure statement (**Document 9.9**).

Questions of persecution, racial bias and unfairness have frequently arisen when African American lawmakers were targets of criminal investigations, ethical reviews or civil suits. For example, writing later about Powell's exclusion from the House for misconduct in January 1967, Rep. William L. Clay Sr., D-Mo., commented:

> In fact, the accusations against him could have been leveled against every chairman of every full committee in the House of Representatives. He did no more, and no less, than any other in terms of exercising traditional legal privileges that accompanied the powerful position of committee chairman. His private life, including intimate relations with numerous and glamorous women, was routine activity for many members of Congress, committee chairmen or not.[2]

In challenging his 1978 payroll-kickback–related conviction, Diggs asserted that the government had singled him out for prosecution. A federal appeals court rejected that argument, ruling that prosecutors may exercise selectivity in choosing which suspects to charge, as long as such selectivity is not based on discriminatory or arbitrary criteria such as race or religion. The court noted that one of three white representatives who had placed no-show employees on their payrolls had also been convicted.

Controversies have ranged from the relatively inconsequential to the intensely serious. At one end of the spectrum was Rep. Cynthia A. McKinney's March 2006 physical scuffle with a white Capitol police officer who failed to recognize her without her congressional identification pin and attempted to prevent her from entering a congressional office building when she passed a security checkpoint. The incident attracted national press attention. The Georgia Democrat claimed that general racism and her status as a black woman were responsible for the confrontation, telling a news conference, "The whole incident was instigated by the inappropriate touching and stopping of me: a female, black Congresswoman." [3] In a House floor speech the following month, however, McKinney apologized, expressing "my sincere regret about the encounter with the Capitol Hill Police . . . There should not have been any physical contact in this incident . . . I am sorry that this misunderstanding happened at all, I regret its escalation, and I apologize." [4] A grand jury investigation of the incident produced no criminal charges, but McKinney failed to win renomination in the Democratic primary later that year.

In 1998 the Republican New York attorney general filed a civil suit accusing Democratic representative Charles B. Rangel and other directors of the nonprofit Apollo Theatre Foundation of mismanaging the historic Harlem landmark. Critics of the suit called the allegations politically motivated, and Demo-crat Eliot Spitzer dropped the case as meritless after becoming attorney general in 1999. After Spitzer's decision, the *Amster-dam News*, an African American weekly, lambasted the *New York Daily News*, which had won a Pulitzer Prize for its editorials about the Apollo Theatre board, accusing the daily newspaper of "fraud and deception" and call-ing one editorial board member an "acid tongue little devil." [5] Rangel said, "The relentless ef-forts of political adversaries and

Rep. William J. Jefferson, D-La., makes a statement to reporters out-side federal court in Alexandria, Virginia, on June 8, 2007, after pleading not guilty to charges of soliciting more than $500,000 in bribes while using his office to broker business deals in Africa. Source: AP Images/Charles Dharapak

the editorial board of the *New York Daily News* to impugn my integrity and the reputations of my colleagues on the Board have failed." [6]

In another instance, a federal grand jury indicted Rep. Floyd H. Flake, D-N.Y., in 1990 on charges of fraud, tax evasion and conspiracy to misappropriate tens of thousands of dol-lars from the church where he was pastor. He denied wrongdoing, and some constituents and other supporters alleged that the prosecution was partly motivated by race or politics. Part-way through trial, the case was dismissed at the prosecution's request. Similarly, race and pol-itics were proffered as prosecutorial motives for conspiracy and fraud charges leveled in 1987 against Rep. Harold E. Ford, D-Tenn. (**Document 9.6**). Ford, like Flake, maintained his innocence, and Ford was ultimately acquitted.

However, not all perceived persecution involves criminal charges, civil suits or ethics inves-tigations. In 1971, for instance, President Richard M. Nixon's staff compiled a list of politi-cal opponents to be targeted for tax audits and other forms of harassment. Only two members of Congress appeared among the original twenty names on the list compiled by White House chief counsel Charles Colson, and both were African American. Ranked thirteenth in prior-ity was Rep. John Conyers Jr., D-Mich., described in Colson's memo as "Coming on fast. Emerging as a leading black anti-Nixon spokesman. Has known weakness for white females." Rep. Ronald V. Dellums, D-Calif., placed sixteenth with this notation: "Had extensive EMK-Tunney [Sen. Edward M. Kennedy, D-Mass., and Sen. John V. Tunney, D-Calif.] support in his election bid. Success might help in California next year." [7] Eventually, Nixon aides put together an enemies list with thousands of names, including ten other African American rep-resentatives. Conyers would later play a prominent role in the House Judiciary Committee hearings on whether Nixon deserved to be impeached (**Document 6.5**).

Some cases considered in this chapter concern significant constitutional issues. In Powell's situation, the question was the power of Congress to bar duly elected members who meet all the constitutional requirements for a seat. And a 2006–2007 corruption probe of Rep. William J. Jefferson, D-La.—ongoing at the time of publication—raised the question of whether law enforcement agencies have the constitutional authority to search congressional offices (**Document 9.12**).

The earliest controversy presented in this chapter focused on Rep. William L. Dawson of Illinois, who was favored by Chicago's Democratic machine for a cabinet seat—postmaster general—when John F. Kennedy won the presidency (**Document 9.1**). Dawson's potential nomination generated strong editorial opposition amid questions about ethics, ties to the city's political machine and organized crime, age, diligence and ability. The chapter also examines the fate of Florida's first African American federal judge, Alcee L. Hastings, who was impeached by the House and convicted in the Senate of corruption in 1989 (**Document 9.4**). Despite—or because of—Hastings's removal from the bench, the Democrat was elected to the House in 1992.

Document 9.1 in Context
"He Has Enormous Power. Mayors Don't Tell Him What to Do; He Tells Mayors": Rep. William L. Dawson Discussed as Prospective Postmaster General

Like many urban politicians, black and white, Rep. William L. Dawson, D-Ill., owed his political career to machine politics: he started as a Democratic party functionary and rose to Chicago city alderman before winning a U.S. House seat in 1942. Dawson was the senior African American in Congress when John F. Kennedy was elected president in 1960 after narrowly carrying Illinois—and amid allegations of Democratic vote-tampering in Chicago. After the election, there was speculation that Dawson was under consideration for a cabinet seat as postmaster general in appreciation for the crucial support Kennedy had received from the Chicago machine and from black voters. The prospect generated some public support but also drew strong criticism on a variety of grounds, including Dawson's close connection to the political machine of Mayor Richard J. Daley, rumored ties to numbers racketeers and organized crime, and lax attitude toward his congressional responsibilities.

As Kennedy put together his administration, he faced opposition to the prospective appointment from the press and in letters he received as the president-elect; excerpts from some of these pieces follow. Representing the other side, however, the vice president of the Freedom for All Foundation, a community-based organization in Chicago, wrote to Kennedy:

> It is hoped that with the long record of service of William L. Dawson . . . that he will be among those represented in your cabinet. Congressman Dawson has made an imme[a]surable record of good service to his country and to his party. It is altogether fitting and proper that he be accorded this opportunity.[8]

Kennedy's advisers were uneasy about the nomination, so they made arrangements to offer the post to Dawson on the condition that he reject the offer. The president-elect's brother and soon-to-be attorney general, Robert F. Kennedy, later wrote that the rumors and pressure from Democratic organizations were embarrassing to his brother:

> And the President decided that he didn't want him. He didn't have—just looking into his background—the right kind of background that we wanted in the administration, and secondly, he just didn't have the capacity for this position. So we arranged at that time—I think, with Dick Daley and others—that he would come meet with the President, and then go out and say the President had offered him the job but he turned it down because of his health and age.[9]

Ultimately, Kennedy appointed Edward Day, a California business executive and former Illinois insurance commissioner, as postmaster general. Dawson went on to chair the House committees on Expenditures in Executive Departments and Government Operations before his death in 1970.

▬ Document 9.1a ▬
Editorial and Letter to the Editor Opposing Rep. William L. Dawson, D-Ill., as Potential Postmaster General, *Chicago Daily News,* December 1960

"We Can't Believe It: Dawson's Record Should Keep Him Out of Cabinet,"
Editorial, December 10, 1960

SOME PARTISAN Republicans would be delighted if President-elect John Kennedy did in fact appoint Rep. William [L.] Dawson Postmaster General. They would have a good issue for 1964.

It was reported some time ago that Dawson was under consideration for this post. This seemed to us so improbable that we did not discuss it seriously. But within the last couple of days it has again been reported by able correspondents as a possibility—even a probability—that Dawson might get this job.

When the City Council committee investigating crime and politics was operating, it turned up records of four telephone calls from a Chicago telephone to an unlisted Washington telephone in Rep. Dawson's office. The Chicago phone was commonly used by Tony Accardo, Jake Guzik, and persons associated with them. From that telephone many long-distance calls went to prominent underworld characters all over the United States.

Dawson denied that he, personally, had ever received any calls from that phone or had talked by phone to any such persons as Accardo and Guzik.

THERE WOULD be special irony in appointing Dawson Postmaster General. A few years ago Dawson's own secretary was convicted and served time for selling nine civil service jobs in the Chicago post office for $3,508 in bribes.

Otto Kerner, then U.S. district attorney, prosecuted the case, but he said he had no evidence connecting Dawson with this corruption.

The 1954 report of the Chicago Crime Commission reported a conversation that two of its investigators had had with Dawson. They said he had on his desk a pile of arrest slips about five inches high relating to gambling offenses.

Dawson was quoted as saying he intended to see Mayor [Martin H.] Kennelly about these slips, but expected to get no satisfaction from him. However, he was quoted as saying he formerly got along fine with Mayor [Edward J.] Kelly. Dawson was also quoted as saying he never hesitated to take money for political purposes from "policy operators."

After this was printed, Dawson denied he had said anything of the kind, adding that he had never talked to Virgil Peterson, operating director of the Crime Commission. It had never been said he had talked to Peterson: the printed report was supposed to be a conversation with two unnamed investigators from the Crime Commission's office.

MORE DETAILS of the same kind could be reported. But more particulars would be pointless. Everybody in or near Chicago knows Dawson's political role on the South Side.

Here he has enormous power. Mayors don't tell him what to do; he tells mayors, and it is to Kennelly's credit that he didn't respond. This cost Kennelly a third term.

Richard J. Daley was still telling people what a great mayor Kennelly was, and how richly Kennelly deserved a third term, when Dawson served notice on the Democratic central committee that Kennelly had to go. He was defeated.

Dawson has absolute political power over an area which has the most crime in Chicago in proportion to its population; the most "errors," "intentional" and otherwise, in counting votes; the most fraud in the registration of voters; and traditionally, at least, the most corruption among the police serving the area.

It is impossible for Sen. Kennedy or his brother to have gone through the Senate racket hearings without knowing all these things. The two Kennedys are neither stupid nor ignorant. Some of their Chicago friends have told them about Dawson.

We cannot believe that the next President will appoint Dawson. If he does, it would indicate that the next President likes the way Dawson runs Chicago's South Side. It would encourage similar conduct in other big cities.

"He Also Dislikes Dawson," Letter to the Editor, December 14, 1960

YOUR EDITORIAL REVIEW of Rep. William Dawson's qualifications for the post of Postmaster General was excellent but incomplete. Dawson, as a Negro, poses as a representative of his people. Nothing could be further from the truth.

His voting record in Congress, when he bothers to be there to vote, leaves much to be desired. His role at Democratic party conventions has been that of an Uncle Tom—a compromiser of Negro aspirations.

His power is based on Chicago's Negro ghetto. It will be interesting to see how his handpicked aldermen vote on Ald. [Leon M.] Despres' Open Occupancy Ordinance. This ordinance is supported by virtually every Negro in Chicago—but it would, if passed, also spell the end of Dawson's political power. It is noteworthy that it had to be introduced by a white.

Dawson took over, and quieted, the Chicago Branch of the NAACP—because it was becoming too active and militant and thus embarrassing "his" city administration.

Much more could be said, and documented, of Dawson's role as a "representative" of Chicago's Negro population. Suffice it to say that the civil rights struggle goes on despite Dawson, not because of him.

He represents, really, only the most corrupt and self-seeking minority segments of the Negro community.

It would be extremely gratifying to have a Negro appointed to the Cabinet. Such an appointment is long overdue and many qualified Negroes exist.

Dawson is not such a man.

SCOTT ARDEN.
Chicago.

Source: "We Can't Believe It: Dawson's Record Should Keep Him Out of Cabinet," *Chicago Daily News,* December 10, 1960; "He Also Dislikes Dawson," *Chicago Daily News,* December 14, 1960, from the John F. Kennedy Presidential Library.

▬ Document 9.1b ▬
Letters to President-elect John F. Kennedy, Opposing Consideration of Rep. Dawson as Possible Postmaster General, December 1960

Commonwealth Edison Company
Chicago-Central Division
5059 West Polk Street, Chicago 44, Illinois
December 1960

Senator Kennedy—
. . . Mr. Wm. Dawson's record in Chicago, Ill. Should keep him out of your Cabinet.

I would suggest you surround yourself with men who will be a credit to your administration.

My best wishes to you in keeping this Country on top.

Sincerely,
Victor Hamlin

Mrs. Edmund D. Soper
1202 Maple Avenue
Evanston, Ill.
Dec. 14, 1950

President-elect John F. Kennedy
Washington, D.C.

Dear Sir,

This letter has just one message: *Please don't appoint Rep. William Dawson of Chicago to anything!* . . .

I cannot give you expert opinion nor specific information on Mr. Dawson. I only know that around here I get only the reaction: Sure he's a Negro and Daly man (or a mid-westerner) but if Kennedy has debts to pay or needs a symbol he certainly can find a *much* better one. His age is also against him.

I speak as a Democrat in this rabid, reactionary Republican suburban area, where my husband and I have been proud to align ourselves with [Adlai] Stevenson [,] Paul Douglas, Otto Kerner, and our local Tyler Thompson (who lost to Marguerite Stitt Church after a magnificent, stirring campaign.)

Also, I speak as one deeply interested in Human Relations and Civil Rights. I would very much like to see able Negroes in places of service to their country. And able mid-Westerners too, for that matter.

With every good wish, and assurance of our constant support,

Sincerely yours,
Moneta T. Soper

Source: John F. Kennedy Presidential Library, Boston, Massachusetts.

Document 9.2 in Context
"Resolved—That the Speaker Administer the Oath of Office to the
Said Adam Clayton Powell": The Exclusion and Reinstatement of
Rep. Powell, D-N.Y.

Adam Clayton Powell Jr., a Harlem minister and civil rights activist, was first elected to the U.S. House of Representatives in 1944. Speaker of the House Sam Rayburn, D-Texas, advised the new member to move slowly and watch how things operate. Powell replied, "Mr. Speaker, I've got a bomb in each hand, and I'm going to throw them right away." [10] He immediately launched into sponsorship of civil rights and labor legislation, and in 1956 he authored what would become the Powell Amendment to a school construction aid bill prohibiting federal funds for projects and programs where racial discrimination existed.

With longevity at the polls and the seniority system in the House, he rose beyond his initial assignments on the Indian Affairs, Invalid Pensions and Labor committees to chair the influential Education and Labor Committee for six years, starting in 1961 when John F. Kennedy took office as president. Shortly after his inauguration, Kennedy wrote a testimonial letter predicting that Powell "will play an important role in carrying through the program of the new Administration. I know he will succeed in this as he has succeeded in so many past efforts to protect and advance the human and civil rights of all Americans." [11] And in the years of Kennedy's New Frontier and Lyndon B. Johnson's Great Society, Powell indeed played a key role in pushing the two presidents' legislative agendas on education, Head Start, job training and related social issues.

But Powell's personal problems had already begun. He was indicted in 1958 on tax evasion charges, and although a jury deadlocked in 1960, he eventually paid $27,833 in penalties and back interest. Also, a widow with organized crime ties whom he had described in a broadcast interview as a "bag woman"—somebody designated to make the payoffs of bribe money to corrupt police officers—successfully sued him for defamation. In 1963 a civil jury awarded the woman $211,500 in damages, and Powell was cited for civil contempt after refusing to pay. There were also complaints that Powell misused $40,000 in committee funds for payments that included the salary of his third wife, whom he kept on the congressional payroll although she had moved to Puerto Rico in 1961. In addition, many of his colleagues were angry about how seldom he showed up in Washington for committee meetings and House sessions.

In January 1967, at the start of the new Congress, fellow Democrats who were unhappy about Powell's absenteeism ousted him as chair of the Education and Labor Committee, a move Powell described as "lynching, northern style." [12] Then the House passed a resolution, pushed by House minority leader and future president Gerald R. Ford, R-Mich., to exclude, or bar, him from taking his seat pending investigation. A Judiciary Committee inquiry followed, and the committee recommended that he be sworn in but censured, stripped of seniority and fined. Instead, however, the House voted 307–116 to exclude him—the first representative excluded in 47 years.

New York held a special election that April to fill the vacancy created by Powell's exclusion, and Powell won that election with overwhelming voter support. He chose, however, not to appear in the House chamber to be sworn in for the remainder of the term. Then, he ran in and won the November 1968 election for a full term.

When Congress returned for its new session in January 1969, the issue of whether to seat Powell arose. Moments before the vote on that question, Rep. Albert W. Watson, R-S.C., took the floor to oppose Powell's return:

> What kind of double standard is this? What manner of hypocrisy? Are we to say to the American taxpayer that $40,000 of his hard-earned money goes as a gift to a flamboyant Congressman who happens to enjoy the good life while at the same time warning that taxpayer not to fudge on his deductions?
> ADAM CLAYTON POWELL is not on trial here. The House of Representatives is on trial. A mere slap on the wrist, a directive to pay back the $40,000—all of these efforts at making a haughty man atone for past sins are absolutely superfluous.[13]

The following resolution to seat Powell passed 252–160, with Gerald Ford among the majority voting to seat Powell.

Later, in a landmark decision in June 1969, the Supreme Court held that the exclusion had been unconstitutional because Powell met all the constitutional requirements for office. Even so, his political career was nearing its end; he would be defeated in the 1970 Democratic primary.

▬▬ Document 9.2 ▬▬
House Resolution to Seat Rep. Adam Clayton Powell Jr., D-N.Y., January 3, 1969

The Clerk reread the resolution, as follows:

H. RES. 2

Resolved—

1. That the Speaker administer the oath of office to the said Adam Clayton Powell, Member-elect from the Eighteenth District of the State of New York.
2. That as punishment Adam Clayton Powell be and he hereby is fined the sum of $25,000, said sum to be paid to the Clerk to be disposed of by him according to law. The Sergeant-at-Arms of the House is directed to deduct $1,150 per month from the salary otherwise due the said Adam Clayton Powell, and pay the same to said clerk until said $25,000 fine is fully paid.
3. That as further punishment the seniority of the said Adam Clayton Powell in the House of Representatives commence as of the date he takes the oath as a Member of the 91st Congress.
4. That if the said Adam Clayton Powell does not present himself to take the oath of office on or before January 15, 1969, the seat of the Eighteenth District of the State of New York shall be deemed vacant and the Speaker shall notify the Governor of New York of the existing vacancy.

The SPEAKER. The question is on the resolution . . .

The yeas and nays were ordered.

The question was taken; and there were—yeas 252, nays 160, answered "present" 6, not voting 17 . . .

Source: Congressional Record, 91st Cong., 1st sess., January 3, 1969, H21.

Document 9.3 in Context
"We Hold That the Case Was Proved and the Conviction Is Affirmed": Rep. Charles C. Diggs Jr., D-Mich., Is Convicted of Fraud

During his twenty-five years on Capitol Hill, Rep. Charles C. Diggs Jr., a Detroit Democrat and former state legislator, moved steadily up the seniority ladder and, at the same time, witnessed growth in the number of black representatives. He first won the seat by defeating a fellow Democrat in the 1954 primary and was one of only three black members sworn in the following January.

In the House, he chaired the Committee on the District of Columbia and the Foreign Affairs Committee's Subcommittee on African Affairs. In addition, he served as the first chair of the Congressional Black Caucus, which he cofounded in 1971 (**Document 6.2**).

In 1978 a grand jury in Washington, D.C., indicted him for running a payroll-kickback scheme in which he took an estimated $66,000 from staffers. According to trial testimony, he used some of the money for personal expenses, some for expenses of his funeral home, the House of Diggs, and the rest for congressional expenses. Evidence showed that some of the funds were spent on life insurance premiums and home mortgage payments, for example, while other money covered rent for his district office and political contributions. One of his former congressional employees testified that she had spent 80 percent of her time working on his funeral home business and only 20 percent on congressional matters.

Even so, Diggs's constituents reelected him the month after his October 1978 conviction. His House colleagues, however, stripped him of committee and subcommittee leadership positions, and in a letter to the Ethics Committee—formally the Committee on Standards of Official Conduct—he admitted misusing public funds and agreed to repay more than $40,000. During the subsequent debate in the full House, nobody spoke in his defense, and on July 31, 1979, the chamber voted 414 to 0 to censure him. The Internal Revenue Service also assessed unpaid taxes on the kickbacks.

On the criminal front, in 1979 the U.S. Court of Appeals for the District of Columbia Circuit upheld his jury conviction on all twenty-nine charges. One appeals judge, Harold Leventhal, dissented in part, saying the jury should have been allowed to differentiate between charges related to personal use of the funds and charges involving use of part of the money to cover Congress-related expenses.

Only when the U.S. Supreme Court refused to review the case did Diggs resign from Congress and go to prison. He spent seven months of his three-year term behind bars before his release. He died in 1998. A year later, his biographer and former press secretary Carolyn DuBose wrote that "Diggs was a visionary" for his role in cofounding the Congressional Black Caucus.[14]

Document 9.3
Appeals Court Affirms the Corruption Conviction of Rep. Charles C. Diggs Jr., D-Mich., in *U.S. v. Diggs*, November 14, 1979

[Malcolm R.] WILKEY, Circuit Judge.

The defendant Charles C. Diggs, Jr. . . . appeals from a conviction on eleven counts of mail fraud . . . and eighteen counts of making false statements to a United States agency . . .

The indictment alleged that between 1 July 1973 and 2 March 1977 the defendant devised a scheme to defraud the United States by misapplying funds allotted for the compensation of congressional employees. On this appeal, the defendant does not challenge the sufficiency of the evidence but contends rather that he lacked the requisite intent to defraud and that he acted within the bounds of his discretion to set the duties and salaries of his congressional employees . . .

. . . Briefly summarizing the counts of the indictment, counts 1 through 4 alleged that Congressman Diggs engaged in a scheme to defraud the United States by inflating the salary of Felix R. Matlock, a congressional employee, as a means of paying various personal, business, and House of Representative expenses; counts 5 through 7 and 8 through 11 charged that Congressman Diggs placed on the congressional payroll Jeralee Richmond and George Johnson as compensation for services rendered either to defendant Diggs personally or to the family business, the House of Diggs. Counts 12 through 29 alleged that the defendant filed materially false and misleading Payroll Authorization Forms with the House of Representatives Office of Finance: counts 12 through 20 charged that he concealed from the agency the fact that he inflated the salaries of Jean G. Stultz, Felix Matlock, and Ofield Dukes with the intention of using the increase in their salaries to meet his own personal and congressional obligations; and counts 21 through 23 and 24 through 29 charged that the defendant placed George Johnson and Jeralee Richmond on the payroll to compensate them for services that were unrelated to the defendant's congressional duties.

I. FACTUAL BACKGROUND

At different periods from October 1973 to January 1977, three of defendant Diggs' congressional employees . . . paid out of the salary allotted to them from the congressional clerk-hire allowance various personal, business, or official expenses of the defendant . . . What is disputed by the defendant are the questions of whether the clerk-hire allowance could be used to defray his congressional expenses and whether the employees' expenditures were made at his direction . . .

Finally, the indictment alleges that Jeralee Richmond and George Johnson performed no congressionally related work while they were compensated from the congressional payroll. Defendant placed Jeralee Richmond on the congressional payroll in July 1974 at a salary of $8,500.00. She was employed at the House of Diggs' Funeral Home in Detroit as a bookkeeper, and she was also expected to deal with problems of constituents who came to the funeral home. Richmond testified that while on the House rolls from July 1974 to August 1976, approximately twenty percent of her time was apportioned to handling constituents' problems and eighty percent to bookkeeping matters of the funeral home . . .

II. ANALYSIS

The scheme to defraud set forth in the indictment has two subparts: (1) the allegation that the defendant "inflated the salaries of Jean G. Stultz, Felix R. Matlock and Ofield Dukes in order to pay for various personal, business and House of Representatives' expenses of defendant Diggs," and (2) the allegation that the defendant placed on the House of Representatives' payroll Jeralee Richmond and George Johnson "who performed no work for the House of Representatives" . . .

A. The Scheme to Defraud: Inflated Salaries of Congressional Employees

1. The Clerk-Hire Allowance

(1) The Government tried its case against the defendant on the rationale that using clerk-hire funds to pay either the Congressman's personal and business expenses or his official expenses was illegal. The Government combined in the same counts of the indictment transactions relating to both types of expenditures. Although defendant admits that it "may have been improper for an employee to be compensated from the clerk-hire allowance for the payment of personal expenses," he asserts that use of the clerk-hire allowance to pay certain of the district office expenses was entirely proper. Thus, putting aside for a moment the question of the defendant's intent in increasing his employees' salaries, we must decide in the first instance whether drawing on clerk-hire funds to meet either the defendant's personal or congressional expenses was illegal. We hold that it was . . .

The clerk-hire allowance is an appropriation by Congress providing compensation "(f)or staff employed by each Member in the discharge of his official and representative duties." On hiring an employee or on adjusting the amount of compensation that an employee will receive, a congressman must submit a "Payroll Authorization Form" to the House of Representatives Office of Finance, marking on the form either the entry entitled "Appointment" or the one designated "Salary Adjustment" . . .

In Diggs' case the defendant submitted the payroll forms to the House Office of Finance approving the increases in the salaries of Stultz, Matlock, and Dukes with the knowledge, undeniable after the first remittitur, that the increment would be used to pay his personal and official expenses. These payments benefited not the employees but the defendant himself. Obviously the defendant directly benefited from the payments to his personal creditors and to the creditors of his business, the House of Diggs. It is equally clear that the defendant profited from the payment of his congressional expenses. Payment of these bills enabled the defendant to provide services to his constituents and thus furthered his prospects for reelection . . . Defendant argues nevertheless that using clerk-hire funds to compensate employees for paying district office expenses fell within his discretion to determine both the salaries and responsibilities of his employees, provided those responsibilities relate to the Congressman's "official and representative duties." The phrase "official and representative duties," so the argument goes, is sufficiently broad to encompass an employee's responsibility for paying congressional expenses. We disagree . . .

The defendant's argument erroneously equates a congressman's discretion to define the duties of an employee with the unfettered power to divert monies intended for one purpose to another, completely unauthorized purpose. During the period relevant to the indictment, the Committee on House Administration had fixed an allowance for district office expenses at $500 per quarter or $2,000 per annum. Thus the allowance for clerk-hire and the allowance for district office expenses were separate and distinct. No House regulation or order authorized the commingling of these funds, either directly, or, as in this case, indirectly . . .

Second, we find that the actual scheme to defraud has clearly been established. No House regulation or order authorized the use of the clerk-hire allowance for purposes other than the sole use and benefit of the staff of a congressman; the money was to go to individual employees for their personal salaries and subsequent personal use or it was not to be expended at all . . .

The defendant defrauded the public of not only substantial sums of money but of his faithful and honest services . . .

III. CONCLUSION

In conclusion, we hold that the case was proved and the conviction is
Affirmed . . .

[Harold] LEVENTHAL, Circuit Judge (dissenting in part):

. . . There was convincing evidence that he did receive kickbacks which were then applied to his personal debts and the business expenses of his Detroit funeral home (the House of Diggs). If the case had been tried on that basis alone, there would have been no problem on appeal.

But there is a problem, one traceable to the government's theory in this prosecution. The government alleged that there were also kickbacks which appellant used to defray his Congressional office expenses . . .

. . . Appellant sought a good faith instruction that if appellant acted with a good faith belief in his right to compensate his employees for paying official congressional expenses, he should be acquitted of the pertinent counts. The court declined to give such an instruction unless it included a statement to the effect that the Congressman could not have acted in good faith unless he believed that the salary described in the employee's payroll authorization forms would be solely for the personal use of the employee, and not compensation for a personal or congressional expense . . .

In facing up to reality, we must confront the underlying question, whether it was widely understood on Capitol Hill that there was an ambiguity in the rules governing use of clerk-hire funds which permitted Congressmen to use the mechanism of inflated allowances to cover congressional expenses. While such use was not explicitly authorized at the time, if it was in some vogue, however uneasy, we must seriously question whether the broad fraud-false statement laws are fairly applicable to reach a practice that is not specifically covered by House rules. There is a fundamental difference between breach of ethics and criminal violations. What is shenanigans, bad taste, and borderline is not the same as what is criminal . . .

. . . The jury should have been allowed to separately consider whether or not appellant acted with fraudulent intent in using the clerk-hire funds for congressional expenses.

Source: U.S. v. Diggs, 613 F.2d 988 (D.C. Cir. 1979).

Document 9.4 in Context
"Guilty of an Impeachable Offense Warranting Removal from Office": Judge Alcee L. Hastings Becomes Rep. Hastings, D-Fla.

When the U.S. House of Representatives impeached U.S. District Judge Alcee L. Hastings of Florida and the Senate convicted him and removed him in 1989 from a lifetime appointment to the bench, their actions unwittingly set in motion the ousted judge's congressional career. In 1992 he won election to the House as a Democrat, where he would sit among many colleagues who had deemed him corrupt.

President Jimmy Carter named Hastings to the bench in 1979 as Florida's first black federal judge. In 1981 a federal grand jury indicted him on bribery and conspiracy charges for allegedly illegal conduct in connection with the prosecution of racketeers Frank and Thomas Romano. Hastings was acquitted; however, his alleged coconspirator, disbarred criminal defense lawyer William Borders, was convicted in a separate trial.

The articles of impeachment voted by the House accused Hastings of soliciting a $150,000 bribe to keep the Romanos out of prison and to enable them to recover most of the $1.2 million in assets that the government had seized. The articles also charged Hastings with committing perjury at his criminal trial.

Hastings's trial brief to the Senate professed his innocence and integrity, and argued that senators were being asked to repudiate a jury verdict merely because they felt uncomfortable with an acquitted judge remaining on the bench. Even so, the Senate convicted him of eight of seventeen articles of impeachment. Hastings then sued to force the government to restore him to office, but a federal judge ruled that the courts lack constitutional authority to review Senate processes for impeachment trials.

Later, when President Bill Clinton faced impeachment in the House in 1998 (**Documents 7.5** and **10.9**), Hastings defended him in a floor speech:

> Today, we have reached the zenith of unfairness. Our military, under the aegis of our President, is attempting to downgrade weapons of mass destruction in Iraq, and we are en masse, as a body, degrading the institution of the Presidency. It's not sad; it's irrational . . .
>
> Our nation is divided. And the House tomorrow will exacerbate that division. We're being unfair and unwise. We are being harsh to the institution of the Presidency, harsh to our troops in harm's way, harsh to each other as colleagues, and extremely harsh to this great country of ours.
>
> This is not a debate for the ages; rather, it is a debate of the stages—partisan political stages.[15]

After Democrats recaptured the House in the 2006 election, Hastings was in line to chair the Intelligence Committee, but Speaker-designate Nancy Pelosi, D-Calif., passed him over. Her official statement, which mentioned neither the bribery prosecution nor impeachment, merely said:

> Congressman Alcee Hastings and I have had extensive consultations, and today I advised him that I would select someone else as Chairman of the House Intelligence Committee. Alcee Hastings has always placed national security as his highest priority. He has served our country well, and I have full confidence that he will continue to do so.[16]

In response, the chair of the Congressional Black Caucus, Melvin L. Watt, D-N.C., praised Hastings's qualifications for the post: "an unequivocal commitment to our nation's security, selflessness and true statesmanship. He would have made an outstanding Intelligence Chairman and we still hope he will at some point in our nation's future."[17] In April 2007 Hastings asserted that, for the good of the Democratic party, he had asked Speaker Pelosi not to appoint him.[18]

▬▬ Document 9.4 ▬▬
Articles of Impeachment against Judge Alcee L. Hastings, October 20, 1989

ARTICLE I

From some time in the first half of 1981 and continuing through October 9, 1981, Judge Hastings and William Borders, then a Washington, D.C. attorney, engaged in a corrupt conspiracy to obtain $150,000 from defendants in United States v. Romano, a case tried before Judge Hastings, in return for the imposition of sentences which would not require incarceration of the defendants.

Wherefore, Judge Alcee L. Hastings is guilty of an impeachable offense warranting removal from office.

ARTICLE II

From January 18, 1983, until February 4, 1983, Judge Hastings was a defendant in a criminal case in the United States District court for the Southern District of Florida. In the course of the trial of that case, Judge Hastings, while under oath to tell the truth, the whole truth, and nothing but the truth, did knowingly and contrary to that oath make a false statement which was intended to mislead the trier of fact.

The false statement was, in substance, that Judge Hastings and William Borders, of Washington, D.C., never made any agreement to solicit a bribe from defendants in United States v. Romano, a case tried before Judge Hastings.

Wherefore, Judge Alcee L. Hastings is guilty of an impeachable offense warranting removal from office.

ARTICLE III

From January 18, 1983, until February 4, 1983, Judge Hastings was a defendant in a criminal case in the United States District court for the Southern District of Florida. In the course of the trial of that case, Judge Hastings, while under oath to tell the truth, the whole truth, and nothing but the truth, did knowingly and contrary to that oath make a false statement which was intended to mislead the trier of fact.

The false statement was, in substance, that Judge Hastings never agreed with William Borders, of Washington, D.C., to modify the sentences of defendants in United States v. Romano . . . from a term in the Federal penitentiary to probation in return for a bribe from those defendants.

Wherefore, Judge Alcee L. Hastings is guilty of an impeachable offense warranting removal from office.

ARTICLE IV

. . . The false statement was, in substance, that Judge Hastings never agreed with William Borders, of Washington, D.C., in connection with a payment on a bribe, to enter an order returning a substantial amount of property to the defendants in United States v. Romano . . . Judge Hastings had previously ordered that property forfeited.

Wherefore, Judge Alcee L. Hastings is guilty of an impeachable offense warranting removal from office . . .

ARTICLE VIII

. . . The false statement was, in substance, that Judge Hastings' October 5, 1981, telephone conversation with William Borders, of Washington, D.C. . . . was a coded conversation in furtherance of a conspiracy with Mr. Borders to solicit a bribe . . .

Wherefore, Judge Alcee L. Hastings is guilty of an impeachable offense warranting removal from office . . .

ARTICLE XVI

From July 15, 1985, to September 15, 1985, Judge Hastings was the supervising judge of a wiretap . . . The wiretap was part of certain investigations then being conducted by law enforcement agents of the United States.

As supervising judge, Judge Hastings learned highly confidential information obtained through the wiretap. The documents disclosing this information, presented to Judge Hastings as the supervising judge, were Judge Hastings' sole source of the highly confidential information.

On September 6, 1985, Judge Hastings revealed highly confidential information that he learned as the supervising judge on the wiretap, as follows: On the morning of September 6, 1985, Judge Hastings told Stephen Clark, the Mayor of Dade County, Florida, to stay away from Kevin "Waxy" Gordon, who was "hot" and was using the Mayor's name in Hialeah, Florida.

As a result of this improper disclosure, certain investigations then being conducted by law enforcement agents of the United States were thwarted and ultimately terminated.

Wherefore, Judge Alcee L. Hastings is guilty of an impeachable offense warranting removal from office.

ARTICLE XVII

Judge Hastings, who as a Federal judge is required to enforce and obey the Constitution and laws of the United States, to uphold the integrity of the judiciary, to avoid impropriety and appearance of impropriety, and to perform the duties of his office impartially, did through—

(1) a corrupt relationship with William Borders, of Washington, D.C.;
(2) repeated false testimony under oath at Judge Hastings' criminal trial;
(3) fabrication of false documents which were submitted as evidence at his criminal trial; and
(4) improper disclosure of confidential information acquired by him as supervisory judge of a wiretap;

undermine confidence in the integrity and impartiality of the judiciary and betray the trust of the people of the United States, thereby bringing disrepute on the Federal Courts and the administration of justice by the Federal Courts.

Wherefore, Judge Alcee L. Hastings is guilty of an impeachable offense warranting removal from office.

Source: U.S. Senate, "Articles of Impeachment Voted by the House of Representatives since 1974: Alcee L. Hastings," in *Impeachment of President William Jefferson Clinton: The Evidentiary Record Pursuant to S. Res. 16,* 106th Cong., 1st sess., S. Doc. 106-3 (Washington, D.C.: U.S. Government Printing Office, 1999), vol. 19, 9–14, www.access.gpo.gov/congress/senate/sd106-3.html.

Document 9.5 in Context
"Be It Resolved, That This Committee Conduct a Preliminary Inquiry": Investigation of Rep. Gus Savage, D-Ill., for Sexual Harassment

Rep. Gus Savage, D-Ill., a former journalist and political activist in Chicago, lost his first contest for the House in 1970 but won a seat ten years later.

His ethics problem arose in March 1989, when he was accused of sexually harassing a female Peace Corps volunteer in Zaire while on an official trip to Africa. The alleged misconduct occurred after a dinner at the home of the U.S. ambassador, when Savage and the volunteer were in a car and he became aggressive, both verbally and physically. The ambassador learned of the incident and confronted Savage, who denied any impropriety. After the *Washington Post* reported the incident in July 1989, members of the House asked the Ethics Committee—formally the Committee on Standards of Official Conduct—to investigate, and the State Department's inspector general told the newspaper that the incident was "pretty egregious." [19]

On August 3, 1989, the committee authorized an investigation. Its report concluded that Savage had subjected the woman, whom it did not identify, to unwanted sexual advances that included forcibly kissing her and asking her several times to have sex.

On November 20, 1989, Savage sent the woman a short written apology. In its report, the committee said that it disapproved of Savage's behavior but that his self-initiated letter made it unnecessary for the committee to order an apology. The letter, coupled with public disclosure of the incident, led the committee to conclude that it need not take any other action.

In a later speech on the House floor, Savage attacked white Democratic colleagues who had complained about him: "And believe it or not, among these self-appointed guardians of personal morality there was one who since has admitted keeping and prostituting a homosexual," he said of Rep. Barney Frank of Massachusetts, who is gay and had been reprimanded for his involvement with a lover who ran a prostitution business from Frank's apartment. "As for the other two so-called liberals," Savage said, referring to Reps. Matthew F. McHugh of New York and Patricia S. Schroeder of Colorado, "I urge them to review their sensitivity to racism and respect for fairness." [20] Savage blocked the *Congressional Record* from printing his remarks.

However, the ethics inquiry, coupled with redistricting and anti-Semitic remarks Savage later made during the 1990 primary campaign, ultimately spelled the end of his political career. Although he narrowly won renomination in the 1990 Democratic primary over challenger Mel Reynolds, Reynolds trounced him in 1992. Reynolds later would be convicted of sexual assault and fraud charges and be forced to resign from Congress in disgrace (**Document 9.7**).

▬ Document 9.5 ▬
Resolution of House Committee on Official Standards Authorizing an Investigation of Rep. Gus Savage, D-Ill., August 3, 1989, and Savage's Letter of Apology, November 20, 1989

RESOLUTION

WHEREAS, the Committee on Standards of Official Conduct has been presented with complaints concerning the actions of Representative Gus Savage while that Member traveled to Africa in connection with his official duties and responsibilities in March 1989; and

WHEREAS, if shown to be true, the actions of Representative Savage implicate the Code of Official Conduct or a law, rule, regulation or other standard applicable to Representative Savage's conduct in the performance of his duties or in the discharge of his responsibilities, and

WHEREAS, pursuant to Committee Rules 10(b) and 13, the Committee determines that the matters merit further inquiry;

NOW, THEREFORE, BE IT RESOLVED, that this Committee conduct a Preliminary Inquiry pursuant to Committee Rule 11(a) to determine whether violations have occurred; and

BE IT FURTHER RESOLVED, that the Chairman and Ranking Minority Member are authorized to issue subpoenas on behalf of the Committee, either for the taking of depositions or the production of records, and that all testimony taken by deposition or things produced pursuant to subpoena or otherwise shall be deemed to have been taken, produced, or furnished in Executive Session; and

BE IT FURTHER RESOLVED, that Representative Savage be immediately notified of this action and informed of his rights pursuant to the Rules of this Committee.

HOUSE OF REPRESENTATIVES
WASHINGTON D.C. 20515

November 20, 1989

While in Zaire earlier this year, if you felt personally offended by any words or actions of mine, I apologize, because I never intended to offend and was not aware that you felt offended at that time.

Sincerely,
Gus Savage, M.C.

Source: House Committee on Standards of Official Conduct, *In the Matter of Representative Gus Savage,* 101st Cong., 2d sess., 1990, H. Rep. 101-397.

Document 9.6 in Context
"Defendants' Motions to Dismiss the Indictment on Double Jeopardy Grounds . . . Are Denied": Rep. Harold E. Ford, D-Tenn., Is Tried, Retried and Acquitted in Corruption Case

It took six years and two trials, but Rep. Harold E. Ford, D-Tenn., was ultimately cleared of fraud and conspiracy charges stemming from an alleged scheme to take bribes from two Tennessee bankers. In April 1987 a federal grand jury accused Ford of conspiring with financiers Jacob Butcher, a twice-unsuccessful Democratic candidate for governor, and his brother C. H. Butcher Jr. to commit tax, bank and mail fraud. The indictment alleged that the Butchers, who once controlled an empire of twenty-seven banks that failed, paid the member of Congress more than $1 million in bribes disguised as business loans that Ford was not expected to repay. The purported plot included the formation of a dummy corporation that funneled payoffs to Ford for his personal use. In a separate case, the Butchers were convicted of defrauding depositors of $20 million and imprisoned.

A former state legislator, Ford belonged to a politically influential Memphis family and chaired a House Ways and Means subcommittee at the time of the indictment. He denied all charges and asserted that Reagan administration prosecutors were politically and racially motivated. Members of the Congressional Black Caucus committed themselves to raise $250,000 toward his defense.

Ford's first trial in 1990 ended when the jurors deadlocked along racial lines and U.S. District Judge Odell Horton declared a mistrial, clearing the way for prosecutors to try the case again. At that point, Ford and his codefendants asked the judge to dismiss the indictment and acquit them, arguing that a retrial would violate the Fifth Amendment prohibition against double jeopardy. The codefendants—two lawyers and an accountant—were accused of facilitating the alleged illicit transactions. In the following excerpt from Horton's decision denying their motion, the judge cites indications of juror misconduct and explains why a retrial was not constitutionally barred.

The issue of political motivations arose again in advance of Ford's second trial before a different judge. Ford, with the backing of the Clinton administration's Justice Department, unsuccessfully objected to the selection of jurors from a predominantly white, rural area of the state. Together, they asked that the jury be chosen from predominantly black Memphis, where the trial was to take place, but the judge rejected that request. In April 1993 the eleven white jurors and one black juror acquitted Ford.

Ford remained in Congress until 1996, when he chose not to run for reelection. His son, Harold E. Ford Jr., won the seat that year.

▬ Document 9.6 ▬
Judge's Decision Upholding Mistrial in Criminal Case against Rep. Harold E. Ford, D-Tenn., in *U.S. v. Ford,* April 10, 1991

. . .

Manifest Necessity

It has long been established in the constitutional jurisprudence of this nation that a federal trial judge may discharge a jury before a verdict is reached, even over the objection of a defendant, where there is a manifest necessity for its declaration or if the ends of public justice would otherwise be defeated . . .

The Court declared a mistrial in this case and discharged the jury, over the defendants' objections, because of 1) manifest necessity and 2) the ends of public justice . . .

Ends of Public Justice

The Court's decision to declare a mistrial in this case was also supported by its considerations of the ends of public justice. Juror misconduct permeated the trial of this case. Two selected jurors were excused from service on the jury by the Court, after extensive questioning, because of their failure during the jury selection process to answer truthfully questions bearing upon their qualifications to serve as jurors. There were strong indications of improper juror contact with outside persons during jury deliberations. Persons sympathetic to one or more defendants visited the courtroom and, throughout the trial, conducted themselves at times in a discourteous manner, obviously and blatantly attempting to influence the jury, despite the best efforts of the Court to discourage such misconduct. Defense counsel did virtually nothing to assist the Court in this effort. Subsequent interviews with discharged jurors by the FBI revealed evidence not only of possible juror misconduct, but also indicated that problematically two jurors were unwilling to follow the law—even though they had faithfully promised to do so during voir dire. One of the excused jurors indicated there was probably guilt on some counts but she could not vote guilty. One juror was reported asleep under the table in the jury room during deliberations. The jury foreman reported to the Court the jury had reached verdicts. Yet, when asked to read the verdicts, he read, before the Court stopped him, not verdicts but the divided vote of jurors on one defendant.

Considering these circumstances, it is clear to the Court the public's interest in a fair trial designed to end in a just judgment has not been served.

The Government, like the defendant, is entitled to resolution of the case by verdict from the jury, and jeopardy does not terminate when the jury is discharged because it is unable to agree. Regardless of the sufficiency of the evidence at petitioner's first trial, he has no valid double jeopardy claim to prevent his retrial . . .

Defendants' motions to dismiss the indictment on double jeopardy grounds as to all defendants are denied. The mistrial was dictated by reasons of 1) manifest necessity and 2) the ends of public justice . . .

Source: U.S. v. Ford, 812 F.Supp. 761 (April 10, 1991).

Document 9.7 in Context
"False and Fraudulent Pretenses, Representations and Promises":
Rep. Melvin J. Reynolds, D-Ill., Is Convicted of Sexual, Financial Crimes

It took Rep. Melvin J. Reynolds, D-Ill., three tries to launch his congressional career, a career that would self-destruct in less than three years in office. He lost primary races for the House in 1988 and 1990 before defeating incumbent Rep. Gus Savage in the 1992 Democratic primary. At the time, Savage had been tainted by a sexual harassment scandal and had been subject to a House ethics investigation (**Document 9.5**).

In June 1994, partway through Reynolds's first term, a teenager complained to police that she had had consensual sex with Reynolds when she was sixteen and seventeen years old. An investigation followed, and a Cook County grand jury indicted Reynolds on charges of aggravated sexual abuse, sexual assault, child pornography and obstruction of justice. He disputed the allegations and initially asserted that the charges were racially motivated. Despite the pending felony charges, voters reelected him in 1994.

At trial, the teenager testified that Reynolds had introduced himself to her on the street a few months before the November 1992 election, and they had had sex several times weekly through the campaign and less often afterward. She told the jury that Reynolds generally paid her $100 or $150 each time they were together. Other witnesses claimed that Reynolds induced the teen to lie to police. Under oath, Reynolds admitted to engaging in "phone sex" or "fantasy sex" with the teenage girl but denied any criminal activity.

Reynolds was convicted in August 1995 and sentenced to prison. An appeals court upheld the conviction, finding evidence that Reynolds had betrayed "a position of trust, authority or supervision" over the teen, who had worked as a campaign volunteer. Also, the court noted, Reynolds "was the person the school would call when [the teen] had problems there." [21] Reynolds resigned his House seat on October 1, 1995.

Reynolds's legal problems ran deeper, however. While he was behind bars in the sex case, a federal grand jury indicted him and his wife for misusing campaign funds for personal purposes, cheating lenders and filing false campaign finance statements. He was sentenced to seventy-eight months behind bars and ordered to pay $20,000 in restitution for bank and wire fraud, making false statements and related charges. The federal appeals court that affirmed his conviction characterized the scheme as "extensive" and noted that "the conspiracy lasted over five years, involved millions of dollars, involved sham ward [political] organizations designed to launder money from unions, and required deceiving the Federal Election Commission, the Internal Revenue Service, and the general public." [22]

Before leaving office, President Bill Clinton commuted the balance of Reynolds's prison sentence in January 2001, enabling him to serve the rest of his time in a community corrections center.

A few days after his release from a halfway house, Reynolds told the *Chicago Reporter:*

> I made mistakes and I regret those mistakes tremendously because . . . they brought a lot of wrath down on my family. My three babies had to suffer . . . But once a person makes a mistake he does not lose his right as a United States citizen to be treated fairly. And race and poverty should not come into any punishment when it comes to someone who had made mistakes. I think in my case it came into it. And it's not fair.[23]

▬ Document 9.7 ▬
Federal Indictment of Rep. Melvin J. Reynolds, D-Ill., in *U.S. v. Melvin J. Reynolds and Marisol C. Reynolds,* November 7, 1996

COUNT ONE
The SPECIAL MARCH 1995 GRAND JURY charges:

. . . 2. From in or about January 1993, continuing until at least in or about January 1994, at Chicago and Riverdale, in the Northern District of Illinois, Eastern Division, and elsewhere, MELVIN J. REYNOLDS, defendant herein, knowingly executed and attempted to execute a scheme and artifice to defraud four financial institutions, namely Amalgamated Bank of Chicago, American National Bank, Citibank, and Riverdale Bank (collectively "the lending banks"), and to obtain moneys, funds, and credits by and under the custody and control of the lending banks, by means of false and fraudulent pretenses, representations and promises.

3. It was part of the scheme that from on or about January 14, 1993 through on or about January 5, 1994, defendant MELVIN J. REYNOLDS fraudulently sought and obtained unsecured personal loans totaling approximately $150,000 from the lending banks by falsely representing his financial condition in order to deceive the lending banks about his ability to repay the loans. As a result of the scheme, the lending banks suffered losses of approximately $95,000 . . .

COUNT TWO
The SPECIAL MARCH 1995 GRAND JURY further charges:

On or about January 13, 1993, at Chicago, in the Northern District of Illinois, Eastern Division, MELVIN J. REYNOLDS, defendant herein, for the purpose of influencing the action of Amalgamated Bank of Chicago, the deposits of which were insured by the Federal Deposit Insurance Corporation, in connection with the issuance of a loan for $15,000, knowingly made a false statement and report of material fact in that he falsely stated in a personal financial statement and loan application submitted to the bank that his total liabilities were $10,000, when in fact his total liabilities far exceeded $10,000 . . .

COUNT TWELVE
The SPECIAL MARCH 1995 GRAND JURY further charges:

. . . 2. Beginning in or about 1989 and continuing until in or about August 1994, at Chicago, in the Northern District of Illinois, Eastern Division, and elsewhere, MELVIN J. REYNOLDS, and MARISOL C. REYNOLDS, defendants herein, did knowingly agree and conspire with each other and with others known and unknown to the Grand Jury: (1) to defraud the United States, and in particular the FEC [Federal Election Commission], by impeding, impairing, obstructing and defeating the lawful functions and duties of the FEC . . . ; and (2) to knowingly and willfully make, and cause others to make, false statements to the FEC . . .

3. It was part of the conspiracy that defendant MELVIN J. REYNOLDS solicited approximately $85,000 from the HEREIU [Hotel Employees and Restaurant Employees International Union] . . . HEREIU notified defendant MELVIN J. REYNOLDS that none of these funds could be used in conjunction with his federal campaign for Congress, because they were from HEREIU's non-federal PAC [political action committee]. Defendant MELVIN J. REYNOLDS caused the funds received from HEREIU's non-federal PAC to be used in connection with his federal campaign for Congress.

4. It was further part of the conspiracy that during 1993 and 1994 defendants MELVIN J. REYNOLDS and MARISOL C. REYNOLDS fraudulently converted to their personal use in excess of $15,000 in checks drawn on the Reynolds Committee checking account,

based upon claims that these funds constituted loan repayments, even though the defendants had not reported such loans to the FEC. The defendants caused two of these checks, for repayments of unreported loans totaling more than $10,000, to bear the forged signature of a worker for the Reynolds Committee . . .

11. It was further part of the conspiracy that the defendants did misrepresent, conceal and hide and cause to be misrepresented, concealed and hidden, the purposes of the acts done in furtherance of the conspiracy . . .

COUNT FOURTEEN

The SPECIAL MARCH 1995 GRAND JURY further charges:

. . . 2. On or about March 3, 1994, at Chicago, in the Northern District of Illinois, Eastern Division, and elsewhere, MELVIN J. REYNOLDS, and MARISOL C. REYNOLDS, defendants herein, knowingly and willfully made and caused the Treasurer for the Reynolds Committee to make false and fictitious statements, representations and writings to the Federal Election Commission, concerning matters within the jurisdiction of the Federal Election Commission, namely the submission of an FEC Form 3 dated February 1, 1994 . . . containing false, fictitious, and fraudulent information regarding the contributions and expenditures made by the Reynolds Committee, knowing the same to contain false, fictitious, and fraudulent statements . . .

Source: U.S. v. Melvin J. Reynolds and Marisol C. Reynolds, Indictment No. 96CM0701, U.S. District Court, Northern District of Illinois, Eastern Division.

Document 9.8 in Context
"The District Court Could Impose a Sentence of '0' Months and Community Service": Rep. Walter R. Tucker III, D-Calif., Is Convicted in an Extortion and Tax Fraud Case

On December 8, 1995, a federal jury convicted Rep. Walter R. Tucker III, D-Calif., of extortion and making false statements in his tax returns. The indictment accused him of soliciting bribes to influence his official actions as mayor of Compton—a position he won after his father died while holding that office—before he was elected to Congress in 1992 and of cheating on his federal income taxes. The focus of the $30,000 bribe scheme was to buy his support for a $250 million waste-to-energy project that a developer hoped to build in the city. The developer, however, was actually an undercover informant for the Federal Bureau of Investigation, which audiotaped and videotaped their conversations and the payoff.

Tucker, a Baptist minister and former deputy district attorney, pleaded not guilty and contended that the money constituted a consulting fee and personal loan, not a payoff:

> If the charge is working seven days a week—I'm guilty . . . If the charge is working for the betterment of my community and for black people—I'm guilty. If the charges are for speaking out against injustices, and how our community was treated during the riots, then I plead guilty.[24]

He also asserted that the government had targeted him because he was African American and Christian.

After nine days of deliberations, the jury rejected his defense and found him guilty of nine felony counts. U.S. District Judge Consuelo B. Marshall imposed a twenty-seven-month sentence, which he began serving in 1996 and appealed while in prison.

On appeal, Tucker contended that authorities had entrapped him and that the prosecution had failed to present enough evidence to prove the charges, thus requiring the convictions be tossed out. The following excerpt from his appellate brief details the third prong of the appeal, Tucker's argument that the judge mistakenly believed she could not sentence him to probation and community service rather than prison and, therefore, he was entitled to be resentenced. The Ninth Circuit U.S. Court of Appeals upheld the conviction and sentence.

In an interview after his release in December 1997, Tucker described prison as a "deep and invaluable" experience:

> I came to one solid conclusion, that is that it was something I would never have asked for, but something that I am so happy I experienced and I would never change . . . if I were given an opportunity to avoid it, to roll the dice again or rewind the tape and say 'Can I do this over god?' I would have to go on and live through it . . . because of what it has done to me as a man, how it has strengthened me . . .
>
> See, what it did for me was to help me understand what it's really like to be a black man . . . because being black from the time we came to this country was always about being subjected to the humility of the master. So (the experience) helped me go back to the slave blocks of the 1700s and understand the price of freedom.[25]

▬ Document 9.8 ▬
Opening Appellate Brief of Former Rep. Walter R. Tucker III, D-Calif., in *U.S. v. Walter R. Tucker*, May 13, 1997

THE DISTRICT COURT ERRED WHEN IT DECIDED THAT IT LACKED AUTHORITY TO SENTENCE MR. TUCKER TO A PERIOD OF PROBATION AND COMMUNITY SERVICE . . .

a) The District Court Believed That A Prison Sentence Was Not Necessary In This Case.

On April 17, 1996, during the sentencing proceedings for Mr. Tucker, the district court judge stated, "So, I don't believe that it's necessary to send him to prison for any additional punishment. Again, that doesn't mean that the Court has the option not to impose a prison sentence, but in terms of just how the Court sees the case, I don't see him as a person that needs to go to prison in order to be punished for the acts he's committed."

The district court believed that Mr. Tucker has already been punished for the activity in which he engaged. "He has lost, at least at this point, his license to practice law . . . He's resigned his position in Congress and, obviously, he and his family have suffered as a result, as he describes it, of a judgment and decisions that he made at the time that these offenses occurred."

The district court believed that the appropriate sentence for Mr. Tucker was to remain in the community and render service as he's done in the past for his community. "I will say on the record here, as I did earlier this morning in a sentence that the Court imposed, the Court believes that this Defendant could certainly serve his sentence in the community. I don't think there's a danger to the community at all. I don't think there's any flight risk. So, if it were up to the Court, if the Court had the authority, based upon this sentence, to permit him to serve it in the community, the Court would feel that he is an appropriate candidate to serve that sentence in the community.

The court continued, "I have also not ordered community service as a condition of probation and some might be curious as to why the Court would not order community service, and that is because I don't believe it's necessary to order this Defendant to perform any service to his community because I think that is something he will do once he is released to the community. There are a lot of projects for which the community needs service and the Defendant has engaged in some of those in the past and the Court would expect that he would do so in the future. And so therefore I don't feel the need to order community service."

However, the district court believed it lacked authority to impose a sentence it felt was appropriate. "We have sentencing rules that govern the sentence that the Court is to impose. One should not believe that it is within the Court's discretion to just impose any sentence that the Court might think appropriate in any given case. Congress has seen fit to enact statutes that were designed to give the Court guidance. There is a Sentencing Commission who has the responsibility to address the sentencing factors, those things that the Commission thinks are important to be considered. The purpose behind this, or at least one of the purposes, is to reduce the disparity in sentencing so that a defendant in one court should not receive a sentence different from a defendant with similar background and involved in similar conduct in another court.

Congress' idea and thought about this was to try to make sure that where conduct is similar, where backgrounds are similar, that sentences should be similar.

The problem, of course, with this approach is that it does not leave much room to consider the human elements and the individual who appears before the Court. But there are these guidelines and the Court believes, having taken an oath to uphold the law, it is the responsibility of the Court to follow the law that has been provided, and that does include the guidelines that I have before me."

The district court concluded, "Based upon the guideline range of this sentence, the court does not have the option to impose probation or any community type placement that would permit the defendant to reside in the community as opposed to in prison." . . .

b) The district court has the legal authority to depart down to a Level 8, Impose a Prison Sentence of Zero (0) months, and Impose A Sentence of Community Service.

1. Normally, A Sentencing Range Falling in Zone D of the Sentencing Table Requires a Minimum Term of Imprisonment

Mr. Tucker was convicted of . . . Extortion Under Color of Official Right which is a Class "C" Felony and . . . False Statement in Tax Return which is a Class "E" Felony . . . a defendant who has been found guilty of Class "D" or "E" felony may be sentenced to a term [of] probation, unless the offense is an offense for which probation has been expressly excluded . . . There is no language . . . which expressly excludes probation as a sentence . . .

2. The District Court Judge Had the Authority to Depart Down to an Imposition of Sentence of Zero Months

The district court did not believe it was necessary to impose a sentence of imprisonment in this case. The district court stated, "If it were up to the court, if the court had the authority, based upon this sentence, to permit him to serve it in the community, the court would feel that he is an appropriate candidate to serve that sentence in the community." . . .

. . . However, the district court had the authority to depart downward to a Offense Level of 8 and a criminal history of 1. The sentencing range would have been 0–6 months.

The district court could have then imposed a prison sentence of zero "0" months and ordered Mr. Tucker to serve in his community during his period of probation. A prison sentence of zero (0) months is recognized as a prison term and not a period of probation . . .

. . . Acknowledging the wisdom, even the necessity, of sentencing procedures that take account individual circumstances . . . Congress allows district courts to depart from the applicable Guideline range if the court finds that there exists an aggravating or mitigating circumstance of a kind, or to a degree, not adequately taken into consideration by the Sentencing Commission in formulating the guidelines that should result in a sentence different from that described . . .

The district court found this case to be unusual and atypical. The Commission intended the sentencing courts to treat each guideline as carving out "heartland" of a set of typical cases. If a sentencing court finds an atypical case, one to which the sentencing guidelines dictates a certain sentencing range, but the conduct significantly differs from the norm, the guidelines authorizes the district court to depart . . .

The district court in the present case believed that Mr. Tucker had already been punished for the activity in which he engaged and that the appropriate sentence was to remain in the community and render service. However, the district court believed it did not have the authority to impose such a sentence. "I will say on the record here, as I did earlier this morning in a sentence that Court imposed, the Court believes that this Defendant could certainly serve his sentence in the community . . . so, if it were up to the Court, if the Court had the authority, based upon this sentence, to permit him to serve it in the community, the Court would feel that he is an appropriate candidate to serve that sentence in the community" . . .

If the district court was aware of its authority to sentence Mr. Tucker to a period of community service, the district court could have "departed downward" . . . Therefore, the case should be remanded for re-sentencing, so that the district court could impose a sentence of "0" months and community service, if it still deemed it appropriate . . .

Source: Appellant's Brief, *U.S. v. Walter R. Tucker*, No. 96-50321, Ninth Circuit U.S. Court of Appeals, May 13, 1997.

Document 9.9 in Context
"A False Statement . . . and the Omission of a Material Liability": Former Del. Walter E. Fauntroy, D-D.C., Is Charged with Filing a False Financial Statement with Congress

Residents of Washington, D.C., had no voice in Congress from March 3, 1875—when Republican delegate Norton P. Chipman's four-year tenure ended—until March 23, 1971, when Democrat Walter E. Fauntroy won a special election for the restored nonvoting seat. Fauntroy, a minister and former member of the District of Columbia City Council, had been a civil rights activist before being elected to Congress.

Fauntroy served in the House for twenty years, championing political rights for the District and chairing the Banking, Finance and Urban Affairs Committee's Subcommittee on International Development, Finance, Trade and Monetary Policy. He also sat on the Select

Committee on Assassinations—established in 1976 and chaired by Rep. Louis Stokes, D-Missouri—that investigated the slayings of President John F. Kennedy and Rev. Martin Luther King Jr. In 1990 he ran unsuccessfully for mayor of the District rather than seeking an eleventh term in Congress.

After leaving office, Fauntroy found himself a subject in a Justice Department task force investigation into illegal and unethical practices concerning the House Bank, which had permitted members of Congress to overdraw their checking accounts without penalty. Eventually, more than 350 representatives were identified as having overdrawn their accounts; more than 75 of them resigned, were defeated in their next election or chose not to seek reelection. Four former representatives were convicted of crimes, as was the former House sergeant at arms.

However, the criminal charge against Fauntroy was unrelated to the House Bank. He was accused of filing a false financial disclosure statement in 1989, while he was still in office. It was alleged that the statement falsely claimed he had made a $23,887 charitable donation to the Washington church where he was pastor as a device to evade limits on outside income for members of Congress.

Fauntroy initially pled guilty to a felony carrying a potential five-year prison term and $250,000 fine, but the charge was reduced to a misdemeanor violation of District of Columbia law after the U.S. Supreme Court ruled in a separate case that the law he was originally charged under did not apply to lying to Congress. U.S. District Judge Paul L. Friedman sentenced Fauntroy to two years of probation, a $1,000 fine and 300 hours of community service, saying, "It is obvious to me that no good would be served by imposing a jail sentence on you." [26]

▬ Document 9.9 ▬
Justice Department Press Release Announces Criminal Case against Former Del. Walter E. Fauntroy, D-D.C., March 22, 1995

FORMER DELEGATE FAUNTROY IS CHARGED, AGREES TO PLEAD GUILTY

WASHINGTON, D.C.—The Department of Justice announced today that Walter E. Fauntroy, former Delegate to the House of Representatives from the District of Columbia, has been charged with one federal felony in an information filed today in the U.S. District Court for the District of Columbia, and that Fauntroy has agreed to plead guilty to the charges.

The information charged Fauntroy, 64, who served in Congress from 1971 to 1991, with violating the false statements statute, Title 18, United States Code, Section 1001, based on a false statement regarding a charitable contribution and the omission of a material liability on his U.S. House of Representatives Financial Disclosure Statement for calendar year 1988, in violation of Title 18, United States Code, Sections 1001 and 2.

The information alleges that Fauntroy filed a false financial disclosure statement required by the Ethics in Government Act with the Clerk of the U.S. House of Representatives in May of 1989. Under the provisions of that Act and under the Rules of the House of Representatives, each member of the House is required to file a financial disclosure statement annually. Fauntroy is charged with having falsely claimed on the financial disclosure statement for 1988 that he had made an end of the year charitable donation in the amount of $23,887.46 to the New Bethel Baptist Church where he serves as pastor to make it appear that he had complied with the Rule of the House of Representatives imposing a cap on outside earned income. Under the rules of the House of Representatives for 1988, no member was permitted to earn more than 30 per cent of the member's salary. Fauntroy also is charged in the information with failure to disclose on the financial disclosure statement a loan he had obtained in June of 1988 in the amount of $24,200. The provisions of the Ethics in Government Act required that Fauntroy disclose the loan.

Fauntroy faces a maximum penalty of five years imprisonment and a $250,000 fine. Under the terms of the plea agreement filed with the court, Fauntroy has agreed to plead guilty to the charge and the government has agreed to recommend that he be sentenced to probation.

The information and plea agreement stem from the Department of Justice's ongoing investigation of the House Bank. This case is being handled by attorneys assigned to the House Bank Task Force, Criminal Division, composed of an Assistant United States Attorney from Philadelphia, Pennsylvania, a Senior Litigation Counsel from the Fraud Section of the Criminal Division, a Senior Counsel in the Criminal Division, and Special Agents of the FBI, Washington, D.C. The Task Force was formed in December 1992 to continue the work of the preliminary inquiry into the House Bank that Malcolm R. Wilkey, retired judge of the United States Court of Appeals for the District of Columbia Circuit, conducted as a special counsel to the Attorney General in 1992.

This is the 10th criminal charge filed to date by the Task Force. The former Sergeant At Arms, Jack Russ, pled guilty to three felonies and is serving a 24-month prison term. Former Member of Congress Carroll Hubbard Jr. pled guilty to three felonies and was sentenced to 36 months in prison. Former Congressman Carl C. Perkins pled guilty to three felonies and was sentenced recently to 21 months in prison. Carol Brown Hubbard, the wife of former Congressman Hubbard, pled guilty to a misdemeanor and was sentenced to five years probation. Martha Amburgey, the secretary to former Congressman Perkins has pled guilty to two felonies and is scheduled to be sentenced on March 28, 1995. Ignatius DeMio, the nephew of former Congresswoman Mary Rose Oakar has pled guilty to one misdemeanor and is scheduled to be sentenced on May 12, 1995. Former Congresswoman Mary Rose Oakar was recently indicted for seven felonies, including conspiracy and filing false statements, and is awaiting trial. Former Congressman Donald "Buz" Lukens was recently indicted on five felony counts alleging acceptance of bribes and is awaiting trial. John P. Fitzpatrick was recently indicted on eight felony counts alleging bribery, conspiracy to defraud the United States, and giving false testimony before the grand jury. The investigation of the House Bank Task Force is continuing.

Source: U.S. Department of Justice, "Former Delegate Fauntroy Is Charged, Agrees to Plead Guilty," press release, March 22, 1995, www.usdoj.gov/opa/pr/Pre_96/March95/153.txt.html.

Document 9.10 in Context
"Lawlessness Alleged by Her Former Employees": Rep. Barbara-Rose Collins, D-Mich., Is Accused of Ethics Violations

Barbara-Rose Collins, D-Mich., who won her seat in 1990, had a reputation for confrontation. For example, she fired a gay staff aide out of fear he might be HIV-positive—two days after the aide's partner died of AIDS. The former staffer filed a House grievance and received back pay and attorney fees, a resolution reached only after Collins lost her 1996 reelection bid. In another instance, she filed a libel suit against a wire service that had interviewed her about racism and against the Detroit newspaper that used the interview in an article; the article had misquoted her as saying, "All white people, I don't believe, are intolerant. That's why I say I love the individuals, but I hate the race." The newspaper acknowledged in a retraction that Collins had actually said "don't like" rather than "hate."

A state appeals court threw out the case, finding no substantial difference between "hate" and "don't like." The court also noted that Collins

> does not contest portions of the article in which she was quoted as saying that "God is going to have to burn [racism] out of white people" or that "the only reason Dr. Martin Luther King was successful was because he said if blood had to flow, let it be my black blood, and not the blood of my white brother, and white people like to hear that kind of stuff." Plaintiff was also quoted as saying that white people "don't even realize how they benefit from racism." [27]

Another set of allegations raised by a watchdog group accused Collins of violating federal law and House ethics rules. In an October 1995 letter, the Congressional Accountability Project asked the House Committee on Standards of Official Conduct to investigate and appoint an outside counsel. The group, founded by consumer activist Ralph Nader, describes its mission as fighting corruption in Congress. The group's letter, excerpted here, was based largely on press reports about how Collins's congressional staff performed political and personal duties on government time and how she misused government resources and bilked her own campaign committee of thousands of dollars.

The group also called for an inquiry into allegations that Collins had accepted "thousands of dollars from a community scholarship fund intended to assist low-income students in her Detroit district" and had used congressional stationary to solicit $2,000 corporate donations to a private community service fund.[28]

The committee voted to conduct a preliminary inquiry, but a subcommittee ultimately recommended no further action after Collins lost her 1996 primary.

Document 9.10
Congressional Accountability Project Letter Accusing Rep. Barbara-Rose Collins, D-Mich., of Ethics Violations, October 3, 1995

Honorable Nancy Johnson, Chairwoman
House Committee on Standards of Official Conduct
U. S. House of Representatives
Washington, DC 29515

RE: Violations of Federal Law and House Rules by Congresswoman
Barbara-Rose Collins

Dear Chairwoman Johnson:

This letter constitutes a formal ethics complaint against Representative Barbara-Rose Collins for violating federal law and House Rules, which prohibit the use of Congressional staff and other official resources for personal and campaign activities. I am writing pursuant to House Rule 10, which authorizes the House Committee on Standards of Official Conduct to investigate "any alleged violation, by a member, officer or employee of the House, of the Code of Official Conduct or of any law, rule, regulation or standard of conduct applicable to the conduct of such member, officer, or employee in the performance of his duties or the discharge of his responsibilities."

In addition, the Committee on Standards of Official Conduct should appoint an outside counsel to investigate whether Rep. Collins has improperly made charges against her campaign account ("Friends of Congresswoman Barbara-Rose Collins"), and improperly accepted monies from a scholarship fund.

A: Rep. Collins' Congressional Staff Regularly Performed Campaign and
Personal Tasks

On August 9, 1995, Sarah Pekkanen of The Hill newspaper wrote that:

. . . a former aide in Collins' Detroit district office told the Hill that she spent up to 80 percent of her time doing work for Collins' 1994 re-election campaign while on the congressional payroll . . .

The former staffer, Edith Lee-Payne, who served as Collins' community affairs liaison during the spring and summer of 1994, charged that Collins routinely instructed her to perform campaign-related work, including fund raising.

Lee-Payne said she and other staffers used Xerox machines in the district office to copy material for bulk mailings for Collins' re-election campaign, served as the "contact person" for local fund raisers, and collected and deposited checks and logged the amounts into a computer before sending copies to Collins.

. . . [Lee-Payne said] "In the weeks surrounding a fund raiser, 80 percent of my time could be spent on campaign or fund-raising activities."

Lee-Payne's allegations were confirmed by four former Collins staffers, who said that they and other staffers performed campaign re-election work in her Washington office as well.

In an August 16, 1995, article in The Hill titled "Collins' Aides Performed Personal, Campaign Duties," Sarah Pekkanen reported that:

Staffers for Rep. Barbara-Rose Collins' Detroit district office were given a list detailing personal and campaign-related work they were told to do while on the Congressional payroll, according to documents obtained by The Hill.

One of the documents details a dozen job duties, including Item number 11, which spells out numerous "campaign-related" chores, such as depositing checks for campaign contributions, preparation of donor lists and paying campaign bills.

. . . item number 12 is identified as "BRC personal," and details "liason [sic] with vendors for her personal accounts, anything related to her apartment (maintenance of her keys)."

B: Call to Investigate Whether Collins' Alleged Misuse of Staff and Official Resources for Campaign and Personal Purposes Violated Federal Law and House Rules

There is a broad prohibition against the use of government resources—including staff time—for political or personal purposes. 31 U.S.C. 1301(a) states that:

Appropriations shall be applied only to the objects for which the appropriations were made except as otherwise provided by law . . .

Similarly, the House Ethics Manual states:

"Funds appropriated to pay congressional staff to perform official duties may be used only for the purposes of assisting a Member in his legislative and representational duties, working on committee business, or performing other congressional functions. Employees may not be compensated from public funds to perform nonofficial, personal, or campaign activities on behalf of the Member, the employee, or anyone else" . . .

Given that Edith Lee-Payne has stated that during some weeks she spent as much as 80 percent of her time on Rep. Collins' campaign work, she could not have "performed official duties commensurate" with the salary she received. Although official staff are permitted to perform campaign duties in their spare time, they may only do so "after the completion of their official duties."

In a May 27, 1995 article titled "Rep. Collins Uses Tax Money For Stamps," Lisa Zagaroli and Carol Stevens of the Detroit News reported that:

House records show Rep. Barbara-Rose Collins has used tax dollars to buy nearly 23,000 first-class postage stamps, valued at $6,600, since taking office in 1991 . . . former staffers in Collins' Washington, D.C., office said the stamps were used for fund-raising letters, personal mail and other activities.

The office "just wasn't using them for what (it) should have been using them for," said former staffer Jon Howard. The office "really had no need for postage stamps in the quantities (it) was getting," he said . . . Other ex-staffers interviewed by The Detroit News reported observing similar uses of office-purchased postage stamps.

Similarly, The Hill article from August 16, 1996 reported that:

Several of Collins' former staffers said the congresswoman routinely purchased postage stamps with taxpayer funds and used them improperly. "Government stamps were frequently used for re-election mailings and the congresswoman's personal mail," said one former staffer. His allegations were confirmed by several other employees.

In addition, the August 9 article in The Hill states that several of Rep. Collins former staff allege that other official resources, including photocopiers, copy paper, and, presumably, computers, were used for campaign purposes. These uses of official resources for campaign purposes are prohibited by federal law . . .

The Committee's "Revised Solicitation Guidelines" state:

Under 31 U.S.C. 1301(a) and under the regulations of the Committee on House Oversight, official resources and allowances may be used only for official activities. Members and House employees are thus prohibited from using any official resources (such as congressional letterhead and telephones, copiers, and fax machines in congressional offices), to solicit campaign funds . . .

Federal law prohibits the filing of false claims with the federal government . . .

Embezzlement of official resources is prohibited by federal law. 18 U.S.C. 641 states that:

Whoever embezzles, steals, purloins, or knowingly converts to his use or to the use of another, or without authority, sells, conveys, or disposes of any record, voucher, money, or thing of value of the United States . . . Whoever receives, conceals, or retains the same with intent to convert it to his use or gain, knowing it to have been embezzled, stolen, purloined, or converted—Shall be fined not more than $10,000 or imprisoned not more than 10 years, or both . . .

Given the statements of former employees of Rep. Collins that she used staff and official resources for campaign and official purposes, we urge the House Committee on Standards of Official Conduct to immediately appoint an outside counsel to investigate the extent of the use and/or embezzlement of official resources for campaign and personal purposes.

C: Call For Investigation to Determine Whether Collins Defrauded Her Campaign Committee

The August 9 article in The Hill reported that:

Rep. Barbara-Rose Collins . . . claimed she spent $8,500 in campaign funds at a New York City specialty store last November to purchase clocks for which she actually paid only $948, according to a store invoice . . .

Store owner Jeff Shin could not find other invoices for the $7,500 in question, and said that he doubted such a large sale existed, since he usually sets aside invoices of more than $1,000 so he can contact the customer in the future.

The House Committee on Standards of Official Conduct should immediately appoint an outside counsel to investigate the discrepancy between the $8,500 that Collins campaign ("Friends of Congresswoman Barbara-Rose Collins") claimed was spent, and the $948 that was apparently spent. What was the disposition of the other $7,552?

Did Rep. Collins defraud her campaign accounts of this money, and then cause her campaign treasurer to file a false campaign disclosure filing with the Federal Election Commission in violation of the reporting requirements of the Federal Election Campaign Act (2 U.S.C. 434(a)(4))?

In an August 19, 1995 article titled "Collins Seen As Lax Lawmaker" in the Detroit Free Press, Lori Montgomery and Marc Selinger wrote that:

Last October, Collins reported paying $1,000 [from her campaign account] to Detroit Edison to reconnect electricity for "constituents" at an address on Ridgemont Street. The only such address in Detroit Edison's service area is in St. Clair Shores—outside Collins' district, said Karl Munzenberger, Detroit Edison's area supervisor of residential credit services. Furthermore, Munzenberger said, there is no record that Collins ever made any payment on the account.

What was the disposition of this supposed $1,000 payment to Detroit Edison? Did Rep. Collins defraud her campaign account of the $1,000 in question? . . .

F: Conclusion

The Code of Ethics of Government Service states that "public office is a public trust." . . . If Congresswoman Barbara-Rose Collins has engaged in the lawlessness alleged by her former employees, then she has violated the trust that her constituents have placed in her. I strongly urge you to immediately appoint an outside counsel to investigate the charges above.

Sincerely,
Gary Ruskin
Director

Source: Congressional Accountability Project to Hon. Nancy Johnson, letter, October 3, 1995, www.essential.org/orgs/CAP/ethics/collins2.html.

Document 9.11 in Context
"I Am No Longer Able to Carry Out My Requisite Duties Effectively": Rep. Frank W. Ballance Jr., D-N.C., Resigns and Is Convicted of Fraud, Money Laundering

After Frank W. Ballance Jr. won a House seat in North Carolina in 2002, his fellow newcomers elected him president of the Democratic Freshman Class of the 108th Congress. However, his tenure ended early and ignominiously after less than a full term.

Ballance's legal woes became public after the North Carolina auditor general found extensive conflicts of interest and large, questionable expenditures by the John A. Hyman Memorial Youth Foundation, a nonprofit organization that had received more than $2 million in state grants over a ten-year period to fund drug abuse prevention and treatment programs. The foundation received the grants while Ballance, then a state senator, was vice chair of the legislative appropriations subcommittee that monitored the Corrections Department budget. During that period, Ballance chaired both the foundation's board of directors and the board of deacons of a church that leased space to the foundation. The audit cited payments from the state grant funds to Ballance's relatives and to foundation members who worked on his political campaigns. The audit recommended that the foundation repay the state $238,926 that had not been spent for substance abuse programs. Investigations by several news organizations disclosed additional wrongdoing involving the foundation.

Ballance resigned from the House in June 2004, citing health problems. His letter of resignation and the response of House Minority Leader Nancy Pelosi, D-Calif., follow.

In September 2004 a federal grand jury indicted Ballance on charges of misusing more than $100,000 in state money. The grand jury also indicted his son, a state court judge, for failing to file an income tax return and not reporting that the foundation had paid him $20,000, which he used as a down payment on a sport utility vehicle. The elder Ballance pleaded guilty to conspiracy to commit mail fraud and money laundering, and U.S. District Judge Terrence Boyle ordered him to prison for four years and fined him $10,000. The plea agreement also required restitution of $61,917 and forfeiture of $203,000 being held in escrow. His son received a nine-month jail sentence on the tax charge.

Interestingly, the foundation was named for North Carolina's first African American representative, former slave John A. Hyman, a Republican who also served less than a full term. Hyman lost a House race in 1872 but won in 1874. However, an ultimately unsuccessful Democratic challenge to the results prevented him from being seated until a few months before the 1876 election, and the Republicans refused to renominate him that year.

Hyman, like Ballance, had been embroiled in scandal originating during his service in the state legislature. While a state senator, Hyman was suspected of corruption, including selling votes. After leaving Congress, he was accused of embezzling from his church and selling whiskey to fellow congregants.

▬ Document 9.11a ▬
Rep. Frank W. Ballance Jr.'s Resignation Letter, June 8, 2004

House of Representatives
Washington, DC, June 8, 2004.

Hon. J. DENNIS HASTERT,
Speaker of the House,
Capitol, Washington, DC.

DEAR SPEAKER HASTERT: Please accept this letter as official notification of my intention to resign my position as United States Representative of the First Congressional District of North Carolina due to my current health condition. The effective date of my resignation will be Friday, June 11, 2004.

Although I appreciate the honor, privilege and opportunity to have served the citizens of the First Congressional District of North Carolina during the 108th Congress, at this juncture I feel that I am no longer able to carry out my requisite duties effectively.

Enclosed herewith please find a copy of the letter that I have tendered to North Carolina's Governor, Mike Easley providing him with notice of my decision to resign.

Respectfully,
FRANK W. BALLANCE, Jr.
Member of Congress

Source: Congressional Record, 108th Cong., 2d sess., June 9, 2004, H3869.

▬ Document 9.11b ▬
Statement of House Minority Leader Nancy Pelosi, D-Calif., on Rep. Ballance's Resignation, June 8, 2004

Washington, D.C. — House Democratic Leader Nancy Pelosi released the following statement today on the resignation of Congressman Frank Ballance of North Carolina:

On behalf of House Democrats, I thank Congressman Ballance for his service, his leadership of the freshman class, and his commitment to his constituents. I am greatly saddened that his health will not permit him to complete his term of office and am praying for his health to recover.

"I look forward to working with the next Democratic representative from North Carolina's First Congressional District."

Source: Office of Rep. Nancy Pelosi, San Francisco, California, Eighth District, "Pelosi Statement on Resignation of Congressman Frank Ballance," www.house.gov/pelosi/press/releases/June04/CongressmanBallance060804.html.

Document 9.12 in Context
"The Search of Congressman Jefferson's Paper Files Violated the Speech or Debate Clause": The Corruption Investigation of Rep. William J. Jefferson, D-La.

William J. Jefferson was elected to Congress from a New Orleans district in 1990 after service in the Louisiana Senate and as a staffer for U.S. senator John Bennett Johnston Jr., D-La. Jefferson came under criminal scrutiny in 2005 for business dealings that allegedly involved soliciting cash and other favors to benefit himself and relatives for using his influence to line up business deals in Nigeria, Ghana and Equatorial Guinea. The investigation culminated in a June 2007 indictment accusing Jefferson of bribery, conspiracy, racketeering, money laundering and violation of the Foreign Corrupt Practices Act. The federal grand jury in Alexandria, Virginia, alleged that Jefferson violated his duty to "perform the responsibilities of his office free from deceit, fraud, concealment, bias, conflict of interest, self-enrichment, and self-dealing."[29] He denied wrongdoing, pleaded not guilty and was awaiting trial as of late summer 2007.

In August 2005 Federal Bureau of Investigation agents raided Jefferson's homes in New Orleans and Washington, D.C. They found $90,000 in marked bills wrapped in foil and hidden in a freezer in his Washington home, money he had received in a sting operation. The FBI also raided the suburban Washington home of the Nigerian vice president, who had ties to Jefferson. Then in January 2006, former Jefferson aide Brett Pfeffer pleaded guilty to conspiracy and aiding and abetting the solicitation of bribes. Pfeffer acknowledged his role in a scheme to lobby Ghanaian and Nigerian officials and to press the U.S. Export-Import Bank to approve loan guarantees for a high-tech telecommunications company in exchange for part ownership of the company. At the time, the Justice Department did not use Jefferson's name but referred to him as "Representative A." In May 2006 the House created an ethics subcommittee to investigate him. In September 2006 the owner of the telecommunications company, Vernon L. Jackson, was sentenced to prison for paying Jefferson more than $400,000 in bribes and stock to push the company's business deals.

On a broader level, however, a constitutional issue was triggered when the FBI raided Jefferson's office in the Rayburn House Office Building in May 2006. That unprecedented raid generated protests from leaders of both parties in the House, who accused the FBI of violating the constitutional separation of powers. Speaker J. Dennis Hastert, R-Ill., supported the Justice Department's duty to "root out and prosecute corruption wherever it is" but said Attorney General Alberto R. Gonzales

> himself was aware that Separation of Powers concerns existed and that the Justice Department was treading on Constitutionally suspect grounds . . . The actions of the Justice Department . . . raise important Constitutional issues that go well beyond the specifics of this case. Insofar as I am aware, since the founding of our Republic 219 years ago, the Justice Department has never found it necessary to do what it did Saturday night, crossing this Separation of Powers line, in order to successfully prosecute corruption by Members of Congress.[30]

Two days later, the speaker and House Minority Leader Nancy Pelosi, D-Calif., demanded the immediate return of the seized papers:

> No person is above the law, neither the one being investigated nor those conducting the investigation.

The Justice Department was wrong to seize records from Congressman Jefferson's office in violation of the Constitutional principle of Separation of Powers, the Speech or Debate Clause of the Constitution, and the practice of the last 219 years. These constitutional principles were not designed by the Founding Fathers to place anyone above the law. Rather, they were designed to protect the Congress and the American people from abuses of power, and those principles deserve to be vigorously defended.[31]

President George W, Bush ordered the documents sealed while the dispute was being resolved. When Jefferson sued for the return of all seized documents, a U.S. district court judge upheld the legality of the search in July 2006.

But in August 2007, a federal appeals court ruled that the raid unconstitutionally allowed federal agents—who are officers of the executive branch of government—to see legislative documents. That, the court held, violated the Speech and Debate Clause which provides that "for any Speech or Debate in either House, [Members of Congress] shall not be questioned in any other Place." The U.S. Court of Appeals for the District of Columbia ordered the government to return all paper files taken in the raid. It allowed the Justice Department to keep copies of computer hard drives and other electronic media because federal agents had not yet seen their contents, which would be reviewed by a federal judge before the criminal trial.

▬ Document 9.12 ▬
U.S. Court of Appeals Decision on the Search of the Capitol Hill Office of Rep. William J. Jefferson, D-La., August 3, 2007

[Judith W.] ROGERS, *Circuit Judge:*

This is an appeal from the denial of a motion . . . seeking the return of all materials seized by the Executive upon executing a search warrant for non-legislative materials in the congressional office of a sitting Member of Congress. The question on appeal is whether the procedures under which the search was conducted were sufficiently protective of the legislative privilege created by the Speech or Debate Clause, Article 1, Section 6, Clause 1 of the United States Constitution . . . Given the Department of Justice's voluntary freeze of its review of the seized materials and the procedures mandated on remand by this court in granting the Congressman's motion for emergency relief pending appeal, the imaging and keyword search of the Congressman's computer hard drives and electronic media exposed no legislative material to the Executive, and therefore did not violate the Speech or Debate Clause, but the review of the Congressman's paper files when the search was executed exposed legislative material to the Executive and accordingly violated the Clause. Whether the violation requires, as the Congressman suggests, the return of all seized items, privileged as well as non-privileged, depends upon a determination of which documents are privileged and then, as to the non-privileged documents, a balancing of the separation of powers underlying the Speech or Debate Clause and the Executive's Article II, Section 3 law enforcement interest in the seized materials . . .

We hold that the compelled disclosure of privileged material to the Executive during execution of the search warrant . . . violated the Speech or Debate Clause and that the Congressman is entitled to the return of documents that the court determines to be privileged under the Clause . . .

I.

On May 18, 2006, the Department of Justice filed an application for a search warrant for Room 2113 of the Rayburn House Office Building, the congressional office of Congressman William J. Jefferson. The attached affidavit of Special Agent Timothy R. Thibault of the Federal Bureau of Investigation ("FBI") described how the apparent victim of a fraud and bribery scheme who had come forward as a cooperating witness led to an investigation into bribery of a public official, wire fraud, bribery of a foreign official, and conspiracy to commit these crimes. The investigation included speaking with the Congressman's staff, one of whom had advised that records relevant to the investigation remained in the congressional office. Based on the investigation, the affiant concluded that there was probable cause to believe that Congressman Jefferson, acting with other targets of the investigation, had sought and in some cases already accepted financial backing and or concealed payments of cash or equity interests in business ventures located in the United States, Nigeria, and Ghana in exchange for his undertaking official acts as a Congressman while promoting the business interests of himself and the targets . . .

The warrant affidavit also described "special procedures" adopted by the Justice Department prosecutors overseeing the investigation. According to the affidavit, these procedures were designed: (1) "to minimize the likelihood that any potentially politically sensitive, non-responsive items in the Office will be seized and provided to the [p]rosecution [t]eam," and (2) "to identify information that may fall within the purview of the Speech or Debate Clause privilege . . . or any other pertinent privilege." Essentially, the procedures called for the FBI agents conducting the search to "have no substantive role in the investigation" and upon reviewing and removing materials from Room 2113, not to reveal politically sensitive or non-responsive items "inadvertently seen . . . during the course of the search." The FBI agents were to review and seize paper documents responsive to the warrant, copy all electronic files on the hard drives or other electronic media in the Congressman's office, and then turn over the files for review by a filter team consisting of two Justice Department attorneys and an FBI agent. The filter team would determine: (1) whether any of the seized documents were not responsive to the search warrant, and return any such documents to the Congressman; and (2) whether any of the seized documents were subject to the Speech or Debate Clause privilege or other privilege. Materials determined to be privileged or not responsive would be returned without dissemination to the prosecution team. Materials determined by the filter team not to be privileged would be turned over to the prosecution team, with copies to the Congressman's attorney within ten business days of the search. Materials determined by the filter team to be potentially privileged would, absent the Congressman's consent to Executive use of a potentially privileged document, be submitted to the district court for review . . . The filter team would make similar determinations with respect to the data on the copied computer hard drives, following an initial electronic screening by the FBI's Computer Analysis and Response Team.

The district court found probable cause for issuance of the search warrant and signed it on May 18, 2006, directing the search to occur on or before May 21 and the U.S. Capitol Police to "provide immediate access" to Room 2113. Beginning on Saturday night, May 20, more than a dozen FBI agents spent about 18 hours in Room 2113. The FBI agents reviewed every paper record and copied the hard drives on all of the computers and electronic data stored on other media in Room 2113. The FBI agents seized and carried away two boxes of documents and copies of the hard drives and electronic data.

On May 24, 2006, Congressman Jefferson challenged the constitutionality of the search of his congressional office and moved for return of the seized property . . .

On July 10, 2006, the district court denied the Congressman's motion for return of the seized materials. Concluding that execution of the warrant "did not impermissibly interfere with Congressman Jefferson's legislative activities," the district court noted that the warrant sought only materials that were outside of the "legitimate legislative sphere." The district court rejected the Congressman's claim that he had a right to remove documents he deemed privileged before execution of the warrant . . .

On June 4, 2007, the grand jury returned a sixteen-count indictment against Congressman Jefferson in the Eastern District of Virginia. The indictment included charges of racketeering, solicitation of (and conspiracy to solicit) bribes, money laundering, wire fraud, and obstruction of justice . . .

II.

The Speech or Debate Clause provides that "for any Speech or Debate in either House, [Members of Congress] shall not be questioned in any other Place . . ." By the time of the Constitutional Convention, the privilege embodied in the Speech or Debate Clause was "recognized as an important protection of the independence and integrity of the legislature," and was to serve as a protection against possible "prosecution by an unfriendly executive and conviction by a hostile judiciary" . . .

. . . The Congressman does not dispute that congressional offices are subject to the operation of the Fourth Amendment and thus subject to a search pursuant to a search warrant issued by the federal district court. The Executive acknowledges, in connection with the execution of a search warrant, that there is a role for a Member of Congress to play in exercising the Member's rights under the Speech or Debate Clause. The parties disagree on precisely when that should occur and what effect any violation of the Member's Speech or Debate rights should have . . .

The search of Congressman Jefferson's office must have resulted in the disclosure of legislative materials to agents of the Executive . . . In order to determine whether the documents were responsive to the search warrant, FBI agents had to review all of the papers in the Congressman's office, of which some surely related to legislative acts. This compelled disclosure clearly tends to disrupt the legislative process: exchanges between a Member of Congress and the Member's staff or among Members of Congress on legislative matters may legitimately involve frank or embarrassing statements; the possibility of compelled disclosure may therefore chill the exchange of views with respect to legislative activity. This chill runs counter to the Clause's purpose of protecting against disruption of the legislative process . . .

The Congressman makes clear in his brief that he is not suggesting advance notice is required by the Constitution before Executive agents arrive at his office. Rather he contends legislative and executive interests can be accommodated without such notice, as urged, for example by the Deputy Counsel to the House of Representatives: "We're not contemplating advance notice to the [M]ember to go into his office to search his documents before anyone shows up," but rather that "[t]he Capitol [P]olice would seal the office so that nothing would go out of that office and then the search would take place with the [M]ember there" . . .

The special procedures outlined in the warrant affidavit would not have avoided the violation of the Speech or Debate Clause because they denied the Congressman any opportunity to identify and assert the privilege with respect to legislative materials before their compelled disclosure to Executive agents. Indeed, the Congressman, his attorney, and counsel for the House of Representatives were denied entry into Room 2113 once the FBI arrived . . . The compelled disclosure of legislative materials to FBI agents executing the search warrant was not unintentional but deliberate—a means to uncover responsive non-privileged materials.

There would appear to be no reason why the Congressman's privilege under the Speech or Debate Clause cannot be asserted at the outset of a search in a manner that also protects the interests of the Executive in law enforcement . . .

Accordingly, we hold that a search that allows agents of the Executive to review privileged materials without the Member's consent violates the Clause. The Executive's search of the Congressman's paper files therefore violated the Clause, but its copying of computer hard drives and other electronic media is constitutionally permissible because the Remand Order affords the Congressman an opportunity to assert the privilege prior to disclosure of privileged materials to the Executive . . .

III.

. . . Clearly a remedy in this case must show particular respect to the fact that the Speech or Debate Clause "reinforces the separation of powers and protects legislative independence" . . .

Although the search of Congressman Jefferson's paper files violated the Speech or Debate Clause, his argument does not support granting the relief that he seeks, namely the return of all seized documents, including copies, whether privileged or not . . .

At the same time, the remedy must give effect not only to the separation of powers underlying the Speech or Debate Clause but also to the sovereign's interest under Article II, Section 3 in law enforcement . . . The Speech or Debate Clause protects against the compelled disclosure of privileged documents to agents of the Executive, but not the disclosure of non-privileged materials. Its "shield does not extend beyond what is necessary to preserve the integrity of the legislative process," and it "does not prohibit inquiry into illegal conduct simply because it has some nexus to legislative functions." This particular search needlessly disrupted the functioning of the Congressman's office by allowing agents of the Executive to view legislative materials without the Congressman's consent, even though a search of a congressional office is not prohibited *per se* . . . Most important, to construe the Speech or Debate Clause as providing an absolute privilege against a seizure of non-privileged materials essential to the Executive's enforcement of criminal statutes pursuant to Article II, Section 3 on no more than a generalized claim that the separation of powers demands no less would . . . "upset the constitutional balance of 'a workable government . . .'"

. . . We conclude that the Congressman is entitled . . . to the return of all materials (including copies) that are privileged legislative materials under the Speech or Debate Clause. Where the Clause applies its protection is absolute . . . [I]t is unnecessary to order the return of non-privileged materials as a further remedy for the violation of the Clause . . . Unlike the Congressman's request for the return of legislative materials protected by the Speech or Debate Clause, the further claim for the return of all non-privileged materials is not independent of the criminal prosecution against him, especially if the legality of the search will be a critical issue in the criminal trial . . . The fact that the prosecution has commenced "will afford . . . adequate opportunity to challenge the constitutionality of the search of his . . . office," and hence "there is now no danger that the [Executive] might retain [the Congressman's] property indefinitely without any opportunity . . . to assert on appeal his right to possession."

Accordingly, we hold that the Congressman is entitled to the return of all legislative materials (originals and copies) that are protected by the Speech or Debate Clause seized from Rayburn House Office Building Room 2113 on May 20–21, 2006 . . .

Source: U.S. v. Rayburn House Office Building, Room 2113, Washington, D.C. 20515, U.S. Court of Appeals for the District of Columbia Circuit, No. 06-3105 (August 3, 2007), http://pacer. cadc.uscourts.gov/docs/common/opinions/200708/06-3105a.pdf.

NOTES

1 House Committee on Standards of Official Conduct, "Statement of the Committee on Standards of Official Conduct in the Matter of Representative Corrine Brown," September 21, 2000, www.house/gov/ethics/Press_Statement_corrineBrownend.html.

2 William L. Clay, *Just Permanent Interests: Black Americans in Congress, 1870–1991* (New York: Amistad Press, 1992), 82.

3 David Stokes, "This Case Has Just Begun," *Atlanta Inquirer*, April 8, 2006, 1.

4 *Congressional Record*, 109th Cong., 2d sess., April 6, 2006, H1578.

5 Wilbert A. Tatum, "The *Daily News* Must Return the Pulitzer Prize," *Amsterdam News*, December 2, 1999.

6 Charles B. Rangel, "A New Beginning for the Apollo Theatre," press release, October 14, 1999.

7 Edward W. Knappman, *Watergate and the White House* (New York: Facts on File, 1974), vol. 1, 96–97.

8 James Lewis Hicklin III to John F. Kennedy, letter, undated, John F. Kennedy Presidential Library, Boston, Massachusetts.

9 Edwin O. Guthman and Jeffrey Shulman, *Robert Kennedy in His Own Words: The Unpublished Recollections of the Kennedy Years* (Toronto, Canada: Bantam Books, 1998), 42.

10 Adam Clayton Powell Jr., *Adam by Adam* (New York: Dial Press, 1971), 72.

11 John F. Kennedy to Angier Biddle Duke, letter, January 28, 1961, John F. Kennedy Presidential Library, Boston, Massachusetts.

12 Congressional Quarterly, *Congressional Ethics: History, Facts, and Controversy* (Washington, D.C.: CQ Press, 1992), 12.

13 *Congressional Record*, 91st Cong., 1st sess., January 3, 1969, H21.

14 Carolyn DuBose, "Diggs' Legacy Still Lives," *Michigan Chronicle*, September 1, 1999.

15 *Congressional Record*, 105th Cong., 2d sess., December 19, 1998, H11823.

16 Nancy Pelosi, "Pelosi Statement on Chairmanship of Intelligence Committee," Press release, November 28, 2006, available at http://www.foxnews.com/story/0,2933,232457,00.html.

17 Congressional Black Caucus, "CBC Chair Comments on Meeting Between U.S. Representative Alcee Hastings and Speaker-elect Nancy Pelosi," press release, November 28, 2006.

18 Jeff Stein, "Exclusive: Hastings Says Bill Clinton Talked Him out of Intelligence Post," Spy Talk, *CQ Homeland Security*, April 27, 2007, http://public.cq.com/docs/hs/hsnews110-000002500119.html.

19 Jim McGee, "Peace Corps Worker Alleges Rep. Savage Assaulted Her," *Washington Post*, July 19, 1989.

20 "Conflicting Accounts of Words in Congress," *New York Times*, October 20, 1990.

21 *People of the State of Illinois v. Melvin Reynolds*, 294 Ill.App.3d 58 (December 31, 1997).

22 *U.S. v. Melvin J. Reynolds,* 189 F.3d 521 (7th Cir., August 27, 1999).

23 Carlos Hernandez Gomez, "Interview with Mel Reynolds," *Chicago Reporter,* January 2001, www.chicagoreporter.com/2001/1-2001/sentencing/Mel.htm.

24 Dennis Schatzman and James Bolden, "Cong. Walter Tucker Digs In, Promises to Fight Charges," *Los Angeles Sentinel,* August 25, 1994.

25 Emanuel Parker, "Walter Tucker: New Found Faith, No Regrets," *Los Angeles Sentinel,* October 21, 1998.

26 Associated Press, "Former Delegate to Congress Is Sentenced," *New York Times,* August 10, 1995.

27 *Collins v. Detroit Free Press, Inc.,* 245 Mich.App. 27, 627 N.W.2d 5 (2001).

28 Congressional Accountability Project, Letter to Rep. Nancy Johnson, October 3, 1995, www.essential.org/orgs/CAP/ethics/collins2.html.

29 *U.S. v. Jefferson,* Criminal No. 1:07CR209 (E.D. Va., June 4, 2007).

30 Office of the Speaker [J. Dennis Hastert, R-Ill.], "Speaker Statement Regarding the Federal Bureau of Investigation Search of Congressional Office," press release, May 22, 2006.

31 Office of the Speaker [J. Dennis Hastert, R-Ill.], "Joint Statement from Speaker Hastert and Minority Leader Pelosi," press release, May 24, 2006.

CHAPTER TEN

African American Women in Congress
A Long Road to Office

The rise of African American women to positions of political power in Congress has been long and arduous. Their efforts to gain political office have long been hindered by twofold discrimination—discrimination based on their race and on their sex.

From the end of the Civil War until the ratification in 1920 of the Nineteenth Amendment (**Document 10.1**), which granted women the right to vote, twenty-two African Americans were elected to Congress, all of them men. But ratification of the Nineteenth Amendment did not quickly open the doors of Congress to women in general or to African American women in particular.

Forty-eight years after women's suffrage was granted, Shirley A. Chisholm, D-N.Y., became the first African American woman to be elected to Congress. Those decades were lean years for all African American political representation; the election of Oscar S. De Priest, R-Ill., in 1928 made him the first

Shirley A. Chisholm, D-N.Y., was elected to the House of Representatives in November 1968 from Brooklyn. She was the first black woman to serve in Congress, and she was reelected six times. She left Congress in January 1983. Source: Library of Congress

African American member of the House of Representatives since 1901, and only nine black men won seats in Congress between 1928 and 1968. Not until 1954 were there as many as three black members of Congress at the same time during the twentieth century. Black congressional representation began to emerge in northern urban centers—Chicago, New York, Detroit—where there were large black populations, while in the South, blacks were effectively barred from voting by discriminatory laws and elections practices.

Then, in 1965, Congress passed the Voting Rights Act (**Document 6.1**), outlawing such discriminatory laws and practices, and the result was a rapid rise in African American representation in Congress. Six blacks were serving in Congress when the Voting Rights Act was passed. The election of 1968—in which Chisholm won her seat—nearly doubled that number to eleven, and by 1975 there were seventeen black members. Black representation continued to rise steadily, if slowly, and by the turn of the century, there were thirty-nine black members of Congress.

African American women were slower to win seats in Congress than were black men. In the first years after the passage of the Voting Rights Act, black women appeared to be making steady gains. Chisholm was joined in Congress in 1973 by three other female black representatives—Yvonne Braithwaite Burke, D-Calif., Cardiss Collins, D-Ill., and Barbara C. Jordan, D-Texas—to bring the total to four for six years. Burke and Jordan left Congress in 1979, and Chisholm retired in 1983. Katie B. Hall, D-Ind., won a single term from 1983 to 1985, but from January 1985 until January 1991, Collins was the only black woman in Congress.

Most political analysts attribute the lag in women's representation in Congress to gender bias in the electorate. As political scientists Dewey M. Clayton and Angela M. Stallings wrote in a 2000 study of black women in Congress:

> Women as political candidates are expected to portray the feminine characteristics ascribed to them in their daily roles as mother, daughter, sister, and wife. The problem, however, is that political candidates are normally expected to be aggressive, tough, ambitious, strong, and rational . . . characteristics normally associated with men.[1]

The difficulty is compounded for black women, Clayton and Stallings argued, because they face race prejudice as well as gender prejudice:

> As a minority within a minority, Black women face sexual discrimination as well as racial discrimination by voters who may expect them to represent only a narrow constituency, Blacks and/or women . . . In addition, Black women have either been largely invisible in the political arena, fading into the larger groups of Blacks or women, . . . or have struggled to overcome negative stereotypes that present them as nonfeminine and tough.[2]

The 1990s, however, witnessed a sharp increase in the number of black women in the House of Representatives. Four newly elected representatives joined Collins in January 1991, and the election of 1992 brought four more black women into the House while Sen. Carol Moseley-Braun, D-Ill., became the first African American woman to serve in the Senate. The 1992 election became known as the "Year of the Woman," because unprecedented numbers of women were running for—and winning—public office all across America. But even though that one election doubled the number of black women in Congress and swelled the size of the Congressional Black Caucus to thirty-nine, black women still accounted for just one quarter of the Caucus.

When they arrived in Congress, black women often encountered demeaning treatment at the hands of colleagues and congressional employees. Administrative employees, for example, attempted to give Moseley-Braun a spouse's ID card, not the senatorial credentials to which she was entitled, and Capitol elevator operators tried to prevent Rep. Cynthia A. McKinney, D-Ga., from using elevators that were reserved for members.[3] Rep. Maxine Waters, D-Calif., recalled that in one of her earliest committee meetings, the committee chair spoke to her condescendingly and called her by her first name in a public session, violating the usual congressional standard of politeness.[4] Rep. Sheila Jackson-Lee, D-Texas, said black women in Congress often feel the pressure of a double standard:

> We're expected to be representatives on economic issues, health issues, housing issues, the issue of incarceration of Black males and drugs. And we lead on some of those issues . . . But at the same time, because of the nature of this job and the nature of our work, it creates the need to be assertive. And sometimes [women lawmakers] are criticized for being too aggressive. Somehow, there is a desire for [women] to be tough, but not show it, or to be aggressive, but to mask it in ways that men are not asked to do.[5]

Rep. Sheila Jackson-Lee, D-Texas, and Rep. Maxine Waters, D-Calif., listen to Independent Counsel Kenneth Starr during the House Judiciary Committee hearing regarding articles of impeachment against President Bill Clinton on November 19, 1998.
Source: CQ Photo/Scott J. Ferrell

From the beginning, African American women in Congress have given much attention to issues revolving around the health, safety, and political and economic concerns of women. Chisholm, for example, was a champion of the proposed equal rights amendment (**Document 10.2**), which sought to write sex equity in civil and political rights into the Constitution. That proposed amendment, though approved by Congress in 1972, narrowly failed to win ratification by the states. More recent efforts to revive the idea have won support from black female members. Collins, whose twenty-four-year congressional tenure remains the longest for any black woman, placed great emphasis on promoting sex equity in employment (**Document 10.3**), and pushed for congressional action on a variety of other family health issues, such as the safety of toys for children (**Document 10.7**). Moseley-Braun worked to gain greater recognition for the suffering of battered women in domestic violence cases (**Document 10.6**).

Female African American members have also worked on a range of legislation beyond women's issues. Hall, for example, played a key role in winning passage of the Martin Luther King Jr. holiday legislation in 1983 (**Document 10.4**). Eleanor Holmes Norton, the Democratic delegate from the District of Columbia, pushed statehood legislation intended to expand the voting power of District residents (**Document 10.12**). And Rep. Carolyn Cheeks Kilpatrick, D-Mich., pushed for increased economic trade with Africa and called for United Nations intervention in the bloody civil war in the Darfur region of Sudan (**Document 10.11**). Women have also held leadership positions within the Congressional Black Caucus. Five women—Burke, Collins, Waters, Rep. Eddie Bernice Johnson, D-Texas, and Kilpatrick—have held the top post of Caucus chair.

Black women have also been at the center of many of the nation's most prominent political battles. Jordan, for example, was thrust into the national spotlight in 1974 when the House Judiciary Committee, on which she served, began considering articles of impeachment against Republican president Richard M. Nixon (**Document 6.4**). Jordan's performance during the committee's hearings won her praise for her oratorical skills and devotion to constitutional principles (**Document 10.8**). After she left Congress, Jordan continued speaking out for what she considered to be fundamental American values. In a 1985 speech, she praised the Great Society objectives of her mentor, President Lyndon B. Johnson, for their appeal to Americans' sense of decency, justice and generosity (**Document 10.5**).

In 1998 Waters and Jackson-Lee were serving on the House Judiciary Committee when the committee was again embroiled in an impeachment controversy, this time involving Democratic president Bill Clinton (**Document 10.9**). Both women strongly opposed impeachment, adding their own personal dissents to the committee's minority report (**Document 7.5**), and as chair of the Caucus, Waters was an outspoken leader of Clinton's defenders. In 2006 Waters engaged aggressively in the debate over the continuing war in Iraq, assailing the Republican administration's policies and denouncing the efforts of GOP lawmakers to put Democrats on the defensive with a resolution that appeared to equate opposition with a lack of patriotism or weakness against terrorism (**Document 10.10**).

This chapter seeks to illustrate both the significance of the role of African American women in Congress and the breadth of their interests and priorities.

Document 10.1 in Context
"The Right of Citizens . . . to Vote Shall Not Be Denied or Abridged . . . on Account of Sex": Women Win the Right to Vote

The ratification in 1920 of the Nineteenth Amendment to the U.S. Constitution (**Document 1.4**) did not merely benefit African American women who wanted to participate in the nation's political process. It was, in significant part, the result of long and energetic activism on the part of African American women who had long agitated for the right of women to vote and to be equal members of American society.

Certainly the majority of suffragists—particularly those recognized by period newspapers and by historians for years afterward—were white. But at least as far back as Maria W. Stewart in the 1830s (**Document 1.7**) and Sojourner Truth in the 1850s, black women had been outspoken advocates for women's rights and equality. As African American women began to found organizations in the 1880s and 1890s to promote community improvement, women's suffrage was a part of their agenda.

The National Association of Colored Women, formed in 1896 under the leadership of Mary Church Terrell, immediately established a department to coordinate efforts to win voting rights for women; that department remained active until the Nineteenth Amendment was ratified. Other black women's organizations—such as the National Baptist Woman's Convention and the Alpha Suffrage Club of Chicago, the latter founded in 1913 by Ida B. Wells—also worked to promote voting rights for women.

A constitutional amendment to grant women the right to vote was first introduced in Congress in 1878, more than forty years before its eventual approval. Some advocates, seeing the difficulty in getting an amendment through Congress, focused on winning women's voting rights on the state level, and by 1912, nine states had adopted legislation to grant women the vote in state elections.

But by 1916 the focus had shifted back to the national level. Pressure for a constitutional amendment grew after New York granted women the right to vote in 1917, and the next year President Woodrow Wilson endorsed the idea. By June 1919 both houses of Congress had approved the amendment; a little more a year later, on August 18, 1920, Tennessee became the thirty-sixth state to ratify the amendment, making it the law of the land.

Ratification, however, did not fling wide the doors to the political process for African American women. "Whites-only" primaries, literacy tests, poll taxes, and violent intimidation continued to disenfranchise most black voters in the South until passage of the Voting Rights Act of 1965 (**Document 6.1**). It was not until January 3, 1969, that Shirley A. Chisholm, D-N.Y., took a seat in the House of Representatives to become the first African American woman elected to Congress.

▬▬ Document 10.1 ▬▬
Nineteenth Amendment to the U.S. Constitution,
Passed by Congress on June 4, 1919, Ratified August 18, 1920

The right of citizens of the United States to vote shall not be denied or abridged by the United States or by any State on account of sex.

Congress shall have power to enforce this article by appropriate legislation.

Source: "Nineteenth Amendment to the U.S. Constitution: Women's Right to Vote (1920)," from the U.S. National Archives and Records Administration, www.ourdocuments.gov.

Document 10.2 in Context
"The Most Subtle, Most Pervasive, and Most Institutionalized Form of Prejudice that Exists": Pressing for Women's Rights

A half century after ratification of the Nineteenth Amendment (**Document 10.1**) granted women the right to vote, another attempt was made to amend the Constitution (**Document 1.4**) to bolster the rights of women. Inspired by the civil rights movement, which had brought important advancements in civil rights protections for African Americans, and determined to eliminate discrimination against women, supporters of the new amendment sought to write the equality of women and men into the Constitution in clear and specific terms.

The proposed equal rights amendment was simple and straightforward. It said: "Equality of rights under the law shall not be denied or abridged by the United States or by any State on account of sex." Although legislation proposing the amendment had been introduced in Congress continually since the late 1940s, it was not until 1970 that Congress gave the legislation serious attention. It took two years to get the amendment through Congress over the objections of traditionalists, but the final vote was overwhelming. Only twenty-four votes were cast against it in the House during a 1971 vote and eight in the Senate during a 1972 vote, giving the amendment far more than the two-thirds support it needed for passage. After passing Congress, however, the measure required ratification by three-fourths of the state legislatures for incorporation into the Constitution.

Within three months of its passage, twenty states had ratified the amendment, and that number grew to thirty by the end of one year. But Congress had attached a time limit of seven years for the proposed amendment to obtain the thirty-eight state ratifications it needed, and support dropped sharply after the first year. Over the next four years, only five more state legislatures voted to ratify the amendment, and during the same period, five states sought to withdraw endorsements they had already given. In 1978 the amendment's supporters sought and won an extension of thirty-nine months in the ratification deadline, but no other states voted to ratify. The amendment expired on June 30, 1982.

Opposition had grown as social conservatives—especially in southern and rural states—attacked the amendment as a radical and potentially dangerous overhaul of the American social structure. They argued that the amendment's unrestricted demand for female equality would require that women be drafted into the military and sent to the battlefield (the United States remained embroiled in the Vietnam War until 1975), could deny women alimony or spousal support in divorces, and could lead to legalization of same-sex marriages.

In a speech on the House floor in the summer of 1970, excerpted here, Rep. Shirley A. Chisholm, D-N.Y., argued in favor of the equal rights amendment. At the time, Chisholm was one of a small but growing number of women in Congress, and she was the first—and only—African American woman in either chamber.

Document 10.2
Rep. Shirley A. Chisholm, D-N.Y., Supports the
Equal Rights Amendment, August 10, 1970

Mrs. CHISHOLM: . . . Mr. Speaker, House Joint Resolution 264, before us today, which provides for equality under the law for both men and women, represents one of the most clear-cut opportunities we are likely to have to declare our faith in the principles that shaped our Constitution. It provides a legal basis for attack on the most subtle, most pervasive, and most institutionalized form of prejudice that exists. Discrimination against women, solely on the basis of their sex, is so widespread that is seems to many persons normal, natural and right. Legal expression of prejudice on the grounds of religious or political belief has become a minor problem in our society. Prejudice on the basis of race is, at least, under systematic attack. There is reason for optimism that it will start to die with the present, older generation. It is time we act to assure full equality of opportunity to those citizens who, although in a majority, suffer the restrictions that are commonly imposed on minorities, to women.

The argument that this amendment will not solve the problem of sex discrimination is not relevant. If the argument were used against a civil rights bill, as it has been used in the past, the prejudice that lies behind it would be embarrassing. Of course laws will not eliminate prejudice from the hearts of human beings. But that is no reason to allow prejudice to continue to be enshrined in our laws—to perpetuate injustice through inaction.

The amendment is necessary to clarify countless ambiguities and inconsistencies in our legal system. For instance, the Constitution guarantees due process of law, in the 5th and 14th amendments. But the applicability of due process of sex distinctions is not clear. Women are excluded from some State colleges and universities. In some States, restrictions are placed on a married woman who engages in an independent business. Women may not be chosen for some juries. Women even receive heavier criminal penalties than men who commit the same crime.

What would the legal effects of the equal rights amendment really be? The equal rights amendment would govern only the relationship between the State and its citizens—not relationships between private citizens.

The amendment would be largely self-executing, that is, and Federal or State laws in conflict would be ineffective one year after date of ratification without further action by the Congress or State legislatures.

Opponents of the amendment claim its ratification would throw the law into a state of confusion and would result in much litigation to establish its meaning. This objection overlooks the influence of legislative history in determining intent and the recent activities of many groups preparing for legislative changes in this direction.

State labor laws applying only to women, such as those limiting hours of work and weights to be lifted would become inoperative unless the legislature amended them to apply to men. As of early 1970 most States would have some laws that would be affected.

However, changes are being made so rapidly as a result of title VII of the Civil Rights Act of 1964, it is likely that by the time the equal rights amendment would become effective; no conflicting State laws would remain.

In any event, there has for years been great controversy as to the usefulness to women of these State labor laws. There has never been any doubt that they worked a hardship on women who need or want to work overtime and on women who need or want better paying jobs, and there has been no persuasive evidence as to how many women benefit from the archaic policy of the laws. After the Delaware hours law was repealed in 1966, there were no complaints from women to any of the State agencies that might have been approached.

Jury service laws not making women equally liable for jury service would have to be revised.

The selective service law would have to include women, but women would not be required to serve in the Armed Forces where they are not fitted any more than men are required to serve. Military service, while a great responsibility, is not without benefits, particularly for young men with limited education or training.

Since October 1966, 246,000 young men who did not meet the normal mental or physical requirements have been given opportunities for training and correcting physical problems. This opportunity is not open to their sisters. Only girls who have completed high school and meet high standards on the educational test can volunteer. Ratification of the amendment would not permit application of higher standards to women.

Survivorship benefits would be available to husbands of female workers on the same basis as to wives of male workers. The Social Security Act and the civil service and military service retirement acts are in conflict.

Public schools and universities could not be limited to one sex and could not apply different admission standards to men and women. Laws requiring longer prison sentences for women than men would be invalid, and equal opportunities for rehabilitation and vocational training would have to be provided in public correctional institutions.

Different ages of majority based on sex would have to be harmonized.

Federal, State, and other governmental bodies would be obligated to follow nondiscriminatory practices in all aspects of employment, including public school teachers and State university and college faculties.

What would be the economic effects of the equal rights amendment? Direct economic effects would be minor. If any labor laws applying only to women still remained, their amendment or repeal would provide opportunity for women in better-paying jobs in manufacturing. More opportunities in public vocational and graduate schools for women would also tend to open up opportunities in better jobs for women.

Indirect effects could be much greater. The focusing of public attention on the gross legal, economic, and social discrimination against women by hearings and debates in the Federal and State legislatures would result in changes in attitude of parents, educators, and employers that would bring about substantial economic changes in the long run.

Sex prejudice cuts both ways. Men are oppressed by the requirements of the Selective Service Act, by enforced legal guardianship of minors, and by alimony laws. Each sex, I believe, should be liable when necessary to serve and defend this country.

Each has a responsibility for the support of children.

There are objections raised to wiping out laws protecting women workers. No one would condone exploitation. But what does sex have to do with it. Working conditions and hours that are harmful to women are harmful to men; wages that are unfair for women are unfair for men. Laws setting employment limitations on the basis of sex are irrational, and the proof of this is their inconsistency from State to State. The physical characteristics of men and women are not fixed, but cover two wide spans that have a great deal of overlap. It is obvious, I think, that a robust woman could be more fit for physical labor than a weak man. The choice of occupation would be determined by individual capabilities, and the rewards for equal works should be equal.

This is what it comes down to: artificial distinctions between persons must be wiped out of the law. Legal discrimination between the sexes is, in almost every instance, founded on outmoded views of society and the pre-scientific beliefs about psychology and physiology. It is time to sweep away these relics of the past and set further generations free of them.

Federal agencies and institutions responsible for the enforcement of equal opportunity laws need the authority of a Constitutional amendment. The 1964 Civil Rights Act and the 1963 Equal Pay Act are not enough; they are limited in their coverage—for instance, one excludes teachers, and the other leaves out administrative and professional women. The Equal Employment Opportunity Commission has not proven to be an adequate device, with its power limited to investigation, conciliation, and recommendation to the Justice Department. In its cases involving sexual discrimination, it has failed in more than one-half. The Justice Department has been even less effective. It has intervened in only one case involving discrimination on the basis of sex, and this was on a procedural point. In a second case, in which both sexual and racial discrimination were alleged, the racial bias charge was given far greater weight.

Evidence of discrimination on the basis of sex should hardly have to be cited here. It is in the Labor Department's employment and salary figures for anyone who is still in doubt. Its elimination will involve so many changes in our State and Federal laws that, without the authority and impetus of this proposed amendment, it will perhaps take another 194 years. We cannot be parties to continuing a delay. The time is clearly now to put this House on record for the fullest expression of that equality of opportunity which our founding fathers professed. They professed it, but they did not assure it to their daughters, as they tried to do for their sons.

The Constitution they wrote was designed to protect the rights of white, male citizens. As there were no black Founding Fathers, there were no founding mothers—a great pity, on both counts. It is not too late to complete the work they left undone. Today, here, we should start to do so . . .

Source: Congressional Record, 91st Cong., 2d sess., August 10, 1970, 28028–28029.

Document 10.3 in Context
"A Concerted and Determined Effort to Recruit and Hire Women": Pushing the Federal Government for Sex Equity

In 1973—with the election of Barbara C. Jordan, D-Texas, Yvonne Braithwaite Burke, D-Calif., and Cardiss Collins, D-Ill.—Shirley A. Chisholm, D-N.Y., had ceased to be the lone black woman in the House. By the early 1980s, however, the presence of African American women in Congress was beginning to wane. Jordan and Burke left Congress in 1979 and Chisholm decided not run for reelection in 1982. Katie B. Hall, D-Ind., joined the House after a special election very late in 1982, but served only one full term after that. For most of the 1980s, therefore, Collins was the only black woman in Congress.

Collins, who had succeeded her husband in the House following his death in a plane crash, served twelve terms in the House. The main focus of her legislative interest was health care, particularly as it affected women and families. She worked to promote a range of health and safety issues (**Document 10.7**), and served as chair of the Congressional Black Caucus in 1979–1980.

Collins also worked with the Congressional Caucus for Women's Issues to promote equity for women. The document that follows is a letter sent by that caucus to President Ronald Reagan in 1982 to urge more equitable advancement of women into supervisory positions within the federal government. The letter was prompted by the passage of legislation, supported by the president, that authorized the hiring of more than 3,300 new employees by the Internal Revenue Service. The caucus was prodding the president to use the opportunity to promote more women into managerial positions.

Collins was one of forty-four Women's Issues Caucus members to sign the letter; four other members of the Congressional Black Caucus also signed the letter. It is interesting to note, however, that the list of signatories reflects the relatively sparse presence of women in Congress itself. Only eight of the letter's signers were women.

▬ Document 10.3 ▬
Letter to President Reagan from the Congressional Caucus on Women's Issues, September 28, 1982

DEAR MR. PRESIDENT: The Tax Equity and Fiscal Responsibility Act of 1982, as passed by the Congress, includes your proposal for an increase of 3,310 positions in the Internal Revenue Service for Fiscal Year 1983.

Currently, 54.5 percent of the full time workforce for the Internal Revenue Service are women. In some of the ten Service Centers, up to 85 percent of the employees are women. Yet, the agency's average grade level for women employees is 6.32 while the average grade level for men employees is 9.99. Women hold only nine of the 257 senior executive positions. There are ten Service Center Directorships, yet only one of these positions is occupied by a woman. In addition, of the 60 District Directorships, women hold only two of these positions.

We know that you have frequently expressed your commitment to bring qualified women into positions of responsibility within the Federal government, and we share your concern in this area. We view the creation of these 3,310 IRS positions as an excellent opportunity for you to demonstrate this commitment by placing women in senior and mid-level positions to serve as revenue officers, investigators, examiners and in a variety of supervisory and management positions.

We urge you, Mr. President, to instruct the Internal Revenue Service to make a concerted and determined effort to recruit and hire women for these newly created positions and to require accountability through followup reports.

Sincerely,

[Signed by forty-three members of Congress, including Cardiss Collins]

Source: Congressional Record, 97th Cong., 2d sess., September 29, 1982, 21680–21681.

Document 10.4 in Context
"A National Commitment to Dr. King's Vision and Determination for an Ideal America": A Federal Holiday Honoring Rev. Martin Luther King Jr.

One of the signal accomplishments of the Congressional Black Caucus was the legislation passed by Congress in 1983 (**Document 6.9**) establishing a national holiday honoring Rev. Martin Luther King Jr. Caucus members began introducing bills aimed at establishing the holiday shortly after King's death in 1968, but they had faced resistance and sometimes outright hostility in the House of Representatives. Some opponents of the legislation questioned the economic advisability of creating another holiday that would mandate time off for workers, while others denounced the idea of honoring King, whom they accused of being a communist.

Although there were only two African American women in Congress at the time, they played a central role in winning passage of the King holiday legislation during the 1983 session. Rep. Katie B. Hall, D-Ind., cosponsored the legislation and was floor manager for the bill during the House debate. Rep. Cardiss Collins, D-Ill., was active in the debate over the bill.

A former Indiana state senator, Hall had been elected simultaneously in November 1982 to complete the final weeks of her predecessor's term, the late Adam Benjamin, in the Ninety-seventh Congress and to a full term of her own in the Ninety-eighth Congress. Hall was defeated in her attempt to win reelection in 1984, losing to a Democratic opponent in the primary election.

During her single term in Congress, however, Hall was selected to chair the Census and Population Subcommittee of the House Post Office and Civil Service Committee. In her role as subcommittee chair, she had overseen preparation of the King holiday legislation. As floor manager for the bill, she led off the debate and oversaw the order and time allocations of the members who spoke in support of the bill. This excerpt from the *Congressional Record* contains Hall's opening remarks.

▬ Document 10.4 ▬
Rep. Katie B. Hall, D-Ind., Leads Debate on Bill to Establish a National Holiday Honoring Rev. Martin Luther King Jr., August 2, 1983

Mrs. HALL of Indiana: . . . Mr. Speaker, H.R. 3345 designates the third Monday in January of each year a legal public holiday to commemorate the birthday of Dr. Martin Luther King, Jr., to take effect on the first January that occurs 2 years after enactment.

Martin Luther King gave to this great Nation a new understanding of equality and justice for all. He taught us that our democratic principles could be seriously impaired if they were not applied equally, and that tailoring these principles through non-violence would have a lasting effect.

Mr. Speaker, the legislation before us will act as a national commitment to Dr. King's vision and determination for an ideal America, which he spoke of the night before his death, where equality will always prevail.

Next year marks the 20th anniversary of Dr. Martin Luther King's Nobel Peace Prize Award, where he was recognized by all people of the world for bringing about a peaceful social revolution which changed the hearts and minds of men and women everywhere.

Mr. Speaker, the time is before us to show what we believe, that justice and equality must continue to prevail, not only as individuals, but as the greatest Nation in this world. It is

America's turn to say thank you to Dr. Martin Luther King, Jr., and it is our duty as elected Representatives to nationalize this tribute.

H.R. 3345 has received overwhelming support from both the Committee on Post Office and Civil Service and the Subcommittee on the Census and Population, by reporting this bill to the House of Representatives with only one dissenting vote. I urge my colleagues to recognize the bipartisan support this legislation carries.

Mr. Speaker, let us all hold the memory of Dr. King and his vital contributions to this country in the highest esteem by supporting the Martin Luther King, Jr., public holiday . . .

Source: Congressional Record, 98th Cong., 1st sess., August 2, 1983, 22208.

Document 10.5 in Context
"The Enemy Was Not Government": Assessing the Values of the Great Society

Few women have had as great an impact as Rep. Barbara C. Jordan, D-Texas, on the political empowerment of African American women. Jordan was a dominant figure in the first generation of black women to capture public office after passage of the Voting Rights Act of 1965 (**Document 6.1**), and her commitment and idealism inspired many other women—white as well as black— to pursue elective office.

Born and raised in Houston, Jordan graduated from Texas Southern University and the Boston University School of Law before returning to her hometown to practice law in 1960. Jordan became politically active in the 1960 presidential campaign of Democrat John F. Kennedy and his running mate, Lyndon B. Johnson. Johnson, a fellow Texan, later became her political mentor.

Soon after the Voting Rights Act was passed, Jordan won her first elective office. She ran for and won a seat in the Texas Senate in 1966, to become the first black woman ever to serve in that body and the first African American state senator in Texas since 1883. It was a remarkable achievement in a state that had for decades excluded blacks from the political process (**Document 5.2**).

Jordan ran for reelection in 1968 and held her seat until 1972, when she was elected to the U.S. House of Representatives. In her autobiography, *Barbara Jordan: A Self-Portrait* (1979), she describes how Johnson helped arrange her assignment to the House Judiciary Committee—an unusually prestigious assignment for a first-term member of Congress. Slightly more than a year after joining the committee, Jordan found herself deeply involved in one of the most intense political dramas of the twentieth century, as the committee considered articles of impeachment against President Richard M. Nixon. Her firm and measured discussion of constitutional responsibility during the committee's impeachment debate (**Document 6.4**) drew widespread praise for her oratorical skills and solidified her reputation for clear judgment and passionate integrity.

In the following speech, delivered as the keynote for a two-day symposium in 1985 at the University of Texas at Austin, Jordan reflects on the legacy of President Johnson and his Great Society initiatives. Her admiration for her mentor is evident in the speech, as are the values to which she committed her own political career.

Document 10.5
Rep. Barbara C. Jordan, D-Texas, Reflects on President Lyndon B. Johnson's Great Society, April 1985

Each generation is different. Each has its actors in the present, its predecessors and its successors. Its leakages are described by the quality of its inheritance. Each generation is marked by its people, its program, its promise. It is marked by its failures and achievements. Each generation leaves a legacy to succeeding generations. That legacy may be solid, etched as if in stone, or that legacy may be very fragile, house of cards, tumbling in the first gust of wind. Each generation has benchmarks which identify its essence. For some, those benchmarks are sabers and new ways to destroy the planet Earth. For others, those benchmarks may be reaping a harvest of hate, greed, avarice. And then there are those generations whose benchmarks are hope and opportunity and a passion for justice.

The successor generation has a right to expect that its predecessor will leave for it its best institutions, its highest ideals, the most enduring of values. This expectation exists because there is a continuum of reciprocal rights, duties, obligations. Those reciprocal duties begin long before the birth of man and continue without ceasing. To guarantee this reciprocity is honored, people consent to come together—for what? People consent to come together for the protection of their person and effects, for an exchange of ideas, for safety, for creativity. People agree to come together to joint venture the future.

There are two value strains which are common running throughout each generation. Those two value strains are liberty and justice. Freedom, liberty to be preferred over coercion. It is the individual who must be released to soar to the outer limits. Justice, or right, is always to take precedence over might. Governments, presidents, Congresses, executive and legislative branches, the governors the people choose must never cease in their search for right. The imperative is to find what is right and do it.

The Great Society is the benchmark of the presidency of Lyndon Johnson and of his generation. No one described the Great Society more eloquently than President Johnson himself. On the 22nd of May, 1964, when he made that graduation speech at the University of Michigan, he said, "Your imagination, your initiative, your indignation will determine whether we build a society where progress is the servant of our needs or a society where old values and new visions are buried under unbridled growth. For in your time," the president continued, "we have the opportunity to move not only toward the rich society and the powerful society but upward to the Great Society."

"The Great Society," President Johnson said, "rests on abundance and liberty for all. It demands an end to poverty and racial injustice, to which," he added, "we are totally committed in our time." Do you believe a president of the United States said that?

"But that is just the beginning," he continued. "The Great Society is a place where every child can find knowledge to enrich his mind and to enlarge his talents. It is a place where leisure is a welcome chance to build and reflect, not a feared cause of boredom and restlessness. It is a place where the city of man serves not only the needs of the body and the demands of commerce but the desire for beauty and the hunger for community.

"It is a place where man can renew contact with nature. It is a place which honors creation for its own sake and for what it adds to the understanding of the race. It is a place where men are more concerned with the quality of their goals than the quantity of their goods.

"But most of all, the Great Society is not a safe harbor," he said, "a resting place, a final objective, a finished work. It is a challenge constantly renewed, beckoning us toward a destiny where the meaning of our lives matches the marvelous products of our labor."

That's the way Lyndon Johnson described the Great Society, and as an idea, it did not come with him fully matured. The idea of the Great Society grew out of the soil of his soul. You know, at that time Michael Harrington had recently written *The Other America* and informed us that there were between forty and fifty million poor people in America. It was shortly before that that John Kenneth Galbraith had completed his book, *The Affluent Society*. That book pictured us as an uncomfortable captive of wealth and the consequent derangement of values.

And then there were Lyndon Johnson's own roots, a land once barren and forbidding transformed. The president, President Johnson, in his State of the Union message in January of 1965 restated his commitment to a great future and he reminded us that a president does not constantly reinvent the wheel in proposing new ideas and new programs. President Johnson stated it this way in that State of the Union message: "A president does not shape a new and personal vision of America, he collects it from the scattered hopes of American past. It existed when the first settlers saw the coast of the New World and when the first pioneers moved westward. It has guided us every step of the way. It sustains every president. But it is also your inheritance and it belongs equally to all people. It must be interpreted anew," President Johnson said, "by each generation for its own needs, as I have tried," he added, "in part, to do tonight. It shall lead us as we enter the third century of the search for a more perfect union. This, then, is the state of the union: free, restless, growing, full of hope. So it was in the beginning and so it shall always be, while God is willing and we are strong enough to keep the faith" . . .

The Great Society programs were different from conventional welfare programs. Lyndon Johnson made them different. He addressed root causes and tried to bring resolution at the point of beginning. Lyndon Johnson did not simply say, let's provide children with better education and the unemployed with jobs. Lyndon Johnson wanted to *prepare* children to *receive* an education. He wanted to provide those without work employability. These programs are not mere words, friends. There are flesh and blood examples of what these programs meant . . .

The legacy of Lyndon Johnson continues to enrich our lives. He saw the enemy, and the enemy was not government. The enemy was ignorance, poverty, disease, ugliness, injustice, discrimination. He believed that it was the duty of government to defeat the enemy.

Panelists today and tomorrow will discuss and debate the programs of the Great Society, what failed, what succeeded. That verdict may interest some of you but it really is not very important. The Great Society is larger than numbers. The Great Society was larger than number crunching and graphs and charts. It was a commitment of mind and spirit. It was a feeling about governance. And I looked for an expression of the feeling about governance and I found it in the last paragraph of Joseph Califano's book on *Governing America*.

Joseph Califano was describing his feelings as he left H.E.W. [Califano was Secretary of Health, Education and Welfare under President Jimmy Carter.] He said, "I left and remained full of hope with an intuitive and empirical conviction that we can govern with competence and compassion. Too many of us, including some in government, don't try because the task seems too difficult, sometimes impossible. Of course, those who govern will make mistakes, plenty of them, but we must not fear failure. What we should fear above all is the judgment of God and history if the most affluent people on Earth, free to act as they wish, choose not to govern justly, distribute our riches fairly and help the most vulnerable among us—or worse, choose not to even try."

That's the worst judgment. The generation of Lyndon Johnson escaped that judgment. The overarching question is, shall we?

Source: Barbara Jordan, "The Great Society and Its Markings," April 1985, speech delivered at the University of Texas at Austin's symposium on "The Great Society: A Twenty-Year Critique." Audio recording from UT KUT Longhorn Radio Network Records, Center for American History, University of Texas at Austin, Box 95-260/4; transcription by Stephen A. Jones.

Document 10.6 in Context
"To Allow Battered Women to Introduce Evidence of Their Abuse . . . as Part of Their Claims of Self-Defense": Protecting Women from Violence

In 1991 the Senate's confirmation hearings on the nomination of Clarence Thomas to the Supreme Court ignited a firestorm of controversy over the issue of sexual harassment (**Document 7.1**). Liberals were already concerned that Thomas, if confirmed, might shift the political balance on the Court and help reverse earlier decisions on such issues as affirmative action and abortion. Then Anita Hill accused Thomas of sexual harassment when he was her superior at the Equal Employment Opportunity Commission. The ensuing debate and the withering cross-examination Hill faced in the hearings angered many women—including Carol Moseley-Braun, the recorder of deeds and a former state legislator in Cook County, Illinois.

Incensed by the confirmation of Thomas and what she considered the Senate's mistreatment of Hill, Moseley-Braun ran for the Democratic nomination to the Senate in 1992, challenging and defeating the two-term incumbent, Democrat Alan J. Dixon. Her victory, which made her the first African American woman to serve in the Senate, along with the addition of three other women to the Senate in that fall's general election, prompted some to call 1992 the "Year of the Woman."

Moseley-Braun was keenly aware of her position as one of just six female senators and the only African American. "I have a special interest in racial issues," she said. "I'm African American. It goes without saying that I have a special interest in gender issues. I'm a female. And there's precious few of us on the Senate floor at this point." [6] Not surprisingly, women's issues were high on her legislative agenda.

She demonstrated that early in her first months in the Senate by introducing a resolution to encourage state courts to admit expert testimony on the effects of domestic violence on battered women in criminal cases where a women was accused of killing a spouse who had abused her. The resolution, which was eventually approved by the Senate but died in the House, sought to counteract "myths, misconceptions, and victim-blaming attitudes" that might be held by jurors and be reinforced by a criminal justice system that "traditionally has failed to protect women from violence at the hands of men." [7]

The document that follows is the *Congressional Record*'s report of Moseley-Braun's comments in the Senate on introducing the resolution.

▬▬ Document 10.6 ▬▬
Sen. Carol Moseley-Braun, D-Ill., Pleads the Case of Battered Women, March 30, 1990

Ms. MOSELEY-BRAUN: Mr. President, I am here today to talk about an issue which until very recently was ignored by the press, the medical community, and the criminal justice system. I am speaking about the battered woman's syndrome and its sometimes fatal consequences. Women who are regularly beaten by their husbands or boyfriends often exhibit behavior that does not fit the general definition of 'normal'. When women are involved in an abusive relationship over a period of time, physical and psychological deterioration can result. Many women come to believe that they are deserving of their mate's treatment. They end up believing the apologies of their abuser and the endless assertions that the abuse will end. Their lives are an emotional rollercoaster—abuse may happen at any moment.

The National Clearinghouse of the Defense of Battered Women estimates that there is a domestic violence-related assault reported every 15 seconds. The clearinghouse also reports that every year 860 women kill men who have abused them—between 75 and 90 percent kill in self defense. Some believe that domestic violence only affects the poor and uneducated. In reality domestic violence knows no boundaries. Its victims, as its perpetrators, include all races, ages, and socio-economic levels.

Most women who kill their abuser have tried desperately to leave, but in many instances their abusers won't let them go. There have been countless stories of women being locked in, deprived of cash, telephones, car keys, or their lives being threatened, and of being physically forced to return to an abusive situation.

To illustrate what can happen to a person who has been repeatedly physically and psychologically abused, I offer a story, which is unfortunately not at all atypical.

A woman, let's call her Sara, is taken into custody. Her husband to the morgue. Earlier that evening they had had a big fight. The police were called by a neighbor, and although Sara had been beaten badly she declined to press charges. Several nights later while he is sleeping, however, she calmly loaded her husband's 357 magnum and shot him dead. In the ensuring trial Sara is sentenced to 15 years for killing her husband even though she had been a victim of abuse for several years.

The jury was not permitted to hear testimony on the history of abuse, however, because Sara lives in one of 41 States that do not, by statute, allow the jury to hear evidence of a history of abuse. It is time that we ensure that juries hear the whole story, and make their decisions based on all of the facts.

For these reasons, I am introducing a resolution that encourages States to allow battered women on trial in criminal cases to not only present evidence of past abuse, but also have expert witnesses testify about the battered woman's syndrome.

After hearing chilling tales of abuse over prolonged periods many ask 'Why didn't she just walk away?'. I think the Nation is just beginning to understand the dimensions of domestic violence and its terrible implications. This has been evidenced by actions by the Governors of Ohio, Maryland, Massachusetts, and Missouri who have granted clemency to several battered women imprisoned for killing their abusers.

In addition, nine States now by statute allow juries to hear a battered woman's history. Several other State legislatures are considering similar laws. This is a good start, but it is insufficient given the scope and extent of the problem. Too many States have not acted, thus leaving it up to the individual judge to decide on a case-by-case basis whether information on a history of battering will be admissible. We must exert leadership on the national level, and we must do it now.

This resolution does not seek to circumvent the jury process nor does it substitute Federal for State law. It does encourage States to allow battered women to introduce evidence of their abuse and its psychological effects as part of their claims of self-defense.

Sara could be your daughter or a friend. Domestic violence causes untold suffering. The stories that we hear so often are simply horrifying. Rather than reacting with shock and horror to each isolated case we must be proactive and seek solutions to the broader problem. This resolution will help to assure that our legal system ensures that all battered women receive a fair trial.

I urge my Senate colleagues to consider this resolution carefully and support it wholeheartedly.

Source: Congressional Record, 103d Cong., 1st sess., March 30, 1993, S4031–24032.

Document 10.7 in Context
"Let Us Show Our Children that We Are Listening": Protecting Children from Injury

African American women in Congress have regularly given special attention to issues that are of particular concern to female voters. In addition, they have sought to promote a variety of legislation on family-related issues, among others.

Rep. Cardiss Collins, D-Ill., spent much of her twelve terms in Congress working to promote legislation protecting the health of women and families. She won her seat in 1973 in a special election to replace her husband, Rep. George Washington Collins, D-Ill., who had been killed in a plane crash. Although she was not the first woman to arrive in Congress in such fashion, many of the women who have been similarly elected have not won—or even stood for—reelection. Few have managed to carve out congressional careers comparable to Collins's nearly twenty-four years in the House.

Collins was a consistent supporter of universal health insurance. In 1991 she cosponsored the Universal Health Care Act and the Family and Medical Leave Act. She also pushed for legislation to expand Medicare coverage to include mammography screening for elderly and disabled women and PAP smears to promote early detection of cervical and uterine cancers.

One example of Collins's health and safety focus was the Child Safety Protection Act of 1994, which established federal safety standards for bicycle helmets and required manufacturers to place warning labels on toys that posed dangers for small children. In the following excerpt from House floor discussion of the final version of the bill, Collins describes the benefits of the legislation, which took more than three years to get through Congress.

▬ Document 10.7 ▬
Rep. Cardiss Collins, D-Ill., Urges the House to Approve the Child Safety Protection Act, May 23, 1994

Mrs. COLLINS of Illinois: . . . Mr. Speaker, I have made child safety a priority since I became chairwoman of the Subcommittee on Commerce, Consumer Protection and Competitiveness over 3 years ago. Last Congress, I introduced H.R. 4706, the Child Safety Protection and Consumer Product Safety Commission Improvement Act, which passed the House but was not considered by the Senate before adjournment. Today, Mr. Speaker, I am pleased to come before the House to support the adoption of the conference report to accompany H.R. 965, the Child Safety Protection Act, which is the successor to H.R. 4706.

The conference report to accompany H.R. 965 includes the toy safety labeling and bicycle standards provisions that have already been passed by the House. Under the bill, toys that present a choking hazard to young children must have a label to warn parents of the choking danger. Bicycle helmets will eventually have to meet a Federal safety standard—initially based upon current voluntary standards—to ensure that the helmets will adequately protect against head injury. In addition, the conference report includes a provision added by the Senate to encourage children to use bicycle helmets.

This legislation has drawn bipartisan support as well as support from a broad array of outside groups. I particularly want to commend the National Safe Kids Campaign for its work in developing this bill which is also supported by the U.S. Public Interest Research Group, Consumer Federation of America, Consumers Union, Public Citizen's Congress Watch as well as The Toy Manufacturers of America.

Mr. Speaker, many individuals helped craft this legislation. I want to thank the distinguished chairman of the Energy and Commerce Committee, Mr. [John D.] DINGELL [D-Mich.], the ranking member of the full committee, Mr. [Carlos J.] MOORHEAD [R-Calif.], and the ranking member of the subcommittee, Mr. [Clifford B.] STEARNS [R-Fla]. I also want to commend two important members of the subcommittee, the gentleman from New York [Mr. Edolphus TOWNS, D-N.Y.] and the gentleman from New Jersey [Mr. Frank PALLONE Jr., D-N.J.] for their work in helping to shape this legislation.

I also thank Chairman [Norman Y.] MINETA [D-Calif.] of the Committee on Public Works and Transportation and the ranking member, Mr. [E. G.] SHUSTER [R-Pa.], for their work on the bicycle helmet provision.

On the Senate side, I was particularly fortunate to have the assistance of Senators [Richard H.] BRYAN [D-Nev.] and [Thomas S.] GORTON [III, R-Wash.] who were cosponsors of companion legislation and whose hard work was essential to moving this bill forward. I also want to commend Senators [John C.] DANFORTH [R-Mo.], [Christopher J.] DODD [D-Conn.], and [Howard M.] METZENBAUM [D-Ohio] for their important contributions and for helping to bring attention to these child safety issues.

In conclusion, Mr. Speaker, I would be remiss if I did not mention some of the most important people of all—our children.

A couple of weeks ago, 102 children, ranging in age from 8 to 15 every State and the District of Columbia, were making their rounds on Capital Hill. They were the National SAFE KIDS Summit Representatives. They did not come to simply tour, but to discuss the importance of injury prevention with Congress and the administration. Summit representatives, Tor Harper, an 11-year-old from Oregon, Marcus Young a 14-year-old from Missouri and Katie Manchester a 10-year-old from Maine, who were saved from severe injury because they were wearing bicycle helmets, are some of the children that know from personal experience the importance of wearing bicycle helmets.

At a hearing of the Subcommittee on Commerce, Consumer Protection and Competitiveness 2 years ago, sixth grader from the Old Donation Center for the Gifted and Talented in Virginia testified about the need for warning labeling on toys that pose a choking hazard to young children.

In an age of passivism and cynicism, it is inspiring to see children that are trying to make a change in our country. When our children come all the way to Washington to talk to us about matters of literally life and death—we must listen. Let us show our children that we are listening by sending H.R. 965 to the President . . .

Source: Congressional Record, 103d Cong., 2d sess., May 23, 1994, H3809.

Document 10.8 in Context
"A Friend to Many, a Mentor, and an Icon": Paying Tribute to Rep. Barbara C. Jordan

On January 17, 1996, Barbara C. Jordan, a former Democratic representative from Texas, died in Austin at age fifty-nine after a long struggle with multiple sclerosis and leukemia. Although her three terms in Congress had ended seventeen years earlier, her political career continued to resonate deeply with women in general and African American women in particular.

Jordan began her political career years before the Voting Rights Act of 1965 (**Document 6.1**) reshaped the nation's political landscape by guaranteeing African Americans the right to vote. As a young lawyer in Houston in 1960, she was an active supporter of Democrat John F. Kennedy's presidential campaign. Two years later, she made the first of two unsuccessful attempts to win a seat in the Texas House of Representatives. The changes wrought by the Voting Rights Act helped propel her to victory in 1966, when she became the first black woman ever to be elected to the Texas Senate and the first African American state senator in Texas since 1883. She served in the state senate until 1972, when she was elected to the U.S. House of Representatives. She and Rep. Yvonne Braithwaite Burke, D-Calif., joined Shirley A. Chisholm, D-N.Y., as the only African American women to serve in Congress up to that point.

The move to Washington soon thrust her onto the center of the national political stage where she was favorably regarded as a member of the House Judiciary Committee that began considering articles of impeachment against Republican President Richard M. Nixon in May 1974 (**Document 6.5**). At the Democratic National Convention in 1976, Jordan's speech-making skills drew high praise from many in her party when she delivered a keynote address (**Document 15.5**) that emphasized public officials' responsibility to lead in the development of a national sense of community.

Jordan retired from politics at the end of her congressional term in January 1979 and spent her remaining years as a professor in the Lyndon B. Johnson School of Public Affairs at the University of Texas at Austin. As an educator and as a trailblazer in politics, Jordan inspired many women to pursue political careers. A week after she died, another African American congresswoman from Houston, Sheila Jackson-Lee, D-Texas, rose in the House of Representatives to lead a tribute to Jordan. The following document is an excerpt of Jackson-Lee's comments.

━━ Document 10.8 ━━
Rep. Sheila Jackson-Lee, D-Texas, Eulogizes Rep. Barbara C. Jordan, January 24, 1996

Ms. JACKSON-LEE of Texas: . . . Mr. Speaker, last week we lost an American hero. Barbara Jordan died last week on Wednesday, January 17, 1996, a friend to many, a mentor, and an icon. The late honorable Congresswoman, Barbara Jordan, who not only represented the 18th Congressional District of Texas that I am now privileged to serve, was one of the first two African-Americans from the South to be elected to this august body since reconstruction. She was a renaissance woman, eloquent, fearless, and peerless in her pursuit of justice and equality. She exhorted all of us to strive for excellence, stand fast for justice and fairness, and yield to no one in the matter of defending this Constitution and upholding the most sacred principles of a democratic government. To Barbara Jordan, the Constitution was a very profound document, one to be upheld.

The lady, Barbara Jordan, the first black woman elected to the Texas Senate, was born February 21, 1936, the daughter of Benjamin and Arlene Jordan. The youngest daughter of a Baptist minister, she lived with her two sisters in the Lyons Avenue area of Houston's Fifth Ward. The church played an important role in her life. She joined the Good Hope Baptist Church on August 15, 1953, under the leadership of Rev. A. A. Lucas, graduating with honors from Houston's [Phillis] Wheatley High School in the Houston Independent School District.

Ms. Jordan went on to Texas Southern University, where she majored in government and history. While at Texas Southern University, Barbara Jordan was an active student and a member of the debate team for 4 years, and a member of Delta Sigma Theta Sorority. She got her tutelage under Dr. Thomas Freeman, who gave her the inspiration and certainly the training to formulate both her words and her tone, and to make her one of this world's greatest orators.

It was her involvement with the debate team that began for her a series of firsts that will become the hallmark of her professional life. Ms. Jordan was a member of the first debate team from a black university to compete in the forensic tournament held annually at Baylor College University in Texas. On that occasion, she won first place in junior oratory, one of many first place trophies in a career as a debater. We must remember at those times there were not many black debate teams from across the Nation competing in integrated tournaments. This was a first. Ms. Jordan was outstanding.

After graduating magna cum laude from Texas Southern University in 1956, she received her law degree from Boston University in 1959. This Constitution became part of Barbara Jordan's life, and she carried it everywhere she went. We already knew Barbara Jordan before the 1974 impeachment hearings, but her undaunted courage on that somber occasion etched her name in our memories forever.

Those of us who have been honored by having the public place its trust in us know the onerous burden and the weight of passing a vote destined to alter our history forever. We know what it took for Barbara Jordan to say 'yea, aye' when the House Committee on the Judiciary roll was called on July 30, 1974, and we are still admiring her for it. That was the day we realized that she was much more than the gilded, persuasive voice that always held sway when she spoke.

I remember her talking about this momentous day and her participation in the Watergate hearings. This young woman, newly elected to Congress, took these responsibilities extremely seriously. She was concerned that people across the country felt that this Government was being undermined, that we were in the throes of a potential revolution, that all would be lost.

Barbara Jordan, concerned about the moment, the history, the impact, seriously studied all of the Watergate hearings in review, listened attentively, and indicated to all of us that she viewed this Constitution as a serious document and would not view it and see it be diminished. She took this role seriously, and she was concerned that she speak in measured words and tone, so those who might be looking would still have faith in the Constitution and in this Government. It was the honorable Barbara Jordan that calmed the fears of most Americans, saying that if she was there with her faith in this Constitution, albeit that she had not been included in this Constitution as an African-American when it was written, then they knew that all might be well.

We realize that Barbara Jordan was a tremendous moral force and was calling upon all of us to account to our conscience as a Nation. Her untimely death leaves a great void in our national leadership, and she will be sorely missed as we grapple with the great moral issues of the day.

Barbara Jordan was a lawyer, legislator, scholar, author, and presidential adviser. She was immensely gifted, and used every bit of her talent and skill to address, improve, and dignify the conditions of human life. In the tradition of Frederick Douglass, Martin Luther King, and Thurgood Marshall, she challenged the Federal Government and the American people to uphold the principles set forth in the American Constitution.

Congresswoman Jordan began her public career as a Texas State Senator. Might I say to you, she was a first then, for there had never been an African-American in the Texas Senate, and she stood tall and proud. Her voice, although eloquent and resonating throughout the halls, was full of passion, and she felt compelled to represent those, the least of her sisters and brothers, individuals who might never have gone outside of the realm of their neighborhood, who might not be able to read or write, did not have a job. She has spoken on behalf of small businesses. She was very concerned about civil rights, employment discrimination, equality and justice, even in the Texas Senate. She served her country with great distinction as a Member of Congress and chairwoman of the U.S. Commission on Immigration Reform. Her extraordinary impact on our country will be felt for many generations.

She gained national prominence in the 1970's as a member of the House Committee on the Judiciary during the impeachment hearings of President Richard Nixon. Again, her eloquent statement regarding her faith in the Constitution helped the Nation to focus on the principle that all elected officials, including the President of the United States, must abide by the mandates of the Constitution.

During her tenure in Congress, Congresswoman Barbara Jordan was a leader on issues relating to voting rights, consumer protection, energy, and the environment. Might I add that she was particularly forceful in including language minorities in the Voting Rights Act of 1965, which then covered Texas, and also allowed for Hispanics and others to be included so that they would have equal justice under the law as right, and have full participation in this Nation, and a full part of this Constitution.

Additionally, Congresswoman Jordan played an active role in the Democratic Party. She served as a keynote speaker at the 1976 and 1992 Democratic National Conventions, and constantly challenged the Democratic Party to be a catalyst for progress and make the American dream a reality for all Americans.

After retiring from Congress, Congresswoman Jordan was appointed a distinguished professor at the Lyndon B. Johnson School of Public Affairs at the University of Texas at Austin. This position enabled her to have a major influence on the next generation of public officials. She impressed her students with her intellect and ability to inspire them to achieve excellence in the classroom, and to be committed to public service.

Mr. Speaker, Barbara Jordan was buried on January 20, 1996. She was buried at the Texas National Cemetery. She was the first African-American in the history of the national State cemetery to be buried there, in her death a first, but making a statement that she was laid to rest among Texas heroes. They benefited because an American hero was laid to rest with them . . .

Congresswoman Barbara Jordan leaves the American people, particularly Members of Congress, a powerful legacy of commitment to freedom, integrity, government, and belief in human progress . . .

. . . Nothing was too hard for her to accept as a challenge, and nothing was too hard for her to overcome; a great American. We lost her, but not her words and her message.

Source: Congressional Record, 104th Cong., 2d sess., January 24, 1996, H822–H824.

Document 10.9 in Context
"The Contrast to the Watergate Experience Could Not Be More Striking": Defending a President Under Fire

When Congress became embroiled in the fight over the impeachment of Democratic President Bill Clinton in 1998, all but one of the African American members of the House opposed removing Clinton from office. The only African American member of the House to vote for impeachment was the sole black Republican, J. C. Watts Jr. of Oklahoma. The forty members of the Congressional Black Caucus—all Democrats—opposed impeachment.

The support Clinton received from Caucus members was not based just on partisan politics. Black Democrats in the House had fought with Clinton over budgetary priorities and his decision to withdraw the nomination of Lani Guinier for a key civil rights post in the Justice Department. But they also perceived Clinton as a social progressive who was committed to the values of civil rights and economic justice that were their priorities at a time when the general political atmosphere of the country appeared to be moving to the right.

Consequently, black Democrats in the House were among Clinton's most intense and vocal supporters in the impeachment fight. Five members of the Black Caucus served on the House Judiciary Committee, which considered—and ultimately recommended—the articles of impeachment that later were adopted by the House and sent Clinton to trial in the Senate. The committee votes on the impeachment articles divided along party lines, and several of the black members added their own personal dissents to underscore the minority report issued by the committee's Democrats (**Document 7.5**).

One of those committee members was Sheila Jackson-Lee, D-Texas, then in her sixth term in the House. She also took an active part in debate on the issue. The document that follows is an excerpt from her discussion of the impeachment question during floor debate on October 6, 1998.

▬▬ Document 10.9 ▬▬
Rep. Sheila Jackson-Lee, D-Texas, Argues against Impeaching President Bill Clinton, October 6, 1998

Ms. JACKSON-LEE of Texas: Mr. Speaker, rising behind my very able colleague, I would be remiss in not joining him in saying that this is an issue of great concern. It is a bipartisan issue. It warrants the attention of the Nation and of this Congress, and it warrants a collaborative effort between the executive and the legislative branch.

It is for that very reason that I thought it was almost imperative that, 1 day after the proceedings in the House Committee on the Judiciary, I come to the floor to discuss these issues that now seem to take the majority of the time, of the thought and analysis and the conscience of America. Today, Mr. Speaker, I rise as an American, and I speak on the issue of constitutional impeachment.

I am an American who happens to be a member of the House Committee on the Judiciary and, as well, a Democrat. But as I speak about constitutional impeachment, I hope that those who may engage in this debate or listen to this debate will not be thwarted by the fact that I serve on this Nation's House Committee on the Judiciary, may not be thwarted by the fact that I am a Democrat, may not label my remarks because I am an African American or because I am a woman.

Frankly I welcome agreement and disagreement. But I would hope in this hour we would be able to get away from what has been the characterization of this debate over the last couple of weeks, partisan, full of labels and misinformation . . .

So first of all, Mr. Speaker, I would like to be able to elaborate on how we got here. First of all, we understand we have got a Constitution. In the wisdom of the Founding Fathers, they established a provision dealing with the removal of the President and Vice President of the United States and other civil officers. In Article 2, Section 4, it reads very simply, 'The President, Vice President and all civil officers of the United States shall be removed from office on impeachment for, and conviction of, treason, bribery or other high crimes and misdemeanors.' Let me emphasize 'high crimes and misdemeanors.' Different from the time that we are in today, our Founding Fathers knew that the word 'high' meant very serious, very high, very important, very troubling, very difficult. They did not want us to entertain frivolous concerns, because they were particularly concerned about us understanding the value of preserving this sovereign Nation. And so as the debate has been played out in the eye of the American public, there are those who would claim impeachable offenses for the President's allegations, or alleged lying to the American people. I say alleged, for some would listen and say, 'That's already a given,' because the House Judiciary Committee's work has not been done; but yes, it is well recognized that the President's behavior was reprehensible. The President has admitted an untruth and admitted improper relations.

Mr. Speaker, even with that, the challenge for those of us who are given this high calling is frankly to abide by the Constitution and not to presume. Now, I can say tonight that from the minimal work and the minimal documentation, I am very uncomfortable with even believing that there is any premise for reaching the level of this unconstitutional allegations or unconstitutional effort, if you will, to proceed against the President for offenses that may not rise to the level of constitutional offenses.

Let me clarify what I said, for I would never want to suggest that we have reached an unconstitutional level at this point. But if we follow through in the mode in which we are now proceeding, I would think the Founding Fathers would say that we are acting unconstitutionally, because we are rushing to judgment on offenses that on their face clearly do not appear to be constitutionally based as offenses that would warrant a constitutional impeachment.

Martin Luther King, whom I call a legal scholar, trained legally, if you will, in fighting injustices, not one that had a law degree, but certainly received his scholarship from being on the front line in fighting against injustice, said in his letter from a Birmingham jail, which many of us are familiar with, 'Injustice anywhere is a threat to justice everywhere. Whatever affects one directly affects all indirectly.'

So it is important for me to share with the American public how we got to where we are today. Frankly, we are operating or operated under H. Res. 525. This was a resolution that came to the floor of the House September 11, 1998. It came after my appearance and several others who appeared in the Rules Committee on September 10, 1998 and argued vigorously that if we were to proceed, suggesting that we should move under Article 2, Section 4, we should move with a very fine standard in the backdrop, and that was that of the Watergate proceedings; chaired by Chairman Rodino, then the Democrats in the minority, then a Republican President, and, of course, Republicans in the minority on that committee. But even with that backdrop, Chairman Rodino, and history paints him well, provided a very fair and evenhanded process. Debating, yes. A difference of opinion, yes. Political in some sense, yes. But remember, now, in contrast to where we are today, on October 6, 1998, there had been a Senate Watergate proceedings under Sam Ervin, there had been at least 3 months of review of the materials that had been laid out before the public eye through those proceedings, even before the House Judiciary Committee considered this thing called inquiry. And so I argued September 10 not as a Democrat, not as a member of the House Judiciary Committee already predisposed, not as a defender of President William Jefferson Clinton. More importantly, I think, I hope that I was defending at that time or at least proceeding to comment both constitutionally and as an American. I argued that fairness dictated that we follow a very good track record, and that was a track record of the Watergate proceedings which moved into executive session and reviewed the documentation that might have been presented then by the special prosecutor and allowed the President's counsel to review, and argued vigorously that we were making a very serious mistake by opening the door to dissemination of materials of which no one had reviewed.

Frankly, the arguments were not wholly listened to, and a resolution came out of the Rules Committee that moved to the House on September 11, 1998 . . .

So when we voted on September 11, and I voted enthusiastically against the release of these documents, including the 445 pages, we in essence gave authority to the House Judiciary Committee not to do as I believe we should have been doing, which is to deliberate, to study and to review and to move carefully into a process that may result in a very considered vote on an impeachment inquiry. But what we did is to throw into a House Judiciary Committee that seemed hell-bent, if you will, on releasing documents with minimal review. Yes, the staff has indicated that they have reviewed every single piece of paper. Review may be taken in a more general term. They have touched it, they have looked at it. Frankly, I would take great issue in that, Mr. Speaker, because I believe if people of good will had been able to review extensively all of the documents that were released, they would not have released such salacious, pornographic materials not for the Nation to see but for the world to see . . .

The contrast to the Watergate experience could not be more striking. In that earlier case it will be recalled the Watergate special prosecution force did not send to Congress an argumentative or inflammatory document, but rather a simple road map which merely summarized and identified the location of relevant evidence. Moreover, this document was submitted for review by Judge Sirica, the supervising judge of the grand jury before it was sent to the House of Representatives. Counsel for President Nixon was given notice and an opportunity to be heard before the report was sent to Congress.

This is not an attempt for cover-up. This is an attempt to appreciate the basic fairness upon which we operate and the constitutional premise of due process . . .

My friends, this is extremely, extremely important because the OIC, the Office of Independent Counsel, is not the judiciary, it is not the legislative branch. In fact, it is not the executive. It is almost a fourth arm of government and bears extensive review itself. It is a frightening element of which this Congress should surely review for its fairness and its properness . . .

This strikes at the very premise of constitutionality and the basis upon which I frankly think that we should proceed . . .

Source: Congressional Record, 105th Cong., 2d sess., October 6, 1998, H9669–H96670.

Document 10.10 in Context
"It Is a Sham Debate": Criticizing President George W. Bush's Iraq War Policy

The dominant political issue of 2006 was the continuing war in Iraq. News reports highlighted ongoing American military casualties and escalating sectarian violence between Iraqis that manifested in suicide bombings, kidnappings and a vicious cycle of murders and revenge killings. In the United States, the public debate intensified as the mid-term elections approached. Opinion polls showed rising public dissatisfaction with the progress of the war and President George W. Bush's methods of prosecuting it.

Democrats, sensing an important shift in voters' sentiments and seeing an opportunity to gain seats in Congress, intensified their criticism of the president's war policies. Congressional debates became heated as Republicans sought to marshal public support by labeling their opponents "Defeatocrats" and accusing them of promoting a policy of "cut and run."

African American women readily engaged in the debate. Rep. Maxine Waters, D-Calif., was in her eighth term in the House when she rose on the floor to assail a GOP resolution declaring that the United States would prevail in the war on terror. Waters, who had served as chair of the Congressional Black Caucus in 1997–1998 during the battle over the impeachment of President Bill Clinton, had a reputation as an aggressive and fiery speaker.

Democrats were angered by the resolution, which they considered GOP grandstanding and an attempt to portray Democrats as unpatriotic. Many Democrats feared that voting against the resolution would open them to accusations that they were not supporting the troops in the field or were not tough enough on terrorism. Conversely, a vote for the resolution would be seen as endorsing the policies of the president and the Republicans.

In the end, the resolution passed the House, largely along party lines. But the difficulty that the resolution presented to Democrats was apparent in the final vote. Among Republicans,

214 voted for the resolution while only 3 voted against; 42 Democrats voted in favor of the resolution, while 149 voted against it. Waters voted against the resolution and explained her reasons emphatically during the debate.

<hr>

▬▬ Document 10.10 ▬▬
Rep. Maxine Waters, D-Calif., Attacks Republicans on Iraq War Policies in House Debate, June 14, 2006

Ms. WATERS: Mr. Speaker, I come this evening to share information that I think the American public must know and understand about what is going on in the Congress of the United States of America and what is going on with this war in Iraq. It is important that I do that this evening because tomorrow there will be on the floor of Congress a so-called debate. But it is a sham debate. This is a debate formed around a resolution, H. Res. 861, that the Republicans have put together in an attempt, one more time, to fool the American people about what they are doing. This resolution was dreamed up after the Republicans determined that the polls were consistently against the way this war is being managed. This resolution was put together after they went home on break and they heard over and over again that the American public is getting fed up with this war, the amount of money that is being spent, the number of lives that are being lost, and so they come to the floor, after having done no oversight, never explaining to the American public how billions of dollars are being spent, never taking the time to find out about the corruption and the mismanagement in Iraq, never investigating the lies and the lack of intelligence and all that has been happening. They have the audacity to come before the public in a so-called debate with the resolution simply designed to trap the Democrats.

It is a resolution that says all kinds of things. Do you love the soldier or don't you? If you don't support our resolution, you are not for the soldiers in Iraq. And so many Democrats are going to get trapped because they claim that in their districts they have half of their constituents for it, this war, and half against it, and they don't know what to do. And so when they have to confront a phony debate and a phony resolution, they may just say yes because they don't want to be criticized for not being patriotic and loving the soldiers and supporting them.

Well, I am here to say tonight it is a sham. And I would hope, overnight, that my colleagues on this side of the aisle would see the light and have the courage to vote against it, to not participate in the sham. But I don't know if they will or not.

But let me just give you the background and the backdrop of why all of this is happening. This war started March 19, 2003. Total number of U.S. troops in Iraq today, about 133,000. Number of soldiers dead, 2,499, as of June 14. Number of soldiers injured, 18,490, as of June 14. Total amount appropriated, including latest supplemental, $320 billion. The cost of the war per month, $6.1 billion, almost $11 million an hour. There were 1,398 reported killings in May alone, more than any other month since the war began in 2006, and that figure doesn't include slain soldiers or civilians killed in bombings. Yet, the President of the United States would make you believe we are winning the war. We are advancing. We are going to be able to turn this mess over to the Iraqis and they are going to be able to contain what is now a civil war.

According to the Pentagon, there are about 600 insurgent attacks each week since the new government took over in February. The rate of insurgent attacks is higher now than it was in 2004. Our soldiers are being killed. It is difficult for them to protect themselves against these bombings, these suicide bombings, these bombings that are set off in cars along the road and dead dogs and on and on and on.

And why are they dying? We are in this war because the President of the United States said that there were weapons of mass destruction that we had to protect against. All that we have encountered is mismanagement, corruption, missteps, a lack of winning this crazy thing. Soldiers dying and some of our young people now being charged with killing innocent people because they put guns in their hands and they told them to go and kill them because they hated it.

These soldiers should not be charged. The President of the United States should be charged. The Republicans should be charged and the Democrats should get some courage and come to this Chamber and make sure that they oppose this war . . .

Source: Congressional Record, 109th Congress, 2d sess., June 14, 2006, H3978–H3979.

Document 10.11 in Context
"I Join My CBC Colleagues This Evening and Ask That America Rise Up": The Crisis in Darfur

In the area of foreign policy, Africa has been a high priority for many African American members of Congress. Rep. Charles C. Diggs, D-Mich., who was the first chair of the Congressional Black Caucus, was particularly concerned with Africa and U.S. relations with African nations. That interest has been shared by most black members who followed him, women as well as men.

Rep. Carolyn Cheeks Kilpatrick, D-Mich., for example, became involved in U.S.–African policy issues during her first term in Congress in 1997–1998. She pushed for bills to promote trade with Africa and helped host a conference on U.S.–African trade in 1998. She also became a member of the House Appropriations Committee's Subcommittee on Foreign Operations, which oversees spending on U.S. foreign assistance programs throughout the world. As a member of the subcommittee and of the Congressional Black Caucus, Kilpatrick made a number of trips to Africa to examine such issues as economic development, education and health programs, hunger and disaster relief, and efforts to combat the AIDS epidemic.

Of special concern to Kilpatrick—and many others both in and out of Congress—was the brutal violence that erupted in the Darfur region of Sudan in 2003 and was still raging four years later. Tens of thousands of people were killed and several million people were displaced by the interethnic fighting that the U.S. government labeled genocide. But while the killing shocked the international community, effective action to stop it proved difficult to come by.

Kilpatrick and several other representatives spoke out on the House floor in July 2004, criticizing the U.S. government and the international community for failing to protect the lives of innocent victims in Darfur and calling on the United Nations to send an international force immediately. Two years later, with the killing in Darfur unabated, Kilpatrick again addressed the House, demanding action to end the bloodshed. Her remarks are excerpted here.

Document 10.11
Rep. Carolyn Cheeks Kilpatrick, D-Mich., Pleads for Action on Darfur Crisis, September 20, 2006

Ms. KILPATRICK of Michigan: Mr. Speaker, the world is in total crisis. The conflict and the devastation in the Darfur region of Sudan is abominable. I call on the President of the United States, who named Andrew Natsios at the U.N. to be the Special Envoy, that we put the full might and credibility of what we have left in our country behind the genocide that is taking place in Darfur.

You have heard the numbers. Atrocities, government-sponsored terrorism, where the President of Sudan does not even acknowledge not only the U.N. forces, not only the African coalition that is there to help secure his people, but that genocide and the killings really exist.

I was on one of the delegations that went to Sudan earlier this year in a bipartisan, bicameral visit. It was outrageous what we saw. Yet, today, as the heightened conflict, killings, this government in Khartoum is now dropping bombs on the civilian population in the refugee camps. Just think about it. They have run them out of their villages. They have burned their villages. They have raped the women. They killed the men and had the children in total chaos and asking for help.

We are the most powerful Nation in the world today. We say that all the time. We must rise up to save the young children, the women, and the men for the sake of their own country.

President al-Bashir has turned his head on it. The Janjaweed, men on horses who ride herd on those villages, kill people, innocent civilians, it could be you, but you are living in another country.

I am asking tonight that we recognize the genocide, the horrific conditions that are going on in Darfur, which is in the southwest region of Sudan. Sudan is the largest country geographically in Africa. It has black Africans, African Arabs and others in the country.

Khartoum in the northern part of the country is where the seat of government is. They just recently signed a southwest agreement in Darfur that they might be better, and better take care of their people, which they are not doing.

The security is deteriorating. There is a credible threat of famine that exists. More and more people are going hungry and starving, and the world relief food efforts are not able to get to the people who have been run off of their land.

The cease-fire is in shambles . . .

Rise up. We need the Nations that surround the Sudan to speak up.

Egypt President Mubarak, I have been a strong supporter of Egypt, and I still will be, but you must speak up. You must do more. You and I have talked about this. You must do more.

Jordan, King Abdullah, you have got to get involved. You have got to get involved. People are dying as we speak.

The region must rise up. How can you let this happen one more time in any part of the world? These are people who cultivate and live and grow food before this atrocity which now has outlasted any other, including Rwanda, in terms of its devastation and loss of life.

The Chad-Sudan border that I visited on another occasion is overwhelmed by the people who are fleeing Sudan. Do we want to keep the chaos going? Do we not really have to sign up as God's people, one Nation under God and treat all of His people the same?

We have the authority, we have the power, and we have the partnerships to bring this to a conclusion. So I join my CBC colleagues this evening and ask that America rise up, that the Middle East region speak out to help people who cannot help themselves.

I want to thank Congressman DONALD PAYNE who is the author of a resolution that we sponsored and passed, H.R. 3127. We passed it in April. We sent it to the Senate, where they sat on it. Now, I understand a Senator does not want to pass it because it was too strong. How can a resolution be strong, too strong when it is about the very subsistence of life for a people?

So I call on all good men and women of the world, Darfur needs us to step up, the people, the children, the women, the men, the villages. We can do better.

I ask that we stand and fight and speak and work, that the people in Darfur can have life and have it more abundantly . . .

Source: Congressional Record, 109th Cong., 2d sess., September 20, 2006, H6815–H6816.

Document 10.12 in Context
"The District's Long Struggle for Democracy": Fighting for Voting Rights in the Nation's Capital

For the two African Americans who have represented Washington, D.C., in Congress since the District was awarded a nonvoting delegate to the House of Representatives in 1971, one issue has been a constant: the status of voting rights and representation for District residents.

The U.S. Constitution (**Document 1.4**) gave Congress authority over a federal district that was to be established as the nation's capital. Since that time, the political status of the District of Columbia's residents has been a source of frequent discussion and debate. While race has always been central to the District's political and social activities, sensitivities of African Americans were heightened in the decades after passage of the Voting Rights Act of 1965 (**Document 6.1**). Increased attention to protecting the voting rights of African Americans and the growth of an African American majority in the city came in conflict with the District's lack of autonomy and full voting representation in Congress.

The District's status has been altered several times since ratification of the Constitution. In 1820, after some years of congressional experimentation with governance, Congress approved a system of home rule in which the voters directly elected their mayor and the District was given expanded legislative authority. That system lasted until 1871, when Congress put the capital's government into a territorial format. By 1878, however, Congress had abolished the territorial system and established a three-member board of commissioners appointed by Congress to run the city, effectively eliminating local control and depriving residents of a voice in both local and national government.

In the late 1960s the D.C. government was reformed again in a modest step toward home rule: the District was granted a nonvoting delegate to the U.S. House of Representatives. Many members of Congress opposed granting any political power to the District, which by the early 1970s had a black-majority population, because it was assumed the strong Democratic allegiance of a majority of the city's voters would shift the relative strength of the parties in Congress. However, legislation to authorize home rule was passed by Congress in 1973. The authorization reserved for Congress the right to veto any legislation approved by the elected D.C. City Council as well as control over the District's budget.

Congress drew back from expanding home rule for the District in the 1990s after Republicans took control of Congress and after local voters reelected Mayor Marion Barry despite the release of a videotape that showed him using illegal drugs. In 1995 Congress established a control board to manage the District's troubled financial affairs, a move that limited home rule and was resented by many D.C. residents.

Eleanor Holmes Norton, the District's delegate since 1991, continued to push for greater autonomy, proposing legislation to grant statehood and full voting rights in Congress. In March 2007 Norton and Rep. Tom M. Davis, R-Va., introduced a new, bipartisan proposal that linked a voting House seat for the overwhelmingly Democratic District with adding a House seat for heavily Republican Utah. In introducing the bill, Norton explained the link between her push for the legislation and her family's longstanding connection with the District.

The legislation passed easily in the House in April but failed on a procedural vote in the Senate in September.

══ Document 10.12 ══
Del. Eleanor Holmes Norton, D-D.C., Introduces the D.C. House Voting Rights Bill of 2007, March 12, 2007

Ms. NORTON: Madam Speaker, the bipartisan bill we introduce today is a culmination of four years of during which Democrats and Republicans have worked together to accomplish a common goal for Utah and the District of Columbia. This effort has been worth every minute, as we are poised to clear the high hurdle to equal citizenship in the People's House—the House of Representatives. Representative TOM DAVIS (R-VA) and I have worked together on many tough bills and have gotten a fair number passed. Still, the bill we introduce today has surely been the toughest, has required the most work for us both, and has taken the most time. I am most grateful to Representative DAVIS who found the balance that makes this bill possible, modeled most recently on Alaska and Hawaii, both admitted to the Union in 1959 after Congress assured itself that their entry would benefit both parties. TOM DAVIS did not stop with his good idea but has worked relentlessly to reach this milestone. Speaker NANCY PELOSI has long fought for the rights of D.C. residents. It was she who personally insisted that this legislation go forward without delay as a bill of historic importance. Majority Leader STENY HOYER, my regional friend for years, has been an especially outspoken champion of this bill. Throughout this process Chairman HENRY WAXMAN (D-CA) has been a central figure, making every possible effort to ensure we would reach this day. From the very beginning, Chairman JOHN CONYERS (D-MI) as a founding member of the Congressional Black Caucus and a member of the Judiciary Committee has fought for our full rights throughout his years in Congress, pressing all along until as chair he will now preside over the committee that will send this bill to the floor. Governor Jon Huntsman Jr. and the entire Utah delegation have been steadfast and determined throughout.

TOM and I have understood that the essential metric required bringing both parties with us, not only bipartisanship in the usual sense but equivalence, that is no partisan gain and no partisan disadvantage. We have gone through many variations, beginning with TOM's original proposal, where the D.C. House seat would have included some Maryland residents. TOM then accepted our notion that a D.C. stand-alone seat would be best and less controversial all around, and the talks and proposals proceeded. We since have tried several scenarios for moving the bill. I continued to keep my bill, the No Taxation Without

Representation Act for the full representation that will never abandon until a bill agreeable to all could be fashioned.

The District of Columbia has waited 200 years to gain the equal citizenship rights they deserve and seek. The framers were clear that American citizens are entitled to equal representation in the House. Our status as second in the United States in federal income taxes that support our government argues indisputably for equivalent rights. However, in this time of war with residents serving in Iraq and Afghanistan, our bill for congressional voting rights for D.C. residents must and I believe will not be denied.

Finally, I hope I can be forgiven a personal moment. Throughout this process, I have never referred to the District's vote as my vote or what the vote would mean to me personally because it will not belong to me. I have never mentioned the special reason I personally wanted to be the first to cast that vote because this bill is for D.C. residents now and in the future, not for me. However, my 16 years in Congress has been defined by the search for some way to get full representation for the city where my family has lived since before the Civil War . . . I cannot deny the personal side of this quest, epitomized by my family of native Washingtonians, my father Coleman Holmes, my grandfather, Richard Holmes, who entered the D.C. Fire Department in 1902 and whose picture hangs in my office, a gift from the D.C. Fire Department, but especially my great-grandfather, Richard Holmes, a slave who walked off a Virginia plantation in the 1850s, made it to Washington, and settled our family here. By definition, subliminal motivation is unknown and unfelt. However, when TOM and I knew that we had reached the best agreement we could, I thought openly of my family. I thought especially of the man I never knew. I thought of Richard Holmes, a slave in the District until Lincoln freed the slaves here nine months before the Emancipation Proclamation. I thought of my great grandfather who came here in a furtive search for freedom itself, not the vote on the House floor. I thought of what a man who lived as a slave in the District, and others like him would think if his great-grand-daughter becomes the first to cast the first full vote for the District of Columbia on the House floor. I hope to have the special honor of casting the vote I have sought for 16 years. I want to cast that vote for the residents of this city whom I have had the great privilege of representing and who have fought and have waited for so long. Yes, and I want to cast that vote in memory of my great-grandfather, Richard Holmes.

Source: Congressional Record, 110th Cong., 1st sess., March 12, 2007, E517.

NOTES

1 Dewey M. Clayton and Angela M. Stallings, "Black Women in Congress: Striking the Balance," *Journal of Black Studies* 30, no. 4 (March 2000): 576.
2 Ibid., 578–579.
3 Lisa Jones Townsel, "A Woman's Place Is in the House and Senate: Part II," *Ebony,* March 1997, 36–40.
4 Kay Mills, "Maxine Waters: 'I don't pretend to be nice no matter what . . .' " *The Progressive,* December 1993.
5 Townsel, "A Woman's Place," 36–40.
6 LaVerne McCain Gill, *African American Women in Congress* (New Brunswick, N.J.: Rutgers University Press, 1997), 147.
7 *Congressional Record,* 103d Cong., 1st sess., March 3, 1993, S4031.

CHAPTER ELEVEN

African American Lawmakers Fight Racism
Representatives of an Excluded People

Race has defined the African American experience and has constantly shaped the activities of the black legislators who have served in Congress since Hiram R. Revels, Jefferson F. Long and Joseph H. Rainey took their oaths of office in 1870. Race is what excluded blacks from Congress before Reconstruction, was the basis on which black representation was diminished by discriminatory election practices after Reconstruction, and has deeply influenced the shifting seas of partisan politics that black officials have had to navigate while seeking to attain and wield power. America's racial divisions have not only defined aspects of the African American congressional agenda, but also the common experience of black legislators—in the halls of the Capitol as well as in the communities from which they were elected.

From the beginning of their service, African Americans in Congress spoke out as the representatives of an excluded people to demand political, economic and social justice. They took part in debate over the Fourteenth Amendment (**Document 3.2**) that was intended to guarantee political and civil rights for the newly freed slaves. Senator Revels argued against the segregation of schools in Washington, D.C. (**Document 3.5**). Rep. Robert C. De Large, R-S.C., helped push through legislation aimed at reining in the violent abuses of the Ku Klux

A banner erected by the National Association for the Advancement of Colored People reminds New Yorkers in the 1920s of the ongoing lynching of African Americans. There were no African American legislators in office between 1901 and 1929, so the NAACP prevailed upon sympathetic white representatives, who introduced unsuccessful anti-lynching legislation in 1918. Such legislation was repeatedly introduced in Congress for thirty years afterward, to no avail.
Source: The Granger Collection, New York

Klan (**Document 3.6**). When Rep. George W. Murray, R-S.C., argued in 1893 for changing U.S. monetary policy to help the common citizen (**Document 14.2**), he spoke openly of his position as the only black representative in Congress.

Black members of Congress also saw their mission in much broader terms, and they resisted the notion that they were in Congress to represent the interests of African Americans alone. In 1880, for example, Sen. Blanche K. Bruce, R-Miss., argued for reform of the nation's policy toward American Indians (**Document 11.1**) to treat them with greater respect and fairness. In 1884 Rep. James E. O'Hara, R-N.C., fought for a measure to end discriminatory practices on interstate railroads (**Document 11.2**), arguing that it would prevent discrimination against both blacks and lower-class whites. And Rep. Thomas E. Miller, R-S.C., pressed for legislation in 1891 to protect voting rights (**Document 11.3**) with a similar argument, saying during House debate that the legislation was important for all citizens:

> Mr. Chairman, it is not alone for the negro that this law is needed; it is necessary to protect the white citizens of the South. It is not the fear of negro supremacy in the South that causes the Southern election officers to suppress the negro vote, but it is the fear of the rule of the majority regardless of race. The master class does not want to surrender to the rule of the people, and they use the frightful bugbear of negro rule to scare the white man and drive him under the yoke that has been bearing heavily upon him for more than a century.[1]

Voting rights, however, remained a sore point for African American legislators for well over a century because they were a crucial tool in the fight against racial discrimination. Despite ratification of the Fourteenth Amendment in 1868 and, two years later, the Fifteenth Amendment (**Document 3.3**), southern states found ways to evade the constitutional requirements and prevent blacks from voting. Even passage of the Voting Rights Act of 1965 (**Document 6.1**)—as successful as it was in opening the political process to African Americans—did not eliminate concerns on the issue, which continue today. For example, the intense debate that arose over the presidential election of 2000 and the efforts of the Congressional Black Caucus to challenge the electoral votes from Florida (**Document 7.6**) were inspired by voting irregularities that echoed, in the opinion of Caucus members, more than a century of southern racial bias at the polls.

One of the more persistent racial problems confronted by African American legislators was the issue of lynchings. As Reconstruction ended, and whites in the South sought to undo the political gains blacks had made since the end of the Civil War, violence became a powerful and increasingly common tool of racial intimidation. Between 1890 and 1923, lynching killed an average of at least one black person a week in America. The Ku Klux Klan Act that De Large had supported in 1871 sought to address the issue, but in 1900, with lynchings only slightly abated, Rep. George H. White, R-N.C., introduced legislation aimed at making lynching a federal crime (**Document 4.9**). Congress failed to pass the bill, and southern white legislators defeated subsequent efforts to pass anti-lynching legislation up into the 1950s. Sometimes, the proposals died in committee; on other occasions, when bills passed the House, southerners used the filibuster to block action in the Senate (**Document 11.4**).

Southern opponents of the legislation pointed to statistical data showing that the annual number of lynchings was on the decline and charged that passing such legislation would put white women in greater danger being assaulted by black men. In 1931 J. E. Andrews, president of the Women's National Association for the Preservation of the White Race, raised the concern in a letter to President Herbert Hoover attacking the efforts of the Southern Commission on the Study of Lynchings, with whom Hoover had met. Andrews enclosed a copy of a letter she had written to the commission's chairman, claiming that

> the white woman and her natural male protectors of her own race daily become more and more cowerd and helpless. God forbid that we should ever raise our voice against a helpless, innocent creature—man or woman, black or white. But God forbid that we shall become such craven cowards as to enter into an alliance with another race to ruthlessly sacrifice the innocent, helpless girls of our own race.[2]

Elected to the Senate from Illinois in 1993, Carol Moseley-Braun was the first, and so far the only, African American woman to serve in that chamber of Congress. During a spate of 1996 arson attacks primarily targeting African American churches, she called for a resolution to condemn the burnings and launch a federal investigation. Here she speaks during the 2004 Democratic National Convention. Source: CQ Photo/Scott J. Ferrell

Lynchings may have been in decline, but killings for the purpose of racial intimidation continued to be common for another three decades. One such incident, the murder of fourteen-year-old Emmett Till in Mississippi (**Document 11.7**) played a pivotal role in sparking the civil rights movement.

While black members of Congress could confront the issues of racism, segregation and discrimination via the legislative process, they continued to encounter racism on a personal level. Opposition to Revels taking his seat in the Senate in 1870, for example, included openly racist comments from some Senate colleagues (**Document 3.4**). In 1929, when Oscar S. De Priest, R-Ill., became the first African American to serve in Congress in nearly three decades, he found himself at the center of a storm of racial controversy after his wife was invited to tea at the White House—as were the wives of all members of Congress—by First Lady Lou Henry Hoover (**Document 11.5**). In 1934 De Priest became the focus of another racial controversy when he challenged the exclusionary policies of the Capitol restaurant (**Document 5.3**).

De Priest's successor, Rep. Arthur W. Mitchell, D-Ill., experienced a particularly humiliating encounter with racism in April 1937. During a break in the congressional schedule, Mitchell was traveling by train to Hot Springs, Arkansas. He had paid for a first-class ticket, but when a conductor came through the Pullman car, he was shocked to see Mitchell among the white passengers and told the congressman he would have to move to the Jim Crow car that Arkansas law mandated for all black passengers, or he would face arrest. When Mitchell identified himself as a congressman, the conductor replied, "It don't make a damn bit of difference who you are as long as you are a nigger you can't ride in this car!" [3]

The passage of decades brought changes to both society and Congress, modifying but not erasing issues of race and racism. The Civil Rights Act of 1964 (**Document 5.11**) and the Voting Rights Act of 1965 eliminated most types of overt discrimination, such as those that had put De Priest in conflict with the Capitol restaurant and forced Mitchell into a segregated railroad car. But new issues emerged. In the wake of the civil rights movement, new challenges were mounted to capital punishment, such as one in 1995 (**Document 11.9**), on grounds that it was disproportionately applied to blacks. A wave of arson attacks on black churches in the 1990s attracted congressional attention (**Document 11.10**), as did concerns that the practice of "racial profiling" was subjecting blacks and other minorities to excessive and inappropriate police scrutiny (**Document 11.11**).

Further, African American legislators continued to encounter insensitivity and racism within the halls of Congress and in the federal government. During World War II, Rep.

William L. Dawson, D-Ill., responded angrily (**Document 11.6**) after a colleague read aloud on the House floor a letter from the secretary of war impugning the quality of African American soldiers. And in February 1970, Rep. Charles C. Diggs Jr., D-Mich., had an angry confrontation in the House dining room with Georgia governor Lester Maddox, who was passing out pick handles—a trademark symbol of his segregationist beliefs. Some years before, when he was ordered to desegregate his Atlanta restaurant, Maddox had threatened to use pick handles to repel black customers. When Diggs confronted him in the House dining room, Maddox called Diggs an "ass" and a "baboon." [4] Black representatives also challenged the display of a prominent segregationist's portrait in a committee hearing room in 1995 (**Document 11.8**), and led the call for Sen. Trent Lott, R-Miss., to resign as Senate majority leader in 2002 after he publicly praised the 1948 segregationist presidential candidacy of Strom Thurmond, then the Democratic governor of South Carolina (**Document 11.12**). Lott stepped down, but he returned to the GOP's Senate leadership team as minority whip in 2007.

The documents in this chapter illustrate some—though far from all—of the race-related issues that black members of Congress have dealt with since 1870. Certainly, not all of the subjects to come before African American representatives have dealt directly with race. As these documents suggest, however, race and racism have seldom been far below the surface.

Document 11.1 in Context
"The Vigor, Energy, Bravery, and Integrity of This Remnant Entitle Them to Consideration": Sen. Blanche K. Bruce, R-Miss., on American Indian Policy

By 1880 the United States was busily expanding its control over the territories and resources of the West. The end of the Civil War had allowed the nation, with the help of a rapidly expanding transcontinental railroad network, to accelerate western settlement, resource exploitation and land speculation. Within a decade, six new states would be admitted to the Union, stretching from the northern Great Plains, across the northern Rocky Mountains to the Pacific Coast.

The greatest barrier to this development, however, was the continued presence, hostility and resistance of indigenous peoples. American Indians found themselves in a bitter struggle to retain access to their ancestral lands and continue the way of life that had sustained them for untold generations. White prospectors, cattlemen, farmers and speculators paid little heed to treaties that had supposedly guaranteed the land entitlements of Indian peoples, and their incursions onto Indian land frequently led to violent confrontations.

Federal authorities sought to intervene, through negotiation where possible but more often through military action. American Indians were driven off whatever lands were desired by whites and forced onto ever smaller reservations. Reformers, among them Sen. Blanche K. Bruce, R-Miss., tried to get the government to adopt a more generous and respectful approach to Indian affairs, with limited success.

During Senate debate over Indian policy, Bruce argued for an approach that would encourage assimilation of Indians into American society. He criticized the nation's treatment of the Indians, arguing that the government treated them as a group in a society based on the concept of individual rights. He supported the legislation under consideration because it promoted land ownership by individual Indians, rather than by tribal units, and would give them a stake in American society as citizens.

At the time he spoke, Bruce was nearing the end of his single term in the Senate, and he was the sole African American member of Congress. Interestingly, while his role as a representative of people who had faced oppression and discrimination may have made him more sensitive to the Indians' right to fair treatment, he was not immune to the common characterization of Indians as "noble savages." Later critics have seen the policy he supported—land ownership by individual Indians—as contradictory to Indian cultural traditions and a source of great damage to Indian societies.

▬▬ Document 11.1 ▬▬
Sen. Blanche K. Bruce, R-Miss., Discusses American Indian Policy on the Senate Floor, April 6, 1880

Mr. BRUCE: . . . Our Indian policy and administration seem to me to have been inspired and controlled by a stern selfishness, with a few honorable exceptions. Indian treaties have generally been made as the condition and instrument of acquiring the valuable territory occupied by the several Indian nations, and have been changed and revised from time to time as it became desirable that the steadily growing, irrepressible white races should secure more room for their growth and more lands for their occupancy; and wars, bounties, and beads have been used as auxiliaries for the purpose of temporary peace and security for the whites, and as the preliminary to further aggressions upon the red man's lands, with the ultimate view of his expulsion and extinction from the continent . . .

The political or governmental idea, underlying the Indian policy, is to maintain the paramount authority of the United States over the Indian Territory and over the Indian tribes, yet recognizing tribal independence and autonomy and a local government, un-American in structure and having no reference to the Constitution or laws of the United States, so far as the tribal government affects the persons, lives, and rights of the members of the tribe alone. Currently with the maintenance of a policy thus based, under treaty obligations, the Government of the United States contributes to the support, equipments, and comforts of these Indians, not only by making appropriations for food and raiment but by sustaining blacksmiths, mechanics, farmers, millers, and schools in the midst of the Indian reservations. This Government also, in its treaties and its enforcement thereof, encourages and facilitates the missionary enterprises of the different churches which look to the Christianization and education of the Indians distributed throughout the public domain. The effort, under these circumstances, to preserve peace among the Indian tribes in their relations to each other and in their relations to the citizens of the United States becomes a very onerous and difficult endeavor, and has not heretofore produced results that have either satisfied the expectations and public sentiment of the country, vindicated the wisdom of the policy practiced toward this people, or honored the Christian institutions and civilizations of our great country.

We have in the effort to realize a somewhat intangible ideal, to wit, the preservation of Indian liberty and the administration and exercise of national authority, complicated an essentially difficult problem by surrounding it with needless and equivocal adjuncts; we have rendered a questionable policy more difficult of successful execution by basing it upon a political theory which is un-American in character, and which, in its very structure, breeds and perpetuates the difficulties sought to be avoided and overcome . . .

. . . There must be a change in the Indian policy if beneficent, practical results are expected, and any change that gives promise of solving this red-race problem must be a change based upon an idea in harmony, and not at war with our free institutions. If the Indian is expected and required to respond to Federal authority; if this people are expected to grow up into organized and well-ordered society; if they are to be civilized, in that the best elements of their natures are to be developed to the exercise of their best functions, so as to produce individual character and social groups characteristic of enlightened people; if this is to be done under our system, its ultimate realization requires an adoption of a political philosophy that shall make the Indians, as an individual and as a tribe, subjects of American law and beneficiaries of American institutions, by making them first American citizens, and clothing them, as rapidly as their advancement and location will permit, with the protective and ennobling prerogatives of such citizenship.

I favor the measure pending, because it is a step in the direction that I have indicated. You propose to give the Indian not temporary but permanent residence as a tribe, and not tribal location, but by a division of lands in severalty you secure to him the individual property rights which, utilized, will sustain life for himself and family better than his nomadic career. By this location you lay the foundation for that love of country essential to the patriotism and growth of a people, and by the distribution of lands to the individual, in severalty, you appeal to and develop that essential constitutional quality of humanity, the disposition to accumulate, upon which, when healthily and justly developed, depends the wealth, the growth, the power, the comfort, the refinement, and the glory of the nations of the earth.

The measure also, with less directness, but as a necessary sequence to the provisions that I have just characterized, proposes, as preliminary to bringing the red race under the operations of our laws, to present them the best phases of civilized life. Having given the red man a habitat, having identified the individual as well as the tribe with his new home, by securing his individual interests and rights therein; having placed these people where law can reach them, govern them, and protect them, you propose a system of administration that shall bring them in contact not with the adventurer of the border, not a speculative Indian agent, not an armed blue-coated soldier, but with the American people, in the guise and fashion in which trade, commerce, arts—useful and attractive—in the panoply that loving peace supplies, and with the plenty and comforts that follow in the footsteps of peace, and for the first time in the Indian's history, he will see the industrial, commercial, comfortable side of the character of the American people; will find his contact and form his associations with the citizens of the great Republic, and not simply and exclusively its armed men—its instruments of justice and destruction. So much this measure, if it should be a type of the new policy, will do for the Indian, and the Indian problem—heretofore rendered difficult of solution because of the false philosophy underlying it, and the unjust administration too frequently based upon it—a policy that has kept the Indian a fugitive and a vagabond, that has bred discontent, suspicion, and hatred in the mind of the red man will be settled—not immediately, in a day or a year, but it will be put in course of settlement, and the question will be placed where a successful issue will be secured beyond a peradventure.

Mr. President, the red race are not a numerous people in our land, not equaling probably a half million of souls, but they are the remnants of a great and multitudinous nation, and their hapless fortunes heretofore not only appeal to sympathy and to justice in any measure that we may take affecting them, but the vigor, energy, bravery, and integrity of this remnant entitle them to consideration on the merits of this question . . .

. . . The Indian is a physical force; a half million of vigorous physical intellectual agents ready for the plastic hand of Christian civilization, living in a country possessing empires of untilled and uninhabited lands. The Indian tribes, viewed from this utilitarian stand-point, are worth preservation, conservation, utilization, and civilization, and I believe that we have reached a period when the public sentiment of the country demands such a modification in the Indian policy, in its purposes, and in its methods, as shall save and not destroy these people . . .

The Indian is human, and no matter what his traditions or his habits, if you will locate him and put him in contact, and hold him in contact with the forces of our civilization, his fresh, rugged nature will respond, and the fruit of the endeavor, in his civilization and development, will be the more permanent and enduring because his nature is so strong and obdurate. When you have no longer made it necessary for him to be a vagabond and a fugitive; when you have allowed him to see the lovable and attractive side of our civilization as well as the stern military phase; when you have made the law apply to him as it does to others, so that the ministers of the law shall not only be the executors of its penalties but the administrators of its saving, shielding, protecting provisions, he will become trustful and reliable, and when he is placed in position in which not only to become an industrial force—to multiply his comforts and those of his people—but the honest, full sharer of the things he produces, savage life will lose its attractions and the hunter will become the herdsman, the herdsman in his turn the farmer, and the farmer the mechanic, and out of the industries and growth of the Indian homes will spring up commercial interests and men competent to foster and handle them . . .

Source: Congressional Record, 46th Cong., 2d sess., April 6, 1880, 2195–2196.

Document 11.2 in Context
"Protection of the Rights of American Colored Citizens": Opposing Segregated Railroad Travel

In December 1884, as the House considered legislation involving interstate commerce, Rep. James E. O'Hara, R-N.C., proposed an amendment to the bill to eliminate discrimination against black passengers on interstate rail lines. O'Hara's amendment was simple and direct:

> And any person or persons having purchased a ticket to be conveyed from one state to another, or paid the required fare, shall receive the same treatment and be offered equal facilities and accommodations as are furnished all other persons holding tickets of the same class without discrimination.[5]

Despite the passage of the Fourteenth Amendment (**Document 3.2**) that had ostensibly guaranteed equal rights to all citizens, it was common practice throughout the South—and even in some places in the North—to segregate black passengers in separate "Jim Crow" cars on trains. Those segregated cars were always the worst of accommodations, and black passengers could not improve their circumstances, even if they were able to afford a first-class ticket.

O'Hara argued that all passengers should be entitled to whatever accommodations they could afford, regardless of race or social status. He pointed out that Congress had passed legislation regulating the conditions under which sheep, swine, cattle and other animals could be transported—requiring periodic respites for water, rest and feeding. Congress, therefore, had not only the power, but the duty, he declared, to regulate the conditions under which human passengers were transported and to protect all passengers from discrimination. In offering his amendment, he emphasized that it was about equity:

> This is not class legislation. It is not a race question, nor is it a political action. It rises far above all these. It is plain, healthy legislation, strictly in keeping with the enlightened sentiment and spirit of the age in which we live; it is legislation looking to; and guarding the rights of every citizen of this great Republic, however humble may be his station in our social scale.[6]

O'Hara's proposal, however, came under attack, primarily from southern representatives who accused him of seeking to create an issue for political gain in the next election by exploiting racial matters. The document that follows is O'Hara's response to his critics during House debate on the proposal.

▬ Document 11.2 ▬
Rep. James E. O'Hara, R-N.C., Seeks to End Segregation on Railroads, December 17, 1884

Mr. O'HARA: I regret exceedingly, Mr. Speaker, that this color question has arisen in this debate. [Laughter.] I for one, sir, hold that we are all Americans; that no matter whether a man is white or black he is an American citizen, and that the aegis of this great Republic should be held over him regardless of his color. The day is too late, public sentiment and the healthy influence of the nineteenth century all stare us in the face—it is too late, sir, for the American Congress to legislate on the question of color.

My amendment proposes nothing sir, in regard to color; it merely says the white man who may not occupy so high a social position as some of his more favored brethren shall not be discriminated against. It says that the colored man shall not be discriminated against. It is an amendment in a healthy direction, an amendment appealing to the common sense and patriotism of the entire people of this land.

The gentleman from Alabama [Hilary A. HERBERT] has suggested that I introduced the amendment or rather inserted the words in it "without discrimination" for a political purpose. Mr. Speaker, I am not in the habit of raising a political issue two years before a campaign begins. The campaign has ended, and I and others who believe with me politically will abide by the result. And far be it from me at this period to raise anything for political purpose. All I ask of the American Congress is that while you are protecting the property of men, while you are protecting dumb brutes, while you are protecting every other interest, you shall at the same time give voice and expression to the protection of the rights of American colored citizens. [Applause on the Republican side.]

Mr. Speaker, "without discrimination" seems to be the words that hurt. If, as the gentleman has said, upon the statute-book of Georgia and upon the statute-book of Alabama there are laws which provide no discrimination can be made, or in substance the same thing, then why in the name of common consistency, why in the name of fairness and justice should there be a desire now to place this "rider" upon my amendment? Why, you gentlemen of the North, you gentlemen of Ohio, of New York, of Indiana, and of every other Northern State, yea, gentlemen from my own State of North Carolina, we ride together, we ride according to the fare we pay or feel able and disposed to pay. If I am not able or disposed to pay for or buy a first-class ticket I buy a second-class ticket, and I go right along and there is no trouble.

If the gentlemen mean what they say, that it is the idea and the firm conviction of every man in the length and breadth of this land to accord to all men their rights and privileges, why then is this amendment to the amendment needed? The very amendment itself bears a negative assertion on its very face. When gentlemen come here and say the words "without discrimination" should be stricken from my amendment, it shows a deliberate purpose to discriminate. I do not believe there is a single railroad in the land, I do not believe there is a single corporation in this country which desires to foster any discrimination. Let the man be white or black, humble or great, plebian or aristocratic, if he pays his fare, if he decently behaves himself, he is entitled to the same right as his money and desire prompt him. [Applause on the Republican side.]

Source: Congressional Record, 48th Cong., 2d sess., December 17, 1884, 317.

Document 11.3 in Context
"To Hold Office Is a Precious Gift . . . but There Are Gifts Superior to Office": Rep. Thomas E. Miller, R-S.C., Calls for Civil Rights Protections

Despite winning two elections, Thomas E. Miller, R-S.C., served only slightly more than five months in the House of Representatives. He was declared the winner in the 1888 election, but only after a protracted challenge by his white Democratic opponent, who alleged election fraud had occurred. Miller's apparent victory in the 1890 election was overturned by the South Carolina Supreme Court because of alleged voting irregularities; the court ruled that the color and size of ballots cast by Miller's supporters did not meet state election requirements.

In the short time that he served, however, he spoke out repeatedly against the abuses that were depriving African Americans of the civil rights guaranteed them by the Fourteenth Amendment (**Document 3.2**). He also defended African Americans against his southern white colleagues' allegations that blacks were the source of many of the South's problems. In a February 1891 speech, Miller assailed the claims of Sen. Alfred H. Colquitt, D-Ga., that the presence of blacks was retarding economic growth in the South.

"It is not the negro, Mr. Chairman, that keeps Northern capital and Western energy from within the borders of the South land, but it is the . . . clannishness of the white citizens, it is the petty prejudices of the white citizens," Miller declared. He said that the Negro "assimilates readily" into American society. "Full of gratitude, trained to obey, it is his nature to lovingly serve those by whom he is employed; he never attempts to cross the boundary of established social lines; but, like the hewer of wood that he is in the South, he toils, obeys, and develops his section." [7] The reward for African Americans, he commented, was to be denied their rights, excluded from political participation, accused unjustly of criminality, and subjected to regular violence, including lynching.

The following document is a January 1891 speech by Miller during a debate over federal election laws. Miller acknowledged that blacks were eager to vote and to hold public office, but he noted that a more crucial issue for his African American constituents was the lack of protection for their fundamental civil rights: they had to confront the constant fear of violence in their daily lives and faced arbitrary injustices at the hands of the legal system.

▬ Document 11.3 ▬
Rep. Thomas E. Miller, R-S.C., Calls for Civil Rights Protections, January 12, 1891

Mr. MILLER: . . . It is late in the day and in the session, but some things are being said to which I should like to reply. To hold office is a precious gift, and the race to which I belong are desirous of it, but there are gifts superior to office. Gentlemen talk about the North and about its not giving negroes representation on their tickets. That is not the thing we are suffering most from in the South.

There are other things of more importance to us. First is the infernal lynch law. That is the thing we most complain of. It is a question of whether when we go to work we will return or not. Second, they have little petty systems of justices who rob us of our daily toil, and we can not get redress before the higher tribunals. Third, we work for our task-masters, and they pay us if they please, for the courts are so constructed that negroes have no rights if those rights wind up in dollars and cents to be paid by the white task-masters.

They speak about pure elections and call the election law a force law. Do not gentlemen from the South boast here in their speeches that it is the white man's right to rule and to control elections, and if they cannot control them by a majority vote they will control them by force or fraud? Take the speech delivered by my colleague from South Carolina [John J. Hemphill], and you will see his brazen-faced boast that it is his right to remain here even without votes; and then when we have an appropriation bill the North is to be taunted with not giving negroes representation upon their tickets.

Yes, gentlemen, we want office; but the first and dearest rights the negro of the South wants are the right to pay for his labor, his right of trial by jury, his right to his home, his right to know that the man who lynches him will not the next day be elected by the State to a high and honorable trust; his right to know that murderers shall be convicted and not be elected to high office, and sent abroad in the land as grand representatives of the toiling and deserving people.

These are rights that we want; and we call upon you gentlemen of the North to speak for us and ask the Chamber over yonder to give us an election law—not a force law [Miller is referring here to a distinction between a "force law" concerning violence used against blacks, such as lynching, and an "election law" addressing only voting rights]—a national law, Mr. Chairman, that will compel the people of the South to register the votes of the negro and the white man alike, and count them as they are cast, and let the wishes of those people in this American country be expressed here by duly elected Representatives of their States. [Applause on the Republican side.]

The sickly sentiment about not giving negroes positions in the North! The negroes of the North have their schoolhouses. Taxes are levied and schoolhouses supported. What do we find in South Carolina, where the Democrats rule? First, the newly elected governor, who claims to stand upon the platform of Jefferson's principles, denies that all men are born free and equal and endowed with equal rights by their Creator. In his annual message to the Legislature he asks for the annihilation of the public-school system which is bringing South Carolina out of the bog of ignorance that she is in to-day and fast placing her along in the phalanx of other States in prosperity . . .

. . . The governor in his annual message, to re-establish ignorance, desires to close the schoolhouse door against the poor children by creating class schools. Yes; that is the way. What does he recommend? He recommends that the constitutional guaranty of a 2-mill tax be abolished; that communities be left to themselves to levy school taxes; and to the community shall also be left the right to say whether the education of the rich man's son or the education of the poor man's son shall be supported by the taxes levied. How do they seek to do it? The largest taxpayers are those people generally who have not many children and as they are compelled by the State law to pay a tax, it is to be left to them whether it shall be used to educate the poor man's child or whether it shall be used to educate their children. It amounts to having no educational system at all and is the destruction of the school system down there. Then they come North and speak about the bitterness of sectionalism, while right there in our Southland country, for want of experience, the governor of South Carolina recommends the destruction of the school system, which has been erected upon the promise of universal education.

What else does he do? He recommends the abolishment of two colleges established, by my assistance, to educate white young men that they may know how to lead the old State up out of poverty and ignorance. Ah, gentlemen, what we need in this land is not so many offices. Offices are only emblems of what we need and what we ought to have. We need protection at home in our rights, the chiefest of which is the right to live. First, the right to live, and next the right to own property and not have it taken from us by the trial justices. I will read you an illustrative chapter, if gentlemen will allow me the time. A Democratic lawyer from my state, Mr. Monteith, speaking about the trial-justice system as sustained by the Democratic Party of that State, says that under it no man is secure in his rights, and he gives a picture like this.

I hope gentlemen will listen. A negro was employed to plow for a white man for $10 a month. This man had a game hen. The hen was lost, and simply because the negro was plowing there he was assumed to be guilty of stealing her, was tried and sentenced to imprisonment, and they chained him by his hands to the plow, but before the thirty days of his sentence expired the good old game hen, with fourteen chicks, came out from under the barn where she had been "setting." [Laughter and applause.] The same gentleman gives another illustration which will bring the blush of shame to the face of every white man. A negro woman, in the absence of her husband, got into a dispute with a white neighbor concerning a boundary line, a question which the trial justices have no right to settle; but they take such a question when it comes before them and whip it around and whip it around until they manage to work it into a criminal case. They put this woman on trial in his absence, and, although her attorney pleaded that she was in a condition in which women can not go to court, she was tried, convicted, and sentenced; and a white constable went to her house, two hours after she had become a mother, dragged her from a sick bed and carried her 15 long miles, to the very seat and center of the intelligence of our State, old Columbia. There, to the honor of the jailer and his white wife, they called together several women, white and black, and they ran that inhuman constable away from the jail and took the poor woman and made her an object of charity.

These are some of the outrages that are inflicted upon my people in the Southland which this "force" bill, as you call it, will protect them from; because, if we get it, instead of seeing South Carolina represented as she has been in this Congress by seven Democrats, you will find six or seven Republicans here. The offices will not go around among the Democrats, and then the spirit of fight that made them secede will make them break up the Democratic Party and we shall have peace. [Applause on the Republican side.]

Source: Congressional Record, 51st Cong., 2d sess., January 12, 1891, 1216.

Document 11.4 in Context
"This Bill Is Not in the Interests of That Good Feeling between the Two Races": The Struggle to End Lynchings

Most African American representatives have seen it as their special duty to speak out against injustice aimed at African American citizens. For too long, that injustice was expressed in brutally violent murders of black people—lynchings that over a fifty-year period from the mid-1880s to the mid-1930s killed several thousand African Americans.

Black members of Congress never had enough votes or enough influence—even with the support of some northern white legislators—to push specific anti-lynching legislation through both houses of Congress and get it signed into law by the president. It was not for lack of trying, however. During Reconstruction, black members focused on bills, such as the Ku Klux Klan Act of 1871 (**Document 3.6**), that were aimed at enforcing the civil rights protections of the Fourteenth Amendment (**Document 3.2**) and ending the violence and intimidation that had been used to reestablish white supremacy in the South. By 1900 an average of two to three black citizens were being lynched per week nationwide. In response, Rep. George H. White, R-N.C., introduced a bill that sought specifically to make lynching a federal crime (**Document 4.9**).

White's bill died in committee and White left office in 1901, marking the start of a twenty-eight-year period in which no African American was elected to Congress. But starting in 1918, following an intensive publicity campaign by the National Association for the Advancement of Colored People (NAACP), sympathetic white legislators sponsored anti-lynching bills in every Congress for at least thirty years. Three of those bills—one sponsored by Leonidas C. Dyer, R-Mo., in 1922 and two sponsored by Joseph A. Gavagan, D-N.Y., in 1937 and 1940—passed the House of Representatives but died in the face of filibusters by southern opponents in the Senate. As late as 1957, Charles C. Diggs Jr., an African American Democrat from Michigan, introduced anti-lynching legislation in the House, only to see it die in committee.

The following document—comprising excerpts from the Senate filibuster of the Gavagan Bill in 1938—illustrates the opposition faced by the proponents of anti-lynching legislation. The bill's opponents mixed assurances that they were concerned with the well-being of black citizens with arguments that the proposed legislation infringed upon states' rights, was unnecessary because of declining numbers of lynchings, and might even inspire irresponsible blacks to commit crimes.

One particular crime was the greatest and most sensitive concern: rape. Alluded to in the closing passage of this excerpt as "the crime which in most cases causes lynching," sexual assaults by black men against white women—sometimes real, but often unfounded or highly exaggerated—had inspired countless lynchings and even a number of deadly race riots. The Atlanta riot of 1906, which killed more than 20 blacks, was fueled by incendiary, and inaccurate, newspaper reports of alleged sexual assaults. Bloody riots that devastated the African American communities of Wilmington, North Carolina, in 1898 (an estimated 50–100 blacks killed) and Tulsa, Oklahoma, in 1921 (an estimated 150–200 blacks killed) were also sparked by lurid and sensationalized newspaper reports of alleged sexual attacks.

═══ Document 11.4 ═══
Opponents Filibuster Gavagan Anti-Lynching Bill, January 7, 1938

Mr. [William E.] BORAH [R-Idaho]: . . . Notwithstanding anything that has been said or that may be said to the contrary, this is a sectional measure. It is an attempt upon the part of States practically free from the race problem to sit in harsh judgment upon their sister States where the problem is always heavy and sometimes acute. It is proposed to condemn these States and the people in them because it is claimed that they have failed properly to meet and adjust this most difficult of all problems. No more drastic condemnation could be offered by a measure than that which is offered by the measure now before the Senate.

It proposes to authorize the national Government to enter into the States, and to take charge of and prosecute as criminals the duly elected officials of the States, from the governor down. It proposes that the Federal Government shall be the sole judge of the guilt or innocence of State officials . . .

. . . I shall contend that the southern people have met the race problem and dealt with it with greater patience, greater tolerance, greater intelligence, and greater success than any people in recorded history, dealing with a problem of similar nature . . .

It is not in the interest of national unity to stir old embers, to arouse old fears, to lacerate old wounds, to again, after all these years, brand the southern people as incapable or unwilling to deal with the question of human life. This bill is not in the interests of that good feeling between the two races so essential to the welfare of the colored people . . .

. . . History has proven that it will be a failure, and those who suffer most will be the weaker race . . .

Lynching is the one crime, Mr. President, that is distinctly and markedly on the decrease in the United States . . .

. . . Last year the number was eight. In many of the Southern States lynching has practically disappeared. Virginia had only one case in 10 years. West Virginia had none during the past 5 years. South Carolina had none during the past 3 years. Oklahoma had one in 10 years. North Carolina had two in 7 years. Arkansas had three in 9 years. Maryland had two in 10 years, and none for the past 3 years . . .

Mr. [Kenneth D.] McKELLAR [D-Tenn.]: . . . In the 21 years I have been in the Senate, it has fallen to me to oppose bills of this kind on three occasions. In 1922 substantially the same bill was introduced, and I think I may say without fear of contradiction that it was then introduced largely for political purposes. I opposed it at that time with all the vigor and determination of which I was capable, and the bill was not passed.

Later on, in 1935, substantially the same bill was again introduced. There was a long contest, and the bill was not passed.

In my judgment, Mr. President, no better conclusion could possibly have been reached in either of those instances than the failure of the bills to pass at those times. I think it was better for the Nation, better for all its people, but especially better for the people of the colored race, that the bills did not pass. So today I agree with the Senator from Idaho that this bill, if passed, will be injurious to the entire Nation, but more especially will it be injurious to the people of the colored race, for whose benefit it is asserted that it should pass . . .

Before I enter upon a discussion of the merits of the bill I wish to say that I was born and reared on a farm in southern Alabama, in the heart of what is generally known as the "black belt" of that State. In the county in which I lived when I was a boy, if I recall aright, there were between 10 and 15 Negroes to one white person. I was reared among Negroes, with Negroes all around, and, so far as I can recall, I never had a difference with a Negro in my life. I have no unkind feelings of any kind, nature, or description toward the Negroes, never have had, and never expect to have. I have the greatest sympathy and consideration for them. I played with them when a boy. My father and mother were both slave owners, and they treated the Negroes with the utmost consideration and the utmost care. They taught their sons to take the same attitude, and I hope I have never abandoned that teaching, and that I have always treated these people with the greatest consideration. I have nothing against the Negroes as a race and nothing against them as a people. I would not do them a wrong for anything in the world . . .

Forty-five years ago there were 231 lynchings, but the number has constantly decreased, year by year, until last year only 8 lynchings occurred.

When we have solved the problem so far as lynching of white people is concerned, and have almost solved the problem in its entirety, what do we find? We find probably a majority of the Senate of the United States paying no attention to other crimes, tying up the business of the Senate in order to inflict a wrong and injury upon the Southern States that have done so much to eradicate the crime. I challenge any Senator on the floor . . . who thinks that there is some other crime that has been decreased more rapidly than has the crime of lynching to stand up and interrupt me, and I will gladly yield . . .

I know that every man who is going to vote on this bill is conscientious about it. I will not say anything to the contrary on that; but I have never seen a more misguided lot of men in my life, because I know the Members of this body, and I know that each and every one of them has enough sense to know that there is no necessity for stirring up race prejudice at this time. There is no necessity or even reason for stirring up race prejudice at this time in the interest of the colored people when this crime is about to pass out of existence. It is down to its last ebb. What you are going to do, Senators, is not to decrease the number of lynchings, but my fear is that you will increase the number. Why? Because the ignorant members of the colored race—not the more intelligent members, but the less intelligent members, especially among the men of that race—will believe that they may commit any crime with impunity and that the Federal Government will protect them by the overlordship provisions of this bill. I am not a prophet, but it would not surprise me at all if there were more than eight lynchings next year, should this bill be enacted . . .

. . . The crimes for which lynchings occur in most cases are being decreased. You gentlemen may not know it, but you are playing with fire. If you let the country generally know that the Federal Government is taking steps in this matter by the passage of a bill of this kind, you will find that ignorant Negroes, learning about it, will be more and more inclined to commit the crime which in most cases causes lynching . . .

Source: Congressional Record, 75th Cong., 2d sess., January 7, 1938, 137–161.

Document 11.5 in Context
"You Are Now Embarking on a Perilous Course": Rep. Oscar S. De Priest, R-Ill., Addresses Social Equity

When Oscar S. De Priest was elected in 1928 as a Republican representative from Chicago, he became the first African American to sit in Congress in nearly three decades. He soon found himself enmeshed in a national controversy, barely six months after taking office, when his wife, Jesse, was invited to tea at the White House by First Lady Lou Henry Hoover.

The First Lady's teas were an annual formality—the wives of all members of Congress were invited—but the addition of a black woman to the guest list deeply offended the social sensibilities of many, particularly southerners. Washington was still, in a cultural sense, a southern city. Mrs. Hoover sought to minimize the possible fallout: the tea was divided into a number of separate sessions on different days, Mrs. De Priest was invited to the last and smallest of the individual sessions, and the other guests at that session were carefully selected to avoid conflict. But when Mrs. De Priest's attendance became public knowledge, southerners were outraged, and they began venting their anger in letters to the First Lady and President Herbert Hoover, and in newspapers across the South.

"Mrs. Hoover is a great favorite socially in the capital," wrote the editors of the *Tallahassee Daily Democrat,* "but even her best friends say that she has committed a grave error, and one that will do her husband lasting political injury." [8] The Texas Legislature, meanwhile, went so far as to pass a resolution rebuking Mrs. Hoover and declaring that, "we bow [our] heads in shame and regret and express in the strongest and most emphatic terms at our command our condemnation and humiliation." [9]

A Hoover backer from Texas wrote to the president to express his personal disappointment:

> The unfortunate incident of entertaining a negro congressman's wife socially in the White House has resulted in embarrassment to your Southern friends and supporters. Such precedents make our negro problem much more difficult and is even calculated to cause a recurrence of race riots in the South.[10]

De Priest's response to the furor was pugnacious. He thumbed his nose at the criticism by organizing a fund-raising party and announcing that the money raised would be used to promote social equality between the races. He also pointedly refused to invite fellow Republicans who had been critical of Mrs. Hoover's action. The following letter to De Priest from House colleague J. C. Shaffer, R-Va., declining his invitation to the party, reflects the atmosphere De Priest faced in Congress.

═══ Document 11.5 ═══
Letter to Rep. Oscar S. De Priest, R-Ill. from Rep. J. C. Shaffer, R-Va., June 18, 1929

Dear Sir:

Your invitation to attend a musical and reception to be given at the Washington Auditorium June 21 has been received.

I decline the invitation.

Permit me to say that I am a Republican Member of Congress and that I have observed your course in the House, and it has been retiring and exemplary. The continuance of this course would have won you the admiration and respect of your colleagues and of the country. Every courtesy has been accorded to you to which you are entitled by virtue of your high office.

You are now embarking on a perilous course which will, if you continue, disturb relations which have long been amicably settled in the South. The people of the country are in sympathy with the development and advancement of your race, and I strongly favor this course.

Any movement or attempt by you in the direction of social equality is not a true interpretation of the attitude of both peoples. It will not be tolerated by the white people of the country, nor is it desired by the negro race.

The white people have their position, and are respected in it. The colored race has its place, and is respected in it. No one desires to disturb these relations. To do so might lead to disaster.

I make this statement in the interest of and because of my friendship for the colored people of the Southland.

Respectfully,

J. C. Shaffer

Source: J. C. Shaffer to Oscar S. De Priest, June 18, 1929, Herbert Hoover Presidential Library, West Branch, Iowa, Presidential Papers, Box 106, Subject File: Colored Question, De Priest Incident Correspondence, 1929, June 16–20.

Document 11.6 in Context
"A Gratuitous Slap in the Face to Many Thousand Negro Soldiers":
Rep. William L. Dawson, D-Ill., Responds to Statements by Secretary of War Henry L. Stimson

Since the American Revolution, African Americans have faced discrimination in the nation's military. Although black soldiers had fought with distinction at Lexington, at Concord and in other early battles, George Washington refused to allow additional black volunteers to enlist in July 1775 when he organized the Continental army, and he refused to permit those blacks already in service to reenlist. Eventually military necessity forced the Continental Congress and the colonial militias to reconsider the policy and accept black recruits, but the habit of rejecting blacks from service—and discriminating against those who were accepted for service—persisted into the middle of the twentieth century.

During the early months of the Civil War, African Americans were barred from service and only gradually won the ability to enlist. Although President Abraham Lincoln eventually acknowledged that black combat soldiers had played a pivotal role in Union victory, they spent much of the war relegated to support services—such as building roads and fortifications—and routinely received the worst uniforms, food and equipment. The same was true of the famed Buffalo Soldiers who served in the West in the closing decades of the nineteenth century, and of the black units during the Spanish-American War and World War I. A number of black units, such as the 365th Infantry in World War I, distinguished themselves in combat, but they often struggled with inadequate equipment and training and a reluctance among senior white officers to give them the opportunity to fight.

Rep. William L. Dawson of Illinois, the only black member of Congress through most of World War II, was keenly sensitive to the issue of discrimination in the military. During World

War I, Dawson served in Europe from 1917 to 1919 as a lieutenant with the 365th Infantry, so he had firsthand experience of military segregation. He was also well aware of the efforts of the NAACP and others to press for integration of the military as World War II progressed. William H. Hastie, for example, had resigned in January 1943 as a civilian adviser to Secretary of War Henry L. Stimson because of persisting racial discrimination in the military.

In early 1944 Dawson was outraged when Rep. Hamilton Fish, R-N.Y., read on the House floor a letter from Stimson that was critical of the performance of black troops. Dawson wrote the letter that follows to John J. McCloy, Stimson's assistant, demanding further information about the training of black units and registering his own indignation at the secretary's comments. Dawson noted that the units most heavily criticized by Stimson were units led by black officers, which Dawson saw as a way of limiting the African Americans' advancement up the ladder of military leadership.

▬▬ Document 11.6 ▬▬
Rep. William L. Dawson's Letter to Assistant Secretary of War John J. McCloy, February 28, 1944

My dear Mr. McCloy:

Yesterday Representative Hamilton Fish of New York addressed the House of Representatives on the matter of the utilization of Negro troops in combat. In the course of his remarks, he read a letter that had been sent him over the signature of the Secretary of War.

The above was the beginning of a letter which I intended to send to you the day after Congressman Fish made his speech and inserted the letter of Secretary Stimson into the Congressional Record. I thought better of the matter, however, and waited until I could view the entire situation in a calmer mood because I was so indignant at the unfair implication of the letter that what I said might have seemed unfair. I am glad that I did wait. Since that date I have received hundreds of communications from every section of this country, denouncing the statements made by the Secretary of War, and demanding that I see the President to ask for the removal of the Secretary of War, or demanding that I immediately introduce a resolution for a sweeping investigation of the entire military situation with a [v]iew of finding out what the sources responsible for the information upon which the Secretary of War based his letter.

I do appreciate the attitude that you have shown in the past, and I sincerely believe that you have the moral courage to stand up for your convictions, either pro or con; so before taking any other step, I thought I would bring it to your attention and, if possible, get your views on the matter. The letter of the Secretary of War is widely regarded as a direct insult to every Negro in the country and a gratuitous slap in the face to many thousand Negro soldiers in the Army. It represents the attitude with which I, an officer in a combat regiment in the last war, am all to[o] familiar.

In view of my former experiences, it is not a strange phenomena that the units selected for conversion were all officered by Negro officers. The evident attempt now to discredit units officered by Negroes seems to be but a move to strike at the Negro officer. Negro units have been taken out of combat and Negro officers have been put up against an impossible situation. Consequently, I would appreciate being informed of the existing plans for the utilization of the Negro officers now in the units which the War Department letter states have failed so miserably. I would further appreciate some amplification of this generalization particularly in view of the long training these units have undergone. In addition, please let me have a statement of the service schools attended by the officers of the 795th Tank Destroyer Battalion and the 930th, 931st Field Artillery Battalions also the bases from which they were formally certified for combat service and who certified them for such service.

This whole situation which has been developed by the letter of the Secretary of War is an unfortunate one and is the gravest danger to the morale of the Negroes in the Army and out of the Army. I would appreciate any views you have upon this matter.

Respectfully yours,
WILLIAM L. DAWSON

Source: Harry S. Truman Presidential Museum and Library, Online Documents: Desegregation of the Armed Forces, www.trumanlibrary.org.

Document 11.7 in Context
"Nothing More Graphically Illustrates the Immediate Need for Corrective Legislation": Rep. Charles C. Diggs Jr., D-Mich., Comments on the Emmett Till Murder Trial

In late August 1955 Emmett Till, a fourteen-year-old African American boy from Chicago, was brutally murdered near the Mississippi Delta town of Money. Till was abducted from the home of his great-uncle, whom he had been visiting, by at least two white men outraged by Till's behavior toward a white woman in a local grocery store. The discovery of Till's mutilated body, weighted down in the Tallahatchie River by a heavy fan from a cotton gin tied around his neck, created a national sensation.

Rep. Charles C. Diggs Jr., D-Mich., was determined to use public outrage over the case to prod the federal government into taking more action to protect the rights of black citizens. He called on the Justice Department to intervene in cases where the civil rights of African Americans had been violated because of their race, and he threatened to challenge the credentials of Mississippi's representatives in Congress because restrictions on black voters also prevented them from serving on juries in cases like the Till murder (**Document 5.10**).

In September 1955, when the woman's husband, Roy Bryant, and his half brother, J. W. Milam, were put on trial for Till's murder, Diggs traveled to Mississippi to observe the proceedings. Mississippi's white residents and officials were less than pleased by Diggs's appearance at the trial, but when some suggested that it would make race relations more tense, Diggs responded that it was "obvious that relations are already strained, and my being on the scene would not make the situation any worse." [11] Nonetheless, his physical safety while he was in Mississippi was far from assured.

Diggs's presence had an impact, according to a reporter who covered the trial: "When he went down there, people lined up to see him. They had never seen a black member of Congress. Blacks came by the truckloads. Never before had a member of Congress put his life on the line protecting the constitutional rights of blacks." [12]

Bryant and Milam were acquitted of Till's murder by an all-white jury, but within four months, *Look* magazine published a report that amounted to an admission by Milam that he and Bryant had killed Till—though they could not be tried again for the murder. The following document presents Diggs's comments on the floor of the House as he submits a copy of the *Look* article to be published in the *Congressional Record*.

▬ Document 11.7 ▬
Rep. Charles C. Diggs Jr., D-Mich., Comments on Emmett Till Murder Trial as He Enters *Look* Magazine Article into the *Congressional Record*, January 12, 1956

Mr. DIGGS: Mr. Speaker, the following article from Look magazine, dated January 24, 1956, relives the infamous Emmett Till case of last year. The stunning revelations are so detailed and stated so positively, the magazine's journalistic integrity and knowledge of libel law is so well established there is no doubt in my mind that the information came directly from the killers themselves, J. W. Milam and Roy Bryant. Safe within the legal confines of immunity from another trial for the same offense provided by the very Constitution which they and others of their breed have challenged, these men apparently grasped at the opportunity of selling this exclusive story for an undoubtedly handsome financial reward.

Their revolting attempt to justify the murder of the Till boy by emphasizing his alleged familiarity with Mrs. Milam and other white women is the product of incurably prejudiced minds.

The substance of this unsigned confession confirms the observations and investigations I made during my attendance at the trial for the defendants last September. I said, following their acquittal, that in my judgment the testimony of the defense witnesses was replete with perjury. The case itself had become obscured by obvious efforts to defy any criticism of Mississippi racial custom. Nothing more graphically illustrates the immediate need for corrective legislation by the Congress of the United States. Negroes must be guaranteed the right to vote without interference, intimidation, or unwarranted restrictions so they may qualify to serve on juries and exercise influence in the election of fair-minded public officials. Armed with this weapon, considering their numerical strength in Mississippi, the problems which confront them could probably be resolved on a local level, which is not inconsistent with the position of those who support the theory of States rights. The Attorney General must be granted sufficient power to intervene in those cases where individual States refuse to provide equal protection of the law to all citizens. This should not preclude, however, such action as he can pursue under present statutes . . .

Source: Congressional Record, 84th Cong., 2d sess., January 12, 1956, A247.

Document 11.8 in Context
"It Has Been Said That a Picture Speaks a Thousand Words": Fighting the Symbols of Segregation

Republicans' return to control of Congress in 1995 brought a host of changes that were of concern to African American members of Congress. The new Republican majority in the House launched the new session of Congress with a flurry of activity, introducing sweeping legislation they had promised in their "Contract with America" (**Document 7.2**) during the 1994 election. In the view of many Congressional Black Caucus members, the legislation—which called for tax cuts, welfare reform, term limits on legislators and tough anticrime measures, among other things—threatened many of the social gains that had been made for African Americans in the 1960s and 1970s.

But the black representatives were disturbed by the small symbols of shifting power, too—even changes in decoration of committee meeting rooms. The document below comprises three statements by Congressional Black Caucus members concerning a confrontation that arose over the hanging of a portrait in the meeting room of the House Rules Committee. The committee's new chairman, Republican Gerald B. H. Solomon of New York, had chosen to install a portrait of Howard W. Smith, a Virginia Democrat who had chaired the committee from 1955 to 1967.

The hanging of the portrait offended Caucus members, however, because Smith had been an ardent supporter of segregation and had resisted passage of the Civil Rights Act of 1964 (**Document 5.11**) and the Voting Rights Act of 1965 (**Document 6.1**). In 1956 Smith had been among the southern representatives and senators who signed the "Southern Manifesto," repudiating the U.S. Supreme Court's rulings against school segregation in the *Brown v. Board of Education* case (**Document 5.9**). Only two southern legislators—Sen. Lyndon B. Johnson of Texas and Sen. Albert Gore Sr. of Tennessee—had refused to sign the manifesto.

Caucus members protested the hanging of Smith's portrait in a dignified demonstration led by Rep. John R. Lewis, D-Ga. Thirty years earlier, Lewis had been a key proponent of the landmark civil rights legislation that Smith had so strenuously opposed.

▰▰▰ Document 11.8 ▰▰▰
African American Lawmakers Oppose the Hanging of Rep. Howard W. Smith Portrait in House Rules Committee Room, January 24 and 25, 1995

A Picture Speaks a Thousand Words

(Mr. LEWIS of Georgia asked and was given permission to address the House for 1 minute.)

Mr. [John R.] LEWIS of Georgia: Mr. Speaker, I read with great sadness and sorrow in this morning's papers that the new chairman of the Rules Committee has replaced the portrait adorning that committee's wall.

The portrait that had hung on that site was of Claude Pepper, one of the most revered and respected Members ever to serve in this institution, a man long associated with protecting the rights and dignity of senior citizens.

The portrait that replaces it, one of Howard W. Smith, a man perhaps best remembered for his obstruction in passing the country's civil rights laws. A man who in his own words 'never accepted the colored race as a race of people who had equal intelligence and education and social attainments as the white people of the South.'

Mr. Speaker, it has been said that a picture speaks a thousand words. I know the gentleman from New York meant no offense, meant no harm. He should change his mind. Symbols in our society are important. We do not need angels on our walls, but certainly we can do better. Mr. Chairman, please take down that picture. Take it down now.

Two Men Worthy of Praise

(Mr. LEWIS of Georgia asked and was given permission to address the House for 1 minute.)

Mr. LEWIS of Georgia: Mr. Speaker, I rise today to commend two individuals who yesterday performed acts worthy of praise, one a Democrat, and one a Republican.

The first, Mr. Speaker, is President Clinton, who last night delivered a State of the Union Address in this Chamber that laid out a vision for our Nation. It is a vision in which lawmakers put aside their partisan differences and work together for the common good, for the well-being of the American people. It is a vision he calls the new covenant.

The second individual I want to commend, Mr. Speaker, is Congressman GERALD SOLOMON, the chairman of the Committee on Rules in this House. Yesterday, in the spirit of the new covenant, Mr. SOLOMON decided to remove from the wall of his committee room the portrait of Howard W. Smith, a portrait that many Members of this House felt was unworthy to hang in a place of such distinction.

I want to thank Chairman SOLOMON. He is a man of honor, integrity, and good will.

These two men, President Clinton and GERALD SOLOMON, deserve our thanks and our praise.

Do Not Return to Ugliness of the Past

(Mr. PAYNE of New Jersey asked and was given permission to address the House for 1 minute and to revise and extend his remarks.)

Mr. [Donald M.] PAYNE of New Jersey: Mr. Speaker, yesterday members of the Congressional Black Caucus took a stand against allowing a symbol of segregation and racial division to be honored in the House of Representatives. I refer to the decision which was made earlier by Members of the new majority party to replace the portrait of Claude Pepper, a great humanitarian and champion of civil rights and older Americans, with a painting of a renowned segregationist and outspoken defender of slavery, former Representative Howard W. Smith. I commend Representative LEWIS of Georgia for speaking out on this issue, and let me also point out that the new chairman of the Rules Committee, our colleague GERALD SOLOMON of New York, to his credit, heard our grievance and agreed to remove the portrait. We appreciate his response, but I am disturbed by what appears to be a pattern of turning back the clock on the progress in racial relations. This incident comes on the heels of the controversy over the hiring of the House Historian, Christine Jeffrey, who insisted that schoolchildren must be fair to the Ku Klux Klan, a secret society who appears in white sheets and who have terrorized African-Americans, Jews, Roman Catholics, and others they find unacceptable.

Mr. Speaker, I hope these incidents are just the result of errors made in haste during the rush of the first 100 days, and not a more sinister campaign to return to the ugliness of the past.

Sources, in order of appearance: Congressional Record, 104th Cong., 1st sess., January 24, 1995, H552; January 25, 1995, H597; January 25, 1995, H601.

Document 11.9 in Context
"The Cause of Justice Will Not Be Served": Fairness, Justice and the Death Penalty

Capital punishment has long been controversial in the United States. While supporters see it as a just penalty for murder and other heinous acts as well as a deterrent to crime, opponents object that its deterrent effects are overrated and that it violates the Constitution's ban on cruel and unusual punishment. The issue has been of special concern to African American legislators because statistics show that black defendants are more frequently convicted of capital crimes and sentenced to death than are white defendants.

Challenges to capital punishment prompted a series of U.S. Supreme Court decisions in the early 1970s that rejected the procedural application of the death penalty in several states and halted executions nationwide from 1973 to 1976. Executions resumed in 1977 after the Court's procedural concerns had been addressed. Additional Court decisions in the late 1980s ruled that statistical analysis showing an uneven application of the death penalty to white and black defendants was insufficient to warrant a ban on capital punishment.

Since 1977 the debate over capital punishment has intensified. Concerns about rising crime rates in the 1980s and 1990s prompted death penalty advocates to call for expanded use of capital punishment and streamlining of the appeals process to produce swifter executions. Opponents have increasingly focused their arguments on advances in DNA-testing techniques that have led to the release of a number of death row prisoners by establishing their innocence. In the most highly publicized incident, Illinois governor George H. Ryan commuted the death sentences of all death row inmates in Illinois in January 2000 and placed a moratorium on use of the death penalty in the state: "We have now freed more people than we have put to death under our system—13 people have been exonerated and 12 have been put to death . . . There is a flaw in the system, without question, and it needs to be studied." [13]

Congressional Black Caucus member Bobby L. Rush, D-Ill., cited Ryan's action as he held a field hearing in February 2003 to examine flaws in the death penalty nationwide. "I have always believed that using the death penalty as a form of punishment is not punishment at all, but rather murder executed by the state," Rush said in a statement announcing the hearing. "That is why I want to build on the momentum of reexamination that exists here in Illinois and develop national legislation that will protect innocent people from a faulty system." [14]

The following document excerpt is from a House Judiciary Committee report on death penalty legislation promoted by the new Republican majority in Congress in 1995 as a way to get tougher on crime. The passage outlines dissent by the six Democratic members of the committee, including three Caucus members—John Conyers Jr. of Michigan, Melvin L. Watt of North Carolina, and Robert C. Scott of Virginia—and elaborates on their opposition to the bill.

▬ Document 11.9 ▬
Democrats Express Their Opposition to the Effective Death Penalty Act of 1995, February 8, 1995

. . .

DISSENTING VIEWS
We strongly oppose this bill.

It sacrifices the last hope of the falsely accused and the wrongly convicted—the Great Writ of Habeas Corpus—to a facile expediency driven by misguided passion for 'finality.'

The enthusiasm for hasty review and swift execution embodied in this bill grotesquely diminishes the historic role of the federal writ of habeas corpus in ensuring justice.

Pursuit of habeas corpus relief by the guilty may inconvenience judicial administration. It may also irritate a society vexed by the persistence of violent crime. But the federal writ's enduring value is that over and over again it frees the falsely accused from jail, the wrongly convicted from prison, and the innocent from horribly mistaken execution.

This federal bulwark against State injustice is priceless. Its value cannot be measured in days 'saved' by rigid timetables, nor by the convenience of short cuts to execution.

The ultimate test of any proposal to reform federal habeas corpus proceedings, therefore, is not whether it will make the trains of judicial administration run on time. This bill may do that.

The true test is whether the reform advances justice. It is whether it protects innocent men and women from being imprisoned and killed by a human process that—especially in death penalty cases—is too often flawed by emotion, subverted by prejudice, and bungled by incompetence . . .

This bill does not address this fundamental and pervasive problem of criminal justice. It neither advances justice nor protects the innocent. It is therefore flawed not only by what it does poorly, but by what it does not do at all.

It is upon this high ground that we stand against this bill.

BACKGROUND

Habeas corpus had a long and distinguished history in England before it was imported to the American colonies. Both the courts at Westminster and Parliament contributed to the development of habeas as the Great Writ of Liberty—the means by which English courts could enforce the 'law of the land' against governmental power. The American colonists also linked habeas corpus with due process of law. Moreover, the Constitution in 1787 assumed that habeas corpus would be available and thus provided that the privilege of the writ could not be 'suspended' except in 'Cases of Rebellion or Invasion' . . .

The Great Writ figured early and often in national affairs. In the wake of Reconstruction, habeas corpus was turned to the task of adjusting the relations between the Federal Government and the states. Most importantly, the writ provided the means by which the federal courts came to have ultimate authority to vindicate federal claims arising in state criminal cases. The sweeping text of the 1867 Act invited such an interpretation. No one would contend that the Reconstruction Congress 'intended' that the federal courts would defer to state judgments . . .

In this century, it has long been settled that the federal courts' jurisdiction in habeas corpus provides the judicial machinery by which fourteenth amendment rights are enforced in the federal judicial system. Justice Oliver Wendell Holmes put the point squarely in his celebrated opinion for the Court in *Moore v. Dempsey*, 261 U.S. 86, 91 (1923), when he declared that even 'perfection in the machinery' of adjudication in state court cannot insulate an unconstitutional conviction from reconsideration by the federal courts in the exercise of their habeas corpus jurisdiction. The *form* of state court process is, accordingly, insufficient—however full and fair it might have been . . .

COMPETENT COUNSEL

On the face of it, this bill is largely procedural. It (1) establishes a general one-year period within which petitioners from State court judgments—capital and non-capital alike—must file for habeas corpus relief; (2) creates a special 180 day limit and accelerated procedure in death penalty cases for States that 'opt in' by choosing to provide *post-conviction* counsel to persons convicted of capital offenses and sentenced to death; (3) limits all petitioners to one federal habeas corpus review—the so-called 'one bite at the apple'—except under the most extraordinary of circumstances; (4) sets rigid timetables within which federal courts must act on petitions; and (5) requires the federal government to award grants to States to help them oppose petitions for federal habeas corpus.

Each of these provisions shaves, calcifies, and truncates existing law so as to tightly limit the ability of non-capital prisoners and persons sentenced to death alike to seek federal review of Constitutional questions raised by their cases.

However, in all of its 21 pages, this 'reform' legislation contains not a single sentence directed toward reforming the greatest single cause of *successful* petitions for federal writs of habeas corpus—incompetent counsel at trial. Although some States commendably have instituted systems to ensure competent counsel in death penalty cases, far too many have not.

By stark contrast, bills reported out of this committee in past Congresses have taken care to ensure that those who face the death penalty will be guaranteed not simply counsel, but *competent* counsel.

Proponents of this bill argue that the procedural reforms it proposes are necessary to ensure that the trial—as opposed to post-conviction appeals and proceedings—is 'the main event.' Yet this bill ignores the fact that 'main events' flawed by shoddy counsel not only wreak injustice upon defendants, but will continue to generate grounds upon which review will be sought, judgments set aside, and justice delayed . . .

In short, not only does simply fairness require that capital defendants be provided good, experienced, aggressive defense counsel, smart judicial administration demands it . . .

The point in all of these cases remains the same, however: if justice is truly to be served, we must not only execute punishment swiftly. We must also ensure that the trial itself is fair.

INNOCENCE

A fatal flaw in H.R. 729 that goes to the heart of due process and fundamental fairness if the failure to ensure that an innocent person should never be executed.

The McCollum bill permits habeas claims only in the difficult-to-imagine situation where there is 'clear and convincing' evidence of innocence and 'no reasonable juror' would find the petitioner guilty. A Democratic amendment to substitute 'preponderance of the evidence' instead of the more restrictive standard was defeated.

Claims of 'innocence' in habeas proceedings are not part of a far-fetched scenario that can never happen in this day and age. The truth is this is all too common. In fact, the Supreme Court decided a case just this January 23, 1995, that shows how easily this can occur.

The facts in *Schlup v. Delo* are that a prison inmate accused of murder argued that a videotape and interviews in the possession of prosecutors showed he could not have committed the murder but the information was not revealed to him until six years after his conviction. The Court ruled that Mr. Schlup should be allowed to raise his claims of innocence.

There is case after shocking case of similar horror stories:

James Dean Walker had served 20 years in prison when one of his co-defendants confessed that he had pulled the trigger that killed a Little Rock police officer. Walker's gun had not been fired but he had been convicted on the testimony of a witness who said she had seen him shoot the officer. The Eighth Circuit, which had denied his first habeas petition 16 years earlier, agreed in 1985 that he should be freed.

Ruben 'Hurricane' Carter was convicted of murder in 1967 and served in prison for 18 years even though the witnesses whose identification led to his conviction later recanted their identifications. The conviction was reversed after a federal judge ordered prosecutors to turn over evidence, including failed polygraph tests, which showed the witnesses were lying. Carter was set free.

Robert Henry McDowell was almost executed for a crime that the victim initially told police was committed by a white man. McDowell was black. The North Carolina Supreme Court reversed a trial court order granting him a new trial but the Fourth Circuit ordered him to be released after the police reports were made public.

False identifications, witnesses recanting, death-bed confessions: these are all too familiar to those who defend Death Row inmates. Access to federal courts is vital.

The federal courts should also be available to hear claims of innocence when based on newly-discovered evidence. This bill is a sly smokescreen to cut off all claims based on innocence.

The bill may achieve the goal of speedier executions but the cause of justice will not be served. It is an admission of failure to pursue one without the other.

For all these reasons, we strongly dissent.

Source: House Committee on the Judiciary, *Effective Death Penalty Act of 1995,* H. Rep. 104-23, 104th Cong., 1st sess., February 8, 1995.

Document 11.10 in Context
"A Rash of Evil Afoot in the Land": Probing a Wave of Church Arsons

During the 1990s, the United States witnessed a dramatic outbreak of arson against African American churches. Although many of the crimes occurred in the states of the old South, they were by no means limited to that region. The United Methodist Church alone recorded 162 arsons at member churches in thirty-two states between 1990 and 2000. The southern states of Texas, South Carolina, Alabama, Florida, North Carolina and Tennessee each had ten or more Methodist church fires, but Pennsylvania had the most at sixteen, and Indiana was close behind with ten.[15]

Methodist churches were not the only ones targeted, nor did all of the churches belong to black congregations, but there was a strong racial bias to the incidents. According to a report by the National Council of Churches U.S.A., between June 1996 and December 1997 alone, "233 burned churches in 18 states have come to the attention of the NCC. Most are African American and a majority, but not all, are in the Southeast." The Rev. Joan Brown Campbell, general secretary of the council, explained the crimes:

> There are people in jail for some of the burnings . . . although the sad story is that often, these crimes are committed by young people who are intentionally used by hate groups. Most are very poor. The church burnings exemplify the lack of opportunity for the poor, both blacks and whites.[16]

In June 1996, at the peak of the outbreak, Sen. Carol Moseley-Braun, D-Ill., introduced a resolution in the Senate condemning the arson attacks against African American churches and calling for federal investigation of all suspicious church fires and prosecution of all individuals found to be involved. The resolution did not emerge from the Judiciary Committee, to which it was referred. The following document presents Moseley-Braun's call for action when she introduced the legislation in the Senate.

═══ **Document 11.10** ═══
Sen. Carol Moseley-Braun, D-Ill., Argues for Resolution on Church Burnings, June 13, 1996

Ms. MOSELEY-BRAUN: Yesterday, Mr. President, I came to the floor and spoke about what I called the domestic terrorism that we are suffering in this country with the burning of churches and other hate crimes in our Nation. I spoke at some length about it and mentioned a time that I will submit a resolution pertaining to the church burnings. I am submitting that legislation now, Mr. President. I would like it held at the desk until the time of adoption.

Mr. President, I know there will be other legislative activity associated with this issue in the days to come. But as the Chair is no doubt aware, since yesterday, when I first took to the floor, there has been yet another church burning in this country.

As I said yesterday, the people who are perpetrators of this rash of hate crimes and church burnings are no more than cowardly domestic terrorists. These are people who work under cover of darkness and anonymity to intimidate some and encourage others, and it is out of cowardice.

However, in spite of the objective of these actions, which it has been suggested are intended to start a race war, there is every indication that these arsonists are confused about the country in which their crimes are taking place.

Most Americans—I reiterate, most Americans—are appalled and outraged. The fact of the matter is, there is in this darkness some light coming through. The light relates, Mr. President, to the efforts of Americans, from the President of the United States down to ordinary people, to stand up, to speak out, to be heard and to demonstrate that this kind of crime, this kind of heinous crime and this kind of domestic terrorism is not to be tolerated in this America.

I have been encouraged, Mr. President, by some of the reports from my home State. In Glenn Carbon, IL, there had been a cross burning. In one of the newspapers in Illinois, the headline there was 'Neighbors Comfort Black Family Who Found Cross in Yard.' The story goes on to say that the people, white and black alike, who live in the community came to the aid of the individuals who suffered the cross burning to indicate their support, to indicate their reassurance that the racial hatred that was symbolized by the cross burning did not reflect the feelings of the neighborhood or of that community. I think that is a very positive and powerful thing.

Another article, Mr. President, from the Alton Telegraph, 'Neighbors show good will to victims of cross burning,' makes the same point. This article goes on to say that neighbors delivered flowers and food, cards, plants and other gifts to the family on Monday, people reaching outside of themselves to stand up against hatred, to stand up against racism, to stand up against the evil that this church burning represents.

I think therein lies the key. We can take action here in this U.S. Congress, the Senate and the House, and the President can take action. We can all come together as a collective community through our Government to take leadership in showing that in this America this kind of criminality will not be tolerated, but we can only do that, and it only takes real meaning when we are joined in our official capacity by individual, unofficial action, when the churches, themselves, come together to participate in ceremonies and services and marches and demonstrations in favor of unity and in favor of love.

When we really focus in on the fact that this rash of hate crimes is just that, a rash of evil afoot in the land, and that good people of all races will make it a point to be heard, not to sit back in silence and to allow this evil to take seed among us, but, rather, that we will all stand up as individual citizens to say, 'This America, in this time, is putting the ugly legacy of racism and racial hatred behind. We will not go back to the days when these kinds of things can happen with impunity.'

We will engage every asset, every resource at our disposal to see to it that these criminals are brought to justice, that the truth is uncovered, that no stone will be left unturned in our efforts to prosecute the perpetrators of these crimes, because they are criminals. We will make it very clear as a national community, all of us, that we will not tolerate this kind of conduct, and that the people who have tried to foist this horror on our community, on our country, will be prosecuted to the fullest extent of the law.

Mr. President, I also say after the speech that I gave yesterday, which is already in the RECORD, I was just really taken personally by the expressions of support, expressions of concurrence and the expressions from my colleagues on both sides of the aisle, people coming up to say, 'We think it is just terrible what is going on. We want to do something about it. We want to be heard. We want to make certain that everybody understands that this kind of activity has no place in America.' I am encouraged and heartened by that, because I think, if anything, that change of heart, that change of collective consciousness, that change in the climate of opinion is precisely the victory that reflects the moral victory that the civil rights movement achieved.

We have a mindset in this country that does not tolerate this kind of horror, that not only does not tolerate it, but is ashamed by it. Out of our repudiation, out of our rejection of these expressions of evil, I believe we will find a new birth as an American community. We will find a new level, frankly, of coming together and of working together, and of unity in this country, and will, I think, set the stage so the young people that are here today will begin to ask the question, in their time: 'I remember the days when race was a debate in the United States, but we got past that. We got smarter, we matured, we moved beyond that.' That is my hope for these young people.

If anything, I think with the expressions of support, the expressions of love, the expressions of unity, the good will that is being shown all over this country in reaction and in response to the hatred we have seen, the cross burnings and the church burnings, the moral victory will be ours as a Nation, and we will move forward as a Nation together, a stronger country because of it.

Mr. President, I understand the resolution will be adopted or can be adopted later this evening. I wanted to bring to my colleagues' attention the fact that this resolution is pending. I understand there will be other legislative initiatives in this regard. I am delighted to join with those, as well, because I think it is very important as a body we speak with one voice, that these people who are doing this are not Americans. Their activities fly in the face of the America that we believe in, fly in the face of the values that this America represents to the world, and that we will not allow their evil to shame all of us, and we will not allow them to get away with it. From that, Mr. President, I believe we will be a greater Nation, and we will have found, out of this horror, some light, and from that light we will be able to build a stronger Nation.

I commend my colleagues who have already joined me. Again, thanks to everyone who has stepped up and said something. One other word: There is a tradition that the only thing that allows evil to prevail is for good people to say nothing. Now is the time for good people to be heard. Now is the time for good people to stand up and say, 'The America that we know and the America we believe in is an America that cherishes the value of brotherhood and love and unity.'

Source: Congressional Record, 104th Cong., 2d sess., June 13, 1996, S6246–S6247.

Document 11.11 in Context
"Eliminating This Last Disgraceful Scar of Overt Discrimination": A Response to "Driving while Black"

In the 107th Congress (2001–2002), members of the Congressional Black Caucus attempted to enact legislation to combat the practice of racial profiling by law enforcement agencies and officials. Racial profiling, in essence, is the practice of subjecting African Americans, Hispanics or other racial or ethnic minorities to greater scrutiny based on the assumption that they are more likely than whites to be involved in illegal activity. For African American members of Congress, racial profiling was a persistent and pernicious example of the sort of racial discrimination that the Civil Rights Act of 1964 (**Document 5.11**) had been intended to outlaw so many years before.

Caucus members sponsored hearings on the issue and pointed to results of a 1999 Gallup poll, which found that almost half of all Americans belonging to minority groups believed they had been stopped by police because of their race. For African American men between the ages of 18 and 34, the rate was much higher—72 percent. The same study found that only 6 percent of whites believed that they had been treated by police in a racially biased manner.

In an article he wrote for the *Afro-American,* a black-owned newspaper based in Baltimore, Rep. Elijah E. Cummings, D-Md., explained the need for the hearings:

> We must challenge the incorrect—but genuine—belief on the part of too many police officers that racial profiling is *justified* as a public safety strategy.
>
> They stop and search us for "driving while Black" (or Brown) because they incorrectly believe that we are more likely to be carrying drugs or committing some other crime. Racial profiling may occur, they acknowledge, but it is a necessary cost of protecting our communities from crime.
>
> The evidence demonstrates, however, that this belief in our greater propensity to break the law is false.[17]

The following document presents the comments of Eleanor Holmes Norton, Democratic delegate from Washington, D.C., on the introduction of the Racial Profiling Prohibition Act of 2001. Although the legislation attracted dozens of cosponsors well beyond the membership of the Caucus and was reintroduced in two subsequent Congresses, it languished in committee.

▬ Document 11.11 ▬
Del. Eleanor Holmes Norton, D-D.C., Speaks on
Racial Profiling Prohibition Act, May 17, 2001

Ms. NORTON: Mr. Speaker, today we introduce the Racial Profiling Prohibition Act of 2001 (RPPA). Congress is decades late in doing its part to insure that law enforcement officers no longer stop or detain people on the street because of their color or their apparent nationality or ethnicity.

It was not until 37 years ago that Congress passed the first civil rights law that had any teeth. The 1964 Civil Rights Act finally barred discrimination against people of color in employment, public accommodations and funding of public institutions. Yet, today, irrefutable, and widespread evidence from every state confirms racially and ethnically motivated stops by police officers and shows that Congress has urgent, unfinished business to update the nation's civil rights laws.

This bill, which is overwhelmingly supported by both the Congressional Black Caucus (CBC) and the Congressional Hispanic Caucus (CHC) as original co-sponsors, seeks to eliminate both legal and constitutional problems that arise when a person is stopped by a police officer because of skin color, nationality or ethnicity. Title VI of the 1964 Civil Rights Act (CRA), enacted in part to implement the 14th Amendment requirement of equal protection, forbids the use of public money for discriminatory purposes. The bill we introduce today, is based on both the 14th Amendment, which gives power to Congress to implement its equal protection responsibilities and on the spending clause of the Constitution, which allows Congress to put conditions on the receipt of federal funds.

The federal funds that are the focus of our bill today are the vast sums contained in our transportation legislation. The last transportation bill, known as TEA-21 (Transportation Equity for the 21st Century Act) authorized $172 billion for highways in 1998. The new transportation bill, which Congress will enact next year, will authorize at least $250 billion in highway funding. By introducing our racial profiling bill today, we serve notice that Congress must not authorize another huge highway bill that does not effectively bar the use of transportation money to fund racial profiling stops on those highways.

The strength of our bill lies in what it requires and what it would do. The bill requires three important obligations if states are to qualify for federal transportation funds. First, law enforcement officers may not use race, national origin, or ethnicity in making decisions concerning a stop unless they are relying on a physical description that may include race to determine that a particular individual may be the person sought. Second, states must adopt and enforce standards prohibiting the use of racial profiling on streets or roads built with federal highway funds. Third, states must maintain and allow public inspection of statistical information on the racial characteristics and circumstances of each stop. Only three states even prohibit racial profiling today; ten others require only racial and ethnic data collection.

As important as information concerning who gets stopped is, what makes our bill effective is its sanction: the withholding of federal funds from states that fail to meet the three obligations of the statute. Money for streets, roads, bridges and other infrastructure is ardently pursued in the Congress. Each state and locality receives funds that are indispensable to building and maintaining major parts of its infrastructure. Next year's authorization will mean nearly 50 percent more in transportation funding to states and localities. These funds will either reinforce pervasive racial profiling or help eliminate it.

The power of transportation funding to command the necessary attention and bring quick results has been repeatedly demonstrated. Congress has successfully used federal highway funding to compel states to attack some of our most urgent problems, for example, reducing drunk driving among minors; requiring the revocation or suspensions of driving licenses of convicted drug offenders; and establishing a national minimum drinking age. Police stops of people on the streets because they are black or Hispanic or of any other non-majority national origin requires the same urgent action.

Withholding federal highway funds works because it hurts. The threat of losing highway funds has proven to be a powerful incentive. We saw the power of this incentive as recently as last year's Transportation appropriation. Congress enacted a provision requiring states to enact .08 blood alcohol content (BAC) laws by 2004 or [forfeit] their highway funds. In only the first six months after that provision was enacted, six states have already passed .08 BAC laws. Many more are sure to follow in order to preserve precious highway funds. A racial profiling provision in the 2003 federal highway funding bill would give the same set of alternatives to the states—effective enforcement of racial profiling legislation or loss of federal funds. If Congress is serious about eliminating this last disgraceful scar of overt discrimination in our country, let us put our money where our mouth is.

I urge my colleagues to support this bill.

Source: Congressional Record, 107th Cong., 1st sess., May 17, 2001, E833–E834.

Document 11.12 in Context
"A Matter of Values, Morality, and Bipartisan Politics": The Lingering Legacy of Segregation

America's history of racial discrimination and segregation has long echoed through the halls of Congress. One of the more surprising echoes, however, was the controversy that erupted in December 2002 and drove a senator from a top party leadership post over casual comments about a fifty-four-year-old political campaign.

The controversy began at the 100th birthday party for Sen. Strom Thurmond, R-S.C., when Senate Majority Leader Trent Lott, R-Miss., remarked on Thurmond's 1948 presidential campaign. At that time, Thurmond was the Democratic governor of South Carolina, but he ran for president as candidate of the breakaway States Rights Democratic Party—known as the Dixiecrats—with a segregationist platform. During Thurmond's birthday party, Lott said, "I want to say this about my state: When Strom Thurmond ran for president, we voted for him. We're proud of it. And if the rest of the country had followed our lead, we wouldn't have had all these problems over all these years, either." [18]

When a furor erupted over the comments, Lott issued a statement apologizing for what he called "a poor choice of words," and denying that he clung to "the discarded policies of the past." [19] But as critics, led by members of the Congressional Black Caucus, continued to assail Lott, evidence came to light suggesting that he may have made similar comments on other occasions. The Jackson, Mississippi, *Clarion-Ledger* reported that Lott had said much the same thing at a 1980 rally in Jackson where Thurmond had been in attendance: "After Thurmond spoke against federal pre-emption of state laws, Lott told the more than 1,000 people present, 'You know, if we had elected this man 30 years ago, we wouldn't be in the mess we are today.' " [20] The storm of criticism eventually forced Lott to drop his plans to seek reelection as Senate majority leader.

The document that follows is a speech on the controversy by Rep. Jesse Jackson Jr., D-Ill., that was delivered before the RainbowPUSH Coalition on December 14, 2002. In this excerpt, Jackson attacks what he sees as a pattern of insensitive comments that render Lott unsuitable for a leadership position in Congress. Lott resigned the post of majority leader about a week later. He remained in the Senate, however, and following the 2006 elections was elected by his fellow Republican senators to the post of minority whip, the party's second-highest leadership position in the Senate.

▬ Document 11.12 ▬
Rep. Jesse Jackson Jr., D-Ill., Attacks the Comments Made by Sen. Trent Lott, R-Miss., December 14, 2002

. . . This week the nation has again been brought face-to-face with its history through the insensitive remarks of Senator Chester Trent Lott, Republican of Mississippi. While it's gradually changing, the problem, so far, has been that the media has focused almost exclusively on the words Senator Lott used at the 100th birthday party celebration for Senator Strom Thurmond (R-SC), and similar words spoken in Mississippi during Ronald Reagan's 1980 presidential campaign.

If those were the only two statements, that might merely reflect two "mistakes." But Senator Lott has a pattern and long history of such statements, and parallel actions. And, so far, there's been little media focus on the pattern . . .

. . . There was no such word as "racism" until 1936. Whether it was Abraham Lincoln, Frederick Douglass, Booker T. Washington or Dr. W. E. B. DuBois, none of them used the word racism to describe the experience of blacks in America. The word didn't exist until 1936. And it didn't derive its original meaning from the African American experience. Racism was used to describe the plight of Jews under Hitler's Nazi Germany and Mussolini's Fascist Italy. African Americans then embraced and adopted the word to describe their own situation. But States' rights versus Union—not racism—is what, historically, has defined our experience and struggle in America.

I have deliberately not called Senator Trent Lott a racist. I haven't because: (a) that's a heavy word to drop on someone and it shouldn't be thrown around lightly; and (b) for me, it has at least five levels of meaning, and I want to make sure if I use the word that the American people understand what I mean.

First. There are philosophical racists. The gentleman in downstate Illinois who openly preaches that whites are genetically superior and Blacks, Jews, Asians, Hispanics and Native Americans are genetically inferior is, philosophically, a racist.

Second. Racism sometimes takes the form of prejudice. Prejudice is a pre-judgment about an individual on the basis of a group stereotype . . .

Third. There are racist actions. When African American churches are burned to the ground; when Black men in chains are dragged behind trucks; when Jewish synagogues have swastikas painted on them; and when Islamic Mosques are physically violated; those are all racist actions.

Fourth. There is such a thing a cultural racism. Most Americans have high morals. They work hard and play by the rules. They try to treat everyone fairly. They're sincere. They don't want to be racist. But some Americans just have limited knowledge, limited experiences and limited exposure. They are simply uninformed and sometimes say insensitive things out of ignorance. They just lack information and knowledge. So they can only be as good as they know to be within the bounds of cultural racism.

Finally, there is institutional racism. We've actually made significant progress as a country on the first four levels of racism as I've defined them. The most insidious level of racism, however, is institutional racism. When the unemployment rate for Blacks is more than twice that of Whites, that's institutional racism. When the infant mortality rate for Black babies is several times that of White babies, that's institutional racism. When they want to tear down and rebuild an airport and put 195,000 new jobs and $20 billion of economic activity in a predominately White area that already has an over-abundance of both, and then put most of the Section 8 housing in an area where we live with few jobs, few services and high taxes, then you know you're looking at institutional [—] well, unbalanced economic growth.

Now how does this apply to Senator Lott? Let me suggest that Senator Lott's words have to be put in an historical context and prioritized.

Yes, I'm deeply concerned about the words expressed by Senator Lott at Strom Thurmond's birthday party. But I'm even more concerned about the words he used to EXPLAIN them. He said he wasn't praising Senator Thurmond's past racial stance, but he liked his commitment to a "strong defense" and his "fiscal conservatism."

Before the Civil War the Democratic slave masters used to have anti-black conventions where they called us "out-our-names." But after the Civil War, when they had lost power and were trying to get it back, they knew they had to change their language. So instead of holding anti-black conventions, the same former Democratic slave masters had anti-taxpayer conventions - since they were being taxed to pay for the new freedmen's education, health care, and housing. They were known as fiscal conservatives, and they called the Radical Republicans of that day—who were supporting such programs—"tax and spend liberals." That's the origin of the phrase!

But what about the "defense" part that Senator Lott liked? Well, these fiscal conservatives aren't fiscally conservative when it comes to spending $400 billion annually on the military. They're not fiscally conservative when it comes [to] spending $200 billion or more to invade Iraq. They're not fiscally conservative when it comes to granting the top 1% of wealthy Americans the lion's share of a $1.35 trillion tax cut, and making it permanent, which will create record deficits as far as the eye can see.

They're only fiscally conservative when it comes [to] providing all Americans with high quality health care, providing all Americans with a high quality public education, providing all Americans with affordable housing, or providing all Americans with a clean environment.

So when these politicians get up and say they're fiscal conservatives, they're calling you "out-your-name" again . . . only this time it's by another, more clever name. So I'm more concerned about the EXPLANATION Senator Lott gave than I am about the original words that stirred all the controversy! . . .

Let's look at the party of "FAMILY VALUES!"

Trent Lott is the Republican Party's Monica Lewinsky—except worse.

Jesse, Jr., what do you mean? Worse!

Let me explain.

Monica Lewinsky reflected Bill Clinton's PRIVATE moral failure. Trent Lott reflects the Republican Party's POLITICAL moral failure. Both Monica Lewinsky and the issue now confronting Trent Lott and the Republican Party are moral issues. One involves personal morality and the other involves public morality.

The so-called party of "family values" said Monica Lewinsky was the NATURAL and INEVITABLE result of the Democratic Party's LIBERAL POLITICAL VALUES.

Trent Lott and the Republican Party of "personal morality" and "family values" is worse than Monica Lewinsky because, if the Democratic Party had known about Monica Lewinsky before the November elections of 1996—we would not have re-nominated Bill Clinton; and if the American people had known about it, they would not have re-elected him President! Bill Clinton's personal moral failure did not reflect the conservative, the moderate, or the liberal values of the Democratic Party—or the American people. Both would have rejected him as their leader.

On the other hand, all of this information about Trent Lott is coming out before he assumes the office of Senate Majority Leader in January, 2003. But the Republicans still want him to be their leader. All of the Republicans so far—President George W. Bush, House Speaker Dennis [Hastert], House Majority Leader Tom DeLay, all the Republicans in the House and Senate—have either said he should still be the Senate Majority Leader or they have remained silent.

You say, but the Democrats didn't impeach Bill Clinton! And that's right. Why? Because, as a matter of law, his personal moral failure did not reach the constitutional standard for impeachment, or conviction in an impeachment trial.

Trent Lott's predicament is not a constitutional matter. It's a matter of values, morality, and bipartisan politics. On June 28, 1984, Senator Don Nickles (R-OK) put together a bipartisan coalition of senators to condemn racially insensitive statements made by Minister Louis Farrakhan. Senator Nickles was joined by senators Carl Levin (D-MI), Orrin Hatch (R-UT), Jacob Chic Hecht (R-NV), Joseph Biden (D-DE), Frank Lautenberg (D-NJ), Jeremiah Denton (R-AL), John Chafee (R-RI), and Bill Bradley (D-NJ) as co-sponsors. Together, they got the U.S. Senate to vote 95-to-0 to rightfully condemn Minister Farrakhan's intemperate remarks.

What do we want? The Congressional Black Caucus wants Senator Nickles to treat Senator Lott like he treated Minister Farrakhan! We want Senator Nickles to put together a bipartisan coalition and formally censure Senator Lott for his intemperate words. We want equal treatment under the law! . . .

The people of Mississippi may be satisfied with Trent Lott—and that's fine. That's why he was elected. Trent Lott may reflect their interests and values—and that's OK. He may even reflect the values of the Republican Party!

But the United States Senate deserves better leadership than Trent Lott. The American people deserve a leader that reflects their highest values . . .

Source: Rep. Jesse Jackson Jr., "Trent Lott is the Republicans' Monica Lewinsky," December 14, 2002, www.jessejacksonjr.org/issues/i1214026434.html.

NOTES

1 *Congressional Record,* 51st Cong., 2d sess., February 14, 1891, 2694.

2 Mrs. J. E. Andrews, President, Women's National Association for the Preservation of the White Race, to George Fort Milton, Chairman, Southern Commission on Lynching, letter, November 15, 1931, from the Herbert Hoover Presidential Library, West Branch, Iowa, Presidential Papers, Box 106, Subject File: Colored Question, Correspondence, 1931—January–August.

3 Dennis S. Nordin, *The New Deal's Black Congressman* (Columbia: University of Missouri Press, 1997), 250.

4 Saul Friedman, "Diggs, Maddox Clash over 'Slur' in Dining Room," *Detroit Free Press,* February 25, 1970.

5 *Congressional Record,* 48th Cong., 2d sess., December 17, 1884, 297.

6 Ibid.

7 *Congressional Record,* 51st Cong., 2d sess., February 14, 1891, 2691.

8 "White House Has Negress as Tea Guest," *Tallahassee Daily Democrat,* Sunday, June 16, 1929, newspaper clipping from the Herbert Hoover Presidential Library, West Branch, Iowa, Presidential Papers, Box 106, Subject File: Colored Question, DePriest Incident Correspondence, 1929, June 16–20.

9 "Relating to Entertainment by Mrs. Hoover," *House Journal,* Forty-First Legislature, Second Called Session, Austin, Texas, Tuesday, June 18, 1929, from the Herbert Hoover Presidential Library, Presidential Papers, Box 106.

10 John L. Denson, M.D., to President Herbert Hoover, letter, June 19, 1929, from Herbert Hoover Presidential Library, Presidential Papers, Box 106.

11 "Representative Diggs at Till Trial Scene," *Michigan Chronicle,* September 24, 1955.

12 Carolyn P. DuBose, *The Untold Story of Charles Diggs* (Arlington, Va.: Barton Publishing House, 1998), 50.

13 "Illinois Suspends Death Penalty," CNN.com, January 31, 2000, http://archives.cnn.com/2000/US/01/31/illinois.executions.02/.

14 Office of Rep. Bobby L. Rush, "Rep. Rush Holds Congressional Hearing on Flawed Death Penalty System," news release, February 3, 2003, www.house.gov/list/press/il01_rush/pr_030203_deathpenalty.html.

15 United Methodist Church, General Board of Global Ministries, "Burned Methodist Churches: National Church Arson Registry, 1990–2000," http://gbgm-umc.org/advance/church-burnings/.

16 National Council of Churches USA., "NCC Matches Leona Helmsley's Promised $500,000 for Burned Churches," 1998 NCC News Archives, http://ncccusa.org/news/newsfour.html.

17 Elijah E. Cummings, "Ending Racial Profiling in America," *Baltimore Afro American Newspaper,* May 26, 2001, from www.house.gov/cummings/articles.

18 "Black Leaders Denounce White Senator's Racist Remarks," *Jet,* January 6, 2003.

19 Ibid.

20 Ana Radelat and Jon Frandsen, "Critics Reject Lott Apology," *Clarion-Ledger* (Jackson, Miss.), December 11, 2002.

CHAPTER TWELVE

African American Lawmakers Address War
Peace, War and Patriotism

The Civil War provided early exposure to the military for a number of African Americans who would go to Congress during and immediately after Reconstruction. Among them was Rep. Robert Smalls, R-S.C., who had been in combat with the Confederate navy, involuntarily, and then the Union navy, voluntarily (**Document 2.4**). Also on the Union side, Rep. Charles E. Nash, R-La., had enlisted as an army private and rose to sergeant major. Rep. John M. Langston, R-Va., had recruited black solders for regiments in Massachusetts and Ohio, and Sen. Hiram R. Revels, R-Miss., had done the same in Maryland and served as chaplain to a black regiment.

Military service in war and peace would continue as a hallmark. Rep. William L. Dawson, D-Ill., served as an infantry lieutenant overseas in World War I, and Sen. Edward W. Brooke III, R-Mass, was an infantry captain in Europe in World War II. Shaped in large part by their own experiences, other veterans including Reps. Louis Stokes, D-Ohio (Army); Ronald V. Dellums, D-Calif. (Marines); Charles B. Rangel, D-N.Y. (Army); and John Conyers Jr., D-Mich. (National Guard and Army) became some of Congress's most vocal proponents of peace. Dellums rose to chair the House Armed Services Committee—a panel he had had to fight to serve on (**Document 6.4**). The generation of Congressional Black Caucus members first elected in the 1990s and later also included veterans,

Soon after his election to Congress in 1970 as an anti-Vietnam War candidate, Rep. Ronald V. Dellums, D-Calif., a former Marine, convened high-profile hearings on war crimes. In 1973 Dellums won a seat on the House Armed Services Committee, which he later chaired. In 1991 Dellums and fifty-three other members of Congress unsuccessfully challenged President George H. W. Bush's power to launch the Persian Gulf War without congressional authorization.
Source: CQ Photo/Scott J. Ferrell

among them Reps. Lucien E. Blackwell, D-Pa. (Army); Sanford D. Bishop Jr., D-Ga. (Army); and Frank W. Ballance, D-N.C. (National Guard).

For Caucus members, a common theme from the Cold War and Vietnam eras to the war in Iraq and other recent conflicts has been the interrelationship between increased military spending and the reduced funds available for domestic programs and nonmilitary foreign assistance. In a 1969 floor speech that denounced war as the business of America, Rep. Shirley A. Chisholm, D-N.Y., pointed out that President Richard M. Nixon had announced his decision to build an antimissile defense system the same day that the Head Start program in Washington, D.C., was cut for financial reasons. Similarly, more than three years into the war in Iraq (**Document 12.10**), Rep. Major R. O. Owens, D-N.Y., noted that the United States already had spent more than $400 billion "on the quagmire in Iraq" but Congress had cut almost $3.5 billion from the 2007 budget for educational programs like No Child Left Behind.[1]

While advocating a strong national defense and endorsing the power of the United States to defend itself and its allies, Caucus members called for adequate weaponry, protective equipment and pay for U.S. troops and criticized waste and abuse in military spending. They also argued that the very structure of the federal government encouraged war and military spending; as one partial solution, some sponsored legislation to create a cabinet-level Department of Peace. In addition, they emphasized their belief that the U.S. government was blatantly disregarding human rights—and damaging the nation's reputation around the world—in its imprisonment and treatment, including torture, of suspected terrorists who were captured in Afghanistan, Iraq and elsewhere and denied access to U.S. courts and due process of law. That concern was by no means new: during his first term in Washington, when the Vietnam War was still underway, Dellums convened special hearings to investigate suspected war crimes committed by U.S. troops in Southeast Asia—a highly sensitive and politically unpopular topic that the leadership of his own party refused to tackle (**Document 12.3**).

Some Caucus members have drawn attention to the inequity of the military's racial and ethnic makeup in wartime, when blacks, other minorities and the poor have provided a disproportionately large proportion of the armed services. One controversial proposed solution to that imbalance was a revived draft for military or other national public service (**Document 12.9**). Racial injustices in the armed forces had been evident since the Civil War (**Document 2.7**), during Reconstruction (**Document 12.1**) through 1948, when President Harry S. Truman formally ordered desegregation of the military (**Document 5.8**), and beyond. In 1971 the Caucus held hearings into racism and repression in the military. Rep. William L. Clay Sr., D-Mo., later wrote of that inquiry: "After twenty-five years of 'official' military desegregation, too many of the nearly 300,000 black Americans in uniform—at home and abroad—were still subjected to overt and subtle manifestations of racism."[2] The Caucus turned over its findings to the Defense Department, which appointed a special task force to look into the situation.

In addition, these lawmakers emphasized that the First Amendment guarantees of free speech, freedom of the press and the right to petition the government to correct grievances are at the core of American values and individual rights—even in times of war. Thus during House Internal Security Committee hearings into student protests against the Vietnam War (**Document 12.2**), Rep. Stokes defended the students' right of dissent. Since the early 1970s, many African American representatives have sponsored unsuccessful legislation to allow conscientious objectors to earmark their federal taxes for nonmilitary purposes (**Document 12.6**).

When Congress quickly debated and passed antiterrorism legislation soon after the September 11, 2001, attacks on the World Trade Center and Pentagon, members of the Caucus took to the floor to warn against governmental intrusion into the personal rights and privacy of American citizens while, at the same time, calling for strong action against those responsible for the attacks (**Documents 12.7** and **12.8**).

When President George W. Bush announced in March 2003 that he intended to invade Iraq, numerous African American legislators contributed to the debate concerning the constitutional responsibilities of Congress. Later, in an October 2003 news conference, Congressional Black Caucus chairman Elijah E. Cummings, D-Md., and Caucus members Diane E. Watson, D-Calif., Maxine Waters, D-Calif. (speaking), Danny K. Davis, D-Ill. (obscured), Donna M. C. Christensen, D-V.I., Barbara Lee, D-Calif., Kendrick B. Meek, D-Fla., and Melvin L. Watt, D-N.C., expressed their opposition to the Bush administration's $87 billion supplemental spending request for activities in Iraq and Afghanistan.
Source: CQ Photo/Scott J. Ferrell

Caucus members have played critical roles in shaping national security policies and programs in the wake of those attacks on U.S. soil. While Republicans controlled Congress, for example, Rep. Bennie G. Thompson, D-Miss., was the senior Democrat on the House Homeland Security Committee. In that capacity, he cosponsored bipartisan legislation intended to impede access to ammonium nitrate fertilizer, a component of deadly improvised explosives, including those used in the 1995 bombing of the Murrah Federal Building in Oklahoma City. With the Democratic victory in the 2006 congressional elections, Thompson became chair of the committee—which had five other African American members at the start of 2007—and pushed quick House action to implement recommendations of the National Commission on Terrorist Attacks upon the United States—the 9-11 Commission. African American lawmakers had been actively involved in addressing antiterrorism issues decades before September 11, 2001, including the continuing problem of weak airline security systems that made hijacking possible (**Document 12.4**).

Legislation is not the only way to challenge war policies. African American members of Congress headed for the courthouse—although unsuccessfully—to seek judicial intervention to stop military involvement in Vietnam, Grenada and the 1990 Persian Gulf War (**Document 12.5**).

Document 12.1 in Context
"If He Were My Enemy, and I Desired to Inflict a Severe Punishment upon Him, I Would Send Him to West Point": Racial Bias in the Armed Forces

Racial bias in the armed forces has been an issue since the Civil War when black soldiers first joined the military in significant numbers, playing an important role in the Union victory (**Document 2.7**). Not until 1948 would the U.S. government officially outlaw segregation in the military, through President Harry S. Truman's executive order (**Document 5.8**), and it would take another six years before the last black-only unit was disbanded and soldiers of all races served side by side.

During the Spanish-American War, the New York *Independent* recounted the treatment of African American soldiers in the South:

> On arriving in Nashville, the black chaplain and his family were given plainly and forcefully to understand, as they entered the railroad dining-saloon, that they could not eat with the other officers of the regiment under a Southern sky. [A] United States commission could not make clean what the South pronounces unclean . . . A glorious dilemma that will be for the Cuban Negro, to usher him into the condition of the American Negro.[3]

During World War I, the *Christian Advocate* noted that the strong performance of black troops had drawn official notice in the reports of the enemy German commanders. The newspaper, published by the African Methodist Episcopal Church in the United States, discussed the bias that black soldiers still experienced in the army despite their professionalism in the face of war: "The racial discriminations which so largely prevail in civil life have reappeared in the camps, resulting in criticism and irritation on the part of 'race-conscious' Negroes who feel that the army should at least live up to the principles of human equality which are inscribed on its banners." [4]

The continuum of discrimination during the Spanish-American War, World War I and later conflicts was deeply rooted in past practices and policies. In 1880 Sen. Blanche K. Bruce, R-Miss., supported an investigation of why one of West Point's first African American cadets, Johnson Whittaker, had been court-martialed after three masked men slashed him with a razor in the barracks and why he had been expelled, even though his conviction was overturned on appeal. In the following floor speech on a resolution to require the secretary of war to report to the Senate about the incident, Bruce derides the West Point officials' theory that Whittaker had faked the attack and mutilated himself. In 1995, with the backing of Rep. James E. Clyburn, D-S.C., President Bill Clinton posthumously commissioned Whittaker as a second lieutenant, saying: "He was ostracized by his white peers. Few spoke to him except to issue orders and commands . . . Johnson Whittaker was a rare individual, a pathfinder—a man who, through courage, example and perseverance, paved the way for future generations of African American military leaders." [5]

▬ Document 12.1 ▬
Sen. Blanche K. Bruce, R-Miss., Condemns the Mutilation of a Black Cadet at West Point, April 9, 1880

Mr. BRUCE: . . . Now, a theory is being advanced that this young man has mutilated himself. If he did, the country ought to know it, and he should be promptly expelled from the institution. But it is asking entirely too much of me when I am called upon to believe that young [Cadet Johnson] Whittaker, or any other man under similar circumstances, would thus mutilate himself. To use a very significant cant phrase, this theory is entirely "too thin." We have for several days been engaged very industriously, and legitimately, I think, in an attempt to pass a bill that will more effectively civilize and Christianize the Indians. I think the Senate would do well if it would devote a little time to the civilization of West Point. For six or seven years scandalous stories have emanated from that institution relative to the treatment received by young men sent there, I know one instance in which a young man voluntarily abandoned the institution because he was unwilling to be subjected to the outrages that were obtained therein.

The Senator from Rhode Island [Mr. Ambrose E. BURNSIDE] says that West Point is not worse than other institutions. I hope it is not; but I fear that West Point has retrograded in some respects, in administration at least, since the Senator left it.

I once said to a young colored man who asked me for my influence to secure him an appointment to this institution, that if he were my enemy, and I desired to inflict a severe punishment upon him, I would send him to West Point. But in cases of this sort it makes no difference whether the cadet is white or colored, and I have not for a moment stopped to consider that phase of the question, and I am glad to see that the Senator from Indiana [Daniel W. VOORHEES] has not done so. We support this resolution upon higher grounds, and rest it upon considerations of humanity and the good order and efficiency necessary to the administration of this important public trust. The Senate ought to know all the facts in the case, and if any of the parties who belong to the corps of which this young man is a member, or if other persons not connected with the institution are the criminals, the country should know it, and the guilty parties should be promptly and adequately punished.

I do not propose to institute a comparison between this and other institutions of learning as to their methods of administration; I do not know that there are other institutions as vicious in the direction under discussion as West Point; but I do know that we are more directly connected with the control of this, a Government and national institution, than of any other of similar character in the country, and that public opinion holds us responsible for the conduct of its affairs. It is hard to conceive that such excesses as have sometimes occurred at West Point, in the matter of hazing and other irregularities and personal indignities, could happen in a military institute with its exact and stringent discipline, unless there was a vice somewhere in the methods of governing the institution, and I believe this investigation will have a healthy influence upon the officers charged with the administration and control of West Point.

Source: Congressional Record, 46th Cong., 2d sess., April 9, 1880, 2249.

Document 12.2 in Context
"Turmoil on the Nation's Campuses": Protests, Antiwar Dissent and Students for a Democratic Society

During the late 1960s and early 1970s, growing opposition to the Vietnam War and concern about social issues such as poverty and injustice sparked mass protests and demonstrations. The sometimes-violent reactions by authorities gave birth to new, occasionally radical, organizations. In May 1970 members of the Ohio National Guard shot at demonstrators at Kent State University during a protest against the U.S. invasion of Cambodia; four students died and nine were wounded. The same month, Mississippi state and local police fired on student protestors at Jackson State College, killing two and injuring twelve.

Students for a Democratic Society was one of the most prominent groups protesting the war in Southeast Asia and supporting civil rights and economic justice. In its 1962 manifesto, known as the Port Huron Statement, SDS advocated the creation of "a new left" that would work for change through universities rather than through political parties. The movement would rely on "younger people who matured in the postwar world" and "include liberals and socialists, the former for their relevance, the latter for their sense of thoroughgoing reforms in the system." The manifesto continued: "A new left must start controversy across the land, if national policies and national apathy are to be reversed. The ideal university is a community of controversy, within itself and in its effects on communities beyond." [6]

That philosophy—and SDS-organized demonstrations—provoked criticism, including charges that the organization was pro-communist, disloyal, unpatriotic and anti-American. In 1969 the House Internal Security Committee, formerly the House Un-American Activities Committee, held hearings into SDS activities at Georgetown, American and George Washington universities in Washington, D.C.; Kent State University in Ohio; and the University of Chicago.

One hearing focused on a March 1969 incident at Georgetown University, where demonstrators disrupted a scheduled lecture by San Francisco mayor Joseph Alioto. The university's academic vice president, Father Thomas R. Fitzgerald, told the committee in a letter how a "small delegation of hairy strangers" had kept the area "under surveillance" and how the corridor outside the auditorium "was fairly well filled with a rather hostile group of young men and women." [7] To escape the protestors, Alioto fled down a fire escape. A column in the student newspaper, the *Hoya,* accused SDS of having the "simple goal" of disruption and of being "antithetical to the goal of being a university." [8]

The committee chair, Rep. Richard H. Ichord II, D-Mo., explained in his opening remarks that the inquiry was looking into the extent to which SDS incited or used terrorism, violence and force to obstruct or oppose the government. Rep. Louis Stokes, D-Ohio, a committee member known for defending civil liberties, emphasized that only a few students had participated in the incident, and he challenged the premise that Congress should curb SDS and other groups' exercise of their constitutional rights to free expression and assembly. In questioning Fitzgerald, Stokes stressed that the young protestors had ample legitimate cause for concern about war, poverty and other challenges facing the nation. Excerpts from the hearing transcript follow.

The House abolished the Internal Security Committee in 1975. Back in 1939 the sole black member of Congress—Illinois Democrat Arthur W. Mitchell—was one of only twenty-one representatives who voted unsuccessfully to abolish its predecessor, the House Un-American Activities Committee.

<hr />

▓▓▓ Document 12.2 ▓▓▓
House Committee on Internal Security Hearings about Students for a Democratic Society, July 1969

The CHAIRMAN [Richard H. Ichord II, D-Mo.]: . . . According to the news media, much of the turmoil on the Nation's campuses has been attributed to Students for a Democratic Society. And within the last year this organization has been reported to have enlarged its field of endeavors to high schools, business, and industry. The reports indicate that while the organization often appears to seize upon some issues which could be legitimate subjects of advocacy or dissent, it also seems to espouse a tactical-militancy which readily disregards the rights of others and which is violative of democratic processes . . .

TESTIMONY OF REV. THOMAS R. FITZGERALD, S.J. . . .

Mr. [Louis] STOKES: . . . Father Fitzgerald, let me, for a point of clarification, check back with you regarding the number of students in your school. I understand you to say it is over 4,000.

Rev. FITZGERALD: All told we have about 7,500 students, but that includes the professional schools. There are a little over 4,000 undergraduates.

Mr. STOKES: Excluding the outsiders who participated in the Alioto incident, approximately how many students would you say participated in that fracas? . . .

Rev. FITZGERALD: I would expect that the number was less than 15 . . . But from what I have heard, the number of students inside the hall who were seriously disruptive was a small number.

Mr. STOKES: So we are talking about less than 15, from your information?

Rev. FITZGERALD: I think less than 15.

Mr. STOKES: Out of the 15, only 3 were charged with disciplinary action, were they not?

Rev. FITZGERALD: That is correct.

Mr. STOKES: And only one of the three was convicted. What is the total strength of SDS on your campus?

Rev. FITZGERALD: I think about 15.

Mr. STOKES: Then we are talking about something that is less than the minimal, really, aren't we, proportionately? . . .

. . . I serve on another congressional committee that has been inquiring into unrest on the campuses throughout the Nation this year. We have had the benefit of the testimony of Dr. [Samuel Ichiye] Hayakawa of San Francisco State. We had Dr. [Nathan M.] Pusey of Harvard. We had Dr. [Robbin Wright] Fleming of the University of Michigan. We had Mr. [John] Mitchell, the Attorney General of the United States. By and large and substantively, they say to us that the young people of this country are rather disaffected with the society in which they live. They tell us that they have three major concerns regarding that society. Those three concerns are: Number one, racism; number two, the war, which includes an inequitable Selective Service system; number three, poverty in the midst of plenty . . .

I have heard this afternoon in testimony before us certain of these same charges leveled towards Georgetown University. I would be interested in having your observations as to the validity of the concerns of these young people.

Rev. FITZGERALD: Let me begin by saying I think, looking at the national picture, there is some basis for their concerns. I don't accept much of the rhetoric which we hear, but I think we do live in an imperfect society . . .

I feel that personally I have not always been as aware of these problems as I should have been. In my few years on the university campus I have learned a great deal about this. I think that my learning process in microcosm is the learning process that my university is going through and that many universities are going through . . . But I think we should admit candidly that there is much to be improved and that we somehow must do considerably better than we have done in the past.

Frankly, I think we will lose the younger generation unless we are willing to go that far.

Mr. STOKES. I think we may have already lost large numbers of them, Father.

Let me ask you this: The same men whom I stated appeared before us in their effort to try and give Congress some idea where they should or should not take the legislative process have urged us to not be reactionary in this Congress, not to be repressive. They have, in effect, said to us that this is a matter that should largely be handled and controlled through our academic institution, through the institution of free learning. The Attorney General of the United States said to us that he already had enough laws on the books to deal adequately with these situations. He also said this, that, in his opinion, for Congress to enact such laws aimed at this kind of situation well might play into the hands of organizations such as SDS and might be exactly what they would want . . .

Rev. FITZGERALD. I think I am in basic agreement with that position . . .

At this date it is not clear to me that the Congress could take any specific action beyond the laws already on the books to assist in this matter . . .

Source: House Committee on Internal Security, *Investigation of Students for a Democratic Society: Part 1-A (Georgetown University),* 91st Cong., 1st sess., 1969, 2, 49–51.

Document 12.3 in Context
"We Have to Deal with the Racism, Militarism and Sexism in This Country and . . . Our Foreign Policies Abroad": Investigating War Crimes by U.S. Forces in Vietnam

As public opposition to U.S. military involvement in Vietnam grew in the late 1960s and early 1970s, so did the number of antiwar African American candidates elected to Congress. Among the most vocal was California Democrat and self-described radical Ronald V. Dellums, a Marine Corps veteran. Rep. William L. Clay Sr., D-Mo., would describe him as "the most outspoken opponent of U.S. intervention in the Indochina war."[9] In February 1971, the month after he took office, Dellums introduced a resolution calling for a full-scale House-Senate inquiry into possible war crimes in Southeast Asia; the next month, twenty-one cosponsors joined him in an identical resolution. The House's Democratic leadership had no interest in such a public inquiry, and the House Rules Committee failed to act on the resolution.

As a result, Dellums convened ad hoc hearings in April 1971 with the assistance of a group called the Citizens Commission of Inquiry on U.S. War Crimes in Vietnam. Among the panel members were Reps. Parren J. Mitchell, D-Md., and John Conyers Jr., D-Mich. A series of witnesses who had served in the U.S. armed forces in Vietnam testified about the atrocities they admitted participating in and witnessing, as well as about the policies they were trained and ordered to follow regarding the treatment of civilians and actual and suspected enemy combatants. Dellums pointed out when he wrote to Secretary of Defense Melvin R. Laird asking for "the generals, potential people who might be named in these hearings, to come forward," that none did.[10] Nor did other Nixon administration policymakers testify. On the final day of the hearings, Dellums renewed his call for a full congressional investigation of war crimes, and he criticized his colleagues' unwillingness to conduct official hearings:

[I came] to the United States Congress as an idealist, but at this moment [am] feeling very pessimistic about the plastic nature of the Congress . . . There are men who will vote to send young people into Southeast Asia to kill, by conscription, but they are too cowardly to sit before them to hear about the insanity that has been churning and drummed into the very young people that are conscripted into the Army.[11]

The ad hoc hearings were but one of a number of actions that Congressional Black Caucus members took in opposition to the war, including voting against Defense Department appropriations despite arguments by supporters of the war that cutting off funds would endanger the lives of U.S. troops. In 1973 Dellums won a spot on the House Armed Services Committee (**Document 6.4**), and eventually rose to chair it.

▬▬ Document 12.3 ▬▬
Dellums Committee Hearings on U.S. Military Policy and War Crimes in Vietnam, 1971

MR. [Ronald V.] DELLUMS [D-Calif.]: . . . This is the first open set of hearings on war atrocities in Indochina . . .

MR. [Parren J.] MITCHELL [D-Md.]: We have begun hearings today to investigate the military policy used in Vietnam which appears to us to foster war crimes. We are concerned with such schemes as free-fire zones, search and destroy missions, mass resettlement of peasantry and the so-called "body count mania."

Since the Department of Defense acknowledges the use of these tactics, we wish to illustrate graphically what happens when such tactics are translated into action. Vietnam has been the ultimate modern war of attrition where civilians die by the score for every combat soldier killed. Our interest here is the suspect military policy, not in uncovering war tallies, but it is likely that we shall hear testimony as repugnant to the national conscience as My Lai.

We do not do so to demean the military or to undermine the national confidence, but we must bring the nature of the Vietnam war home to the American people, for it is they in the final analysis who must reject and end it.

The men who testify before us, and I know some of them personally, display great courage, and we commend them. In order to speak about these atrocities they have discarded careers and jeopardized their future security. But they speak out of a deep moral conviction that demands respect.

This nation will be shocked by what it hears, but America will be better for having heard it . . .

MR. [John] CONYERS [Jr., D-Mich.]: . . . First of all, I want to emphasize that this Congress has displayed a complete lack of moral responsibility and legislative integrity in not having the courage to openly look at the actions that we are forced to do as an ad hoc committee through the failure of anyone to act on the Joint Resolution 409 or to have hearings under one of the several committees that this could have been done under the rules of the House . . .

STATEMENT OF NATHAN HALE
23, Spec. 5, 198th Brigade . . .

MR. HALE: My name is Nathan Hale.

I was an interrogator with Americal Division in Vietnam from December, '67 until December, '68.

Upon my arrival in Vietnam, I was assigned to the 1st Cavalry—it is an armored unit. When I arrived at the unit, I was told by my S-2 [intelligence officer] my job would be to elicit information from detainees. He also told me I could elicit information by any means possible. I personally have used boards, rifle butts, pistol-whipped people, just used sheer human brutality for information that my superiors wanted to hear.

I also have a series of slides, if you want to see them, of an operation I was on south of Danang with the Marine Corps. The name of the operation was Daring Endeavor. The date was October, 1968. On this operation two men were hanged by the national field police, and also people were tortured as illustrated in the slides. But during the whole time the Lieutenant Colonel was present at all times, either him or the company commanders . . .

STATEMENT OF MICHAEL J. UHL
First Lieutenant, Counter Intelligence officer . . .

MR. UHL: I am Michael Uhl from Babylon, Long Island. I have served with the 11th Brigade of the Americal Division, as the Military Intelligence Team Chief of the First Military Intelligence Team from November, 1968, until late April of 1969, at which time I was evacuated.

The primary mission of the Military Intelligence Team on the brigade level was to interrogate suspects, people suspected of being Viet Cong sympathizers, prisoners of war and also the collection of tactical and combat intelligence . . .

During my five months in Vietnam I witnessed many, many, many incidents of brutality, brutalization and torture of prisoners. Torture was a policy that existed when I got there, continued after I left . . .

STATEMENT OF DANIEL NOTLEY
E/6, 1/20 Battalion, 11th Brigade, Americal Division . . .

MR. NOTLEY: My name is Daniel Notley, and my home right now is St. Paul, Minnesota . . .

MR. CONYERS: Where did this massacre that you are reporting to us take place?

MR. NOTLEY: Truoung Khanh II hamlet, Quang Ngai Province.

MR. CONYERS: On or about April 18, 1969?

MR. NOTLEY: Yes.

MR. CONYERS: Approximately 30 people were killed?

MR. NOTLEY: That's right, women and children.

MR. CONYERS: Who was the highest ranking officer that you know had knowledge of this?

MR. NOTLEY: A lieutenant colonel. He must have known, he was in the village the next day. Unless he just couldn't smell. I mean, you could smell bodies from the napalm and unless he was absolutely stone blind—which I know he was not—there was no way he could have kept from knowing that. Everybody knew that in the battalion. Everybody . . .

STATEMENT OF DAVID BRESSEM
Warrant Officer, 1/9 Air Cavalry . . .

Mr. BRESSEM: I am a student at Springfield College in Springfield, Massachusetts.

I served in Vietnam from April of '67 until September '67. I was a helicopter pilot. I flew a gunship from Bravo 2, 1/9 Air Cavalry.

Bravo 2 is a reconnaissance unit, whose main function is to find the enemy, usually by making contact with them . . .

One rule was if we were to spot a suspect we had to call back for clearance in order to fire upon him. If we saw a man running across a field with a rifle and pack, or if we just suspected an individual, it was necessary to call back for clearance. However, if we were to call back for clearance, normally a man running across a field can dive into a ditch in a matter of seconds, so what we normally do, we always flew in teams of two aircraft and the higher aircraft would go ahead and call back for clearance, while the lower aircraft would go ahead and try to kill the individual.

And if we received clearance, then we would report it as a kill. If we did not receive clearance, we would just forget about it. This happened all of the time. We were working under these rules.

MR. DELLUMS: I am sorry, I am trying to follow that.

If your activity ended in the death of Vietnamese people and it was not cleared, then you—

MR. BRESSEM: We would not report it.

MR. DELLUMS: You would not report it?

MR. BRESSEM: See, in order to fire on an individual under the rules, we had to obtain clearance. If we did not obtain that clearance, you know, we were not permitted to kill.

MR. DELLUMS: And if you received the clearance, you reported it as a kill.

MR. BRESSEM: As a body count, yes.

MR. DELLUMS: But sometimes you killed and it wasn't cleared and you just didn't report it.

MR. BRESSEM: Right . . .

STATEMENT OF ELLIOTT L. MEYROWITZ
E/4, C/2/502, 1st Brigade, 101st Airborne Division . . .

MR. MEYROWITZ: While in Vietnam, operating north of Tuy Hue in the Two Corps area in August, September and November of 1966 I personally have committed the following crimes . . .

We have developed a country wherein violence has been the sole means and sole justification for doing anything, to such an extent that we have reduced all responsibility for our actions to some structure called the system, the establishment or the institutions involved . . .

MR. DELLUMS: . . . I think there are many conclusions that can be drawn, but I would like to allude to four tentative conclusions after sitting here for four days. It appears to me that it is the psychology of our involvement in Indochina to annihilate the Vietnamese people, whether South Vietnamese, Viet Cong, North Vietnamese, as subhuman beings, and the racism that is pervasive in this country is obviously pervasive in Southeast Asia. That Asian people are perceived as less than human, and therefore, there is no effort to make a real distinction between who is a civilian, and who is a combatant, who is a friend, and who is an enemy . . .

Secondly, it is my considered opinion that conventional warfare in a people's struggle such as our engagement in Southeast Asia, ends up in daily atrocities. People, old women and children thrown down wells and grenaded, for what military purpose? Innocent women and children shot down in a village, for what military purpose? Bombs dropped on innocent human beings, for what military purpose? . . .

Thirdly . . . if we are to assume any responsibility, then that responsibility in my estimation must be laid at the highest military level, civilian policy-making level.

But I think to stop there would be to stop extremely short of where I think this country has to go, and that is to a close examination of the institutional factors that give rise to our absurd involvement in Indochina . . .

We have to deal with the racism, militarism and sexism in this country and how that gets extended to our foreign policies abroad. It is not enough to lay blame on a given individual . . .

Source: Citizens Commission of Inquiry, ed., *The Dellums Committee Hearings on War Crimes in Vietnam: An Inquiry into Command Responsibility in Southeast Asia* (New York: Vintage Books, 1972), 5–7, 85, 91, 179, 197, 282–283, 325, 327, 333–335.

Document 12.4 in Context
"The Passengers Have Rights": Airline Security and Anti-Air Piracy Legislation

Long before al-Qaida operatives hijacked four commercial passenger jets on September 11, 2001, serious weaknesses in airline security were evident. In 1961 the first U.S. airplane was hijacked. During a six-month period in 1968–1969, authorities reported twenty-eight actual or attempted hijackings of U.S. aircraft.

In 1973 Congress debated legislation intended to tighten security and enable the United States to implement the 1970 Convention for the Suppression of Unlawful Seizure of Aircraft, an international treaty addressing air piracy and terrorism. Rep. Ralph H. Metcalfe, D-Ill., sat on the House Interstate and Foreign Commerce Committee's Subcommittee on Transportation and Aeronautics, which was studying the issue. During subcommittee hearings, Metcalfe questioned the sponsor of some of the legislation, Rep. Robert C. Eckhardt, D-Texas, who appeared as a witness. As the following excerpt from their colloquy illustrates, Metcalfe had concerns about existing and proposed security measures, including the arbitrary ways in which officials and airlines applied those measures, the limits of technology and the constitutional right of passengers to be free from unreasonable search and seizure under the Fourth Amendment.

Public concern about airline security was new, but Metcalfe's questioning foretold sensitive issues that would rise again in the decades leading up to and following the September 11 attacks—such as allegations of ethnic profiling against Muslims, even those who were U.S. citizens or legal residents; passenger privacy; and the high costs and inconveniences that security regulations impose on travelers, airlines, airport authorities, shippers and law enforcement agencies. For example, a 1987 General Accounting Office investigation found a wide variation across U.S. airports in the effectiveness of screening passengers for weapons. In 1989 Rep. Cardiss Collins, D-Ill., chaired a Government Operations subcommittee investigating aviation security. In 1990 the President's Commission on Aviation Security and Terrorism—created after the 1988 bombing of a Pan American World Airlines flight over Lockerbie, Scotland—found serious flaws in the aviation security system, vulnerabilities that the General Accounting Office again cited in a 1994 report. In the aftermath of the 2001 attacks (**Document 12.7**), at a time of raw national emotions, Congress and the Bush administration again wrestled with how to balance the interests of airline security, the costs and benefits of enhanced security measures, individual rights and the smooth operation of the air travel system. More than five years later, in January 2007, the General Accountability Office (formerly the General Accounting Office) found that improvements had been made but warned that the commercial aviation system remained a highly visible target for terrorists.

▬ Document 12.4 ▬
Rep. Ralph H. Metcalfe, D-Ill., Questions Rep. Robert C. Eckhardt, D-Texas, about Passenger Searches before the House Interstate and Foreign Commerce Committee's Subcommittee on Transportation and Aeronautics, February 27, 1973

. . .

Mr. METCALFE: In following your testimony it appears as though you are saying that there are guidelines for search and seizure. Am I right in that?

Mr. ECKHARDT: Yes, sir.

Mr. METCALFE: Now are these guidelines specifically defined? Have you seen them and do you know what they are?

Mr. ECKHARDT: There are guidelines in the court decisions interpreting the Fourth Amendment?

Mr. METCALFE: Let me get a little personal.

I travel frequently, as do all other Congressmen. Most of the time when I go through the gates, my bags are searched and I am not searched.

Then on occasion, I have to empty my pockets out and I usually carry a lot of change and I wonder how it is that I can go through sometimes and not have to empty my pockets out and I usually carry a substantial amount of keys, at least a couple of packages of keys but they are in leather cases, therefore I want to know whether or not there are specific guidelines.

I know that sometimes a policeman who may be accompanying me to the gate shows his identification and he is permitted to pass; his badge and his identification.

There are other occasions when they are asking him to check his side arms there at the check point which is against police regulations in the city of Chicago. That is the reason

I would like to know whether or not there are specific guidelines or isn't it in the discretion of the personnel?

Mr. ECKHARDT: I must say to my distinguished colleague from Illinois that I have had exactly the same experience and it seems rather difficult to ascertain from the experience what the guidelines are.

Mr. METCALFE: Do you not think, Congressman, that we ought to be specific because this is the sort of thing that I think irks some of the passengers—it has irked me—to have somebody go beyond whatever the guidelines are. I think they ought to specify what those guidelines are.

Am I really tripping the detector and they know who I am when I go through with my change in my pocket and with a couple of packages of keys in leather containers and they are not saying anything about it, or is that that they just can't detect that?

I have seen some individual go through and have to come back again and take off a pin and anything that has metal in it.

Mr. ECKHARDT: I certainly agree that there ought to be uniformity with respect to what is done in order to search a person and in order to permit him to fly.

The question though is just exactly where that uniformity should be established. It is my view that there should be a certain degree of flexibility with respect to the actual techniques of detecting weapons or explosives.

Indeed, I see no real reason why these methods should be totally disclosed in advance either by a written rule or by a statute.

For instance, after the recent hijacking from the Houston Airport in which a clerk for Eastern Airlines was killed, I had suggested that it was a very bad thing to put the metal-detecting device within only a few feet of the opening to the aircraft, because obviously the persons attempting to stop the man in that short area could be overrun, as they were in that case.

The man was armed. He was only a few feet from the aircraft. Even if there had been anyone to stop him, a shootout in that accordion fold area would have been just as bad as a shootout on the plane . . .

If there is a failure, it is a failure in uniform enforcement. I suggest that the way to avoid this failure of uniform enforcement is to place the general authority in the hands of a Federal police presence and I suggest the FBI.

Mr. METCALFE: I have no objection to that. I am concerned about the flexibility that you want to allow them.

I notice in most of the airports, you have to go through the screening, the detection point, way before you get to your gate—as a matter of fact, before you get to the first gate which everybody has to go through, which is something new and which I think is very highly desirable.

As far as giving them additional liberties, I think we need to have a review of that so that we will really know whether or not they are going beyond them.

The passengers have rights. I think thus far the airlines have had good cooperation from the passengers. They recognize it is for their own benefit. I would like to see it continued.

Sometimes if certain people who are assigned to make the inspection are overzealous, I don't think that helps the trade of that particular airline or the flying public . . .

Source: House Committee on Interstate and Foreign Commerce, *Anti-Hijacking Act of 1973: Hearings before the Subcommittee on Transportation and Aeronautics,* 93d Cong., 1st sess., 1973, 198–200.

Document 12.5 in Context
"Members of Congress Who Request an Injunction Directed to the President": Opposition to the 1991 Persian Gulf War

After Iraqi president Saddam Hussein invaded oil-rich Kuwait in August 1990, U.S. president George H. W. Bush significantly escalated the number of American troops stationed in Saudi Arabia and elsewhere in the Persian Gulf region. With war looming, Rep. Ronald V. Dellums, D-Calif., led fifty-three other legislators, including more than a dozen African American representatives, in filing a 1990 lawsuit challenging Bush's constitutional power to take the nation to war without congressional authorization. On January 12, 1991, only one member of the Congressional Black Caucus—Connecticut Republican Gary A. Franks—voted for a resolution authorizing the president to deploy troops against Iraq. Five days later, Operation Desert Storm began.

That was not the first time African American lawmakers had turned to the judicial system in an effort to block the start of, or force an end to, a war. For example, in 1971 Rep. Parren J. Mitchell, D-Md., and twelve other House members sued President Richard M. Nixon and the secretaries of state, defense, the army, the navy and the air force, alleging that the ongoing war in Indochina was illegal without either a declaration of war or explicit congressional authorization. A federal appeals court in Washington, D.C., upheld the lawmakers' right to sue—their legal standing—but ruled that the case involved a "political question" that falls outside the power of the judiciary under the Constitution. In a comment that presaged future debates over military appropriations for other wars, however, the appeals court wrote:

> This court cannot be unmindful of what every schoolboy knows: that in voting to appropriate money or to draft men a Congressman is not necessarily approving of the continuation of a war no matter how specifically the appropriation or draft act refers to that war. A Congressman wholly opposed to the war's commencement and continuation might vote for the military appropriations and for the draft measure because he was unwilling to abandon without support men already fighting. An honorable, decent, compassionate act of aiding those already in peril is no proof of consent to the actions that placed and continued them in that dangerous posture.[12]

Later, Rep. John Conyers Jr., D-Mich., and ten other members of Congress challenged the constitutionality of President Ronald Reagan's October 1983 military invasion of Grenada and sought an injunction requiring the immediate withdrawal of all U.S. troops. The administration had justified that operation as necessary to protect about 1,000 Americans in the Caribbean island nation after the assassination of its prime minister and the seizure of political power by the new Revolutionary Military Council. In June 1985 a federal appeals panel dismissed the case as moot, or stale, because U.S. combat forces had been withdrawn within two months after the invasion. Also, the Reagan administration had already announced plans to remove noncombat personnel, who were helping maintain order and train Grenadian police, by September 30, 1985.

In December 1990, U.S. District Judge Harold H. Greene refused to block President Bush's military actions in the Persian Gulf. Excerpts of his decision follow.

▬ Document 12.5 ▬
U.S. District Court Decision in *Dellums v. Bush*, December 13, 1990

This is a lawsuit by a number of members of Congress who request an injunction directed to the President of the United States to prevent him from initiating an offensive attack against Iraq without first securing a declaration of war or other explicit congressional authorization for such action . . .

I [BACKGROUND]

On August 2, 1990, Iraq invaded the neighboring country of Kuwait. President George Bush almost immediately sent United States military forces to the Persian Gulf area to deter Iraqi aggression and to preserve the integrity of Saudi Arabia. The United States, generally by presidential order and at times with congressional concurrence, also took other steps, including a blockade of Iraq, which were approved by the United Nations Security Council, and participated in by a great many other nations.

On November 8, 1990, President Bush announced a substantial increase in the Persian Gulf military deployment, raising the troop level significantly above the 230,000 then present in the area. At the same time, the President stated that the objective was to provide "an adequate offensive military option" should that be necessary to achieve such goals as the withdrawal of Iraqi forces from Kuwait . . .

The House of Representatives and the Senate have in various ways expressed their support for the President's past and present actions in the Persian Gulf. However, the Congress was not asked for, and it did not take, action pursuant to Article I, Section 8, Clause 11 of the Constitution "to declare war" on Iraq. On November 19, 1990, the congressional plaintiffs brought this action, which proceeds on the premise that the initiation of offensive United States military action is imminent, that such action would be unlawful in the absence of a declaration of war by the Congress, and that a war without concurrence by the Congress would deprive the congressional plaintiffs of the voice to which they are entitled under the Constitution . . .

II POLITICAL QUESTION

. . . The congressional power to declare war does not stand alone, however, but it is accompanied by powers granted to the President. Article II, Section 1, Clause 1 and Section 2 provide that "[t]he executive powers shall be vested in a President of the United States of America," and that "[t]he President shall be Commander in Chief of the Army and Navy . . ."

The question whether an offensive action taken by American armed forces constitutes an act of war (to be initiated by a declaration of war) or an "offensive military attack" (presumably undertaken by the President in his capacity as commander-in-chief) is not one of objective fact but involves an exercise of judgment based upon all the vagaries of foreign affairs and national security.

. . . If the Executive had the sole power to determine that any particular offensive military operation, no matter how vast, does not constitute war-making but only an offensive military attack, the congressional power to declare war will be at the mercy of a semantic decision by the Executive. Such an "interpretation" would evade the plain language of the Constitution, and it cannot stand . . .

While the Constitution grants to the political branches, and in particular to the Executive, responsibility for conducting the nation's foreign affairs, it does not follow that the judicial power is excluded from the resolution of cases merely because they may touch upon such affairs . . . In fact, courts are routinely deciding cases that touch upon or even have a substantial impact on foreign and defense policy . . .

The Court has no hesitation in concluding that an offensive entry into Iraq by several hundred thousand United States servicemen . . . could be described as a "war" within the meaning of Article I, Section 8, Clause 11, of the Constitution . . .

III STANDING

. . . Plaintiffs further claim that their interest guaranteed by the War Clause of the Constitution is in immediate danger of being harmed by military actions the President may take against Iraq . . .

The right asserted by the plaintiffs in this case is the right to vote for or against a declaration of war . . .

With close to 400,000 United States troops stationed in Saudi Arabia, with all troop rotation and leave provisions suspended, and with the President having acted vigorously on his own as well as through the Secretary of State to obtain from the United Nations Security Council a resolution authorizing the use of all available means to remove Iraqi forces from Kuwait, including the use of force, it is disingenuous for the Department to characterize plaintiffs' allegations as to the imminence of the threat of offensive military action for standing purposes as "remote and conjectural." . . . For these reasons, the Court concludes that the plaintiffs have adequately alleged a threat of injury in fact necessary to support standing . . .

V RIPENESS

. . . It has long been held that . . . the Judiciary will undertake to render decisions that compel action by the President or the Congress only if the dispute before the Court is truly ripe, in that all the factors necessary for a decision are present then and there . . . The principle that the courts shall be prudent in the exercise of their authority is never more compelling than when they are called upon to adjudicate on such sensitive issues as those trenching upon military and foreign affairs. Judicial restraint must, of course, be even further enhanced when the issue is one—as here—on which the other two branches may be deeply divided . . .

A. Actions by the Congress

No one knows the position of the Legislative Branch on the issue of war or peace with Iraq . . . It would be both premature and presumptuous for the Court to render a decision on the issue of whether a declaration of war is required at this time or in the near future when the Congress itself has provided no indication whether it deems such a declaration either necessary, on the one hand, or imprudent, on the other . . .

It would hardly do to have the Court, in effect, force a choice upon the Congress by a blunt injunctive decision, called for by only about ten percent of its membership, to the effect that, unless the rest of the Congress votes in favor of a declaration of war, the President, and the several hundred thousand troops he has dispatched to the Saudi Arabian desert, must be immobilized. Similarly, the President is entitled to be protected from an injunctive order respecting a declaration of war when there is no evidence that this is what the Legislative Branch as such—as distinguished from a fraction thereof—regards as a necessary prerequisite to military moves in the Arabian desert . . .

In short, unless the Congress as a whole, or by a majority, is heard from, the controversy here cannot be deemed ripe; it is only if the majority of the Congress seeks relief from an infringement on its constitutional war-declaration power that it may be entitled to receive it . . .

B. Actions Taken by the Executive

. . . Plaintiffs assert that the matter is currently ripe for judicial action because the President himself has stated that the present troop build-up is to provide an adequate offensive military option in the area . . .

The Department of Justice, on the other hand, points to statements of the President that the troops already in Saudi Arabia are a peacekeeping force to prove that the President might not initiate more offensive military actions . . .

Given the facts currently available to this Court, it would seem that as of now the Executive Branch has not shown a commitment to a definitive course of action sufficient to support ripeness . . .

Should the congressional ripeness issue . . . be resolved in favor of a finding of ripeness as a consequence of actions taken by the Congress as a whole, there will still be time enough to determine whether, in view of the conditions as they are found to exist at that time, the Executive is so clearly committed to early military operations amounting to "war" in the constitutional sense that the Court would be justified in concluding that the remainder of the test of ripeness has been met. And of course an injunction will be issued only if . . . the Court could find that the controversy is ripe for judicial decision. That situation does not, or at least not yet, prevail, and plaintiffs' request for a preliminary injunction will therefore not be granted . . .

Source: Dellums v. Bush, 752 F.Supp. 1141 (D.D.C. 1990).

Document 12.6 in Context
"To Affirm the Religious Freedom of Taxpayers Who Are Conscientiously Opposed to Participation in War": Peace Tax Proposals

The concept of war resisters and pacifists withholding their tax dollars from military spending in America dates back to colonial times. Since then, hundreds of citizens, predominantly Quakers, have been jailed or fined or have had their property seized for refusing to pay taxes as a matter of conscience. The most famous of them was the essayist Henry David Thoreau, who was imprisoned for refusing to pay a Massachusetts tax imposed to finance the Mexican-American War.

While the selective service laws recognize the right of conscientious objectors to perform alternative, nonmilitary service rather than being drafted into the armed forces, there is no parallel legal alternative for taxpayers. In the early 1970s, lawmakers began looking for a way to allow taxpayers who opposed the Vietnam War to fulfill their financial obligations to the government with the assurance that their money would not be spent to support the war effort. In April 1972 Rep. Ronald V. Dellums, D-Calif., introduced the first World Peace Tax Fund bill to create a legal mechanism for conscientious objectors to channel their income, gift and estate taxes for nonmilitary purposes only.

In the decades that followed, African American lawmakers continued to lead the push for such legislation. The following document, the Religious Freedom Peace Tax Fund Act, is the version introduced in October 1997, with Rep. John R. Lewis, D-Ga., as lead sponsor and a number of Congressional Black Caucus members among the cosponsors. The legislation tied together the concepts of religious freedom and conscientious objection to war and was designed to apply to spending for such agencies as the Defense Department, Central Intelligence Agency, Selective Service System, National Security Council and military-related expenditures of the Energy Department and National Aeronautics and Space Administration. In reintroducing the bill in 1999, Lewis, a Baptist minister, noted that seventeen percent of federal spending was dedicated to military purposes and said, "This military spending is inconsistent with the religious beliefs of hundreds and thousands of Americans. Because of their strong beliefs, these people would rather disobey their government than disobey their God or their beliefs."[13] Later, Lewis said the September 11, 2001, attacks on the World Trade Center and Pentagon (**Document 12.7**) should not restrict the rights of conscientious objectors, adding, "Look at the military budget. We have enough bombs, we have enough missiles, we have enough guns." [14]

Hearings took place on the legislation, but it never emerged from the House Ways and Means Committee.

━━ Document 12.6 ━━
Religious Freedom Peace Tax Fund Act, October 9, 1997

A BILL To affirm the religious freedom of taxpayers who are conscientiously opposed to participation in war, to provide that the income, estate, or gift tax payments of such taxpayers be used for nonmilitary purposes, to create the Religious Freedom Peace Tax Fund to receive such tax payments, to improve revenue collection, and for other purposes.

Be it enacted by the Senate and House of Representatives of the United States of America in Congress assembled,

SECTION 1. SHORT TITLE.
This Act may be cited as the "Religious Freedom Peace Tax Fund Act".

SEC. 2. FINDINGS.
Congress finds that—

(1) the framers of the United States Constitution, recognizing free exercise of religion as an unalienable right, secured its protection in the First Amendment of the Constitution; and Congress reaffirmed it in the Religious Freedom Restoration Act of 1993;
(2) taxpayers who are conscientious objectors recognize and affirm their civic and legal responsibilities to pay their full share of Federal taxes, and seek to do so without violation of their moral, ethical, or religious beliefs;

(3) for more than 25 years, these taxpayers have sought legal relief from either having their homes, automobiles, and other property seized, bank accounts attached, wages garnished, fines imposed, and threat of imprisonment for failure to pay, or violating their consciences;

(4) conscientious objection to participation in military service based upon moral, ethical, or religious beliefs is recognized in Federal law, with provision for alternative service; and

(5) the Joint Committee on Taxation in 1992 and 1994 has certified that a tax trust fund, providing for conscientious objector taxpayers to pay their full taxes for non-military purposes, would increase Federal revenues.

SEC. 3. DEFINITIONS.

(a) DESIGNATED CONSCIENTIOUS OBJECTOR.—For purposes of this Act, the term "designated conscientious objector" means a taxpayer who is opposed to participation in war in any form based upon the taxpayer's deeply held moral, ethical, or religious beliefs or training (within the meaning of the Military Selective Service Act (50 U.S.C. App. 450 et seq.)), and who has certified these beliefs in writing to the Secretary of the Treasury in such form and manner as the Secretary provides.

(b) MILITARY PURPOSE.—For purposes of this Act, the term 'military purpose' means any activity or program which any agency of the Government conducts, administers, or sponsors and which effects an augmentation of military forces or of defensive and offensive intelligence activities, or enhances the capability of any person or nation to wage war, including the appropriation of funds by the United States for—

(1) the Department of Defense;

(2) the Central Intelligence Agency;

(3) the National Security Council;

(4) the Selective Service System;

(5) activities of the Department of Energy that have a military purpose;

(6) activities of the National Aeronautics and Space Administration that have a military purpose;

(7) foreign military aid; and

(8) the training, supplying, or maintaining of military personnel, or the manufacture, construction, maintenance, or development of military weapons, installations, or strategies.

SEC. 4. RELIGIOUS FREEDOM PEACE TAX FUND.

(a) ESTABLISHMENT.—The Secretary of the Treasury shall establish an account in the Treasury of the United States to be known as the "Religious Freedom Peace Tax Fund", for the deposit of income, gift, and estate taxes paid by or on behalf of taxpayers who are designated conscientious objectors. The method of deposit shall be prescribed by the Secretary of the Treasury in a manner that minimizes the cost to the Treasury and does not impose an undue burden on such taxpayers.

(b) USE OF RELIGIOUS FREEDOM PEACE TAX FUND.—Funds in the Religious Freedom Peace Tax Fund shall be allocated annually to any appropriation not for a military purpose.

(c) REPORT.—The Secretary of the Treasury shall report to the Committees on Appropriations of the House of Representatives and the Senate each year on the total amount transferred into the Religious Freedom Peace Tax Fund during the preceding fiscal year and the purposes for which such amount was allocated in such preceding fiscal year. Such report shall be printed in the Congressional Record upon receipt by the Committees.

(c) SENSE OF CONGRESS.—It is the sense of Congress that any increase in revenue to the Treasury resulting from the creation of the Religious Freedom Peace Tax Fund shall be allocated in a manner consistent with the purposes of the Fund.

Source: Religious Freedom Peace Tax Fund Act, H.R. 2660, 105th Cong., 1st sess., October 9, 1997.

Document 12.7 in Context
"Though the Color of Our Skin and the Religions That We Preach May Differ, Americans . . . Stand United": Lawmakers Respond to the September 11, 2001, Attacks on the World Trade Center and Pentagon

On the morning of September 11, 2001, al-Qaida operatives galvanized the world by hijacking four commercial passenger jets, crashing two into the World Trade Center in New York City and a third into the Pentagon in Arlington, Virginia, just outside Washington, D.C. After passengers struggled with the hijackers, the fourth jet crashed in rural Pennsylvania. An estimated 3,000 people died in the attacks.

Many black lawmakers served on key committees that in the following weeks and months tried to bolster laws and policies to improve national security and combat terrorism while attempting to prevent the erosion of civil rights and civil liberties.

Many of the victims lived in districts represented by Congressional Black Caucus members from New York, New Jersey and Washington, D.C. During the House session immediately after the attacks, a number of black lawmakers spoke about not only the events of the moment but also the long-term implications for the nation. Their speeches expressed sympathy for victims and their families and admiration for the sacrifices made by police, firefighters, emergency medical technicians and other rescue workers; their themes included patriotism, national unity and a determination to bring the perpetrators to justice.

Even members from states far from the attack sites could tie the shocking events to their own districts. For example, Rep. Melvin L. Watt, D-N.C., took to the House floor to "pay special tribute to the family of Sandy Bradshaw," a constituent who was a flight attendant on United Airlines flight 93, which crashed in Pennsylvania.[15] Rep. Alcee L. Hastings, D-Fla., told about the call he had received from a constituent, whose nephew died at the World Trade Center: "I was stunned and had little that I could say to him. America changed . . . and it is changed for all time to come." [16]

Two days after the hijackings, Rep. Edolphus Towns, D-N.Y., warned about what he called a "disturbing element" in some Americans' reaction, describing religion-based hatred and violence in his district and elsewhere:

> A number of Sikhs have been attacked by ignorant people seeking to vent their anger at what happened. In New York, an old Sikh man was beaten with baseball bats . . . Sikh businesses have been stoned and cars have been burned. Apparently, these Sikhs were targeted because of their turbans and beards, which are required by their religion.

It would be grossly unfair to attack Muslims, although Mr. bin Laden, who appears to be the prime suspect, claims to be an adherent of the Muslim faith . . . Yet what makes these attacks even stranger is that Sikhs are not Muslims. They don't wear a turban the same way. Sikhism is an independent religion.[17]

Here are excerpts of speeches given on the House floor in the immediate aftermath of the attacks by Reps. Carrie P. Meek, D-Fla.; Sheila Jackson-Lee, D-Texas; Bobby L. Rush, D-Ill.; J. C. Watts Jr., R-Okla.; Alcee L. Hastings, D-Fla.; Eddie Bernice Johnson, D-Texas; Corrine Brown, D-Fla.; and Chaka Fattah, D-Pa.

▬ Document 12.7 ▬
African American Lawmakers Speak on the House Floor about the Attacks of September 11, 2001

Mrs. [Carrie P.] MEEK of Florida: . . . On December 7, 1941, I was a young student when I heard about the sneak attack on Pearl Harbor, the feelings I felt then, frustration and helplessness, sadness for those whose lives where cut short, and for their spouses, their children and their families, anger against those despicable persons who would inflict such unspeakable pain and suffering on so many innocent and helpless people.

Mr. Speaker, I feel today just as I felt after Pearl Harbor. But this country is changing, Mr. Speaker; and I feel personally bound, as all of my colleagues do, to take action and to stem the flow of violence in this country and around the world. I feel more determined than ever to protect our democratic ideals . . .

Ms. [Sheila] JACKSON-LEE of Texas:. Mr. Speaker, today we as Americans must reaffirm our allegiance to the United States of America, and as we stand here today, men and women all over this Nation are drawn to New York and drawn to Virginia and the Pentagon helping to recover, helping to discover and find our loved ones.

But we must resolve that this terrorism and this terrorist act will not undermine our constitution, will not undermine our resolve and will not undermine our faith . . .

We ask people of all faiths all over the world to take us to the level of weeding out these terrorists because we will not attack recklessly but we will attack with purpose . . .

Mr. [Bobby L.] RUSH [of Illinois]: . . . In spite of the ugliness of this tragedy, I witnessed the beauty of the American spirit rising Phoenix-like out of the ashes; beauty that was demonstrated by those who were attacked, those who rescued, and those who led; beauty that was demonstrated in the form of strength of character, unity in spirit, and a willing spirit.

I believe that today, because of our pain, America is stronger than it has ever been. God bless America.

Mr. [J. C.] WATTS [Jr.] of Oklahoma: . . . The tragedy that Americans experienced was a blemish on our Nation's history. It was a day that will be remembered by families in New York City and Washington, D.C., and every town throughout the country. Unlike momentous days of joy that we tell our children and grandchildren about, September 11, 2001, will be a day that we will recall for years to come with sadness and with sorrow.

Like Pearl Harbor and the Oklahoma City bombing in 1995, the surprise attack on the people and sites that run the country, our economy, our military and government will not be the final word. There can be no justice without peace, but there can be no peace without justice.

Over 6 years ago I stood on this floor and condemned the bombing of the Federal Building in Oklahoma City. Today, like 1995, we should remain strong. We should not succumb to fear. If we succumb to fear and paranoia, the terrorists have won. In this time of emergency and mourning, let us open our hearts to those that need our help . . .

Mr. Speaker, politics has taken a day off. Today Congress recognizes and remembers the afflicted and the sorrowing and those who came to the aid of their fellow man.

Mr. [Alcee L.] HASTINGS of Florida: . . . But we stand here today to say to the citizens of our Nation and the world at large, America is taller than the World Trade Center, bigger than the Pentagon, and mightier than any destructive device. America is an idea. This idea will never be extinguished by despicable acts of terrorism . . .

Today, we say to the rest of the world, though the color of our skin and the religions that we preach may differ, Americans throughout this great country stand united as one against anything that seeks to destroy the liberty and freedom we enjoy. When American liberty and freedom is threatened, we do not recoil but we rise up . . . This is our history, and it is our destiny.

Ms. EDDIE BERNICE JOHNSON of Texas: . . . Let it be known, that the United States Congress will stop at nothing, and at no time, to protect our citizens. Let it be known, that the United States of America will never, ever, cower to terrorists and never give up our way of life. Let it be known that Americans may disagree as Americans, but we are all one American family. Most importantly, let it be known that we will, we will, we will bring those responsible for the horrors of terrorism to complete justice. Our flags are at half-mast, but our heads are high as Americans.

Ms. [Corrine] BROWN of Florida: . . . This was a well-organized and thought-out attack and it demands a well-organized and powerful response. Members of these fanatical groups cannot go unpunished, nor will this nation support them. Those nations that give them shelter, weapons, support and training, we will deliver a swift and immediate response to this horrible act.

Congress and the Committee on Transportation and Infrastructure must take steps to implement new safety standards for air travel and, in fact, all modes of transportation. I have received numerous calls today from pilots saying that we have to absolutely secure the cockpits on our airplanes and that we need to put U.S. marshals on each and every plane again just as we did in the 1990s . . .

In closing, I want to make it clear, whether we are a Democrat, a Republican, male or female, black or white, we stand behind the Commander in Chief. War has been declared against the American people, and you are either with us or against us. There is no in between.

Mr. [Chaka] FATTAH [of Pennsylvania]: . . . We must act, not just speak. Action is our Nation's heavy burden tonight.

Let us beg[i]n first, care for the wounded, rescue any survivors, bury the dead, heal New York and begin to rebuild the Pentagon.

Second, think and work to prevent further immediate attacks on our people and infrastructure of all kinds.

Finally, determine who is responsible for these attacks and for past acts that have gone unpunished and make them pay their debt to this country. Avoid harm to innocent people but pursue justice for those who have lost their lives. We can do no less.

Source: Congressional Record, 107th Cong., 1st sess., September 11, 2001, H5499, H5501, H5502, H5519–H5520, H5531, H5542–H5543, H5562.

Document 12.8 in Context
"Any Legislative Action We Take Must Ensure That Our Traditions of Civil Liberty Continue to Stand Strong": Congress Enacts the USA PATRIOT Act

President George W. Bush and Congress reacted with legislative proposals almost immediately after the shock of the September 11, 2001, attacks (**Document 12.7**). "National security" and "homeland security" became the buzzwords in the swift legislative response to acts that the U.S. government labeled terrorism. The Uniting and Strengthening America by Providing Appropriate Tools Required to Intercept and Obstruct Terrorism (USA PATRIOT) Act of 2001 quickly emerged "to deter and punish terrorist acts in the United States and around the world" and "to enhance law enforcement investigatory tools." [18]

The sweeping measure included key provisions concerning domestic security, surveillance procedures, intelligence-gathering, international money laundering and financing of terrorism, bank secrecy, border security, protection of critical infrastructure and stronger criminal penalties. It also changed existing immigration, foreign intelligence surveillance and banking laws. Congress moved quickly on the legislation. The House and Senate initially passed different versions of the bill, with the House's more sensitive to individual rights, but the final version of the USA PATRIOT Act became law only a month and a half after the attacks.

While there was no dispute that the United States needed to respond to demonstrated weaknesses in national security, some members of the Congressional Black Caucus feared an overreaction that would jeopardize civil liberties and encourage action based on ethnicity and religion, especially discrimination against Muslims. These excerpts from the House debate reflect those fears.

Ultimately, the Senate passed the USA PATRIOT Act with only one dissenting vote, while the House passed it 357–66. The president signed it October 26, 2001. Some sections were later found to be unconstitutional infringements on civil liberties; in March 2006 Congress extended the law in modified form.

During her unsuccessful campaign for the Democratic presidential nomination in 2004, former senator and ambassador Carol Moseley-Braun, D-Ill., criticized the legislation at a debate in Baltimore:

> This administration has pandered to fear and frightened the American people at every turn. And the Patriot Act is just part of that. We would do a disservice to our people and our generation if we gave the next generation less liberty, less opportunity, less hope than we inherited from the last generation. [19]

Document 12.8
Congressional Black Caucus Members Engage in House Debate on the USA PATRIOT Act, October 12, 2001

Ms. [Sheila] JACKSON-LEE of Texas: . . . It is important that we say to the American people the truth, that we are in a crisis. But we can be in a crisis and be of sane mind of cautiousness and of balance. . .

Just a few days ago, the FBI called in a practicing physician from San Antonio of Muslim faith to come all the way across country and determine that he was not engaged in any activities. If we have this bill where there would be no opportunity for judicial review in that process, innocent persons would be involved . . .

This bill was called the PATRIOT Bill, and I want to remind my colleagues of what a patriot was in the early stages of this Nation. It was an individual who was willing to lay down his or her life so that the civil liberties and the Bill of Rights and the Constitution could be protected. It was people who ran away from a despotic government in order to seek freedom in the United States. Yes, there is terrorism; and might I say that there is sufficient terrorism that the Department of Justice saw fit to put a random Web site indicating that this Nation would face terrorist acts. I wonder whether that was put on to simply threaten the United States Congress into not doing its job, but rather to be frightened into passing an antiterrorist bill that really does not balance the rights of the American citizens along with the rest of the needs that we have . . .

Mr. [Bobby L.] RUSH [of Illinois]: . . . Mr. Speaker, I cannot forget the abuses of the fourth amendment by Federal agencies in the not so distant past.

Mr. Speaker, it is an indisputable fact that during the 1970s, the FBI kept information in its files covering the beliefs and activities of at least 1 in every 400 Americans. It is a fact that the FBI Director, J. Edgar Hoover, created the COINTEL program whereby they spied on and violated the constitutional rights of thousands of American citizens. It is a fact that during the 1960s, the U.S. Army created files on about 100,000 civilians. It is a fact that between 1953 and 1973, the CIA opened and photographed almost 250,000 first class letters within the United States, and from these photographs it created a database of over 1.5 million names.

Mr. Speaker, it is a fact that great Americans, such as Dr. Martin Luther King, Jr. were subjected to illegal and frivolous wiretaps by the FBI. And, Mr. Speaker, it is a fact that amongst the most absurd Federal wiretaps have been those extended to Members of Congress.

Mr. Speaker, temporary or not, this is very dangerous ground that we are treading on; and without a balanced, open and fair process, I feel that we may not be living up to the promise that all Americans have made to preserve the things which make America great. I fear that we may be returning to the dark days of McCarthyism and Hooverism . . .

Ms. [Maxine] WATERS [of California]: . . . The bill before us today is a faulty and irresponsible piece of legislation that undermines our civil liberties and disregards the Constitution of the United States of America.

This bill takes advantage of the trust that we have placed in this administration. Our law enforcement and intelligence community have all of the laws and all of the money that they need to do their job. Mr. Speaker, they failed us; and now this Attorney General is using this unfortunate situation to extract extraordinary powers to be used beyond dealing with terrorism, laws that he will place into the regular criminal justice system.

The question to be answered today is can we have good intelligence and investigations and maintain our civil liberties? This bill says no. I say yes. Let us not give away our privacy. Let us not undermine our constitutional rights . . .

Mrs. [Donna M. C.] CHRISTENSEN [of the Virgin Islands]: . . . I remember hearing someone say shortly after September 11th in response to something I cannot remember now, that the first casualty of this war must not be the U.S. Constitution.

Well it wasn't the first, but if this bill is passed, it will perhaps be the most devastating one, certainly the most far-reaching one, one that will not honor those whose lives were lost in the terrorist attack, and one that all of us in this body—those who voted for it and those who did not—will rue to our dying day.

This will be the crowning glory and the golden key of all of the most extreme radical conservatives in this country. With the right to wiretap, with the right to hold without due process, with the right to even punish dissent, the very worst of infringements on the civil liberties that we have worked so hard to extend to all and protect and preserve, will reign, and threaten not just the terrorists, but all Americans.

When I think of all our forefathers fought for to create this independent Nation, with freedom and justice for all; when I think of the struggle to end slavery, to win the right to vote and to ensure that all Americans fully participate in this society, and all the lives that were given in these efforts, it makes me sick to think that today we might pass this travesty of justice and freedom and fairness, and in doing so undermine the government of checks and balances that they in their wisdom constructed, relinquish our responsibilities in this body, and dishonor their memory and their legacy . . .

Ms. [Carolyn Cheeks] KILPATRICK [of Michigan]: . . . While the current circumstances require expedited action, we must also be deliberate and circumspect in our action. I know these aims run counter to one another, but at this juncture in our history it is critical that we think before we act. The attacks on our nation have changed us forever causing strong demands for action to improve our security. Our response to terrorism, however, must not thwart the very democratic values that this nation was founded upon.

Any legislative action we take must ensure that our traditions of civil liberty continue to stand strong—anything less would serve the goals of those who attacked us.

Unfortunately, we are now poised to consider a measure that grants our federal government broad sweeping powers to investigate not only terrorism, but all crimes. We are now poised to consider legislation that may jeopardize the civil liberties that we hold dear . . .

We must not repeat the mistakes of our past. We must not revert to the age of McCarthyism when accusation and innuendo operated with the force of law. I am concerned that those who support today's process and the measure before us today have not learned the lessons of history well enough . . .

I am particularly concerned about those who suggest that our current situation justifies the practice of racial profiling or search and seizure procedures without clear standards that are subject to thorough review of our nation's judges. As an African American, I know all too well the ills of racial profiling. The President has proclaimed that our war on terrorism is not a war on Islam. He has proclaimed that our nation takes pride in its diversity, which is strengthened by our brothers and sisters of the Islamic faith. I suggest that if our policy is to focus our heightened investigative efforts solely on those who look Middle Eastern, or foreign, then we dishonor the President's noble proclamations . . . Our outcry and efforts against foreign terrorism should be just as zealous against domestic terrorism. Our outcry against the Osama bin Ladens of the world should be just as strong against the Timothy McVeighs . . .

Source: Congressional Record, 107th Cong., 1st sess., October 12, 2001, H6710–H6711, H6716–H6717, H6762–H6763, H6769–H6770, H6771.

Document 12.9 in Context
"The Disproportionate Burden of Service on the Poor Is Dramatic": The Controversy over Reviving the Draft

The United States had a military draft during the Civil War (**Document 2.6**), World Wars I and II, and from 1948 to 1973; currently, all male citizens aged 18–25 must register with the Selective Service System. When Rep. Charles B. Rangel, D-N.Y.—a high school dropout who won a Purple Heart and Bronze Star in the army during the Korean War—proposed in December 2002 that the United States revive the draft for all men and women between the ages of 18 and 26, the idea enlisted few congressional allies but did set off a national debate. Explaining his position, Rangel wrote:

> I believe that if those calling for war knew that their children were likely to be required to serve—and to be placed in harm's way—there would be more caution and a greater willingness to work with the international community in dealing with Iraq. A renewed draft will help bring a greater appreciation of the consequences of decisions to go to war.[20]

Rangel contended that such a requirement, with an alternative for civilian service, would bring the realities of war home to Americans. The military component of his proposed Universal National Service Act drew the most attention, but the measure would have provided two options to fill the two-year requirement: "(1) as a member of an active or reserve component of the uniformed services; or (2) in a civilian capacity that, as determined by the President, promotes the national defense, including national or community service and homeland security." [21] It eventually drew more than a dozen cosponsors—including Reps. Sheila Jackson-Lee, D-Texas; Corrine Brown, D-Fla.; Elijah E. Cummings, D-Md.; and Jesse L. Jackson Jr., D-Ill.

A month before the 2004 presidential election, Republican opponents used parliamentary rules to force a House floor debate and vote, despite the sponsors' objections and without committee hearings. Rep. Robert ("Robin") Hayes, R-N.C., belittled the bill as "an incredible insult to the men and women who wear the uniform." [22] Rep. Major R. O. Owens, D-N.Y., retorted, "It is insulting and disgusting for the Republican Majority to make a joke of serious war and peace policy by bringing draft legislation to the floor as a frivolous matter, as a joke." [23] The bill lost with a vote of 402–2.

In February 2006 Rangel revised the proposal to apply to all men and women between the ages of 18 and 42. The higher age limit, he explained, was because the army had raised its top age for volunteers to 42.

Rangel revived the issue after the Democrats won control of the House in the November 2006 elections, declaring on CBS News's *Face the Nation* that President George W. Bush would not have invaded Iraq if the United States had a draft that put children of members of the administration and Congress "in harm's way." [24] He expanded on his position in the postelection statement that follows.

There was again widespread criticism. For example, in a column distributed by the National Newspaper Publishers Association, the president of the National Black Chamber of Commerce attacked what he called the "nouveau draft" idea: "America, please wake up to this scheme and call it what it is: A plain old evil and despicable draft that is no better than the previous one . . . There are no merits." [25] The *Philadelphia Inquirer* editorialized that "Rangel didn't expect an actual vote on his plan. He was more interested in making his tiresome—and dubious—rhetorical point that Iraq is a rich man's war but a poor man's fight." [26] In reality, the editorial continued, low-income and minority soldiers did not account for a disproportionately high share of casualties in the war in Iraq, unlike during the Vietnam War.

▭ Document 12.9 ▭
Rep. Charles B. Rangel, D-N.Y., Justifies Resumption of the Military Draft, November 21, 2006

WASHINGTON—The question of whether we need a universal military draft will be important as long as this country is placing thousands of young men and women in harm's way in Iraq. As long as Americans are being shipped off to war, then everyone should be vulnerable, not just those who, because of economic circumstances, are attracted by lucrative enlistment bonuses and educational incentives.

Even before the first bomb was dropped, before the first American casualty, I have opposed the war in Iraq. I continue to believe that decision-makers would never have supported the invasion if more of them had family members in line for deployment.

Those who do the fighting have no choice; when the flag goes up, they salute and follow orders. So far, more than 2,800 have died and 21,000 wounded. They are our unrecognized American heroes.

The great majority of people bearing arms for this country in Iraq are from the poorer communities in our inner cities and rural areas, places where enlistment bonuses up to $40,000 and thousands in educational benefits are very attractive. For people who have college as an option, those incentives—at the risk to one's life—don't mean a thing.

In New York City, the disproportionate burden of service on the poor is dramatic. In 2004, 70 percent of the volunteers in the city were Black or Hispanic, recruited from lower income communities such as the South Bronx, East New York, and Long Island City.

The Bush Administration, the Pentagon, and some Republicans in Congress are considering deploying up to 20,000 more troops to Iraq, above the 141,000 already on the ground. Among the planners are Army General John Abizaid, head of the U.S. Central Command, who has admitted the difficulty of finding additional combat troops for the war without expanding the size of the active duty military.

If Abizaid is right, increasing troop strength will mean dipping further into the reserves and national guard units which are already carrying an unfair burden of multiple deployments. The over-stretched active duty Army is filling the ranks in Iraq with stop loss orders, and extended deployments, and even recalls of the Individual Ready Reserves, active duty veterans who have time remaining on the military obligations.

These facts lead me to ask anyone who supports the war how can they not support the military draft when the growing burden on our uniformed troops is obvious, and the unfairness and absence of shared sacrifice in the population cannot be challenged.

If this war is the threat to our national security that the Bush Administration insists it is, then the President should issue a call for all Americans to sacrifice for the nation's defense. If there must be a sacrifice, then the burden must be shared fairly.

That is why I intend to reintroduce legislation to reinstate the military draft, making men and women up to age 42 eligible for service, with no exemptions beyond health or reasons of conscience. I believe it is immoral for those who insist on continuing the conflict in Iraq, and placing war on the table in Iran and North Korea to do so only at the risk of other people's children.

Source: Charles B. Rangel, "Reinstate the Draft: It's a Matter of Fairness," news release, November 21, 2006.

Document 12.10 in Context
"Whether or Not This Congress Has the Sole Responsibility to Declare War": Congressional Black Caucus Members Oppose the War in Iraq

African Americans in Congress strongly opposed President George W. Bush's policies toward Iraq, just as they had his father's invasion of the same country in 1991's Operation Desert Storm (**Document 12.5**). For example, they voted against an October 2002 resolution authorizing the president to combat terrorism and seek enforcement of United Nations Security Council resolutions regarding Iraq. In March 2003 Bush announced that the United States would invade Iraq because Iraqi president Saddam Hussein allegedly possessed weapons of mass destruction and had ties with the perpetrators of the September 11, 2001, attacks on the Pentagon and World Trade Center (**Document 12.7**). The president insisted that he did not need a formal declaration of war from Congress to launch the operation. In response, several members of the Congressional Black Caucus took to the House floor, under the leadership of John Conyers Jr., D-Mich., to debate the constitutional responsibilities of Congress under such circumstances. The following excerpts come from speeches by Reps. Danny K. Davis, D-Ill., Major R. O. Owens, D-N.Y., and Sheila Jackson-Lee, D-Texas (also see **Document 10.10**).

As the war in Iraq continued, Caucus members vociferously attacked the administration's policies and practices. Their major concerns included the detention and abuse of prisoners in military custody; the increasingly sectarian and civil war–like nature of the conflict among Iraq's Sunni Arabs, Shiite Arabs and Kurds; inadequate weaponry and protective equipment for U.S. troops; the limited burden carried by allied nations in what the president had characterized as a "coalition of the willing"; rising U.S. military and Iraqi civilian casualties;

and the escalating economic cost of the war that was increasing the U.S. budget deficit and diverting resources from other domestic and international priorities.

Critics of the war in Iraq differentiated between their opposition to the war and military policies and their support for U.S. troops serving there, as they had during the Vietnam War and other conflicts. In a radio address on the third anniversary of the U.S. military engagement in Iraq, Rep. Elijah E. Cummings, D-Md., recalled how the Caucus had opposed the war from the start, saying, "Tragically, all that we foresaw three years ago has come to pass. Yet, even as we challenged the wisdom of this war, we have also supported the brave Americans who have fought with such valor and skill." [27]

Opposition to the war extended beyond direct issues of the economics of the war and the withdrawal of U.S. troops. For example, Rep. Charles B. Rangel, D-N.Y., introduced a resolution in May 2004 to impeach Secretary of Defense Donald Rumsfeld for overseeing the "preemptive invasion and occupation of Iraq," asserting that Rumsfeld had done so under false premises, had failed to adequately protect U.S. troops and had misled Congress.[28] In April 2006 Rep. Harold E. Ford Jr., D-Tenn., called on Rumsfeld to resign and urged Bush to appoint former secretary of state Colin Powell as his replacement; Powell had left Bush's cabinet in large part because he disagreed with the president's Iraq policy. Rumsfeld did resign several months later, immediately after Republicans lost control of Congress in the November 2006 election, but he was replaced by Condoleezza Rice, the president's national security adviser, who also vigorously defended the war effort.

▬ Document 12.10 ▬
Members of the Congressional Black Caucus Participate in the House Debates on U.S. Military Intervention in Iraq, March 19, 2003

Mr. [Danny K.] DAVIS of Illinois: . . . The Constitution places the power to declare war squarely and solely in the Congress. This issue arises far above partisan politics . . .

As the American people are attempting to make sense of this complex situation, it is the duty of the Congress to ask some hard questions. One, is there an immediate threat to the United States? In my judgment, the answer is no. We have not received evidence of immediate danger. We have not received evidence that Iraq has the means to attack the United States, and we have not received evidence that the danger is greater today than it was last year.

Will the use of military force against Iraq reduce or prevent the spread or use of weapons of mass destruction? All evidence is that Iraq does not possess nuclear weapons today. The use of chemical or biological weapons or the passage of such weapons to terrorist groups would be nothing less than suicide for the current Iraqi leadership . . .

Mr. [Major R. O.] OWENS [of New York]: . . . War is hell. War is hell. The question is, Do we have to plunge into hell in order to accomplish what we are seeking to accomplish? . . .

Saddam Hussein, I have no case to make for. The man finances suicide bombers in Palestine. The big question is why? Why did we let him continue to sell oil all over the world so that he could finance suicide bombers in Palestine and continue building his arms industry? Where does he get the money from to continue to build up his arms industry? We talk about weapons of mass destruction. He has a big army. He has a big army with conventional weapons. The money to buy those weapons and to keep that army going has continued to flow, despite the fact that we have sanctions imposed on Iraq. Why did we not enforce the sanctions? What oil barons did we bow to to let them make a profit by not enforcing the sanctions? Why did we not, if France was trafficking in oil and Russia was trafficking, why did we not come down on our partners and really make the sanctions stick? They have never stuck. He has continued to get money, as much as he wants, to do what he wants to do.

People say, well, we are responsible for a lot of deaths of children in Iraq. No. That is ridiculous. He has the money. He does not spend it for the nutrition of children; he does not spend it for medicine. He spends it on building up his weapons and his power, and we let him do it. Why do we have to go all the way to a war, mobilizing 300,000 American troops, when we did not bother to do what we could have done on the seas? We control the sea lanes. We could have stopped the oil from being sold and transmitted all over the world, but we did not . . .

Our armed services and our military might can be put to good use. I like to think of myself as a follower of Martin Luther King. But I am not a pacifist in the sense that I think military force is necessary. There are times that military force is necessary. Thank God we have force. Our professional soldiers are the best in the world. My brother was a sergeant major in the Army for 20, 26 years. We have a very professional group of people now that run the military, and they are determined to do a good job for our Nation. We cannot fault them for the decisions that were made.

The problem is at the top; and the White House and the decision-making here in Washington, it is all wrong and dangerously off course. We are at a pivotal moment in American history, and instead of going one way with our military might and our wealth and our power, and our influence, most people in the world love us. I do not believe Americans are hated by ordinary people anywhere in large numbers . . .

Ms. [Sheila] JACKSON-LEE [of Texas]: . . . It is appropriate that we are on the floor, because we are filling in the gap of really what the Congress should be doing at this moment; that is, a somber, decided, and deliberative debate on the constitutional question of whether or not this Congress will declare war against Iraq.

Through the course of our interaction, we have pressed the issue of not whether one is for or against this war, but whether or not this Congress has the sole responsibility to declare war.

Frankly, Mr. Speaker, and, frankly, with respect to this debate, I do not believe we should be silenced on this issue. I will tell the gentleman why; because even as America is hovering and preparing for the worst, the Constitution is being shredded. It is being ignored, and it is being taken lightly, because it is clear that the Founding Fathers wrote this document to respect the three branches of government, to recognize that we are strong as a democracy if those three branches are interrelated.

The Constitution does enunciate that the President, whoever that is, is the Commander in Chief and can deploy troops. Many will suggest that a resolution debated in October 2002, satisfied the question. It did not, because it gave more power to the President than has ever been given to any President in the United States, Democratic or Republican, meaning that actions might be able to be perpetrated without coming back to the United States Congress.

Clearly, it is well known that if the Congress does not use its power, it does not give up its power. So going back to the Constitution, whether or not it takes us 6 hours or 24 hours, it is clear that this body could debate that question. It is not, as I said, a question of winning or losing, it is a question of the sanctity of process. A President cannot singly and should not singly take the Nation into war . . .

I am not asking the President to give up everything and to suggest that Saddam Hussein should be given flowers, but I am saying that war should be the last option. I believe there will be a third option . . .

But we have options, and we will be discussing this in the context of reaching out: One, convene an international tribunal, war crimes tribunal, with the United Nations Security Council and indict Saddam Hussein and his party leaders, and try him for war crimes; two, leave 50,000 troops on the border and bring home at least 200,000 of our young men and women; a vigorous, strong 50,000-person coalition, troops that are in a coalition, vigorously allowing the U.N. inspections to go forward; humanitarian aid now. Reinvigorate the Mideast peace process, fight the war against terrorism, and restore the coalition. These are key elements that could be done.

I believe, Mr. Speaker, that we can do something more than stand in silence. Frightening, deadening silence is appalling for this body that had the likes of the great leaders that we have known that have gone on before us . . .

Source: Congressional Record, 108th Cong., 1st sess., March 19, 2003, H2120–H2123.

NOTES

1 Congressional Black Caucus, "U.S. Representative Major Owens to Deliver Weekly CBC 'Message to America,' " press release, August 11, 2006.

2 William L. Clay, *Just Permanent Interests: Black Americans in Congress, 1870–1991* (New York: Amistad Press, 1992), 235.

3 "A Negro Chaplain on Jim Crow, 1898" (*The Independent,* April 28, 1898), in *A Documentary History of the Negro People in the United States,* ed. Herbert Aptheker (New York: Citadel Press, 1969), 822–823.

4 "The Negro Soldier," *Christian Advocate* 93 (September 12, 1918): 1146–1147.

5 White House, Office of the Press Secretary, "Remarks by the President at Johnson Chestnut Whittaker Commissioning," July 24, 1995.

6 Kathlyn Gay and Martin K. Gay, *Encyclopedia of Political Anarchy* (Santa Barbara, Calif.: ABC-CLIO, 1999), 152–153.

7 Thomas R. Fitzgerald to House Committee on Internal Security, letter, June 3, 1969, in House Committee on Internal Security, *Investigation of Students for a Democratic Society: Part 1-A (Georgetown University),* 91st Cong., 1st sess., 1969, 151.

8 Don Casper, "The SDS Cancer," *Hoya,* March 20, 1969, in House Committee on Internal Security, *Investigation of Students for a Democratic Society,* 250.

9 William L. Clay, *Just Permanent Interests,* 118.

10 Citizens Commission of Inquiry, ed., *The Dellums Committee Hearings on War Crimes in Vietnam: An Inquiry into Command Responsibility in Southeast Asia* (New York: Vintage Books, 1972), 332.

11 Ibid.

12 *Mitchell v. Laird,* 488 F. 2d 611 (D.C. Cir. 1973).

13 *Congressional Record,* 106th Cong., 1st sess., April 15, 1999, E679.

14 Felicia R. Lee, "War Resisters: 'We Won't Go' to 'We Won't Pay,' " *New York Times,* August 3, 2002, B7.

15 *Congressional Record,* 107th Cong., 1st sess., September 11, 2001, H5519.

16 Ibid., H5531.

17 *Congressional Record,* 107th Cong., 1st sess., September 13, 2001, E1644.

18 *Uniting and Strengthening America by Providing Appropriate Tools Required to Intercept and Obstruct Terrorism (USA PATRIOT Act) Act of 2001,* Public Law 107-56, 115 STAT. 272 (2001).

19 "Moseley-Braun and Sharpton Take Spotlight at Black Caucus' Presidential Debate," *Jet,* September 29, 2003, 4.

20 Charles B. Rangel, "Bring Back the Draft," *New York Times,* December 31, 2002.

21 *Universal National Service Act of 2003,* H.R. 163, 108th Cong., 1st sess., January 7, 2003.

22 *Congressional Record,* 108th Cong., 2d sess., October 5, 2004, H8122.

23 Ibid.

24 John Heilprin, "Congressman Rangel Will Seek to Reinstate Draft," Associated Press, November 19, 2006.

25 Harry C. Alford, "A Drafty Draft Proposal," *Chicago Defender,* December 1, 2006.

26 "U.S. Military Makeup Is Representative and Fair," *Philadelphia Inquirer,* November 27, 2006.

27 Congressional Black Caucus, "U.S. Congressman Elijah Cummings to Deliver Weekly CBC 'Message to America,' " press release, March 17, 2006.

28 *Impeaching Donald Rumsfeld, Secretary of Defense,* H. Res. 629, 108th Cong., 2d sess., May 6, 2004.

CHAPTER THIRTEEN

African American Lawmakers and International Affairs
America as a World Power

Like many of their white colleagues, African Americans in Congress paid little attention to foreign affairs during Reconstruction and the post-Reconstruction era. Instead, they focused their attention inward, toward problems within the borders of the United States. In the nineteenth century, their legislative efforts mainly addressed civil rights, public projects within their districts and individual constituent problems like pensions. Although African American members did not sit on foreign relations committees during the nineteenth century, Rep. Josiah T. Walls, R-Fla., did speak on Cuban independence from colonial Spain (**Document 13.1**), and Rep. George H. White, R-N.C., backed U.S. expansionism after the Spanish-American War (**Document 13.2**).

Again like many of their white colleagues of those times, most black members came to Congress with little or no personal experience abroad. The most notable exception was Rep. John M. Langston, R-Va., who had served as President Rutherford B. Hayes's appointed minister and consul general in Haiti and chargé d'affaires in Santa Domingo in the

In March 2001 Del. Eleanor Holmes Norton, D-D.C., addressed her House colleagues concerning strategies for combating the AIDS epidemic in Africa via prevention and increased drug availability. Here she comments on the 2004 elections during a news conference.
Source: CQ Photo/Scott J. Ferrell

Dominican Republic. The other prominent exception was Rep. Robert B. Elliott, R-S.C., who had been born and educated in England.

There were no African Americans in Congress during the critical years of World War I and the postwar period when the League of Nations struggled unsuccessfully to maintain peace. Democrat Arthur W. Mitchell of Illinois arrived in 1935, while the militarists in Japan, the Nazis in Germany and the fascists in Italy were consolidating power and gearing up for war. Mitchell made several goodwill trips to the Caribbean on behalf of President Franklin D. Roosevelt, including a ten-week trip through the predominantly black West Indies in 1935, but he had no significant impact on foreign policy.

William L. Dawson, D-Ill., and Adam Clayton Powell Jr., D-N.Y., served in the House during part of World War II, but they were not assigned to committees dealing with international relations. Yet the situation for black Americans at home was directly relevant to world events. During the war, Walter White, executive secretary of the National Association for the Advancement of Colored People (NAACP), studied Japanese and German propaganda broadcasts to Asia, Africa and Latin America; he found that those broadcasts played up racial tensions in the United States, including killings and mistreatment of black soldiers in southern training camps and the government's refusal to abolish segregation in the armed forces. He reported:

> In one form or another this moral was driven home. See what the United States does to its own colored people; this is the way you colored people of the world will be treated if the Allied nations win the war! Be smart and cast your lot with another colored people, the Japanese, who will never mistreat fellow colored people![1]

Although Dawson did belong to the Interior and Insular Affairs Committee, which had jurisdiction over U.S. territories, in 1951–1952, no black representative sat on the House Foreign Affairs Committee until Charles C. Diggs Jr., D-Mich., did so in 1959. And not until 2005 was a black senator, Barack Obama, D-Ill., assigned to such a committee.

As their numbers, seniority and assertiveness grew, members of the Congressional Black Caucus not only won more foreign affairs committee assignments but also engaged themselves in a diverse range of international issues. Some of these related to Africa and the Caribbean, with their large black populations—apartheid in South Africa (**Document 6.11**), another racist regime in Rhodesia, AIDS (**Document 13.5**), turmoil in Haiti (**Document 13.6**), humanitarian aid (**Document 13.7**) and ethnic violence in Sudan's Darfur region (**Document 13.9**). The Caucus's 1975 legislative agenda (**Document 6.7**) included provisions about fair employment practices for U.S. businesses in South Africa, funding for development in Africa and trade in Rhodesian chrome. Rep. George ("Mickey") Leland, D-Texas, who chaired the House Select Committee on Hunger, died when his plane crashed on a mission to feed the hungry in Ethiopia in 1989. Rep. J. C. Watts Jr., R-Okla., wrote of his third trip to Africa as a journey to his roots and an effort to better understand U.S.-African relationships and "the terrible problems of poverty and disease facing many of these countries."[2]

Other interests spanned the globe, such as human rights, foreign aid programs and promoting democracy overseas. For example, Rep. Parren J. Mitchell, D-Md., testified at a 1971 House Foreign Affairs subcommittee hearing about religious persecution of Jews in the Soviet Union. He drew parallels between their plight and the treatment of blacks in the United States, and he called for support of the right of Jews to emigrate to other countries under the United Nations Declaration of Human Rights. Rep. Ralph H. Metcalfe, D-Ill., who chaired the House subcommittee on the Panama Canal, played a key role in winning congressional ratification of a 1978 treaty turning the canal over to Panamanian control. The Middle East has also long been a region of interest to congressional African Americans, who generally have expressed overwhelming support for the survival of Israel and an end to violence and terrorism in that part of the world (**Document 13.10**). In 1979 Caucus members criticized President Jimmy Carter for firing their former House colleague, Andrew J. Young Jr., D-Ga., as ambassador to the United Nations (**Document 6.8**), reportedly for secretly meeting with Palestine Liberation Organization representatives without Carter's approval.

Through the administrations of Ronald Reagan, George H. W. Bush, Bill Clinton and George W. Bush, Caucus members continued to address international topics such as environmental treaties, free trade agreements, relations with authoritarian regimes, human rights and arms contro; (**Document 13.4**). For example, although Rep. Gwen S. Moore, D-Wis., voted for State Department appropriations in 2005, she took issue with "several ill-conceived" provisions of the legislation, includ-

Members of the Congressional Black Caucus, from left, Rep. Al Green, D-Texas, Rep. John R. Lewis, D-Ga., Rep. Barbara Lee, D-Calif., Rep. Eddie Bernice Johnson, D-Texas (obscured), Rep. Gwen S. Moore, D-Wis., Del. Eleanor Holmes Norton, D-D.C., and Rep. Melvin L. Watt, D-N.C., hold a press conference regarding Darfur on Tuesday, May 16, 2006, at the Sudanese Embassy in Washington, D.C. Source: AP Images/Lauren Victoria Burke

ing one that could cut U.S. contributions to the United Nations by 50 percent and "handicap our ability to work with other countries to make the U.N. a stronger and more effective organization." [3] And with North Korea testing nuclear weapons despite U.S. and multinational objections in 2006, Rep. Gregory W. Meeks, D-N.Y., described the tense situation as "the newest link" in President George W. Bush's "long chain of foreign failures" and warned that "North Korea has a very unpredictable regime. Either we manage this crisis effectively now or we will have to manage it in a much bigger and more costly way in the future." [4]

For Caucus members, foreign policy encompasses many issues directly linked to problems within their own districts and states. Among them are international drug smuggling (**Document 13.3**) and related crime; international trade (**Document 13.8**) and related loss of jobs within the United States; and immigration (**Document 13.11**) and related demand for scarce resources for health care, job training, public education and other taxpayer-supported services.

Document 13.1 in Context
"The Spanish Government Insults the Christian World by Perpetuating Human Slavery": U.S. Policy toward Cuba, 1874–2007

When on January 24, 1874, Rep. Josiah T. Walls, R-Fla., called for the United States to back Cuban independence and attacked Spain for its continued practice of slavery, he was the first of many African American lawmakers to publicly express an interest in Cuba. His remarks, drawing on the experiences of the American Revolution and emancipation, came little more than midway through the Caribbean island's Ten Years War as Spain struggled to keep a presence in the Western Hemisphere long after most former European colonies had won independence. Representing a state located just ninety miles from Cuba, Walls cited the

Florida legislature's resolutions supporting the Cuban people's struggle for "their national existence" and "a free government for themselves and their children." [5] It would be another twenty-four years, however, until Spain lost Cuba—by losing the Spanish-American War in 1898.

From then until Fidel Castro became president in a 1959 revolution, the United States and Cuba were close allies and economic partners. But during the early 1960s, faced with an alliance between Castro's communist regime and the Soviet Union, the United States imposed an economic embargo that continues in 2007. However, as the Cold War abated and then ended, the embargo came under growing criticism. In 1989, for example, Rep. George "Mickey" Leland, D-Texas, introduced legislation to lift the embargo on the export of medicines and medical equipment, saying, "The advent of glasnost has broadened the opportunities to extend humanitarian aid previously impossible due to existing tensions between the superpowers." [6]

Rep. Maxine Waters, D-Calif., visited Cuba in 1999 and 2000 to examine health care and medical training. Her second trip coincided with the international debate over the fate of Elián González, a boy whose mother died while fleeing with him from Cuba to Florida. The Cuban government demanded that Elián be returned to his father in Cuba, despite impassioned objections from his relatives in Miami. Waters called for his immediate return, saying, "This child should not be deprived of his father . . . This political spectacle that is being created in Miami in unconscionable. There is no reason a little child should be a political pawn. This is not about whether or not we like Castro." [7]

During a 2006 hearing before the House International Relations Subcommittee on the Western Hemisphere, Rep. Barbara Lee, D-Calif., called the embargo a "failed 40-year policy" [8] and said it "hasn't done anything in terms of helping to normalize relations with the people of Cuba." [9] At the same hearing, Rep. Gregory W. Meeks, D-N.Y., criticized recommendations by the Commission for Assistance to a Free Cuba to tighten the embargo and to establish an $80 million fund to promote opposition to Castro's rule. He also contrasted U.S. policy toward the communist regimes in China and Cuba:

> It seems as though we are trading now with a country that is much bigger than Cuba ever was and is as Communist as Cuba ever was in a little place called China, but because of being able to talk to them and work with them, we are doing much better than we did say 20, 30 years ago. Wouldn't it then be logical to say that we should change the policy that we've had over close to 50 years with Cuba currently and not exclude or prevent people from getting visas to visit this country?[10]

▬ Document 13.1 ▬
Rep. Josiah T. Walls, R-Fla., Speaks on Cuban Belligerency, January 24, 1874

On the joint resolution declaring the right of the Cuban republic to recognition as a belligerent.
Mr. WALLS: . . . Mr. Speaker, I feel moved to press the adoption of this joint resolution in obedience to what I understand as the prevailing sentiment of the American people—that sentiment which soars above the selfishness of traditional dynasties, or the soulless ordinances of international law. The progress of the human family is indicated all along the line of its march by bright epochs, embodied in the heroic endeavor of peoples in the upbuilding effort of self-government, and in opposition to the pernicious habit of government

under the extinct prerogative of divine right. Experiments in the establishment of governments of the people have met with almost uninterrupted failure in the past, down to the time when the continental patriots of our own land arose in their honesty, their might and majesty, and their devotion to truth and justice, to throw off the yoke of a tyranny less odious than that under which the Cuban patriots suffer at this moment, and pledged their lives, their fortunes, and their sacred honor to the maintenance of the principle that "all men were created equal," and entitled to life, liberty, and the pursuit of happiness; and that when governments are subversive of these ends, they ought to be altered or abolished . . .

It is a fact beyond controversy, that the erection of a republic on this continent placed the possessions of European powers on our soil beyond the possibility of rehabilitation, and created the desire for liberty in the hearts of all peoples to whom the glad tidings went, that in this endless waste of the western world, whither the star of empire takes its way, the full fruition of the hopes of mankind was fully realized. Even in the breasts of chattel slaves of Hayti, supposed to be brutalized by the oppression of centuries, the divine inspiration sprouted into patriotism, and out of the revolt there came a brain-power and a capacity which successfully secured emancipation, enfranchisement, the defeat of the great Napoleon, and the final establishment of the Haytian Republic.

Then came the struggle of the peoples of the Spanish possessions in South and Central America to throw off the yoke of the tyranny under which the Cuban republic now suffers without encouragement or assistance . . .

That this Congress will immortalize itself by following the traditions of the past, and obey the behests of civilization and humanity, by conceding belligerent rights to the republic of Cuba, there is little doubt; and the friends of Cuban liberty and emancipation are willing to rest their case and trust to the magnanimity and love of equity, individually and collectively characteristic of the war-making power of the land.

Aside from the claims of the brave patriots of Cuba, battling for national existence, there are half a million of people whose race this American nation has started on the high road to equality, and whom they are teaching the world to respect as citizens of the best government on earth, suffering under the galling chains of an abject serfdom, upon which we have placed the stamp of our condemnation in our land, and which continues in all its horrors under Spanish rule in Cuba, in spite of the kindly offices of Christian nations and in flagrant violation of the most sacred treaty obligations.

The course of Spain in the matter of emancipation has been one of continued duplicity and fraud, and the institution of slavery is as flourishing to-day in the Spanish possessions in America as before the time when God, in His mercy, waked this nation to light and life. Existing a foul blot at our doors and a disgrace and a reproach to the institutions of which we are representative, and a foul stigma upon the civilization of the time, Spain has reveled in the blood-bought wealth of this heinous traffic for more than three centuries; and even now, when Russia and even Brazil have followed in our footsteps in the noble work of emancipation, the Spanish government insults the Christian world by perpetuating human slavery.

The Cuban patriots first incurred the hatred of Spanish officials, and incited their persecution, by their outspoken hostility to the African slave trade, which Spain had solemnly agreed with Great Britain to prohibit, and their advocacy of emancipation in some shape . . .

The contest in Cuba is waged on the part of Spain for continued supremacy in her possessions on this continent, pride in the prospective dominance of the Latin races in America, and the perpetuation of African slavery in the western world as a continued menace to our institutions. The existence of the so-called republic of Spain, professing to be inspired by the *magna charta* of American liberty, which pronounced "all men created equal," is a travesty upon humanity and a libel upon civilization while it extends the protection of the Spanish government to the most pronounced slave oligarchy that has ever existed among men . . .

Spain insists that there is no war in Cuba, and proceeds to place her construction upon international law as applied to neutrals in a state of war, and gracefully permits us to reha-bilitate her navy, furnish arms and ammunition, and legal opinions if you will, to enable her to prosecute a war which is no war, and suppress a rebellion which is no rebellion. The tide of events so well developed by the gallant Cubans persuades us there is a war of some dimen-sions in Cuba, to suppress which Spain has repeatedly violated the rules of civilized war-fare, and to exterminate the men who dare to die rather than accept a questionable liberty under Spanish tyranny, and reforge the chains of slavery on the limbs of half a million human beings who will never bask in the sunlight of freedom till this Government asserts in its power that no slave shall exist upon this continent. While the republic of Cuba is strug-gling against the fearful odds of the wealth and munitions of war freely furnished Spain by the peoples of the world without hinderance, with no sympathy but that cheap and safe kind which emanates from mass-meetings and is couched in resolutions; shut out from the light of the world, as it were; fighting like Spartans in the fastnesses of Cuba; decimated and dying, but never surrendering; the footsteps of her sympathizers are dogged by Spanish spies—even followed within the jurisdiction of neutral powers, and on the high seas captured and mur-dered in cold blood for the crime of sympathizing with the heroic struggle of a brave peo-ple who demand liberty or death.

The Spanish government has continued to suppress the Cuban rebellion, which they per-sist is no rebellion, every year since its inception, at the cost of twenty thousand lives and hundreds of thousands in treasure; and if no argument and no plea will reach this Congress from the voice of the struggling patriots or of the oppressed slaves of Cuba, in God's name let us interpose to save Spain and the so-called Spanish republic. If the continued violation of all law, the confiscation of the property, and the imprisonment of American citizens, and their indiscriminate murder; the unblushing protection of the institution of slavery in its most repulsive form, repugnant to every instinct of free government; the insult to our flag, and the brutal murders of women and children without the forms of law, do not arouse this nation to duty and to action, then, in the name of the Spanish republic, if such an anomaly can exist in the present state of affairs in that unhappy country, I appeal to this Congress to relieve her of one of the insurrections on her hands so that she can have a fair trial in her new-found republican experiment . . .

Source: Congressional Record, 43d Cong., 1st sess., January 24, 1874, Appendix, 27–29.

Document 13.2 in Context
"Let the Christian Civilization Make Happy Those Poor, Half-Civilized People": American Expansionism and the Spanish-American War

U.S. victory in the short-lived Spanish-American War of 1898 created a policy dilemma: choos-ing between expansionism and anti-imperialism. On one hand, the country had long ago shed its own colonial masters and supported the liberation of colonies elsewhere, particularly in the Western Hemisphere. On the other hand, the country had just acquired overseas territories through the Treaty of Paris of 1898, which the Senate narrowly ratified in February 1899. Under the treaty, Spain relinquished all claims to Cuba and authorized U.S. occupation of the island. Spain also ceded Puerto Rico and Spanish holdings in the West Indies, plus the Philippine Islands.

It took U.S. troops six years to suppress a guerrilla movement in the Philippines. During that time, the *Indianapolis Freeman,* a weekly African American newspaper, quoted a black soldier stationed in the Philippines:

> I was struck by a question a little boy asked me, which ran about this way—"Why does the American Negro come from America to fight us when we are much friend to him and have not done anything to him? He is the same as me, and me all the same as you. Why don't you fight those people in America that burn the Negroes, that made a beast of you, that took the child from its mother's side and sold it? [11]

Rep. George H. White, a North Carolina Republican who was then the sole African American in Congress, used a House debate concerning army reorganization legislation to endorse U.S. sovereignty over the Philippines, Cuba and Puerto Rico—as well as the Hawaiian Islands, a former monarchy and independent republic annexed by the United States in 1898, separately from the Spanish-American War. In the following excerpts from his January 1899 speech, White lays out his support for U.S. expansionism. However, he devoted the bulk of his sharply worded speech to criticizing racism in the United States and among some congressional colleagues. In a subsequent February 1900 speech about tariffs for Puerto Rico, White again tied together the two themes of the U.S. government's responsibility for recently acquired territories and for continued racial injustice at home.

White did not seek reelection in 1900 when the pro-expansionist president, Republican William McKinley—who had initially opposed going to war with Spain—defeated the anti-imperialist candidate, Democrat William Jennings Bryan.

There was little black representation in Congress during the subsequent decades in which colonies changed hands—defeated nations like Germany and Italy gave them up to the victors in World Wars I and II—and the few African Americans who served during that time concentrated primarily on domestic issues rather than foreign affairs. Later, in the post–World War II era, black members of Congress sided strongly with the movement for independence among European colonies, particularly those in Africa and Asia. They related the new struggles with the American Revolution. In calling for the United States to recognize the independence of Guinea-Bissau from Portugal in 1973, for example, Rep. Charles C. Diggs Jr., D-Mich., wrote:

> Just as the United States [did] in the revolutionary war, the people of Guinea-Bissau . . . are fighting for the right to independence against an alien colonial regime . . .

> The interest of the United States must be on the side of the principles which we have pledged in the United Nations charter . . .

> Further, an enlightened view of our foreign policy, economic and geo-political interests makes clear that our interests lie in recognizing the new state.[12]

▰ Document 13.2 ▰
Rep. George H. White, R-N.C., Calls for Annexation of the Philippines, January 26, 1899

Mr. WHITE of North Carolina: Mr. Chairman, I supported very cheerfully all measures tending to bring about the recent war for liberating a very much oppressed and outraged people. I supported with equal cheer all appropriations that were necessary for the successful prosecution of that war to a final termination. I thought it was necessary then; I think now that it was a necessity. It has been the province of the people of the United States at all times to extend a helping hand to the oppressed, to the outraged—I mean, of course, without the borders of the United States.

Being a member of this great Republic and one of the Representatives on this floor, I gave my support in voice and in every way that I could to all measures tending to the liberation of these poor people in Cuba. I now favor the acquisition of all of the territory that is within our grasp as a result of that war. [Applause.]

To say that we will not accept, to say that we will not take these acquisitions, and to say that we will not extend to the people thereof the civilization of our country, the Christian manhood and womanhood we enjoy, is to do them a wrong and to take steps backward. I therefore favor the annexation of the Philippine Islands, and I also favor the bill now pending before this House for the extension of our standing Army commensurate with our new conditions . . .

In times of peace it is well to prepare for war. We are now at peace, but it may not be thirty days before we shall be thrown into another war. Who can tell? Certainly if this discussion goes on, the treaty being considered in the other end of the Capitol being transferred, in part, to this end of the Capitol, and being of such character so as to encourage and inflame those of the Philippines opposed to annexation, it is most likely that it will not be thirty days before we will be at war again. Therefore I favor action upon this bill and extending our Army so that it will be ample for all emergencies that may arise . . .

Recognize your citizen at home, recognize those at your door, give them the encouragement, give them the rights that they are justly entitled to, and then take hold of the people of Cuba and help establish a stable and fixed government among them; take hold of the Porto Ricans, establish the government there that wisdom predicated, which justice may dictate. Take hold of the Philippine Islands, take hold of the Hawaiian Islands, there let the Christian civilization go out and magnify and make happy those poor, half-civilized people; and then the black man, the white man—yes, all the riff-raff of the earth that are coming to our shores—will rejoice with you in that we have done God's service and done that which will elevate us in the eyes of the world. [Prolonged applause.]

Source: Congressional Record, 55th Cong., 3d sess., January 26, 1899, 1124, 1126.

Document 13.3 in Context
"All of This Talk . . . Has to Be a Lot of Poppycock": Combating Illegal Drug Use and Trafficking

The scourge of illegal drugs smuggled into the United States has long been a major concern for blacks in Congress, particularly those from urban districts. On the home front, issues have included the availability and affordability of treatment programs, inadequate prevention efforts, drug-related crime and penalties, police corruption, the health impacts of drug abuse, the economic ramifications of narcotics and the failure of the nation's prisons and jails to rehabilitate inmates with addiction and abuse problems. Some black lawmakers have also become entangled in controversial proposals to legalize or decriminalize some drugs.

On the international front, drug-related issues relate to American foreign policy and relationships with countries—some of them allies—that produce or transship drugs and the failure of U.S. customs and law enforcement agencies to intercept narcotics smuggled into the country. In the late 1960s and early 1970s, much attention focused on Turkey as a grower of opium poppies and on France as a processing center for heroin. Later, the Golden Triangle of Southeast Asia became a major source of heroin heading for the United States. Afghanistan lost its status as a major poppy-growing nation under the Taliban government of fundamentalist Sunni Muslims from 1996 until 2001. But following the U.S. invasion of Afghanistan and ouster of the Taliban after the September 11, 2001, attacks on the United States (**Document 12.7**), large-scale poppy production resumed. The United Nations Office on Drugs and Crime reported that in 2007, "Afghanistan produced an extraordinary 8,200 tons of opium"—one-third more than in 2006—"becoming practically the exclusive supplier of the world's deadliest drug . . . Afghanistan's opium production has thus reached a frighteningly new level" [13]

In Latin America, the megasource of cocaine, narcotics traffickers wield considerable political and economic power. Government-run crop substitution programs have had only marginal success in dissuading farmers from growing illegal drugs, while drug trafficking has bred extensive corruption among all levels of government and law enforcement officials, up to national leaders such as former Panamanian leader Manuel Noriega, who was convicted and imprisoned in the United States on cocaine trafficking, money laundering and racketeering charges.

Congressional Black Caucus members have advocated a comprehensive national drug strategy and accused both Republican and Democratic administrations of doing too little. They have investigated international drug cartels and corruption, and they have sponsored legislation to cut foreign aid to nations that fail to act decisively to control drug production and exports. Based on newspaper reports in 1996, for example, they called for a formal inquiry into allegations that the Central Intelligence Agency used profits from cocaine sold to street gangs in Los Angeles to underwrite Contra rebels seeking to overthrow the elected, leftist government of Nicaragua. (The CIA denied such involvement, and subsequent congressional inquiries failed to prove the allegations.) In a March 2005 House debate, Rep. Gregory W. Meeks, D-N.Y., argued that the Caucus's alternative budget proposal would increase foreign aid so developing countries in the Caribbean could reduce drug trafficking.

In the following excerpt from a 1977 House Select Committee on Narcotics Abuse and Control hearing on Southeast Asian narcotics, two top-level Carter administration officials— Director Peter Bourne of the Office of Drug Abuse Policy and Director Robert L. DuPont of the National Institute on Drug Abuse—answer questions from Rep. Charles B. Rangel, D-N.Y.

⬛ **Document 13.3** ⬛
Rep. Charles B. Rangel, D-N.Y., Questions Administration Witnesses during House Committee Hearings on Southeast Asian Narcotics, July 1977

TESTIMONY OF DR. PETER BOURNE, DIRECTOR, OFFICE OF DRUG ABUSE POLICY . . .

Dr. BOURNE: . . . The suppression of illicit narcotics traffic is a high priority of this administration. The President has a personal interest and deep concern about the effects of narcotics as they continue to drain our human resources, particularly the youth of our Nation, and, as a result of that special interest, has taken a number of steps designed to impact on the problem . . .

. . . Our current estimate of worldwide illicit opium ranges between 900 and 1,000 tons. Included in this estimate is 100 tons in Mexico, 400 tons in South Asia—Afghanistan and Pakistan—up to 100 tons in smaller producing areas, and 400 tons, or 40 percent of the total, in Southeast Asia—Burma, Thailand, and Laos . . .

Mr. RANGEL: . . . I don't have any problem with the President's concern. I do have a serious problem with his priorities. I have been waiting to see when this situation was going to surface before I treat this as any other administration that talks about the degree of cooperation.

It is my understanding that the International Narcotics Committee in the U.N. is a complete disaster, but diplomatically we are not supposed to talk about this.

My colleague from Texas talked about the cooperation with Mexico. It has not been that long ago that soldiers ran out with broomsticks and knocked off poppies. The State Department said that is cooperation. I assume we are moving ahead of that position. Drug rehab centers are closing down in my district. I know that this is inconsistent with the priority, as you say, that the best we do is supplement Mexican heroin for Asian heroin . . .

I am very sensitive to the efforts we are making in Burma. The Mexican Government has always been extremely cooperative. I have no problems with the Turkish government cooperating. But my kids are dying. The addict population is exploding, the centers are closing and I have all the confidence that there is some priority with President Carter and I don't see a damned thing . . .

. . . I don't want to embarrass any foreign governments, but as long as we are sending military and economic assistance to these governments and as long as the Ways and Means Committee is working out preferential trade treaties with these governments and our tourists are spending money with these governments, I don't know how long you would ask us, to wait, that come from afflicted communities until the President is able to articulate the priorities that he shared with you . . .

Dr. BOURNE: Also, the President will be sending a message to the Congress on the drug abuse problem fairly shortly. We have been working on this very diligently. I think that it will have a series of specific suggestions, recommendations covering the entire range of the drug field from international aspects to law enforcement, treatment, prevention . . .

TESTIMONY OF ROBERT L. DuPONT, M.D., DIRECTOR, NATIONAL INSTITUTE ON DRUG ABUSE

Dr. DuPONT: . . . Furthermore, it seems to me that Southeast Asia is an area of unique priority to us because of the large opium and heroin production in that area and the obvious, active connection to the international narcotics trafficking. This production and trafficking is, in a sense, a gun pointed at our Nation. There is no other area of the world where those two conditions pertain . . .

Mr. RANGEL: All of this talk about the successes that we had with Turkey without any external pressures has to be a lot of poppycock . . .

You take some airplanes away from a Turkish general? That is like taking heroin away from an addict. There were pressures placed. They didn't do it just because it was the right and moral thing to do. During that period of time we had everything going for us at one time. We had a step-up in law enforcement . . . We had prevention programs. We were moving ahead. Whether it was a rhetorical move against narcotics, it certainly was as it related to the military government of Turkey, the concern we had . . .

Source: House Select Committee on Narcotics Abuse and Control, *Southeast Asian Narcotics*, 95th Cong., 1st sess., July 12–13, 1977, 9–10, 22–23, 76, 81.

Document 13.4 in Context
"Plaintiff's Claims Would Seriously Impinge on the Powers of the Legislative and Executive Branches": Challenging U.S. Foreign Policy in Central America

United States policy toward Latin America during the Cold War often included support of right-wing political regimes and opposition to leftist regimes with actual or alleged communist ties. In 1973, for example, the CIA backed a military junta that assassinated leftist Chilean president Salvador Allende. Later, during the Reagan administration, the United States intervened in several Central American conflicts: In El Salvador, the United States supplied military advisers, military equipment and financial aid to the government—the Salvadoran Revolutionary Government Junta—which was engaged in a civil war with the leftist Democratic Revolutionary Front. In Nicaragua, U.S. assistance went to insurgent forces known as the Contras, who sought to oust the elected leftist Sandinista government; some of that money came from illegal U.S. arms sales to Iran.

In an effort to assert the constitutional authority of Congress in formulating foreign policy and to curb what they regarded as abuses of power by the president, Cold War–era members of the Congressional Black Caucus turned to the legal system—as they had in challenging past U.S. military actions and would do again in future times of conflict and war (**Document 12.5**). In the early 1980s, Rep. George W. Crockett Jr., D-Mich., led twenty-nine representatives, including eleven Caucus members, in a suit accusing President Ronald Reagan and his secretaries of defense and state of violating the War Powers Clause of the Constitution, as well as the War Powers Resolution and the Foreign Assistance Act, by aiding the government of El Salvador. The suit also asserted that the government of El Salvador was engaged in large-scale human rights violations, including political assassinations of innocent civilians, disappearances, torture and arbitrary arrests. It asked the court to order the immediate with-drawal of U.S. military personnel, equipment and aid.

In the first decision that follows, *Crockett v. Reagan,* U.S. District Judge Joyce Hens Green of Washington, D.C., sides with the administration and dismisses the suit. She concludes that the issue is "non-justiciable," meaning that it is a political question that cannot be reviewed by judges. The U.S. Court of Appeals for the District of Columbia Circuit unanimously affirmed Green's decision.

In a separate case, twelve members of Congress, including ten African Americans, sued over U.S. policies in Nicaragua. They argued that the Reagan administration was unconsti-tutionally engaged in acts of war without congressional authorization, and they requested a court order to stop what they contended was an undeclared war against the democratically elected government of Nicaragua and its people. That suit also accused the administration of violating a prohibition against CIA and Defense Department funding for military activities intended to overthrow the Nicaraguan government.

In the second decision that follows, *Sanchez-Espinoza v. Reagan,* U.S. District Judge Howard F. Corcoran of Washington, D.C., dismisses their arguments. He also rejects claims by the co-plaintiffs—twelve Nicaraguan citizens, who sought damages for injuries caused by osten-sibly U.S.-backed terrorist attacks in their country, and two Florida residents, who wanted to force the closure of U.S.-sponsored paramilitary training camps in their state.

The lawmakers failed to persuade the courts to force policy changes on the White House. However, their legal challenges were significant because they explored crucial issues involv-ing the country's constitutional system of checks and balances among the three branches of government.

<hr>

▬ Document 13.4a ▬
Court Decision in *Crockett v. Reagan* Rejects Challenge to U.S. Policy in El Salvador, October 4, 1982

Joyce Hens Green, District Judge.

. . . Plaintiffs seek declaratory judgments that the actions of defendants have violated the above-described provisions of law, and a writ of mandamus and/or an injunction directing that defendants immediately withdraw all United States Armed Forces, weapons, and mili-tary equipment and aid from El Salvador and prohibiting any further aid of any nature . . .

Defendants have urged several grounds for dismissal: that the complaint presents a non-justiciable political question, that plaintiffs have not established standing, that the Court should exercise its equitable discretion to dismiss, and that there is no private right of action under the statutory provisions invoked by plaintiffs . . .

THE WAR POWERS RESOLUTION

. . . The Court concludes that the factfinding that would be necessary to determine whether U.S. forces have been introduced into hostilities or imminent hostilities in El Salvador ren-ders this case in its current posture non-justiciable. The questions as to the nature and extent of the United States' presence in El Salvador and whether a report under the WPR [War Powers Resolution] is mandated because our forces have been subject to hostile fire or are taking part in the war effort are appropriate for congressional, not judicial, investigation and determination. Further, in order to determine the application of the 60-day provision, the

Court would be required to decide at exactly what point in time U.S. forces had been introduced into hostilities or imminent hostilities, and whether that situation continues to exist. This inquiry would be even more inappropriate for the judiciary . . .

However, the question presented does require judicial inquiry into sensitive military matters. Even if the plaintiffs could introduce admissible evidence concerning the state of hostilities in various geographical areas in El Salvador where U.S. forces are stationed and the exact nature of U.S. participation in the conflict, . . . the Court no doubt would be presented conflicting evidence on those issues by defendants. The Court lacks the resources and expertise (which are accessible to the Congress) to resolve disputed questions of fact concerning the military situation in El Salvador.

. . . The subtleties of factfinding in this situation should be left to the political branches. If Congress doubts or disagrees with the Executive's determination that U.S. forces in El Salvador have not been introduced into hostilities or imminent hostilities, it has the resources to investigate the matter and assert its wishes. The Court need not decide here what type of congressional statement or action would constitute an official congressional stance that our involvement in El Salvador is subject to the WPR, because Congress has taken absolutely no action that could be interpreted to have that effect . . .

Even if the factfinding here did not require resolution of a political question, this Court would not order withdrawal of U.S. forces at this juncture. At most, it could order that a report be filed. This conclusion is based upon the structure and legislative history of the WPR.

The War Powers Resolution, which was considered and enacted as the Vietnam war was coming to an end, was intended to prevent another situation in which a President could gradually build up American involvement in a foreign war without congressional knowledge or approval, eventually presenting Congress with a full-blown undeclared war which on a practical level it was powerless to stop . . .

Here, plaintiffs' concern that aid is being given to a country which is engaging in a consistent pattern of gross violations of human rights has been directly addressed by Congress. In Section 728 of the International Security and Development Cooperation Act of 1981, assistance to El Salvador was conditioned upon certification by the President, 30 days after enactment and every 180 days thereafter, that the government of El Salvador is making a concerted and significant effort to comply with internationally recognized human rights, is achieving substantial control over all elements of its own armed forces so as to bring an end to the indiscriminate torture and murder of Salvadoran citizens by these forces, is making continued progress in implementing essential economic and political reforms, including the land reform program, and is committed to the holding of free elections. Since its enactment, the President has made two certifications under the Act. Congress has taken no action to end aid to El Salvador . . . Whatever infirmities the President's certifications may or may not suffer, it is clear that under these circumstances plaintiffs' dispute is primarily with their fellow legislators who have authorized aid to El Salvador while specifically addressing the human rights issue, and who have accepted the President's certifications . . .

Source: Crockett v. Reagan, 558 F. Supp. 893 (D.D.C. 1982).

▬ Document 13.4b ▬
Federal Judge Rebuffs Challenge to U.S. Policy in Nicaragua in *Sanchez-Espinoza v. Reagan*, August 1, 1983

Howard F. Corcoran, District Judge.

. . . Because we find that (1) this case involves significant factual and policy questions for which there are no judicially discoverable and manageable standards, and (2) resolution of plaintiff's claims would seriously impinge on the powers of the Legislative and Executive branches to establish and carry out foreign policy, as well as provide for national security, we conclude that this lawsuit is not justiciable. As a result, defendants' motion to dismiss this case in its entirety will be granted . . .

II. DISCUSSION

This lawsuit is another cog in the wheel of controversy currently surrounding U.S. government involvement in Central America, particularly in Nicaragua, Honduras and El Salvador. The federal defendants strenuously argue that adjudication of plaintiffs' claims would impermissibly interfere with the constitutional powers of the Executive and Legislative branches of our government to conduct foreign affairs and attend to national security concerns. As a result, they argue, this case presents a non-justiciable political question. We agree.

The political question doctrine insures that the judiciary exhibits appropriate concern for the separation of powers under our tri-partite system of government . . .

In the present context, we are mindful that "matters intimately related to foreign policy and national security are rarely proper subjects for judicial intervention" inasmuch as they are "so exclusively entrusted to the political branches of government as to be largely immune from judicial inquiry or interference" . . .

First, this Court lacks judicially discoverable and manageable standards for resolving the dispute presented . . . Moreover, the covert activities of CIA operatives in Nicaragua and Honduras are perforce even less judicially discoverable than the level of participation by U.S. military personnel in hostilities in El Salvador . . .

A second reason for finding this matter non-justiciable is the impossibility of our undertaking independent resolution without expressing a lack of the respect due coordinate branches of government. President Reagan has stated on numerous occasions, to the Congress and to the public at large that he is *not* violating the spirit or letter of the Boland Amendment, or any other statutes, in Nicaragua. By all media accounts, members of both Houses of Congress strenuously disagree with the President's assertion. Were this Court to decide, on a necessarily incomplete evidentiary record, that President Reagan either is mistaken, or is shielding the truth, one or both of the coordinate branches would be justifiably offended. At this stage, therefore, it is up to Congress and the President to try to resolve their differences and jointly set a course for U.S. involvement in Central America.

Finally, there is a real danger of embarrassment from multifarious pronouncements by various departments on one question. As previously noted, the Executive urges that his actions are legal and necessary to national security . . . Congressional debate is ongoing, and the result will be some legislative pronouncement as to the proper role, if any, of U.S. military and CIA officials in Nicaragua. Judicial resolution of the Congressional plaintiffs' claims unnecessarily might provide yet a third view on U.S. activities in Central America. Such an occurrence would, undoubtedly, rattle the delicate diplomatic balance that is required in the foreign affairs arena . . .

Sanchez-Espinoza v. Reagan, 568 F. Supp. 596 (D.D.C. 1983).

Document 13.5 in Context
"We Have Got to Tailor Strategies for Combating AIDS": African Americans, Africa and AIDS

As the worldwide HIV/AIDS epidemic has expanded, African American lawmakers have worked to keep the issue at the forefront of the public's attention and the U.S. government's policy agendas. Their interest has been twofold. First, African Americans have suffered disproportionately from the disease, with more than 40 percent of new cases in the United States affecting blacks. Second, the epidemic has had its most brutal impact in Africa, a region at the top of the Congressional Black Caucus's foreign policy agenda, where millions of adults have died of the disease and millions of children have been orphaned, many of whom also contracted HIV/AIDS from their mothers.

"I am concerned about how this global public health challenge has devastated sub-Saharan Africa," Rep. Carolyn Cheeks Kilpatrick of Michigan, a Democratic member of the House Appropriations Committee's Foreign Operations Subcommittee, said in 1999. "AIDS not only affects a nation's health, it has a devastating effect on its ability to build economic and social investment." [14]

Kilpatrick and other Caucus members have pushed for greater public awareness and greater federal commitment to combating AIDS in the United States. Concerns raised by the Caucus in 1998 prompted President Bill Clinton's administration to allocate $156 million to fight HIV/AIDS in minority communities.[15] In 2002 the Caucus criticized President George W. Bush's administration for its handling of the African AIDS crisis. "We cannot win the war against AIDS without greater financial resources and a clear plan of action for the United States," Caucus members wrote in a letter to Bush. "Each day we delay in mounting a comprehensive—and compassionate—response to the global AIDS and TB pandemics, the cost in human, social, and economic terms grow." [16]

In March 2004 Del. Eleanor Holmes Norton of Washington, D.C., addressed her House colleagues on the importance of drug availability and preventive measures in dealing with the AIDS epidemic in Africa. Her comments follow.

▬▬ Document 13.5 ▬▬
Del. Eleanor Holmes Norton, D-D.C., Discusses Fighting AIDS in Africa on the House Floor, March 14, 2001

Ms. NORTON: Mr. Speaker, recently drug companies announced that they would sell anti-AIDS drugs in southern Africa at a considerable discount. This would still entail hundreds of dollars per person. The recent experience of Bristol-Myers Squibb gives me caution. A $100 million, 5-year initiative that was meant to donate money for AIDS drugs in Africa has boiled down to almost nothing. The reasons are not entirely clear. Although this was to be a charitable gift, the money has come down to $1.3 million per year to five participating countries.

I recall that when Prime Minister Mbeki of South Africa was here for a visit last year, we all wondered why Mbeki was embroiled in a torturous notion about the cause of AIDS. I wish he had been more forthright about what his real problem was, and when he met with the Congressional Black Caucus I believe I was able to extract from him what his real problem was. South Africa offers free medical care, and on cross-examination it became clear that if South Africa were to even use the rather inexpensive drugs to combat mother-to-infant transmission it would use up its entire medical budget.

We must not forget that with the great importance we attach to drugs and especially the agreement of some of these companies to offer drugs at discount rates in southern Africa, that in developing countries nothing can replace prevention. In this country, Medicaid is overwhelmed with the costs of AIDS, but it is an entitlement, so people are going to get it. In developing countries, where there is TB and malaria and hundreds of other diseases, to superimpose our notion of how to combat the disease is not going to work. I hate to consider it, but it is true. It seems to me that it is time to face the importance of continuing to stress prevention as the most important strategy not only in this country but especially in developing countries.

Developing countries are being set back decades because of the AIDS crisis. To the great credit of some of the companies and others around the world, we want drugs to be made available to developing countries as well. It will be important to prioritize which drugs to which people. Mother-to-children drugs that are especially effective in keeping children from getting AIDS at all would be very, very important. But, beyond that, we have got to tailor strategies for combating AIDS to the environment in which those strategies are expected to work.

In Africa, we greet the decision of the drug companies to offer drugs at discount rates. At the same time, we must remind ourselves that most of our effort must go into preventing AIDS, which has already become a catastrophe of epidemic proportions in southern Africa.

Source: Congressional Record, 107th Cong., 1st sess., March 14, 2001, H904–H905.

Document 13.6 in Context
"Another Sad Chapter of the Painful History of the World's First Black Independent Nation": U.S. Foreign Policy and Haiti

Since 1791, when Toussaint L'Ouverture led the slave rebellion that resulted in the creation of the world's first independent black republic, African Americans have had a special interest in Haiti. The success of the rebellion and the establishment of Haitian independence in 1804 sparked fear among slaveholders in the states of the antebellum South, and inspired many African Americans—free and slave, northern and southern—with the possibilities of freedom and self-determination. In the early twentieth century, Haiti was among the few foreign service consular positions open to African American political appointees. Despite its history of violence and extreme poverty, Haiti remains for many black people a powerful symbol.

But the relationship between the United States and Haiti—the first two independent nations of the Western Hemisphere—has long been troubled. Concerns about German influence and violence within the country prompted the United States to invade Haiti in 1915—an action condemned by the NAACP—and to occupy it until 1934. In 1994, during the Clinton administration, the United States invaded Haiti again to restore to power Jean-Bertrand Aristide, a former priest who had been popularly elected but then deposed in a coup by the Haitian military. The Congressional Black Caucus accused the administration of racially motivated treatment of people fleeing Haiti—they were denied the political refugee status that would have allowed them to enter the United States.

In November 2001 members of the Caucus urged President George W. Bush to increase humanitarian aid to Haiti and to revise policies that Caucus members said were contributing to Haiti's economic and social crisis. In a letter to Bush, they wrote:

> Mr. President, the people of Haiti are suffering . . . In Haiti, AIDS and HIV are rising at alarming levels. The illiteracy rate remains at over 45%. In addition, the country's infrastructure is in dire straits. Haiti has very few, if any, decent roads, very little potable water, and the fuel situation is catastrophic. It is imperative that the US remove its blockade of essentially all aid to Haiti, particularly the loans currently held up at the Inter-American Development Bank.[17]

Much of the U.S. government's reluctance to offer aid revolved around Aristide, who had handed over the Haitian government to his duly elected successor in 1996 but had won reelection to the presidency in 2001. Although Aristide remained popular among the people, his leftist political orientation, his unwillingness to privatize government-owned companies and his disbanding of the Haitian military after U.S. forces returned him to power in 1994 had alienated many people in both countries. In early 2004 a new uprising forced Aristide to flee to exile in the Central African Republic and then South Africa amid circumstances that were the focus of much controversy. Aristide claimed that he had been forced into exile by the U.S. and French governments in what amounted to a kidnapping; U.S. and French authorities countered that Aristide left Haiti voluntarily.

Caucus members were intensely skeptical of the government's statements. In the following document, New York representative Gregory W. Meeks expresses his concern about the situation during a subcommittee hearing on the issue.

▬ Document 13.6 ▬
Rep. Gregory W. Meeks, D-N.Y., Attacks U.S. Role in the Ouster of Haitian President Jean-Bertrand Aristide, March 3, 2004

Early Sunday morning, Haitian President Jean-Bertrand Aristide resigned his office and went into exile. His final destination is unknown. Thus, a tragic page has been turned in another sad chapter of the painful history of the world's first Black independent nation. Americans should take no joy in what has occurred. They should be very concerned about what lies ahead, bearing in mind that whatever happens to Haiti from this point indirectly happens to America.

More than 1,000 Haitians have sought refuge in the United States, only to be returned to their deeply troubled nation. More refugees are sure to come as the wide-spread looting, street violence, and killings already under way during the past week intensifies in the wake of Aristide's departure.

President Bush has sent in a contingent of U.S. Marines. Other nations are contributing troops to an international peacekeeping force authorized by the United Nations Security Council.

Hopefully, these steps will quell the violence and anarchy. Hopefully, they will expedite the restoration of order and put into place a government acceptable to all Haitians. President Bush is staking a lot on hope. Unfortunately, hope is a poor substitute for policy—especially good policy.

Which is why Americans should not take comfort in what has transpired, nor pride in the role of their own government. The Bush administration is deeply complicit in the ouster of a democratically elected president of an independent country. The long term interests of the American people as opposed to the immediate interests of the Bush Administration demand that Wednesday's congressional hearing on Haiti find answers to three questions: Why did developments in Haiti take the course they have? What are the implications of yet another U.S.-backed coup? Where will things go from here?

While it cannot be said that Aristide played no role in the demise of his presidency, it is also true that withholding badly needed U.S. and international aid made it doubly difficult for the Aristide government to fulfill its responsibilities to the Haitian people. Over the past several weeks, as gangs of armed thugs, former torturers and death squad leaders, coup plotters, drug dealers, and convicted murderers—to paraphrase Colin Powell's words, mounted an armed rebellion against the duly elected government, the Administration rejected Aristide's call for international assistance. The Administration only supported the Caribbean Community's (CARICOM) plan of action for resolving the crisis in response to intense pressure from the Congressional Black Caucus—a plan to which Aristide agreed but the opposition rejected.

The Administration's posture assured the opposition that it would not have to reach a compromise. They could simply hold out and let the thugs do their dirty work. In effect, the Administration promised to send in the marines if and only if Aristide resigned. Lacking sufficient internal forces to restore law and order, Aristide—facing the specter of revenge killings, more looting, and massive waves of refugees fleeing to the United States—had no choice. The Administration claims the resignation was consistent with Haiti's constitution. That may be formally true, but in essence we are witnessing the 33rd coup d'etat in Haiti's history—most of them engineered by the United States.

The Administration suggests that the crisis was solely Aristide's fault. It also accuses the ousted Haitian president of electoral fraud. I have been among those who criticized Aristide for autocratic governance, for failure to develop democratic institutions, and for insufficient steps to improve the material conditions of the Haitian people.

But, in a democracy, elections should be the principal means by which leaders are replaced. Instead, President Bush has strengthen[ed] undemocratic and anti-democratic methods, while further weakening Haiti's already fragile democratic institutions. Moreover, what exactly is the agenda of the opposition and of the armed rebels that our government tacitly supports? What costs will the American people incur? What will [happen] when the marines leave? What message are we sending to other countries in the hemisphere experiencing internal political difficulties? Will these nations be more or less inclined to tolerate dissent?

What Haiti needs most is the rule of law and an orderly constitutional process. It urgently needs large scale humanitarian assistance in the form of food, clothing, medical care, and shelter. It also needs stability, sustained help in creating a coherent civil society, and a long term economic development commitment from the United States, the UN, CARICOM, the Organization of American States, and the international community. CARICOM is to be commended for its balanced approach to resolving this crisis. Let us hope the UN maintains a peacekeeping presence and when the time comes contributes election monitors.

The Administration has once again demonstrated that it is fully capable of ousting a head of state that it does not like. It has shown itself to be far less capable when it comes to reconstruction and nation-building. Yet, it is precisely on these questions that once again the credibility of the United States hinges.

Source: House Committee on International Relations, *The Situation in Haiti: Report of Hearing before the Subcommittee on the Western Hemisphere,* 108th Cong., 2d sess., March 3, 2004, 106–107.

Document 13.7 in Context
"Members of the Congressional Black Caucus Commend Your Bold Efforts": Promoting Humanitarian Aid for Africa

In June 2005 the Congressional Black Caucus took an unusual step by writing directly to British prime minister Tony Blair, praising and encouraging his efforts to increase international humanitarian aid to the nations of Africa. Caucus members had a longstanding interest in Africa, especially when it came to humanitarian concerns regarding poverty, hunger, disease and natural disasters. But their efforts most often focused on influencing U.S. government policy toward the region or calling on the United Nations or the international community to take action.

Blair, however, had launched a concerted effort to push the international community to increase its assistance to Africa. He announced in late 2004 that he would give African concerns—development aid, fair trade and debt relief—a prominent place on the agenda when Britain chaired the G8 summit meeting of economic powers in 2005. He also organized the Commission for Africa, which issued a report in March 2005, addressed to the leaders of the G8 nations, calling for billions of dollars in international investment to reduce poverty, improve infrastructure, and expand economic development.

The Caucus's praise for Blair was a genuine acknowledgement of his efforts, but it was also intended to pressure the administration of President George W. Bush to follow Blair's lead and increase U.S. humanitarian assistance to Africa. The Caucus chided Bush for pledging significantly less funding for famine relief than Blair had requested of Parliament. In the letter to Blair, which follows, the Caucus states that the debt relief proposed by Blair is a key element in responding to Africa's many problems: "Africa's debt crisis is the single biggest obstacle to the continent's development, to the fight against HIV/AIDS and represents a crippling load that undermines economic and social progress . . . The idea of 100 percent debt relief is not about handouts, but about mutual interest and mutual security."

Document 13.7
Congressional Black Caucus's Letter to British Prime Minister Tony Blair, June 7, 2005

Dear Prime Minister Blair:

The 43 members of the Congressional Black Caucus commend your bold efforts to achieve major debt relief and a significant increase in aid for Africa. We wholeheartedly support your efforts to reduce the debilitating effects of poverty in Africa by encouraging new policies toward Africa.

2005 is indeed a vital year for Africa and significant poverty reduction will be impossible without considerably more aid and attention to Africa in the near future. As you and your government have recently acknowledged, time is not on our side and this is not a time for timidity or a time to fear reaching too high.

As the report released by the Commission for Africa confirmed, Africa remains the only part of the developing world that remains no better off than it was 25 years ago. More than 25 million of sub-Saharan Africa's 700 million people are infected with HIV, and life expectancy, which peaked at about 50 years in 1992, has since fallen to about 46 years. Child malnutrition, illiteracy, and lack of access to clean water are serious problems throughout the continent. A January 2005 report issued by the United Nations Millennium Project indicated that Africa stood no chance of meeting the Millennium Development Goals without a massive infusion of aid.

Africa's debt crisis is the single biggest obstacle to the continent's development and to the fight against HIV/AIDS. Debt represents a crippling load that undermines economic and social progress. Many poor countries in Africa spend 30 to 40 percent of their annual budgets on repaying their foreign-held debt, spending more on interest and debt than they spend on their own country's health and education budgets combined.

Furthermore, most of Africa's foreign debt is illegitimate in nature, as much of it was incurred by unrepresentative regimes. Sadly, the Heavily Indebted Poor Countries Initiative has not reduced the debts of African countries to sustainable levels, and today it is clear that Africa's creditors must move beyond this framework. The idea of 100 percent debt relief is not about handouts, but about mutual interest and mutual security.

We strongly support your efforts to ensure that debt cancellation is a critical item on the agenda during the July G-8 Summit in Scotland. In addition, we commend you for having the wisdom to insist that the risk of increasing aid to Africa is worth taking, particularly since the amounts of aid you are proposing can readily be afforded by all the Summit participants and all of them would gain new markets and help create an environment in which violence and terrorism are much less likely.

The Congressional Black Caucus stands firmly with you in fighting for a partnership with Africa that is based on mutual respect and solidarity, one that will require the most serious reevaluation of Western policy on Africa in a generation. Although there is much work to be done to convince some stakeholders (including the Bush Administration) of all the steps that need to be taken, the momentum for change you are helping to fuel is real. We believe that there is common ground that needs to be found between your government and the other G-8 participants on securing debt relief, increasing aid, and removing trade-distorting subsidies and other barriers to trade in Africa.

Marshalling the resources needed to significantly reduce poverty in sub-Saharan Africa will not be easy. However, if we work closely together, a new deal for Africa can be negotiated. These are big goals, but the stakes could not be higher. Therefore, as we pledged to Nelson Mandela, the former President of South Africa during his recent visit to the United States, we join you in committing our energy, capability and resolve to shaping a new future for Africa.

Sincerely,
Melvin L. Watt, *Chairman*
Donald M. Payne, *Co-Chair, Task Force on International Relations*

Source: Congressional Black Caucus, "Congressional Black Caucus Applauds British Prime Minister Tony Blair for His Bold Efforts to Achieve Major Debt Relief and a Significant Increase in Aid for Africa," news release, June 7, 2005, http://www.house.gov/list/press.

Document 13.8 in Context
"American Workers Suffer with Anxiety . . . Each Time We Pass Another Free Trade Agreement": Free Trade and American Jobs

In the mid-1990s, Congressional Black Caucus members became increasingly concerned with international trade policy as the United States engaged in a series of negotiations aimed at eliminating trade barriers between the United States and other nations in the Western Hemisphere. The biggest concern for Caucus members was the impact of international trade agreements on workers, particularly manufacturing workers, in the United States.

Congress ratified the North American Free Trade Agreement, known as NAFTA, in 1994. That agreement among the United States, Canada and Mexico had been signed by President George H. W. Bush two years earlier and called for the removal of a wide range of trade restrictions, the cutting of tariffs and the protection of intellectual property rights. The agreement faced stiff opposition from foes, who said it would eliminate U.S. jobs by exploiting low-wage workers in Mexico.

When President George W. Bush's administration negotiated a new agreement that extended the NAFTA model to cover trade between the United States, the Dominican Republic and five Central American nations, resistance in Congress was again strenuous. The new agreement, called CAFTA, was presented to Congress in 2005, where it won ratification by very narrow margins in both the House and Senate. Key Caucus member Charles B. Rangel, D-N.Y., criticized the agreement, saying it did not do enough to protect the wages and conditions of Central American workers:

> Some of the working conditions . . . are below common decency in terms of lack of pay and lack of health care. And we've met with some of those people. We've met the Catholic Bishops that service these areas. And, from a spiritual point of view, they think it's immoral not to include the workers in these agreements . . . We don't want the stealing of our intellectual property rights but we don't want management just to ignore human rights.[18]

Other Caucus members took issue with CAFTA, including Rep. Carolyn Cheeks Kilpatrick, D-Mich. She expressed her disappointment at the ratification of the CAFTA, which did not include as much worker protection as did NAFTA. Even with the limited protections, she argued, NAFTA was responsible for the loss of thousands of U.S. manufacturing jobs.

▨ Document 13.8 ▨
Rep. Carolyn Cheeks Kilpatrick, D-Mich., Criticizes CAFTA Trade Legislation, July 27, 2005

Washington, DC—Congresswoman Carolyn Cheeks Kilpatrick (13th District, MI) is extremely displeased the majority of the Members of the U.S. House decided to pass H.R. 3045, the Central American Free Trade Agreement (CAFTA) with a vote of 217-215.

"Recent statistics from the Labor Department indicate that America has lost more than 2.5 million manufacturing jobs since the passage of NAFTA. In my home state of Michigan, we have experienced a net job loss of more than 200,000 manufacturing jobs due to exports.

Throughout the U.S., American workers suffer with anxiety about the elimination of their jobs each time we pass another free trade agreement. They know that factories are being relocated to foreign countries where they will be immune from paying U.S. taxes, and will be able to pay workers a fraction of U.S. hourly wages that range from $14 to almost $18. Each time we pass another trade agreement, their worst fears are realized," said Congresswoman Kilpatrick.

"The United Nations International Labor Organization (ILO) reports, the average hourly wage earner in Nicaragua makes 95 cents; $1 in Guatemala, and $1.25 in El Salvador. Such miniscule wages pose a tremendous incentive to Asian and U.S. manufacturers to build factories and strategic alliances in Central America. The same factories that will be created in Central America will be able to avoid strong environmental laws that exist in the U.S., thereby contributing to environmental degradation throughout Central America," added Congresswoman Kilpatrick.

"I am a very concerned that worker protection provisions throughout Central America will be weakened. The legislation omits an important protection that was included in NAFTA—that labor enforcement proceedings not be unnecessarily complicated. I reject the hypocrisy of a trade agreement that would sanction placing the welfare of low wage earners in jeopardy. In my state of Michigan, we have strong worker protections in place. I cannot in good conscience support a measure that would pose potential harm to workers throughout countries in Central America," stated Congresswoman Kilpatrick.

"Supporters of CAFTA say its passage will facilitate the elimination of tariffs and quotas and will ultimately result in increased trade and long-term growth. In reality, consumers and laborers in Central America will not be able to afford American manufactured goods. They will, however, be able to manufacture goods in Central America that will be sold in America with a profit margin that could not be realized if the same item were manufactured domestically," concluded Congresswoman Kilpatrick.

Source: Rep. Carolyn Cheeks Kilpatrick, "Kilpatrick Statement On CAFTA," news release, July 27, 2005, www.house.gov/kilpatrick.

Document 13.9 in Context
"An End to the Continuing Genocide and the Plight of Millions": Black Caucus Members Address the Humanitarian Crisis in Sudan

The longstanding interest of Congressional Black Caucus members in African issues and concerns drew them quickly into the effort to halt a devastating outbreak of violence in the Darfur region of Sudan. Sudan had been torn by civil war for years, but the violence in Darfur took on a new and more desperate character in the summer of 2003 as the government-backed Arab Janjaweed militias began attacking the villages of non-Arab peoples in the Darfur region. By the end of 2006, more than 400,000 people had been killed and others—estimates by international agencies reached more than two million—had been displaced by the violence. Many of the refugees fled over the border into neighboring Chad.

In the summer of 2004, Caucus members helped push through Congress a resolution that declared the situation a genocide, called on the United Nations to act to halt the killings and urged the administration of President George W. Bush to keep pressuring the international community to intervene. The resolution won overwhelming approval but had little impact. The Sudanese government resisted international intervention and the United Nations was unable to negotiate an end to the violence. Caucus members continued their efforts to keep the situation in the public eye. The Caucus released a statement in December 2005 in which it again called for action:

> Eighteen months after first declaring that genocide was occurring in Darfur, the Congressional Black Caucus once again is calling for immediate action by the Bush Administration and the international community to end the violence and the humanitarian nightmare in that region.

> As security continues to deteriorate rapidly in Darfur, threatening hundreds of thousands of innocent civilian lives, the CBC feels it is the moral obligation of the United States and the international community to provide and deploy all necessary resources to protect innocent civilians and humanitarian operations throughout Darfur.[19]

As the killing continued into the spring of 2006, the Caucus intensified its efforts, turning to the tactics of civil disobedience that had guided the civil rights movement of the 1960s and had been employed in the 1980s to pressure the South African government to end apartheid. The following document is a news release from the Caucus, issued after a demonstration at the Sudanese Embassy in Washington, D.C., at which seven of its members were arrested for blocking the embassy entrance. Although the United Nations Security Council authorized deployment of a peacekeeping force in Darfur in late July 2007, by September 2007 the force had not yet been deployed and the violence continued.

▆▆ Document 13.9 ▆▆
Congressional Black Caucus Members Are Arrested in Darfur Protest, May 16, 2006

(Washington, D.C.)—"It's time for the members of the Congressional Black Caucus (CBC) and the world community to raise the ante on Sudan," U.S. Representative Melvin L. Watt (D-NC), CBC Chair, said today at a press conference and demonstration in front of the Sudanese Embassy to dramatize the urgency of the crisis in Darfur. The protest resulted in the arrest of seven members of the CBC for disorderly conduct for obstructing the entrance to the Sudanese Embassy.

Chairman Watt was joined by U.S. Representatives Barbara Lee (D-CA), John Lewis (D-GA), Eddie Bernice Johnson (D-TX), Gwen Moore (D-WI), Al Green (D-TX) and D.C. Delegate Eleanor Holmes Norton in calling for an end to the continuing genocide and the plight of millions of people who have been slaughtered and displaced by violence in Sudan.

"The situation in Darfur has deteriorated significantly," noted Rep. Lee. "People are dying and are in misery. Countless women and girls are raped daily, there is no food, conditions are unsanitary and there is an inadequate supply of water in the region."

To date, an estimated 450,000 Darfurians have died since the beginning of the genocide in 2003, more than 2.5 million have been displaced from their homes and nearly 3.5 million people are currently in need of emergency humanitarian assistance as a result of the crisis orchestrated by the Government of Sudan and its allied Janjaweed militias.

Rep. John Lewis said: "We must not forget that while we consider what to do, the situation on the ground is worsening for the millions of people affected by the crisis. The CBC plans to build on the level of civic action and attention around the genocide in Darfur and will work to keep the world community engaged."

"After Rwanda, we said 'never again' but the genocide and rapes have not diminished and never again has come and gone," noted D.C. Delegate Norton. "We have no less an obligation here than we had in South Africa to do much more to heighten awareness. If anything, the continuation of unabated genocide and unthinkable abuse of women and children creates an even greater urgency."

Recently, a peace agreement was reached in Abuja, Nigeria between the Government of Sudan and the Sudanese Liberation Movement (SLM). The CBC thinks that the agreement falls short of expectations to provide protection to civilians on the ground, more political representation for Darfur in the central government and adequate mechanisms for ensuring disarmament of the Janjaweed.

During the press conference, Chairman Watt and the CBC listed the following demands to stop the genocide in Darfur:

- Cessation of Violence—The government of Sudan and its Janjaweed militias must immediately stop the violence against Darfurians;
- UN Peacekeepers—A Chapter 7 UN peacekeeping mission to assist the African Union Mission;
- Accountability—Accountability for government officials and Janjaweed responsible for genocide;
- Emergency Food—President Bush must push the Government of Sudan to release its 300,000–500,000 metric tons of grain reserves to feed the starving people of Darfur;
- Civilian Protection—Protection of civilians who remain vulnerable;
- Refugee Return—The Administration must work to ensure the Government of Sudan does all it can for the internally displaced and the refugees of Darfur to restore security so they can return to their homes soon, and;
- Full Implementation of Peace Agreements—Full implementation of the Darfur Peace Agreement and the Comprehensive Peace Agreement between the North and South.

A growing number of members of Congress are pushing for a measure passed in the House recently to be signed into law. House Resolution 3127 seeks to hold Sudanese government officials and Janjaweed commanders accountable for their involvement in the genocide. U.S. Rep. Donald Payne, CBC member and head of the CBC African Task Force, is the chief co-sponsor of this legislation.

The CBC was the first to highlight the crisis in Darfur and on June 24, 2004 introduced H. Con Res 467, declaring genocide in the region.

Source: Congressional Black Caucus, "CBC Members Arrested During Protest at Sudanese Embassy Say Its Time to Raise the Ante on Sudan," news release, May 16, 2006, www.house.gov/list/press/nc12_watt/pr_cbc_051606.html.

Document 13.10 in Context
"I Rise in Support of Israel's Right to Protect and Defend Itself": African American Lawmakers and the Middle East

Historically, African Americans in Congress have been strong defenders of U.S. diplomatic, economic and military support for Israel and critical of nations and groups that have sought its destruction. Even so, some black lawmakers have been criticized for taking stands viewed as anti-Israel, pro-Arab or pro-Palestine. For example, challenger Artur Davis defeated Rep. Earl F. Hilliard of Alabama and challenger Denise L. Majette defeated Rep. Cynthia A. McKinney of Georgia in their 2002 Democratic primaries based in part on the incumbents' positions on the Middle East, which were depicted as anti-Israel.

In July 2006, the House of Representatives condemned attacks on Israel shortly after the country had obeyed a United Nations Security Council resolution to withdraw completely from neighboring Lebanon. The resolution condemned the militant groups Hamas and Hezbollah "for engaging in unprovoked and reprehensible armed attacks against Israel on undisputed Israeli territory, for taking hostages, for killing Israeli soldiers, and for continuing to indiscriminately target Israeli civilian populations with their rockets and missiles" and demanded that the Iranian and Syrian governments "direct Hamas and Hezbollah to immediately and unconditionally release Israeli soldiers which they hold captive." [20]

During the debate, as the following excerpts show, Rep. Al Green, D-Texas, steadfastly supported Israel's right of self-defense, while Rep. Barbara Lee, D-Calif., combined her backing for Israel's continued survival with a caution against U.S. support for the use of military force against Iran and Syria; she also called for advancing the peace process. Earlier that year, after Hamas won a parliamentary majority in the elections for the government of the Palestinian Authority, Green had said the United States should not give aid to the Palestinian Authority "should any political party holding a majority of Parliamentary seats advocate for the destruction of the state of Israel." [21] Later that summer, Green traveled to the Middle East with a congressional delegation and met with a member of the Israeli Knesset (parliament), a member of the Palestinian Authority in the West Bank, the prime minister of Lebanon and a senior Jordanian government official.

▬▬ Document 13.10 ▬▬
Rep. Barbara Lee, D-Calif., and Rep. Al Green, D-Texas, Speak about Attacks on Israel, July 19, 2006

Ms. [Barbara] LEE [of California]: . . . Madam Speaker, I join with those who condemn the recent kidnapping of Israeli soldiers and the rocket attacks into Israel, and also, I rise in support of Israel's right to protect and defend itself from attacks in accordance with international law, including Article 51 of the United Nations Charter.

However, this resolution goes much further than that, and it also omits any mention, and I think this is so critical at this stage, it omits any mention of how and why the United States should exert its leadership in stopping the violence. Too many people, Israelis Lebanese and Palestinians, have been killed, and there is no end in sight. Very seldom do I cast a "present" vote, but in this instance I will, and let me explain why.

This resolution reaffirms our support for Israel, demands that the Government of Lebanon do everything in its power to find and free the kidnapped Israeli soldiers and to gain control of its borders in order to prevent future attacks. It also condemns Hamas and Hezbollah for killing Israeli soldiers and for indiscriminately targeting Israeli civilians, and it recognizes the plight of the families of the innocent victims. These provisions warrant our strong support and certainly sends a strong message in support of Israel, in behalf of Israel and on behalf of Israel.

But on the other hand, there are provisions in this resolution that are totally unfinished or missing and leave this resolution very much incomplete.

Such a course of action, I believe, ought to make it clear that in no uncertain terms will the United States support a strategy of the use of force against Iran or Syria. This resolution leaves the door open for this.

This resolution ought to make it clear that the only way to remove the threat to Israel and to the larger region is to resolve these issues through an immediate cease-fire and commit the United States, through the cease-fire, to high-level and sustained diplomacy. We need to be doing that right now in support of many of the initiatives such as the road map. This resolution does not really address how to end the escalating violence that really, quite frankly, does more violence and harm to Israel's long-term interests and living in peace and security with her neighbors.

This resolution should offer concrete steps on how to achieve peace and security for Israel and the region, and the resolution says nothing about the peace process.

The bottom line is there is absolutely no military resolution to the issues confronting the Middle East, notwithstanding the acts of self-defense to which Israel is entitled in accordance with international law.

If we do not put a stop to all of the hostilities today, what is to stop future violence with more technologically advanced weapons systems, rockets with even longer ranges? Where does it end? Is war the only answer?

Israel's security and a sustained peace that includes a two-state solution cannot be achieved militarily. The only option, and the only hope, is a political solution to this crisis and for a sustained peace.

That is why, Madam Speaker, it is imperative that all parties return to internationally recognized borders and for all parties to resume urgent, multilateral diplomatic efforts, including a return to the road map and a full engagement by the quartet.

What we should be doing today is imploring all sides to agree to a cease-fire, insist on the return of the hostages, and agree to an international security force.

If we can reach the end of that road that we are walking down right now, then our ally, I believe, Israel will find the peace and security that she and her people rightfully deserve.

So, Madam Speaker, I intend to vote "present" on this resolution because, while I believe there are some provisions that warrant our support, I do not believe it goes far enough in addressing the immediate security needs and the violence that is taking place right now in the Middle East.

Mr. AL GREEN of Texas: . . . Madam Speaker, I want peace for both Palestinians and Israelis. I want justice for both Palestinians and Israelis. And I support House Resolution 921 condemning the recent attacks on Israel and supporting Israel's right to defend herself.

Madam Speaker, Hezbollah has killed more Americans than any other terrorist group, save al Qaeda: 257 Americans killed in the 1983 bombings of the U.S. embassy and barracks in Beirut; 19 Americans killed in the 1996 bombings of the Khobar Towers.

Hezbollah has more than 13,000 rockets capable of hitting Israeli cities and towns and killing innocent persons. Does anybody think that these rockets will just go away? Hezbollah wasn't getting weaker. Hezbollah was getting stronger.

Israel must defend herself or there will be no Israel to defend . . .

Source: Congressional Record, 109th Cong., 2d sess., July 19, 2006, H5468–H5469, H5474.

Document 13.11 in Context
"If We Think That Putting Up a Few More Miles of Fence Is . . . the Whole Answer": Immigration, Immigrant Rights and Border Security

The urban districts that traditionally send most African Americans to the Capitol often have significant immigrant populations, both legal and undocumented. The U.S. system of immigration policies, strategies and controls—developing criteria on who may come to the country and who may not, determining how to enforce the laws and how much money to spend doing so—has long been a topic of Congressional Black Caucus concern and legislative initiatives.

In a 2006 radio address, Rep. Jesse Jackson Jr., D-Ill., put a face rooted in black history on the issue while calling for comprehensive changes in the law, not simply a focus on law enforcement:

> African Americans came here as slaves, not as immigrants, so why should we identify with the immigrant cause? We should identify out of principle, and the principle should be: *human rights for all human beings.* No other human being is an "illegal alien." No human being should have his or her human rights violated. No human being should be treated any less than as a full human being and in a humane way.[22]

Legislation that fails to legalize those immigrants who are currently illegal is unrealistic, according to Rep. Maxine Waters, D-Calif., because "we simply cannot arrest, detain, jail and/or deport 11 million undocumented immigrants." [23] In April 2006, she called for an immigration policy that:

1. Secures our borders to curtail the influx of undocumented immigrants from the North and the South and develops security policies that address *all* illegal immigration.
2. Provides for the deportation of undocumented criminals and violent gang members.
3. Allows 11 million undocumented immigrants in this country to gain legal status under a comprehensive policy—with criteria.
4. Includes a livable wage standard for all workers and punishes employers who violate the law.[24]

In a 2006 article, Rep. Sheila Jackson-Lee, D-Texas, criticized as ineffective and unrealistic the Bush administration's proposed guest worker program and the government's efforts to manage undocumented immigrants now in the United States and to seal the borders. Jackson-Lee, then the senior Democrat on the Judiciary Committee's Subcommittee on

Immigration, Border Security and Claims, advocated permanent legal status for "honest, hard-working undocumented immigrants" who have lived in the country at least five years and adding 15,000 Border Patrol agents over a five-year span.[25]

Some African American politicians have pushed for a tougher approach to immigration, including Alan Keyes, the 2004 GOP Senate nominee in Illinois (**Document 8.8**). During one campaign debate with Democratic candidate Barack Obama, Keyes said:

> We need to have guarded borders. We need to make clear that the states and localities are not gonna extend privileges to aliens . . . And I think, if we take all those steps, in order to make sure we're enforcing strictly and can enforce our immigration laws, so that we've applied to both borders what's necessary for immigration and national security, we can then move forward.[26]

Immigration remained a major issue in the 2006 election season when the House, Senate and President George W. Bush failed to agree on comprehensive new laws. Less than two months before the election, Congress passed the controversial Secure Fence Act, authorizing construction of a 700-mile fence along the U.S.-Mexico border. In the following Senate floor speech, Obama acknowledges that the fence might help control the influx of illegal immigrants but warns that it will fall far short of addressing other key issues, such as penalties for employers that hire those aliens. Obama voted for the bill, although his Caucus colleagues in the House voted against it.

═══ Document 13.11 ═══
Sen. Barack Obama, D-Ill., Speaks about the Secure Fence Act, September 21, 2006

Mr. OBAMA: . . . The bill before us will certainly do some good. It will authorize some badly needed funding for better fences and better security along our borders, and that should help stem some of the tide of illegal immigration in this country. But if we think that putting up a few more miles of fence is by any means the whole answer to our immigration problems, then I believe we are seriously kidding ourselves.

This bill, from my perspective, is an election-year, political solution to a real policy challenge that goes far beyond November. It is great for sound bites and ad campaigns, but as an answer to the problem of illegal immigration, it is unfinished at best.

Yes, we need tougher border security and stronger enforcement measures. Yes, we need more resources for Customs and Border agents and more detention beds. Democrats and Republicans in both the House and the Senate agree on these points. But immigrants sneaking in through unguarded holes in our border are only part of the problem.

As a host of former Bush immigration officials and Members of Congress said in today's *Washington Post*, we must "acknowledge that as much as half of the illegal-immigration problem is driven by the hiring of people who enter the United States through official border points but use fraudulent documents or overstay visas."

This serves as a reminder that for the last 15 years, our immigration strategy has consisted of throwing more money at the border. We have tripled the size of the Border Patrol and we strengthened fences. But even as investments in border security grew, the size of the undocumented population grew as well. So we need to approach the immigration challenge from a different perspective.

This is why for months Democrats and Republicans have been working together to pass a comprehensive immigration bill out of this Congress because we know that in addition to greater border security, we also need greater sanctions on employers who illegally hire people in this country. We need to make it easier for those employers to identify who is legally eligible to work and who is not. And we need to figure out how we plan to deal with the 12 million undocumented immigrants who are already here, many of whom have woven themselves into the fabric of our communities, many of whom have children who are U.S. citizens, many of whom employers depend on. Until we do, no one should be able to look a voter in the face and honestly tell them that we have solved our immigration problem.

A model for compromise on this issue is in the Senate bill that was passed out of this Chamber. In the new electronic employment verification system section of that bill that I helped write with Senator *Grassley* and Senator *Kennedy,* we agreed to postpone the new guest worker program until 2 years of funding is made available for improved workplace enforcement. We could extend that framework and work together to first ensure the money is in place to strengthen enforcement at the border and then allow the new guest worker program to kick in. We can do all of that in one bill, but we are not.

So while this bill will probably pass, it should be seen only as one step in the much greater challenge of reforming our immigration system. Meeting that challenge will require passing measures to discourage people from overstaying their visas in the country and to help employers check the legal status of the workers applying for jobs.

It seems it was just yesterday that we were having celebratory press conferences and the President and the Senate leadership were promising to pass a bill that would secure our borders and take a tough but realistic approach to the undocumented immigrants who are already here.

Today that promise looks empty and that cooperation seems like a thing of the past. But we owe it to the American people to finish the job we are starting today. And we owe it to all those immigrants who have come to this country with nothing more than a willingness to work and a hope for a better life. Like so many of our own parents and grandparents, they have shown the courage to leave their homes and seek out a new destiny of their own making. The least we can do is show the courage to help them make that destiny a reality in a way that is safe, legal, and achievable. So when we actually start debating this bill, I hope the majority leader will permit consideration of a wide range of amendments.

Source: Congressional Record, 109th Cong., 2d sess., September 21, 2006, S9879–S9880.

NOTES

1 Walter White, *A Rising Wind* (Garden City, N.Y.: Doubleday, 1945), in *The Black Experience 1865-1978: A Documentary Reader,* ed. Anthony J. Cooper (Kent, United Kingdom: Greenwich University Press, 1995), 225.

2 J. C. Watts Jr., *What Color Is a Conservative? My Life and My Politics* (New York: HarperCollins, 2002), 256.

3 *Congressional Record,* 109th Cong., 1st sess., July 20, 2005, E1572.

4 Congressional Black Caucus, "U.S. Congressman Gregory W. Meeks to Deliver Weekly CBC 'Message to America,' " press release, July 7, 2006.

5 *Congressional Record,* 43d Cong., 1st sess., January 24, 1874, Appendix, 29.

6 *Congressional Record,* 101st Cong., 1st sess., April 12, 1989, E1168.

7 *Congressional Record,* 106th Cong., 2d sess., January 27, 2000, H15

8 House Committee on International Relations, *Report of the Commission for Assistance to Cuba: Hearing before the Subcommittee on the Western Hemisphere,* July 27, 2006, 43.

9 Ibid., 9.

10 Ibid., 48.

11 "Negro Soldiers on the Filipino Insurrection, 1901" (*Freeman,* May 11, 1901), in *A Documentary History of the Negro People in the United States,* ed. Herbert Aptheker (New York: Citadel Press, 1969), 825–826.

12 Charles C. Diggs Jr., "Statement on the Proclamation of Independence of the Republic of Guinea-Bissau," *Issue: A Journal of Opinion* 3, no. 3 (Fall 1973): 30, 33.

13 United Nations Office on Drugs and Crime, *Afghanistan Opium Poppy Survey 2007,* August 2007, iv.

14 Rep. Carolyn Cheeks Kilpatrick, "Kilpatrick to Examine AIDS Policies of Three African Nations during Presidential Mission March 27–April 5," news release, March 26, 1999, www.house.gov/kilpatrick/pr032699_aids.html.

15 Jennifer Brooks, "The Minority AIDS Crisis: Congressional Black Caucus Prompts Administration to Launch $156 million HIV/AIDS Initiative for Racial and Ethnic Minorities," April 1999, U.S. Department of Health and Human Services, Office of Minority Health Resources Center, www.omhrc.gov.

16 Rep. Barbara Lee, "Congressional Black Caucus Leaders Demand that President Bush Provide Greater Resources for HIV/AIDS Epidemic," news release, December 20, 2002, http://lee.house.gov/index.cfm?.

17 "Congressional Black Caucus Asks President Bush to Resume Aid to Haiti," letter from Congressional Black Caucus members to President George W. Bush, November 8, 2001, from National Coalition for Haitian Rights, www.nchr.org/hrp/cbc_open_letter.htm.

18 Rep. Charles B. Rangel, "Rep. Charles B. Rangel Opening Statement Mark Up of Bush Administration CAFTA Legislation," news release, June 30, 2005, www.house.gov/list/press/wm31_democrats/063005.

19 Congressional Black Caucus, "The Congressional Black Caucus Urges Immediate Action Be Taken to End the Genocide in Darfur," news release, December 15, 2005, www.house.gov/list/press/nc12_watt/pr_cbc_121505b_genocideindarfus.html.

20 "Condemning the Recent Attacks against the State of Israel, Holding Terrorists and Their State-Sponsors Accountable for Such Attacks, Supporting Israel's Right to Defend Itself, and for Other Purposes," H. Res. 921, *Congressional Record,* 109th Cong., 2d sess., July 19, 2006, H5451.

21 *Congressional Record,* 109th Cong., 2d sess., February 17, 2006, E195.

22 Congressional Black Caucus, "Congressman Jesse Jackson, Jr. to Deliver Weekly CBC 'Message to America,'" press release, May 5, 2006.

23 Maxine Waters, "U.S. Rep. Maxine Waters' Statement on Illegal Immigration," press release, April 13, 2006.

24 Ibid.

25 Sheila Jackson-Lee, "Why Immigration Reform Requires a Comprehensive Approach that Includes Both Legalization Programs and Provisions to Secure the Border," *Harvard Journal on Legislation* 43, no. 2 (Summer 2006): 267.

26 Debate between Alan Keyes and Barack Obama, sponsored by WTTW and the City Club of Chicago, October 26, 2004; transcript from Renew America, www.renewamerica.us/archives/media/debates/04_10_26debate3.htm.

CHAPTER FOURTEEN

At the Heart of the African American Experience

The Struggle for Economic Justice

Economics have long been at the heart of the African American experience. It was white Europeans' desire for economic profit that led them to transport Africans across the Atlantic to toil as slaves on the plantations and farms of America. It was the labor of those slaves that made the Cotton Kingdom of the American South an economic powerhouse before the Civil War. And it was the desire of white supremacists to return to that race-based prosperity that drove efforts, during Reconstruction and after, to exclude African Americans from the political process and to limit their ability to work independently and profitably.

Rep. Charles B. Rangel, D-N.Y., authored a 1973 article titled "The Verbal Cure" that was published in the liberal-leaning magazine The Nation. *In it, he attacked the Nixon administration's shift away from government programs designed to help the poor. Thirty-four years later, when Democrats took control of Congress in 2007, Rangel became chairman of the influential House Ways and Means Committee. He is pictured here during the committee's markup of the Katrina Housing Tax Relief Act of 2007.*
Source: CQ Photo/Scott J. Ferrell

At every turn, African Americans have found themselves enmeshed in the economic inequities of American society. Nearly a century and a half after emancipation, blacks are still disproportionately represented among the poor. Over the years, they have had to struggle against laws that effectively forced them to sign unfair labor contracts with white landowners; against discrimination in the workplace that kept them from getting desirable jobs and ensured that they would be the first to be fired in times of economic downturn; and against the indifference and shifting priorities of a society that often saw programs to aid the poor as expendable. The documents in this chapter illuminate some of the ways in which African Americans in Congress addressed the many facets of economic injustice.

In the late nineteenth century, the U.S. economy was still largely agrarian. As the industrialization of America accelerated, many thousands of African Americans moved to the cities of the South as well as the North, seeking jobs that paid more than farm labor. For many, farm work was inextricably tied to the memories of slavery and freedom somehow seemed "freer" in the cities. But the majority of black Americans still lived and worked on farms. The few who obtained small farms of their own faced an endless struggle to retain them in the face of crop failures, declining market prices for their crops, burdensome taxes and discriminatory banking practices. Most blacks, however, especially in the South, were forced to continue to work for white landowners as wage laborers, tenant farmers or sharecroppers.

The late nineteenth century was a time of great uncertainty and unrest in America's farming regions. Concerns over federal trade and monetary policies, and over the market dominance of eastern banks and investors, gave rise to a number of organizing efforts among the nation's farmers—white as well as black. Organizations such as the Grange and the Farmers' Alliance emerged in an attempt to give farmers a unified voice on public policies that affected them. Black farmers—barred from the Farmers' Alliance—formed their own organization, the Colored Farmers' Alliance, to voice their concerns as well. In the political realm, the Populist Party sought to tap into the anger of farmers and, to some extent, appealed for the support of black as well as white farmers.

Though black representation in Congress was never large in the late nineteenth century and sharply declined with the end of Reconstruction, those African Americans who served in Congress frequently argued for policies that would benefit black farmers and farm laborers. Benjamin S. Turner, R-Ala., in his 1872 appeal for the refund of a cotton tax that had been levied for several years just after the Civil War, argued that the tax had resulted in a glut of cheap foreign cotton that drove down prices in the international cotton market (**Document 14.1**). The big loser, he argued, was the farm laborer, most often black, who "gathered the cotton with his bloodstained fingers from the pods." George W. Murray, R-S.C., waded into the monetary policy debate in 1893 between backers of the gold standard and "free silver"—a key Populist position—to argue for a middle course that would benefit farm workers more than bankers or mining interests (**Document 14.2**). Four years later, George H. White, R-N.C., argued for tariffs to protect southern industries and the jobs of southern laborers—many of whom were black (**Document 14.3**). At the time, White was the only African American in Congress, and his speech expressed a keen awareness that he was the sole spokesman for a people whose economic interests were not sufficiently protected.

During the long gap between White's departure from Congress in 1901 and the arrival of the next black representative, Oscar S. De Priest, R-Ill., in 1929, the job market of the nation, and the role of blacks in that job market, changed dramatically. The booming growth of the nation's cities, particularly those in the North; the continuing acceleration of industrialization, spurred on by World War I; and the great migration of southern blacks to the cities of the North combined to make blacks a substantial component of the growing legions of manufacturing workers. Some industrialists, such as Henry Ford, even recruited in the South to attract black workers to their northern factories. But black manufacturing workers often faced pay discrimination, and many were shunted into the least desirable jobs. Ford may have been progressive in his willingness to hire blacks for his sprawling Ford Rouge complex in Dearborn, Michigan, but most of them were assigned to the foundry—the hottest, dirtiest and most dangerous part of the complex.

When the economy slumped, black workers were often the first to suffer layoffs. Early in the Great Depression, as millions of workers lost their jobs, the impact fell most heavily on black workers. The severity of the nation's economic collapse prompted some political leaders to consider extreme measures. As Congress debated legislation in early 1932 to provide federal relief to unemployed workers and their families—help for the needy was still widely viewed as a local, rather than federal, responsibility—one suggestion was to have the federal government pay for trains that would carry unemployed black workers from northern cities back to the rural southern communities from which they had migrated over the previous decades. As Walter White, executive secretary of the National Association for the Advancement of Colored People (NAACP), pointed out in a sharply worded letter to President Herbert Hoover (**Document 14.4**), such a plan would not only violate African Americans' rights as citizens and condemn many to starvation, but it would also return them to "a condition of actual peonage—of debt slavery" that still prevailed for many blacks in the South.

Decades later, in 2005, Del. Eleanor Holmes Norton, D-D.C., proposed a Fair Pay Act (**Document 14.9**), arguing that the workplace continued to be a focal point for race and gender discrimination. The job market had changed dramatically since the 1930s, with less reliance on manufacturing jobs and more on service-industry jobs. But while women were a growing portion of the workforce, wage rates remained lower for women, especially black women, Norton said. She pointed out that, as a result of stereotypes and employers' hiring practices, three-quarters of African American working women were concentrated in sales and clerical, service, and factory jobs that restricted their ability to make full use of their skills and maximize their earnings. The need

Rep. Barbara Lee, D-Calif., was among Congressional Black Caucus members who continued to advocate for greater federal support of recovery efforts months after Hurricane Katrina devastated the Gulf Coast of Mississippi and Louisiana in 2005, displacing numerous poor and minority residents.
Source: CQ Photo/Scott J. Ferrell

for economic equity for women also was the subject of a campaign speech by Rep. Shirley A. Chisholm, D-N.Y., in her 1972 run as the first African American presidential candidate (**Document 14.5**).

A constant difficulty for African Americans has been sustaining America's attention to the issue of economic inequality in the face of competing priorities, particularly during times of war. In a 1973 magazine article, Rep. Charles B. Rangel, D-N.Y., criticized the lack of support for poverty programs while the United States was still spending millions on the Vietnam War (**Document 14.6**). Thirty years later, in a rap poem, Rep. Major R. O. Owens, D-N.Y., challenged American spending on the war in Iraq, as well as the extent to which poor and working-class Americans were called upon to fight the war (**Document 14.8**).

Members of the Congressional Black Caucus challenged America's priorities in August 2005 in the aftermath of Hurricane Katrina. In a speech during debate on legislation to assist with rebuilding the Gulf Coast communities that were devastated by the storm, Rep. Barbara Lee, D-Calif., spoke for many in the Caucus when she said that the storm's victims had been abandoned by their government during the disaster because they were poor and mostly black (**Document 14.10**). In January 2007 Caucus members were among those who accused President George W. Bush of ignoring the storm's victims when he did not refer to the continuing recovery efforts in his State of the Union address.

Hovering over all of these issues is the great unresolved question that has lingered since ratification of the Thirteenth Amendment (**Document 2.8**) banned slavery in America: Does the United States owe economic compensation to descendants of the former slaves? Gen. William Tecumseh Sherman's Special Field Order No. 15, which provided land and the use of army mules to freed slaves along the Atlantic Coast between Charleston, South Carolina, and Jacksonville, Florida, was an early—and rescinded—effort to provide for the emancipated slaves' economic needs. Bills to provide pensions to former slaves were introduced in Congress in the 1890s and early 1900s but died in committee. Since 1989 Rep. John Conyers Jr., D-Mich., has repeatedly introduced legislation to study the possibility of providing reparations to the descendants of African American slaves (**Document 14.7**). Support for the idea—which is controversial even within the African American community—appeared to be growing after the turn of the twenty-first century, and Conyers's ascendancy to chair the House Judiciary Committee in January 2007 raised the possibility that he might be in a position to promote the bill more effectively. But with or without passage, the proposed legislation served as a reminder that economic justice remained an unresolved and tender issue in the history of African Americans and the nation.

Document 14.1 in Context
"This Tax Was Unjust, Inequitable, and Unconstitutional": Rep. Benjamin S. Turner, R-Ala., and the Cotton Tax

The end of the Civil War brought tremendous political, economic and social turmoil. President Andrew Johnson fought with the Radical Republicans in Congress over the requirements governing the southern states' restoration to the Union and representation in Congress. At the same time, southern whites struggled to reassert political supremacy despite the emancipation of 4.5 million slaves and the Reconstruction rules imposed by Congress that required the inclusion of African Americans in the political process. The southern economy, meanwhile, had been devastated by four years of warfare conducted mainly on southern soil, and the emancipation of the slaves on whose labor the Cotton Kingdom had been created made the resurrection of the southern economy a complicated undertaking.

As blacks began to vote, participate in the rewriting of southern state constitutions and be elected to public office, they used their newfound political voice to call for reforms to help those who were newly freed cope with uncertainties of freedom and diminish the continuing inequities they faced. Many severe inequities were economic. Though thousands of African Americans began leaving the South soon after the war, the majority remained and continued to do the agricultural work with which they were most familiar—growing cotton. Annual labor contracts pressed on them by the Freedmen's Bureau (**Document 2.10**), white planters and southern vagrancy laws regularly put black agricultural workers at an economic disadvantage, and the beginning of the sharecropping system launched millions of black farmers into a pattern of ever-growing debt that would keep them tied to the land.

In May 1872, Rep. Benjamin S. Turner, R-Ala., one of the first African Americans elected to Congress, called for the refund of a cotton tax that had been levied between 1866 and 1868. The result of the tax, Turner argued, was to depress the price of cotton on world markets and reduce the incomes of southern cotton growers. Although the tax had hurt all growers—and its spin-off effects were felt across the southern economy—the weight of the tax had fallen most heavily on poor farmers and agricultural workers, especially blacks. From the House floor, Turner called for justice by refunding the tax to those he said were most harmed by it. Excerpts of his remarks follow.

▬▬ Document 14.1 ▬▬
Rep. Benjamin S. Turner, R-Ala., Proposes a Refund of the Cotton Tax on the House Floor, May 31, 1872

Mr. TURNER: . . . I had the honor on the 20th day of February last to present a petition and memorial to Congress praying Congress and the country to refund the cotton tax. The understanding of the people is that this tax fell upon a certain section and class. It did not fall upon the owner of the land, nor upon the merchant, nor upon the consumer, but directly upon the laborer who tilled the soil and gathered the cotton with his bloodstained fingers from the pods. The seventh section of the Constitution of the United States authorizes Congress to levy a uniform tax. Our understanding of uniformity is that every State in the Union shall pay a tax in proportion to its population and wealth; hence we claim that the cotton tax falling upon a special section of the country and upon a certain class of citizens is unconstitutional; because, in the first place, it is detrimental to one section of the country and beneficial to another; next, it is a direct tax upon industry in that part of the country where cotton is made. And, instead of paying the people a premium for their industry it is a direct prohibition of cotton making.

In 1866, 1867 and 1868 there was a cotton tax levied amounting to $70,000,000. We claim that this tax was unjust, inequitable, and unconstitutional . . . This tax wrought a more serious influence and destructive consequence than seems to be understood by Congress and the people in general.

The war through which we have passed stopped cotton making for a time, and thus caused cotton to be scarce and high in other markets of the world. Other nations, looking upon cotton as one of the chief necessities of life, went into cotton making in self-defense, and continued so to do till the war was over in the United States . . .

These nations, by their energy, industry, and success, glutted the markets of the world with cotton so much so that it reduced the cotton of the United States from forty-three cents in 1866 to thirty-one cents in 1868.

And when the cotton tax was repealed in 1868, the outside influence began to decrease and the price of our cotton to increase, and has been getting higher and higher ever since.

. . . A fair calculation will show that if there had been no tax upon cotton, the minimum value would never have gone below thirty-five cents per pound.

. . . And, sir, as I have said before, the Government collected $70,000,000 upon cotton, thereby bringing about the influence of which I have spoken before, namely, increasing competition, glutting the markets and reducing the price of our cotton to an additional amount of $250,000,000, besides the $70,000,000 paid on cotton. This $250,000,000 fell into the hands of other nations by the prohibitory influence of our own Government, consequently the whole loss to the cotton-making section of the country by the direct tax and its indirect influence amounts to $320,000,000.

To prove my argument to be true, I will refer to other products of industry than cotton. For instance, take away the tariff from iron and place a prohibitory tax of three cents per pound for making iron. What would be the effect? I am satisfied that such would be the effect that iron-masters from all parts of the world would be bringing iron to the United States, while ironmasters in our country would have to abandon their business or starve. This I know, Mr. Speaker, will not be disputed by the tariff men of Pennsylvania upon this floor.

. . . I will place any other article in the same situation that cotton has been placed. Salt, for instance. Take away the tariff and impose a tax of one cent per pound, and the effect will be the same as upon cotton. Or take sugar, and impose the prohibitory tax of three cents per pound upon it, and the effect upon it will be the same as that upon cotton.

According to the Constitution, I deny that this tax is uniform, since it would have been as fair to tax either of the just-named articles, as it was to tax cotton, for custom and the present status of civilization recognize these articles to be the prime necessities of life. Cotton is a necessity according to custom, decency, civilization, and under rules and regulations of society. There are no rules nor regulations laid down by law, neither constitutional, statute, common, nor municipal law, that compels any man to eat or drink; but, on the other hand municipal law, moral customs, and influences of every civilized community compel every man to properly clothe himself, making it a penal offense for him to appear in the street unless his nakedness is thoroughly concealed; nor does custom stop with a mere concealing of nakedness, but even a superfluity of clothing is necessary, so as to add to his personal appearance. Cotton, therefore, being an indispensable article of dress, and an absolute necessity to protect us from the many changes of weather, should not be placed in the same category with tobacco and whiskey, recognized and acknowledged poisonous luxuries of life.

Again I refer to the class of people who make cotton. The statistics will show that twenty-nine bales of cotton out of every thirty made in the United States are made directly by the Negroes in the southern states, and to them . . . this tax is due. I will say for them that when they were set free they found themselves without homes, without clothes and without bread; with all their means of subsistence in the North and northwestern states, thousands of miles from them, slandered and abused, said to be too lazy to make cotton unless a will superior to their own were placed over them to control, they united themselves and determined to make cotton under their own direction in order that they might refute the base slanders which had been heaped upon them. And but for this tax which I have mentioned they would have been able to purchase one-eighth of the land upon which this cotton was made. Further, this three cents per pound came directly from the labor of the man who made the cotton. In addition to this tax, he pays large freights upon all substances, meat, bread, and other articles, such as are shipped to him from the great distances above mentioned. He must pay the freights on cotton to and from the New England mills, also the manufacturer's percentage and the merchant's profit.

Now , Mr. Speaker, I plead in behalf of the poor people of the South, regardless of caste or color, because this tax had its blighting influence. It cut the jugular vein of our financial system, bled it near unto death, and wrought a destructive influence upon every line of business. It so crippled every trade and industry that our suffering has been greater under its influence than under that of the war. That tax took away all the income and left us no profit and very little circulating medium. I therefore beg Congress to correct the error and refund the cotton tax to that class of people from whom it was taken and for whom I wish to please in my imperfect way . . .

Mr. Speaker, I ask Congress to make this appropriation, and I ask it in behalf of the land-less and poor people of our country. In that section of country that I have the honor in part to represent upon this floor the people are extremely poor, having been emancipated from slavery after hundreds of years of disappointment and privation. These people have struggled longer and labored harder, and have made more of the raw material than any peo-ple in the world. Notwithstanding the fact that they have labored long, hard, and faithfully, they live on little clothing, the poorest food, and in miserable huts. Since they have been free they have not slackened their industry, but have materially improved their economy. While their labor has rewarded the nation with larger revenue, they have consumed less of the substance of the country than any other class of people. If dressing less, eating little, and hard and continued labor means economy, these people are the most economical in the world. And, it is a universal understanding among themselves that they are not to live in any extravagant way so far as eating and dressing is concerned. They are laboring and making every effort to secure land and houses. It is next to impossible that this generation will accomplish it without such aid, as I now ask from the Government . . .

Source: Congressional Globe, 42d Cong., 2d sess., May 31, 1872, Appendix, 540–541.

Document 14.2 in Context
"I Represent the Largest Constituency of Any Member": Seeking the Middle Monetary Path

On August 24, 1893, Rep. George W. Murray, R-S.C., stepped into a political debate over U.S. monetary policy that raged throughout the 1890s. The issue was closely tied to the rising political activism of farmers who had been hurt by depressed agricultural prices since the mid-1870s. The Farmers' Alliance, organized in Texas in 1876, had agitated for collective action to break the power of railroads, brokers and merchants over the transportation and sale of agricultural goods. Black farmers, who had generally suffered even more than white farm-ers, were barred from joining the Farmers' Alliance. So they formed their own organization, the Colored Farmers' Alliance, which supported many of the same policies and tried, when possible, to cooperate with the white Farmers' Alliance.

That activism gave rise to the Populist Party, which captured the electoral college votes of four states (Colorado, Idaho, Kansas and Nevada) for its presidential candidate, James B. Weaver, in 1892. Four years later, the Populist Party nominated William Jennings Bryan, who was also the presidential nominee of the Democratic Party. A keystone of Bryan's platform was a rejection of the gold standard for currency—which he said benefited eastern banking interests at the expense of farmers—in favor of free coinage of silver. In his speech to the 1896 Democratic National Convention, Bryan famously denounced the nation's bankers and com-mercial interests, declaring that they "shall not crucify mankind upon a cross of gold."[1]

Murray, in the following speech to the House of Representatives, seeks to steer a middle course in the gold versus silver debate. He identifies not two interests in the conflict, but three: the capitalists and bankers, who were promoting the gold standard; the mining companies and their owners, who were promoting free silver coinage; and average working people, who would benefit, he argues, from some mixture of the two. According to Murray, a monetary policy that balanced the perspectives of the gold and silver promoters would be more equitable and would not give any of the parties economic advantage over the others.

▬▬ Document 14.2 ▬▬
Rep. George W. Murray, R-S.C., Discusses Impact of Monetary Policy, August 24, 1893

Mr. MURRAY: . . . The speeches on this floor remind me of the custom among persons of the Methodist persuasion, when called upon in experience meetings to give expression to the reasons upon which their faith is predicated.

As my first important vote in this House will be on the pending bill, I deem it necessary to give expression to the reasons impelling me to cast it, as I shall.

The casual observer very readily perceives that upon the settlement of the pending question the American people are divided into three distinct and somewhat antagonistic elements.

Upon its settlement the miner, producer, and laborer are becoming no less interested than the merchant prince and millionaire.

The first class is composed of capitalists, bankers, and commercial men, who own and control nearly all the currency, and are desirous of making and keeping it dear by keeping this volume as small as possible.

The second class is composed of those who own the silver mines and all the un-coined bullion not in possession of the Government, and are using all their power to establish free coinage, I fear, mainly to enhance the value of their possessions.

The third class is composed of the toiling and producing millions, who are neither gold bugs nor silver bugs, and who realize so little from their labor and investments that each year finds them less able to meet the obligations of the former, in consequence of which they are forced to sink deeper and deeper under threatening billows of mortgages and debts, beneath which many of the giant ships of their fellows, bringing the bread and necessities of life from the shores of nothingness, have sunk to rise no more, leaving their overburdened barks in raging seas of debts. I am in favor of a change in our monetary policy, but not such a one as has been suggested by the advocates of the gold standard.

To the last-named class nearly all of my constituents, and the whole race of which I am the sole representative, belong.

In two respects I represent the largest constituency of any member of this House, a district of two hundred and seventy thousand, and a race of nearly eight million.

Speaking for them I do not believe that the great evils with which they are afflicted are owing to the operations of the so-called Sherman Law.

They had been hurtfully feeling the mailed hand of the unrighteous financial policy of their country long before the silver-purchasing bill of 1890 became a law.

They believe and know that the primary cause of the direful disease which has been making paupers of them and their children for more than a dozen years lies deeper than the recent superficial, and in some respects, designing unrest in money circles.

They trace it to a contraction of the circulating medium that, like a viper with its victim in its coils, has been drawing its cords tighter around their prosperity, until it is dead. I am of the opinion that the only sure and permanent remedy is a lengthening of the cords, an enlargement of the volume of money.

Unlike the other classes, my constituents combine patriotism with self-interest.

They want the volume of money increased by the use of those substances in which their Government would have the greatest security.

While they want and must have more and cheaper money, they demand that it be made of such substances as have the greatest intrinsic value, and as the supply of gold is inadequate and growing less, are in favor of making up the deficiency with silver, and to that extent favor free coinage and bimetalism, and no one, in the course of this debate, has even pretended to prove that there is more than a sufficiency of both gold and silver obtainable to supply the monetary use of the world.

I submit that the true measure of the superabundance or insufficiency of the circulating medium is the price of labor and productions of one period compared with those of another . . .

The negro, as patriotic and devoted as when dying on the plains of Boston, bleeding on Bunker Hill, or suffering the horrors of war through cold and heat, in hunger and nakedness, amidst northern snows or the malarial swamps of the South, under the lead of Marion, Sumter, and Washington, or repelling the formidable army of Lord Packenham, under the lead of the gallant and indomitable Jackson, in the war of 1812, or turning the tide of war in favor of the Stars and Stripes, under the commands of Butler, Hunter, Shaw, Logan, Hancock, and Grant, in the Civil War, in such a way as caused each star to assume such brilliancy and each stripe such strength as to daze the eyes and successfully resist the great battering rams of the Confederacy, is in favor of the remonetization of silver as a means of increasing the circulating medium, because it would tend to make America the happy home of all Americans. [Applause.]

I feel so proud of being able to say that history does not reveal the fact where a black hand was ever voluntarily raised to strike down the flag of its country, nor is the vote of the black man ever knowingly cast against its interest.

Notwithstanding the ill treatment received at the hands of his countrymen, he is always found voting and shouting for America and Americans, and on this currency question he is in favor of an American, instead of and English, German, French, or Belgian policy.

I am especially in favor of silver because it so fittingly illustrates the condition of the colored Americans.

Driven out of competition with gold in paying custom dues and the principal and interest on the bonded debt, which it so largely aided in making, and is not even allowed to redeem its creature, the silver certificate, there are those who ask why, does it not stand up on terms of equality in the marts of trade with gold?

It is dishonest to ask, or expect, a slave to compete on terms of equality with a free man.

I remember seeing, in my peregrinations through my native State, placarded in many nooks and corners, "White is king," which I was inclined to believe. But in the case of gold and silver it seems that that doctrine has been exploded. The little, yellow, gold man, so small and circumscribed, has, by special training and baneful education in later years, become so strong and malevolent that he is spitefully driving this large, useful, humane, and philanthropic white man (silver) from nearly every place of honor, usefulness, and amusement . . .

. . . Standing before you to-day, the lone spokesman for my race, I hear voices that you do not hear; I see faces that you cannot see.

I have visited the farmer in his cabin; have tilled the soil and followed the furrow side by side with the humblest; I have spoken and discussed with the businessmen, and the ruling class of my State. I see their wants and I feel their needs, and every fiber of my body vibrates in sympathy with the people—the common people. [Applause.]

They call to us today for help; call from the mines that close them out and deny them bread; call from the factories that have hushed their busy hum, but have not stilled the cry of the child for bread.

I shall be criticized for the stand which I have taken on this question, but as between the monopolist and the gold bugs on the one side and the common people on the other I stand with the people, feeling myself their creature and their servant and ready to do their bidding . . .

Source: Congressional Record, 53d Cong., 1st sess., August 24, 1893, 858–862.

Document 14.3 in Context
"We Want Pay for an Honest Day's Work": Protecting Workers in the South

Throughout the nineteenth century, the circumstances of the southern laborer were a major concern for the African American representatives in Congress. Not only did the majority of black workers still reside in the South, but their wages and working conditions lagged behind those of workers in the North. As with Rep. Benjamin S. Turner in his plea to refund the cotton tax in 1872 (**Document 14.1**), and with Rep. George W. Murray in his discussion of U.S. monetary policy in 1893 (**Document 14.2**), Rep. George H. White, R-N.C., sought in 1897 to ease the struggle of southern black workers by influencing federal trade policy.

In a March 1897 speech in the House of Representatives, White argued in favor of a trade bill that included tariffs aimed at protecting southern goods and industries. The core of his argument was that the legislation would benefit southern workers by protecting them from competition from cheaper foreign labor. Such protection was necessary, he argued, to enable the workers to earn a decent living.

But White's speech resonated with other issues as well. He spoke of his position as Congress's sole representative of the nation's 9 million African Americans, "90 percent of whom are laborers." He also noted that his colleagues had used racist language in their debate on the bill. Moreover, he alluded to the increasing disenfranchisement of black voters in the South.

Although White was the only black member of Congress in 1897, more than twenty years earlier, black representation had peaked at eight—seven representatives and one senator—in the Forty-fourth Congress. That number was cut in half in the election of 1876, and since 1891 there had been only one black member in each Congress. Since the end of Reconstruction, the southern states had been working aggressively—and effectively—to disenfranchise black voters. White's awareness of his political isolation and of the economic and political suppression of blacks in general is vividly apparent in his speech, which is excerpted here.

▬▬ Document 14.3 ▬▬
Rep. George H. White, R-N.C., Supports Tariffs to Protect Southern Laborers, March 31, 1897

Mr. WHITE of North Carolina: . . . I rise to supplement what my colleague [Romulus Z. LINNEY] said during the five minutes I have. I desire not only to add a word in behalf of the articles mentioned by him—coal, iron, mica, cotton, wool, cattle, hogs, etc.—but wish especially to emphasize a word in behalf of the people of eastern North Carolina on that part of this bill which includes lumber. Under the Wilson bill the contracts which had been entered into by the mill men had in many instances to be forfeited; the mills that had been running day and night, giving employment to thousands and thousands of operatives, were shut down, and those operatives were thus shut out. These men, the heads of families, were forced to see their loved ones pinched with want, with no way for them to earn a dollar. This bill, because of this lumber schedule, as well as others, commends itself especially to the southern people who have to labor to get bread and meat for their families. [Laughter and applause on the Republican side and in the galleries.]

I have been amused, Mr. Chairman, by my Democratic friends, though not surprised, because I have heard that old yarn before [laughter], in their advocacy of "free trade." Why, they have from time to time advocated "free whiskey" also; and in the last campaign their shibboleth was "free silver." In fact, the Southern element of the Democratic party had advocated "free" everything except free ballots and free Negroes.

It is wonderful, Mr. Chairman, how solicitous those gentlemen are about the future welfare of the Republican party. The bone and sinew of their arguments are their fears that the place that now knows us will, if we pass this bill, soon know us no more forever. Well, gentlemen, we will take care of this side of the House. We have heard of the devil teaching scriptures, but never to save a soul. If we are contented, you ought not to be troubled. [Laughter.]

Mr. Chairman, gentlemen on the other side of this Chamber have felt themselves called upon to resent some imputations of incompetency that went from this side of the House. Well, I am a Southerner to the manner born and reared, and am usually in sympathy with the South, but when Democratic members on the other side of this House drag into this great Congress of the United States the expressions of the southern plantations in regard to "the darky and heels of a mule," then I think the imputation is a correct one.

Mr. Chairman, I am here to speak, and I do speak, as the sole representative on this floor of 9,000,000 of the population of these United States, 90 percent of whom are laborers. Under this bill they are protected; they are given an opportunity to earn their living. Bread and butter are what we want, not fine-spun Democratic campaign theory. We have had enough of that. We want something now upon which soul and body can be kept together. We want an honest dollar. We want pay for an honest day's work. We believe that this bill may bring about these things or that such may be largely the effect. We are therefore willing to rest our case here . . . When, as the gentleman from Indiana [Henry U. JOHNSON] suggests, it shall have passed under the scrutinizing eye of the United States Senate, we shall have, as I believe, a measure of which every American citizen ought to be proud.

My friend from South Carolina said that my colleague [Mr. LINNEY] did not represent the popular sentiment of the South when he advocated the protective tariff features enunciated in this bill. I think, Mr. Chairman, that it comes with bad grace from the gentleman to talk of misrepresentation of the Southern people when he considers the fact that 130,000 people in his State are not allowed to vote at all. [Applause on the Republican side.]

I want to say to him that while I know but little of South Carolina as it now is—I used to know something of it when it was a State in the Union, with the privileges of sister States of the Union—yet I do know something of the sentiment in my own State of North Carolina, and many other States, and I can tell the gentleman from my own knowledge that there is a growing sentiment prevailing with the development of that country that the industries and the labor of America shall be protected against the pauperism and the cheap labor of foreign countries, Democratic campaign thunder to the contrary notwithstanding. [Prolonged applause on the Republican side.]

Source: Congressional Record, 55th Cong., 1st sess., March 31, 1897, 550–551.

Document 14.4 in Context
"This . . . Vicious Method of Putting upon Negro Americans": A Depression-Era Plan to Relocate African Americans Back to the South

By the winter of 1931–1932, economic conditions in the United States had reached disastrous proportions. The Great Depression had seemingly put the nation's economy into free fall. Businesses all over the country were plunging into bankruptcy, closing and throwing millions of employees out of work. As the situation became more desperate, a swelling chorus of voices—labor leaders, local officials, newspaper editors and average citizens—called on the federal government to provide some kind of relief for the suffering of the unemployed.

In late January 1932, American Federation of Labor president William Green issued a statement outlining the scope of the problem and urging the federal government to take action:

> Ever since October unemployment has been rising rapidly. Winter lay-offs on farms have cost the jobs of about 1,250,000 wage earners, and some 1,100,000 more have been laid off in industry and salaried positions. The army of unemployed has risen to 8,300,000 (approximately) at the 1st of January.[2]

Green estimated the cost of feeding, clothing and housing the unemployed for 1932 alone at between $3.5 billion and $5.7 billion, a cost that he said could be borne only by the federal government.[3]

The escalation of suffering brought with it the fear of chaos that hunger and desperation might spark. An editorial in the *Chicago Daily News* declared that

> stark hunger brushes aside like flimsy the ordinary safeguards of society. You can bring in soldiers to keep order, but soldiers bring with them bullets, not bread. The cost of supplying the necessities of life to those who are destitute . . . would be a mere fraction of the cost of 24 hours of hunger-driven disorder.[4]

In the midst of the crisis, Sens. Robert M. La Follette Jr., R-Wis., and Edward P. Costigan, D-Colo., proposed legislation to provide $375 million in federal relief for the unemployed. Some in Congress opposed the idea—as did President Herbert Hoover—because they saw unemployment relief as essentially a state and local responsibility. Others were not deterred from suggesting more extreme measures. A report on the congressional debate in the

February 4, 1932, *New York Herald Tribune* asserted that some members of Congress were preparing to propose a "hard-boiled" plan:

> It has been suggested that money to provide trains to take indigent Negroes from New York, Detroit and Chicago back to the South, from which they were lured by the ill-balanced prosperity of a few years ago, would be the best solution of that part of the problem.[5]

On seeing that report, Walter White, executive secretary of the National Association for the Advancement of Colored People (NAACP), fired off the letter that follows to President Hoover, repudiating the proposal and vowing to resist it if it were enacted.

<hr>

▬▬ Document 14.4 ▬▬
NAACP Executive Secretary Walter White's Letter to President Herbert Hoover, February 4, 1932

My dear Mr. President:

A dispatch special to the New York *Herald-Tribune* from Washington by Mark Sullivan reports that in the consideration of the Costigan-La Follette Bill to provide federal relief to the unemployed a suggestion has been made that the United States Government provide money for trains to take "indigent Negroes from New York, Detroit and Chicago back to the South from which they were lured through the ill balanced prosperity of a few years ago" as the best solution of unemployment in large cities.

The National Association for the Advancement of Colored People, speaking in behalf of twelve million American Negro citizens and in behalf of intelligent and fair-minded citizens of other races, takes this means of going on record most emphatically against any such proposal, for the following reasons:

1. The economic unsoundness of the proposal consists in attempting to return Negroes to communities which they left because in those communities they could not earn a decent living. The Negroes and whites yet remaining on the farms of the South are now suffering from the collapse of the cotton industry due to the boll weevil, drought, and the low price of cotton. To add to their numbers will be merely to add to the numbers already facing starvation.

2. The argument that Negroes will be "better off in the farming communities from which they came" entirely ignores the fact that multitudes of Negroes still live in a condition of actual peonage—of debt slavery maintained through commissary stores and the system of share-cropping which prevails, by which Negroes are kept in perpetual debt to their landlords and thus are held bound to the land. This proposal amounts to a deportation by federal subsidy of thousands of United States citizens into peonage.

3. The argument further ignores the fact that Negroes, like any other group of citizens, are entitled to seek advancement in whatever part of the country they may find it. Why should this proposal to return Negroes to the land be confined to one race. The vast preponderance of those who have left the farms is white.

4. Besides the economic unsoundness of the project, it ignores the social conditions confronting Negroes in southern communities, which furnished a main motive for their departure. I refer to lynching, mob violence, injustice in the courts, insult, denial of equal educational opportunity, segregation in public places and in general inhuman and

degrading and insulting proscription. To propose to return Negroes, against their will, to such conditions is to invite the united opposition of the colored citizens of the nation.

The National Association for the Advancement of Colored People, through its 327 branches, the Negro press numbering more than 200 newspapers, church and fraternal organizations both north and south, as well as fair-minded Americans of other races, will vigorously oppose any such discriminatory action as that which is being proposed. Every legitimate means will be resorted to in opposing this economically unsound and essentially vicious method of putting upon Negro Americans even greater handicaps than those from which they are already suffering.

> Respectfully yours,
> [Walter White]
> Secretary

Source: Walter White to President Herbert Hoover, February 4, 1932, Herbert Hoover Presidential Library, West Branch, Iowa, Presidential Papers, Box 106, Subject File: Colored Question, Correspondence, 1932, January–June.

Document 14.5 in Context
"Anti-feminism Is Destructive Both to Those Who Perpetrate It and to Its Victims": Economic Justice for Women

Shirley A. Chisholm's arrival in Congress in January 1969 was a first on at least two levels: she was the first African American woman elected to Congress, and she arrived with the first class of new legislators to feel the full effects of the Voting Rights Act of 1965 (**Document 6.1**). Six African Americans had been members of the two previous Congresses; the election of 1968 increased black membership in Congress to eleven, including Chisholm a Democrat. The next two elections raised that number to fourteen and then seventeen.

As a founding member of the Congressional Black Caucus, Chisholm was a strong advocate for African Americans, particularly those living in urban areas like her district in Brooklyn, New York. Before entering politics, she had worked for eighteen years as a nursery school teacher and director, and as an educational consultant with New York City's Division of Day Care. She supported increased federal spending on social services, such as education and health care, and she served on the House Education and Labor Committee.

Chisholm also was an advocate for women in their struggles against discrimination, especially in the workplace. Women's issues were an important element of her Democratic political platform in 1972 when she became the first African American to seek a major party's nomination for president of the United States, and the National Organization for Women was one of her key supporters. In her 1970 autobiography, *Unbought and Unbossed,* Chisholm wrote of the difficulty involved in breaking down the stereotypes that underlay discrimination against women:

> The cheerful old darky on the plantation and the happy little homemaker are equally stereotypes drawn by prejudice. White America is beginning to be able to admit that it carries racial prejudice in its heart, and that understanding marks the beginning of the end of racism. But prejudice against women is still acceptable because it is invisible. Few men can be persuaded to believe that it exists.[6]

The document that follows is a standard speech that Chisholm used regularly during her presidential campaign. It outlines her view of the economic impact caused by discrimination against women.

▓ Document 14.5 ▓
Rep. Shirley A. Chisholm, D-N.Y., Campaigns for the Democratic Party's Presidential Nomination, 1972

At one time or another we have all used the phrase "economic justice." This afternoon I would like to turn your attention to economic justice for women. Of course this is only an illusory phrase, as it is an undeniable fact that economic justice for American women does not exist.

As I look back over the years of my own lifetime, the transformation in the economic, social and political role we women play in American life has been almost incredible. But we are still quite a long way from anything like equality of opportunity. We are still in a highly disadvantaged position relative to men. This is revealed by our earnings. On the average, women who are full-time, year-round workers receive only about 60 per cent of what men who are similarly employed earn. The median income for full-time, year-round women workers was $3,973, compared to $6,848 for men . . .

The factors that have narrowed our opportunities are multiple and complex. There are restrictive hiring practices. There is discrimination in promotions. Many myths, which run entirely counter to the facts, maintain that women make poor supervisors, or that they have substantially higher rates of absenteeism and labor turnover. A recent Department of Labor survey revealed that women are more reliable and are absent less frequently than the male population of our labor force. The myth about the unreliability of women is somewhat like the one about women being bad drivers. That one has been disproven lately also by the insurance companies—women pay lower rates.

The claim is often made, and without the slightest justification, that even women with more than adequate training and knowledge lack the ability to assume higher-level positions in industry. As the late President Kennedy declared in December, 1961, in the opening words of his executive order establishing a Commission on the Status of Women, "These continuing prejudices and outmoded customs act as barriers to the full realization of women's basic rights, which should be respected and fostered as part of our nation's commitment to human dignity, freedom and democracy." When President Nixon's first nomination for the Supreme Court was rejected, it appalled and disturbed me greatly that he did not even consider nominating a woman. Our women have too long been overlooked for positions of importance in policy-making and decision areas.

The under-utilization of American women is one of the most senseless wastes of this century. It is a waste our country can no longer afford. David Deith, a financial reporter, wrote that the Swedish national income could be 25 per cent higher if women's labor potential was fully utilized. The standard of living in France would rise 35 per cent if women were as professionally active as men. To my knowledge no comparable studies have been made in the U.S. on women, but Federal Reserve Board member Andrew Brimmer once estimated that racial bias costs our nation $20 billion a year and there are five times more women in America than there are blacks.

Meeting the challenge presented by a dynamic, expanding economy in the '70s and beyond will require that American business employ all the financial, material and human resources at its command. We are expected to maintain and improve a high standard of living for a rapidly growing population. We are called upon to meet greater demands for American goods abroad.

The greatest domestic problems of today—poverty in our urban ghettos, inadequate housing, substandard housing, the lack of meaningful, rewarding jobs for many thousands of our citizens—are all challenges that the business sector is being asked to take up. At the same time, we must maintain a growing economy in which all can participate.

In mobilizing our resources for the task, we must make sure that none are overlooked; particularly we must train, develop and use effectively the knowledge and skills of all our people. It is not enough that we talk of the nation's manpower needs; we are going to need "womanpower" as well . . .

When I decided to run for Congress, I knew I would encounter both anti-black and anti-feminist sentiments. What surprised me was the much greater virulence of the sex discrimination. It seems that while many, many Americans still harbor racist emotions, they are no longer based on so-called racial characteristics. Paternalism has to a great extent disappeared from racial bias. But I was constantly bombarded by both men and women exclaiming that I should return to teaching, a woman's vocation, and leave politics to the men.

Like every other form of discrimination, anti-feminism is destructive both to those who perpetrate it and to its victims. Male schoolteachers, for example, are well aware of this. They have had to fight against both men and women who cast aspersions on their maleness because of their vocation. No one knows how many men have declined careers in teaching jobs they would have enjoyed because of the "female" character of that profession. When one group of society is as oppressed as American women are, no one can be free. Males, with their anti-feminism, maim both themselves and their women.

Like black people, women have had it with this bias. We are no longer content to trade off our minds and abilities in exchange for having doors opened for us by gallant men. While most men laugh jeeringly at the fledgling "women's liberation groups" springing up across the nation, they should know that countless women—including their cohorts, their wives and their daughters—silently applaud such groups. We—American women—are beginning to respond to our oppression. While most of us are not yet revolutionaries, we are getting in tune with the cry of the liberation groups. Women are not inherently passive or peaceful; we're not inherently anything but human. And like every other oppressed people rising today, we're out for freedom—by any means necessary.

Such is the predicament of all American women; the problem is multiplied for those of us who operate also under racial prejudice. So far most of the feminine revolution has been directed at the problems of professional women whose skills are not recognized or rewarded. However, this very fact that professional ladies have spokesmen who will protest their condition gives them hope of alleviating their suffering. I turn now to the specific dilemma of the black woman.

The feminine revolution has been headed mostly by middle-class white professional women and aimed toward the higher-level jobs. More of our attention should be directed toward those women who comprise the menial working force of our country. Particularly, the black woman, who usually has to find employment as a maid, housekeeper, day worker, cafeteria helper, etc. These are dead-end jobs, jobs inherently degrading and humiliating, jobs which barely provide a subsistence existence. Today young women are revolting against this kid of subservient employment. They refuse to take a job which robs them of their self-respect and dignity in exchange for a few dollars. They want the opportunity to prove their worth, to show, to both whites and black men, that they are women, black women, and that they are proud.

Most of these black women lack the academic training to compete for professional and white-collar jobs. Our society must begin to give them training. But in the meantime, there are definite steps which can be taken now to utilize the talents of black women and to provide them with an income above the poverty line, steps which will eliminate the discrimination on the basis of race and sex.

Some of you may be thinking, "How can she say that this discrimination is so virulent? Isn't she the first black female member of Congress? That proves that the bias isn't really too great." On the contrary, my battle was long, incredibly hard and continual. Because I pushed, I encountered the strongest prejudice of less competent males, both black and white. That I won is a tribute to the women in my neighborhood who are finally saying no to the system. They are fed up. And as each day goes by and the awareness of women to our plight grows, there will be more and more women who will say no.

We live in revolutionary times. The shackles that various groups have worn for centuries are being cast off. This is evidenced by the "developing" nations of the world, which we consider, for the most part, underdeveloped. Countries such as India, Ceylon [Sri Lanka] and Israel have women for Prime Ministers and in other decision-making positions. American women must stand and fight—be militant even—for rights which are ours. Not necessarily on soapboxes should we voice our sentiments, but in the community and at the polls. We must demand and get day care centers, better job training, more opportunities to enter fields and professions of our choosing and stop accepting what is handed to us.

Source: Shirley Chisholm, *The Good Fight* (New York: Harper & Row, 1973), 188–192.

Document 14.6 in Context
"Defined Out of Existence": Rep. Charles B. Rangel, D-N.Y., on the Government Approach to Poverty

In the spring of 1973, the United States was wracked by social and political turmoil. The nation was still struggling, amid mass protests, to extricate itself from the war in Vietnam as it plunged headlong into the Watergate scandal that eventually forced the resignation of President Richard Nixon. Not surprisingly, the nation's attention was not as focused as it once had been on America's other war—the War on Poverty.

President Lyndon B. Johnson's decision to declare the War on Poverty in his 1964 State of the Union address was a combination of progressive reformism and partisan political calculation. On the one hand, the undertaking "appealed to Johnson because, like many southerners, he believed that the nation's racial problems were essentially economic in nature. If blacks only had good jobs and decent incomes, whites would, in his view, respect them and let them exercise their civil rights." [7] It also made political sense: Johnson sought to appeal to black voters in the 1964 presidential election. Therefore, the president called for a comprehensive and cooperative effort by all levels of government to eradicate poverty, a key element of his Great Society program.

But Johnson, a Democrat, left office in January 1969, and Nixon, who succeeded him, was a conservative Republican who did not share Johnson's liberal, expansive view of the government's role. Although Nixon initially agreed to support a proposed Family Assistance Plan, which would have guaranteed a minimum income for poor families, the legislation did not muster the necessary votes for passage in the Senate, and Nixon backed away from the idea after the 1972 election. His 1974 budget proposal called for the elimination of most of Johnson's Great Society programs.[8]

In the May 1973 article from *The Nation* reprinted here, Rep. Charles B. Rangel, D-N.Y., attacks the shift in the nation's priorities away from helping those in need, especially the urban poor.

▬▬ Document 14.6 ▬▬
Rep. Charles B. Rangel, D-N.Y., Calls for Greater Attention to the Needs of the Poor, May 1973

Poverty may soon disappear, if not from the country, at least from the vocabulary of official bureaucratese. There have been reports that a federal interagency committee is quietly studying the possibility of ending government use of the word. It would little surprise the 25.6 million poor Americans if they were, in fact, defined out of existence. Observing White House policies and priorities, they already question whether the President knows they are really here.

When the Subcommittee on Equal Opportunities of the House Committee on Education and Labor held hearings on the planned budget cuts, witness after witness decried the impact of Administration proposals on human needs. The word "adminicide" was used to describe the cutbacks in health, housing, job training, day care, education and senior citizen programs.

Poor Americans know how it feels to be put at the end of the line, to be forced to ride in the back of the bus of the country's conscience. They saw the Administration spend $425 million to bomb Hanoi for seventeen days during the 1972 Christmas season, while spending only $398 million a year for the entire community-action program in the United States. They are aware that the amount spent by the Pentagon on nuts and candy in the 1971-72 budget ($16.7 million) would fund the community action programs in eight New York City neighborhoods. So there is not great shock in the nation that their very existence will be erased by the bureaucrats. There is outrage, though.

The current official definition of the poverty line for a nonfarm family of four in our country is a cash income of $4,137 a year. Maximum welfare payments for a family of four, COPE reports, range from $700 annually in Mississippi to more than $3,600 in a handful of Northern states. Even with rent subsidies, food stamps and Medicaid, poverty-level families fight a daily battle for survival. Mollie Orshansky, a HEW statistician, pointed out recently that the gap between poor and nonpoor Americans would be even greater if certain benefits received by middle-class families were computed as income: expense accounts, vacation pay, commodity discounts.

• Abolish welfare for the rich? There is no word yet from the Administration on an end to tax loopholes and corporate subsidies.

- A sweep of the White House wand and the Office of Economic Opportunity vanishes. It is uncertain whether the magic of the courts will be stronger than White House magic.

- Abracadabra, and officials responsible for the Watergate espionage team are hidden in a puff of smoke. The magic of public opinion may blow the smoke away.

- Presto, and the air bombardment of Cambodia is not an "act of war." Does Congress have anything up its sleeve?

- My Lai, General Lavelle's unauthorized bombing missions over North Vietnam, broken Indian treaties—White House magic tries to wish them all away.

It is true, as the Administration contends, that "poverty" is a politicized, value-laden word. It is, however, the most accurate word for portraying what poor people face daily. Euphemisms cannot convey the reality of the slum housing where so many of my Harlem and East Harlem constituents live. Or the despair in New York City's public schools where reading levels continue to fall. Or the fear caused by the heroin plague, which feeds on unemployment and racial discrimination. White House magic can't make *them* disappear overnight.

Source: Rep. Charles B. Rangel, "The Verbal Cure," *The Nation*, May 21, 1973, 654.

Document 14.7 in Context
"To Acknowledge the Fundamental Injustice, Cruelty, Brutality, and Inhumanity of Slavery": Rep. John Conyers Jr., D-Mich., and the Slavery Reparations Movement

Ever since Gen. William Tecumseh Sherman's Field Order No. 15—allowing freed slaves forty acres of confiscated Confederate farmlands along the south Atlantic Coast and the use of army mules—was rescinded by President Andrew Johnson in 1865, the question of compensation for the injustices of slavery has troubled the American body politic. The Radical Republicans in Congress tried to make some land available to freed farmers with the Southern Homestead Act of 1866, but much of the public land set aside was unfit for farming, and many of those who received land did not have the resources necessary to farm it.

A generation later, between 1890 and 1903, legislation was introduced nine times in Congress for the purpose of providing pensions to former slaves. Each time, however, the bill died in committee. Periodically, such prominent black leaders as Marcus Garvey and Malcolm X demanded that the U.S. government compensate African Americans—with land or cash—for the injustice of slavery, but those demands were generally dismissed as impractical or even extremist. Interest in reparations for slavery revived in 1987 after a bill passed by Congress and signed by President Ronald Reagan set aside about $200 million to compensate Japanese Americans for their internment in camps in the United States during World War II.

In 1989 Rep. John Conyers Jr., D-Mich., introduced a bill, excerpted here, to establish a commission that would study the impact of slavery on African Americans and make recommendations to Congress about remedies. Though he introduced it in every session from the 101st through the 109th Congress, the legislation remained in committee. One difficulty was that public opinion—even among African Americans—was divided on the issue. An ABC News poll in 1997 found that just 10 percent of whites and 65 percent of blacks supported the idea of reparations.[9] And almost a quarter of the members of the Congressional Black Caucus—including Rep. John R. Lewis, D-Ga., who was a leader of the civil rights movement during the 1960s—declined to sign on as cosponsors.[10] Even sympathetic critics considered the idea too divisive and too expensive to be practical.

In the opening years of the twenty-first century, however, an increasing number of prominent black leaders began to talk again about reparations. In 2001, the National Association for the Advancement of Colored People (NAACP) put reparations on its list of top priorities. It was unclear whether the election of 2006, which gave Democrats the majority in both chambers of Congress and elevated Conyers to chair the House Judiciary Committee, would help move the legislation any closer to passage.

▬ Document 14.7 ▬
Commission to Study Reparation Proposals for African Americans Act, Introduced in House November 20, 1989

A BILL To acknowledge the fundamental injustice, cruelty, brutality, and inhumanity of slavery in the United States and the 13 American colonies between 1619 and 1865 and to establish a commission to examine the institution of slavery, subsequent de jure and de facto racial and economic discrimination against African Americans, and the impact of these forces on living African Americans, to make recommendations to the Congress on appropriate remedies, and for other purposes.

Be it enacted by the Senate and House of Representatives of the United States of America in Congress assembled,

SECTION 1. SHORT TITLE.
This Act may be cited as the 'Commission to Study Reparation Proposals for African Americans Act'.

SEC. 2. FINDINGS AND PURPOSES.
(a) FINDINGS- The Congress finds that—
> (1) approximately 4,000,000 Africans and their descendants were enslaved in the United States and the colonies that became the United States from 1619 to 1865;
> (2) the institution of slavery was constitutionally and statutorily sanctioned by the Government of the United States from 1789 through 1865;
> (3) the slavery that flourished in the United States constituted an immoral and inhumane deprivation of Africans' life, liberty, African citizenship rights, and cultural heritage, and denied them the fruits of their own labor; and
> (4) sufficient inquiry has not been made into the effects of the institution of slavery on living African Americans and society in the United States.

(b) PURPOSE- The purpose of this Act is to establish a commission to—
> (1) examine the institution of slavery which existed from 1619 through 1865 within the United States and the colonies that became the United States, including the extent to which the Federal and State governments constitutionally and statutorily supported the institution of slavery;

(2) examine de jure and de facto discrimination against freed slaves and their descendants from the end of the Civil War to the present, including economic, political, and social discrimination;

(3) examine the lingering negative effects of the institution of slavery and the discrimination described in paragraph (2) on living African Americans and on society in the United States;

(4) recommend appropriate ways to educate the American public of the Commission's findings;

(5) recommend appropriate remedies in consideration of the Commission's findings on the matters described in paragraphs (1) and (2); and

(6) submit to the Congress the results of such examination, together with such recommendations.

SEC. 3. ESTABLISHMENT AND DUTIES.

(a) ESTABLISHMENT- There is established the Commission to Study Reparation Proposals for African Americans (hereinafter in this Act referred to as the 'Commission').

(b) DUTIES- The Commission shall perform the following duties:

(1) Examine the institution of slavery which existed within the United States and the colonies that became the United States from 1619 through 1865. The Commission's examination shall include an examination of—

(A) the capture and procurement of Africans;

(B) the transport of Africans to the United States and the colonies that became the United States for the purpose of enslavement, including their treatment during transport;

(C) the sale and acquisition of Africans as chattel property in interstate and intrastate commerce; and

(D) the treatment of African slaves in the colonies and the United States, including the deprivation of their freedom, exploitation of their labor, and destruction of their culture, language, religion, and family.

(2) Examine the extent to which the Federal and State governments of the United States supported the institution of slavery in constitutional and statutory provisions, including the extent to which such governments prevented, opposed, or restricted efforts of freed African slaves to repatriate to their home land.

(3) Examine Federal and State laws that discriminated against freed African slaves and their descendants during the period between the end of the civil war and the present.

(4) Examine other forms of discrimination in the public and private sectors against freed African slaves and their descendants during the period between the end of the civil war and the present.

(5) Examine the lingering negative effects of the institution of slavery and the matters described in paragraphs (1), (2), (3), and (4) on living African Americans and on society in the United States.

(6) Recommend appropriate ways to educate the American public of the Commission's findings.

(7) Recommend appropriate remedies in consideration of the Commission's findings on the matters described in paragraphs (1), (2), (3), and (4). In making such recommendations, the Commission shall address, among other issues, the following questions:

(A) Whether the Government of the United States should offer a formal apology on behalf of the people of the United States for the perpetration of gross human rights violations on African slaves and their descendants.

(B) Whether African Americans still suffer from the lingering affects of the matters described in paragraphs (1), (2), (3), and (4).

(C) Whether, in consideration of the Commission's findings, any form of compensation to the descendants of African slaves is warranted.

(D) If the Commission finds that such compensation is warranted, what should be the amount of compensation, what form of compensation should be awarded, and who should be eligible for such compensation.

(c) REPORT TO CONGRESS- The Commission shall submit a written report of its findings and recommendations to the Congress not later than the date which is one year after the date of the first meeting of the Commission held pursuant to section 4(c).

SEC. 4. MEMBERSHIP.

(a) NUMBER AND APPOINTMENT-

(1) The Commission shall be composed of 7 members, who shall be appointed, within 90 days after the date of enactment of this Act, as follows:

(A) Three members shall be appointed by the President.

(B) Three members shall be appointed by the Speaker of the House of Representatives.

(C) One member shall be appointed by the President pro tempore of the Senate.

(2) All members of the Commission shall be persons who are especially qualified to serve on the Commission by virtue of their education, training, or experience, particularly in the field of African American studies . . .

SEC. 8. AUTHORIZATION OF APPROPRIATIONS.

To carry out the provisions of this Act, there are authorized to be appropriated $8,000,000.

Source: Commission to Study Reparation Proposals for African Americans Act, H.R. 3745, Congressional Record, 101st Cong., 1st sess., November 20, 1989.

Document 14.8 in Context
"Let the Rich Go First": Rep. Major R. O. Owens Attacks Inequities in the War in Iraq

America's commitment to economic justice is often tested in time of war. Wars are expensive, and African American members of Congress have regularly sought to underscore the way in which spending on the nation's military undertakings has undercut America's ability to support a wide range of social programs. In a 1973 critique of the federal government's handling of the War on Poverty, Rep. Charles B. Rangel, D-N.Y., noted that the declining commitment to the poor ran parallel to growth in spending on the Vietnam War (**Document 14.6**).

The connection between war and economic justice involves more than comparative spending, however. During the Vietnam War and again during the war in Iraq, critics charged that the majority of fighting and dying was being done by men and women from lower socioeconomic backgrounds—poor or working-class minorities and whites. In the case of Vietnam, the military draft system included a range of deferments that benefited the affluent. Public anger over the inequities of the draft and the way the draft kept providing troops for an unpopular war eventually prodded the military to switch to an all-volunteer system.

Bitterness over the Vietnam draft was still intense thirty years later, when President George W. Bush launched the invasion of Iraq to topple its leader, Saddam Hussein. Opponents in 2003 charged that Bush had used family connections to serve in an Air National Guard unit, which kept him from being sent to Vietnam. Bush's vice president, Dick Cheney, who was a strong advocate for the war in Iraq, had been granted deferments that kept him out of the service during the Vietnam War.

In July 2003, about four months after the start of the war in Iraq, Rep. Major R. O. Owens, D-N.Y., attacked the ability of the rich and powerful to avoid military service and criticized the government's increasing military spending while working people were struggling economically. Owens's casting of his critique in the form of a rap poem injected a note of personal creativity but also helped him make his point. By adopting a mode of expression popular among young people from poor, working-class, urban and minority backgrounds, he emphasized the perspective of those he said carried the greatest burden in the war effort.

▬ Document 14.8 ▬
Rep. Major R. O. Owens, D-N.Y., Raps about the War in Iraq on the House Floor, July 18, 2003

Mr. OWENS: Mr. Speaker, the July 10th vote to allow the expenditure of funds to implement radical changes in the overtime provisions of the Wage and Hour Act was an outrageous and devastating attack on working families. Compounding the horror of this action is the recent announcement that our present complement of soldiers in Iraq, ninety percent of whom come from working families, will be forced into combat overtime for the indefinite future. Not even the one year rotation rule of Viet Nam will be applied to relieve their long ordeal under extreme heat and guerrilla warfare duress. Overtime in the dangerous defense of the nation is being mandated without controls while at the same time overtime wages to feed working families is being subjected to new schemes which reduce take-home pay. This is an unacceptable continuation of the gross exploitation and oppression of working families by the Republican's Scrooges who presently dominate the Congress and the White House. This nation faces a tragic predicament: An elite group of juvenile old men have plunged us into a war where great suffering and pain is being inflicted on working families who bear the brunt of the casualties on the front lines as well as the fallout from economic dislocations and recession here at home. It appears that the Republican well-to-do decision makers have great contempt for those who do the dangerous and dirty work for our nation. All Americans must remember the debt we owe to those who risk their last full measure of devotion. Or perhaps the powerful and the rich should go to the front lines first. The RAP poem below is a summary of my indignation on this critical action:

LET THE RICH GO FIRST
    Working Families
    Keep your soldiers at home,
    For overtime in Iraq

No cash
No comp time
Not even gratitude,
Republicans intrude
To exempt all heroes,
No combat rotation
Life on indefinite probation
Scrooges running the nation.
To the front lines
Let the rich go first—
For blood they got a thirst,
Let the superstars drink it
In the glorious trenches;
Leave the disadvantaged on the benches.
Working Families
Let the rich go first:
The battlegrounds they always choose
Their estates have the most to lose;
Send highest IQs to
Take positions at the front,
Let them perform their best
High tech warfare stunt;
Working Families
Keep your malnourished sons home—
Harvard Yale kids should roam
The world with guns and tanks,
Reserve gold medals
For the loyal Ivy League ranks.
O say you can see
Millionaire graduates
Dying for you and me?
Welfare Moms
Have a message for the masters:
Tell Uncle Sam
His TANF pennies he can keep
For food stamps we refuse to leap
Through your hoops like beasts;
Promise to leave our soldier alone
And we'll find our own feasts.
To Uncle Sam we offer a bargain—
Don't throw us dirty crumbs
Don't treat us like bums
And then demand
The full measure of devotion;
Our minds are now in motion
Class warfare

Is not such a bad notion;
Your swindle will not last
Recruiters we won't let pass,
Finally, we opened our eyes—
Each family is a private enterprise,
Each child a precious prize;
We got American property rights,
Before our children die in war
This time we'll choose the fights.
Let the rich go first:
They worry about
The overtime we abuse;
The battlefields they always choose
Their estates have the most to lose.
Let the rich go first!

Source: Congressional Record, 108th Cong., 1st sess., July 18, 2003, E1509.

Document 14.9 in Context
"Men and Women . . . Should Be Paid a Comparable Wage": Del. Eleanor Holmes Norton on Employment Discrimination in a Changing Job Market

As American society has changed, efforts to combat discrimination have adjusted. When the Fair Labor Standards Act was passed by Congress in 1938, for example, the job market was overwhelmingly dominated by men and a large portion of the economy's jobs involved routine physical labor for which little training or education was required.

By the first decade of the twenty-first century, however, the job market looked very different. In 2006 women represented 46 percent of the nation's workforce and U.S. Department of Labor estimates projected that percentage to increase over the next decade.[11] The nature of work had also had changed dramatically. Manufacturing jobs had been declining in number for several decades, while jobs in the service sector of the economy had been increasing. Employers were also setting higher education requirements, and many of the jobs in the new economy required college degrees or at least some advanced technical training.

The document that follows is legislation introduced in the House in April 2005 by Eleanor Holmes Norton, Democratic delegate from the District of Columbia, and was aimed at amending the Fair Labor Standards Act to make it more responsive to the realities of the contemporary workplace. In announcing the legislation, Norton said the old law had become "creaky with age" and needed revision to overcome stereotyping of women that tended to steer them into particular kinds of jobs that resulted in "pay according to gender and not according to the skills, efforts, responsibilities and working conditions necessary to do the job." [12] She called for more aggressive action:

> We introduce the Fair Pay Act because the pay problems of most women today stem mainly from this sex segregation in the jobs that women and men do. Two-thirds of white women, and three quarters of African American women work in just three areas: sales and clerical, service and factory jobs. Only a combination of more

aggressive strategies can break through the ancient societal habits present throughout human time the world over as well as the employer steering of women into
women's jobs that is as old as paid employment itself. The FPA recognizes that if men
and women are doing comparable work, they should be paid a comparable wage.[13]

The legislation died in committee.

▰▰▰ Document 14.9 ▰▰▰
Fair Pay Act of 2005, Introduced April 19, 2005

A BILL To amend the Fair Labor Standards Act of 1938 to prohibit discrimination in the
payment of wages on account of sex, race, or national origin, and for other purposes.

*Be it enacted by the Senate and House of Representatives of the United States of America in
Congress assembled,*

SECTION 1. SHORT TITLE AND REFERENCE.

(a) Short Title- This Act may be cited as the 'Fair Pay Act of 2005'.

(b) Reference- Except as provided in section 8, whenever in this Act an amendment or repeal
is expressed in terms of an amendment to, or repeal of, a section or other provision, the
reference shall be considered to be made to a section or other provision of the Fair Labor
Standards Act of 1938 . . .

SEC. 2. FINDINGS.

Congress finds the following:

(1) Wage rate differentials exist between equivalent jobs segregated by sex, race, and
national origin in Government employment and in industries engaged in commerce or in
the production of goods for commerce.

(2) The existence of such wage rate differentials—

(A) depresses wages and living standards for employees necessary for their health and
efficiency;

(B) prevents the maximum utilization of the available labor resources;

(C) tends to cause labor disputes, thereby burdening, affecting, and obstructing commerce;

(D) burdens commerce and the free flow of goods in commerce; and

(E) constitutes an unfair method of competition.

(3) Discrimination in hiring and promotion has played a role in maintaining a segregated
work force.

(4) Many women and people of color work in occupations dominated by individuals of
their same sex, race, and national origin.

(5) A 2000 study conducted by the Census Bureau of 400 fields that employed 10,000
full-time, year-round workers found that women were able to earn at least as much as men
in just 5 fields: hazardous material removal, telecommunications line installation and
repair, meeting and convention planning, food preparation, and construction trade assistant work.

(6) In 2004, an Institute for Women's Policy Research analysis of data collected in the
Current Population Survey by the Bureau of Labor Statistics found that women were paid
only 76 cents for every dollar that a man is paid.

(7) Section 6(d) of the Fair Labor Standards Act of 1938 . . . prohibits discrimination in compensation for 'equal work' on the basis of sex.

(8) Title VII of the Civil Rights Act of 1964 . . . prohibits discrimination in compensation because of race, color, religion, national origin, and sex. The Supreme Court, in its decision in County of Washington v. Gunther, 452 U.S. 161 (1981), held that title VII's prohibition against discrimination in compensation also applies to jobs that do not constitute 'equal work' as defined in section 6(d) of the Fair Labor Standards Act of 1938 . . . Decisions of lower courts, however, have demonstrated that further clarification of existing legislation is necessary in order effectively to carry out the intent of Congress to implement the Supreme Court's holding in its Gunther decision.

(9) Artificial barriers to the elimination of discrimination in compensation based upon sex, race, and national origin continue to exist more than 3 decades after the passage of section 6(d) of the Fair Labor Standards Act of 1938 . . . and the Civil Rights Act of 1964. Elimination of such barriers would have positive effects, including—

(A) providing a solution to problems in the economy created by discrimination through wage rate differentials;

(B) substantially reducing the number of working women and people of color earning low wages, thereby reducing the dependence on public assistance; and

(C) promoting stable families by enabling working family members to earn a fair rate of pay.

SEC. 3. EQUAL PAY FOR EQUIVALENT JOBS.

(a) Amendment- Section 6 (29 U.S.C. 206) is amended by adding at the end the following:

'(h)(1)(A) Except as provided in subparagraph (B), no employer having employees subject to any provision of this section shall discriminate, within any establishment in which such employees are employed, between employees on the basis of sex, race, or national origin by paying wages to employees in such establishment in a job that is dominated by employees of a particular sex, race, or national origin at a rate less than the rate at which the employer pays wages to employees in such establishment in another job that is dominated by employees of the opposite sex or of a different race or national origin, respectively, for work on equivalent jobs.

'(B) Nothing in subparagraph (A) shall prohibit the payment of different wage rates to employees where such payment is made pursuant to—

'(i) a seniority system;

'(ii) a merit system;

'(iii) a system that measures earnings by quantity or quality of production; or

'(iv) a differential based on a bona fide factor other than sex, race, or national origin, such as education, training, or experience, except that this clause shall apply only if—

'(I) the employer demonstrates that—

'(aa) such factor—

'(AA) is job-related with respect to the position in question; or

'(BB) furthers a legitimate business purpose, except that this item shall not apply if the employee demonstrates that an alternative employment practice exists that would serve the same business purpose without producing such differential and that the employer has refused to adopt such alternative practice; and '(bb) such factor was actually applied and used reasonably in light of the asserted justification; and

'(II) upon the employer succeeding under subclause (I), the employee fails to demonstrate that the differential produced by the reliance of the employer on such factor is itself the result of discrimination on the basis of sex, race, or national origin by the employer.

'(C) The Equal Employment Opportunity Commission shall issue guidelines specifying criteria for determining whether a job is dominated by employees of a particular sex, race, or national origin . . . Such guidelines shall not include a list of such jobs.

'(D) An employer who is paying a wage rate differential in violation of subparagraph (A) shall not, in order to comply with the provisions of such subparagraph, reduce the wage rate of any employee.

'(2) No labor organization or its agents representing employees of an employer having employees subject to any provision of this section shall cause or attempt to cause such an employer to discriminate against an employee in violation of paragraph (1)(A).

'(3) For purposes of administration and enforcement of this subsection, any amounts owing to any employee that have been withheld in violation of paragraph (1)(A) shall be deemed to be unpaid minimum wages or unpaid overtime compensation under this section or section 7.

'(4) In this subsection:

'(A) The term 'labor organization' means any organization of any kind, or any agency or employee representation committee or plan, in which employees participate and that exists for the purpose, in whole or in part, of dealing with employers concerning grievances, labor disputes, wages, rates of pay, hours of employment, or conditions of work.

(B) The term 'equivalent jobs' means jobs that may be dissimilar, but whose requirements are equivalent, when viewed as a composite of skills, effort, responsibility, and working conditions . . .

Source: Fair Pay Act of 2005, H.R. 1697, *Congressional Record*, 109th Cong., 1st sess., April 19, 2005.

Document 14.10 in Context
"Six Months after Katrina, Virtually Nothing Has Changed": American Poverty, American Disaster

Few American natural disasters have had the emotional or economic impact that Hurricane Katrina had when it slammed into New Orleans and the Gulf Coast in late August 2005. One of the most powerful hurricanes ever to hit the United States, Katrina—and the flooding associated with the storm—killed at least 1,300 people, caused more than $80 billion in damage, dislocated hundreds of thousands of people and left large portions of New Orleans submerged for weeks. Months after the storm, several thousand people remained missing.

As Americans watched television coverage of the devastation, and of the suffering and growing desperation of survivors in New Orleans, they became increasingly critical of the government's response to the disaster. Federal, state and local authorities criticized each other for the slow pace of rescue efforts that left people on the roofs of flooded homes for days following the storm. The brunt of the criticism, however, fell on the federal government, which critics said was unprepared and slow to react despite advance warning that the storm was likely to overwhelm communities along the Gulf Coast.

Although the suffering and loss inflicted by Hurricane Katrina—and Hurricane Rita, which pounded the Gulf Coast of Texas less than a month later—was not limited to a single ethnic group or socioeconomic class, many perceived that the poor, particularly minorities, suffered extra hardships because of their inability to flee the storm. The largely black neighborhoods of New Orleans' Lower Ninth Ward, were especially hard-hit, and many of the most potent televised images showed poor African Americans stranded in the heat and chaos of a devastated New Orleans with little food and water.

That connection between poverty and the suffering of disaster victims was made clear about two months after the storm, when members of the Congressional Black Caucus introduced legislation aimed at providing increased federal support for recovery efforts along the Gulf Coast. At a news conference announcing the measure, Caucus members "called on President Bush and on Democratic and Republican members of the House and Senate to support its comprehensive legislative response to the devastation of Hurricane Katrina, and to make a commitment to eradicate poverty." [14]

As debate over the legislation continued, and as the efforts to rebuild the Gulf Coast dragged on, Caucus members continued to emphasize that theme. The document that follows is an excerpt of comments made by Rep. Barbara Lee, D-Calif., during House debate in March 2006, nearly seven months after Hurricane Katrina hit.

▬ Document 14.10 ▬
Rep. Barbara Lee, D-Calif., Urges Relief for Hurricane Katrina Victims, March 14, 2006

Ms. LEE: . . . Let me just say tonight, Madam Speaker, that we know the entire world watched the wealthiest, most powerful country on earth, quite frankly, turn its back on those who couldn't afford to evacuate this horrific hurricane called Katrina. People were left to fend for themselves on rooftops trying to save their lives and the lives of their families. And the majority of these people were African American. And we cannot sweep under the rug the faces of those who were disproportionately abandoned by their government because unfortunately, today, 6 months after the storm, the majority of these people are still fending for themselves.

If we don't deal with this up front we will continue to be in denial about the unfinished business of America in addressing the issues of race and class.

Now, 2 months ago, I had the opportunity to visit New Orleans and Mississippi as part of the first congressional field hearing which was held in the gulf coast. We toured New Orleans. We saw the Ninth ward, New Orleans East, Lakeview and other areas. We went to Mississippi and passed through Waveland, Bay St. Louis and Gulfport. And I tell you, like others who have visited the region, it takes a visit to the region to really fully understand the impact and the devastation that this hurricane brought upon the people of that region.

We saw firsthand this devastation and quite frankly, I will never, ever be able to sleep as well ever again in life based on what I saw during those 2 days.

We heard from victims of the storm who lost their homes and were displaced, who were living with friends and relatives or staying in hotels or motels mostly waiting for their FEMA trailers. They wanted to know that they would have a place to stay so that they could call someplace, just someplace their own. They wanted to know that FEMA wouldn't terminate housing assistance for people living in motels or hotels. They wanted to know that they wouldn't be discriminated against in seeking housing because of their race, ethnicity, age or disability. They wanted to know that the levees would be rebuilt so that they could go back to their homes and their communities to rebuild. And they wanted to know that they wouldn't be evicted from their homes or be gouged.

And we heard of the price gouging over and over and over again. And they wanted us to help them to make sure that they would not be gouged by the high rental prices or that some opportunistic developer wouldn't buy up their land and gentrify their communities. And they wanted to know that they would be hired to carry out Federal contracts to clean up and rebuild the gulf so that they could work, they could work and get a steady paycheck and participate in the equitable development of the region. They wanted to know that their kids could go back to school and still be children. And they wanted to know that they could go to a clinic or a hospital if they got sick.

In short, they wanted to know that they mattered and that their government would do all that it could to take care of them and put them back on their feet quickly.

And, Madam Speaker, the survivors of Hurricane Katrina are still wondering the exact same things today. 6 months after Katrina, virtually nothing has changed. Only now, our government is about to add insult to injury by disenfranchising over 300,000 displaced survivors from New Orleans, who will not be given the right to vote in elections that will determine the future of their city.

And tomorrow, we have learned that FEMA will boot out probably another 7,000 families that are still living in hotels and motels and have no other place to go.

This is a disgrace. The administration failed to prepare a plan of action to respond to Hurricane Katrina, and they have failed to put together a coherent plan to rebuild and restore the gulf coast region.

H.R. 4997, a comprehensive bill to help the gulf coast rebuild, which is supported by Katrina survivors and introduced by the Congressional Black Caucus under the leadership of Congressman MEL WATT [D-N.C.] should be supported. This bill provides for housing rights, a victim restoration fund in the spirit of 9/11 Victims Fund, expanded opportunities in rebuilding the gulf coast and voting rights for all.

We also work very closely with Mr. [Rep. Richard H.] BAKER [R-La.] and improved upon his will to rebuild New Orleans and to help the region recover; got bipartisan support in the Financial Services Committee for that bill. But the administration has rejected both of these plans.

And now we are 3 months away from the start of the new hurricane season. And we can not afford to allow the continued incompetence of this administration to hinder the recovery and rebuilding process any longer.

Tomorrow, when we vote on the supplemental appropriations bill, I will offer an amendment to basically block FEMA from using, any money to evict people living in hotels or motels as a result of Katrina. We should not allow FEMA to kick people out on the streets. That is just plain and simple. That should not be done. So I urge my colleagues to support my amendment.

And we must continue to stand with the people of New Orleans and gulf coast and send a clear signal to the rest of the world that we must take care of all people. We must put people first regardless of their race or their income or their age or their disability. We have got a lot of work to do, and we don't have a lot of time to do it, Madam Speaker.

And so I just want to thank my colleagues from the region for their tenacity, their continued support for staying strong in the midst of a storm and for allowing those of us from other areas to try to help and try to do something.

I am very proud of my congressional district, immediately raised money to send to the gulf coast region and to New Orleans. The Ninth Congressional District, like other Congressional Districts and other nonprofit organizations and charitable groups, should be commended for stepping up to the plate.

But our government must do more and we must do more now.

Source: Congressional Record, 109th Cong., 2d sess., March 14, 2006, H955–H956.

Notes

1 William Jennings Bryan, "Cross of Gold," speech delivered at the Democratic National Convention, July 9, 1896, from Douglass Archives of American Public Address, http://douglassarchives.org/brya_a26.htm.

2 "Statement of Mr. William Green, President of the American Federation of Labor, Regarding the Unprecedented Unemployment Crisis, Based on Reports Received from Affiliated Organizations—Winter Unemployment," in *Congressional Record,* 72d Cong., 2d sess., January 28, 1932, 2855–2856.

3 Ibid.

4 "Hunger Calls," *Chicago Daily News,* January 23, 1932, in *Congressional Record,* 72d Cong., 2d sess., January 28, 1932, 2855–2856.

5 Mark Sullivan, "Fate of U.S. Aid to Jobless Held to Rest in House," *New York Herald Tribune,* February 4, 1932.

6 Shirley Chisholm, *Unbought and Unbossed* (Boston: Houghton Mifflin, 1970), 163–164.

7 Carl M. Brauer, "Kennedy, Johnson, and the War on Poverty," *Journal of American History* 69, no. 1 (June 1982): 115.

8 Lester C. Thurow, "The Political Economy of Income Redistribution Policies" *Annals of the American Academy of Political and Social Science* 409, Income Inequality (September 1973): 146–155.

9 Melissa R. Michelson, "The Black Reparations Movement: Public Opinion and Congressional Policy Making," *Journal of Black Studies,* 32, no. 5 (May 2002): 578.

10 "Six White Congressmen Endorse Reparations for Slavery," *Journal of Blacks in Higher Education,* no. 27 (Spring 2000): 20–21.

11 U.S. Department of Labor, Women's Bureau, "Quick Stats 2005," www.dol.gov/wb/stats/main.htm.

12 Del. Eleanor Holmes Norton, "Norton, Harkin, Clinton, DeLauro Introduce Fair Pay Legislation On Equal Pay Day," news release, April 19, 2005, www.norton.house.gov.

13 Ibid.

14 Congressional Black Caucus, "Congressional Black Caucus Introduces Hurricane Katrina Relief Legislation to Help Gulf Coast Residents," news release, November 3, 2005, www.congressionalblackcaucus.net.

CHAPTER FIFTEEN

Visions of America
The Dream and the Reality

O n a hot, sunny day in late August 1963, Rev. Martin Luther King Jr. stood on the steps of the Lincoln Memorial in Washington, D.C.—within sight of the Capitol, where Congress resides—and delivered one of the most famous speeches in American history. The moment was rich in symbolism, coming as it did 100 years after President Abraham Lincoln signed the Emancipation Proclamation (**Document 2.3**). The crowd of marchers listening to King, estimated at more than 200,000, was one of the largest the city had ever seen.

Already noted for her role in the House Judiciary Committee hearings that considered the impeachment of President Richard M. Nixon, Rep. Barbara C. Jordan, D-Texas, right, spoke of her vision for America at the 1976 Democratic National Convention in New York's Madison Square Garden. She is seen here with future president Jimmy Carter, center, and former vice president Hubert H. Humphrey, left. Source: AP Images

King's inspirational eloquence that day, along with his earnestness, passion and commitment to American ideals of justice and equality, captivated the crowd and, eventually, the nation. In the years following his death, that speech became a staple of the annual celebrations marking the national holiday that was declared in his honor (**Document 6.10**). It is widely admired, both for its rhetorical brilliance and for its vision of America, which King cast in the metaphor of a dream:

> So I say to you, my friends, that even though we must face the difficulties of today and tomorrow, I still have a dream. It is a dream deeply rooted in the American dream that one day this nation will rise up and live out the true meaning of its creed—we hold these truths to be self-evident, that all men are created equal.[1]

King's speech was a declaration of loyalty to U.S. constitutional government, but it was also a challenge to the nation's conscience. Though it is widely remembered for the ringing idealism of his "dream," it is crucial not to overlook the indictment of American injustice earlier in the speech. Noting the 100th anniversary of Lincoln's proclamation, King said:

But one hundred years later, the Negro still is not free; one hundred years later, the life of the Negro is still sadly crippled by the manacles of segregation and the chains of discrimination; one hundred years later, the Negro lives on a lonely island of poverty in the midst of a vast ocean of material prosperity; one hundred years later, the Negro is still languished in the corners of American society and finds himself in exile in his own land.[2]

Part of the speech's greatness came from the grace with which King encompassed themes that had been common in the speeches and writings of African Americans for nearly 200 years. Since Phillis Wheatley's book of poems was first published in 1773, countless African American writers and orators have declared their own visions of America. Over and over again, they have articulated dreams of an America that lived up to its ideals of justice, equality and freedom for all. They have emphasized their loyalty to the United States, and they have described the struggle of African Americans to claim their freedom with hope, dignity and faith. Speaking more than a century before King, Frederick Douglass, the greatest African American orator of the nineteenth century, called on America to live up to the that profound declaration of the founders that "all men are created equal" (**Document 1.12**).

The documents in this chapter assemble the visions of a range of African American political leaders from the Reconstruction era through the early twenty-first century. The chapter begins with the comments of Rep. Josiah T. Walls, R-Fla., on the plans for celebrating the nation's centennial (**Document 15.1**). During that 1874 congressional debate, Walls rejected the arguments of his colleagues who criticized plans for a major exposition in Philadelphia to honor the centennial as excessive or unnecessary; he viewed the plans as entirely fitting and proper. Like Douglass before him and King after, Walls traced the genius of the American system of government to "the organic and paramount doctrines of the Declaration ascribing to every man born of woman an entire and absolute equality of political rights." And in a stylized allusion that was common to the oratory of the time, he acknowledged that he owed his presence in Congress to the support of blacks who had been enabled to vote by "the tardy but in the end full and complete vindication of the sublime and sublimely simple announcements of the Declaration."

That same year, Rep. Richard H. Cain, R-S.C., declared his own faith in the principles of the Constitution and his belief that most Americans were willing to accept that the Constitution protected the rights of African Americans as well as whites (**Document 15.2**). During debate over what became the Civil Rights Act of 1875 (**Document 3.9**), Cain insisted that African Americans—who had been helping to build the nation's wealth for two centuries—deserved to enjoy the same freedom and rights as all other citizens.

Nearly a century later, the nation's ideals and values were again at issue, as the civil rights movement and the war in Vietnam inspired a generation of activist youth to challenge America's leaders. As she wrote in her autobiography, *Unbought and Unbossed*, Rep. Shirley A. Chisholm, D-N.Y., examined her interactions with young people during her campaigns, considered the future of leadership in America and examined the disconnect between the nation's ideals and the common attitudes toward activist youth of the late 1960s and early 1970s. The political dialogue of that time was often drenched in the rhetoric of revolution, particularly among young people; Chisholm argued for an understanding of young people's anger that recognized their idealism and called for a renewed commitment to renewal and reform of the nation's institutions (**Document 15.3**).

Rep. Adam Clayton Powell Jr., D-N.Y., had a perspective on the revolutionary rhetoric of the same period that more specifically focused on racial issues: the philosophy of the Black Power movement, which had taken a more militant and confrontational stance toward white America than had the movement led by King. In his autobiography, *Adam by Adam*, he sought to define the idea of Black Power and laid out a fifteen-point program for promoting black autonomy and empowerment (**Document 15.4**).

The speech Rep. Barbara C. Jordan, D-Texas, gave before the 1976 Democratic National Convention was a landmark: it was the first such address by an African American or a woman. Jordan had captured national attention as a member of the House Judiciary Committee as it considered the impeachment of President Richard M. Nixon in 1974 (**Document 6.5**). Her convention speech, which emphasized the responsibility and accountability of public officials in building a unified national community, was deeply rooted in the ideals of the Declaration and the Constitution and received widespread praise for its articulation of how contemporary American society should live up to its democratic principles (**Document 15.5**).

Fourteen years later, when Rep. Louis Stokes, D-Ohio, rose to address America's budgetary priorities during House debate, the world situation was undergoing radical change. The Berlin Wall—the symbolic division between Eastern and Western Europe and a focal point of tensions between the United States and the Soviet Union for nearly three decades—had been dismantled, and the Soviet Union was on its way toward collapse and dissolution. Some U.S. lawmakers began to ask how the government should spend the "peace dividend" many thought would result from a declining fear of military confrontation with the Soviets. Stokes insisted that any peace dividend should be used to reorder American priorities toward helping the homeless, the elderly and those in need of health care (**Document 15.6**).

But while economic and political values have always been central to the social vision of African Americans, black leaders have not always agreed on economic and political priorities. Rep. Gary A. Franks, R-Conn., a conservative, urged a renewed emphasis on entrepreneurship by African Americans and harkened back to the philosophy of economic self-reliance advanced by Booker T. Washington in the late nineteenth and early twentieth centuries (**Document 15.7**).

Rep. J. C. Watts Jr., R-Okla., offered another conservative take on American values in his 1996 speech to the Republican National Convention (**Document 15.8**). He emphasized the traditional values of small-town America, where family and community blend individual responsibility with concern for people suffering from poverty or hunger. Watts's speech offered the compassion of committed individuals and communities as an alternative to government programs for solving problems.

In contrast, Rep. John R. Lewis, D-Ga., emphasized the need for leadership from governmental officials in building a sense of national unity, arguing that the United States must measure its strength in the world "not just materially or militarily . . . but morally." According to Lewis, writing in his memoir, *Walking with the Wind*, that strength comes from the recognition that "we are one people, one family, one house—the American house, the American family" (**Document 15.9**).

Likewise, in January 2007, Sen. Barack Obama, D-Ill., called for a renewal of Americans' shared commitment to moral principles by establishing a system of universal health care for all Americans (**Document 15.10**). Citing the examples of Presidents Harry S. Truman and Lyndon B. Johnson, Obama stressed the need for bold leadership to resolve a crisis that has left tens of millions of Americans without insurance or the ability to pay for health care: "In a country that spends more on health care than any other nation on Earth, it's just wrong."

What emerges from these disparate visions are some common threads. Black leaders express their dissatisfaction at the ways in which America has failed to live up to its promises, especially to African Americans, but also their abiding faith in the principles contained in the Declaration of Independence and the Constitution. Time and again, African Americans in Congress speak to a desire for unity, hope, compassion, justice, equality, a commitment to human dignity and faith—a faith in God and a faith in the ideals that are the root of American freedom.

Rep. John R. Lewis, D-Ga., speaks at a July 20, 2006, news conference following the Senate vote on renewal of the Voting Rights Act. Behind him, left to right, are former judge Greg Mathis of Detroit, Rev. Jesse Jackson, Ted Shaw (head of the NAACP's legal defense fund) and Rep. Melvin L. Watt, D-N.C. Lewis was a leader of the 1965 "Bloody Sunday" protest in Selma, Alabama, which helped propel passage of the landmark Voting Rights Act of 1965. Source: CQ Photo/Scott J. Ferrell

Document 15.1 in Context
"The Promotion of Human Happiness and Progress": African Americans Observe the Nation's Centennial

During the 1874 House debate over plans for celebration of the nation's centennial, Rep. Josiah T. Walls, R-Fla., voiced his strong support for the celebration as a recognition of the great principles of democratic government expressed in the Declaration of Independence. Walls's defense of those principles was particularly significant in light of the difficulties he had faced taking his rightful place in Congress.

Walls was the only black representative from Florida to serve in Congress during Reconstruction. He was born a slave in Virginia in 1842 and was forced to work as a servant in the Confederate army during the Civil War until he was captured by Union troops. Eventually, he enlisted in the Union army and rose to the rank of sergeant by war's end.

Walls entered politics in Florida after the war, serving as a delegate to the state's constitutional convention in 1868 and a term in the Florida Senate before his election to Congress in 1870. His congressional career, however, was disrupted and abbreviated by challenges to his credentials. Walls's first term was cut two months short, in January 1873, when he was unseated in favor of a Democratic candidate who had contested the 1870 election. Walls won reelection in 1872 and served his full term, but his victory in the 1874 election triggered another challenge that resulted in his replacement in April 1876 by another Democratic opponent.

His experience was not unique. Sen. Hiram R. Revels, R-Miss., the first African American elected to either house of Congress, faced an intense challenge when he arrived in the capital in 1870 to take his seat (**Document 3.4**). And would-be representative and senator Pinckney B. S. Pinchback, R-La., was denied a seat in Congress, even though he had been elected to both chambers—to the House by popular vote in the 1872 election and to the Senate by the Louisiana Legislature (**Document 3.8**). In the case of each man, much of the opposition was overtly racist.

Yet, in his speech supporting the centennial celebration, Walls declares his faith in the constitutional process and the ideals espoused by the founders. He calls on his colleagues and his fellow citizens to consider the centennial "an appropriate occasion to manifest our gratitude to our fathers and our pride in the quality of their work."

▬ Document 15.1 ▬
Rep. Josiah T. Walls, R-Fla., Discusses America's Centennial Celebration, May 7, 1874

Mr. WALLS: . . . From what I have seen of the wide discussion of the proposed centennial exposition in the public press, and from the course of the debates upon the subject in these Halls, it seems to me that a misapprehension of the origin and character of the enterprise has from the beginning taken largely from the dignity of the discussion, and has largely and without necessity added acrimony and bitterness to the evident feeling attending it.

The exposition has in the press, even of this capital, been sneeringly alluded to as "The Philadelphia Job," as though it were an evident attempt on the part of the people of Pennsylvania, and especially of the city of Philadelphia, in an improper and unwarrantable manner, from motives of selfish greed, to foist upon an indifferent and an unwilling people a scheme foreign to their interests and in opposition to their wishes, and all for the petty gains and notoriety that by the adoption of the proposed plan would inure to the local benefit of a particular section. It is only upon the supposition of the existence of some such opinion that I can account for an acerbity of feeling and a harshness of language in the newspaper discussion of the centennial that to me seemed utterly uncalled for and unworthy of the theme . . .

From the very first, then, a dominant and not discreditable feature of the centennial seems to have been that it contemplated a public, emphatic, and comprehensive expression by a whole people, who for a hundred years had enjoyed a more than usual share of the ordinary blessings of human life under the genial but powerful influences of an essentially popular government based upon the organic and paramount doctrines of the Declaration ascribing to every man born of woman an entire and absolute equality of political rights, of their gratitude for the blessings attending their lot, and their profound appreciation of the adequacy of a free government to the protection of the social, political, and personal rights of all within its scope.

Such recognition of advantages received from the practical operation of existing systems of government has characterized the people of all the various known governments that have existed from time immemorial, so much so as to have become a custom well-nigh universal.

Recognized thus as proper and becoming under monarchical and even despotic governments, will any say that it is any less proper and becoming to the happy people who exult in the possession of the only literally free government upon the face of the broad earth?

Indeed, there would seem to be a peculiar propriety in such a national exhibition to the nations of the world of our own satisfaction with the capacities and excellencies of our own system of government thus approved, tested, and favored, to be both sufficient and satisfactory, by the dangers and reverses as well as the sometimes more dangerous successes of a century of practical trial.

It may all be very true that no absolutely new truth and no unheard of discovery in political science was announced in the Declaration as a novel and starting base upon which to found governmental structure that challenge the admiration of the nation. Such admitted fact in no whit derogates from the value or force of that noble document. Right there, in the very fact that in the Declaration was nothing intrinsically new, but that it simply gathered up and arranged in systematic order and for a practical purpose in the promotion of human happiness and progress those simple, forcible, and undoubted political truths which had long been acknowledged as true in the abstract, but never practically embodied in any actual and existing form of government, consists the real power of the Declaration.

It was this very novelty of making practical application of what had previously been considered only abstract prepositions for the discussion of philosophers, and to serve as themes for sentimental preachers and visionary theorists, to the protection of every-day rights and privileges, and their incorporation into an actual system of government for living men, which aroused the skeptical curiosity, and awakened the incredulous but zealous attention of the political world.

Thus proclaiming nothing actually new to philosophers and theorists the announced determination to base upon the truths of the Declaration an actual government of living men, and to place it in competition with existing governments of a variously but totally different character, startled and at first alarmed the nations.

Organically strange, and, in its application, of necessity essentially aggressive and practically threatening, the newly organized Government met with but chary courtesy from other nations, and early excited an alarm and a proclivity to opposition that to this day has not entirely disappeared.

While other nations thus so gladly welcome and celebrate those memorial days which remind them of the glorious deeds of their own noble and beloved ancestry, and delight to sound their praise, shall we, a happy and prosperous nation of forty millions, exulting in the possession of a Government by the people, for the people, of the people, entirely adequate to all our wants, and, however otherwise differing, united in common satisfaction without political heritage, decline upon an appropriate occasion to manifest our gratitude to our fathers and our pride in the quality of their work? . . .

Does any man suppose that the founding fathers of 1776, with the halter dangling before their eyes, affixed signatures to the Declaration from deliberate conviction that pecuniary gain to them would there-from result? Was greed the animus of that ever-memorable political announcement of "Millions for defense, but not one cent for tribute?"

. . . So I believe that when from every corner of this broad land, from every State and Territory, thousands and millions of the free citizens of a free government shall assemble in the very cradle and place of the birth of all that politically they hold dear, and exchange with each other the mutual grasp and the meaningful glances of a common citizenship, there will be aroused in the bosoms of all a higher and purer sense of the honest and sincere attachment cherished by all in common for those free institutions whose origin and beneficent sway they are now to celebrate than they have ever before been permitted to feel, and which will strengthen all the bonds which can unite freemen to their native land, and kindle a blaze of patriotic feeling in whose dazzling light all questions of minor differences and all hurtful recollections of past disagreements will be blotted out.

Recognizing fully the obligations of a large majority of those to whose suffrages I owe my official presence in this Hall to the tardy but in the end the full and complete vindication of the sublime and sublimely simple announcements of the Declaration, I am willing that others should find amusement in contemplating the centennial as "an overgrown and spread-eagle Fourth of July"; while for myself and at least four millions of the new freemen of this land of liberty, I will hope that, in the mercy of God, my own life may be spared till, among the crowding thousands of exulting freemen, I may on the 4th of July, 1876, stand in the very shadow of Independence Hall, and with glowing heart read the undying words of Webster:

> When my eyes shall be turned to behold, for the last time, the sun in heaven may I not see him shining on the broken and dishonored fragments of a once glorious Union; on states disseevered, discordant, and belligerent; our land rent with civil feuds, or drenched, it may be, in fraternal blood! Let their last feeble and lingering glance rather behold the gorgeous ensign of the Republic now known and honored throughout the earth, still full high advanced, its arms and trophies streaming in their original luster, not a stripe erased or polluted, not a single star obscured, bearing for its motto no such miserable interrogatory as "What is all this worth?" nor those other words of delusion and folly, "Liberty first and Union afterwards," but everywhere spread all over it in characters of living light, blazing on all its ample folds, as they float over the sea and over the land, and in every wind under the whole heavens, that other sentiment, dear to every true American heart—Liberty and Union, now and forever, one and inseparable!

Entertaining such sentiments and cherishing the hope that the day of the termination of one hundred years from the birth of our Government may by common consent and by universal adoption be fixed upon as the day of the definite and emphatic termination of all feelings of harshness and bitterness arising from our recent contentions, I shall not apologize for them, however unfashionable they may be held to be but still continue to hold them, hoping for them a wider adopting and a more commanding prevalence . . .

Source: Congressional Record, 43d Cong., 1st sess., May 7, 1874, Appendix, 250.

Document 15.2 in Context
"I Appeal to You in the Name of God and Humanity to Give Us Our Rights": The Civil Rights Act of 1875

In 1874, in the midst of a yearlong debate over legislation that eventually became the Civil Rights Act of 1875 (**Document 3.9**)—the last major civil rights bill to pass Congress for three-quarters of a century—Rep. Robert B. Vance, a white North Carolina Democrat, derided blacks while denouncing the legislation as an infringement on states' rights and a violation of the Constitution. Rep. Richard H. Cain, R-S.C., responded, defending the legislation as a straightforward attempt to guarantee the Constitution's protections of all citizens' rights.

Cain was born in Virginia in 1825 but was raised in Ohio, where he attended Wilberforce University. After he and other black students were rebuffed by the governor of Ohio in their efforts to enlist in the Union army at the start of the Civil War, Cain moved to Brooklyn, New

York, where he was a pastor from 1861 to 1865. At the war's end, Cain moved to Charleston, South Carolina, and became active in politics. He served as a delegate to the state's postwar constitutional convention in 1868 and was a member of the state senate during 1868–1872. He also managed a newspaper in Charleston.

Cain was elected to the U.S. House of Representatives for the first time in 1872. He served from March 1873 to March 1875, but he was not a candidate for reelection in 1874. In 1876 he ran again and was elected; his March 1877–March 1879 term was his last as he did not run again. He was appointed a bishop of the African Methodist Episcopal Church in 1880, a position he held until his death in 1887.

Cain supported the Civil Rights Act of 1875, asserting a strong faith in the constitutional principles of citizens' rights and the belief that most white Americans—even those in the South—were willing to accept the application of those constitutional principles to African Americans. He articulated a vision of America in which the divisions of the Civil War would be healed by ensuring the protections of the Constitution for all.

▰▰ Document 15.2 ▰▰
Rep. Richard H. Cain, R-S.C., Speaks on Civil Rights Legislation, January 10, 1874

Mr. CAIN: Mr. Speaker, I feel called upon more particularly by the remarks of the gentleman from North Carolina [Mr. Robert B. VANCE, D-N.C.] on civil rights to express my views . . . It has been assumed that to pass this bill in its present form Congress would manifest a tendency to override the Constitution of the country and violate the rights of the States.

Whether it be true or false is yet to be seen. I take it, so far as the constitutional question is concerned, if the colored people under the law, under the amendments to the Constitution, have become invested with all the rights of citizenship, then they carry with them all rights and immunities accruing to and belonging to a citizen of the United States. If four, or nearly five, million people have been lifted from the thralldom of slavery and made free; if the Government by its amendments to the Constitution has guaranteed to them all rights and immunities, as to other citizens, they must necessarily therefore carry along with them all privileges enjoyed by all other citizens of the Republic . . .

Mr. Speaker, the colored men of the south do not want the adoption of any force measure. No; they do not want anything by force. All they ask is that you will give them, by statutory enactment under the fundamental law, the right to enjoy precisely the same privileges accorded to every other class of citizens.

The gentleman, moreover, has told us that if we pass this civil-rights bill we will thereby rob the colored men of the South of the friendship of the whites. Now, I am at a loss to see how the friendship of our white friends can be lost to us by simply saying we should be permitted to enjoy the rights enjoyed by other citizens. I have a higher opinion of the friendship of the southern men than to suppose any such thing. I know them too well . . .

I cannot understand how it is that our southern friends, or a certain class of them, always bring back this old ghost of prejudice and of antagonism. There was a time, not very far distant in the past, when this antagonism was not recognized, when a feeling of fraternization between the white and the colored races existed, that made them kindred to each other. But since our emancipation, since liberty has come, and only since—only since we have stood up clothed in our manhood, only since we have proceeded to take hold and help advance the civilization of this nation—it is only since then that this bugbear is brought up against us again. Sir, the progress of the age demands that the colored man of this country shall be lifted by law into the enjoyment of every right, and that every appliance which is accorded to the German, to the Irishman, to the Englishman, and every foreigner, shall be given to him; and I shall give some reasons why I demand this in the name of justice.

For two hundred years the colored men of this nation have assisted in building up its commercial interests. There are in this country nearly five million of us, and for a space of two hundred and forty-seven years we have been hewers of wood and drawers of water; but we have been with you in promoting all the interests of the country. My distinguished colleague, who defended the civil rights of our race the other day on this floor, set this forth so clearly that I need not dwell upon it at this time.

I propose to state just this: that we have been identified with the interests of this country from its very foundation. The cotton crop of this country has been raised and its rice-fields have been tilled by the hands of our race. All along as the march of progress, as the march of commerce, as the development of your resources has been widening and expanding and spreading, as your vessels have gone on every sea, with the stars and stripes waving over them, and carried your commerce everywhere, there the black man's labor has gone to enrich your country and to augment the grandeur of your nationality. This was done in the time of slavery. And if, for the space of time I have noted, we have been hewers of wood and drawers of water; if we have made your cotton fields blossom as the rose; if we have made your rice fields wave with luxuriant harvests; if we have made your corn fields rejoice; if we have sweated and toiled to build up the prosperity of the whole country by the productions of our labor, I submit, now that the war has made a change, now that we are free—I submit to the nation whether it is not fair and right that we should come in and enjoy to the fullest extent our freedom and liberty . . .

All we ask is that you, the legislators of the nation, shall pass a law so strong and so powerful that no one shall be able to elude it and destroy our rights under the Constitution and laws of our country. That is all we ask . . .

We believe in the Declaration of Independence, that all men are born free and equal, and are endowed by their Creator with certain inalienable rights, among which are life, liberty, and the pursuit of happiness. And we further believe that to secure those rights governments are instituted. And we further believe that when governments cease to subserve those ends the people should change them . . .

I think it is proper and just that the civil-rights bill should be passed. Some think it would be better to modify it, to strike out the school clause, or to so modify it that some of the State constitutions should not be infringed. I regard it essential to us and the people of this country that we should be secured in this if in nothing else. I cannot regard that our rights will be secured until the jury-box and the school-room, those great palladiums of our liberty, shall have been opened to us. Then we will be willing to take our chances with other men.

We do not want any discriminations to be made. If discriminations are made in regard to schools, then there will be accomplished just what we are fighting against. If you say that the schools in the State of Georgia, for instance, shall be allowed to discriminate against colored people, then you will have discriminations made against us. We do not want any discriminations. I do not ask any legislation for the colored people of this country that is not applied to the white people. All that we ask is equal laws, equal legislation, and equal rights throughout the length and breadth of this land.

The gentleman from North Carolina [Mr. VANCE] also says that the colored men should not come here begging at the doors of Congress for their rights. I agree with him. I want to say that we do not come here begging for our rights. We come here clothed in the garb of American citizenship. We come demanding our rights in the name of justice. We come, with no arrogance on our part, asking that this great nation, which laid the foundations of civilization and progress more deeply and more securely than any other nation on the face of the earth, guarantee us protection from outrage. We come here, five millions of people— more than composed this whole nation when it had its great tea-party in Boston Harbor, and demanded its rights at the point of the bayonet—asking that unjust discriminations against us be forbidden. We come here in the name of justice, equity, and law, in the name of our children, in the name of our country, petitioning for our rights . . .

Let the civil-rights bill be passed this day, and five million black men, women, and children, all over the land, will begin a new song of rejoicing, and the thirty-five millions of noble hearted Anglo-Saxons will join in the shout of joy. Thus will the great mission be fulfilled of giving to all the people equal rights . . .

Our wives and our children have high hopes and aspirations; their longings for manhood and womanhood are equal to those of any other race. The same sentiment of patriotism and of gratitude, the same spirit of national pride that animates the hearts of other citizens, animates theirs. In the name of the dead soldiers of our race, whose bodies lie at Petersburg and on other battle-fields of the South; in the name of the widows and orphans they have left behind; in the name of the widows of the confederate soldiers who fell upon the same fields, I conjure you let this righteous act be done. I appeal to you in the name of God and humanity to give us our rights, for we ask nothing more . . .

Source: Congressional Record, 43d Cong., 1st sess., January 10, 1874, 565–567.

Document 15.3 in Context
"To Insist That This Nation Deliver on the Promise It Made": Youth and America's Future

Rep. Shirley A. Chisholm, D-N.Y., was widely recognized for her elective accomplishments, many of which were firsts: she was the first African American woman elected to Congress, the first African American woman to run for a major party's presidential nomination. But she was also remarkable for the thoughtful and humane way in which she approached politics. She was outspoken in her rejection of stereotypes and traditional roles for women and African Americans, calling on women to become revolutionaries, and she refused to be pigeonholed as the candidate of black Americans, insisting that her aim was to represent all the people.

During the 1972 presidential primary campaign she took the astonishing step of visiting Alabama governor George Wallace in the hospital after he had been shot while making his own run for the Democratic presidential nomination. The visit shocked and angered many of her supporters because Wallace had long been a prominent opponent of civil rights. His efforts to block integration at the University of Alabama had, in fact, catapulted him into the national spotlight just a few years earlier. But Chisholm saw the visit as simply the decent thing to do. As Chisholm recalled the incident, "He said, 'What are your people going to say?' I said, 'I know what they are going to say. But I wouldn't want what happened to you to happen to anyone.' He cried and cried."[3]

Chisholm was particularly concerned with young people and the problems that they faced. The Vietnam War had sparked intense turmoil on America's college and university campuses, and Chisholm often spoke before student groups. Her interest in children and education predated her political service: she had worked as a nursery school teacher and as a child care center director for thirteen years, beginning in the mid-1940s, and served as an educational consultant for New York City's Division of Day Care for another five years before being elected to the state legislature in 1964.

She was elected to the U.S. House of Representatives in 1968, where she served seven terms before retiring from Congress in 1983. She taught at Mount Holyoke College for several years after leaving office. The following excerpt from her 1970 book, *Unbought and Unbossed,* illustrates Chisholm's struggle to understand and accommodate the concerns of protesting youth—and the importance of making the effort.

Document 15.3
Rep. Shirley A. Chisholm, D-N.Y., Addresses the Needs of America's Young People, 1970

One question bothers me a lot: Who's listening to me? Some of the time, I feel dishearteningly small and futile. It's as if I'm facing a seamless brick wall, as if most people are deaf to what I try to say. It seems so clear to me what's wrong with the whole system. Why isn't it clear to most others? The majority of Americans do not want to hear the truth about how their country is ruled and for whom. They do not want to know why their children are rejecting them. They do not dare to have to rethink their whole lives. There is a vacuum of leadership, created partly by the bullets of deranged assassins. But whatever made it, all we see now is the same tired old men who keep trucking down front to give us the same old songs and dances.

There are no new leaders coming along. Where are they? What has happened suddenly? On the national level, on the state level, who commands respect, who is believed by a wide enough cross section of the population to qualify as a leader? I don't see myself as becoming that kind of a leader. My role, I think, is more that of a catalyst. By verbalizing what is wrong, by trying to strip off the masks that make people comfortable in the midst of chaos, perhaps I can help get things moving.

It may be that no one can have any effect on most adults in this society. It may be that the only hope is with the younger generation. If I can relate to them, give them some kind of focus, make them believe that this country can still become the America that it should have been, I could be content. The young may be slandered as "kooks" and "societal misfits" by frightened, demagogic old men, but that will not scare them. They are going to force change. For a while they may be beaten down, but time is on their side, and the spirit of this generation will not be killed. That's why I prefer to go around to campuses and talk with the kids rather than attend political meetings. Politicians tell me I'm wasting my time and energy. "They don't vote," I'm told. Well, I'm not looking for votes. If I were, I would get the same kind of reception that a lot of political figures get when they encounter younger people, and I would deserve it.

There are many things I don't agree with some young zealots about. The main one, I suppose, is that I have not given up—and will not give up until I am compelled to—my belief that the basic design of this country is right. What is essential is to make it work, not to sweep it away and substitute—what? Something far worse, perhaps.

Most young people are not yet revolutionary, but politicians and police and other persons in power almost seem to be conspiring to turn them into revolutionaries. Like me, I think, most of them are no more revolutionary than the founders of this country. Their goals are the same—to insure individual liberty and equality of opportunity, and forever to thwart the tyrannous tendencies of government, which inevitably arise from the arrogance and isolation of men who are securely in power. All they want, if it were not too unfashionable for them to say so, is for the American dream to come true, at least in its less materialistic aspects. They want to heal the gaping breach between this country's promises and its performance, a breach that goes back to its founding on a Constitution that denied that black persons and women were full citizens. "Liberty and justice for all" were beautiful words, but the ugly fact was that liberty and justice were only for white males. How incredible that it is nearly 200 years since then, and we have still to fight the same old enemies! How is it possible for a man to repeat the pledge of allegiance that contains these words, and then call his fellow citizens "societal misfits" when they are simply asking for liberty and justice? . . .

Whenever I speak to student groups, the first question they ask me is "Can't you do something about the war?" The next one usually is "How can you stand to be part of this system?" They mean, "How can you stay in Congress and keep talking about progress, about reconciliation, after all that this society has done to you and your people?" It is the hardest question I could be asked, and the answer is the most important one I can offer. I try to explain to them:

"You can be part of the system without being wedded to it," I say. "You can take part in it without believing that everything it does is right. I don't measure America by its achievement, but by its potential. There are still many things that we haven't tried—that I haven't tried—to change the way our present system operates. I haven't exhausted the opportunities for action in the course I'm pursuing. If I ever do, I cannot at this point imagine what to do next. You want me to talk to you about revolution, but I can't do that. I know what it would bring. My people are twelve percent of the population, at most fifteen percent. I am pragmatic about it: revolution would be suicide."

What is the alternative? What can we offer these beautiful, angry, serious, and committed young people? How are we all to be saved? The alternative, of course, is reform—renewal, revitalization of the institutions of this potentially great nation. This is our only hope. If my story has any importance, apart from its curiosity value—the fascination of being a "first" at anything is a durable one—it is, I hope, that I have persisted in seeking this path toward a better world. My significance, I want to believe, is not that I am the first black woman elected to the U.S. Congress, but that I won public office without selling out to anyone. When I wrote my campaign slogan, "Unbossed and Unbought," it was an expression of what I believe I was and what I want to be—what I want all candidates for public office to be. We need men and women who have far greater abilities and far broader appeal than I will ever have, but who have my kind of independence—who will dare to declare that they are free of the old ways that have led us wrong, and who owe nothing to the traditional concentrations of capital and power that have subverted this nation's ideals.

Such leaders must be found. But they will not be found as much as they will be created, by an electorate that has become ready to demand that it control its own destiny. There must be a new coalition of all Americans—black, white, red, yellow and brown, rich and poor—who are no longer willing to allow their rights as human beings to be infringed upon by anyone else, for any reason. We must join together to insist that this nation deliver on the promise it made, nearly 200 years ago, that every man be allowed to be a man. I feel an incredible urgency that we must do it now. If time has not run out, it is surely ominously short.

Source: Shirley Chisholm, "Youth and America's Future," in *Unbought and Unbossed* (Boston: Houghton Mifflin, 1970), 170–177.

Document 15.4 in Context
"These Are the Steps I Urge All of America's 25 Million Black People to Take": Black Power and the Future of Black America

Rep. Adam Clayton Powell Jr., a Democrat from New York, was as controversial as he was charismatic. The son of a minister, Powell was himself an accomplished preacher, newspaper publisher, community activist and teacher before he ventured into elective politics in New York City, where he won a seat on the city council in 1941. Three years later he was elected to the first of his thirteen sometimes-tumultuous terms in Congress.

Powell's arrival in Washington doubled African American representation in Congress because the only other black member at the time was William L. Dawson, D-Ill. But where Dawson's relatively quiet but effective approach reflected an older generation of leadership, Powell's outspoken attacks on racial segregation and discrimination in America were more in tune with the younger generation's growing black militancy that erupted into the Black Power movement of the 1960s.

Just a year after taking his seat in Congress, Powell's first book was published. Entitled *Marching Blacks,* its first chapter declared that the United States was in the midst of a second Civil War and called on all African Americans to leave the southern states (**Document 5.7**). The provocative suggestion drew criticism even among the African Americans community, but Powell's willingness to challenge the white power structure endeared him to many.

In 1971, after losing his bid for a fourteenth term in Congress, Powell published his autobiography, in which he included a discussion of the Black Power movement that was injected into the public consciousness during the 1966 March against Fear in Mississippi led by Rev. Martin Luther King Jr. Younger activists at the march, most notably Stokely Carmichael, were tiring of King's commitment to nonviolence in the face of racist attacks, and they attracted enormous attention when they began chanting the slogan, "Black Power." The new militancy divided the civil rights movement and frightened many whites. In this excerpt, Powell offers his own explanation of Black Power and uses it as the basis of a proposed fifteen-point program for black political and social activism.

▰▰▰ Document 15.4 ▰▰▰
Rep. Adam Clayton Powell Jr., D-N.Y., Explains Black Political and Social Activism, 1971

. . . During 1968, 1969, and 1970 I made more than one hundred speeches all over the United States. I spoke to entirely white audiences in the South and to entirely black audiences in the North. And I found that no phrase strikes more terror to the hearts of white Americans than Black Power.

Black Power was founded half a century ago by Marcus Garvey, the semiliterate immigrant from Jamaica, at whose feet I sat as a youngster and listened while he talked. I held the first National Black Power Conference in this Republic. Therefore I write with authority.

Black Power does not mean antiwhite unless whites make blacks antiwhite.

Black power does not mean violence, but it does not mean total nonviolence. It does not mean that you walk with a chip on your shoulder, but you walk letting the chips fly where they may.

Black Power means black dignity. Pride in being black. Pride that black is beautiful. Pride that blacks are not second-class citizens as our forefathers were.

Black Power means a complete separation from Negroes. Especially the Negro bourgeoisie or, as I call them, Negro bushies.

Black Power means pride in heritage. Pride in knowing that before the first white man, a savage in what is now England, could ever comb his matted locks, black men were carving statues, painting, creating astronomy, mathematics, and the alphabet.

Black Power means pride that the first man who died on Boston Common that America might be free was a black man, Crispus Attucks. Pride that a black man, Benjamin Banneker, planned the city of Washington, the capital of the Republic—and before him another black man from France, Pierre L'Enfant.

Black Power means that blacks have a willingness to die for their cause—no cause has ever been successful without the willingness of people who believe in it to die for it, whether they died or not.

Black Power means we are no better—and above all no less—in terms of equality with any other ethnic group in the United States.

Black Power means we are going to lead our own black group and do not want any white leadership. Whites can help us with troops, maybe a corporal or sergeant, but above all no white generals. We will command our destiny. We ask those who want to help us to help us. With our without you, we're going to win.

Black Power means that we have paid the price in Watts, in Newark, in Detroit, in Harlem, in a hundred and three cities after Martin Luther King, Jr., was assassinated.

Black Power means we're not afraid of anyone even though others may have the weapons that we do not have—although some of the Black Power groups do have weapons.

Black Power means we are proud of our Black Panthers. We may not agree with them, because few people really understand them. But we are proud of any group that's willing to die for its cause.

Black Power means we are searching for truth always. Not the truth of J. Edgar Hoover's wiretapping of Black Panther Headquarters and infiltration of Black Power movements. It means the kind of truth that we discovered on the scene in Chicago when we went to the Black Panther Headquarters . . .

The truth about [Black Panther leader] Fred Hampton's assassination by the police of the city of Chicago. We saw the truth—the door with every bullet hole made from the outside in. Not one shot fired from inside out. We saw the truth—that Fred Hampton was killed while he was sleeping; they came through an outside door on the back porch and shot him in the top of his head.

Black Power calls on all Americans to stop the genocide against the Black Panthers and black people everywhere.

Black Power says don't forget the executive secretary of the NAACP who was murdered in Mississippi. Don't forget the two white boys from Manhattan and a black soul brother who were bulldozed into the earth in Mississippi. Don't forget the assassination of Jack Kennedy. Don't forget the assassination of Bobby Kennedy.

Black Power says power to the people. The gaunt man who walked at midnight on Pennsylvania Avenue said it once—power to the people. He said the only government that would not perish from the earth would be a government of the people (power to the people), by the people (power to the people), and for the people (power to the people). But what does this power, this Black Power come from? Let me tell you what I have been telling my brothers, what I call a Black Position Paper.

1. Black organizations must be black-led. To the extent to which black organizations are led by whites, to that precise extent is their black potential for ultimate control and direction diluted.

2. The black masses must finance their own organizations; at least such organizations must derive the main source of their funds from black people. No other ethnic group in America permits others to control their organizations . . .

3. The black masses must demand and refuse to accept nothing less than that proportionate percentage of the political spoils, such as jobs, elective offices, and appointments, that are equal to their proportion of the population and their voting strength. They must reject the shameful racial tokenism that characterizes the political life of America today . . .

4. Black people must support and push black candidates for political office first, operating on the principle of "all other things being equal" . . .

5. Black leadership in the North and the South must differentiate between and work within the two-pronged thrust of the black revolution: economic self-sufficiency and political power. The Civil Rights Act of 1964 had absolutely no meaning for black people in New York, Chicago, or any of the Northern Cities. De jure school segregation, denial of the right to vote, or barriers to public accommodations are no longer sources of concern to Northern blacks. Civil rights in the North means more jobs, better education, manpower retraining, and development of new skills . . .

6. Black masses must produce and contribute to the economy of the country in strength proportionate to their population. We must become a race of producers, not consumers. We must rid ourselves of the welfare paralysis that humiliates our human spirit.

7. Black communities of this country—whether New York's Harlem, Chicago's South and West Sides, or Philadelphia's North Side—must neither tolerate nor accept outside leadership, black or white. Each community must provide its own local leadership, strengthening the resources within its own local community.

8. The black masses should follow only those leaders who can sit at the bargaining table with the white power structure as equals and negotiate for a share of the loaf of bread, not beg for some of its crumbs . . .

9. This black leadership—the ministers, politicians, businessmen, doctors and lawyers—must come back to the blacks who made them in the first place or be purged by the black masses. Black communities all over America today suffer from "absentee black leadership" . . .

10. Blacks must reject the white community's carefully selected "ceremonial Negro leaders" and insist that the white community deal instead with the black leadership chosen by black communities . . .

11. Blacks must distinguish between desegregation and integration. Desegregation removes all barriers and facilitates access to an open society. Integration accomplishes the same thing but has a tendency to denude the Negro of pride in himself . . .

12. Demonstration and all continuing protest activity must always be nonviolent. Violence, even when it erupts recklessly in anger among our teen-agers, must be curbed and discouraged.

13. No black person over twenty-one must be permitted to participate in a demonstration, walk a picket line, or be part of any civil rights or community activity unless he or she is a registered voter.

14. Black people must continue to defy the laws of man when such laws conflict with the law of God . . .

15. Black people must discover a new and creative total involvement with ourselves. We must turn our energies inwardly toward our homes, our churches, our families, our children, our colleges, our neighborhoods, our businesses and our communities. Our fraternal and social groups must become an integral part of this creative involvement by using their resources and energy toward constructive fund-raising and community activities. This is no time for cotillions and teas. These are the steps I urge all of America's 25 million black people to take as we begin the dawn of a new day by walking together. And as we walk together hand in hand, firmly keeping the faith of our black forebears, we glory in what we have become and are today.

Source: Adam Clayton Powell Jr., "The Future of Black America," in *Adam by Adam: The Autobiography of Adam Clayton Powell Jr.* (New York: Kensington Publishing Corp., 1971), 245–250.

Document 15.5 in Context
"Who Then Will Speak for the Common Good?" Rep. Barbara C. Jordan's Vision for America

When Rep. Barbara C. Jordan, D-Texas, walked to the rostrum to deliver the keynote address at the 1976 Democratic National Convention, she was a rising political star. In just her second term in Congress, she was widely recognized and admired for her role in the House Judiciary Committee hearings that considered impeachment of Richard M. Nixon (**Document 6.5**).

Jordan was among the first wave of African Americans to win major political offices at the state and national levels after the reforms of the Civil Rights Act of 1964 (**Document 5.11**) and the Voting Rights Act of 1965 (**Document 6.1**). She had run twice, in 1962 and 1964, for a seat in the Texas House of Representatives but lost both elections. In 1966, however, she won election to the Texas Senate, becoming the first African American since 1883 and the first black woman ever to hold that office. She served as a state senator until 1972; during her tenure, she was the first black woman to serve as president pro tem of that body, and she also served one day as acting governor of Texas.

In 1972 Jordan won a seat in the Congress. As she described in her 1979 autobiography, *Barbara Jordan: A Self-Portrait,* it was the friendship and patronage of Lyndon B. Johnson, the former president and a fellow Texan, that enabled her to win appointment to the prestigious House Judiciary Committee during her first term in Wahington. She served three terms in the House and then taught for several years at the Lyndon B. Johnson School of Public Affairs at the University of Texas in Austin.

In the following excerpt from her speech to the Democratic National Convention in 1976 Jordan expresses her vision of America: a nation of interwoven rights and responsibilities that depends on the commitment of each citizen—and each political leader—to build a community of justice and freedom and trust.

▰▰▰ Document 15.5 ▰▰▰
Rep. Barbara C. Jordan, D-Texas, Delivers the Keynote Speech at the 1976 Democratic National Convention

One hundred and forty-four years ago, members of the Democratic Party first met in convention to select a Presidential candidate. Since that time, Democrats have continued to convene once every four years and draft a party platform and nominate a Presidential candidate. And our meeting this week is a continuation of that tradition.

But there is something different about tonight. There is something special about tonight. What is different? What is Special? I, Barbara Jordan, am a keynote speaker.

A lot of years passed since 1832, and during that time it would have been most unusual for any national political party to ask that a Barbara Jordan deliver a keynote address . . . but tonight here I am. And I feel that notwithstanding the past that my presence here is one additional bit of evidence that the American Dream need not forever be deferred.

Now that I have this grand distinction what in the world am I supposed to say?

I could easily spend this time praising the accomplishments of this party and attacking the Republicans but I don't choose to do that.

I could list the many problems which Americans have. I could list the problems which cause people to feel cynical, angry, frustrated: problems which include lack of integrity in government; the feeling that the individual no longer counts; the reality of material and spiritual poverty; the feeling that the grand American experiment is failing or has failed. I could recite these problems and then I could sit down and offer no solutions. But I don't choose to do that either.

The citizens of America expect more. They deserve and they want more than a recital of problems.

We are a people in a quandary about the present. We are a people in search of our future. We are a people in search of a national community.

We are a people trying not only to solve the problems of the present: unemployment, inflation . . . but we are attempting on a larger scale to fulfill the promise of America. We are attempting to fulfill our national purpose; to create and sustain a society in which all of us are equal . . .

What is it, what is it about the Democratic Party that makes it the instrument that people use when they search for ways to shape their future? Well I believe the answer to that question lies in our concept of governing. Our concept of governing is derived from our view of people. It is a concept deeply rooted in a set of beliefs firmly etched in the national conscience, of all of us.

Now what are these beliefs?

First, we believe in equality for all and privileges for none. This is a belief that each American regardless of background has equal standing in the public forum, all of us.

Because we believe this idea so firmly, we are inclusive rather than an exclusive party. Let everybody come . . .

We believe that the people are the source of all governmental power; that the authority of the people is to be extended, not restricted. This can be accomplished only by providing each citizen with every opportunity to participate in the management of the government. They must have that.

We believe that the government which represents the authority of all the people, not just one interest group, but all the people, has an obligation to actively—underscore, actively—seek to remove those obstacles which would block individual achievement . . . obstacles emanating from race, sex, economic condition. The government must seek to remove them.

We are a party of innovation. We do not reject our traditions, but we are willing to adapt to changing circumstances, when change we must. We are willing to suffer the discomfort of change in order to achieve a better future.

We have a positive vision of the future founded on the belief that the gap between the promise and reality of America can one day be finally closed. We believe that.

This my friends, is the bedrock of our concept of governing. This is a part of the reason why Americans have turned to the Democratic Party. These are the foundations upon which a national community can be built.

Let's all understand that these guiding principles cannot be discarded for short-term political gains. They represent what this country is all about. They are indigenous to the American idea. And these are principles which are not negotiable.

In other times, I could stand here and give this kind of exposition on the beliefs of the Democratic Party and that would be enough. But today that is not enough. People want more. That is not sufficient reason for the majority of the people of this country to vote Democratic. We have made mistakes. In our haste to do all things for all people, we did not foresee the full consequences of our actions. And when the people raised their voices, we didn't hear. But our deafness was only a temporary condition, and not an irreversible condition.

Even as I stand here and admit that we have made mistakes I still believe that as the people of America sit in judgment on each party, they will recognize that our mistakes were mistakes of the heart. They'll recognize that.

And now we must look to the future. Let us heed the voice of the people and recognize their common sense. If we do not, we not only blaspheme our political heritage, we ignore the common ties that bind all Americans.

Many fear the future, Many are distrustful of their leaders, and believe that their voices are never heard. Many seek only to satisfy their private work wants. To satisfy private interests.

But this is the great danger America faces. That we will cease to be one nation and become instead a collection of interest groups: city against suburb, region against region, individual against individual. Each seeking to satisfy private wants.

If that happens, who then will speak for America?

Who then will speak for the common good?

This is the question which must be answered in 1976.

Are we to be one people bound together by common spirit sharing in a common endeavor or will we become a divided nation?

For all of its uncertainty, we cannot flee the future. We must not become the new puritans and reject our society. We must address and master the future together. It can be done if we restore the belief that we share a sense of national community, that we share a common national endeavor. It can be done . . .

As a first step, we must restore our belief in ourselves. We are a generous people so why can't we be generous with each other? We need to take to heart the words spoken by Thomas Jefferson:

"Let us restore to social intercourse the harmony and that affection without which liberty and even life are but dreary things."

A nation is formed by the willingness of each of us to share in the responsibility for upholding the common good.

A government is invigorated when each of us is willing to participate in shaping the future of this nation.

In this election year we must define the common good and begin again to shape a common good and begin again to shape a common future. Let each person do his or her part. If one citizen is unwilling to participate, all of us are going to suffer. For the American idea, though it is shared by all of us, is realized in each one of us.

And now, what are those of us who are elected public officials supposed to do? We call ourselves public servants but I'll tell you this: we as public servants must set an example for the rest of the nation. It is hypocritical for the public official to admonish and exhort the people to uphold the common good. More is required of public officials than slogans and handshakes and press releases. More is required. We must hold ourselves strictly accountable. We must provide the people with a vision of the future.

If we promise as public officials, we must deliver. If we as public officials propose, we must produce. If we say to the American people it is time for you to be sacrificial; sacrifice. If the public official says that, we (public officials) must be the first to give. We must be. And again, if we make mistakes, we must be willing to admit them. We have to do that. What we have to do is strike a balance between the idea, the belief, that government ought to do nothing. Strike a balance.

Let there be no illusions about the difficulty of forming this kind of a national community. It's tough, difficult, not easy. But a spirit of harmony will survive in America only if each of us remembers that we share a common destiny . . .

Source: Barbara C. Jordan, "Who Then Will Speak for the Common Good?" Keynote speech delivered at the Democratic National Convention, July 12, 1976, from the LBJ School of Public Affairs, University of Texas at Austin, www.utexas.edu/lbj/barbarajordanforum.

Document 15.6 in Context
"We Cannot Move Forward Unless We Reorder Our Priorities": Rep. Louis Stokes, D-Ohio, on the Federal Budget

In November 1989, after authorities announced the relaxation of travel restrictions between East and West Germany, enthusiastic Germans with sledgehammers began tearing apart the Berlin Wall that had divided the city since 1961. The wall was an icon of the Cold War between the United States and its Western European allies on one side, and the Soviet Union and its Eastern European client states on the other. The collapse of the physical representation of the metaphoric "iron curtain" that Winston Churchill had described in 1946 was viewed as a symbolic end to the Cold War.

Within two years, the Soviet Union had dissolved, leaving the United States as the world's sole superpower. Though the four decades of tension between the two great powers had not brought them into direct and open warfare, the period had been characterized by enormous military spending on both sides. The question that arose, even as the wall fell, was what the end of the Cold War would mean for U.S. spending priorities.

American social liberals had long been critical of the impact of military spending on the budgets of programs for health, education and other social services. Many of them saw the decline of tensions with the Soviet Union as an opportunity to shift funding priorities away from the military and toward social programs to help people in need.

During the debate in February 1990 on the federal budget Rep. Louis Stokes, D-Ohio, discussed how to use the so-called peace dividend. At the time, Stokes was in his eleventh term in the House. He had served in the U.S. army during World War II, but he was critical of what he considered excessive spending on expensive weapons programs, arguing that the military needed to accept its fair share of budget cuts if the nation were to meet its responsibilities to "the poor, the elderly, and minorities."

Document 15.6
Rep. Louis Stokes, D-Ohio, Comments on the "Peace Dividend," February 7, 1990

Mr. STOKES: . . . Now that the walls of oppression have come tumbling down all over the world, the United States no longer needs to carry the burden of protecting the entire world. We should now be able to direct our efforts inward to ensure that this country has the resources to meet the challenges of the 21st century. Unfortunately, President [George H. W.] Bush and his administration do not seem interested in preparing America for these challenges.

President Bush recently presented the Congress with a $1.23 trillion budget plan for fiscal year 1991. For those of us who were hoping for a windfall or dividend resulting from a decrease in defense spending, and who believed that this President might be in touch with the needs of this country, the President's budget is a bitter disappointment. According to the President, there is no dividend for peace.

The President's budget does not reflect the dramatic events in Eastern Europe and the Soviet Union. The President's request for the Defense Department totals $295.1 billion in budget authority. It does not propose canceling or reducing any of the new generation of strategic weapons. In fact, large increases are included in the budget for the Stealth bomber, star wars and the MX missile. If we continue to support all of these weapons systems and not choose among them, we will see expenditures for these already expensive weapons increase significantly in a few years, when they will reach full production stage. Yet, OMB Director Richard Darman did not include these out-year costs among the 'pacmen' that threaten to gobble up our budgetary resources.

I, too, am concerned about the magnitude of the Federal deficit. If the President's budget were adopted, the deficit would be reduced to $61.4 billion, under the Gramm-Rudman target of $64 billion. The military, however is not being asked to assume a fair share of spending reductions that must be made in order to reduce the deficit. The budget includes over $16.1 billion in spending reductions. Four-fifths of this amount is expected to come from domestic programs. Defense contributes only one-fifth of the total amount of the reduction package. A large portion of these cuts would come from entitlement programs, such as Medicare and child nutrition programs.

I question the priorities expressed in the President's budget. Under the President's plan, the National Aeronautics and Space Administration would receive the largest increase in the budget—$2.9 billion. This represents an increase of nearly 24 percent for this agency. The program being asked to absorb the largest cut is the Medicare Program, which provides health care to some 35 million elderly and handicapped Americans. A cut of nearly $5.5 billion could result in reduction of services to this vulnerable population and would exacerbate the health care crisis facing this Nation.

Apparently, the President feels that we should use the peace dividend to support space exploration. Here in America, on planet Earth, we have 3 million homeless people. Their needs are not addressed in this budget. The President states that he is increasing funding to combat homelessness by 66 percent in fiscal year 1991. At the same time, he declined to request funds to develop new public housing units. The waiting list nationwide for public housing now includes nearly 1 million people.

Cuts in important domestic spending programs have been justified by the administration as necessary to reduce the budget deficit. Reduction of the budget deficit, however, only seems to be a priority when the administration considers programs that affect certain populations—the poor, the elderly, and minorities. This policy is embodied in the resurrected capital gains tax cut proposal. A report of the Joint Economic Committee indicates that this type of tax cut will result in a loss of revenue to the Government in the long run.

The budget proposal that the President has asked us to consider demonstrates that despite the outbreak of peace, his administration is still functioning in a military mode. It does not devote enough resources to vital domestic programs, such as health care, and education. The 1990's symbolize the gateway to the 21st century. This is the time to ensure that as we face the challenges of this new century, we go forward with a healthy and well-educated citizenry, and that our cities provide a safe and enriching environment for our children. This is the ideal that America has always stood for. We must fulfill it, if we expect to prosper in the 21st century. We cannot move forward unless we reorder our priorities.

Source: Congressional Record, 101st Cong., 2d sess., February 7, 1990, H350.

Document 15.7 in Context
"If We . . . Show but a Fraction of the Courage and Resolve of Our Esteemed Ancestors": African Americans and Economic Empowerment

In early 1993 Democrat Bill Clinton had just taken over the White House after twelve years of Republican control under Presidents Ronald Reagan and George H. W. Bush. Although Reagan had been enormously popular and Bush had received widespread support for his handling of the Persian Gulf War, Clinton won the November 1992 election in significant part because a declining economy had eroded support for Bush.

As in all economic recessions, African Americans suffered disproportionately because they were more heavily represented in the nation's lower income levels. In late February 1993 Rep. Gary A. Franks, R-Conn., took the occasion of Black History Month observances in the House to address the disparity of economic conditions in the United States and to assert his own views on the need for—and the path to—black economic empowerment. At the time, Franks was the sole black Republican in Congress, and he was only the second to serve since the early 1930s, when African Americans began their historic shift in political affiliation from the party of Abraham Lincoln to the party of Franklin Delano Roosevelt.

Franks, a northern conservative, served five years on the Waterbury County Board of Aldermen before being elected to Congress in 1990. He served three terms in the House before losing a reelection bid in 1996, and he also tried unsuccessfully to win election to the Senate in 1998.

His economic philosophy was strongly in the vein of traditional conservative Republican theory. In his address to the House reproduced here, he argues that the economic problems facing African Americans cannot be solved by more government programs and asserts that those problems stem from "social pathologies" within the African American community, not merely racism. He emphasizes the need for self-reliance and praises the approach of Booker T. Washington.

Washington, who was the most widely recognized and influential black leader of the late nineteenth and early twentieth centuries, devoted his life to promoting an educational system based on teaching work skills he believed would result in economic independence and advancement for African Americans. Many blacks, however, criticized him as too willing to accept racial segregation and discrimination. Franks believed a renewed emphasis on economic self-reliance would empower African Americans in ways no government program ever could.

▬ Document 15.7 ▬
Rep. Gary A. Franks, R-Conn., Discusses Black Empowerment, February 24, 1993

Mr. FRANKS of Connecticut: Mr. Speaker, I am pleased to join my colleagues in celebrating Black History Month. Our history is rich and diverse and one that reflects the greatness of America. However, I hasten to add, that no abstract of statistics is needed to see the vast disparities in economic advantage which separate the urban or inner-city black poor from the rest of the Nation. Mr. Speaker, as we look at the state of black America the expression 'when white America sneezes black America catches a cold' comes to mind.

A long and crippling recession has driven many of our African-American families deeper and deeper into an existence marked by destitution and impoverishment. The recession has aggravated one of the most stubborn problems faced by African-Americans—disproportionate employment. This is highlighted by the fact that since the beginning of the recession black unemployment has climbed by over 16 percent. During the third quarter of 1992 black unemployment was in excess of 14 percent, which was more than double the white unemployment rate!

I have long advocated the idea that many of the answers to our problems lie in the empowerment of African-Americans via entrepreneurial pursuits. The approach of 'all we need is more money for more programs, and eventually our problems will be solved' is simply not realistic—as history has so vividly shown us.

Currently African-Americans own fewer businesses, and the businesses that are owned tend to be very small in comparison to all businesses. For example, African-Americans were 12.1 percent of the population in 1987 but owned only 2.4 percent of the businesses. African-American businesses accounted for only 0.19 percent of total receipts.

The notion of empowerment via entrepreneurship is an intricate concept that if properly implemented will yield individual financial wealth, community capital formation, and even political power.

The problems that we face as a nation continue to be aggravated by the consistent decaying of our urban areas where the vast majority of the bottom stratum of African-Americans reside. The black community has problems which can no longer be blamed solely on racism and which force us to confront our most fundamental failures.

There is no way for us to ignore the social pathologies that beset our urban areas. We are faced with over one quarter of young African-Americans in the crucial ages of 20 to 24 years old, according to one survey, having fallen from the economy—they are not working, they are not in school, and not actively looking for work. In our urban areas more than half of all African American babies are born out of wedlock; approximately one-half of all African American children are sustained by transfers from the State and Federal Governments.

Unfortunately, there are no easy answers. As we view our history, in many instances we see those who stressed the need for African Americans to become economically self-reliant were often maligned by the black establishment of their times.

One such man was Booker T. Washington, the distinguished educator, who stressed the importance of property ownership. He was maligned and sneered at as he promoted his 'bootstrap' approach wherein he called for African Americans to use the resources in their possession to elevate themselves.

We have to approach old problems with new, result-oriented programs and solutions. Choices have to be tied to an improved economy as well as an improved social order. School choice must be made available to everyone, especially those in our most blighted urban areas. We have to enact welfare reform that does more than offer a young single mother a surrogate husband, but instead provides a means to develop marketable skills and offers an avenue to employment. Perhaps she can be employed by an urban entrepreneur, who has received financial support and incentives to locate a business within an urban enterprise zone.

I celebrate Black History Month with my colleagues and I am encouraged by the thought, that if we, within these Chambers show but a fraction of the courage and resolve of our esteemed ancestors we will enact the type of legislation that will solve the aforementioned problems faced by African Americans.

Source: Congressional Record, 103d Cong., 1st sess., February 24, 1993, E477–E478.

Document 15.8 in Context
"The Republican Definition of Compassion": Rep. J. C. Watts Jr., R-Okla., Speaks for the Republican Party

From 1935, when Rep. Oscar S. De Priest, R-Ill., left office, through the elections of 2006, only four black Republicans were elected to Congress: Edward W. Brooke III of Massachusetts in the Senate and Del. Melvin H. Evans of the Virgin Islands and Reps. Gary A. Franks of Connecticut and J. C. Watts Jr. of Oklahoma in the House. Watts, who had been a popular standout quarterback at the University of Oklahoma, was elected in 1994.

Watts rose quickly in the ranks of the House Republican leadership. He was elected chairman of the GOP House Conference, the number-four party leadership post, in just his third term. By then, however, he had become a highly visible Republican Party figure, having been selected in January 1997 to deliver the party's nationally broadcast response to President Bill Clinton's State of the Union address (**Document 7.4**).

Watts's rise in the Republican Party was partly a reflection of his personal charisma and straightforward political style; his presence gave him a broad appeal to conservative voters. Unlike many of his African American colleagues in Congress, he had won in a district that was predominantly white. But the GOP was also happy to highlight Watts as it attempted to attract a larger share of black voters. Watts was among an increasingly visible and vocal number of African Americans in the 1990s who believed the solution to America's social problems lay less in governmental action than in a return to the traditional conservative values of devotion to family, country and personal responsibility to which the GOP laid claim.

Watts's first major appearance on the national political stage came at the 1996 Republican National Convention in San Diego. He delivered one of the most prominent speeches at that convention, outlining his vision of those traditional values that he saw at the root of American greatness. The speech is excerpted here.

══ Document 15.8 ══
Rep. J. C. Watts Jr., R-Okla., Describes His Vision of the American Dream, August 13, 1996

Let me start by saying, I'm thrilled Bob Dole has chosen the second best quarterback in the Republican party, Jack Kemp as his running mate.

When it comes to the American dream, no one has a corner on the market. All of us have an equal chance to share in that dream. In my wildest imagination, I never thought that the fifth of six children born to Helen and Buddy Watts—in a poor black neighborhood, in the poor rural community of Eufaula, Oklahoma—would someday be called Congressman. But then, this is America, where dreams come true. I never thought I would have the privilege of addressing the American people but this is America where dreams still come true. One of the Republicans major products is dream making. People are dying to get into this country—not out of it.

It is still the greatest, most prosperous, most powerful nation on the face of the earth and it produces hundreds of thousands of dreams come true every day.

Tom Lewis had a dream. As a police officer walking the streets of D.C.'s toughest neighborhoods, time after time, kids would come up to him, father-less children, and ask, "Will you be my daddy?" So, when Tom retired from the D.C. police force, he took his life savings, bought a house and turned it into a center where kids could go for tutoring and nurturing and a warm meal, he calls this the Fishing School. Tom understands that what we build, nourish, and encourage the youth of America to be today, is what our country will be 20 years from now. Tom is joined by countless other unsung heroes.

This past year I had the opportunity to travel the country and meet the people who are changing lives, one heart at a time. In my own home state of Oklahoma, there's the Resurrection House in Chickasha that takes care of the homeless in a rural community. There's an organization called TEEM, the education and employment ministry, where Doc Benson restores people with a job and a future. I celebrated with Freddy Garcia at Victory Fellowship in San Antonio who not only met the challenge of his own drug addiction but has a ministry serving others with success rates that the social scientists can only dream about.

These people working in the trenches and suffering with those who suffer understand compassion. They understand compassion can't be dispensed from a safe distance by a faceless bureaucrat sitting in an air conditioned office in Washington D.C. And while we are on the subject of compassion, it was just about four years ago that I was privileged to address the GOP convention.

It was at that time I talked to you about the Republican definition of compassion. We don't define compassion by how many people are on welfare, or AFDC, or living in public housing. We define compassion by how FEW people are on welfare, AFDC, and public housing because we have given them the means to climb the ladder of success. At that time, welfare reform was a distant hope, but I am pleased to tell you that just two weeks ago, the historic Republican Congress passed, over the objections of Bill Clinton, welfare reform that will restore compassion and dignity to those less fortunate. Compassion can't be measured in dollars and cents. It does come with a price tag, but that price tag isn't the amount of money spent. The price tag is love—being able to see people as they can be and not as they are. The measure of a man is not how great his faith is, but how great his love is. We must not let government programs disconnect our souls from each other. Bob Dole understands. Bob Dole knows that it's people like Tom Lewis, the folks at the Resurrection House, Freddy Garcia, and Doc Benson—it's these people, not the government that can provide folks with tools they need to become productive citizens with dignity.

Bob Dole understands Washington can't teach people right from wrong, dry their tears, or help a child with his homework. Bob Dole understands it's people helping people, neighbor helping neighbor. In fact, I have a special message for the kids in your house tonight. I'd ask you to get them, and while you do, let me tell you that the years I spent as a youth minister were glorious years that made an investment in eternity.

In addition, there is one title I cherish a great deal more than Congressman and that is the title of—Dad. So, indulge me while I say a word to the kids in the audience tonight.

Young people, America needs you. If our country is going to continue to be great, if it is going to continue to be strong, you are going to have to do your part. You are going to have to fight for America. Fight against skipping school and cheating on your papers. Fight against driving too fast and disobeying your parents. Fight against cursing and smoking. And fight, fight with every fiber of your being against drugs and alcohol. I know, I know you've heard all this before and you probably think that J. C. Watts is just another old fashioned grown-up and if you're thinking that, you're right, just ask my five kids . . .

I know it's tough. That's why I'm asking you to fight and be counted as a leader. You can help your friends find the courage to say no to the things that make them weak. And yes to the things that make them strong. You see character does count. For too long we have gotten by in a society that says the only thing right is to get by and the only thing wrong is to get caught. Character is doing what's right when nobody is looking. And I want to make a promise to you. We will do our best to leave this country in better shape financially, environmentally, and most of all, spirituality.

Parents and adults I don't just challenge the youth tonight. I challenge you. For what we build and nourish and encourage in our youth today, is what our country will look like 20 years from now.

The American Dream is about becoming the best you can be. It's not about your bank account, the kind of car you drive, or the brand of clothes you wear. It's about using your gifts and abilities to be all that God meant for you to be. Whether your dream is to be a doctor, teacher, engineer, or Congressman. If you can dream it, you can do it. The American Dream is the promise that if you study hard, work hard and dedicate yourself you can be whatever you want to be.

Make America proud by keeping the American Dream alive. You can do it. You are America's greatest resource. And one more thing—if a poor black kid from rural Oklahoma can be here tonight, this great country will allow you to dream your dreams too!

God bless you all.

Source: Rep. J. C. Watts Jr., speech at the Republican National Convention, August 13, 1996; available at Public Broadcasting Service, *NewsHour*, www.pbs.org/newshour/convention96/ floor_speeches/watts.html.

Document 15.9 in Context
"Reaching over the Fences": The Legacy of the Rev. Martin Luther King Jr.'s "Beloved Community"

Rep. John R. Lewis, D-Ga., comes to any discussion of America's racial atmosphere and the struggle of African Americans for civil rights with a unique perspective. As a young man, Lewis played a central role in the civil rights struggle of the 1960s. In 1961 he was among the Freedom Riders who were beaten and arrested while protesting the segregation of interstate buses in the South. He helped plan and was among the speakers at the 1963 March on Washington where Martin Luther King Jr. delivered his famous "I Have a Dream" speech. And he was a leader of the famous march that was attacked by Alabama state troopers as the protestors crossed the Edmund Pettus Bridge in Selma in 1965.

Born in 1940, Lewis graduated in 1961 from the American Baptist Theological Seminary in Nashville, Tennessee, and then received a bachelor's degree in religion and philosophy from Fisk University in 1967. From 1963 to 1966 he chaired the Student Nonviolent Coordinating Committee, an influential and militant youth organization that was active in organizing civil rights protests. In the 1980s he entered elective politics, serving four years on the

Atlanta City Council before winning his first term in Congress in 1986. He was continuously reelected through the election of 2006.

Lewis was deeply influenced by King's vision of the "Beloved Community," a nation and a world transformed by nonviolent confrontation of hatred, bigotry and injustice into a society of reconciliation and understanding. Lewis wrote in his 1998 memoir, *Walking with the Wind:*

> Dr. King was more than just a teacher or a preacher. He was a man of action . . . This is where we can start, in our own backyards, on our own blocks, down our own streets, from one section of a town into another, from white neighborhoods into black and vice versa. This is where integration truly begins, not by government mandate, but by literally reaching over the fences around our own homes.[4]

In the document that follows—an excerpt from his 1998 memoir—Lewis explores his own vision of the way toward that Beloved Community, thirty years after King's death.

▬ Document 15.9 ▬
Rep. John R. Lewis, D-Ga., Discusses the "Beloved Community," 1998

. . . The path that remains to lead us to the Beloved Community is no longer racial alone. It is one, I believe, marked by the differences, divisions and canyons created by class. There hasn't been a time in America—certainly not since World War II—that the classes have been pushed as far apart as they are today, with vast numbers of poor at one end, a small number of wealthy at the other and a middle class in danger of completely disappearing as most of it is pushed toward the lower end of the spectrum. Measurements of economic well-being are misleading. The overall economy might be healthy, but where is most of that wealth going? Vastly and disproportionately, it is funneled to the relatively few at the top. America's total wealth, jobs and productivity might be growing, but the benefits are being enjoyed primarily by a small minority.

We cannot let this continue. We cannot have a very few people visibly and luxuriantly living in excess while the rest of the nation lives in fear and anxiety. We cannot afford to have two societies, moving further apart. The famous 1968 Kerner report warned that America was in danger of becoming "two societies . . . separate and unequal." At that time those societies were defined by race. Now, I believe the division is both class and race.

And such disparity is a recipe for disaster. It creates a climate of cynicism and discouragement. It encourages people at all ends of the spectrum to turn away from one another, to insulate themselves and, yes, even to arm themselves, for both defense and attack. It makes the political system seem distant, incomprehensible, irrelevant, monolithic and insensitive to the needs of the people. If we are going to begin turning back toward one another, to humanize one another, we need to humanize the political system, we need to make it respond directly to the problems of the people—not just to the people in power, or to the people who are loudest, but to *all* of the people, including, crucially, those who have no power, those who have no voice.

The poor, the sick, the disenfranchised. We cannot run away from them. We're all living in this house. When we move away from community and connection and live instead in a climate of "every man for himself," we are sowing the seeds that will lead to the destruction of American society as we know it. If we are not going to become divided and balkanized, like Northern Ireland or Lebanon or Rwanda or so much of Eastern Europe, we must push and advocate and make real the policies and decisions that can pull us together, that recognize our dependence on one another as members of a family. If we continue to allow hundreds of thousands of our young people—black, Hispanic, Asian, Native American, white—to grow up without a feeling that they have a stake in this society, if we let them come into young adulthood without ever holding a meaningful job, without any sense of hope, I think we are asking for trouble. We can't retreat from them. We can't turn our backs on them. We can't circle the wagons in suburban developments with armed guards at the gates and believe that we are safe. The people, the masses, will eventually arrive at those gates, angry and upset, and then it will be too late. We must reach out to one another *now*. We must realize that we are all in this together. Not as black or white. Not as rich or poor. Not even as Americans or "non"-Americans. But as human beings.

I believe in America. I love this country. That's why I've tried so hard over the years to make it better. This is unquestionably the greatest nation on earth, a land of limitless opportunity and possibility, not just in material terms but in moral, ethical and spiritual terms. I believe the next frontier for America lies in the direction of our spiritual strength as a community. This is the place where we must move if we are to continue to lead the rest of the world. It is not just materially or militarily that we must measure our might, but morally.

Somewhere, sometime—and I hope in the not too distant future—someone must take the lead. At the highest level—in the White House, in the Senate, in the House of Representatives—somebody needs to say, forcefully and with complete conviction, that we are one nation, we're one society, we're one people. We're one house, the American house. We're one family, the American family. We don't speak that way anymore. I'm not sure we even *think* that way.

But we must. And those of us in government must lead the way. It must create the climate, create the environment and set the agenda for these changes. We must insist that the government form policies, legislation, programs—whatever is needed—to nurture the environment in which we can narrow that gap instead of allowing it to continue to grow. We must develop a just and sensible way of redistributing our resources so that no one, but no one, will be left out of society.

The resources are there. We are a wealthy nation, a bountiful nation. Unfortunately, much of that wealth and bounty has been gathered by a very few, who have then used that wealth and power to shape the political system to benefit them. A lot of people made a lot of money during the 1980s, and those same people are now enjoying massive tax breaks. I think they should be required to pay up, to contribute their proportionate share, to invest in the areas of our nation that are falling down—the inner cities, the rural communities—providing the resources for large numbers of their fellow Americans to begin building meaningful lives.

That is one thing that can be done with the people inside the walls of power. As for those on the outside, they need to push, to agitate, to create a climate in which the government cannot ignore them. This is what we did during the movement. We *made* the government listen. We *made* the government respond . . .

There is an old African proverb: "When you pray, move your feet." As a nation, if we care for the Beloved Community, we must move our feet, our hands, our hearts, our resources to build and not to tear down, to reconcile and not to divide, to love and not to hate, to heal and not to kill. In the final analysis, we are one people, one family, one house—the American house, the American family.

Source: John Lewis with Michael D'Orso, "Home," in *Walking with the Wind: A Memoir of the Movement* (New York: Simon & Schuster, 1998), 460–475.

Document 15.10 in Context
"We Have It within Our Power to Shape History": Sen. Barack Obama, D-Ill., Calls for Universal Health Care

No one was surprised when, in February 2007, Sen. Barack Obama, D-Ill., announced that he was running for the 2008 Democratic presidential nomination. Obama's announcement had been expected for months, and he was already drawing large crowds at his public appearances. An engaging and impressive speaker, he had attracted a great deal of attention when he delivered a speech at the 2004 Democratic National Convention.

Obama was then only a candidate for the U.S. Senate. He had served seven years in the Illinois Senate and had spent most of his career as a civil rights lawyer and community organizer. The 2004 convention was his first real exposure to a national political audience. But almost immediately, he became the focus of speculation involving the 2008 presidential campaign. Many thought that he was the first African American candidate who would be popular enough among white voters to have a real chance of winning the nomination and perhaps even the presidency.

Born in 1961 in Hawaii, Obama was the son of a black man from Kenya and a white woman from Kansas. His parents separated when he was two, and he later moved to Indonesia with his mother and her second husband. He attended schools in Indonesia and Hawaii, then enrolled at Occidental College in Los Angeles. He also attended Columbia University in New York before earning a law degree from Harvard University. At Harvard, he was the first African American president of the Harvard Law Review.

The document that follows is an excerpt from a speech he delivered to the Families USA Conference in Washington, D.C., on January 25, 2007, two weeks before he announced his candidacy for president. In the speech, Obama examines the debate over America's health care crisis, urging his audience to demand bold action from their leaders.

Document 15.10
Sen. Barack Obama, D-Ill., Discusses the Importance of Leadership and Universal Health Care, January 25, 2007

. . . On this January morning of two thousand and seven, more than sixty years after President Truman first issued the call for national health insurance, we find ourselves in the midst of an historic moment on health care. From Maine to California, from business to labor, from Democrats to Republicans, the emergence of new and bold proposals from across the spectrum has effectively ended the debate over whether or not we should have universal health care in this country.

Plans that tinker and halfway measures now belong to yesterday . . .

In the 2008 campaign, affordable, universal health care for every single American must not be a question of whether, it must be a question of how. We have the ideas, we have the resources, and we will have universal health care in this country by the end of the next president's first term.

I know there's a cynicism out there about whether this can happen, and there's reason for it. Every four years, health care plans are offered up in campaigns with great fanfare and promise. But once those campaigns end, the plans collapse under the weight of Washington politics, leaving the rest of America to struggle with skyrocketing costs.

For too long, this debate has been stunted by what I call the smallness of our politics—the idea that there isn't much we can agree on or do about the major challenges facing our country . . .

Well we can't afford another disappointing charade in 2008. It's not only tiresome, it's wrong. Wrong when businesses have to layoff one employee because they can't afford the health care of another. Wrong when a parent cannot take a sick child to the doctor because they cannot afford the bill that comes with it. Wrong when 46 million Americans have no health care at all. In a country that spends more on health care than any other nation on Earth, it's just wrong.

And yet, in recent years, what's caught the attention of those who haven't always been in favor of reform is the realization that this crisis isn't just morally offensive, it's economically untenable. For years, the can't-do crowd has scared the American people into believing that universal health care would mean socialized medicine and burdensome taxes—that we should just stay out of the way and tinker at the margins.

You know the statistics. Family premiums are up by nearly 87% over the last five years, growing five times faster than workers' wages. Deductibles are up 50%. Co-payments for care and prescriptions are through the roof.

Nearly 11 million Americans who are already insured spent more than a quarter of their salary on health care last year. And over half of all family bankruptcies today are caused by medical bills.

But they say it's too costly to act.

Almost half of all small businesses no longer offer health care to their workers, and so many others have responded to rising costs by laying off workers or shutting their doors for good. Some of the biggest corporations in America, giants of industry like GM and Ford, are watching foreign competitors based in countries with universal health care run circles around them, with a GM car containing twice as much health care cost as a Japanese car.

But they say it's too risky to act.

They tell us it's too expensive to cover the uninsured, but they don't mention that every time an American without health insurance walks into an emergency room, we pay even more. Our family's premiums are $922 higher because of the cost of care for the uninsured.

We pay $15 billion more in taxes because of the cost of care for the uninsured. And it's trapped us in a vicious cycle. As the uninsured cause premiums to rise, more employers drop coverage. As more employers drop coverage, more people become uninsured, and premiums rise even further.

But the skeptics tell us that reform is too costly, too risky, too impossible for America.

Well the skeptics must be living somewhere else. Because when you see what the health care crisis is doing to our families, to our economy, to our country, you realize that caution is what's costly. Inaction is what's risky. Doing nothing is what's impossible when it comes to health care in America.

It's time to act. This isn't a problem of money, this is a problem of will. A failure of leadership. We already spend $2.2 trillion a year on health care in this country . . .

So where's all that money going? We know that a quarter of it—one out of every four health care dollars—is spent on non-medical costs; mostly bills and paperwork. And we also know that this is completely unnecessary. Almost every other industry in the world has saved billions on these administrative costs by doing it all online . . . Another, more controversial area we need to look at is how much of our health care spending is going toward the record-breaking profits earned by the drug and health care industry. It's perfectly understandable for a corporation to try and make a profit, but when those profits are soaring higher and higher each year while millions lose their coverage and premiums skyrocket, we have a responsibility to ask why.

At a time when businesses are facing increased competition and workers rarely stay with one company throughout their lives, we also have to ask if the employer-based system of health care itself is still the best for providing insurance to all Americans. We have to ask what we can do to provide more Americans with preventative care, which would mean fewer doctor's visits and less cost down the road. We should make sure that every single child who's eligible is signed up for the children's health insurance program, and the federal government should make sure that our states have the money to make that happen . . .

But regardless of what combination of policies and proposals get us to this goal, we must reach it. We must act. And we must act boldly. As one health care advocate recently said, "The most expensive course is to do nothing." But it wasn't a liberal Democrat or union leader who said this.

It was the president of the very health industry association that funded the "Harry and Louise" ads designed to kill the Clinton health care plan in the early nineties.

The debate in this country over health care has shifted . . . Leaders no longer have a reason to be timid. And America can no longer afford inaction. That's not who we are—and that's not the story of our nation's improbable progress.

Half a century ago, America found itself in the midst of another health care crisis. For millions of elderly Americans, the single greatest cause of poverty and hardship was the crippling cost of health care and the lack of affordable insurance. Two out of every three elderly Americans had annual incomes of less than $1,000, and only one in eight had health insurance.

As health care and hospital costs continued to rise, more and more private insurers simply refused to insure our elderly, believing they were too great of a risk to care for.

The resistance to action was fierce. Proponents of health care reform were opposed by well-financed, well-connected interest groups who spared no expense in telling the American people that these efforts were "dangerous" and "un-American," "revolutionary" and even "deadly."

And yet the reformers marched on . . . And finally, after years of advocacy and negotiation and plenty of setbacks, President Lyndon Johnson signed the Medicare bill into law on July 30th of 1965.

The signing ceremony was held in Missouri, in a town called Independence, with the first man who was bold enough to issue the call for universal health care—President Harry Truman.

And as he stood with Truman by his side and signed what would become the most successful government program in history—a program that had seemed impossible for so long—President Johnson looked out at the crowd and said, "History shapes men, but it is a necessary faith of leadership that men can help shape history."

Never forget that we have it within our power to shape history in this country. It is not in our character to sit idly by as victims of fate or circumstance, for we are a people of action and innovation, forever pushing the boundaries of what's possible.

Now is the time to push those boundaries once more. We have come so far in the debate on health care in this country, but now we must finally answer the call first issued by Truman, advanced by Johnson, and fought for by so many leaders and Americans throughout the last century. The time has come for universal health care in America . . .

Source: Sen. Barack Obama, "The Time Has Come for Universal Health Care," speech to Families USA Conference, Washington, D.C., January 25, 2007, http://obama.senate.gov/speech/070125-the_time_has_co/.

NOTES

1 Martin Luther King Jr., "I Have A Dream," in *A Testament of Hope: The Essential Writings and Speeches of Martin Luther King Jr.,* ed. James M. Washington (New York: HarperCollins, 1991), 219.
2 Ibid., 217.
3 John Nichols, "Shirley Chisholm's Legacy," The Online Beat, *The Nation,* www.thenation.com.
4 John Lewis with Michael D'Orso, *Walking with the Wind: A Memoir of the Movement* (New York: Simon & Schuster, 1998), 459.

Appendix A
Chronology of Major Events

1581 First African slaves arrive in North America, in Spanish Florida.

1619 First African slaves arrive in British North America, in Virginia.

1776 The Declaration of Independence is signed, proclaiming "all men are created equal."

1780 Black residents of Massachusetts petition the state for voting rights.

1787 The Northwest Ordinance bans slavery in the Northwest Territories.

1789 The Constitution takes effect, tacitly recognizing slavery as the status quo but allowing Congress to ban the importation of slaves after 1808.

1812 The United States and Britain fight the War of 1812.

1820 The Missouri Compromise admits Missouri as a slave state but bans slavery in additional western territories north of latitude 36°30".

1850 The Compromise of 1850 admits California as a free state, bans slave trafficking in Washington, D.C., and strengthens the fugitive slave law.

1857 The Supreme Court rules in *Dred Scott v. Sandford* that blacks have no legal rights and that Congress lacked authority to ban slavery in federal territories.

1859 The Supreme Court upholds the Fugitive Slave Act of 1850.

1860 Abraham Lincoln is elected president, becoming the first Republican to hold that office. South Carolina is the first of eleven Southern states to secede from the Union.

1861 Fort Sumter in the harbor off Charleston, South Carolina, is shelled, setting off the Civil War. The seceding states form the Confederate States of America.

1862 Congress outlaws slavery in the District of Columbia.

1863 President Lincoln's Emancipation Proclamation bans slavery in areas of rebellion and authorizes African Americans to serve in the Union army and navy. Anti-draft riots erupt in Northern cities.

1865 President Lincoln is assassinated. The Confederate armies surrender, ending the Civil War. Reconstruction begins. The Thirteenth Amendment, prohibiting slavery, is ratified. "Black Codes" are passed by Southern legislatures. Radical Republicans take control of Congress in midterm elections and clash with Democrat Andrew Johnson, who became president upon Lincoln's death.

1866 The Civil Rights Act of 1866 is enacted over President Johnson's veto.

1867 The Tenure of Office Act is enacted over President Johnson's veto. Secretary of War Edwin M. Stanton indicates that he will enforce the Civil Rights Act of 1866.

1868 President Johnson fires Secretary Stanton. Johnson is impeached by the House of Representatives and acquitted by the Senate. The Fourteenth Amendment, guaranteeing equal protection, is ratified. Former Union general Ulysses S. Grant is elected president.

1869 The House of Representatives refuses to seat J. Willis Menard of Louisiana, who would have become the first African American in Congress.

1870 The Fifteenth Amendment guaranteeing voting rights is ratified. Hiram R. Revels of Mississippi becomes the first African American senator and Joseph H. Rainey of South Carolina becomes the first African American representative.

1871 Congress passes the Ku Klux Klan Act, which is intended to enforce the Fourteenth Amendment's guarantee of equal protection.

1872 Congress passes the Amnesty Act of 1872, restoring voting rights and the opportunity to run for office to most Confederate civilian officials and military officers.

1873 Panic of 1873 launches five-year economic depression.

1874 Democrats take control of the House of Representatives in midterm elections, reducing the power of the Radical Republicans. This marks the beginning of the end for Reconstruction.

1875 The Civil Rights Act of 1875 is enacted. It is the last major civil rights statute until 1957.

1876 Republican Rutherford B. Hayes is declared the winner of the contested presidential election.

1877 Remaining Federal occupation troops withdraw from the former Confederate states. West Point graduates its first African American cadet.

1879 Sen. Blanche K. Bruce of Mississippi becomes the first African American to chair a select congressional committee.

1883 The Supreme Court invalidates most provisions of the 1875 Civil Rights Act.

1884 The Supreme Court upholds the convictions of Ku Klux Klan members for violating the voting rights of African Americans.

1896 The Supreme Court upholds segregation under the "separate but equal" principle in its *Plessy v. Ferguson* decision.

1898 The Spanish-American War begins. Rep. George H. White, R-N.C., is the sole African American in Congress.

1901 Rep. White leaves office, marking the start of a twenty-eight year absence of African Americans from Congress.

1913 The Seventeenth Amendment, allowing popular election of senators, is ratified. Previously, senators were elected by their state legislatures.

1917 The United States enters World War I, with no African Americans in Congress.

1929 Oscar S. De Priest of Illinois becomes the first African American representative since 1901. The Great Depression begins.

1935 Rep. Arthur W. Mitchell of Illinois becomes first African American Democrat in Congress. The Supreme Court rules that political parties can discriminate on the basis of race.

1937 The Supreme Court rules that poll taxes are constitutional.

1941 The United States enters World War II. Rep Arthur W. Mitchell, D-Ill., is the only African American in Congress. President Franklin D. Roosevelt signs an executive order banning employment discrimination in defense industries.

1948 President Harry S. Truman signs an executive order desegregating the armed forces.

1949 Rep. William L. Dawson of Illinois becomes the first African American to chair a standing congressional committee.

1950 Korean War begins, with two African Americans in Congress.

1954 The Supreme Court outlaws public school segregation in *Brown v. Board of Education*.

1957 The Civil Rights Act of 1957 is signed by President Dwight D. Eisenhower.

1964 The Civil Rights Act of 1964 is signed by President Lyndon B. Johnson.

1965 The Voting Rights Act of 1965 is signed by President Johnson.

1967 Edward W. Brooke III of Massachusetts takes office as the nation's first popularly elected African American senator. Adam Clayton Powell Jr. of New York is excluded from the House of Representatives. Thurgood Marshall becomes the first African American Supreme Court justice.

1968 Rev. Martin Luther King Jr. is assassinated.

1969 Shirley A. Chisholm of New York becomes the first African American woman in the House of Representatives. The Democratic Select Committee, the forerunner of the Congressional Black Caucus, is established.

1971 The Congressional Black Caucus is incorporated as the successor to the Democratic Select Committee and meets with President Richard M. Nixon.

1972 Rep. Chisholm runs for the Democratic presidential nomination.

1973 The United States withdraws its military forces from Vietnam, with seventeen African Americans in Congress.

1974 The House Judiciary Committee, including all three of its African American members, votes to impeach President Nixon, who resigns.

1978 Rep. Charles C. Diggs Jr. of Michigan becomes the first African American convicted of a felony while a member of Congress.

1983 Rev. Martin Luther King Jr.'s birthday is declared a national holiday.

1991 Gary A. Franks of Connecticut becomes the first African American Republican elected to the House of Representatives since the Great Depression.

1993 Carol Moseley-Braun of Illinois becomes the first African American woman in the Senate.

1994 The Republicans' "Contract with America" helps the GOP win control of Congress for first time in 40 years.

1999 The House votes to impeach President Bill Clinton, but the Senate acquits him after his trial.

2001 Al-Qaida operatives hijack commercial passenger jets and crash them into the World Trade Center, the Pentagon and a Pennsylvania field. Approximately 3,000 people die in the attacks.

2003 The United States invades Iraq with thirty-nine African Americans in Congress.

2004 Illinois is the first state to have an African American Democrat (Barack Obama) and Republican (Alan Keyes) competing for a Senate seat. Obama wins the election.

2006 Congress renews the Voting Rights Act of 1965. The legislation is signed by President George W. Bush.

2007 Democrats regain control of Congress, following their victories in the 2006 elections.

Appendix B
African American Members of the 110th United States Congress

There were forty-two African Americans serving in the House of Representatives—including two of the cofounders of the Congressional Black Caucus—and one in the Senate as of September 2007. All were Democrats and members of the Congressional Black Caucus. Together, they represented twenty-one states, the Virgin Islands and the District of Columbia.

U.S. SENATE

Barack Obama, D-Ill.[a]

U.S. HOUSE OF REPRESENTATIVES

Sanford D. Bishop Jr., D-Ga.
Corrine Brown, D-Fla.
G. K. Butterfield, D-N.C.
Julia M. Carson, D-Ind.
Donna M. C. Christensen, D-V.I.
Yvette D. Clarke, D-N.Y.[b]
William L. Clay Jr., D-Mo.
Emanuel Cleaver II, D-Mo.
James E. Clyburn, D-S.C.
John Conyers Jr., D-Mich.[d]
Elijah E. Cummings, D-Md.
Artur Davis, D-Ala.
Danny K. Davis, D-Ill.
Keith Ellison, D-Minn.[b]
Chaka Fattah, D-Pa.
Al Green, D-Texas
Alcee L. Hastings, D-Fla.
Jesse L. Jackson Jr., D-Ill.
Sheila Jackson-Lee, D-Texas
William J. Jefferson, D-La.
Eddie Bernice Johnson, D-Texas
Hank Johnson, D-Ga.[b]

Stephanie Tubbs Jones, D-Ohio
Carolyn Cheeks Kilpatrick, D-Mich.
Barbara Lee, D-Calif.
John R. Lewis, D-Ga.
Kendrick B. Meek, D-Fla.
Gregory W. Meeks, D-N.Y.
Juanita Millender-McDonald, D-Calif.[c]
Gwendolynne S. Moore, D-Wis.
Eleanor Holmes Norton, D-D.C.
Donald M. Payne, D-N.J.
Charles B. Rangel, D-N.Y.[d]
Laura Richardson, D-Calif.[e]
Bobby L. Rush, D-Ill.
David Scott, D-Ga.
Robert C. Scott, D-Va.
Bennie G. Thompson, D-Miss.
Edolphus Towns, D-N.Y.
Maxine Waters, D-Calif.
Diane E. Watson, D-Calif.
Melvin L. Watt, D-N.C.
Albert R. Wynn, D-Md.

Sources: Congressional Black Caucus, http://congressionalblackcaucus.net; U.S. Congress, *Biographical Directory of the U.S. Congress, 1774–Present*, http://bioguide.congress.gov.

[a] First elected in 2004 to a six-year term.
[b] First elected in 2006 to a two-year term.
[c] Died April 22, 2007.
[d] Original member of Congressional Black Caucus, founded in 1971.
[e] Took oath of office September 4, 2007, to succeed the late Juanita Millender-McDonald after special election victory.

Appendix C

African American Members of Congress, 1870–2007

As of September 2007, 121 African Americans had served in Congress; 5 in the Senate and 116 in the House. Following are the names of the black members, their political affiliations and the states they represent, listed according to the Congress to which they were first elected. Some members did not take office until the Congress under which they are listed was already under way, due to election challenges, special elections and other circumstances. Some served nonconsecutive terms. This list includes those elected to serve as nonvoting delegates.

U.S. SENATE

41st Congress (1869–1871)
Hiram R. Revels, R-Miss.

44th Congress (1875–1877)
Blanche K. Bruce, R-Miss.

90th Congress (1967–1969)
Edward W. Brooke III, R-Mass.

103d Congress (1993–1995)
Carol Moseley-Braun, D-Ill.

109th Congress (2005–2007)
Barack Obama, D-Ill.

U.S. HOUSE OF REPRESENTATIVES

41st Congress (1869–1871)
Jefferson F. Long, R-Ga.
Joseph H. Rainey, R-S.C.

42d Congress (1871–1873)
Robert C. De Large, R-S.C.
Robert B. Elliott, R-S.C.
Benjamin S. Turner, R-Ala.
Josiah T. Walls, R-Fla.

43d Congress (1873–1875)
Richard H. Cain, R-S.C.
John R. Lynch, R-Miss.
Alonzo J. Ransier, R-S.C.
James T. Rapier, R-Ala.

44th Congress (1875–1877)
Jeremiah Haralson, R-Ala.
John A. Hyman, R-N.C.
Charles E. Nash, R-La.
Robert Smalls, R-S.C.

48th Congress (1883–1885)
James E. O'Hara, R-N.C.

51st Congress (1889–1891)
Henry P. Cheatham, R-N.C.
John M. Langston, R-Va.
Thomas E. Miller, R-S.C.

53d Congress (1893–1895)
George W. Murray, R-S.C.

55th Congress (1897–1899)
George H. White, R-N.C.

71st Congress (1929–1931)
Oscar S. De Priest, R-Ill.

74th Congress (1935–1937)
Arthur W. Mitchell, D-Ill.

78th Congress (1943–1945)
William L. Dawson, D-Ill.

79th Congress (1945–1947)
Adam Clayton Powell Jr., D-N.Y.

84th Congress (1955–1957)
Charles C. Diggs Jr., D-Mich.

85th Congress (1957–1959)
Robert N. C. Nix Sr., D-Pa.

88th Congress (1963–1965)
Augustus F. Hawkins, D-Calif.

89th Congress (1965–1967)
John Conyers Jr., D-Mich.

91st Congress (1969–1971)
Shirley A. Chisholm, D-N.Y.
William L. Clay Sr., D-Mo.
George W. Collins, D-Ill.
Louis Stokes, D-Ohio

92d Congress (1971–1973)
Ronald V. Dellums, D-Calif.
Walter E. Fauntroy, D-D.C.
Ralph H. Metcalfe, D-Ill.
Parren J. Mitchell, D-Md.
Charles B. Rangel, D-N.Y.

93d Congress (1973–1975)
Yvonne B. Burke, D-Calif.
Cardiss Collins, D-Ill.
Barbara C. Jordan, D-Texas
Andrew J. Young Jr., D-Ga.

94th Congress (1975–1977)
Harold E. Ford Sr., D-Tenn.

96th Congress (1979–1981)
George W. Crockett Jr., D-Mich.
Julian C. Dixon, D-Calif.
Melvin H. Evans, R-V.I.
William H. Gray III, D-Pa.
George T. ("Mickey") Leland, D-Texas
Bennett M. Stewart, D-Ill.

97th Congress (1981–1983)
Mervyn M. Dymally, D-Calif.
Katie B. Hall, D-Ind.
Gus Savage, D-Ill.
Harold D. Washington, D-Ill.

98th Congress (1983–1985)
Charles A. Hayes, D-Ill.
Major R. O. Owens, D-N.Y.
Edolphus Towns, D-N.Y.
Alan D. Wheat, D-Mo.

99th Congress (1985–1987)
Alton R. Waldon Jr., D-N.Y.

100th Congress (1987–1989)
Mike Espy, D-Miss.
Floyd H. Flake, D-N.Y.
John R. Lewis, D-Ga.
Kweisi Mfume, D-Md.

101st Congress (1989–1991)
Donald M. Payne, D-N.J.
Craig A. Washington, D-Texas

102d Congress (1991–1993)
Lucien E. Blackwell, D-Pa.
Eva M. Clayton, D-N.C.
Barbara-Rose Collins, D-Mich.
Gary A. Franks, R-Conn.
William J. Jefferson, D-La.
Eleanor Holmes Norton, D-D.C.
Maxine Waters, D-Calif.

103d Congress (1993–1995)
Sanford D. Bishop Jr., D-Ga.
Corrine Brown, D-Fla.
James E. Clyburn, D-S.C.
Cleo Fields, D-La.
Earl F. Hilliard, D-Ala.
Alcee L. Hastings, D-Fla.
Eddie Bernice Johnson, D-Texas
Cynthia A. McKinney, D-Ga.
Carrie P. Meek, D-Fla.
Melvin J. Reynolds, D-Ill.
Bobby L. Rush, D-Ill.
Robert C. Scott, D-Va.
Bennie G. Thompson, D-Miss.
Walter R. Tucker III, D-Calif.
Melvin L. Watt, D-N.C.
Albert R. Wynn, D-Md.

104th Congress (1995–1997)
Elijah E. Cummings, D-Md.
Chaka Fattah, D-Pa.
Victor O. Frazer, Ind.-V.I.
Jesse L. Jackson Jr., D-Ill.
Sheila Jackson-Lee, D-Texas
Juanita Millender-McDonald, D-Calif.
J. C. Watts Jr., R-Okla.

105th Congress (1997–1999)
Julia M. Carson, D-Ind.
Donna M. C. Christensen, D-V.I.
Danny K. Davis, D-Ill.
Harold E. Ford Jr., D-Tenn.
Carolyn Cheeks Kilpatrick, D-Mich.
Barbara Lee, D-Calif.
Gregory W. Meeks, D-N.Y.

106th Congress (1999–2001)
Stephanie Tubbs Jones, D-Ohio

107th Congress (2001–2003)
William L. Clay Jr., D-Mo.
Diane E. Watson, D-Calif.

108th Congress (2003–2005)
Frank W. Ballance Jr., D-N.C.
G. K. Butterfield, D-N.C.
Artur Davis, D-Ala.
Denise L. Majette, D-Ga.
Kendrick B. Meek, D-Fla.
David Scott, D-Ga.

109th Congress (2005–2007)
Emanuel Cleaver II, D-Mo.
Al Green, D-Texas
Gwendolynne S. Moore, D-Wis.

110th Congress (2007–2009)
Yvette D. Clarke, D-N.Y.
Keith Ellison, D-Minn.
Hank Johnson, D-Ga.
Laura Richardson, D-Calif.

Note: The African American members of the 110th Congress are listed as of September 2007. *Sources:* Mildred L. Amer, *Black Members of the United States Congress: 1870–2007,* Congressional Research Service, Library of Congress, September 5, 2007, Congressional Black Caucus Foundation, "African American Members of the 110th United States Congress," www.cbcfinc.org/About/CBC/members.html; CQ Press, *American Political Leaders, 1789–2005* (Washington, D.C.: CQ Press, 2005); U.S. Congress, *Biographical Directory of the U.S. Congress, 1774–Present,* http://bioguide.congress.gov.

Selected Bibliography

This bibliography includes resources on African Americans in Congress and the African American political experience. Newspapers and journals are listed first, followed by reference books and general works. These are followed by resources related to each chronological or themed chapter.

HISTORICAL AND CONTEMPORARY NEWSPAPERS AND MAGAZINES

Amsterdam News
Atlantic Monthly
Charleston Mercury
Christian Recorder
Cleveland Gazette
Harper's Weekly
Illinois State Register
The Liberator
New York Times
New York World
Washington Post

JOURNALS

American Historical Review
Annals of the American Academy of Political and Social Science
Civil War History
Columbia Law Review
Harvard Law Review
Journal of American History
Journal of Blacks in Higher Education
Journal of Mississippi
Journal of Negro History
Journal of Southern History
Mississippi Valley Historical Review
Pennsylvania History
Phylon
Political Research Quarterly
Political Science Quarterly
Prologue
Review of Politics
Reviews in American History
Virginia Law Review
Western Political Quarterly
Wisconsin Law Review
Yale Law Journal

REFERENCE WORKS

Amer, Mildred L. *Black Members of the United States Congress: 1870–2007*. Prepared by the Congressional Research Service, Library of Congress, Washington, D.C., September 5, 2007.

Aptheker, Herbert, ed. *A Documentary History of the Negro People in the United States*. Secaucus, N.J.: The Citadel Press, 1974.

Berlin, Ira, Barbara J. Fields, Thavolia Glymph, Joseph P. Reidy, and Leslie S. Rowland, eds. *Freedom: A Documentary History of Emancipation 1861–1867, Volume 1*. Cambridge, England: Cambridge University Press, 1985.

Blaustein, Albert P., and Robert L. Zangrando, eds. *Civil Rights and the American Negro: A Documentary History*. New York: Trident Press, 1968.

Boyd, Herb, ed. *Autobiography of a People: Three Centuries of African American History Told by Those Who Lived It*. New York: Anchor Books, 2000.

Bracey, John H., Jr., August Meier, and Elliott Rudwick, eds. *The Afro-Americans: Selected Documents*. Boston: Allyn and Bacon, 1972

Canon, David T., Garrison Nelson, and Charles Stewart III, eds. *Committees in the U.S. Congress, 1789–1946*. Washington, D.C.: CQ Press, 2002.

Chafee, Zechariah, Jr., ed. *Documents on Fundamental Human Rights*. Cambridge, Mass.: Harvard University Press, 1951.

Commager, Henry Steele, ed. *Documents of American History*. Englewood Cliffs, N.J.: Prentice-Hall, 1973.

Cooper, Anthony J., ed. *The Black Experience 1865–1978: A Documentary Reader*. Kent, United Kingdom: Greenwich University Press, 1995.

DuBois, W. E. B. *Black Reconstruction: An Essay toward a History of the Part which Black Folk Played in the Attempt to Reconstruct Democracy in America, 1860–1880*. New York: Russell and Russell, 1935.

Ducas, George, ed., with Charles Van Doren. *Great Documents in Black American History*. New York: Praeger Publishers, 1970.

Fishel, Leslie H., Jr., and Benjamin Quarles. *The Black American: A Documentary History*. Glenview, Ill.: Scott, Foresman and Company, 1976.

Fleming, Walter F., ed. *Documentary History of Reconstruction: Political, Military, Social, Religious, Educational and Industrial, 1865 to 1906*. New York: McGraw Hill, 1966.

Foner, Eric. *Freedom's Lawmakers: A Directory of Black Officeholders during Reconstruction*. New York: Oxford University Press, 1993.

Foner, Philip S., ed. *The Voice of Black America: Major Speeches by Negroes in the United States, 1797–1971*. New York: Simon and Schuster, 1972.

Foner, Philip S., and Ronald L. Lewis, eds. *Black Workers: A Documentary History from Colonial Times to the Present*. Philadelphia: Temple University Press, 1989.

Frazier, Thomas R., ed. *Afro-American History: Primary Sources*. New York: Harcourt, Brace and World, 1970.

Gellman, David N., and David Quigley, eds. *Jim Crow New York: A Documentary History of Race and Citizenship, 1777–1877*. New York: New York University Press, 2003.

Green, Robert P., Jr., ed. *Equal Protection and the African American Constitutional Experience: A Documentary History*. Westport, Conn.: Westwood Press, 2000.

Holt, Thomas C., and Elsa Barkley Brown, eds. *Major Problems in African-American History*. Vol. 1, *From Slavery to Freedom, 1619–1877*. Vol. 2, *From Freedom to "Freedom Now," 1865–1990s*. Boston: Houghton Mifflin, 2000.

Hornsby, Alton, Jr. *Chronology of African American History: From 1492 to the Present*. 2d ed. Detroit: Gale, 1997.

Middleton, Stephen, ed. *Black Congressmen during Reconstruction: A Documentary Sourcebook*. Westport, Conn.: Praeger, 2002.

Mullin, Michael, ed. *American Negro Slavery: A Documentary History*. Columbia: University of South Carolina Press, 1976.

Osofsky, Gilbert. *The Burden of Race: A Documentary History of Negro-White Relations in America*. New York: Harper and Row, 1967.

Ragsdale, Bruce A., and Joel D. Treese. *Black Americans in Congress, 1870–1989*. Office of the Historian, U.S. House of Representatives. Washington, D.C.: U.S. Government Printing Office, 1990.

Ripley, C. Peter, ed. *Witness for Freedom: African American Voices on Race, Slavery, and Emancipation*. Chapel Hill: University of North Carolina Press, 1993.

Rose, Willie Lee, ed. *A Documentary History of Slavery in North America*. New York: Oxford University Press, 1976.

Rowell, Chester H. *A Historical and Legal Digest of All the Contested Election Cases in the House of Representatives of the United States from the First to the Fifty-Sixth Congress, 1789–1901.* Westport, Conn.: Greenwood Press, 1976.

Salser, Mark R. *Black Americans in Congress.* Portland, Ore.: National Book Co., 1991.

Schneider Collection, ed. *African American History in the Press 1851–1899: From the Coming of the Civil War to the Rise of Jim Crow as Reported and Illustrated in Selected Newspapers of the Time.* 2 vols. Detroit: Gale, 1996.

Simmons, William J. *Men of Mark: Eminent, Progressive and Rising.* New York: Arno Press, 1968. 1887 edition available at the University Library of the University of North Carolina at Chapel Hill, *Documenting the American South,* http://docsouth.unc.edu/neh/simmons/menu.html.

Wright, Kai, ed. *The African-American Archive: The History of the Black Experience in Documents.* New York: Black Dog and Leventhal, 2001.

U.S. Congress. Joint Committee on Printing. *Biographical Directory of the U.S. Congress, 1774–2005.* 16th ed. H. Doc. 108-222. Washington, D.C.: U.S. Government Printing Office, 2006. www.gpoaccess.gov/serialset/cdocuments/hd108-222/index.html. Online edition available, updated through the present, at http://bioguide.congress.gov.

GENERAL WORKS

Brooke, Edward W. *The Challenge of Change: Crisis in Our Two-Party System.* Boston: Little, Brown, 1966.

Chisholm, Shirley. *The Good Fight.* New York: Harper and Row, 1973.

———. *Unbought and Unbossed.* Boston: Houghton Mifflin, 1970.

Christopher, Maurice. *Black Americans in Congress.* New York: Thomas Y. Crowell, 1976.

Clay, William L. *Just Permanent Interests: Black Americans in Congress, 1870–1991.* New York: Amistad Press, 1992.

Dellums, Ronald V., and H. Lee Halterman. *Lying Down with the Lions: A Public Life from the Streets of Oakland to the Halls of Power.* Boston: Beacon Press, 2000.

Douglass, Frederick. *Life and Times of Frederick Douglass, Written by Himself.* New York: Pathway Press, 1941. 1892 edition available at the University Library of the University of North Carolina at Chapel Hill, *Documenting the American South,* http://docsouth.unc.edu/neh/dougl92/menu.html.

Drago, Edmund L. *Black Politicians and Reconstruction in Georgia: A Splendid Failure.* Baton Rouge: Louisiana State University Press, 1982.

Edmonds, Helen G. *Black Faces in High Places: Negroes in Government.* New York: Harcourt Brace Jovanovich, 1971.

Franklin, John Hope, and Alfred A. Moss Jr. *From Slavery to Freedom: A History of African Americans.* 7th ed. New York: Alfred A, Knopf, 1994.

Franks, Gary. *Searching for the Promised Land: An African American's Optimistic Odyssey.* New York: ReganBooks, 1996.

Harding, Vincent. *There Is a River: The Black Struggle for Freedom in America.* New York: Vintage Books, 1983.

Haygood, Wil. *King of the Cats: The Life and Times of Adam Clayton Powell, Jr.* Boston: Houghton Mifflin, 1993.

Hine, Darlene Clark, and Kathleen Thompson. *A Shining Thread of Hope: The History of Black Women in America.* New York: Broadway Books, 1998.

Jordan, Barbara, and Shelby Hearon. *Barbara Jordan: A Self-Portrait.* Garden City, N.Y.: Doubleday and Company, 1979.

Levine, Michael L. *African Americans and Civil Rights: From 1619 to the Present.* Phoenix, Ariz.: Oryx Press, 1996.

Lynch, John Roy. *Reminiscences of an Active Life: The Autobiography of John Roy Lynch.* Edited by John Hope Franklin. Chicago: University of Chicago Press, 1970.

McClure, Alexander K. *Colonel Alexander K. McClure's Recollections of Half a Century.* Salem, Mass.: Salem Press Co., 1902.

McCluskey, Audrey Thomas, and Elaine M. Smith. *Mary McLeod Bethune: Building a Better World: Essays and Selected Documents.* Bloomington: Indiana University Press, 1999.

Miller, Edward A., Jr. *Gullah Statesman: Robert Smalls from Slavery to Congress, 1839–1915.* Columbia: University of South Carolina Press, 1994.

Nordin, Dennis S. *The New Deal's Black Congressman: A Life of Arthur Wergs Mitchell.* Columbia: University of Missouri Press, 1997.

Pohlman, Marcus D. *Black Politics in Conservative America.* New York: Longman, 1990.

Powell, Adam Clayton, Jr. *Adam by Adam.* New York: Dial Press, 1971.
———. *Marching Blacks.* New York: Dial Press, 1973.
Rangel, Charles B., with Leon Wynter. *And I Haven't Had a Bad Day Since: From the Streets of Harlem to the Halls of Congress.* New York: St. Martin's Press, 2007.
Smith, Samuel Denny. *The Negro in Congress, 1870–1901.* Port Washington, N.Y.: Kennikat Press, 1940.
Watts, J. C., Jr., and Chriss Winston. *What Color Is a Conservative? My Life and My Politics.* New York: HarperCollins, 2002.

CHAPTER 1: THE ANTECEDENTS OF AFRICAN AMERICAN POLITICAL EMPOWERMENT

Bennett, Lerone, Jr. *Before the Mayflower: A History of Black America.* New York: Penguin Books, 1993.
Blumrosen, Alfred W., and Ruth G. Blumrosen. *Slave Nation: How Slavery United the Colonies and Sparked the American Revolution.* Naperville, Ill.: Sourcebooks, 2005.
Colaiaco, James A. *Frederick Douglass and the Fourth of July.* New York: Palgrave Macmillan, 2006.
Davis, David Brion. *Inhuman Bondage: The Rise and Fall of Slavery in the New World.* New York: Oxford University Press, 2006.
Foner, Eric. *Free Soil, Free Labor, Free Men: The Ideology of the Republican Party before the Civil War.* New York: Oxford University Press, 1970.
Franklin, John Hope. *From Slavery to Freedom: A History of Negro Americans.* 4th ed. New York: Alfred A. Knopf, 1974.
Franklin, John Hope, and Loren Schweninger. *In Search of the Promised Land: A Slave Family in the Old South.* New York: Oxford University Press, 2006.
Jacobs, Donald M., ed. *Courage and Conscience: Black and White Abolitionists in Boston.* Indianapolis: Indiana University Press, 1993.
Jordan, Winthrop D. *White Over Black: American Attitudes toward the Negro, 1550–1812.* New York: W.W. Norton, 1977.
Locke, Mary Stoughton. *Anti-Slavery in America.* Boston: Ginn and Company, 1901.
Loewenberg, Bert James, and Ruth Bogin, eds. *Black Women in Nineteenth-Century American Life: Their Words, Their Thoughts, Their Feelings.* University Park: Pennsylvania State University Press, 1976.
Shields, John C., ed. *The Collected Works of Phillis Wheatley.* New York: Oxford University Press, 1988.

CHAPTER 2: THE SLAVERY DEBATE ERUPTS

Aptheker, Herbert. "Negro Casualties in the Civil War." *Journal of Negro History* 32, no. 1 (January 1947): 10–80.
———. "The Negro in the Union Navy." *Journal of Negro History* 32, no. 2 (April 1947): 169–200.
Bentley, George R. *A History of the Freedmen's Bureau.* Philadelphia: University of Pennsylvania Press, 1955.
Currie, David P. "Through the Looking Glass: The Confederate Constitution in Congress." *Virginia Law Review* 90, no. 5 (2004): 1257–1399.
Douglass, Frederick. *Life and Times of Frederick Douglass, Written by Himself.* New York: Pathway Press, 1941. 1892 edition available at the University Library of the University of North Carolina at Chapel Hill, *Documenting the American South,* http://docsouth.unc.edu/neh/dougl92/menu.html.
Foner, Eric. *Reconstruction: America's Unfinished Revolution, 1863–1877.* New York: Harper and Row, 1988.
Franklin, John Hope. *The Emancipation Proclamation.* Garden City, N.Y.: Doubleday, 1963.
Quarles, Benjamin. *The Negro in the Civil War.* Boston: Little, Brown, 1969.
Uya, Okun Edet. *From Slavery to Political Service: Robert Smalls, 1839–1915.* New York: Oxford University Press, 1971.

CHAPTER 3: RECONSTRUCTION

Benedict, Michael Les. *The Impeachment and Trial of Andrew Johnson.* New York: W.W. Norton, 1973.
Cohen, William and David J. Danelski. *Constitutional Law: Civil Liberty and Individual Rights.* 5th ed. New York: Foundation Press, 2002.
DuBois, W. E. B. *Black Reconstruction: An Essay toward a History of the Part which Black Folk Played in the Attempt to Reconstruct Democracy in America, 1860–1880.* New York: Russell and Russell, 1935.
Ferrell, Claudine L. *Reconstruction.* Westport, Conn.: Greenwood Press, 2003.

Hearn, Chester G. *The Impeachment of Andrew Johnson*. Jefferson, N.C.: McFarland and Company, 2000.
Lynch, John R. *The Facts of Reconstruction*. New York: Arno Press, 1968.
Ostaus, Carl R. *Freedmen, Philanthropy and Fraud*. Urbana: University of Illinois Press, 1976.
Primus, Richard A. "The Riddle of Hiram Revels." *Harvard Law Review* 119 (April 2006): 1681–1734.
Rabinowitz, Howard N. *Southern Black Leaders of the Reconstruction Era*. Urbana: University of Illinois Press, 1982.
Reid, George W. "Four in Black: North Carolina's Black Congressmen, 1874–1901." *Journal of Negro History* 64, no. 3 (Summer 1979): 229–243.
Schweninger, Loren. *James T. Rapier and Reconstruction*. Chicago: University of Chicago Press, 1978.
Shenton, James P., ed. *The Reconstruction: A Documentary History of the South After the War: 1865–1877*. New York: G.P. Putnam's Sons, 1963.
Trefousse, Hans L. *Impeachment of a President: Andrew Johnson, the Blacks, and Reconstruction*. Knoxville: University of Tennessee Press, 1975.

CHAPTER 4: AFTER RECONSTRUCTION

Greener, Richard T. "Defending the 'Negro Exodus.' " *Journal of Social Science* 11 (May 1880): 303–315.
Prather, Leon H. "The Red Shirt Movement in North Carolina, 1898–1900." *Journal of Negro History* 62, no. 2 (April 1977): 174–184.
Wang, Xi. *The Trial of Democracy: Black Suffrage and Northern Republicans, 1860–1910*. Athens: University of Georgia Press, 1997.

CHAPTER 5: THE EARLY TWENTIETH CENTURY TO THE CIVIL RIGHTS MOVEMENT

Aptheker, Herbert. *Afro-American History: The Modern Era*. New York: Citadel Press, 1971.
Carson, Clayborne, David J. Garrow, Gerald Gill, Vincent Harding, and Darlene Clark Hine, eds. *The Eyes on the Prize Civil Rights Reader*. New York: Penguin Books, 1991.
Estell, Kenneth, ed. *The African-American Almanac*. 6th ed. Detroit: Gale Research, 1994.
Flournoy, Craig. "Reporting the Movement in Black and White: The Emmett Till Lynching and the Montgomery Bus Boycott." PhD diss., Louisiana State University, 2003.
Franklin, John Hope, and August Meier, eds. *Black Leaders of the Twentieth Century*. Urbana: University of Illinois Press, 1982.
Hine, Darlene Clark, William C. Hine, and Stanley Harrold. *The African-American Odyssey*. 3d ed. Vol. 2, *Since 1865*. Upper Saddle River, N.J.: Pearson Prentice Hall, 2006.
King, Desmond. *Separate and Unequal: Black Americans and the U.S. Federal Government*. New York: Oxford University Press, 1995.
Odum-Hinmon, Maria E. *The Cautious Crusader: How the Atlanta Daily World Covered the Struggle for African American Rights from 1945 to 1985*. PhD diss., Philip Merrill College of Journalism, University of Maryland, 2005.
Patler, Nicholas. *Jim Crow and the Wilson Administration: Protesting Federal Segregation in the Early Twentieth Century*. Boulder: University Press of Colorado, 2004.

CHAPTER 6: THE CIVIL RIGHTS MOVEMENT AND BEYOND

Albert, Carl Bert. *Little Giant: The Life and Times of Speaker Carl Albert*. Norman: University of Oklahoma Press, 1990.
Quarles, Benjamin. *The Negro in the Making of America*. 3d ed. New York: Macmillan, 1987.
Young, Andrew. *A Way Out of No Way: The Spiritual Memoirs of Andrew Young*. Nashville, Tenn.: Thomas Nelson Publishers, 1994.

CHAPTER 7: THE MODERN ERA

"Affirmative Action in College Admissions: White Men Strike Back." *Journal of Blacks in Higher Education*, no. 6 (Winter 1994–1995): 20–21.

Barnett, Marguerite Ross. "The Congressional Black Caucus." *Proceedings of the Academy of Political Science* 32, no. 1, Congress against the President (1975): 34–50.

Dickson, David A. "American Society and the African American Foreign Policy Lobby: Constraints and Opportunities." *Journal of Black Studies* 27, no. 2 (November 1996): 139–151.

"Don't Walk Away from Your Vote: Consider the Huge Blocking Power of the Congressional Black Caucus." *Journal of Blacks in Higher Education,* no. 13 (Autumn 1996): 38–39.

Gerber, Alan. "African Americans' Congressional Careers and the Democratic House Delegation." *Journal of Politics* 58, no. 3 (August 1996): 831–845.

Hoffman, Adonis E. "Federal Funding Upheaval: The Impact on Blacks." *Journal of Blacks in Higher Education,* no. 2 (Winter, 1993–1994): 123–126.

Jones, Charles E. "United We Stand, Divided We Fall: An Analysis of the Congressional Black Caucus' Voting Behavior, 1975–1980." *Phylon* 48, no. 1 (First Quarter 1987): 26–37.

Pinney, Neil, and George Sera. "The Congressional Black Caucus and Vote Cohesion: Placing the Caucus within House Voting Patterns." *Political Research Quarterly* 52, no. 3 (September 1999): 583–608.

Smith, Robert C. "The Black Congressional Delegation." *Western Political Quarterly* 34, no. 2 (June 1981): 203–221.

Thomas, Dan, Craig McCoy, and Allan McBride. "Deconstructing the Political Spectacle: Sex, Race, and Subjectivity in Public Response to the Clarence Thomas/Anita Hill 'Sexual Harassment' Hearings." *American Journal of Political Science* 37, no. 3 (August 1993): 699–720.

Chapter 8: African Americans Run for Office

Barone, Michael, and Grant Ujifusa. *Almanac of American Politics, 1994.* Washington, D.C.: National Journal, 1994.

Barone, Michael, Grant Ujifusa, and Douglas Matthews. *Almanac of American Politics, 1972.* Boston: Gambit, 1973.

———. *Almanac of American Politics, 1974.* Boston: Gambit, 1975.

Becker, John F., and Eugene E. Heaton. "The Election of Senator Edward W. Brooke," *Public Opinion Quarterly* 31, no. 3 (Fall 1967): 346–358.

Grigg, Delia, and Jonathan N. Katz. "The Impact of Majority-Minority Districts on Congressional Elections." Paper presented at the annual meeting of the Midwest Political Science Association, Chicago, April 2005.

Kleppner, Paul. *Chicago Divided: The Making of a Black Mayor.* DeKalb: Northern Illinois University Press, 1985.

Menard, John Willis. *Lays in Summer Lands.* Enterprise Publishing Co., 1879.

Miller, Alton. *Harold Washington: The Mayor, the Man.* Chicago: Bonus Books, 1989.

Pohlman. Marcus D. *Black Politics in Conservative America.* New York: Longman, 1990.

Travis, Dempsey J. *"Harold": The People's Mayor.* Chicago: Urban Research Press, 1989.

Chapter 9: African Americans Face a Political Reality

Giglio, James N. *The Presidency of John F. Kennedy.* Lawrence: University Press of Kansas, 1991.

Hilty, James W. *Robert Kennedy: Brother Protector.* Philadelphia: Temple University Press, 1997.

Isserman, Maurice, and Michael Kazin. *America Divided: The Civil War of the 1960s.* New York: Oxford University Press, 2000.

Knappman, Edward W., ed. *Watergate and the White House.* Vol. 1. New York: Facts on File, 1974.

Sorenson, Theodore C. *Kennedy.* New York: Harper and Row, 1965.

Tolchin, Susan J., and Martin Tolchin. *Glass Houses: Congressional Ethics and the Politics of Venom.* Cambridge, Mass.: Westview Press, 2001.

Chapter 10: African American Women in Congress

Gill, LaVerne McCain. *African American Women in Congress.* New Brunswick, N.J.: Rutgers University Press, 1997.

Holmes, Barbara A. *A Private Woman in Public Spaces: Barbara Jordan's Speeches on Ethics, Public Religion, and Law.* Harrisburg, Pa.: Trinity Press International, 2000.

Rogers, Mary Beth. *Barbara Jordan: American Hero.* New York: Bantam Books, 1998.

CHAPTER 11: BLACK LAWMAKERS FIGHT RACISM IN AMERICA

DuBose, Carolyn P. *The Untold Story of Charles Diggs*. Arlington, Va.: Barton Publishing House, 1998.

Friedman, Saul. "Diggs, Maddox Clash over 'Slur' In Dining Room." *Detroit Free Press*, February 25, 1970.

Nordin, Dennis S. *The New Deal's Black Congressman; A Life of Arthur Wergs Mitchell*. Columbia: University of Missouri Press, 1997.

Michigan Chronicle, "Diggs, Wilkins Again Ask U.S. Intervention in Emmett Till Case," January 21, 1956.

———. "Representative Diggs at Till Trial Scene," September 24, 1955.

CHAPTER 12: AFRICAN AMERICAN LAWMAKERS ADDRESS WAR

Marzalek, John F., Jr. *Court-Martial: A Black Man in America*. New York: Charles Scribner's Sons, 1972.

Maxwell, Bruce, ed. *Homeland Security: A Documentary History*. Washington, D.C.: CQ Press, 2004.

———. *Terrorism: A Documentary History*. Washington, D.C.: CQ Press, 2002.

Torricelli, Robert, and Andrew Carroll, eds. *In Our Own Words: Extraordinary Speeches of the American Century*. New York: Washington Square Press, 1999.

CHAPTER 13: AFRICAN AMERICAN LAWMAKERS AND INTERNATIONAL AFFAIRS

Cohen, Jon, and Malcolm Linton. "Ground Zero: AIDS Research in Africa." *Science* 288, no. 5474 (June 23, 2000): 2150–2153.

Diggs, Charles C., Jr. "Statement on the Proclamation of Independence of the Republic of Guinea-Bissau." *Issue: A Journal of Opinion* 3, no. 3 (Autumn 1973): 30–33.

Hansen, Keith. "A Plague's Bottom Line." *Foreign Policy* 37 (July–August 2003): 26–27.

Holden, Robert H., and Eric Zolov. *Latin America and the United States: A Documentary History*. New York: Oxford University Press, 2000.

Jackson-Lee, Sheila. "Why Immigration Reform Requires a Comprehensive Approach that Includes Both Legalization Programs and Provisions to Secure the Border." *Harvard Journal on Legislation* 43, no. 267 (Summer 2006): 267–286.

Reid, George W. "Four in Black: North Carolina's Black Congressmen, 1874–1901," *Journal of Negro History* 64, no. 3 (Summer 1979): 229–243.

———. "The Post-Congressional Career of George H. White, 1901–1918," *Journal of Negro History* 61, no. 4 (October 1976): 362–373.

Sweeney, John. "Stuck in Haiti." *Foreign Policy* 102 (Spring 1996): 142–151.

CHAPTER 14: AT THE HEART OF THE AFRICAN AMERICAN EXPERIENCE

Blodgett, Frederick H. "An Evolutionary Democrat." *Scientific Monthly* 21, no. 1 (July 1925): 26–33.

Brauer, Carl M. "Kennedy, Johnson, and the War on Poverty." *Journal of American History* 69, no. 1 (June 1982): 98–119.

Fite, Gilbert C. "The Historical Development of Agricultural Fundamentalism in the Nineteenth Century." *Journal of Farm Economics* 44, no. 5, Proceedings Number (December 1962): 1203–1211.

———. "Republican Strategy and the Farm Vote in the Presidential Campaign of 1896." *American Historical Review* 65, no. 4 (July 1960): 787–806.

Haveman, Robert H. "The War on Poverty and the Poor and Nonpoor." *Political Science Quarterly* 102, no. 1 (Spring 1987): 65–78.

Michelson, Melissa R. "The Black Reparations Movement: Public Opinion and Congressional Policy Making." *Journal of Black Studies* 32, no. 5 (May 2002): 574–587.

"Six White Congressmen Endorse Reparations for Slavery." *Journal of Blacks in Higher Education*, no. 27 (Spring 2000): 20–21.

Sundquist, James L. "Co-Ordinating the War on Poverty." *Annals of the Academy of Political and Social Science* 385, Evaluating the War on Poverty (September 1969): 41–49.

CHAPTER 15: VISIONS OF AMERICA

Carmichael, Stokely, and Charles V. Hamilton. *Black Power: The Politics of Liberation in America*. New York: Vintage Books, 1967.

Carson, Clayborne. *In Struggle: SNCC and the Black Awakening of the 1960s*. Cambridge, Mass.: Harvard University Press, 1981.

Ellis, Catherine, and Stephen Drury Smith, eds. *Say It Plain: A Century of Great African American Speeches*. New York: The New Press, 2005.

Lewis, John. *Walking with the Wind: A Memoir of the Movement*. New York: Simon and Schuster, 1998.

Washington, James M., ed. *A Testament of Hope: The Essential Writings and Speeches of Martin Luther King Jr*. New York: HarperCollins, 1991.

Text Credits

CQ Press and the authors would like to acknowledge the valuable assistance and resources provided by the libraries of Presidents Gerald R. Ford, Herbert Hoover, John F. Kennedy, and Franklin D. Roosevelt.

CHAPTER 1: THE REVOLUTIONARY WAR TO *DRED SCOTT*

Documents 1.1, 1.7: Reprinted courtesy of the Manuscript, Archives and Rare Books Division, Schomburg Center for Research in Black Culture, The New York Public Library, Astor, Lenox and Tilden Foundations. **1.3:** Reprinted courtesy of the Massachusetts Archives. SC1/series 45X, Massachusetts Archives Collection, v.186:p.134–136. **1.8:** Reprinted courtesy of the Samuel J. May Anti-Slavery Collection at the Cornell University Library, http://dlxs.library.cornell.edu/m/mayantislavery/. **1.10:** Reprinted courtesy of the Digital Collection of the University of Detroit Mercy Black Abolitionist Archive. **1.12:** Reprinted courtesy of the Department of Rare Books and Special Collections, University of Rochester Libraries, www.library.rochester.edu.

CHAPTER 2: THE CIVIL WAR

Documents 2.1: Reprinted from The Avalon Project at Yale Law School, www.yale.edu/lawweb/avalon/avalon.htm. **2.2:** Reprinted courtesy of the Hargrett Rare Book and Manuscript Library, University of Georgia Libraries, http://www.libs.uga.edu/hargrett/speccoll.html. **2.6:** Reprinted courtesy of the descendants of Edward Markoe Wright. **2.9:** Reprinted from Freedman and Southern Society Project, University of Maryland, www.history.umd.edu/Freedmen.

CHAPTER 4: AFTER RECONSTRUCTION

Documents 4.1: Reprinted courtesy of the General Research and Reference Division, Schomburg Center for Research in Black Culture, The New York Public Library, Astor, Lenox and Tilden Foundations. **4.6, 4.12:** Reprinted from Herbert A. Aptheker, ed., *A Documentary History of the Negro People in the United States* (Secaucus, N.J.: Citadel Press, 1969). Reprinted by permission of Bettina Aptheker. **4.7:** Reprinted courtesy of The Gilder Lehrman Center for the Study of Slavery, Resistance, & Abolition at the MacMillan Center, Yale University, www.yale.edu/glc. **4.8:** Used with permission of Documenting the American South, The University of North Carolina at Chapel Hill Libraries.

CHAPTER 5: THE EARLY TWENTIETH CENTURY TO THE CIVIL RIGHTS MOVEMENT

Document 5.7: From *Marching Blacks* by Dr. Adam Clayton Powell, Jr., copyright 1946 by Dr. Adam Clayton Powell, Jr. Copyright © 1973 by The Estate of Adam Clayton Powell, Jr. Used by permission of Doubleday, a division of Random House, Inc.

CHAPTER 6: THE CIVIL RIGHTS MOVEMENT AND BEYOND

Document 6.4: From *Lying Down with the Lions* by Ronald V. Dellums. Copyright © 2000 by Ronald V. Dellums. Reprinted by permission of Beacon Press, Boston.

CHAPTER 8: AFRICAN AMERICANS RUN FOR OFFICE

Documents 8.2: From *Reminiscences of an Active Life* by John Roy Lynch. Reprinted by permission of University of Chicago Press. **8.3:** From *The Negro and the Democratic Front* by James W. Ford. Reprinted by permission of International Publishers Co., New York. **8.4** From *The Challenge of Change* by Edward Brooke. Copyright © 1966 by Edward W. Brooke. By permission of Little, Brown, and Co. **8.7:** From *Searching for the Promised Land* by Gary Franks. Reprinted by special arrangement through agent B.K. Nelson, Inc. **8.8:** Reprinted courtesy of ABC 7, Chicago. **8.10:** Reprinted courtesy of NBC News, *Meet the Press.*

CHAPTER 9: AFRICAN AMERICANS FACE A POLITICAL REALITY

Document 9.10: Reprinted courtesy of Gary Ruskin and the Congressional Accountability Project.

CHAPTER 10: AFRICAN AMERICAN WOMEN IN CONGRESS

Document 10.3: Reprinted courtesy of the Center for American History at the University of Texas at Austin.

CHAPTER 14: AT THE HEART OF THE AFRICAN AMERICAN EXPERIENCE

Document 14.6: Reprinted with permission from the May 21, 1973, issue of *The Nation.* For subscription information call 1-800-333-8536. Portions of each week's *Nation* magazine can be accessed at http://www.thenation.com.

CHAPTER 15: VISIONS OF AMERICA

Documents 15.4: Reprinted from *Adam by Adam: The Autobiography of Adam Clayton Powell Jr.* by Adam Clayton Powell Jr. (New York: Kensington Publishing Corp., 1971). All rights reserved. By arrangement with Kensington Publishing Corp. www.kensingtonbooks.com. **15.5:** Reprinted courtesy of the LBJ School of Public Affairs, University of Texas at Austin, www.utexas.edu/lbj/barbarajordanforum. **15.9:** Reprinted with the permission of Simon & Schuster Adult Publishing Group from *Walking with the Wind: A Memoir of the Movement* by John Lewis with Michael D'Orso. Copyright © 1998 by John Lewis.

Index